SECRETARIAL PRACTICE

SECRETARIAL PRACTICE

THE MANUAL OF
THE CHARTERED INSTITUTE OF SECRETARIES
OF JOINT STOCK COMPANIES AND OTHER PUBLIC BODIES

Prepared under the authority of the Council of the Institute

SIXTH EDITION

CAMBRIDGE
W. HEFFER & SONS LTD

First Edition					1912
Second Edition		-	-	-	1923
Third Edition	-	-	-	-	1924
Ditto	(*Reprint*)	-	-		1925
Ditto	(*Revised*)	-	-		1926
Ditto	(*Reprint*)	-	-		1927
Ditto	(*Reprint*)	-	-		1928
Fourth Edition		-	-	-	1930
Ditto	(*Reprint*)	-	-		1931
Ditto	(*Reprint*)	-	-		1933
Fifth Edition	-	-	-	-	1935
Ditto	(*Reprint*)	-	-		1941
Ditto	(*Reprint*)	-	-		1943
Ditto	(*Reprint*)	-	-		1944
Ditto	(*Reprint*)	-	-		1946
Ditto	(*Reprint*)	-	-		1947
Sixth Edition	(*Completely revised*)				1951

Printed in Great Britain at the Works of
W. HEFFER & SONS LTD., CAMBRIDGE, ENGLAND

Foreword

THE Council wishes to place on record its indebtedness to the legal editor and his assistant for the work which they have undertaken and so successfully carried out in connection with this edition. The practical aspects of the book also called for very careful preparation, and a great deal of work devolved upon the 'Secretarial Practice' Committee of the Council, consisting of Mr. Alfred Read, M.B.E. (Chairman), Mr. E. G. Hardman, Mr. H. Ockford, Mr. T. P. Rogers, Mr. P. Lloyd Tanner and the late Mr. Hildred Carlisle. To this Committee the Council expresses sincere thanks and its appreciation of the enthusiasm and unselfish service devoted to the task.

The Council also wishes to acknowledge with gratitude the assistance of those named below for their specific contributions:

Mr. Frank Shackleton, Fellow (Directors and Meetings of Shareholders), Mr. F. R. M. de Paula, O.B.E., F.C.A. (Accounts I), Mr. A. T. Purse, LL.B., Fellow, Barrister-at-Law (generally and Accounts II), Messrs A. S. House, Associate, E. C. Morris, A.C.A., F. V. Tappenden, T. R. Brabazon, Associate, S. W. Singleton, B.Com. (Accounts II), Mr. Herbert Johnson, Fellow, Member of Council (Reconstruction), Mr. G. Godfrey Phillips, C.B.E., of Linklaters & Paines, Solicitors to the Institute (Powers of Attorney), Mr. E. G. Hardman, Fellow, Member of Council (all forms reproduced in Appendix F—involving exceptionally heavy work on Mr. Hardman's part), Mr. L. J. L. Cohen, M.A., Barrister-at-Law (Private Companies and Foreign Companies), Professor J. Boyd, M.A., LL.B., and Mr. J. F. Dempster, Fellow (Scottish Companies), Mr. S. M. Rix, Fellow, Member of Council (Statutory Companies), Mr. Frank Bower, M.A. (Taxation of Trading Companies), Mr. N. P. M. Elles, M.A., Barrister-at-Law (Exchange Control, The Control of Borrowing and Issues of Capital, and Investigations by the Board of Trade, the Index to the book and the Index of Cases), Mr. J. C. Mitchell, J.P., Fellow, Past President (Superannuation), Mr. R. R. Merifield, B.A., B.C.L. (Canada), Mr. C. G. Hovelmeier, B.Com., Associate (South Africa), Mr. R. K. Yorston, B.Com., Associate (Australia), Hon. R. H. Algie, M.P. (New Zealand), and Mr. W. G. Lee, Fellow, who gave great assistance in the early stages of the work.

Special tribute is due to Dr. A. M. Allen, the Secretary of the Institute, and to Mr. E. G. Wallace, Joint Assistant Secretary, who has acted throughout as Secretary of the

'Secretarial Practice' Committee.   They have not only made contributions to the subject matter, but their assistance in collating the various suggestions which have been submitted has been invaluable.

In recording its appreciation the Council is convinced that it speaks on behalf of every member into whose hands this book may come.

E. M. STAPLEY,

President.

December, 1950

Preface to the Sixth Edition

In the preparation of the sixth edition of this book the opportunity has been taken not only of making the very extensive
legal revisions necessitated by the Companies Act, 1948, but
also of reviewing and expanding the sections concerned with
secretarial practice. Lord Justice Cohen, who followed Judge
Shewell Cooper as legal editor for the fourth and fifth editions,
has been succeeded in that capacity by Mr. J. W. Brunyate,
Bencher of Grays Inn, assisted by Mr. N. P. M. Elles, M.A.,
Barrister-at-Law, of the Inner Temple.

In addition to this general revision, new chapters on
Accounts, Exchange Control, The Control of Borrowing and
Issues of Capital, Investigations by the Board of Trade, and
Superannuation have been added, while others, including
chapters on Accounts, Meetings of Shareholders, Resolutions,
Directors, Taxation of Trading Companies, Reconstructions,
and Stamp Duties, have been largely or entirely rewritten.
The number of forms included has been more than trebled, and
the other material in the Appendices has also been completely
revised and appreciably extended. Owing to lack of space
the text of the Companies Act has not been included in this
edition, as in the second and subsequent editions.

ALFRED READ,
Chairman, 'Secretarial Practice' Committee.

December, 1950

·Contents

Appendices

SECRETARIAL PRACTICE

CHAPTER I

COMPANIES IN GENERAL

THE word 'company' throughout this book generally means a body incorporated under one or more of the Acts of Parliament which relate exclusively to companies in general.

This phraseology of daily life happens to accord, with substantial accuracy, with the definitions in the Companies Act, 1948. Section 455 of that Act defines a company as a company formed and registered under that Act, or an existing company; while an 'existing company' means any company formed and registered under the Joint Stock Companies Acts, the Companies Act, 1862, the Companies (Consolidation) Act, 1908, or the Companies Act, 1929, which was not registered under such Acts in Northern Ireland or in the Irish Republic. The Joint Stock Companies Acts are defined to mean the Joint Stock Companies Act, 1856, and certain other Acts before 1862; but the expression does not include the Joint Stock Companies Act, 1844, under which Act companies were first empowered to become incorporated, although without limited liability. The right to register with limited liability was first conferred by an Act of 1855, which was replaced by the codifying Act of 1856, mentioned above.

It must not be overlooked, however, that there are two important classes of companies or corporations to which neither the Joint Stock Companies Acts, nor the Companies Act, 1948, have any direct relation.

The first of these are associations incorporated by royal charter, of which the British South Africa Company and the Hudson's Bay Company may be taken as examples.

The other class comprises companies incorporated under special Acts of Parliament, generally for the purpose of working some undertaking of a public nature, *e.g.* dock companies, water companies, and the like. Companies of this class are commonly described as statutory companies. They are dealt with specially in chapter XXIV.

It must further be borne in mind that companies incorporated in the Irish Republic are only subject to such of the provisions of the Companies Act, 1948, as apply to companies incorporated outside Great Britain and (s. 461) that companies incorporated in Northern Ireland are subject only to the same provisions and to such of the other provisions of the Act as relate expressly to companies incorporated in Northern Ireland.

The Companies Act (Northern Ireland), 1932, follows in the main the provisions of the Companies Act, 1929.

Companies Act, 1948. The vast majority of companies are, however, companies to which the provisions of the Companies Act, 1948, apply.

In considering references in other Acts or in documents to any section of the repealed Acts relating to companies, it will be necessary to bear in mind s. 38 of the Interpretation Act, 1889, and ss. 456–459 of the Companies Act, 1948, under which, in effect, such references will generally be construed as references to the corresponding sections of the Companies Act, 1948.

It must not be forgotten that the Act is a consolidation Act, and not a codifying Act (such as the Bills of Exchange Act, 1882, the Partnership Act, 1890, and the Sale of Goods Act, 1893). Large and important branches of existing company law are practically untouched by it, whilst the law as to debentures, apart from the matter of registration, is only dealt with in a few isolated particulars.

Accordingly, useful though the Act is, all who are connected with the practical working of companies will require to supplement their knowledge of the Act by an acquaintance with a considerable quantity of additional law, for the most part the result of decisions of the courts. Company law, then, is in part statute law, and in part case law; the case law comprising not only decisions upon the present statute and its predecessors, but also on matters in which the statutes play no directly material part.

The Companies Acts, whilst conferring the boon of limited liability, at the same time restricted freedom of action to the extent of prohibiting unregistered partnerships of more than a certain number. Sections 429 and 434 of the 1948 Act, reproducing the older law, in effect make ten the maximum number of persons who may carry on banking business together, and twenty the maximum number who may carry on any other business together, without registration under the Act, or without the sanction of a special Act of Parliament or a charter. Mining companies within the stannaries are, however, excepted.

Under the Act, as under the earlier Acts, various descriptions of companies may be registered (see ss. 1 and 2). These are:—

(a) companies limited by shares;

(b) companies limited by guarantee, which may either

(i) have a share capital; or

(ii) not have a share capital;

(c) unlimited companies, which may either
>   (i) have a share capital; or
>   (ii) not have a share capital.

Companies limited by guarantee are those in which the members undertake, on a winding up, to contribute (up to the limit of their guarantee) to the assets of the company for the payment of its debts and liabilities. The limit of their guarantee is set out in the memorandum of association [s. 2 (3)]. See p. 9, and the First Schedule to the Act, Table C. The same applies whether or not they have a share capital. Few companies limited by guarantee, however, are now registered with a share capital, as such companies have little advantage over an ordinary company limited by shares. **Limited by Guarantee.**

Companies limited by guarantee not having a share capital are chiefly associations for mutual insurance, or charitable purposes, societies, social clubs supported by the subscriptions of their members and not formed for purposes of profit, and other companies of a like nature, which, while not requiring a trading capital, desire to have the advantages conferred by incorporation. There are no shares. The articles prescribe the number of members and usually contain provision for admission and retirement of members. Funds are usually obtained by yearly subscriptions, the guarantee, which is often of quite small amount, being only available in a winding up. These companies sometimes obtain the licence of the Board of Trade to dispense with the word 'limited' (s. 19); such licence can be revoked [s. 19 (5)]. The amounts guaranteed are in the nature of reserve liability (compare s. 60) and cannot be charged [re *Irish Club Co.* (1906), W.N. 127].

Unlimited companies also are far from common, since they furnish small attraction either to the ordinary trader or to the ordinary investor. They do not attract *ad valorem* duty on their capital. **Unlimited Companies.**

The vast majority of registered companies being companies limited by shares, it is not thought necessary in the following pages to refer specially to the other classes of companies. But it must be borne in mind that, unless the provisions of any particular section of the Act are expressly limited to any particular class or classes of companies, they are of general application. Thus s. 5 of the Act (as to alteration of memorandum) and s. 131 of the Act (as to the annual general meeting) apply to all the descriptions of companies which are authorised to register; while s. 130 (as to the statutory meeting) applies only to companies limited by shares and to companies limited by guarantee which have a share capital, and s. 119 (as to keeping a dominion register) applies only to companies having a share capital, *i.e.* to companies limited **Companies Limited by Shares.**

by shares, and also to guarantee companies and unlimited companies if they have a share capital. It should also be borne in mind that many provisions which formerly, before 1929, applied only to companies limited by shares, now apply also to companies limited by guarantee and having a share capital, *e.g.* s. 52 as to return of allotments. (See p. 50 *et seq.*)

Private Companies.   Companies under the Act also fall into two classes, according to whether they are or are not private companies. Further, private companies may or may not be exempt private companies. The special position and privileges of private companies are dealt with in chapter XXIII. The Registrar of Companies will register, as a private company, a company limited by guarantee without a share capital provided that its articles contain the restrictions required by s. 28 of the Act, but see p. 367.

Oversea Companies.   Companies incorporated outside the United Kingdom, which establish a place of business within the United Kingdom, are made subject to certain statutory requirements. The extent of these requirements is shown in chapter XXVI, which deals with foreign companies.

CHAPTER II

THE REGISTRATION OF COMPANIES

THE Registrar of Companies exercises in the matter of registration functions mainly, but not purely, ministerial. The Registrar must refuse to register a company by a name which, in the opinion of the Board of Trade, is undesirable (s. 17, see chapter III); and he should refuse to register as a private company a company the articles of which do not contain the provisions required by s. 28. He also assumes the right to refuse to register in other cases, *e.g.* if the articles of a private company contain provisions as to share-warrants. His duty is to determine whether an association applying for registration is authorised to be registered under the Act. If all of its objects were obviously illegal, he would be bound to refuse registration; and if in such circumstances registration were obtained, the certificate could be cancelled [*Bowman* v. *Secular Society* (1917), A.C. at p. 349]. He cannot, however, hold a judicial enquiry on evidence, and he may be compelled by *mandamus* to register, if he improperly refuses registration [*R.* v. *Registrar of Companies*; ex p. *Bowen* (1914), 3 K.B. 1161].

It will be convenient to enumerate at once the essential **Require-** requirements for the registration of a new company, which **ments.** are as follows:

1. A memorandum of association must be prepared which must contain the particulars required by law (s. 2).

2. The memorandum must be stamped as if it were a deed, and must be subscribed by at least seven persons [except in the case of private companies (see chapter XXIII), when two will suffice], each of whom must sign in the presence of, and have his signature attested by, at least one witness (ss. 1, 3).

3. Each subscriber of the memorandum must take at least one share and write opposite to his name the number of shares he takes [s. 2 (4)].

4. If the memorandum is accompanied by articles (which under s. 6 is obligatory except in the case of a company limited by shares), the articles must be printed (see p. 8) and stamped as if they were contained in a deed, and signed by the subscribers to the memorandum, and be expressed in separate paragraphs numbered consecutively, and the signature of each subscriber must be

5

executed in the presence of, and attested by, at least one witness (s. 9). If there are no articles accompanying the memorandum, the new Table A, which is the model set of articles for a company limited by shares scheduled to the Companies Act, 1948, will constitute the articles of the company (s. 8).* In the case of a private company, the articles must contain provisions (*a*) restricting the right to transfer its shares; (*b*) limiting the number of its members (exclusive of employees and ex-employees) to 50; (*c*) prohibiting any public issue of shares or debentures (s. 28): 'debentures' includes debenture stock, bonds and any other securities of a company, whether constituting a charge on the assets of the company or not (s. 455).

5. The memorandum and the articles (if any) must be delivered to the Registrar (s. 12).

6. A statutory declaration, by a solicitor engaged in the formation of the company, or by a person named in the articles as a director or secretary of the company, of compliance with all or any of the requirements of the Act, in respect of registration and of matters precedent and incidental thereto, must be produced to the Registrar [s. 15 (2)]. (See Appendix F, Form 4.)

7. Except in the case of a private company, every person appointed a director by the articles, or named in the prospectus or statement in lieu of prospectus as a director or proposed director of a company, or, in the case of an intended company, as a proposed director, must by himself or his agent, authorised in writing, sign and deliver to the Registrar for registration a consent to act (see Appendix F, Form 7), and, unless he has already signed the memorandum for a number of shares not less than the qualification (if any), sign and deliver to the Registrar for registration an undertaking in writing to take from the company and pay for his qualification shares (if any) (see Appendix F, Form 9); and a list of the persons who have consented to be directors of the company must be delivered to the Registrar by the applicant for registration (s. 181). (See Appendix F, Form 8.)

8. The prescribed fees must be paid to the Registrar of Companies (s. 425 and Twelfth Schedule). These are set out in Appendix A.

* Table A of the 1948 Act applies only to companies registered after the commencement of that Act. A company registered without other articles before 1948 would continue after 1948 to have as its articles the old Table A of the 1929 (or earlier) Act.

As regards the above requirements, the particulars required by law to be contained in the memorandum of a company limited by shares will be found in chapter III. The deed stamp which the memorandum and the articles are required to bear is in each case an impressed stamp of 10s. (see Appendix A).

The names, addresses, and descriptions of the subscribers, **Signatories.** or signatories, and of the witnesses to their signatures, must be fully and clearly set out.

Women, whether married or single, may be subscribers. A subscriber may sign by an agent [*Whitley Partners Ltd.* (1886), 32 Ch. D. 337], though the Registrar may require evidence of the latter's authority to do so.

A corporate body may be a subscriber and sign by its authorised representative [*Whitley Partners Ltd., supra*]; but for the purpose of forming the minimum number of subscribers the signature must be that of the authorised representative.

Foreign corporate bodies and foreign individuals, even though they be resident abroad [*Princess of Reuss* v. *Bos* (1871) L.R. 5 H.L. 176] may be subscribers and sign. The Exchange Control Act, 1947, s. 8 provides, however, that the subscription of the memorandum by a person resident outside the scheduled territories or by a nominee for another person so resident shall be invalid unless the prior permission of the Treasury is obtained. This does not have the effect of invalidating the incorporation of the company (see chapter XXX).

A signatory induced to sign by the misrepresentation of a promoter has no right of rescission against the company, seeing that the company did not then exist [*Metal Constituents, Lord Lurgan's Case* (1902), 1 Ch. 707].

Since the repeal of the Companies Act, 1867, s. 25, it would appear that the subscribers' shares need not necessarily be paid for in cash; for the general liability of a shareholder is to pay for his shares in money, or, with the company's consent, in money's worth [*Baglan Hall Colliery Co.* (1870), 5 Ch. App. 346].

No limit is imposed by the Act to the number of shares in a company which may be held by a single member, and nothing in the Act requires that the subscribers to the memorandum shall take a substantial interest in the undertaking; a company may therefore consist of one person holding all the shares except six, which may be held for him by his nominees [*Salomon* v. *Salomon & Co.* (1897), A.C. 22]. It follows that in the case of a private company (see chapter XXIII), all the shares except one may be held by one person, and that the one share may be held by his nominee.

No formal allotment of shares to a signatory is necessary [*London & Provincial Coal Co.* (1877), 5 Ch. D. 525].

Certificate of Incorporation. On the registration of the memorandum of a company the Registrar shall certify under his hand that the company is incorporated, and, in the case of a limited company, that the company is limited [s. 13 (1)].

From the date of incorporation mentioned in the certificate of incorporation, the subscribers of the memorandum, together with such other persons as may from time to time become members of the company, shall be a body corporate by the name contained in the memorandum, capable forthwith of exercising all the functions of an incorporated company, and having perpetual succession and a common seal, but with such liability on the part of the members to contribute to the assets of the company in the event of its being wound up as is mentioned in this Act [s. 13 (2)].

The duty of the Registrar, then, is to register the memorandum (with the accompanying articles, if any) and to issue a certificate of incorporation.   The date of the certificate marks the beginning of the existence of the new corporate body, thenceforth a legal entity distinct from the members composing it.   A common seal is, it will be observed, an essential part of its equipment. Express power to hold land without licence in mortmain is contained in the Act, but associations not for profit may not hold more than two acres of land without the licence of the Board of Trade (s. 14).

The Registrar's certificate of incorporation is 'conclusive evidence that all the reqirements of this Act in respect of registration and of matters precedent and incidental thereto have been complied with, and that the association is a company authorised to be registered and duly registered under the Act' [s. 15 (1)] [*Hammond* v. *Prentice* (1920), 1 Ch. 201].

Printing of Articles. It may be noted that although s. 9 requires that the articles of association must be printed, the Registrar will, in fact, accept for registration articles prepared under any of the following processes: (1) lithography of any description, (2) compotype, (3) gammeter multigraph, (4) monotype, (5) multigraph, (6) roneotype, (7) rotaprint.

CHAPTER III

THE MEMORANDUM OF ASSOCIATION

THE memorandum of association, in the case of a company limited by shares, must state the following:

(i) the name of the company, having the word 'limited' as the last word in its name [s. 2 (1) (*a*)], unless a licence to dispense with the word 'limited' has been granted under s. 19;

(ii) whether the registered office of the company is to be situate in England or Scotland [s. 2 (1) (*b*)];

(iii) the objects of the company [s. 2 (1) (*c*)];

(iv) that the liability of the members is limited [s. 2 (2)];

(v) the amount of share capital with which the company proposes to be registered, and the division thereof into shares of a fixed amount [s. 2 (4) (*a*)].

In the case of a company limited by guarantee, clauses (i) to (iv) are identical with those of a company limited by shares, while clause (v) must state 'that each member undertakes to contribute to the assets of the company in the event of its being wound up while he is a member, or within one year after he ceases to be a member, for payment of the debts and liabilities of the company contracted before he ceases to be a member, and of the costs, charges, and expenses of winding up, and for adjustment of the rights of the contributories among themselves, such amount as may be required not exceeding a specified amount,' [s. 2 (3)] *e.g.* £1. If a company limited by guarantee has a share capital, there will be a sixth clause in the memorandum identical in form with clause (v) of a company limited by shares [s. 2 (4)]. If it has no share capital, the articles (not the memorandum) must state the number of members with which it proposes to be registered [s. 7 (2)]. Notice must be given to the Registrar of any increase of membership (see Appendix F, Form 13).

In the case of an unlimited company, whether or not it has a share capital, the memorandum need only have three clauses, which are the same as clauses (i), without the word 'limited,' (ii) and (iii) of the memorandum of a company limited by shares [s. 2 (1) and (4)]. The share capital of such a company, if it has shares, and the number of members with which it proposes to be registered, though not required to appear in the memorandum, must be stated in the articles (s. 7).

The memorandum of association is the charter of the **Nature of** company and defines its powers, while the articles of **Memo-** association form a code of regulations for the internal **randum.**

9

management of the company.   The following extracts from the judgments of the House of Lords in *Ashbury Railway Carriage Company* v. *Riche* (1875), L.R., 7 H.L. 653, 667, 693, show clearly the functions of the memorandum.

Lord Cairns, L.C., says: 'I will ask your Lordships to observe . . . the marked and entire difference there is between the two documents which form the title-deeds of companies of this description—I mean the memorandum of association on the one hand and the articles of association on the other hand. With regard to the memorandum of association, your Lordships will find, as has often already been pointed out, . . . that that is, as it were, the charter, and defines the limitation of the powers of a company to be established under the Act. With regard to the articles of association, those articles play a part subsidiary to the memorandum of association. They accept the memorandum of association as the charter of incorporation of the company, and so accepting it the articles proceed to define the duties, the rights and the powers of the governing body as between themselves and the company at large, and the mode and form in which the business of the company is to be carried on, and the mode and form in which changes in the internal regulations of the company may from time to time be made.   With regard, therefore, to the memorandum of association, if you find anything which goes beyond that memorandum or is not warranted by it, the question will arise whether that which is so done is *ultra vires*, not only of the directors of the company, but of the company itself. With regard to the articles of association, if you find anything which, still keeping within the memorandum of association, is a violation of the articles of association, or in excess of them, the question will arise whether that is anything more than an act *extra vires* the directors but *intra vires* the company.'

Lord Selborne, in the same case, says: 'I only repeat what Lord Cranworth' [in *Hawkes* v. *Eastern Counties Railway* (1885), 5 H.L.C. 331] 'stated to be settled law, when I say that a statutory corporation, created by Act of Parliament for a particular purpose, is limited, as to all its powers, by the purposes of its incorporation as defined in that Act. The present and all other companies incorporated by virtue of the Companies Act of 1862 appear to me to be statutory corporations within this principle.   The memorandum of association is under that Act their fundamental, and (except in certain specified cases) their unalterable law; and they are incorporated only for the objects and purposes expressed in that memorandum.   The object and policy of those provisions of the statute, which prescribe the conditions to be expressed in the memorandum, and make these conditions (except in certain points) unalterable, would be liable to be defeated, if a contract under the common seal, which on the face of it transgresses the fundamental law, were not held to be void, and *ultra vires* of the company, as well as beyond the powers delegated to its directors or administrators. It was so held in the case of the East Anglian Railway Co.' [*East Anglian Railway* v. *Eastern Counties Railway* (1851), 11 C.B. 775], 'and in the other cases upon Railway Acts, which cases were approved in this House in Hawkes' case' [see above] 'and I am unable to see any distinction for this purpose between statutory corporations under Railway Acts, and statutory corporations under the Joint Stock Companies Act of 1862.'

There is a distinction, therefore, between a common law corporation constituted by royal charter on the one hand, and a statutory corporation, such as a water company created by its special Act or a company incorporated under the Companies Acts, on the other hand. The former 'has *prima facie* . . . the power to do with its property all such acts as an ordinary person can do, and to bind itself to such contracts as an ordinary person can bind himself to;' the latter 'is made up of persons who can act within certain limits, but in order to ascertain what are the limits, we must look to the statute. The corporation cannot go beyond the statute, for the best of all reasons, that it is a simple statutory creature' [see per Bowen L.J., in *Baroness Wenlock* v. *River Dee Co.* (1883), 36 Ch. D. 675 (*n*), at p. 685 (*n*)].

As to the name of a company, s. 17 of the Act provides **Name of** that no company shall be registered by a name which in the **Company.** opinion of the Board of Trade is undesirable. This provision gives the Board of Trade an unfettered discretion to refuse registration and there is no right of appeal against the Board's decision. The company may, however, in such a case, with the Board's written approval, change its name with effect from the date of its registration. Section 18 (2) further provides that, if through inadvertence or otherwise a company, on its first registration, or on its registration by a new name, is registered by a name which in the opinion of the Board of Trade is too like the name of an existing company, it may change its name with the sanction of the Board of Trade. The Board also has power within six months of the registration of a company to direct that it shall change its name within six weeks or such longer period as the Board may allow. The current practice of the Board of Trade is summarised in the letters included in Appendix E.

A company must also have its name (i) painted or affixed conspicuously, in letters easily legible, on the outside of every office or place in which its business is carried on; (ii) engraven in legible characters on its seal; (iii) mentioned in legible characters in all business letters and all the company's notices, advertisements, and other official publications; in all bills of exchange, promissory notes, endorsements, cheques and orders for money or goods purporting to be signed by or on behalf of the company; and in all bills of parcels, invoices, receipts, and letters of credit of the company [s. 108 (1)]. There are penalties for default; and further, as regards any bill of exchange, promissory note, cheque, or order for money or goods, 'any director, manager, or officer of a limited company, or any person on its behalf,' who signs or authorises the signing of any such document in which the company's name is not mentioned in legible characters, will, if the company fails duly to pay the same, be personally liable to the holder [s. 108 (2) (3) (4)]. The holder of an order for goods means the person to whom the order is given, whether he be in physical possession of it or not [*Civil Service Co-operative Society* v. *Chapman* (1914), 30 T.L.R. 679].

The provision that the name of the company must be mentioned in all bills of exchange, etc., has been strictly construed, so that, if the name is incorrectly given or abbreviated, the person signing will be personally liable [*Atkins & Co.* v. *Wardle* (1889), 58 L.J. Q.B. 377; *Nassau Steam Press* v. *Tyler* (1894), 70 L.T. 376]. Nor in the case of a limited company must the word 'Limited' be omitted except where a licence has been granted by the Board of Trade under s. 19 of the Act [*Religious Education Press Ltd.* (1942), 86 Sol. J. 262]. It has, however, been held that the use of the abbreviation 'Ltd.' for 'Limited' is sufficient [*Stacey* v. *Wallis* (1912), 28 T.L.R. 209]; and if the company's name is correctly stated by the drawers of a bill of exchange, the acceptors will not be liable if the company's name is not correctly stated in the acceptance.

Registered Office. Notice of the situation of the registered office, and of any change therein, must be given to the Registrar within 14 days after the date of incorporation of the company or of the change, as the case may be [s. 107 (2)]. (See Appendix F, Form 2.) The company cannot remove its registered office from England to Scotland, or *vice versa*, although it may remove it from one part of the country specified in the memorandum to another part. Wales is included in England for the purposes of clause 2 of the memorandum; thus, a company whose registered office is at Swansea should be described in the memorandum as situate in England. The insertion of the correct registered address in the annual return is not a sufficient notice under s. 107.

The registered office is the place at which documents must be served on the company, and they may be so served either by leaving them at, or sending them by post to, the registered office [s. 437 (1)]. The word 'document' includes summons, notice, order and other legal process (s. 455). A summons in criminal proceedings, as well as writs in civil proceedings, must be served at the registered office, as required by the section, and not at a branch establishment [*Pearks* v. *Richardson* (1902), 1 K.B. 91]. Where a company registered in Scotland carries on business in England, the process of any court in England may be served on the company by leaving it at, or sending it by post to, the principal place of business of the company in England, addressed to the manager or other head officer in England of the company, but a copy of the process must be sent by post to the registered office in Scotland [s. 437 (2) (3)].

A verbal notice to the company, *e.g.* of the withdrawal of an application for shares, is good [*Wilson's case* (1869), 20 L.T. 962]. In the absence of the secretary, such notice may be given at the registered office to a clerk in charge, and is then a communication to the company [*Truman's case* (1894), 3 Ch. 272].

As to clause (iii), the objects clause of the memorandum, **Objects.** the objects of the company must not include any that offend either against particular statutes or against the general law, *e.g.* a limited company cannot give itself power to purchase its own shares, for by so doing it reduces its capital without leave of the court contrary to the provisions of the Act.

It has been the practice in the past to state very fully and clearly the objects of the company. Now that the new provisions of the Act (s. 5) make it easier to alter the objects, this practice may to some extent be modified. It must be remembered, however, that the powers of a company to transact business are limited to the objects and purposes specified in the memorandum. Everything which is at variance with, or goes beyond the scope of, the memorandum, is *ultra vires* the company, and absolutely void and incapable of ratification, even though all the shareholders may assent to it [*Ashbury Railway Carriage Co.* v. *Riche* (1875), L.R. 7 H.L. 653]. It is better therefore to err on the side of taking too wide rather than too narrow powers.

To decide whether a particular action is within the company's powers may be a matter of some difficulty. Where the main object is clearly set out in one paragraph of the objects clause, other paragraphs containing powers expressed in general words have sometimes been held to be ancillary only, giving powers to be exercised in carrying out the main object but not enabling the company to carry on any business it likes. [*German Date Coffee Co.* (1882), 20 Ch. D. 169; *Amalgamated Syndicate* (1897), 2 Ch. 600]. To avoid this a paragraph is often introduced to the effect that each of the detailed objects is to be an independent object. The House of Lords has held that such a paragraph does have the effect that a transaction which is within any of the detailed objects is within the powers of the company [*Cotman* v. *Brougham* (1918), A.C. 514]; though if the question were one not of *ultra vires*, but of whether the company should be wound up on the ground that its substratum has gone through its main objects having failed, less attention would be paid to a paragraph of that sort [*Cotman* v. *Brougham* (1918), A.C. 514, at p. 520; *Baku Consolidated Oilfields Ltd.* (1944), 1 All E.R. 24]. The tendency of recent judgments is to give a fairly generous construction to the objects clause, recognising that businesses are organic by nature and change with the times. [*Kitson & Co. Ltd.* (1946), 1 All. E.R. 435; *Taldua Rubber Co. Ltd.* (1946), 2 All. E.R. 763; *Galbraith* v. *Merito Shipping Co. Ltd.* (1947), S.C. 446 at p. 452]. It was held in *Kitson & Co. Ltd.* that the objects clause of a company formed to acquire an existing engineering business implied a paramount purpose to carry on an engineering business generally and not merely the particular business acquired.

The objects clause usually includes the following words: 'To do all such other things as are incidental or conducive to the attainment of the above objects, or any of them.' Such words have been considered of importance [*Simpson* v. *Westminster Palace Hotel* (1860), 8 H.L.C. 712; *Johns* v. *Balfour* (1889), 1 Meg. 191; *Deuchar* v. *Gas Light & Coke Co.* (1925), 41 T.L.R. 563]. Generally speaking, however, they are used to exclude all doubt as to whether a company has power to do such things, and are not 'meant to authorise a company to do any other things than those which have been previously declared to be the "objects" for which the company is established, but to prevent failure in accomplishing those objects by reason of any merely verbal or accidental error or uncertainty in the expressions applicable to those objects' [per Bacon V.C., *London Financial Association* v. *Kelk* (1884), 26 Ch. D. 107, at p. 138]. In *Evans* v. *Brunner, Mond & Co.* [(1921), 1 Ch. 359] these words were held to justify a grant out of the funds of a chemical manufacturing company to universities and other scientific institutions, for the furtherance of scientific education and research.

Although, as has been said above, it is wiser to state fully the objects of the company, and to leave as little as possible to implication, a company has undoubtedly an implied power to do anything that may be reasonably necessary to attain its stated objects. In other words, a commercial corporation has such powers as are expressly or impliedly warranted by its constitution [*Kingsbury Collieries* (1907), 2 Ch. 259]. What may be 'reasonably necessary' depends on the particular objects of the company, *e.g.* the directors of an ordinary trading company have an implied power to borrow money for the purposes of the business of the company [*General Auction Co.* v. *Smith* (1891), 3 Ch. 432]. A company may be impliedly authorised to grant pensions or gratuities to employees retiring from its service or to their dependents if it can be shown that it is for the benefit of the company's business so to do [*Hutton* v. *West Cork Ry. Co.* (1883), 23 Ch. D. 654; *Henderson* v. *Bank of Australasia* (1888), 40 Ch. D. 170]; but if the company has ceased its business, *e.g.* if it is being wound up, such gratuities may well be *ultra vires*, since the company no longer has a commercial interest to secure by making gifts to its employees [*Hutton* v. *West Cork Ry. Co.* (*supra*)].

The limitation of liability clause merely states that the liability of members is limited and is the same in all limited companies.

The share capital is dealt with in chapter V, together with the various methods by which the capital clause can be altered.

The memorandum of association is alterable only in the mode and to the extent for which express provision is made by the Act. Several alterations are, however, permitted by the Act. Section 23 of the Act provides, moreover, that any condition contained in a company's memorandum which could lawfully have been contained in the articles of association instead of in the memorandum may, subject to certain conditions stated in the section, be altered by special resolution. This section, however, does not apply where the memorandum itself provides for or prohibits the alteration of these conditions, and the section does not authorise any variation or abrogation of the special rights of any class of members. It should further be noted that s. 210 of the Act gives the court wide powers to alter a company's memorandum in the case of oppression of minorities. *Alterations to Memorandum.*

A company may change its name by passing a special resolution, and obtaining the written approval of the Board of Trade, whereupon the new name is substituted in the register at Bush House for the old name and an altered certificate of incorporation is issued* (s. 18). This approval will not usually be granted unless satisfactory reasons for the change exist. It is therefore desirable to submit the proposed name to the Board of Trade before passing the special resolution. The change of name does not in any way affect any rights or obligations of the company, or render defective any legal proceedings by or against the company. *(a)* **Name.**

The objects of the company may by the procedure stated below be altered so far as required to enable the company: *(b)* **Objects.**

 (a) to carry on its business more economically or more efficiently; or

 (b) to attain its main purpose by new or improved means; or

* The change of name is not complete until this has been done [*Shackleford, Ford & Co.* v. *Dangerfield* (1868), L.R. 3 C.P. 407].

(c) to enlarge or change the local area of its operations; or

(d) to carry on some business which, in existing circumstances, may conveniently or advantageously be combined with the business of the company; or

(e) to restrict or abandon any of the objects specified in the memorandum; or

(f) to sell or dispose of the whole or any part of the undertaking of the company; or

(g) to amalgamate with any other company or body of persons.

The alteration contemplated by (a) is one which will leave the business of the company substantially what it was before [*Cyclists' Touring Club* (1907), 1 Ch. 269].

In the case of (d), the new business may be wholly different from the existing business, provided it be not destructive of or inconsistent with it; and the question whether the new business can be conveniently and advantageously combined with the existing business is one for the decision of the company's shareholders and managers [*Parent Tyre Co.* (1923), 2 Ch. 222].

The procedure for altering the objects, which has been changed by the Companies Act, 1948 (s. 5), is as follows. A special resolution is passed, notice of which has to be served not only on members but also on debenture holders entitled to object, *i.e.* holders of debentures secured by floating charge and either issued before 1st December, 1947, or belonging to a series some of which were issued before that date. A form of Notice of Application is found in Appendix F, Form 60. An application to the court can then be made by either (a) the holders of at least 15 per cent. in nominal value of the company's issued share capital or any class of it (or, if there is no share capital, 15 per cent. of the members); or (b) the holders of at least 15 per cent. of debentures issued as stated above. A member or debenture holder who has consented to or voted in favour of the special resolution cannot, however, apply to the court. If no application to the court is made within 21 days the special resolution is effective to alter the objects. A print of the altered memorandum must be sent to the Registrar within 15 days after the end of the 21-day period. This print must be certified by a director or secretary to be a true copy of the memorandum as amended. If an application to the court is made, notice of it must be given to the Registrar forthwith by the company, and an office copy of the court's order, with a print of the altered memorandum if the alteration is confirmed, must be sent to the Registrar within 15 days of the order [s. 5 (7)]. The court, on the application, may confirm the alteration wholly or in part, and may impose conditions or make arrangements for the purchase of the interests of dissentient members [s. 5 (4)].

If the company has a Board of Trade licence to omit the word 'Limited' from its name, the notice to members of the proposed special resolution must be sent also to the Board of Trade [s. 5 (6)].

CHAPTER IV

ARTICLES OF ASSOCIATION

WITH the memorandum, there may, in the case of a company limited by shares, and there must, in the case of a company limited by guarantee or unlimited, be registered articles of association, signed by the subscribers and prescribing regulations for the company (s. 6). The articles of a company limited by guarantee must state the number of members with which the company proposes to be registered. The articles of an unlimited company must state the number of members and also, if the company has a share capital, the amount of capital with which the company proposes to be registered (s. 7).

Table A.
In the case of a company limited by shares, registered on or after 1st July, 1948, if no articles are registered, the regulations contained in Table A, in the First Schedule to the Companies Act, 1948, are, so far as they are applicable, the regulations of the company. Many existing companies have as articles an earlier version of Table A.

Table A is a model set of articles, which can be adopted, modified or rejected, as the company or its promoters may please. It has been held that, the original Table A being part of the Companies Act, 1862, placed there by the legislature, no transaction which conforms to its provisions can be *ultra vires* in the sense of illegal [*Lock* v. *Queensland Mortgage Co.* (1896), A.C. 461]. The same principle must apply to the subsequent versions of Table A, including the present Table A. The regulations contained in Table A (as well as any other articles) can be altered by a special resolution passed by the company (s. 10). Table A may be altered by the Board of Trade from time to time, but any alterations so made will not affect any company registered before the date of such alteration [s. 454 (2)].

Table A, 1948, is divided into two parts. Part I contains a model set of articles for a public company. Part II incorporates most of Part I, but adds those articles which are necessary and advisable for private companies generally. Table A, however, does not suit the requirements of all companies. Large companies continue to have special articles of their own, and exclude Table A entirely; small companies may adopt Table A with or without modification; but generally speaking it is more convenient for a company to have articles of its own, and the additional expense is small. Except in very simple cases, hybrid articles, *i.e.* Table A with modifications, are apt to be unsatisfactory. It is inconvenient to have to refer to two separate documents; and there is a risk of ambiguity. Table A is designed to stand as a whole and, if parts of it are cut out, it may well happen that other parts do not work as was intended. Whereas, if not enough of Table A is cut out, it may be found that some new article introduced conflicts with an article of Table A which has been retained.

It may be found useful to notice some of the chief points **Contents of** which require special attention in preparing the articles of **Articles.** association.

The articles should provide for the purchase by the company of the business it is formed to acquire, whether by entering into an agreement already prepared but not executed, or by adopting an agreement already made between the vendors and certain persons as trustees for the proposed company. If any of the vendors are also directors, it is usual and advisable to insert a provision for their protection; but the protection will not be effective unless it covers the facts of the particular case, and the extent of the protection is open to some doubt [*Omnium Electric Palaces* v. *Baines* (1914), 1 Ch. 332, per Sargeant J. at p. 347].

Provision should be made for the payment of commissions for underwriting.

Alteration of share capital in the various ways permitted by the Act should be authorised (see chapter V). A limit should as a rule be placed on the borrowing powers of the company, *e.g.* that the amount borrowed must not exceed the amount of the issued share capital, except with the sanction of a general meeting. If the company requires a quotation on the Stock Exchange its borrowing powers must be so limited that the total amount owing by the company and its subsidiaries (exclusive of inter-company borrowings) shall not exceed a reasonable amount, except with the consent of the company in general meeting. The Stock Exchange preserves a discretion as to what constitutes a reasonable amount in each case, but it is unlikely to be greater than twice the issued share capital of the parent company.

The length of notice required for a general meeting, the quorum, and the conditions under which a poll may be demanded, should be specified; and in framing these articles the provisions of s. 133 (annual and other general meetings), s. 141 (special resolutions), and s. 142 (resolutions requiring special notice, *e.g.* a resolution under s. 184 to remove a director) must be borne in mind (see p. 131). The voting powers of members must be carefully considered; if particular persons are to have control of the company they must be ensured a majority of votes. Provision should be made as to voting by proxy (see chapter XII).

It is convenient to provide for class meetings of share-holders, giving power for a special majority of a class to bind the class, so that variations may, if necessary, be made in the respective rights of the different classes. If these rights have been defined in the memorandum of association, the memorandum should contain a power to modify the rights in manner provided by the articles.

Full provisions as to the number, appointment, qualification, remuneration, disqualification, retirement, and removal of directors should be made, and, if necessary, regulations as to the appointment, etc., of one or more managing directors, and of alternate directors. It is sometimes desirable to make provision for the directors to appoint committees composed not only of members of the board, but of others, such as senior employees or technical experts, because of their special knowledge. Where a director is to be appointed by a general meeting, it should be provided that due notice of intention to propose any candidate other than one recommended by the board must be given to the company. The powers of the directors should be specified, and, in most cases, ample powers of delegation given. Proceedings at board meetings may be fully regulated. An article providing that a resolution signed by all the directors in the United Kingdom is valid without an actual meeting is often convenient in the case of a small company (cf. Table A, clause 106).

It is usual to insert a provision empowering a director to contract with the company, but any such provision must be subject to the restriction that he must declare his interest (s. 199), and is usually subject to the further restriction that he may not vote in respect of such contract. The latter restriction would in any event be implied, and accordingly a director cannot vote on a contract in which he is interested unless expressly authorised by the articles to do so. With the growth of subsidiary companies, particularly when the number of directors is small, difficulties often arise in obtaining an independent quorum to sanction contracts with such subsidiaries, unless all directors are permitted to vote. In such cases interested directors should be allowed to vote, but, in general, only when their interest consists in being a director or a shareholder in the other company. A director's indemnity clause against liabilities incurred in the conduct of the company's business, other than liabilities due to the director's wilful act or default, was often inserted and was effective [*City Equitable Fire Insurance Co. Ltd.* (1925), 1 Ch. 407]. Under s. 205 of the Act, however, the provisions of such a clause are made void except that (1) rights of indemnity in respect of anything done or omitted while such a provision was in force are unaffected, and (2) the company may under any such provision indemnify any officer or auditor against any liability incurred by him in the successful defence of any civil or criminal proceedings, or in connection with any successful application to the court under s. 448 for relief from liability for negligence, default or breach of trust or duty. A provision should, therefore, still be inserted limited to such indemnity as is authorised by the second exception mentioned above.

It is desirable to give the board power to form a reserve fund, subject to whatever special conditions may be advisable in each case. Where power is taken to create redeemable preference shares (s. 58), special provision should be made as to the capital redemption reserve fund referred to in that section.

Among the regulations as to payment of dividends, it should be provided that interim dividends may be paid, that no larger dividend may be declared than is recommended by the board, that no dividend shall bear interest against the company, and that dividends shall be calculated on the paid-up value of the shares.

Articles often contain many clauses which simply reproduce statute law; for example, a repetition of the statutory obligation regarding the balance sheet. Such clauses are strictly speaking unnecessary, being at best only a reminder. Where the whole of a particular subject is dealt with by statute, for example, the appointment of auditors, the modern tendency is not to reproduce the statute in the articles. Where, however, the subject is one dealt with mainly by the articles, it may well be an advantage to refer also in the articles to a statutory provision on the subject which has also to be observed.

For the Stock Exchange requirements as to articles of association, see Appendix D.

The provisions of the articles cannot extend the powers of **Nature of** the company. It is useless, for example, for an article **Articles.** defining the powers of directors to clothe them with a power which the company itself does not possess. Thus, to take a simple instance, if a company, which, not being a trading company, has no implied power to borrow money, has not taken in its memorandum a power to borrow, it is clear that an article giving the directors power to borrow will be wholly inoperative.

Neither can the articles deprive members of rights given to them by statute, and therefore a provision in the articles that, in case of a reconstruction, dissenting shareholders shall not have the rights given them by s. 287 is invalid [*Payne* v. *Cork Co.* (1900), 1 Ch. 308]. Similarly, where shareholders have in certain circumstances a statutory right to present a winding-up petition, an article purporting to deprive them of that right is invalid [*Peveril Gold Mines* (1898), 1 Ch. 122]. In the same way an article seeking to take away the right of shareholders to requisition a meeting, or to inspect the company's books, or to remove directors by ordinary resolution, would be wholly inoperative.

Legal Effect of Articles. The legal effect of articles of association, as a whole, requires to be clearly understood. Section 20 (1) of the Act provides that 'subject to the provisions of this Act, the memorandum and articles shall, when registered, bind the company and the members thereof to the same extent as if they respectively had been signed and sealed by each member and contained covenants on the part of each member to observe all the provisions of the memorandum and of the articles,' and this section as judicially interpreted is the chief source of information on the point. The questions which require to be considered may be stated as follows: (1) What is the effect as between the company and the members? (2) What is the effect as between the members themselves? (3) What is the effect as between the company and outsiders?

Company and its Members. (1) As between the company and its members, it is clear that the members are bound to the company, and a series of decisions has firmly established the proposition that the company is similarly bound to the members. It is to be observed that the relationship of the member to the company is more than a simple contractual relation. He is bound as though he had covenanted with the company under seal. The practical result is that the company can sue a member to enforce the obligations of the member to the company under the articles. Thus the company can sue a member for calls, or to enforce a lien, or for many other purposes. Similarly, a member can sue the company if the company acts in contravention of the articles, *e.g.* in forfeiting shares without complying strictly with the relevant terms of the articles. The rights, however, in respect of which a member can sue the company are merely those with which he is endowed as a member of the company. When, although a member, he acquires rights in another capacity, even as a director, other principles apply [see (3) below].

Members inter se. (2) As between the members themselves the position appears to be different. It is true that in *Wood* v. *Odessa Waterworks Company* (1889), 42 Ch. D. 636, at p. 642, Stirling, J., said that the articles of association of a company constitute a contract not merely between the shareholders and the company, but between each individual shareholder and every other. But the words of the section hardly bear the construction that each shareholder has contracted with every other shareholder, and Lord Herschell, in *Welton* v. *Saffery* (1897), A.C. 299, at p. 315, after stating the words of the section, went on to say: 'The articles thus become in effect a contract under seal by each member of the company and regulate his rights. They cannot, of course, diminish or affect any liability created by the express terms of the statute; but, as I have said, the statute does not purport to settle the rights of the members *inter se;* it leaves these to be determined by the articles (or the articles and memorandum together), which are the social contract regulating those rights. I think it was intended to permit perfect freedom in this respect. It is quite true that the articles constitute a contract between each member and the company, and that there is no contract in terms between the individual members of the company; but the articles do not any the less, in my opinion, regulate their rights *inter se.* Such rights can only be enforced by or against a member through the company, or through the liquidator representing the company; but I think that no member has, as between himself and another member, any right beyond that which the contract with the company gives.' The point, then, is that, there being no contract constituted by the articles between one member and another, although their mutual rights are regulated by the articles, one member cannot in general sue another in respect of a violation of those rights, but the company must do it for him.

(3) As between the company and outsiders the articles do not constitute any contract whatever. This seems to be true even in the case of a member in relationships with the company arising otherwise than purely through membership. It was long ago held that where the articles of a company provided that the preliminary expenses should be paid by the company, this gave the promoter no right whatever to recover them from the company [*Melhado* v. *Porto Alegre Railway Company* (1874), L.R. 9 C.P. 503]. The effect of the article was merely an agreement by the company with each individual shareholder that the company would pay the preliminary expenses; and if the company failed to do so there was no breach of contract with the promoter, but only with the shareholders, who were not damnified. Similarly, in *Eley* v. *Positive Life Assurance Company* (1876), 1 Ex. D. 88, there was an article providing that the plaintiff should be employed for life as solicitor to the company and should only be removable for misconduct. He acted for some time, and then the company discontinued the employment. It was held that he could not sue the company. Lord Cairns, in the Court of Appeal, stated the effect of the article as being that, the articles being an agreement *inter socios,* it amounted to an agreement between the parties to it to employ the plaintiff. This being an agreement to which the plaintiff was in no way a party, he had no right of action upon it. 'This article,' he says, 'is either a stipulation which is binding on the members or else a mandate to the directors;

Company and Outsiders.

in either case it is a matter between the directors and share-holders and not them and plaintiff.' Lord Cairns meant, apparently, that the contract was between the company and each individual member, and also between each individual member and each of his fellow members; but, in view of Lord Herschell's words in *Welton* v. *Saffery* (*supra*), it appears that the latter of these two elements must strictly be excluded. The principle of the decision is not, however, affected by the exclusion.

Appoint-ment under the Articles. The hardship of this decision is more apparent than real. If a man is appointed by the articles as secretary or solicitor of a company, there is, it is true, no binding contract by the company or the members to employ him as such. The prudent and the usual course is for a contract to be entered into between the company and the individual it is desired to employ, wholly apart from the articles, and then his position is clear. Even if no contract has in fact been entered into, and a person appointed by the articles has in fact been employed as, say, secretary, the view taken by the court is that, although the articles do not constitute a contract, it can be ascertained from them upon what terms he is serving. Or, to put the matter in another way, if the company and the secretary act as contemplated by the clause, the court will treat them as though they had entered into a contract in terms of the clause. There have been many cases in which this principle has been acted on, and in some of them the individual was a director, *e.g. ex parte Beckwith* (1898), 1 Ch. 324.

Articles of association are public documents, and a person dealing with a company will be deemed to know and understand the contents of the articles [*Griffith* v. *Paget* (1877), (No. 2) 6 Ch. D. 511 at p. 517]; but he is not bound to do more than make sure that the proposed dealing is not inconsistent with the company's regulations. 'If the directors have power and authority to bind the company but certain preliminaries are required to be gone through on the part of the company before that power can be duly exercised, then the person contracting with the directors is not bound to see that all these preliminaries have been observed. He is entitled to presume that the directors are acting lawfully in what they do' [per Selwyn, L.J. *Land Credit Co. of Ireland* (1869), 4 Ch. App. 460, at p. 469], provided he does not negligently disregard facts which put him on inquiry as to some irregularity [*Liggett* (*Liverpool*) v. *Barclays Bank* (1928), 1 K.B. 48]. If, however, the person is contracting, not with the directors as a board, but with an individual director, he will not be entitled to presume that authority has been conferred on the individual director unless that director has been held out as having authority, *e.g.* he was the managing director, and the contract was within the ordinary ambit of the powers of a managing director [*Houghton & Co.* v. *Nothard Lowe & .Wills* (1927), 1 K.B. 246 at p. 267; *British Thomson Houston* v. *Federated European Bank* (1932), 2 K.B. 176].

The interpretation of articles is a matter which involves **Interpreta-** the most careful attention. To discover the true meaning **tion.** of an article, it is frequently necessary to look, not only at the other articles of the same group, but also at the whole set. A striking instance of this is to be found in the case of *Mosely* v. *Koffyfontein Mines* (1910, 2 Ch. 382, and, on appeal, 1911, 1 Ch. 73), where the decision of the court of first instance as to the construction of an article was reversed by the Court of Appeal, on consideration, in connection with the article in question, of another article which does not appear to have been brought to the notice of the court below. See also *Adair* v. *Old Bushmills Distillery Co.* (1908), W.N. 24.

As to matters which the Act requires to be stated in the memorandum, when there is an inconsistency between the memorandum and the articles, the memorandum must prevail [*Wedgwood Coal and Iron Co., Anderson's Case* (1876), 7 Ch. D. 75, at p. 89]. As to matters which the Act does not require to be stated in the memorandum, if there is an ambiguity, the articles may be permitted to explain the memorandum [*Capital Fire Insurance Association* (1882), 21 Ch.D. 209, at p. 213].

Reference has been made above to the power of alteration **Alterations.** by a company of its articles. The power, which is of the widest description, is conferred by s. 10 of the Act, which provides that: (1) 'Subject to the provisions of this Act and to the conditions contained in its memorandum, a company may by special resolution alter or add to its articles'; and (2) 'Any alteration or addition so made in the articles shall, subject to the provisions of this Act, be as valid as if originally contained therein, and be subject in like manner to alteration by special resolution.'

The liability to alteration is a statutory incident annexed to the articles of a company, and a person who becomes a member of a company must be taken to know that the continued existence of any articles upon which he relies when taking up membership is dependent upon the will of the statutory majority required to effect an alteration. Accordingly no shareholder can have absolute control of a company unless he has secured the control of three-fourths of the voting power. Hence the provisions as to voting powers which sometimes find their way into the articles of companies, *e.g.* that the holders of certain shares shall have four votes for each share held by them, and the holders of the remaining shares one vote for each share. It was held as long ago as

1879 that a company cannot contract out of this power. In *Walker* v. *London Tramways Company* (1879), 12 Ch. D. 705, a particular article dealing with the reserve fund was, by its own provisions, declared to be unalterable, but the court held that the article was to that extent invalid.

As illustrating the extent of the power of alteration, reference may be made to *Andrews* v. *Gas Meter Company* (1897, 1 Ch. 361), where it was held that a company, having no authority under its memorandum or articles to create any preference between different classes of shares, may alter its articles so as to authorise the issue of preference shares by way of increase of capital; to *James Colmer* (1897, 1 Ch. 524), which shows that voting rights conferred by the articles can be altered without restriction on a reduction of capital; to *Allen* v. *Gold Reefs* (1900, 1 Ch. 656), where it was held that an alteration made *bona fide* in the interests of the company as a whole was valid, even though it retrospectively affected existing rights; to *Shuttleworth* v. *Cox Bros. & Co. (Maidenhead)* (1927, 2 K.B. 9) where it was held that it is for the company and not for the court to say whether an alteration is for the benefit of the company provided that it is not of such a character that no reasonable man could so regard it; and to *British Equitable Assurance Company* v. *Baily* (1906, A.C. 35), where a policy-holder in the participating branch of an assurance company having power to alter its by-laws, who had taken his policy on the faith of a prospectus which stated the practice of the company as to the distribution of profits, was held to be validly compelled, by an alteration in the by-laws, to submit to a distribution of profits on a reduced basis. None the less, a company cannot by altering its articles justify a breach of contract [*British Murac Syndicate* v. *Alperton Rubber Co.* (1915), 2 Ch. 186, see also *Southern Foundries* (1926) *Ltd.* v. *Shirlaw* (1940), A.C. 701].

It has been pointed out above that alterations of the articles purporting to enlarge the powers of a company, or to deprive the members of a statutory right, are invalid. There are two other limitations on the power of alteration of articles: (i) articles must not be altered so as to increase the liability of an existing member without his written consent (s. 22), and (ii) as any alteration of articles involves the binding of a minority by a majority, the power must be exercised *bona fide* for the benefit of the company as a whole, and no fraud on, or oppression of, the minority, or want of good faith on the part of the majority, will be permitted. A fictitious case, put by Lord Wrenbury,* well illustrates this. 'Say,' he says, 'that there are one thousand shares of £10 each ranking equally for dividend, a special resolution that shares 1 to 900 shall for the

---

* Buckley on the Companies Acts, 12th Edition, p. 37.

future have twice as much dividend as shares 901 to 1000 must be impossible as against shares 901 to 1000.' It is obvious that it is theoretically possible for the statutory majority of shareholders to pass such a resolution, but it is equally clear that any court would restrain the company from acting upon the resolution, inasmuch as it would result in grossly unfair and oppressive treatment of a helpless minority. Lord Wrenbury sums up the position as follows: 'Possibly the limitation on the power of altering the articles is that the alteration must not be such as to sacrifice the interests of the minority to those of a majority without any reasonable prospect of advantage to the company as a whole.' The above-mentioned resolution could not be passed *bona fide* for the benefit of the company as a whole. In *Brown* v. *British Abrasive Wheel Co.* (1919, 1 Ch. 290), a proposed alteration was restrained by the court as oppressive to the minority; in *Sidebottom* v. *Kershaw Leese & Co.* (1920, 1 Ch. 154) an alteration introducing the principle of compulsory transfer, in the case of a shareholder competing with the company, was held to be made *bona fide* and was permitted. In *Dafen Tinplate Co.* v. *Llanelly Steel Co.* (1920, 2 Ch. 124) an alteration introducing a general power to buy out any member, with one specified exception, at pleasure, was held invalid, as not being genuinely for the benefit of the company as a whole; but see *Shuttleworth* v. *Cox Bros. & Co.* (*Maidenhead*), *supra*.

A secretary should always make careful note of matters in which the articles of his company appear to require amendment; and the opportunity should be taken, when meetings of the company are required for other purposes, to improve the articles and bring them up to date.

A company is bound, under penalty, to send to any member, on his request, a copy of the memorandum and of the articles, if any, and a copy of any Act of Parliament which alters the memorandum, subject to payment in the case of a copy of the memorandum and articles of a sum not exceeding one shilling, and in the case of a copy of an Act of a sum not exceeding the published price thereof (s. 24). If the memorandum has been altered, the copy must be in accordance with the alteration (s. 25).

CHAPTER V

CAPITAL AND SHARES

As has been seen in chapter III, a clause (commonly the fifth) in the memorandum of association of a company limited by shares, must state 'the amount of share capital with which the company proposes to be registered, and the division thereof into shares of a fixed amount' [s. 2 (4)].

The amount of share capital with which a company is registered, or to which that amount is subsequently increased, is generally called the nominal capital, or the authorised capital, of the company. The phrases 'issued capital' and 'paid up capital' must be distinguished, since neither of these is necessarily identical in amount with the nominal capital, or one with the other. Thus a company may have a nominal share capital of £100,000, divided into 100,000 shares of £1 each. If 60,000 shares have been issued and 15s. per share has been paid on them, the issued share capital is £60,000 and the paid-up capital £45,000.

The capital clause, being one of the conditions of the memorandum, can only be altered in the mode and to the extent for which express provision is made in the Act (s. 4). The alterations so provided for are increase of capital, consolidation of shares, conversion into stock and reconversion into shares, subdivision of shares, cancellation of shares (s. 61), and reduction of capital (s. 66). Such alterations are effected by the company in general meeting; but in case of a reduction of capital the sanction of the court is also required. The capital can also be reorganised by a scheme of arrangement under s. 206.

Increase of Capital. A company may, if authorised by its articles, increase its share capital by the issue of new shares of such amount as it thinks expedient. Such increase need not be authorised by the memorandum nor is a power therein effective [*Dexine Co.* (1903), W.N. 82], but it must be authorised by the articles, and if the articles as originally framed do not sanction such increase, they must be altered by special resolution before it can be effected. The power must only be exercised by the company in general meeting [s. 61 (2)]. The articles may require a special or extraordinary resolution; otherwise an ordinary resolution is all that is necessary. A specimen form of resolution will be found in chapter XIV. Every copy of the memorandum of association issued after the date of the alteration must be altered accordingly.

Notice of any increase in the share capital beyond the registered share capital together with a printed copy of the resolution authorising the increase, must be sent to the Registrar within fifteen days from the date of the passing of the resolution by which such increase has been authorised (s. 63). The notice must include the prescribed particulars (see Form No. 10 in the Companies (Forms) Order, 1949) of the classes of shares affected by the increase and must be accompanied by a form of statement of increase of capital (see Appendix F, Forms 57 and 58). The appropriate fees must be paid on the additional capital (Twelfth Schedule attached to Companies Act, 1948), and *ad valorem* duty must be paid under the Stamp Act, 1891 (s. 112), and the amending Acts. (See Appendix A.)

Preference shares may be issued by the way of increase of capital unless forbidden by the memorandum [*Andrews* v. *Gas Meter Co.* (1897), 1 Ch. 361] and such preference shares may be made redeemable under s. 58 (see further p. 36).

The rights attached to the shares in the increased capital must not prejudice any rights unalterably attached by the memorandum to the different classes of shares into which the original capital of the company is divided [*Ashbury* v. *Watson* (1885), 30 Ch. D. 376]. The memoranda, however, of most modern companies give powers which permit modification of the rights attached to the shares in the initial capital with the sanction of class meetings.

A company may, if authorised by its articles, consolidate **Consolidation.** and divide all or any of its share capital into shares of larger amount than its existing shares. The power must be exercised by the company in general meeting [s. 61 (2)]. If the articles of the company do not authorise consolidation, a special resolution is necessary, but two resolutions, one to alter the articles and the other to authorise the consolidation, need not be passed; one will suffice [*Campbell's Case* (1873), 9 Ch. App. 1]. Notice of the consolidation must be given to the Registrar (s. 62) within one month (see Appendix F, Form 59). Consolidation of shares, followed by subdivision of the same shares, may be effected by one and the same resolution [*North Cheshire Brewery Co.* (1920), W.N. 149].

A company can only convert all or any of its paid-up **Conversion** shares into stock, and reconvert that stock into shares of any **into Stock** denomination, if it is authorised by its articles to do so. **and re-** Where the power is not so given, it is not necessary to have **conversion.** the articles varied before the resolution for the conversion is passed. A special resolution passed in the usual way will suffice [*Campbell's Case* (1873), *supra*]. The power to convert and reconvert must be exercised by the company in general meeting [s. 61 (2)], but there seems to be no reason why the articles of a company should not provide that the directors may, at their discretion, with the sanction of the company previously given in general meeting, convert unissued shares into stock as and when such shares are issued and fully paid. Notice of the conversion of shares into stock must be given to the Registrar, as must also notice of re-conversions (s. 62). After conversion and notice to the Registrar, all the provisions of the Act which are applicable to shares only shall cease to apply as to so much of the capital as is converted into stock; and the register, and the list of members to be forwarded to the Registrar, shall show the amount of stock held by each member instead of the number of shares [ss. 110 (1), 124 (1) (b)] (see Appendix F, Form 54). If the company's shares are quoted on the Stock Exchange it is advisable to ensure in advance that the company has complied with Stock Exchange requirements (see Appendix D). Throughout the Act, 'share' includes stock, except where a distinction between stock and share is expressed or implied (s. 455).

Stock. Stock differs from shares in this respect, 'that shares are not necessarily paid up.' 'Shares are not necessarily converted into stock as soon as they are paid up; they may exist either as paid up, or as not paid up shares. But as regards stock, that can only exist in the paid up state.' 'Shares in a company, as shares, cannot be bought in small fractions of any amount (*i.e.* less than the nominal value), but the consolidated stock of a company can be bought just in the same way as the stock of the public debt can be bought, split up into as many portions as you like, and subdivided into as small fractions as you please. . . . Independently of that, however, it possesses all the qualities of shares. It is, in fact, simply a set of shares put together in a bundle' [per Lord Hatherley, in *Morrice* v. *Aylmer* (1875), L.R. 7 H.L. 717, at pp. 724, 725].

Stock is ordinarily transferable in the same manner as shares, but sometimes a minimum amount of stock is fixed, *e.g.* so that dealings in fractions of £1 may not be allowed. Stock units, however, may usually be dealt in in units of any denomination, *e.g.* 1s., 2s. etc. Stockholders have the same rights as regards dividends and voting as shareholders. Preference and other rights in respect of shares are not affected by their conversion into stock. Warrants to bearer may be issued in respect of stock [*Pilkington* v. *United Railways of Havana* (1930), 2 Ch. 108] (see chapter X).

Stock cannot be issued direct; shares must first be issued and then, when fully paid, may be converted into stock. The direct issue of stock is, however, an irregularity which after the lapse of a long time may be waived [*Home and Foreign Investment Corporation* (1912), 1 Ch. 72].

Subdivision. The power of subdivision can be exercised only if authorised by the articles. It must be exercised by the company in general meeting [s. 61 (2)]. The rule in *Campbell's Case* applies also in the case of sub-division. Notice of the sub-division must be given to the Registrar (s. 62) (see Appendix F, Form 59). The shares of the company, or any of them, may be subdivided into shares of smaller amount, but the proportion between the amount paid and the amount, if any, unpaid on each subdivided share must be the same as in the case of the original shares.

The necessity of preserving, in the subdivided shares, the due proportion of unpaid liability existing in the original shares may, however, be avoided on a scheme of arrangement under s. 206 (see chapter XX) involving subdivision [*Vine* v. *General Rubber Trust* (1913), 108 L.T. 709, *Guardian Assurance Co.* (1917), 1 Ch. 431], or on a reduction of capital involving subdivision [*Doloswella Rubber Estates* (1917), 1 Ch. 213].

Cancellation. The power of cancellation of shares, which can be exercised only by the company in general meeting, and then only if authorised by the articles, applies only to shares which have not been taken or agreed to be taken. It is really a method of reducing the nominal capital without the sanction of the court; but only unissued shares can be cancelled. Notice of the cancellation must be given to the Registrar (s. 62).

In the case of any of the alterations in the memorandum dealt with above, copies of the memorandum issued afterwards must contain the alteration [s. 25 (1)].

Reorganisation. Under the 1929 Act any reorganisation of capital which involved an alteration of the memorandum of association could be carried into effect only by a scheme of arrangement under s. 153 of that Act. Section 23 of the 1948 Act provides facilities (within the limitations of the section, see p. 15) for the alteration of the memorandum. If these limitations are exceeded, a scheme of arrangement under s. 206 of the 1948 Act is still necessary.

Reduction. Reduction of capital is effected by the company, provided it is so authorised by its articles, passing a special resolution for the reduction, and then applying to the court by petition* for an order confirming the reduction (ss. 66, 67). The power to reduce may be exercised by a company in any way whatever [see *Poole* v. *National Bank of China* (1907), A.C. 229], although the Act particularises three ways, namely (*a*) by extinguishing or reducing the liability on any of its shares in respect of share capital not paid up; (*b*) either with or without extinguishing or reducing liability on any of its shares, by cancelling any paid-up capital which has been lost or is unrepresented by available assets; and (*c*) either with or without extinguishing or reducing liability on any of its

---

* See 1948, Statutory Instruments Nos. 1756 and 1880.

shares, by paying off any paid-up share capital which is in excess of the wants of the company (s. 66). In general it should be noted that the court has a wide power to refuse to confirm a reduction of capital [*Carruth* v. *I.C.I.* (1937), A.C. 707, 743, 766]. It is usually advisable to couple with the special resolution for the reduction of capital a resolution that the capital be increased to its former level, as no capital duty is payable on an increase of capital made simultaneously with an equivalent reduction.

If the original articles do not give the power they must first be altered in the usual way by special resolution, and the special resolution for reduction subsequently passed [*Patent Invert Sugar Co.* (1886), 31 Ch. D. 166]. A power to reduce contained only in the memorandum is ineffective [*Dexine Co.* (1903), W.N. 82]. The precise procedure to be adopted to effect a reduction depends upon whether or not the reduction involves either the diminution of liability in respect of unpaid capital or the return to shareholders of paid-up capital. If either of these is involved, creditors are clearly affected and may object [s. 67 (2)]; but, in the more common case where paid-up capital has been lost, or is unrepresented by available assets, creditors are not prejudiced, and in such cases, and indeed in any case other than the two specifically mentioned in s. 67 (2), can object only if the court so allows.

The petition is supported by affidavit evidence. An affidavit by the chairman of directors commonly sets out the history of the company, and the circumstances leading to the present position, and the secretary should depose to the due calling of the meetings of the company. Where the reduction is sought to be effected on the ground of capital lost or unrepresented by available assets, evidence of the loss should always be adduced [*Caldwell* v. *Caldwell* (1916), W.N. 70].

On the petition being presented a summons is issued for the directions of the court as to the procedure preliminary to the hearing of the petition. This procedure is governed by Order LIII B, Rules 10 and 11 of the Rules of the Supreme Court. The detailed consideration of this order is beyond the scope of this book; but it may be mentioned that if creditors are affected, the court will require a list of the company's creditors made out at a date fixed by the court, and this list will have to be verified by an affidavit which is usually sworn by the secretary. As the debts due to the creditors appearing in the list will have to be paid off or provided for before the reduction is confirmed unless such creditors consent to the reduction [see ss. 67 (2), 68], it is advisable to present the petition on a date at which the company's indebtedness is at the minimum.

On confirmation by the court of the reduction, a copy of

the order of the court, and an approved minute showing the amount of the reduced capital with its division into shares, must be produced to the Registrar for registration and the reduction takes effect only from the date of registration (s. 69). Copies of the memorandum issued after the registration must embody the minute (ss. 25, 69 (6)], and notice of the registration must be published as the court directs [s. 69 (3)].

If so ordered by the court a company must add the words 'and reduced' to its name for such period as the order may specify [s. 68 (1)]. The Act does not prescribe the events in which the court will direct the addition of the words 'and reduced,' but as a rule no direction is given. Section 68 (2) provides that the court may also require the company to publish the reasons for the reduction or such other information as the court may think expedient with a view to giving proper information to the public, and, if the court thinks fit, the causes which led to the reduction.

As already stated, the memorandum must state the amount **Shares.** of share capital and the division thereof into shares of a fixed amount. Section 73 of the Act provides that 'the shares or other interest of any member in a company shall be personal estate, transferable in manner provided by the articles of the company, and shall not be of the nature of real estate.' Under s. 74 'each share in a company having a share capital shall be distinguished by its appropriate number': provided that, if at any time all the issued shares in a company, or all the issued shares therein of a particular class, are fully paid up and rank *pari passu* for all purposes, none of those shares need thereafter have a distinguishing number (so long as it remains fully paid up and ranks *pari passu* for all purposes with all shares of the same class for the time being issued and fully paid up).

Prior to the coming into force of s. 69 of the Companies Act, 1947 (now s. 74 of the Companies Act, 1948), it was necessary for every share in the capital of a company to be distinguished by its appropriate number. The new section, however, which came into force on the 1st December, 1947, makes the numbering of shares unnecessary if all the issued shares in the company, or all the issued shares of a particular class, are fully paid up and rank *pari passu* for all purposes.

All shares issued before the 1st December, 1947, will of course have been given numbers in accordance with the statutory requirements existing before that date. If, however, shares are fully paid and rank *pari passu* with all other issued shares of the company or all other issued shares of the same class, they may now be 'de-numbered.' This will have the advantage of saving the work involved in entering the distinctive numbers on transfers, certificates, registers of members, etc.

The procedure for 'de-numbering' is a simple one. If, as is invariably the case, it is provided in the articles of association that the administration of the affairs of the company is delegated to the directors except where the Act or the articles of association require a resolution in general meeting, a resolution of the directors on the following lines will be effective:—

'RESOLVED that pursuant to s. 74 of the Companies Act, '1948, the distinguishing numbers at present attaching to 'the...............shares of.........................
'each in the company numbered............to..........
'inclusive be discarded and that henceforth the said shares 'do have no distinguishing numbers.'

The above is all that is required in the case of shares which are not quoted on the Stock Exchange, London. If, however, the shares are quoted, it must be remembered that the effect of 'de-numbering' them will automatically invalidate the existing quotation of the shares and, accordingly, it will be necessary for the company to apply through its brokers to the Share and Loan Department of the Stock Exchange for a quotation for the unnumbered shares in place of the existing quotation for numbered shares.

In practice, it is desirable for the company, through its brokers, to make the necessary arrangements with the Stock Exchange in advance of the resolution 'de-numbering' the shares so that there is no hiatus between the substitution of the new quotation for the existing quotation.

There would appear to be no necessity of calling in share certificates merely for the purpose of deleting the distinctive numbers, as it will be sufficient simply to omit the numbers from certificates subsequently issued. The distinctive numbers should, however, be deleted from the register of members as soon as the resolution referred to above has been passed, or on and from the date from which it becomes effective.

It must be remembered that, in accordance with the proviso of s. 74 of the Act, if unnumbered shares become partly-paid or no longer rank *pari passu* for all purposes with all shares of the same class for the time being issued and fully paid-up, distinctive numbers must be allocated to the shares forthwith. In the case of shares quoted on the Stock Exchange, London, an undertaking that this will be done is required before a quotation of 'de-numbered' shares is granted.

Shares, being personal property, pass on death to the executor or administrator of the deceased in trust for the legatees or next of kin.

They are choses in action, and are therefore not within the order or disposition clause of s. 38 of the Bankruptcy Act, 1914 [*Colonial Bank* v. *Whinney* (1886), 11 A.C. 426]. For a discussion as to the precise nature of a share, and the interest which its possession gives to the shareholder in a company, see *Borland's Trustee* v. *Steel Brothers* (1901, 1 Ch. 279).

Shares may be divided into different classes, and the rights Classes of of each class may be defined by the memorandum or articles, Shares. or, in the case of shares created on an increase of capital, by the resolution effecting the increase.

It is usual to find in the memorandum or, where the capital is not divided into two classes of shares by the memorandum, in the articles, a provision authorising the variation of the rights attached to any class of shares subject to the consent of a specified proportion of the holders of the issued shares of the class or to the sanction of a resolution passed at a separate meeting of the holders of shares of the class. Such a provision is effective, but under s. 72 the holders of not less in the aggregate than 15 per cent. of the issued shares of the class, being persons who did not consent to, or vote in favour of, the resolution for the variation, may apply to the court to have the variation cancelled, and, where any such application is made, the variation will not take effect unless and until it is confirmed by the court. An application under this section must be made within 21 days after the consent was given or the resolution passed. The court must confirm the variation unless it is satisfied that having regard to all the circumstances of the case, the variation would unfairly prejudice the shareholders of the class represented by the applicant, and there is no appeal from an order of the court under this section. A copy of any order of the court under this section must be forwarded by the company to the Registrar of Companies within 15 days after the making of the order. The expression 'variation' in this section includes 'abrogation.' It will be noticed that the onus of proof is on the dissentient minority.

Shares may be divided into any number of classes, *e.g.* preferred, ordinary, 'A' preference, 'B' preference, and so forth.

The preferential right is generally in respect of capital and of dividend, but the right may be of any kind, *e.g.* in respect of voting power. These rights are entirely separate, and the possession, *e.g.* of preferential rights as to dividend, gives no similar right in the distribution of capital [*Simpson* v. *Palace Theatre* (1893), 69 L.T. 70].

Prima facie, where a preferential dividend is provided for, it is cumulative [*Webb* v. *Earle* (1875), L.R. 20 Eq. 556]; *i.e.* a deficiency in one year can be paid out of the profits of a subsequent year before the ordinary shareholders receive anything; but, if it is provided by the memorandum that the holders of preference shares shall be entitled out of the net profits of each year to a preferential dividend at a certain rate, then such dividend is not cumulative [*Staples* v. *Eastman Photographic Materials Co.* (1896), 2 Ch. 303; see also *Adair* v. *Old Bushmills* (1908), W.N. 24].

Whether preference shareholders are entitled to arrears of dividend on a winding-up is a question of some difficulty. Each case must, however, be decided on its own merits [*Wood Skinner & Co.* (1944), Ch. 323; *F. de Jong & Co. Ltd.* (1946), Ch. 211].

Where capital is reduced, the presumption is that the reduction is to be borne as between classes of shareholders in the same way as loss of capital is borne on a winding-up, but the court can sanction any reduction it thinks fair.

The question sometimes arises whether preference shares are entitled, in the absence of express provision, to participate in the distribution of surplus assets after all capital paid up on them has been repaid. In the last analysis this will always be a matter of construction of the memorandum and articles of the company concerned. In the past there has, however, been a considerable conflict of authority as to the principles which should guide this construction. It is thought that this conflict of authority has now been settled by the decision of the House of Lords in *Scottish Insurance Corporation* v. *Wilson's and Clyde Coal Co. Ltd.* (1949), All E.R. 1068, overruling *William Metcalfe & Sons Ltd.* (1933), Ch. 142 (in which the said authorities are well reviewed). The decision of the House of Lords lays down the broad proposition that the articles which determine the rights of preference shareholders are exhaustive and that consequently, unless the articles otherwise provide, preference shareholders will not be entitled to participate in the distribution of surplus assets after the capital paid up on the preference shares has been repaid.

Preference shares are sometimes repayable at a premium on a winding up. Such premium is usually stated in the articles of association as a definite amount per share. An alternative method frequently used is to fix the premium by reference to the average price on the Stock Exchange, London, taken, for example, over the six months prior to the date of the resolution to wind up or the winding up order.

Redeemable Preference Shares. Section 58 of the Act provides that a company may, if so authorised by its articles, issue preference shares which are, or at the option of the company are, liable to be redeemed. This power is, however, subject to the following limitations: (1) only fully paid shares may be redeemed, (2) redemption may only be effected out of profits which would otherwise be available for dividend or out of the proceeds of a fresh issue of shares made for the purposes of the redemption, (3) if the redemption is effected out of profits, there shall be transferred out of profits which would otherwise have been available for dividend to a special 'capital redemption reserve fund' a sum equal to the nominal amount of the shares redeemed, (4) if the shares are redeemed at a premium, the premium must in any event be provided for out of the profits of the company or out of the company's share premium account before the shares are redeemed. Having regard to ss. (2), it would appear to be essential that the actual terms of redemption must be specified in the articles and that an article giving the directors power to fix the terms would be invalid.

Where under this section a company has redeemed or is about to redeem any preference shares, it may issue shares up to the nominal amount of the shares redeemed or to be redeemed as if such latter shares had never been issued, and no capital duty will be payable under the Stamp Act upon such new issue, provided that, where the new issue is made before the redemption of the old shares, the old shares are redeemed within one month after the issue of the new shares [s. 58 (4)].

The provisions of the Act as to reduction of capital apply to the capital redemption reserve fund save that, after new shares have been issued in place of redeemed shares under the above mentioned provision enabling such issue, the capital redemption reserve fund may then be applied in paying up unissued shares of the company to be issued to the members of the company as fully paid bonus shares. Under this section the redemption of preference shares by a company shall not be taken as reducing the amount of the company's authorised share capital.

Shares can only be issued at a discount under the provisions **Restrictions** of s. 57, but whether shares are, or are not, offered for public **as to Issue.** subscription, a commission may be paid subject to the conditions mentioned in s. 53 of the Act (see chapter IX, p. 106).

If shares are illegally issued at a discount, the allottee cannot get rescission when once his name has been registered if he knew that the shares were being issued at a discount and assented to his name being placed on the register for such shares; he has become a member of the company, and remains so with a liability to pay the amount unpaid on his shares [*Railway Time-Tables Publishing Co.*, ex parte *Sandys* (1889), 42 Ch. D. 98].

Shares may be issued at a premium without any special **Share** authority, but a sum equal to the aggregate amount or value **Premium** of the premiums on those shares must be transferred to the **Account.** 'share premium account' [s. 56 (1)]. Further, the provisions of the Act relating to the reduction of share capital apply as if the share premium account were paid-up capital of the company. Section 56 (2), however, expressly authorises the application of the share premium account: (*a*) in paying up unissued shares to be issued as fully-paid bonus shares; (*b*) in writing off preliminary expenses; (c) in writing off the expenses of or commission paid or discount allowed on any issue of shares or debentures, or (d) in providing the premium payable on redemption of debentures or redeemable preference shares.

A company may not purchase its own shares [*Trevor* v. *Whitworth* (1887), 12 A.C. 409]. A power in that behalf reserved by the articles would be void, and so would such a power in the memorandum (same case). If a company purchases its own shares, it reduces its capital in a manner not authorised by the Act.

Prohibition of financial assistance by company for purchase of its own shares. It is illegal under the Act of 1948 (s. 54) for a company to give, directly or indirectly, any financial assistance for the purpose of or in connection with a purchase or subscription made or to be made by any person of any shares in the company or, where the company is a subsidiary, in its holding company unless (i) lending money is part of the ordinary business of the company and the loan is made in the ordinary course of business, or (ii) the loan is made in the manner indicated in the section in connection with a profit-sharing scheme to enable the employees of the company to participate in its profits, or (iii) the loan is made to employees of the company, other than directors, to enable them to purchase fully-paid shares to be held by themselves in *bona fide* ownership.

Reserve Liability. By s. 60 of the Act a limited company may, by special resolution, determine that any portion of its share capital which has not been already called up shall not be capable of being called up except in the event and for the purposes of the company being wound up. The effect of this is that the capital referred to is only available in winding up, and cannot be mortgaged or charged in any way.

Membership. If the number of members of a company falls below the required minimum and it carries on business for more than six months while the number is so reduced, all its members are faced with unlimited liability if they know the facts (s. 31).

The general nature of shares and some of their characteristics having thus been briefly noticed, it becomes material to consider how membership of a company is constituted and who may be a member. Section 26 of the Act defines a member thus: '(1) The subscribers of the memorandum of a company shall be deemed to have agreed to become members of the company, and on its registration shall be entered as members in its register of members; (2) every other person who agrees to become a member of a company, and whose name is entered in its register of members, shall be a member of the company.'

As to subscribers, see chapter II. A director signing and delivering to the Registrar for registration an undertaking to take and pay for his qualification shares is in the same position as a subscriber [s. 181 (2)], and should be entered on the register of members directly the contract to take the shares is filed. No one (except a subscriber to the memorandum of association, who automatically becomes a member) can become a member until his name is entered on the register. The register, however, may be rectified on application to the court, if names are on it which ought not to be on it or if names are not on it which ought to be on it [s. 116].

The agreement to take shares is therefore the true test whether a person is, or can be compelled to accept registration as, a member of the company, with the consequent liabilities of membership. He may apply for shares either personally, or by agent; either in writing, or by word of mouth; he may contract to take shares, *e.g.* as a vendor or an underwriter; he may be estopped from denying the agreement, either by taking no steps to have his name removed from the register, or by his conduct in attending meetings and so forth, although he may have originally made no agreement to take shares; and he may become a shareholder by transfer.

A shareholder ceases to be a member (1) on death, although his estate still remains liable; (2) on transferring his shares to another person, though in this case he retains for one year a contingent liability in respect of shares not fully paid; (3) by a surrender or forfeiture of his shares. In the case of bankruptcy of a member, the shares vest in his trustee subject to a right of disclaimer: as to the effect of exercising this right see *Wise* v. *Lansdell* (1921), 1 Ch. 420.

Subject to the regulations of the company and to the provisions of the Exchange Control Act, 1947 (see chapter XXX), anybody may hold shares. Some companies, however, provide that only persons of a certain nationality, or other special classes of persons, shall be eligible as shareholders, and such provisions are valid. A corporation may hold shares if authorised to do so by its own memorandum, and perhaps even if not so authorised, *e.g.* where shares are taken in payment of a debt [*Lands Allotment Co.* (1894), 1 Ch. 616. As to infants, see chapter IX. Section 27 of the Act now provides that neither a subsidiary company nor its nominee shall be a member of its holding company, and any allotment or transfer of shares in a company to its subsidiary or nominee for its subsidiary is void. There are, however, two exceptions to this rule: (i) where the subsidiary is concerned as personal representative or trustee, unless the holding company or one of its subsidiaries is beneficially entitled under the trust save by way of security for the purposes of a transaction entered into by it in the ordinary course of a business which includes the lending of money; (ii) where a subsidiary at the date of the coming into force of the section is a member of its holding company; but unless it is a case falling within exception (i) it has no voting rights at any meetings of the company. A company

Who may hold Shares.

is not bound to accept a partnership as the holder of shares in the firm's name, and the transfer of shares in a firm's name is not accepted by the Stock Exchange as good delivery. But shares may be allotted to, and registered in the names of, two or more persons jointly, and the articles usually provide that the certificate shall be delivered to the person first named in the register.

Under the Bodies Corporate (Joint Tenancy) Act, 1899, s. 1, a body corporate is placed in the same position as an individual as regards joint tenancy. Articles of association usually provide that dividends are paid to the person first named in the register, and that any one of joint holders may give effectual receipts for such dividends. Upon the death of a joint holder resident in England, his interest passes in accordance with the doctrine of survivorship to the survivor or survivors. A proof of death, *e.g.* original death certificate or official copy, must be furnished to the company accompanied by the relative share certificate and the appropriate fee. Probate or letters of administration can be admitted as evidence of death. The share certificate is endorsed as follows:—

> Certificate of death of...................
> produced the......day of..........19..
>
> (Signed)............Secretary

and the name of the deceased joint holder is deleted from the list of names on the share certificate. The death certificate is marked by a rubber stamp with a note of the registration. Particulars of the death should be entered in the register of documents (or a suitable entry made in the register of probates) and such particulars posted to the share register account: these will include the obliteration of the name of the deceased joint holder. A similar amendment will be made in the index of members and to the addressograph plate. These amendments to the records should receive early attention in order to ensure, in the case of the death of the first-named joint holder in an account, that notices, dividend warrants, circulars, etc., are sent to the new first-named joint holder. The rule of survivorship in a joint holding does not apply in Scotland. When a joint holder dies abroad the company will require production of the original death certificate certified by a notary public or a British consul and accompanied where necessary by an English translation, the latter also being certified by the notary or consul. Under Table A, cl. 132, and most articles, notices directed to be given to the members may be given to the person named first in the register. That person usually also has the right of voting given to him by the articles (see Table A, cl. 63; see also chapter XII, p. 153). One joint holder cannot transfer shares registered in the names of all the joint holders [*Barton* v. *North Staffordshire Railway* (1888), 38 Ch. D. 458]. It is usually provided that the joint holders of a share shall be severally as well as jointly liable for the payment of all instalments and calls due in respect of such share; otherwise the liability is joint only.

Section 80 of the Act provides that every company shall, **Share** within two months after the allotment of any of its shares, **Certificates.** debentures or debenture stock and within two months after the date on which a transfer of any such shares, etc., is lodged with the company, complete and have ready for delivery the appropriate certificates unless the conditions of issue of the shares, debentures or debenture stock otherwise provide. 'A certificate under the common seal of the company specifying any shares held by any member shall be *prima facie* evidence of the title of the member to the shares' (s. 81). 'Share' includes stock (s. 455).

A share certificate under the common seal estops the company from denying that the person to whom a certificate is granted is the registered shareholder entitled to the specific shares included in the certificate [re *Bahia Railway* (1868), L.R. 3 Q.B. 584; *Balkis Company* v. *Tomkinson* (1893), A.C. 396], unless the seal has been affixed without the company's authority, so that the certificate is a forgery [*South London Greyhound Race-courses* v. *Wake* (1931), 1 Ch. 496]. It is not a negotiable instrument, nor a warranty of title on the part of the company issuing it [*Longman* v. *Bath Electric Tramways* (1905), 1 Ch. 646].

If the certificate describes the shares as fully paid, the company cannot, as against a *bona fide* holder without notice, deny that the shares are so paid up [*Burkinshaw* v. *Nicolls* (1878), 3 A.C. 1004; and see *Bloomenthal* v. *Ford* (1897), A.C. 156; *Coasters* (1911), 1 Ch. 86].

To raise a case of estoppel against the company, the holder of the shares must show that he acted on the certificate [*Dixon* v. *Kennaway* (1900), 1 Ch. 833]. If the company refuses to do something which, assuming the certificate to be correct, it ought to have done, it can be sued, and the measure of damages will be the value of the shares at the date of the breach of duty [*Ottos Kopje Mines* (1893), 1 Ch. 618].

In Appendix F will be found forms of share certificate (Forms 35, 36 and 37), a stock certificate (Form 38), a form of fractional certificate (Form 39) and a form of endorsement for fractional certificate (Form 40).

In companies whose shares are actively dealt in it frequently happens that two transfers are simultaneously presented to the board of directors, whereby shares are bought and almost immediately resold. In such a case certificates should be prepared for all transfers lodged for registration, and all of them should be signed and sealed. Certificates in respect of those shares which have been transferred should be marked on the front with the words 'shares transferred'; on the back, particulars of the shares actually transferred and the names of the transferees should be given. Certificates which have been rendered inoperative by the endorsements made thereon are thus presented to the board for signature and the transaction is recorded in the company's share register. This method is recommended because the company's records are thereby rendered complete, and also because most articles of association state that a transfer lodged for registration shall be accompanied by the relative share certificate; further, the regulations of the Stock Exchange, London, require that a certificate should bear the signature of one director and the secretary. This regulation may now be relaxed 'in cases where the directors, being so authorised by the articles (of association) have resolved to adopt some method of mechanical signature which is controlled by the auditors and bankers of the company.' In such cases, however, the prior consent of the Stock Exchange should always be obtained.

No charge is made for the original share certificate issued to a shareholder, and the Stock Exchange regulations forbid any charge, but if the certificate should be worn out or lost it is renewed usually on payment of a small charge. In general a company should insist on the execution of a statutory declaration verifying the loss, supported by a guarantee by a person of standing; but, if the account is a small one, a letter of indemnity should be sufficient. A suitable form of indemnity is given in Appendix F (Form 41). The certificate should be marked 'Duplicate' on its face in a distinguishing colour.

The important subject of the transfer and transmission of shares is dealt with in chapter VIII. Other incidents connected with shares are treated in chapter IX, and the capitalisation of profits in chapter XVIII.

CHAPTER VI

PROSPECTUS AND ALLOTMENT

A COMPANY which wishes to raise money by issuing shares *Commence-* or debentures to the public will issue a prospectus, which *ment of* must comply with various statutory requirements. A pros- *where Public* pectus is defined by s. 455 of the Act as 'any prospectus, *Issue is* notice, circular, advertisement, or other invitation, offering *made.* to the public for subscription or purchase any shares or debentures of a company.' The word is therefore not limited to the formal document ordinarily thought of as being a prospectus, but includes any document, however informal, which offers to the public shares or debentures of the company. In particular, a letter from a company offering shares or debentures to its existing shareholders is strictly a prospectus, if in all the circumstances it is likely to result in shares or debentures becoming available for subscription or purchase by persons other than those receiving the offer (s. 55); such, for example, would usually be the case where a large company offers shares on bonus terms to existing shareholders and gives to them a right to renounce their rights in favour of other persons, the rights being in such a form that they can be sold on the Stock Exchange. Such a letter, being a prospectus, has to comply with certain of the statutory requirements though it is exempt from the more onerous requirements. On the other hand, a letter offering shares to existing shareholders or to other particularly selected people, in circumstances which will not result in the public acquiring shares, is not an offer to the public and not therefore a prospectus.

Prospectuses can conveniently be regarded as falling into three classes, according to the statutory requirements with which they must comply:—

(*a*) prospectuses issued generally [*i.e.* issued to persons who are not existing members or debenture holders of the company (s. 455), and which are not within any statutory exemption]. A typical example would be a prospectus issued by a new company making a public issue of shares on its formation;

(*b*) prospectuses issued generally, but exempt from certain requirements because they are offering shares or debentures uniform with shares or debentures already quoted on a Stock Exchange [s. 38 (5) (*b*)];

(*c*) prospectuses not issued generally, *i.e.* prospectuses issued only to existing members or debenture holders of the company, whether or not the members or debenture holders will have a right of renunciation.

Prospectuses in the class (*a*) mentioned above must comply with the full statutory requirements and in particular with those of s. 38 and the Fourth Schedule to the Act, which prescribe many details that the prospectus must contain. Prospectuses in classes (*b*) and (*c*) do not have to comply with s. 38 or the Fourth Schedule and can therefore be very much shorter documents; but they must comply with certain requirements of other sections: they must be dated (s. 37) and filed with the Registrar (s. 41), together with any expert's consent (ss. 40 and 41 and see below), and they are subject to the provisions of s. 43 (civil liability for mis-statements), s. 44 (criminal liability for mis-statements) and s. 51 (procedure when application has been made for a stock exchange quotation). Prospectuses in class (*b*) mentioned above must also comply with s. 50 which prescribes the earliest date on which allotments may commence.

It should also be noted that under s. 39 a stock exchange can, in certain cases, grant exemption for particular issues from the full requirements of s. 38.

The full statutory requirements for the first class of prospectuses, those issued generally and enjoying no exemption, can now be considered, assuming as a typical example a company whose first active step after incorporation is to make a public issue of shares. Such a company before starting business must comply with ss. 37 to 47 and 109 of the Act, as follows:—

Prospectus.   1. A prospectus must be prepared containing the particulars required under s. 38 (1) and the Fourth Schedule to the Act. These statutory provisions are designed to ensure that the public is given sufficient information about the company and its business to enable a subscriber to judge fairly the merits of the offer. It is not proposed to repeat them here; they are lengthy, and a secretary concerned with a prospectus should refer to the Act. Moreover, a prospectus will not be prepared without obtaining legal advice. It will, however, be the duty of the secretary to supply the legal advisers with the necessary information and material. In doing so he should bear in mind the cardinal principle of preparing a prospectus, that, if there is any point likely to deter subscribers from taking up shares, it is probably a point which the prospectus should mention and full information upon it must be supplied to the legal advisers. More especially, if any person concerned is making a profit, however small or indirect, out of the issue, that is a matter which probably has to be disclosed.

The preparation of the prospectus requires great care, not only to ensure that it complies with s. 38, but also to see that the statements therein are accurate, as under s. 43, directors, promoters and any persons who authorise the issue of the prospectus, are liable, even in the absence of fraud, to compensate any subscriber for shares or debentures who is damaged by any untrue statement therein, unless he can establish one of the defences indicated in the section. Further, s. 44 of the Act provides that, where a prospectus contains any untrue statement, any person who authorised the issue of the prospectus shall be criminally liable, unless he proves either that the statement was immaterial or that he had reasonable grounds to believe and did, up to the time of issue of the prospectus, believe that the statement was true. For the purposes of s. 43 and s. 44 of the Act a statement included in a prospectus shall be deemed to be untrue if it is misleading in the form and context in which it is included; and a statement shall be deemed to be included in a prospectus if it is contained therein or in any report or memorandum appearing on the face thereof, or by reference incorporated therein or issued therewith (s. 46).

2. When a prospectus includes a statement by an expert, *i.e.* an engineer, valuer, accountant or other professional person, a written consent must be obtained from the expert to the issue of the prospectus with the statement included in the form and content in which it is included (s. 40). The object of this provision is no doubt to ensure that a statement by the expert is not made misleading by the content in which it is used.

3. The prospectus must be dated, the date being *prima facie* the date of publication (s. 37), and a copy of it, signed by every director or proposed director named therein, or by his agent authorised in writing, must be delivered for registration to the Registrar. It may then be issued. It must state on the face of it that a copy has been delivered for registration to the Registrar [s. 41 (2) (*a*)]. The prospectus must also have endorsed thereon or attached thereto (i) any expert's consent to its issue, (ii) where issued generally, particulars of contracts as required by the Fourth Schedule to the Act [s. 41 (1)], and must also specify, or refer to statements included in the prospectus which specify, any documents required by s. 41 to be endorsed on or attached to the copy so delivered [s. 41 (2) (*b*)].

4. No person must be named as a director, or proposed director in the prospectus (whether the prospectus is issued by or on behalf of a company already formed or in relation to an intended company), unless before the publication thereof he has, by himself or his agent authorised in writing, signed and delivered to the Registrar for filing (1) a consent to act and (2) an undertaking in writing to take from the company and pay for his qualification shares, if any. This undertaking

will not, however, be required if, before the publication of the prospectus, he has, by himself or his agent authorised in writing, signed the memorandum for a number of shares, not less than his qualification, or taken from the company and paid or agreed to pay for his qualification shares or made and delivered to the Registrar for registration a statutory declaration that a number of shares, not less than his qualification, are registered in his name [s. 181 (1)]. As to the restrictions placed on the circulation of prospectuses under the Control of Borrowing Order, 1947, see p. 429 *et seq.*

Minimum Subscription. 5. In order to ensure that a company shall not commence business unless it has adequate means for its intended operations, s. 47 of the Act requires that before any allotment is made of any share capital offered to the public for subscription there must have been subscribed:—

(*a*) the amount stated in the prospectus as the minimum amount which in the opinion of the directors must be raised by the issue of share capital to provide for

(i) the purchase price of any property purchased or to be purchased which is to be defrayed in whole or in part out of the proceeds of the issue;

(ii) any preliminary expenses or underwriting commission payable by the company;

(iii) the repayment of any moneys borrowed by the company in respect of any of the foregoing matters; and

(iv) working capital;

and (*b*) the sum payable on application for the amount so stated must have been paid to and received by the company. The amount so stated must be reckoned exclusively of any amount payable otherwise than in cash, and is referred to in the Act as the minimum subscription. Before 1929 a sum paid by cheque could not be treated as paid to and received by the company until the cheque had been cleared [*Mears* v. *Western Canada Co.* (1905), 2 Ch. 353], but under s. 47 a sum is to be deemed to have been paid to and received by the company if a cheque for that sum has been received by the company in good faith and the directors have no reason for suspecting that the cheque will not be paid. The amount payable on application in respect of each share must not be less than 5 per cent. of the nominal amount of the share.

6. The allotment having been made, every director must, unless he has already done so, pay to the company on each of the shares taken or contracted to be taken by him, and for

which he is liable to pay in cash, an amount equal to the amount per share payable by the public on application and allotment (s. 109).

7. A statutory declaration by the secretary or one of the directors in the prescribed form (see Companies (Forms) Order, 1949, Form 44] [see Appendix F, Form 11) must be filed with the Registrar (s. 109). This declaration vouches the following facts: (*a*) the amount offered for public subscription; (*b*) the amount of the minimum subscription; (*c*) the allotment of a number of shares not less than the minimum subscription; (*d*) the payment by every director of application and allotment money on each of the shares contracted to be taken by him; (*e*) that no money is or may be repayable to applicants for shares and debentures offered for public subscription by reason of any failure to apply for or obtain permission for the shares or debentures to be dealt in on any stock exchange.

Thereupon the Registrar is to issue his certificate entitling the company to commence business, the certificate being conclusive evidence that the company is so entitled [s. 109 (3)]. **Registrar's Certificate.** It is important to remember that contracts made by a company before the date on which it is entitled to commence business are provisional only, but become binding on that date [s. 109 (4)]. Consequently, if a company is wound up before it becomes entitled to commence business, it is not liable on any of its contracts [*Otto Electrical Manufacturing Co.* (1906), 2 Ch. 390]. Although the company, before obtaining a certificate entitling it to commence business, may not exercise its borrowing powers, it may nevertheless offer to the public debentures, simultaneously with the offer of shares, may receive application money on debentures, and may allot both shares and debentures [s. 109 (5)]. Section 109, however, has no application to private companies.

If a company does not issue a prospectus on or with reference to its formation, but desires to be in a position to allot shares, commence business and exercise its borrowing powers without making a public issue of shares, it must (unless it is a private company) comply with the following formalities:— **Commencement of Business, where no Public Issue is made.**

1. A statement in lieu of prospectus must be completed, and signed by every person named therein as a director or proposed director of the company, or by his agent authorised in writing, and filed with the Registrar. The form of the statement in lieu of prospectus, showing the particulars it must contain, is to be found in the Fifth Schedule to the Act [ss. 48 (1), 109 (2)] (Appendix F, Forms 5 and 6). The restrictions on naming a person as a director or proposed director in a prospectus imposed by s. 181 (1) (see above, p. 45) apply also to a statement in lieu of prospectus.

Statement in lieu of Prospectus.

The particulars required by s. 48 are to a great extent identical with those which a prospectus is required to contain by s. 38 and the Fourth Schedule of the Act; but the draftsman of a statement in lieu of prospectus must adhere to the form set forth in the Fifth Schedule. There is also the same civil and criminal liability for untrue statements [s. 48 (5), (6)].

2. Where a company does not issue a prospectus on or with reference to its formation, or where it has issued such a prospectus, but has not proceeded to allot any of the shares offered to the public for subscription, the statement in lieu must be filed before any allotment of shares or debentures can be made [s. 48 (1)], or the allotment may be void [*Jubilee Cotton Mills* (1924), A.C. 958]. If, however, the statement is filed but is incorrect, a subsequent allotment is not invalid [*Blair Open Hearth Furnace Co.* (1914), 1 Ch. 390].

3. Every director must, unless he has already done so, pay to the company on each of the shares taken or contracted to be taken by him, and for which he is liable to pay in cash, an amount equal to the amount per share payable on application and allotment on the shares payable in cash [s. 109 (2)].

4. A statutory declaration [Form 44A, Companies (Forms) Order, 1949] (Appendix F, Form 12) similar in most respects to that which must be filed by a company making a public issue, but with the necessary differences, must be filed with the Registrar, who will then issue his certificate entitling the company to commence business.

It should be noted that in the case of a company which does not invite public subscriptions, a minimum subscription is not a condition precedent to obtaining a certificate that the company is entitled to commence business.

In this case, also, contracts made by the company before the date at which it becomes entitled to commence business are provisional only, but become binding on that date.

Contracts referred to in a prospectus or statement in lieu of prospectus cannot be varied prior to the statutory meeting (s. 130) except subject to the approval of that meeting (s. 42).

Restrictions as to Allotment.

There are very stringent provisions in the Act as to first allotments. Section 47 (4) provides that, in the case of a company making an initial public issue of shares, if the minimum subscription has not been subscribed, and the application money received, within forty days from the first issue of the prospectus (*i.e. prima facie* the date of the prospectus) all the money subscribed is returnable to the subscribers without interest, and, if any of the money has not been returned within forty-eight days from the issue, the directors are jointly and severally liable to return it with interest at 5 per cent. from the forty-eighth day. A director, however, is not liable if he proves that the default was not due to any misconduct or negligence on his part. Any condition binding an applicant to waive compliance with this sub-section is void [s. 47 (5)]. Section 47 (4) applies only before allotment has taken place; after allotment, the only remedies available are under s. 49 [*Burton* v. *Bevan* (1908), 2 Ch. 240].

Section 47 does not apply to any allotment of shares subsequent to the first allotment of shares offered to the public [s. 47 (6)].

Section 49 (1) provides that an allotment made, in the case of a company making a public issue of shares without the minimum subscription being subscribed, or the necessary application money received, or, in the case of a company not issuing a prospectus or not having allotted any of the shares offered for public subscription, without a statement in lieu of prospectus being delivered to the Registrar, shall be voidable by the applicant at any time up to one month from the holding of the statutory meeting or, where the company is not required to hold a statutory meeting or the allotment is made after the statutory meeting, within one month from the date of allotment, notwithstanding that the company may be in liquidation. Notice of avoidance within the month, followed by prompt legal proceedings, is sufficient; the proceedings need not be actually commenced within the month [*National Motor Mail Coach* (1908), 2 Ch. 228].

By s. 49 (2) a director who knowingly contravenes, or permits or authorises an allotment in contravention of, any of the provisions of ss. 47 or 48 is liable to compensate both the company and the allottee for any loss, damages or costs sustained or incurred thereby. Proceedings to recover any such loss, damages or costs must be commenced within two years from the date of the allotment. It would appear that the amount of damages to which an allottee is entitled is the difference between the price paid for the shares and their real value at the time of allotment, such value being ascertained in the light of subsequent events. The loss to the company would appear to be the total nominal value of the shares if the applicant avoids the allotment.

The meaning of 'knowingly' should not be overlooked. It means 'with knowledge of the facts.' Ignorance or mistake of law cannot be admitted as an excuse for disobeying an Act of Parliament [*Twycross* v. *Grant* (1877), 2 C.P.D. 469]. It would seem, then, that when once it has been proved that a director or other official of a company knows the facts, *i.e.* that shares have been allotted in a particular manner, it must be assumed that he knows whether the particular manner adopted is the right method, and if it contravenes the law he will be liable.

Under s. 50 of the Act, in the case of a prospectus issued generally, no allotment may be made and no proceedings taken on applications until the beginning of the third day after the day on which the prospectus was first issued, or such later time as may be specified in the prospectus. Section 50 also provides that application for shares or debentures made pursuant to a prospectus issued generally shall not be revocable until after the expiration of the third day after the time of opening of the subscription lists (unless before then public notice withdrawing consent to the issue of the prospectus has been given under s. 43). Section 51 imposes another restriction on allotment. Where a prospectus (whether issued generally or not) states that application has been or will be made for permission for the shares or debentures to be dealt in on a stock exchange, any allotment is void (i) if the permission has not been applied for before the third day after the first issue of the prospectus, or (ii) if such permission has been refused before the expiration of three weeks from the date of the closing of the subscription lists, or such longer period (not exceeding six weeks) as may (within the said three weeks) be notified by the Stock Exchange. If, however, the Stock Exchange intimates within the specified period that the application will be given further consideration, this is not to be deemed a refusal of permission. Where permission has not been applied for or is refused, the company must forthwith repay all money received from the applicants. If it is not repaid within eight days, the directors are jointly and severally liable to repay the money with 5 per cent. interest from the eighth day, unless all or any of them can prove that default in repayment was not due to misconduct or negligence on their (or his) part. All money received as above must be kept in a separate account so long. as the company is liable to repay it. Further, any condition attempting to bind an applicant to waive compliance with s. 51 is void.*

This chapter has thus far dealt with first allotments. It now remains to deal with other provisions of the Act, which relate to all allotments.

In the case of a company making an offer of shares to the public, *i.e.* issuing a prospectus, or its equivalent, the provision that the amount payable on application is not to be less than 5 per cent. of the nominal amount of the share [s. 47 (3)] applies to subsequent public issues as well as to the first [s. 47 (6)]. The important requirements of s. 52 apply to all allotments by all public companies. Sub-sections (1) and (2) of that section run as follows:—

Return of Allotments.   (1) Whenever a company limited by shares or a company limited by guarantee and having a share capital makes any

---

* Saturdays, Sundays, and Bank Holidays are disregarded for the purpose of ss. 50 and 51.

allotment of its shares, the company shall within one month thereafter deliver to the Registrar for registration:—

(a) a return of the allotments, stating the number and nominal amount of the shares comprised in the allotment, the names, addresses, and descriptions of the allottees, and the amount (if any) paid or due and payable on each share (see Appendix F, Form 32); and

(b) in the case of shares allotted as fully or partly paid up otherwise than in cash, a contract in writing constituting the title of the allottee to the allotment, together with any contract of sale, or for services or other consideration in respect of which that allotment was made, such contracts being duly stamped; and a return stating the number and nominal amount of shares so allotted, the extent to which they are to be treated as paid up, and the consideration for which they have been allotted.

(2) Where such a contract as above mentioned is not reduced to writing, the company shall within one month after the allotment deliver to the Registrar for registration the prescribed particulars of the contract stamped with the same stamp duty as would have been payable if the contract had been reduced to writing, and those particulars shall be deemed to be an instrument within the meaning of the Stamp Act, 1891, and the Registrar may, as a condition of filing the particulars, require that the duty payable thereon be adjudicated under s. 12 of that Act.

It will be noticed that not only has the contract with the company under which the shares are allotted, fully or partly paid up, to be filed, but also the contract constituting the title of each allottee. As regards the statement of the consideration, it appears that it will suffice if it is stated generally (the nature of the consideration being disclosed) [*Frost & Co.* (1899), 2 Ch. 207].

It is not necessary to include in the return of allotments the names of the subscribers to the memorandum. It is, however, quite normal to include them, particularly where it is desired that they shall continue to hold their shares [*Tufnell's Case* (1885), 29 Ch. D. 421].

The court is enabled to grant relief in certain cases of omission to deliver to the Registrar any document required by this section to be delivered by extending the time for the delivery thereof. The relief may be granted in three cases, *i.e.* when the court is satisfied (1) that the omission to deliver was accidental, or (2) that it was due to inadvertence, or (3) that it is just and equitable to grant relief [s. 52 (3)]. Section 52 states that the return of allotments must be made within one month of allotment. When letters of allotment also include letters of renunciation, the Registrar as a matter of practice, in the case of large issues, is prepared to accept a return of allotment compiled at a date when the company is in a position to know the persons who have accepted an allotment with a view to becoming members of the company. Thus, where letters of renunciation are used, the person in favour of whom the shares are renounced should be shown in the return as the allottee. It is, however, pointed out that the indulgence of the Registrar in this matter should be treated with reserve.

It must be remembered that the omission to deliver the contract or particulars does not render the allottee liable to pay for the shares in cash, but only exposes the officers of the company to penalties. It is not necessary first to obtain an extension of time from the court in order to deliver the documents after the proper time, and therefore the documents should be delivered as soon as the omission is discovered. The object of an application to the court is to secure relief against the penalties.

It will be convenient here to note that under the Act the court is empowered to order the company and any officer thereof to make good any default in filing any return or other document with the Registrar within the time limited by the order and that any order so made will be without prejudice to any liability to penalties under any other section [s. 428]. The company or any of its officers responsible for the default may be ordered to bear the costs of the application to the court for such an order.

Application for Shares. A formal prospectus is always accompanied by appropriate application forms. A form of application requires to be carefully prepared, and may have attached to it a form of receipt for the application money, if it is desired to issue a receipt. It is more usual, especially in the case of large public issues, for the application forms to contain a footnote to the effect that no receipt will be issued for the application money; the receipt being provided in the allotment letter or letter of regret. No form of application can lawfully be issued unless accompanied by a prospectus complying with s. 38, except (1) in connection with a *bona fide* invitation to underwrite, (2) in relation to shares or debentures not offered to the public [s. 38 (3)], (3) having regard to s. 38 (5) (*a*) where the offer is made to existing shareholders or debenture holders of the company concerned, and (4) where the offer relates to shares or debentures which are identical with shares or debentures already issued and for the time being dealt in or quoted on a prescribed stock exchange [s. 38 (5) (*b*)]. The effect of s. 38 (3) is clearly to make the issue of an application form with the usual abridged prospectus published in the newspapers illegal; and a breach of the sub-section involves liability to a penalty of £500 for each breach.

As stated above, the prohibition does not apply to forms of application for private subscriptions, but great care will be necessary to make sure that the invitation cannot be construed as an invitation to the public. This sub-section, unlike the corresponding section applicable to oversea companies [s. 417 (3)], does not contain the words 'or an intended company,' but having regard to s. 38 (1) it will probably be construed as applying to forms of application for shares in an intended company and to forms of application for the purchase of shares as well as to forms of application to subscribe for shares. (See Appendix F, Forms 17, 19 and 23*b*.)

On receipt of the applications, the secretary will have a series of application and allotment sheets prepared by his staff. It need hardly be pointed out that there is need for the greatest accuracy in this work. A form of application and allotment sheet will be found in Appendix F (Form 26).

The board will meet in due course, and, if the minimum **Allotment.** subscription has been reached, and they have no reason for suspecting that the cheques for application money will not be paid, will proceed to allot. A form of resolution to allot will be found in chapter XIV.

The secretary's business will then be to dispatch the allotment letters and letters of regret. Under the rules of the Stock Exchange all letters of allotment must be posted simultaneously.

Form 18 is an example of an allotment letter with receipt for allotment money only attached. Form 19 is an example of an allotment letter with receipts attached both for allotment money and for payment in full, and Form 27 shows an allotment letter constituting an interim certificate, with receipt forms for all subsequent instalments attached.

In the absence of any provision to the contrary in the conditions of issue of any shares, debentures, or debenture stock, a company must within two months after allotment complete and have ready for delivery the certificates for shares or debenture stock, or the debentures, as the case may be (s. 80). It is sometimes more convenient to postpone the issue of certificates until the shares or stock are fully paid, and it is therefore desirable to make provision accordingly. Without any such provision, interim or provisional certificates must be issued, with receipt forms upon them which are signed by the company's bank, upon production of the certificate and payment of the instalments as they become due. Form 27 may be used for the purpose. A failure to comply with s. 80 exposes the officers of the company to pecuniary penalties and the court may limit a time within which the default must be made good [s. 80 (2) (3)].

Allottees who intend to retain their shares will hold their allotment letters until the date upon which they have to be surrendered in exchange for definitive share certificates. The date when the exchange is to be effected is usually stated on the allotment letter. Allottees who desire to renounce all the shares comprised in the allotment letter will be required to complete the form of renunciation and the party or parties in whose favour the shares are renounced must complete the registration application form. Both forms are incorporated in the letter of allotment (see Appendix F, Form 20). Renounced letters of allotment are negotiable in the market until they are finally accepted and delivered to the company for registration.

If the allotment is renounced, the original allottee will never appear on the register, the first name entered on the register in respect of the shares renounced being that of the party in whose favour they were renounced. One of the requirements of the Stock Exchange is an undertaking to split letters of allotment. Where an allottee wishes to sell part of the shares allotted to him before his allotment letter is due for surrender in exchange for a share certificate, the allottee or his broker will request that the letter be split, e.g. an allotment of 1,000 shares may have to be split into four allotments of 250 each. Split letters of allotment are not usually 're-split.' The request for splits should be made in writing to the company and it is usual for the company to charge 1s. for each split issued. On receipt of the request to split, the original letter of allotment (which should be lodged with the request) is cancelled, placed on a special file in the order as received, and the required number of new letters of allotment prepared in accordance with the instructions as to splitting. It is usual to insert the number of the original allotment letter on the new forms together with the additional distinguishing letters (a) (b) etc., and each form should be marked with the word 'SPLIT' by rubber stamp or letterpress. An entry on the original allotment sheet will be made recording the split against the original allotment, and particulars of the splits, with details of instalments paid, should be recorded on a split allotment sheet. When request to split is made personally to the company, a split ticket is issued by way of a receipt which is surrendered in exchange for the split letters of allotment when the latter are ready for delivery. The execution of the letter of renunciation and the signature of the form of acceptance has a similar effect to a transfer of the shares, but it is not in law a transfer of shares attracting *ad valorem* duty, but an assignment of the right of the original allottee to be registered in respect of the shares. [*Pool Shipping Co.* (1920), 1 Ch. 251; *Collins* v. *Associated Greyhound Racecourses* (1930), 1 Ch. 1.] A time limit must be fixed within which letters of renunciation must be lodged or in default the original allottee will be entered in the register. As soon as that time has expired the secretary will have to inspect carefully all the forms that have been lodged. If the forms of renunciation and acceptance have been duly completed, he will enter the acceptor in the register instead of entering the original allottee; if a form is defective, he will have to enter the original allottee. The limit of time fixed by the Stock Exchange for letters of renunciation to be in force is six weeks and, for partly-paid shares, one month from date of the final call.

Upon receipt by the company of the renounced and accepted allotment letters for registration, details of the acceptors will be entered on the renunciation and split allotment lists, and the necessary cross entries made on the original allotment list. The allotment letters will then be marked 'Renunciation registered' and returned to the person by whom they were lodged for exchange for share certificates at the appropriate date. It is the registrar's duty to see that the declarations required to be made on Form D have been completed in accordance with the requirements of the Exchange Control Act, 1947. As soon as possible after the final date for renunciation of allotment letters, arrangements should be immediately put in hand for the register of members to be compiled from the allotment, renunciation and split lists, dividend mandates recorded and stencils or plates prepared for the addressing machines. Concurrently with this work, share or stock certificates, as the case may be, should be prepared in readiness to be exchanged on the due date against the surrender of allotment letters. All allotment letters should be cancelled upon receipt and filed in numerical order. Share or stock certificates must be completed and ready for delivery within two months of allotment, unless the conditions under which the shares were issued otherwise provide (s. 80).

The question of what is the longest period which can safely be limited within which the letters of renunciation must be lodged is one of considerable difficulty. It is usual to issue split allotments up to within a week before the final date fixed for the registration of renounced letters of allotment in order to allow sufficient time for the requisite registration application forms to be completed by the person(s) in whose name(s) the shares are to be registered. There is no statutory provision imposing any limit; but it is obvious that, in the case of shares offered for subscription before the statutory meeting has been held, the period should not be longer than will permit of the register being duly completed before the notice convening the statutory meeting is sent out. Unless this course is adopted, many of the subscribers would not receive the statutory report sent out for the statutory meeting. Again,

c

it is obviously undesirable in view of s. 124 that shares should be issued upon such terms that at the date of the annual return no one is entered on the register in respect thereof. No letters of renunciation should therefore be outstanding when the notice convening the annual meeting is sent out. It must also be borne in mind that, if letters of renunciation were allowed generally to be outstanding for long periods, the law would probably be altered in order to prevent evasion of the *ad valorem* duty payable on transfers. In these circumstances it is thought that as a rule the period allowed should not exceed one month and in any event should not be extended more than a few days after the date for payment of the final instalment on the shares. The period last mentioned will enable issues to be placed, which is the primary and justifiable object of the issue of letters of allotment with letters of renunciation attached.

Where a reconstruction is being carried out and it is desired to secure exemption from stamp duty under s. 55 of the Finance Act, 1927, letters of renunciation should not be used or the benefit of the exemption may be lost [*Tillotson* v. *I.R. Commissioners* (1933), I.K.B. 134].

'Rights' Issues. Companies desirous of raising fresh capital can, and do, offer to classes of members or to members generally, the right to acquire new shares in specified proportions. This type of share dealing is the reverse of the ordinary application and allotment method, as in this procedure the offer by the company is made by way of provisional letter of allotment and the signature on the form of acceptance by the member, or the person in whose favour he has renounced, completes the contract. Shares of the company so offered are sometimes issued at prices below those ruling on the Stock Exchange. Hence the member to whom the shares are offered, if he does not wish to take them up, can sell his 'rights' on the market. The buyer then applies for the shares in the place of the member. A circular letter containing the offer, fully explaining the circumstances and giving details of procedure, is usually issued by the company and is accompanied either by a letter of rights or a provisional allotment letter. (See Appendix F, Forms 21 and 23a.)

Decisions on Application. Inasmuch as agreement to become a member is often constituted by application and allotment, and agreement to become a member followed by entry on the register constitutes membership of a company (s. 26) with all its attendant rights and liabilities, it is important to appreciate the effect of a number of legal decisions on the subjects of application and allotment.

The following are among the chief points to be observed with regard to an application for shares.

It need not be in writing [*Levita's Case* (1867), 3 Ch. App. 36].

It may be withdrawn before acceptance but, subject to the provisions of s. 50 of the Act, it remains open until the letter of revocation is actually received [*Byrne* v. *Van Tienhoven* (1880), 5 C.P.D. 344]. The withdrawal need not be in writing, and may be communicated to the secretary or, in his absence, even to a clerk in charge [*Truman's Case* (1894), 3 Ch. 272]. The doing of some act inconsistent with the continuance of the offer, done to the knowledge of the company, may be an effective withdrawal [*Dickinson* v. *Dodds* (1876), 2 Ch. D. 463]. The application may be made by an agent [*Hannan's Empress Co.* (1896), 2 Ch. 643]; but unless the agent informs the company that he takes the shares as agent and not as principal he may be personally liable in respect of them [*Southampton Steamboat Company* (1864), 4 De G.J. & S. 200]. Moreover, if the allotment is made to the agent and he renounces in favour of an undisclosed principal, the principal may be unable to rescind on the ground of misrepresentation contained in the prospectus issued to the agent [*Collins* v. *Associated Greyhound Racecourses Limited* (1930), 1 Ch. 1]. Application in a fictitious name, followed by allotment, renders the applicant liable, and his real name may be entered on the register [*Hercules Insurance Co., Pugh & Sharman's Cases* (1872), L.R. 13 Eq. 566]. Application by a father in the name of his infant son renders the father liable [*Imperial Mercantile Association, Richardson's Case* (1875), L.R. 19 Eq. 588]. Application subject to a condition precedent will not give rise to a contract unless the condition is performed [*Aldborough Hotel Co.* (1869), 4 Ch. App. 184; where a builder applied on condition that he should have the building contract]. But if the condition is subsequent—in other words, if it can be construed as a separate agreement, collateral to the agreement to take shares, the applicant will be liable on the shares notwithstanding breach of the collateral agreement [*Richmond Hill Hotel Co., Elkington's Case* (1867), 2 Ch. App. 511].

Allotment 'is generally neither more nor less than the acceptance by the company of the offer to take shares' [per Chitty, J., *Nicol's Case* (1885), 29 Ch. D. 421, at p. 426]. **Decisions on Allotment.**

Below are some of the more important decisions on allotment.

An improperly constituted board of directors has no power to act for the company, and therefore an allotment by such a board will be invalid [*Homer District Gold Mines* (1889), 39 Ch. D. 546]. On the other hand, an allotment by an irregularly constituted board may be subsequently ratified by a regular board [*Portuguese Copper Mines, Badman's and Bosanquet's Cases* (1890), 45 Ch. D. 16]. Directors cannot delegate their power to allot [*Leeds Banking Co., Howard's Case* (1866), 1 Ch. App. 561], unless by the articles they are authorised to do so

[*Harris's Case* (1872), 7 Ch. App. 587]. The power of directors to allot is a fiduciary power, which must be exercised *bona fide* for the benefit of the company as a whole, and not for their own ends, *e.g.* to maintain their control, or to defeat the wishes of the majority of the shareholders [*Piercy* v. *S. Mills & Co.* (1920), 1 Ch. 77; see also *Gas Meter Co.* v. *Diaphragm, etc., Co.* (1925), 41 T.L.R. 342].

Allotment must be made within a reasonable time after application; otherwise the allottee may refuse to accept the shares [*Ramsgate Hotel* v. *Montefiore* (1866), 4 H. & C. 164]. It must be communicated, though the communication need not necessarily be in writing [*Gunn's Case* (1867), 3 Ch. App. 40; *Levita's Case* (1867), 3 Ch. App. 36]. Generally the contract is complete as soon as the letter of allotment is posted, even though it is never received [*Household Insurance Co.* v. *Grant* (1879), 4 Ex. D. 216]. Posting means putting the letter under the control of a postal official authorised to receive it [*London and Northern Bank*, ex parte *Jones* (1900), 1 Ch. 220]. To make a complete contract the allotment must correspond with the application; *e.g.* if A applies for 100 shares, and 50 only are allotted to him, he is not bound to take them, unless the application contained such words as 'or such less number as may be allotted to me' [ex parte *Roberts* (1852), 1 Drew, 204]. No fresh condition can be imposed by the allotment. If it is complicated by the addition of a new term or condition, there will be no contract [*Jackson* v. *Turquand* (1869), L.R. 4 H.L. 305].

Shares should never be allotted to an infant, for he can afterwards repudiate the contract, and obtain repayment of the money paid for them, and have his name removed from the register; but he cannot recover money already paid for the shares unless there has been a total failure of consideration, *i.e.* unless it can be shown that the shares could not have been sold [*Steinberg* v. *Scala* (*Leeds*) (1923), 2 Ch. 452, overruling *Hamilton* v. *Vaughan-Sherrin Electrical Co.* (1894), 3 Ch. 589]. But if he is registered and acts as holder of the shares after attaining his majority [*Lumsden's Case* (1868), 4 Ch. App. 31], or does not repudiate within a reasonable time [*Yeoland Consols* (1888), 58 L.T. 922], he will be liable. Knowingly to allot to an infant is a misfeasance [ex parte *Wilson* (1872), 8 Ch. App. 45].

CHAPTER VII

OFFERS FOR SALE AND KINDRED MATTERS

AN offer for sale is a different method of distributing shares Offers for sale under s. 45. or debentures to the public, under which a single person (or syndicate) agrees with the company to subscribe the whole issue and then proceeds to resell the shares or debentures to the public. The offer to the public is thus made by the single subscriber and not by the company. Section 45 of the Act applies to such transactions most of the statutory provisions applicable to prospectuses. Under that section, where a company allots or agrees to allot any shares in or debentures of a company with a view to all or any of such shares or debentures being offered for sale to the public, the document by which such offer for sale is made shall for all purposes be deemed to be a prospectus issued by the company. Accordingly s. 37 (as to dating), s. 38 (1) and the Fourth Schedule (as to particulars to be included in a prospectus), s. 38 (2) (as to the invalidity of a waiver clause), s. 42 (as to restrictions or alterations of terms of contracts mentioned in the prospectus), and s. 43 (as to the liability of directors, etc., for statements in a prospectus) apply to such an offer for sale.

In addition to the matters required by s. 38 to be included in a prospectus the offer for sale must state [s. 45 (3)] (i) the net amount received or to be received by the company in respect of the shares or debentures to which the offer relates, and (ii) the place and time at which the contract for the allotment of such shares or debentures may be inspected. Under s. 45 (2) the fact that the offer for sale of the shares or debentures is made within six months after the allotment or agreement to allot, or that at the date when the offer is made the whole consideration to be received by the company for the shares or debentures has not been so received, is *prima facie* evidence that the allotment or agreement to allot was made with a view to an offer for sale to the public. Of course, if the allotment is in fact made with a view to the shares or debentures being offered to the public, the section will apply to the offer, even though it is made more than six months after allotment and after the whole consideration has been received by the company. Under s. 45 (3) the copy of the offer for sale which is delivered to the Registrar for filing pursuant to s. 41 must be signed by the persons making the offer. Section 45 (4) contains special provisions as to the signature of the offer for sale where the offer is made by a company or firm. The copy of the offer for sale to be delivered for registration must in all cases also be signed by every director or proposed director of the company [s. 41 (1)].

It is not quite clear whether s. 38 (3), which prohibits the issue of application forms without a prospectus complying with s. 38, applies to application forms accompanying offers for sale, but the language of the sub-section appears wide enough to cover such forms of application. Forms of application and acceptance will be found in Appendix F, Forms 22 and 23.

Section 45 applies only to offers for sale of shares by a company as defined by s. 455, where the original allotment or agreement to allot was made with a view to an offer for sale to the public. It does not apply where the shares offered were not allotted or agreed to be allotted with a view to an offer for sale to the public. It would appear, however, that in such a case, if the offer is made to the public, it must be accompanied by a prospectus where the offer is issued with a form of application; for under s. 38 (3) it is unlawful to issue a form of application for shares unless the form is issued with a prospectus complying with s. 38.

The provisions of the Companies Act, 1929, s. 356, which restricted house-to-house canvassing and the issue of circulars, were repealed and extended by the Prevention of Fraud (Investments) Act, 1939. Most of this Act is concerned with the licensing of dealers in securities, but s. 13, which restricts the distribution of circulars relating to investments, has to be borne in mind by an ordinary company. This section and s. 12 are printed in Appendix O. With certain exceptions it is unlawful for a company to distribute any circular inviting persons to acquire, dispose of, subscribe for or underwrite securities. The exceptions include the issue of a prospectus which falls within the prospectus provisions of the Companies Act, and also the issue of circulars by a company to its creditors or employees or to holders of its own securities or to the creditors, employees or security-holders of its subsidiary, if the circulars relate to the securities of the company or its subsidiary. Whenever, therefore, a company proposes to distribute to persons other than its security-holders, employees or creditors, circulars which relate to transactions in securities, and for some reason the circular is not an ordinary prospectus, it is necessary to consider whether it may not fall within the prohibition of this Act.

CHAPTER VIII

TRANSFER AND TRANSMISSION OF SHARES

THE duties of a secretary in connection with the transfer and transmission of shares are among the most difficult and responsible within his province. There is very little statute law on the subject, but a great deal of case law, and a great deal of somewhat complicated practice. It is proposed to deal first with transfers and then with transmission, with special reference to companies under the Companies Act.

Register of Members.

Inasmuch, however, as a company's register of members plays an important part in connection with both transfer and transmission, it may be as well to clear the ground by a few words as to the register and the proper method of keeping it. The register of members is one of the books which a company under the Companies Act is required to keep, provision for that purpose being made by s. 110 of the Act.

The register of members, which may be kept in one or more books, must contain:

(*a*) the names and addresses of the members;

(*b*) a statement of the shares held by each member, distinguishing each share by its number, so long as the share has a number;

(*c*) a statement of the amount paid or agreed to be considered as paid on the shares of each member;

(*d*) the date at which each person was entered in the register as a member;

(*e*) the date at which any person ceased to be a member.

Where the company has converted any of its shares into stock and given notice thereof to the Registrar, the register must show the amount of stock held by each member instead of particulars (*b*) and (*c*) above.

In practice the register, to be of real value, must necessarily show a good deal more than the matters stated above. The transfer of part of a holding must be provided for and the resulting balance shown, and there should be references, both in the case of shares acquired by a member by transfer and in the case of shares transferred by him, to the transfer numbers. Some companies provide also for the numbers of the share certificates issued being shown in the register of members. A form of share register will be found in

Appendix F, Forms 85 and 86. A form of stock register will be found in Appendix F, Form 87. (For further particulars on the register of members see chapter IX, p. 110.)

Share Warrants. In the case of the issue of share warrants, the name of the holder must be struck out of the register, as if he had ceased to be a member, and there must be entered in the register (i) the fact of the issue of the warrant; (ii) a statement of the shares or stock included in the warrant, distinguishing each share by its number, so long as the share has a number; and (iii) the date of the issue of the warrant. Until the warrant is surrendered, these particulars are to be deemed to be the particulars required by the Act to be entered in the register. On the surrender of the warrant the date of the surrender must be entered [s. 112 (4)]. On surrendering the warrant for cancellation the bearer is entitled to be registered as a member in the ordinary way [s. 112 (2)]. (As to share warrants generally see chapter X.)

Joint Accounts. In the case of joint shareholdings, problems frequently arise to which the articles of association give no clear answer, and as each case must be decided on its merits, it is recognised that procedure cannot be uniform. The following are examples of practical points which have arisen in the past few years:

(i) Whether joint shareholders are entitled to have their holdings split into two or more accounts with a different name standing first in each case. Most articles provide that only the first named of joint shareholders is entitled to vote and receive notices, consequently the question is one of importance. It was held in *Burns* v. *Siemens etc. Works* (1919), 1 Ch. 225, that joint shareholdings could be thus split so that voting power could be made more effectively on a show of hands, and the court was empowered under s. 116 of the 1908 Act to order rectification of the company's register. It should also be noted that a transfer to nominees cannot be refused registration on the ground that such transfer would have the effect of increasing the shareholders' voting power, *e.g.* where the voting power decreases as the size of the shareholding increases [*Bell Bros.* (1891), 65 L.T. 245]. In the absence of such transfer, however, it is thought that a company is justified in refusing to split a shareholding.

(ii) Whether a transfer out of a joint account should be rejected if the names are set out in the transfer in an order different from that entered in the register. In a simple case, where there is only one joint shareholding, difference in order is immaterial and

should be disregarded. But where the joint shareholding is split and the names in the separate accounts
are in different orders, then the transfer instrument
must be returned for amendment. The same applies
to dividend mandates.

(iii) Whether a request should be accepted for communications to be sent to a joint holder other than
the first named. In such a case the company may
comply with a request by all the joint shareholders,
but cannot, of course, be compelled to go beyond the
provisions of its articles.

(iv) Whether a formal transfer is necessary for a change in
order of names in a joint shareholding. Normally no
formal transfer is needed and no stamp duty is payable.
A letter signed by all the joint shareholders should
suffice, although it is appreciated that practice
differs on this point. The old share certificate
should be withdrawn and a new one issued with the
order of the names altered to conform with the
register. A formal transfer (by deed if so required by
the articles) is of course necessary where two independent shareholders desire to amalgamate their
holdings.

(v) The question has been raised how far one joint
shareholder can effectively act alone on behalf of
himself and his fellow joint shareholders. It was held
in *Patentwood Keg Syndicate* v. *Pearse* (1906), W.N.
164, that a general meeting was not properly convened
since the requisition was signed by one only of two
joint shareholders. The general rule is that he can
act alone in so far as the articles so provide and not
otherwise. Articles usually provide that one joint
shareholder may vote and give receipts for dividends
on behalf of all.

(vi) Should a company limit the number of joint shareholders for any one holding? It is desirable that the
articles should limit the number of joint shareholders
to four, but in the absence of such a provision, the
names of all joint shareholders (however many)
must be registered.

(vii) Should a company accept a letter of request from
executors to be registered in their own right when
the order of their names in the letter of request
varies from that in the probate? It was decided in
T. H. Saunders & Co. (1908), 1 Ch. 415, that the
company must enter the names in the order desired
by the executors. If more than one account is
allowed in the same name, the shareholder concerned

sometimes desires that his separate account be separately designated, *e.g.* Jones No. 1 Account, Jones No. 2 Account, etc. It is not thought that such designation constitutes an infringement of s. 117 of the Act regarding trusts on the register, nor of s. 28 (1) (*b*) in the case where the separate accounts are nominee shareholdings, although refusal by the company to earmark such accounts is legitimate. Thus companies may, it is thought, safely accept such requests and perform this small additional service to members without involving themselves in an excessive increase in work. None the less it is desirable that companies when accepting such requests should make it clear that they reserve the right at all times to treat all earmarked accounts as one account if they should think fit.

Alterations in Register. As to alterations of names in the register in the case of the marriage of a female shareholder, the marriage certificate should be produced before the necessary alteration is made. If the shareholder refuses to produce the marriage certificate there is no reason why the holding should not remain in the maiden name. In this case, however, all future transfers must be made in the maiden name. A form of request is useful as giving a specimen of the new signature. In other cases of change of surname the deed-poll, or copy of the *London Gazette* containing the notification, should be produced. Any other documentary evidence should be verified by a statutory declaration. In all the above cases no new share certificate need be issued, but the existing certificate should be produced and the new names recorded, preferably on the back thereof. Where notification of change of address is sent by a member, acknowledgment should be sent to both the old and the new address to preclude the possibility of fraud. Further, it should be sent in a plain envelope not disclosing the identity of the sender, and this envelope should be stamped independently of the franking machine (if any).

Trusts. There is a prohibition against the entry of trusts on the register. 'No notice of any trust, expressed, implied, or constructive, shall be entered on the register, or be receivable by the registrar, in the case of companies registered in England' (s. 117). 'The object of the section,' says Lord Wrenbury, 'is (1) to relieve the company from taking notice of equitable interests in shares, and (2) to preclude persons claiming under equitable titles from converting the company into a trustee for them' (*Buckley on the Companies Act*, 12th edition, p. 299).

A company receiving notice of any lien or equitable interest should accordingly decline to recognise it. A suitable form of letter by the company, in reply to a notice of lien or equitable interest, is given in Appendix F (Form 106).

The registration of transfers may, however, be prevented by any person interested giving to the company a notice, in the prescribed form, requiring it to refrain from registering them. Such notice must be accompanied by an affidavit describing the nature of his interest. Payment of dividends may be restrained likewise by the same procedure. This procedure is in accordance with the Rules of the Supreme Court (see Order 46, r. 4), and its effect is to prevent the company from registering a transfer without giving the person claiming to be interested an opportunity of applying to the court to restrain the transfer. Upon the transfer being presented for registration, the company must notify the person who has given the notice, and unless that person proceeds to obtain within eight days an order of the court restraining the transfer, the company may proceed to register the transfer in spite of the notice. Forms of notice by the company to the person on whose behalf the notice and affidavit were lodged, and to the person actually lodging them, will be found in Appendix F (Forms 124 and 125). In the case of debenture stock or redeemable preference shares, where redemption or conversion is to be carried out and a notice in lieu of distringas has been lodged, such redemption or conversion operates as a transfer. Accordingly notice should be served on the party interested, and in the case of conversion he should be informed that the new stock will be treated as free from restraint unless a further notice in lieu of distringas is lodged. A form of notice is given in Appendix F (Form 125a).

Notice in lieu of Distringas.

Articles of association usually contain a provision which goes further than s. 117, and is to the effect that the company shall be entitled to treat the registered holder of a share as the absolute owner, and shall not be bound to recognise any equitable or other claim to, or interest in, such share on the part of any other person (cf. Table A, clause 7). Such an article will not, however, enable a company to disregard entirely all equitable interest in its shares; for notice of the interest in shares by a person, other than the registered holder, will affect the company in its capacity as a trader, although it does not affect it in its duty of keeping the register [*Mackereth* v. *Wigan Coal Co.* (1916), 2 Ch. 293].

It must be noted that, if there is a question whether a company is an exempt private company (see p. 369), the existence of equitable interests in the shares is very material, and cannot therefore be disregarded for this purpose.

The holder of an equitable interest in shares may secure the interference of the court on his behalf [*Binney* v. *Ince Hall Coal Co.* (1866), 35 L.J. Ch. 363], and he can restrain the company from allowing the shares to be transferred by taking proceedings under the Rules of the Supreme Court, Order 46, r. 4, if he so desire (see p. 65). Save as indicated in the preceding paragraphs, the company is not bound by any notice of equitable interests which it may receive, so that successive mortgagees will rank entirely according to priority in date of their respective charges [*Société Générale* v. *Walker* (1884), 11 A.C. 20]. If a company, having a lien over its shares for all debts due from the holder thereof, receives notice that another person holds the shares as security for a debt due, the company cannot claim priority for a debt which became due to the company from the holder after such notice has been received [*Bradford Banking Co.* v. *Briggs* (1886), 12 A.C. 29].

As between the registered shareholder and his *cestui que trust* in their relation to the company, the former is the person who is liable for all payments which have to be made in respect of the shares, and this liability is not limited to the amount of the trust estate [*Muir* v. *City of Glasgow Bank* (1879), 4 A.C. 337]. The beneficial holder is, however, bound to indemnify the registered holder, and at any rate where he is *sui juris* and entitled to the whole beneficial interest in the shares, his personal obligation is not confined to the extent of the trust property [*Hardoon* v. *Belilios* (1901), A.C. 118]. This right to an indemnity cannot be enforced while it is uncertain whether calls will be made [*Hughes-Hallett* v. *Indian Mammoth Mines* (1882), 22 Ch. D. 561], but can be enforced if there is evidence that calls will be made [*Hobbs* v. *Wayet* (1887), 36 Ch. D. 256].

Closing of Register of Members. Section 115 of the Act provides that a company may, on giving notice by advertisement in some newspaper circulating in the district in which the registered office of the company is situate, close the register of members for any time or times not exceeding in the whole 30 days in each year. The object of closing the register is to enable dividend lists to be prepared and to ascertain who are entitled to be present at a forthcoming annual general meeting; also, as during the period the register of members is closed, there is no right of inspection. It will be noted that this section is permissive and that, subject to the 30 days' limit, the articles of association must be complied with. It is not necessary or obligatory to close the books, and some companies never do so, while others only close them before the payment of the final dividend and the annual general meeting, merely announcing that interim dividends will be paid to those persons on the register at a certain date. Closing the 'transfer books' for preparation of dividend warrants, however, really serves no useful purpose, and the consequent holding over of transfers received during the closure is avoided, if, instead of closing the books, a final day is stated in the notice announcing the date up to and including which transfers will be received for the dividend. The work of registering transfers can then proceed as usual, after the number of the last transfer included for the dividend has been ascertained and duly noted. When the members' holdings, as shown by the register of members at the stated date, have been entered on the dividend sheets, the posting of transfers to the register of members can then proceed. The register of members should not in this connection be confused with the register of transfers, for the closing of which no advertisement is obligatory. Table A, clause 27, however, seems to cover both by stating that the registration of transfers may be suspended, etc.

Section III of the Act lays down that every company having **Index to** more than 50 members must, unless the register is in such **Register of** form as to constitute in itself an index, keep an index (which **Members.** may be in the form of a card index) of the names of its members. The index must enable the account of each member in the register to be readily found and, in the event of any alteration in the register of members, the company must, within 14 days thereafter, make any necessary alteration in the index.

It is often a matter of some difficulty to find a simple and reliable method of index to the register, and at the same time, especially in companies having an extensive register, a method whereby reference to the register itself is minimised by the recording of the various notes relative to any particular account in such index. Probably the most usual form is for the register to contain all the necessary particulars, including not only the address of the shareholder as originally registered, but also the various changes of his address from time to time, together with a note as to payment of dividend, and special instructions as to the sending of reports and statements, notes with regard to orders of court, notice in lieu of distringas, powers of attorney, etc., with a simple index of the name with the folio in the register of members.

This method is doubtless sufficient in a small company where the clerk handling the books readily acquires an intimate knowledge of the accounts, and can turn up any particular account without delay; but on a big register it is very cumbersome, and does not lend itself to ready handling when there is work in hand requiring a considerable staff or urgent completion. Loose-leaf registers which already are widely used by companies of any size, will probably be used by an increasing number of companies in the future in view of the requirements of ss. III and 124 of the Act, as thereby the register can be kept in absolute alphabetical order. To safeguard a loose-leaf register the sheets should be numbered serially and a record kept of the number of every sheet taken from stock for use in the register. The printers of the sheets would supply a certificate of the number of sheets in each supply order, and the auditors would check off from it the sheets used.

Another method is to have an index-book to the register of members containing such particulars of the proprietors as to minimise the necessity for reference to the register itself. A form of index to the register of members, showing the particulars it may contain, will be found in Appendix F (Form 88).

Card Index.   A very useful system is the card index which has been introduced by many companies, a form of which is also given (Appendix F, Form 89).

Under the provisions of s. 436 of the Act, it is permissible for a company to keep a register either by making entries in a bound book or by recording details in any other manner, so that a card index register of members could be maintained if desired in place of a bound book or loose-leaf binders. It should, however, be noted that it is provided under the Act that if any register is not kept by making entries in a bound book adequate precautions should be taken for guarding against falsification. When any default is made in complying with this regulation, the company and any officer of the company who is in default is liable to a fine not exceeding fifty pounds and is also liable to a default fine.

Although many large corporations now use a card index system instead of bound or loose-leaf registers, the card index system is generally supplementary to the register of members, and is maintained solely to facilitate easy reference and handling by the registration department.

It will be observed that the card comprises at a glance full particulars of the proprietor's holding in the several classes of shares or stock, together with his full name, original and altered addresses (if any), instructions with regard to dividends, and any other matters of a like nature, with a file number, if the filing system is numerical, where any correspondence relating to his account may be found, and the number of the folio where his account may be found on the register of members.

In the ordinary course the alteration to the card in regard to the proprietor's holding is not done in the same detail as in the register of members. Suppose, for example, that several transfers are dealt with on one date, while they are, of course, posted severally into the register, the card will show simply the date and the total value of the several transfers either into or out of the account as the case may be. It is useful to provide a third column under each heading, where the balance of the account may be entered after every operation.

Under the card index system dividend sheets may be spread over a larger staff than is possible when reference has to be made to the books for the purpose, while, as stated above, the old-time objection to the use of the card is met by the retention of the full particulars in the register of members. Most companies now use an addressing machine which greatly facilitates the work.

Other points of advantage in the card system are (a) the facility for keeping the index of names in strict alphabetical order, and (b) after the annual return has been made to Bush House, the 'dead' cards may be taken out and kept separately, thus starting each year with a clean index.

It is now proposed to deal with the actual transfer of shares. **Right of** There are five provisions of the Act dealing with transfers. **Transfer.** These are set out below:—

S. 73. The shares or other interest of any member in a company shall be personal estate, transferable in manner provided by the articles of the company, and shall not be of the nature of real estate.

S. 75. Notwithstanding anything in the articles of a company, it shall not be lawful for the company to register a transfer of shares in or debentures of the company unless a proper instrument of transfer has been delivered to the company: provided that nothing in this section shall prejudice any power of the company to register as shareholder or debenture holder any person to whom the right to any shares in or debentures of the company has been transmitted by operation of law.

S. 76. A transfer of the share or other interest of a deceased member of a company made by his personal representative shall, although the personal representative is not himself a member of the company, be as valid as if he had been such a member at the time of the execution of the instrument of transfer.

S. 77. On the application of the transferor of any share or interest in a company the company shall enter in its register of members the name of the transferee in the same manner and subject to the same conditions as if the application for the entry were made by the transferee.

S. 78 (1). If a company refuses to register a transfer of any shares or debentures, the company shall, within two months after the date on which the transfer was lodged with the company, send to the transferee notice of the refusal.

Subject to the requirement of s. 75, that there must be a proper instrument of transfer, shares may be transferred in manner provided by the articles of the company, and the right to transfer, unless restricted by the articles, is an absolute right [*Weston's Case* (1868), 4 Ch. App. 20; *Hafner*,

Olhausen v. *Powderley* (1943), I.R. 426, at p. 447 *et seq.*].
The mode of transfer and the restrictions on the right to
transfer may vary in different companies to almost any extent.
There are usually restrictions on the transfer of shares not
fully paid, but in the case of fully paid shares the Stock
Exchange regulations require that there shall be no restrictions if an official quotation, or permission to deal, is to be
obtained. (See Appendix D, p. 537.)

If there are no restrictions in the articles, a member may
transfer to anyone, even though the company be *in extremis*
and the transferee a man of no substance, so long as the
transfer is *bona fide* in the sense that the transferor retains
no interest in the shares, and whether such is the case is
a question of fact [*Mexican and South American Co., De
Pass's Case* (1859), 4 De G. & J. 544; *Discoverers' Finance
Corporation, Lindlar's Case* (1910), 1 Ch. 312]. If, however,
the articles contain a clause authorising the directors to refuse
registration, a transfer which directors have registered may
be set aside, if registration was obtained by the transferor
actively misrepresenting or passively concealing the truth;
and, whether or not the articles contain a clause authorising
the directors to refuse registration, a transferor cannot
escape liability where the opportunity for registration has
been obtained fraudulently, or in breach of some duty owed
to the company [*Discoverers' Finance Corporation, Lindlar's
Case* (1910), *supra*]. Where articles provide that shares
may not be transferred without the consent of the directors,
there is no obligation to obtain their consent before executing
transfers; and a director cannot, by wilfully refusing to
attend board meetings, prevent the registration of a transfer
[*Copal Varnish Co.* (1917), 2 Ch. 349].

The procedure on the transfer of shares, in its simplest
form, is for the seller to execute a transfer, and to hand it
with the relevant certificate to the purchaser, who, after
executing the transfer, properly stamped, lodges it with
the certificate at the company's office for registration.
The transfer, if in order, is then passed by the directors
and the purchaser's name entered on the register in place of the
seller's. The decision in *Birkett* v. *Cowper-Coles* (1919), 35
T.L.R. 298, to the effect that, on a sale of shares, the obligation
to prepare a transfer is, as a general rule, on the purchaser,
was based on a decision in 1843 dealing with the transfer of
shares in a railway company, and appears to be in conflict
with the recognised practice, which practice does not appear
to have been questioned by the courts in the case either
of sales effected personally or of sales effected through brokers
[*Skinner* v. *City of London Marine Insurance* (1885), 14 Q.B.D.
882, at p. 887; *London Founders' Association* v. *Clarke* (1888),
20 Q.B.D. 576].

Since, however, shares are generally bought and sold through brokers, the exigencies of business and the practice of the Stock Exchange have amplified the procedure. When a seller is only disposing of part of his holding, his broker, having effected a sale, presents the transfer with the relative certificate at the company's office, whereupon the secretary or other authorised person certifies on the transfer that the certificate has been lodged (see p. 72 *et seq.*). The transfer, so certificated, is handed by the seller's broker to the purchaser's broker, and it thus becomes good delivery under the rules of the Stock Exchange.

The form of transfer, which it is the duty of the seller's **Form of** broker to prepare, is often prescribed by the articles, and **Transfer.** in that case the directors may refuse to register a transfer not in such form. Where, however, a transfer is required to be 'in the usual common form' (and the Stock Exchange regulations for obtaining permission to deal require that the articles should provide for the common form being used), directors cannot refuse to register it because it omits immaterial particulars, *e.g.* the address of the transferor and the denoting number of the shares, if any, if both are known to the directors and there can be no ambiguity [*Letheby & Christopher* (1904), 1 Ch. 815]. The importance of uniformity in the form of transfers can hardly be over-estimated, and there is a common form which is generally used. This will be found in Appendix F (Form 92).

It has been suggested that an addition should be made to the common form of the words 'being of full age,' after the words 'and I, the said transferee,' in order to avoid the possibility of partly paid shares being registered in the name of a minor. Directors should not sanction a transfer to an infant, for he can repudiate the shares either before or on coming of age, and although, if the infant has not come of age at the commencement of a winding up, the transferor is *prima facie* liable in respect of the shares, the company may have precluded itself by laches from putting the transferor on the register. In view of the difficulties in the way of ascertaining in every case that the transferee is of full age, it is reasonable to assume that it is the case; if, however, there is reason to believe that he is not of full age, his name should not be entered on the register until his age has been ascertained. (See the note at conclusion of chapter IX.)

It is usual for the articles to provide that transfers shall be signed by both the transferor and the transferee; but even in the absence of such a provision, where the articles do not prescribe any particular form of transfer but it has been the practice to require the execution of both the transferor and the transferee, the directors may decline to register a transfer not so executed [*Marino's Case* (1867), 2 Ch. App. 596].

It should also be mentioned that the company may at its discretion waive the transferee's signature, but should never do so if the shares are not fully paid.

The articles may or may not require a transfer to be by deed. This variation is especially important in the case of blank transfers. Where a transfer is required to be by deed a transfer in blank is void at law and not operative as a deed. It will, however, confer on the transferee an equitable title and he may call for the execution of a deed, but the equitable title will be subject to any superior equity. Where a transfer without seal is sufficient, the addition of a seal does not render the instrument less effectual [*Ortigosa* v. *Brown, Janson & Co*. (1878), 47 L.J.Ch. 168]. Where a deed is necessary, the directors have no power to dispense with it [*Murray* v. *Bush* (1873), L.R. 6 H.L. 37].

Certification of Transfers. All companies ought to certificate transfers, for while there is no statutory obligation to certify, if may reasonably be argued that certification is part of the business and incidental to the act of registering transfers. Transfers may be certified although unstamped,* or undated, but not if the transferee's name is not stated. A transfer should be certificated although a call has been made which is not yet payable, but the call must be paid before the transfer is accepted for registration. If the seller is the transferee on a transfer which has not yet been registered, it is the usual practice not to certificate the transfer until after the lapse of a sufficient time to enable the transferor of the first transfer to communicate with the company if necessary, although this rule is usually relaxed if the seller is a stock jobber. (See Appendix F, Form 95.)

Although practice differs, it is recommended that transfers presented for certification should be complete, with the exception of the date, execution by the transferee and the requisite declaration on Form 'D' (Exchange Control Act, 1947) on behalf of the transferee, although in the latter case some indulgence is shown in regard to the full names and addresses of the transferees, since these are not always known. It is also advisable that the deed should be stamped, though

* A secretary so certifying is not enrolling, registering, or entering the transfer within the meaning of s. 17 of the Stamp Act, 1891; but a secretary should, of course, not register an unstamped transfer. Thus it will be right for a secretary to certify an unstamped transfer as it will in any case have to be stamped before it is registered. In the case, however, of a transfer which, though stamped, is insufficiently stamped, although the person lodging the transfer can insist on certification, the secretary will be right in returning the transfer. For if the transfer is not refused on certification it will have to be refused on registration, and no greater delay will ensue by returning it in the first place. On the other hand, if it is not returned on certification, the company runs the risk that on registration the insufficiency in the stamp duty may be overlooked.

the registering official will not render himself liable by certificating an unstamped transfer. See footnote on p. 72.

A rubber stamp is commonly used to certificate transfers, the signature of the secretary or registrar being added in a space left for the purpose. The certification should always be signed and not merely initialled. The date also should be inserted. The following form should be adopted:

Certificate for the within mentioned shares [or stock] has been lodged at the Company's office.

Date

For the   Company, Limited.

, *Secretary.*

(Address).

The following form is used in the case of certification by a stock exchange:—

Certificate for the within mentioned shares [or stock] sent to the Company's office by the   Stock Exchange.

, *Secretary.*

(Address).

When a transfer is presented for certification before the transferor has been registered, the words 'Transfer receipt No. . . . .' should be substituted for the word 'Certificate.' This transfer receipt should then be issued, but a balance receipt in favour of the immediate transferee should not be so issued until the transfer of shares into his name has been registered.

The address of the company should, for the convenience of stockbrokers and others, be included on the certification stamp.

The record of certificated transfers should be kept by endorsement on the back of the certificate or by means of a certification form that can be attached to the certificates. The certificate should immediately be cancelled and the cancelled certificates, on which will be endorsed the record of certification, should be preserved.

It will be found convenient, upon a transfer being presented for certification, to send a notice called a 'seller's notice' to the transferor at once instead of waiting until the transfer is lodged for registration. This method has the advantage of giving the earliest possible notification to the holder of the shares, and effects a greater saving of time and trouble both to the company and the transferor where there are many certifications against one certificate. The Share and Loan Department of the Stock Exchange requires companies to give an undertaking to notify a transferor as soon as a transfer out of his name has been certificated. A form of notice will be found in Appendix F (Form 95).

It is the practice of the Stock Exchange and provincial stock exchanges to certificate transfers of shares as well as of stock. In all cases the certificate is lodged with a stock exchange and a form filled up giving the necessary particulars. This form is sent by the stock exchange with the corresponding certificate to the company concerned by the same day's post. The practice of stock exchanges certifying transfers has become increasingly common in recent years, and is a convenience to stockbrokers, expecially in the provinces, or, in the case of the Stock Exchange, where the transfer office of the company is not in London or is at a distance from the stockbroker's office. On the other hand, obviously stock exchange authorities are not in a position to detect even a gross and clumsy forgery of a share certificate if such should be presented to them, and, to that extent, it may be argued that the practice is not such a safe one, from the public point of view, as when the company's own officials alone certify transfers. It is interesting to note that the 1948 Act, s. 79, makes no provision with regard to a false certification by a stock exchange.

Legal effect of Certification. The legal effect of certification by the company is laid down by s. 79 of the Act. The certification of transfers shall be taken as a representation by the company to any person acting on the facts of the certification that there have been produced to the company such documents as on the face of them show a *prima facie* title to the shares or debentures concerned in the transferor named in the instrument of transfer, but not as a representation that the transferor has any title to the shares or debentures [s. 79 (1)]. An instrument of transfer shall be deemed to be certificated if it bears the words 'Certificate lodged' or words to the like effect [s. 79 (3) (*a*)]. If a false certification is made by a company negligently, the company shall be under the same liability to a person acting on the faith of such certification as if it had been made fraudulently [s. 79 (2)]. Further, the certification shall be deemed to have been made by the company if (i) the person issuing the instrument is a person authorised to issue certificated instruments of transfer on the company's behalf and (ii) the certification is signed by a person authorised to certificate transfers on the company's behalf, or by any officer or servant either of the company or of a body corporate so authorised [s. 79 (3) (*b*)]. A certification is deemed to be signed by a person if (i) it purports to be authenticated by his signature or initials (whether handwritten or not) and (ii) it is not shown that the signature or initials was or were placed there neither by himself nor by any person authorised to use the signature or initials for the purpose of certificating transfers on the company's behalf [s. 79 (3) (*c*)]. The provisions of s. 76 appeared for the first time in the 1948 Act, and although it may be noted that s. 79 (1) almost adopts verbatim the words of Lindley, L.J., in *Bishop* v. *Balkis Co.* (1890), 25 Q.B.D. 512, at p. 519, it has the effect of overruling that case in that a company is now liable for a false certification made by the company negligently. The decisions in *George Whitechurch* v. *Cavanagh* (1902), A.C. 117, and in *Kleinwort Sons & Co.* v. *Associated Automatic Machine Corporation, Ltd.* (1934), 50 T.L.R. 244, are also overruled, as, if an officer or servant of the company has fraudulently certificated a transfer, the company is now bound even if that officer or servant is not authorised to sign certifications. It is therefore advisable for the registrar and one or two named clerks to be made 'authorised persons' by a resolution of the board. It is assumed that the secretary and assistant secretary are authorised.

If the certificate of shares lodged with the transfer for **Balance** certification includes a larger number of shares than is **Receipt.** included in the transfer, the secretary will issue to the seller or his broker a balance receipt. This will entitle the seller in due course to receive a certificate for the unsold balance of his shares. These balance receipts should be in a book with forms for duplicating by means of carbon sheets. They should always be signed by a responsible official. An example is given in Appendix F (Form 96). The practice with regard to the preparation of certificates for the balance of shares varies in different offices. Some companies contend that to make out a balance certificate in respect of the unsold portion of shares on all certificates lodged upon certification of transfers is a waste of time, and they therefore do not make out any certificate in respect of the balance unless and until requested to do so, such balance remaining on the cancelled certificate retained in the office pending delivery of further transfers or an application for a balance certificate. If this procedure is followed, no further transfers in respect of the unappropriated balance must be certificated or accepted for registration, nor must any balance certificates be issued without the surrender of the balance receipt. It is, however, contended by many companies, and also by many auditors, that a balance certificate should be made out in respect of every balance represented by unsold shares on certificates lodged with transfers for certification, as, in that way, it is easier to trace the whole of a particular shareholding should occasion arise; where this method is adopted, such a balance certificate is made out even when it is known that further transfers will be presented for certification or registration in respect of those particular shares. On the further transfer being presented, the balance certificate is immediately cancelled, even though it may not have been before the board for sealing. Where the former practice is adopted, the balance receipt should contain an intimation to the effect that no definitive certificate will be made out in respect of the balance unless a request for the same is made. Where the latter practice is followed, the balance receipt given should contain an intimation as to when the balance certificate will be ready for delivery.

It will be seen from the foregoing that, notwithstanding the provisions of the Act as to the legal effect of certification of transfers, the practice is one which requires to be carried out with the very greatest care. The clerk responsible for the work should be careful to see that the transferor's name is correctly stated, that he has signed the transfer, that the name of the transferee* is inserted, that no more shares are being transferred than are comprised in the certificate, that the distinctive numbers (if any) are correctly stated on the transfer, and that the company's name is correctly stated, and, by reference to the register of members or card index, that no notice in lieu of distringas has been lodged. It occasionally happens that an old address, copied from the share certificate, is inserted in the transfer, and it is therefore necessary to refer to the register or card index to check the address of a transferor so that the notice to him (if such is sent on certification) may be sent to the correct address. Sometimes the transfer contains a new address of which the company has no notice. Confirmation should always be obtained from the transferor before altering the register in such a case. Where an outside audit of the transfers is conducted, it is the usual practice of auditors to enface the certificates with a small rubber stamp or some other distinctive mark, and the clerk responsible for the certification of the transfer should be careful to see that the certificate lodged with the transfer bears such mark, and is, therefore, *prima facie* genuine.

Powers of Attorney. The general law as to powers of attorney is discussed in chapter XXII, but it is convenient to deal here with the practice in connection with transfers. The signature on a transfer, whether that of the transferor or the transferee, may be affixed by an attorney, or agent. In such cases it becomes the duty of the secretary to satisfy himself that the authority of the attorney is properly constituted. Where the transferor has executed the transfer by attorney, the matter should be dealt with upon presentation of the transfer for certification, but when the transfer is lodged for registration, reference should again be made to the records of powers of attorney in order to make sure that no notice of revocation or death has been received since the transfer was certificated. If the transferee has executed the transfer, it is upon lodgment of the transfer for registration that the matter will arise. If the power of attorney has already been lodged for registration at

---

* Otherwise on a series of sales the Inland Revenue may lose stamp duty and the company is facilitating this loss. Further, it is preferable for the company to know for whom it is holding the share certificates.

the company's office, particulars of it will appear in the company's register of powers of attorney, *i.e.* the date of registration, the names of the donor and donee of the power, and some particulars of its scope and duration. It is, however, always advisable to keep a copy of each power for reference. In particular it is not wise to rely on the fact that the power is endorsed as a 'general power,' as there is no accepted form of general power, and a third party is only covered, as against the principal, if the act which the attorney is permitted to carry out is within the authority of the power. If the attorney or his solicitor refuse to supply a copy, one may usually be obtained by informing him that, unless a copy is forthcoming, it will be necessary to call for the production of the original power each time the attorney desires to act. The copy can then be referred to, and unless there is any doubt whether the power is still in force, the transfer may be accepted. If the power is presented for the first time upon a transfer being lodged for certification or registration, it must be carefully inspected in order to see that it is under seal, that it is properly stamped, executed and attested, that it authorises the transaction sought to be effected, whether the sale or purchase of shares, and whether of the particular shares in question, and that it is still effective. If the power of attorney is executed by a corporation, it should be borne in mind that s. 74 (1) of the Law of Property Act, 1925, operates only in favour of a purchaser as defined by s. 205 of that Act, *i.e.* 'a purchaser in good faith and for valuable consideration' including 'a lessee, mortgagee or other person who for valuable consideration acquires an interest in property.' Although a power of attorney is automatically revoked by the death of the principal, if a company registers a transfer executed by the attorney after such death and is itself unaware of the death, it will be protected under the Law of Property Act, 1925, s. 127, if the power is expressed to be irrevocable for a period not exceeding one year from the date of the instrument. The company should, however, refuse to register such a transfer if it has notice of the principal's death. It is usually a wise precaution to obtain from the attorney a declaration that the donor is still alive and has not revoked the power.

On the execution of the transfer by the transferee, it is **Registration** lodged with the company for registration. The depositing **of Transfers.** broker or agent should be asked to write or stamp his name and address on the back of the transfer, and the secretary should give a printed form of receipt to the effect that the transfer has been lodged for registration subject to the approval of the board. A form of receipt to be used when the transfer is handed in over the counter, and when it is sent by post, will be found in Appendix F (Form 94). This form is, it will be observed, bound as a book with carbon copies.

A rubber stamp should be used to stamp each transfer for the purpose of recording the various operations connected with it, and the records should be duly made from time to time until they are complete. A specimen stamp is given in Appendix F (Form 93).

Upon receipt of a transfer for registration, the signature of the transferor should be carefully compared with the record in the office and, unless the transfer has previously been certificated, a notice, in a sealed opaque envelope not bearing the name of the company by which it is sent, should be sent to the transferor stating that the transfer has been lodged, and that, unless objection is received, it will be assumed to be in order. This notice is called a 'seller's notice' and a form thereof is given in Appendix F (Form 95). This will be unnecessary where a notice was sent on certification. In the case of joint holders, the notice should be sent to every holder.

It is important that the secretary should bear in mind the provisions of the Exchange Control Act, 1947, before registering a transfer (see chapter XXX, below).

Transfer Receipts. On receiving a transfer deed for registration a company may adopt one of two practices. It may either issue a returnable transfer receipt or it may issue a non-returnable receipt or a mere acknowledgement. The advantages and disadvantages of these two practices are considered below. The following list (which is not intended to be exhaustive) gives the main variations of both practices in current use:—

(i) Transfer (and balance) receipts are issued, returnable to the company before delivery of new certificates, for which receipts are required.

(ii) As (i) with the addition that transfer receipts have to be signed before being returned to the company, *e.g.* the Parsons system.

(iii) As (i) except that no receipts are required for certificates, the cancelled and endorsed transfer (and balance) receipts being treated as sufficient evidence of issue of certificates.

(iv) Transfer receipts are issued which are not exchangeable for new certificates, but are returnable in the event of further dealing in the stock before the certificates are ready. Balance receipts are issued which are returnable in either event. Certificate receipts are required.

(v) Transfer (and balance) receipts are issued which are not exchangeable for new certificates but are returnable in the event of further dealing in the stock before the certificates are ready. Certificate receipts are required.

(vi) Selective issue of transfer (and balance) receipts, *e.g.* for jobber's dealings, receipts not being issued for direct investment transactions. When issued, receipts are returnable in order to obtain new certificates; certificate receipts are also required.

(vii) Transfer receipts are not issued, formal acknowledgements being sent indicating that new certificates will follow in due course. Certificate receipts are required.

(viii) Transfer (and balance) receipts are not issued. In the case of postal transactions formal acknowledgements are sent as in (vii), but, in the case of counter transactions, tickets are given which have to be surrendered as proof of identity before new certificates are issued. New certificates in respect of transfers received by post, or over the counter, respectively, are issued only in the same manner. Certificate receipts are required in both cases.

Returnable Transfer Receipts.

A returnable transfer receipt usually sets out the details of the stock concerned and the transferee's name and indicates that, subject to the transfer being passed by the directors, a new certificate in the name of the transferee will be ready on a specified date or after a specified period, and also states that such new certificate will only be issued in exchange for the receipt. A receipt of this nature is a temporary scrip and, as such, involves the giving of an indemnity should it be lost. It will, however, be observed that transfer receipts are not accepted as good delivery by any stock exchange, and consequently the question whether they constitute effective documents of title is largely academic.

From the practical angle the treatment of transfer receipts as temporary scrip, *i.e.* making them returnable, has the following merits:—

(a) Receipts are *prima facie* evidence of the right of the parties presenting them to receive stock certificates or to have transfers certificated. Thus the risk of new certificates being issued to parties not entitled to or no longer interested in the stock, or of allowing such parties to deal with the stock, is reduced, if not eliminated.

(b) They give on the face of them all the information necessary to companies or other interested parties to identify the stockholdings concerned.

(c) They continue without break the chain of *prima facie* evidence of title in the hands of stockholders or their agents.

(*d*) They reduce the amount of 'floating stock' at any time in companies' offices. There is always a certain amount of 'floating stock' held to the order of stock exchanges and in connection with deceased estates, in respect of which no temporary scrip is issued, but the volume of this is usually far less than the amount of stock passing on ordinary transfers.

(*e*) The system is simple, straightforward and practical.

The disadvantages are that additional work in companies' and brokers' offices is involved; postages, now a heavy item, are increased; in the event of receipts changing hands, *e.g.* from stockbroker to bank, endorsement is necessary; in the event of receipts being lost in the post or otherwise, indemnities are necessary; and brokers and others sometimes delay or neglect to return receipts, involving the issue of reminders.

Non-returnable Receipts and Acknowledgments. Companies which issue non-returnable receipts, or issue only what are termed acknowledgements of transfers, really fall into the same class, *i.e.* they do not regard the documents they issue as temporary scrip or as evidence of title, but merely as items of business correspondence conveying information. The return of such documents, in the event of intermediate dealing in the stock, does not convert them into scrip; it performs the purely practical office of readily identifying the stock from the companies' point of view. In the same way, the tickets, which in some of these systems are given in exchange for documents received over the counter, merely serve as a means of identity and ready reference to companies' own records. From the time a transfer is lodged with a company for registration until the new certificate in the transferee's name is issued, no evidence of title to the block of stock concerned exists outside the company's domestic records. The merits of the system are as follows:—

(*a*) Saving of work both in companies' and brokers' offices.

(*b*) Saving in postage, though this will vary considerably, depending on the actual system in force.

(*c*) Elimination of the need for indemnities should receipts or acknowledgements be lost in the post or otherwise.

(*d*) Prompt clearance by companies of new certificates.

The disadvantages are that special precautions have to be taken to ensure that new certificates are issued correctly, or, in the event of intermediate dealings, are not issued; companies may be involved in additional work in identifying particular stockholdings should any query arise during the registration period; the chain of evidence of title in the hands of stockholders or their agents is broken; and the amount of 'floating stock' in companies' offices, and, therefore, the possibility of error in issuing new certificates, is considerably increased.

The registration of transfers is, subject to the articles, a **Approval of** matter for the board, for whose approval they must be **Transfers.** submitted; but before the transfers are submitted to the board for approval they should be carefully scrutinised by the secretary or his responsible deputy with a view to seeing:—

(a) that each transfer is accompanied by the relative certificate (unless it has been certificated) and registration fee of 2s. 6d.;

(b) that the name and address of the broker lodging the document for registration is recorded on the back of each transfer;

(c) that the transfer is in respect of only one class of shares or stock—most companies will not accept transfers which deal with more than one class of share or stock, unless their articles provide otherwise;

(d) that the transferor's name and address are in exact accord with the register of members;

(e) that the consideration money bears its proper relation to the fair and reasonable market value of the stock or shares transferred;

(f) that the transferee's full name and address are clearly entered therein;

(g) if the capital of the company is divided into two or more classes of shares or stock, that the class of shares specified in the transfer is the same class as that comprised in the certificate;

(h) that the number of shares or amount of stock is shown correctly in words and figures;

(i) that in the case of shares which are numbered the distinctive numbers are clearly entered and agree with the numbers appearing on the certificate and with the number of shares to be transferred;

(j) that the name of the company is correctly given;

(k) that the document is signed by all parties and their signatures correctly attested. If a corporate company, the common seal of the company should be affixed. Where transfers are executed by illiterate or infirm persons, the attestation clauses must be amended to state the facts. When transfers are executed abroad or in a British colony, the signatures should be attested by some person holding a public position, such as H.M. consul, or vice-consul, a magistrate, notary public or a British chaplain;

(*l*) that the transfer is stamped with an *ad valorem* stamp (impressed) on the consideration money, which should approximate to the market value of the stock or shares being transferred. When the consideration stated on the transfer is below the market value, and in all cases of nominal consideration, the registrar should insist on the adjudication stamp of the Board of Inland Revenue being impressed thereon before accepting it for registration (Stamp Duties—see p. 459 and Appendix A);

(*m*) that the transfer is dated, the day and year being written in words;

(*n*) that the necessary declarations on Form 'D' on the reverse of the transfer are completed in accordance with the requirements of the Exchange Control Act, 1947 (see Appendix F, Form 92);

(*o*) that there is no notice in lieu of distringas or other charge upon the stock or shares therein referred to, or anything which would otherwise invalidate the transfer.

If the name of the transferee has been altered, or another name substituted, the transfer should be refused, unless it is accompanied by a satisfactory written explanation and statement that there has been no sub-sale, or a satisfactory letter of indemnity. Unfortunately, incorrect or incomplete names are sometimes passed to stockbrokers, and a request for the registration of an additional christian name or names may be received. A letter, stating the facts, signed by the new member, should be sufficient, but in case of doubt a letter of indemnity or a statutory declaration may be demanded. A request for the registration of additional christian names should be accompanied by a statutory declaration.

As soon as the directors have passed the transfers for registration, they should be posted in the register of members. All postings in the register of members should be checked by the registrar or a competent member of the staff.

Where the transferee is a corporate body, the secretary should ask for a certified extract from the articles showing how the seal is to be affixed. Transfers to a partnership firm as such should not be registered [*Vagliano Anthracite Collieries* (1910), W.N. 187]; although, if the firm's name is entered on the register, the partners become liable as individual members [*Weikersheim's Case* (1873), 8 Ch. App. 831]. Subject to any contrary provision in the articles, there is no real objection to registering a transfer of shares in the title of the holder of an office without reference to his names. Whenever the shares are dealt with, however, or important instructions are given with regard to them, satisfactory evidence must be produced to establish the identity of the person purporting to deal with them.

The Public Trustee, if separate accounts are necessary, **Public** may be registered with a number, or a letter and number, **Trustee.** *e.g.* 'The Public Trustee, Account No. 3,' or 'The Public Trustee a/c A 40.' [Public Trustee Act, 1906, s. 11 (5)]. Any introduction of a name, *e.g.* 'The Public Trustee, *re* John Jones,' would appear to be contrary to the provisions of s. 117 of the Act, which forbids notice of any trust being entered on the register.

If a transfer signed by the registered holder is presented **Death of** after the death of the transferor and is in order in every **Transferor or** detail, the transfer should be accepted for registration. **Transferee.** But if probate or letters of administration have been registered or the company has otherwise received notice of his death, the secretary should give notice of the lodgment of the transfer to the personal representatives, and a reasonable time should be allowed for objection, if any, to be lodged. The death of the transferor does not by itself entitle the company to refuse registration. Naturally, if the shares have already been registered in the names of the executors or administrators, the transfer should not be accepted. In the case of an alteration in the name of the transferee caused by the death of a transferee before execution of the transfer, it will be necessary, before the company can accept it for registration, for the brokers to make a declaration on the back of the document setting out the facts and stating that there has been no sub-sale.

As regards attestation, a transfer executed out of the **Attestation.** United Kingdom is not usually accepted unless it is attested by H.M. consul, a clergyman, justice of the peace, or notary public, or unless the signature is guaranteed by a bank or a firm of standing. When one of the parties to a transfer is illiterate or infirm, and has executed the deed by making his mark, the attestation should state that the document has been read over and explained to the party, and that it appeared to have been understood by him (see Appendix F, Form 93a); in a case of this kind there should be two witnesses, one of whom should be a doctor, a justice of the peace, a clergyman, a solicitor, or some other person of standing. The wife or husband of a transferor or transferee should not be accepted as a witness, nor should the attestation by one of the parties to the transfer to the signature of the other be allowed. The address and occupation of a witness should be specified. The description of a witness, 'clerk,' or 'married woman,' may be accepted, although the correct form should be 'clerk to   ,' 'wife of   .' In the case of a divorced woman the correct description is 'single woman.' If a witness has signed in the wrong place, it may be accepted if the intention is clear. The same witness may attest both signatures. A transferee who is also a transferor need sign only once.

Surviving holders in a joint account need not be so described on transfers. When shares are being sold by executors in their capacity as executors, they should be so described in the transfer. But if the executors have been registered in their personal capacity, a transfer should not be accepted if they, as transferors, are described as 'executors of . . . deceased.'

More than one account (*e.g.* two or more sellers to the same buyer) should not be allowed on the same transfer form; nor should transfers of more than one class of shares or stock on the same transfer form be accepted unless the articles otherwise provide.

Stamps. The scale of stamps on transfers will be found in the Inland Revenue Circular, dated August, 1949 (see Appendix A). It must be remembered that, by s. 17 of the Stamp Act, 1891, 'if any person whose office it is to enrol, register, or enter in or upon any rolls, books, or records, any instrument chargeable with duty, enrols, registers, or enters any such instrument not being duly stamped, he shall incur a fine of ten pounds.' This makes it incumbent upon the secretary to satisfy himself that transfers are properly stamped. If the consideration accords with the market price, and the stamp with both, there is no difficulty. If the stamp accords with the consideration, but the consideration is less than the market value, but near it, the secretary cannot be expected to do anything further. If the difference is considerable, the transfer should be refused in the absence of a satisfactory explanation and the adjudication mark of the Revenue Stamp Office should be required under s. 12 of the Stamp Act. Transfers executed abroad and attested by H.M. consul or a notary public attract an extra 1s. duty if the seal of either of these officials is attached.

With regard to transfers for nominal consideration and stamp duty rates generally, the Inland Revenue circular, 1949, should be followed (see Appendix A). Where, however, the beneficial interest passes, whether for value or as a gift *inter vivos*, full *ad valorem* duty is payable.

It has been held that directors may refuse to register a transfer not duly stamped, and in determining whether it is duly stamped they may go behind that which appears on the face of the document [*Maynard* v. *Consolidated Kent Collieries* (1903), 2 K.B. 121].

It may occasionally happen that the secretary receives a transfer which, though appearing on its face to be correctly stamped, is known to him, from other information in his possession, to be incorrectly stamped. In such a case he should return the transfer to the broker presenting it, stating the information in his possession, and (unless the matter can be cleared up) requiring the stamp to be adjudicated. The more extreme case has also sometimes arisen of a transfer presented after adjudication, but insufficiently stamped because the information given to the Revenue was untrue. *Prima facie* the secretary is bound to accept an adjudicated stamp, but he must not be a party to a fraud on the Revenue, and, if he has good reason for suspecting such a fraud in the case of an adjudicated stamp, his best course would be to inform the Revenue of the fact and obtain their views before registering the transfer. He should, of course, in such a case consult his directors.

Certificates attached to transfers lodged for registration, as in the case of certificates in respect of transfers left for certification, should be cancelled immediately they are delivered to the company, so as to prevent any chance of their being subsequently used for an improper purpose. The retention of cancelled certificates for an indefinite period is unnecessary. Some companies retain them for three years, some for six, after the transfer is lodged. Practice naturally varies on such a point, but there is no reason why they should not be destroyed after a reasonable time. **Cancellation of Certificates.**

The deed of transfer lodged for registration having been found in order, and being accompanied by a certificate, or bearing on its face the company's certification, is stamped with the date of lodgment, given its consecutive number, and entered in the register of transfers, if such a book is kept [Appendix F (Form 91)].

Where directors are given a discretion as to registering transfers, they must not exercise that discretion capriciously. The court, in the absence of evidence to the contrary, will presume that the directors have done right [*Coalport China Co.* (1895), 2 Ch. 404], and the onus of proof is on those who say the directors have not acted *bona fide* [ex parte *Penney* (1872), 8 Ch. App. 446]. If they have *bona fide* considered the matter and the articles so provide, the directors need not give their reasons for refusing to register a transfer, but if they do give reasons the court will inquire into the sufficiency of such reasons [*Bell Brothers*, ex parte *Hodgson* (1891), 65 L.T. 245, *Hafner Olhausen* v. *Powderley* (1943), I.R. 426]. In this connection it must be remembered that a power to directors to refuse to register transfers of shares varies in accordance with the wording of individual articles; *e.g.* if an article provides that the directors may refuse to register a transfer if 'in their opinion it is contrary to the interests of the company that the proposed transferee should be a member thereof,' a refusal to register is justified only on grounds personal to the proposed transferee [*Bede Steam Shipping Co.* (1917), 1 Ch. 123]. In re *Hackney Pavilion* (1924), 1 Ch. 276, it was held that, in order that the directors may effectively decline to register a transfer, a resolution of **Withholding Registration.**

the board is necessary. As in this case there was equality of voting, registration could in the circumstances be compelled. Directors must not knowingly register a transfer in breach of trust, but they will be liable only if they have knowledge of that breach or that the transfer is in fraud of a person having equitable rights [*Société Générale* v. *Tramways Union* (1884), 14 Q.B.D. 424]. This difficulty can, however, be overcome by the board giving notice to the person interested that the transfer will be passed in the ordinary way, unless he takes action to restrain the company and the directors within seven days. In re *Smith* v. *Fawcett Ltd.* (1942), Ch. 304, 2 All E.R. 542, 544, the articles gave the directors power to refuse the transfer of shares in their absolute and uncontrolled discretion. Such articles are common in private companies (cf. Table A, Part II, clause 3). In this case Lord Greene, M.R., in his judgment said that, where the articles conferred a discretion on directors with regard to the acceptance of a transfer of shares, the directors must exercise their discretion *bona fide* in what they considered, not what a court might consider, to be in the interest of the company, and that in a private company the control of the directors over the membership might be very strict indeed. It may be noted that under such an article a transfer of shares to an existing member may be refused in the same way as to anyone else. If registration is refused, notice must be given to the transferee within two months of the lodgment of the transfer (s. 78). A person in whose favour shares are renounced is not a transferee, so that directors with power to refuse to register transfers are not thereby entitled to refuse to register such a person as the holder of the shares [*Pool Shipping Co.* (1920), 1 Ch. 251]. It therefore appears that, to entitle directors to refuse to register such persons, there must be special provision in a company's articles.

Before the closing of the transfer books for dividend purposes, care should be taken that every transfer lodged for registration be passed and registered. While the books are closed, the certification of transfers should proceed as usual, and transfers presented for registration should be accepted and carefully preserved, and there seems no objection to the usual notice as to lodgment of transfer being immediately sent to the transferor; but apart from this the secretary will not deal with any transfers lodged for registration until the books are once more open. (See p. 66, above.)

Procedure of Transfer Committee. The procedure usually followed by the transfer committee or board in checking the transfers and issuing certificates where there is no transfer audit is as follows:—

The secretary, having carefully checked the transfers for the period under consideration, will prepare a detailed statement for submission to the transfer committee which generally consists of two directors. The directors usually act in rotation as members of the committee. The statement will include the following information:—

(a) that the transfers have been checked with the transferors' certificates and that the latter have been cancelled;

(b) that requests to register executors and administrators as holders in their own right have been checked with the certificates relating thereto, the latter also having been cancelled;

(c) that new share certificates have been prepared and checked for issue.

The statement should in each case gives details of the amount of shares or stock involved.

The members of the committee will check the details given in the secretary's statement with the new certificates, after which the latter will be dated, signed, sealed and checked with the entries on the transfer committee register. The certificates are then ready for issue in exchange for transfer receipts, etc. As soon as the transfers have been passed by the board, the transferees should be placed on the register of members. In some instances it is permissible for the directors to delegate the task of 'passing' transfers, although most boards prefer to examine the documents themselves. It is then customary for the board or a committee appointed for the purpose to pass transfers of all kinds. In the case of partly paid shares or shares in private companies, where some right is given to the directors to refuse to register transfers, the directors owe a duty to the company to scrutinise the documents and to exercise their discretion. In other cases, however, provided that the articles do not state otherwise, the board may delegate the duty of seeing that transfers are correct and there is no need for them to 'pass' the transfers, although a resolution of the board is required to authorise the affixing of the seal to the new certificates. As the transfers represent the titles of the transferees they must be kept in a place of absolute safety, and retained by the company in perpetuity.

In the event of a duplicate certificate having been issued in exchange for an indemnity in respect of a lost, mislaid, or destroyed original certificate, it will be necessary to see that the duplicate certificate is the one lodged with the transfer and not the original, and, should the latter be lodged, to communicate with the transferor to ascertain the reason why he is dealing with the original and not the duplicate.

Should a certificated transfer be lost, the company should, before certificating a duplicate transfer, require an indemnity from the transferee or his stockbroker. This should, in general, be accompanied by a statutory declaration verifying the loss, and a guarantee by a bank or firm of standing, unless

D

the number of shares proposed to be transferred is small. Should a transfer receipt or balance receipt be lost, an indemnity similarly guaranteed should be required.

The Keeping and Closing of Transfer Registers. The view is widely held that under modern practice the keeping of a register of transfers is dispensed with, on the ground that the transfers themselves, when properly bound, form a much better record of the transfer of shares and that the additional work of entering up the register is thus avoided. This is not necessarily the case, especially with regard to the larger companies, where the binding of transfer deeds into volumes for use as a register is far too cumbersome and it is more convenient to keep a register. The keeping of a transfer register also has the advantage of enabling the register of transfers to be closed at dividend time without closing the register of members, unless the articles of association otherwise provide. Table A, clause 27, provides that 'the registration of transfers may be suspended at such times and for such periods as the directors may from time to time determine, provided always that such registration shall not be suspended for more than 30 days in any year.' If, however, the register of members is closed, an advertisement must be inserted in the press in accordance with s. 115 of the Act. A form of register of transfer will be found in Appendix F, Form 91.

Certificates. Great care should be exercised in the preparation of the certificates to see that the number of shares or amount of stock (and in the case of the former, the distinctive numbers, if any) are correctly stated. The address of the holder should be inserted, with courtesy designations, *e.g.* 'Reverend,' 'Mrs.,' 'Miss,' etc.* In joint accounts it is usual to give the address of the first-named holder only, unless otherwise provided for in the articles of association; but there is generally a clause in the articles to the effect that in the case of joint accounts all notices will be addressed to the first-named holder, so that the addresses of the second, third, or other holders in joint accounts are, except for purposes of identification, not required to be set out in the index to the register of members, although it is essential that they should always be fully detailed in the register itself in order to comply with s. 110 of the Act.

By s. 80 of the Act, companies are required to complete and have ready for delivery the certificates of all shares, the debentures, and the certificates of all debenture stock allotted or transferred, within two months after the transfers are lodged for registration, unless the conditions of issue otherwise provide. A failure to comply with this provision exposes the officers of the company to pecuniary penalties and the court may limit a time for making good the default [s. 80 (2) (3)].

---

* The practice of dispensing with courtesy titles is growing and it is not strictly necessary to insert them.

One or two other matters connected with transfers remain **Legal Effect** to be noticed. The legal effect of a transfer, duly completed **of Transfers.** by registration, is important. A transferee does not get a full title until the transfer is registered [*Société Générale* v. *Walker* (1885), 11 A.C. 20]; on that date, and not before, he becomes a shareholder. Until registration, the transferee has only an equitable right, which he may lose by the appearance of some person with a superior equity, or by the registration of a later transfer [*Moore* v. *N.W. Bank* (1891), 2 Ch. 599; *Ireland* v. *Hart* (1902), 1 Ch. 522]. Meanwhile the transferor remains liable to pay calls, but there is an implied contract by the transferee to indemnify him [*Loring* v. *Davis* (1886), 32 Ch. D. 625], and, subject to the articles of association, the transferor can enforce the registration. If a shareholder neglects to have the name of the transferee substituted for his own upon the register of members and a winding-up supervenes, his name must remain there, and he is therefore liable to pay up the amount due upon his shares [*Walker's Case* (1868), 6 Eq. 30, cf. *Sussex Brick Co.* (1904), 1 Ch. 598], although he would be entitled to indemnity by the transferee. The transferor, after registration, is not primarily liable as a contributory [*Hoylake Railway Co.* (1874), 9 Ch. App. 257], but remains liable for one year to be placed on the 'B' List of contributories (see ss. 212 and 257 of the Act). Even after registration, the transferor will be liable to be restored to the register if the transfer was fraudulent, or made without the authority of the transferee, or to a nominee of the company to the knowledge of the transferor; but in the case last mentioned the transferee may be liable [*Cree* v. *Somervail* (1879), 4 A.C. 648]. The entry of the name of a transferee on the register by a secretary, without authority, before the directors have approved the transfer, gives the transferee no title, and the transferor still remains liable on the shares [*Chida Mines* v. *Anderson* (1905), 22 T.L.R. 27].

If the articles provide that a member shall not be entitled to vote while any call or other sum is due and payable to the company in respect of any of the shares of such member, it has been held that, although the calls can be recovered from the original holder, even after forfeiture, the person to whom the shares have been re-sold by the company takes the shares subject to such disqualification, notwithstanding that he acquired them upon the terms that he should be discharged from all calls due prior to his acquisition of the shares [*Randt Gold Mining Co.* v. *Wainwright* (1901), 1 Ch. 184].

The company is not bound to register a transfer at once, but is allowed time for inquiry; if, however, registration is improperly refused, the company will be liable in damages [*Ottos Kopje Diamond Mines* (1893), 1 Ch. 618].

The only duty of the transferor of shares is to execute a valid transfer and hand it to the transferee; it is for the transferee to insist on his right to registration [*Skinner* v. *City of London Insurance Corporation* (1885), 14 Q.B.D. 882], but the transferor is under an implied obligation, arising from the relation of grantor and grantee, not to prevent or delay the registration [*Hooper* v. *Herts* (1906), 1 Ch. 549]. (See also s. 77.)

The vendor of shares is under a duty to deliver a transfer executed by a transferor who is, and continues to be, ready and willing that the subject matter of the transfer shall be duly vested in the person named, or to be named, in the transfer [*Hichens, Harrison Woolston & Co.* v. *Jackson* (1943), A.C. 266, 279].

Blank Transfers.

The effect of blank transfers, *i.e.* transfers in which the name of the transferee is omitted, should be noticed. Blank transfers are usually given in cases where the transferor is desirous of raising money on the shares; and here there is a difference in the legal position according to whether the articles of the company do or do not require a transfer to be made by deed.

1. *Where the articles do not require a transfer by deed.* A form of transfer signed by a vendor of shares, but with the name of the transferee omitted, is equivalent, when delivered to a purchaser, to an authority to him to fill in the blank with any name he likes [*Walker* v. *Bartlett* (1856), 18 C.B. 845], and the vendor is entitled to be indemnified by the purchaser against all calls thereafter made [*Spencer* v. *Ashworth, Partington & Co.* (1925), 1 K.B. 589]. When the name is filled in, the transferee is entitled to be registered as holder of the shares [*Tahiti Cotton Co.*, ex parte *Sargent* (1874), 17 Eq. 273].

2. *Where the articles require a transfer by deed.* The name of the transferee must be inserted before the deed is executed [*Taylor* v. *Great Indian Peninsula Railway Co.* (1859), 4 De G. and J. 559]; otherwise the document is inoperative as a deed [*Hibblewhite* v. *McMorine* (1840), 6 M. & W. 200], and gives the purchaser no right to call upon the company to place his name upon the register. The purchaser however, has, in consequence of the contract of sale, an equitable title to the shares, and he can compel the vendor to aid him to acquire a legal title by executing a proper transfer [*Morris* v. *Cannan* (1862), 31 L.J.Ch. 425]. If there is an obvious addition on the face of the deed in another handwriting, written confirmation that the transfer was completed prior to execution should normally be sufficient.

If a mortgagee of shares, holding a transfer in blank, purports to sell them, and hands over to his purchaser the transfer still in blank, the fact that it is in blank affects the purchaser with notice, and he gets no better interest than his vendor (the mortgagee) had [*France* v. *Clarke* (1884), 26 Ch. D. 257]. If, however, the mortgagee himself fills in the transfer, his transferee, provided he be a *bona fide* purchaser for value without notice, will get a complete title to the shares [*Easton* v. *London Joint Stock Bank* (1886), 34 Ch. D. 95].

A forged transfer gives the alleged transferee no rights to **Forged** the shares [*Barton* v. *London & North-Western Railway* (1889), **Transfers.** 24 Q.B.D. 77]; but where a company acting on a forged transfer has issued a certificate in the name of the transferee and this has been passed on to a *bona fide* holder for value, the company is estopped by its certificate from denying that the person named in such certificate is the proprietor of the shares, and he is entitled to damages against it [*Balkis Co.* v. *Tomkinson* (1893), A.C. 396]. The court will order the company to rectify its register where it has acted on a forged transfer [*Bahia Railway* (1868), L.R. 3 Q.B. 584].

By the Forged Transfers Acts, 1891 and 1892 (54 & 55 Vict. c. 43; 55 & 56 Vict. c. 36), companies are empowered to make compensation for losses arising from forged transfers, or transfers under forged powers of attorney. The Acts are sometimes adopted by a company's articles, but this is unnecessary as they apply whether they are adopted or not. It is, however, emphasised that these Acts merely give a company power to pay compensation, and do not impose any obligation so to do. Compensation is payable out of the company's funds, and the Acts empower the company, by fees or otherwise, to provide a fund to meet claims for compensation, and to impose reasonable restrictions on the transfer of shares and securities (or on powers of attorney for the transfer thereof) as they may consider requisite for guarding against losses arising from forgery. The object of these Acts is to enable a company to give relief to a purchaser who is deprived of his shares owing to the registration of a forged transfer or a transfer under a forged power of attorney.

To provide for the cases of the death, bankruptcy, or **Trans-** insolvency of a member, a transmission clause is almost **mission.** invariably inserted in the articles. It must be remembered that transfer and transmission are two distinct things. Transmission occurs by operation of the law, *e.g.* on death or bankruptcy, when the power of transfer ceases, and secures that there shall be someone entitled to the shares held by the deceased or bankrupt—at any rate, in a representative capacity. The object of the transmission clause is that the representative capacity shall be changed into a responsible capacity, as between the holder and the company, whatever may be the rights as between the holder and the beneficiary.

In the case of companies under the Companies Acts, the

circumstances in which persons entitled to shares in a representative capacity (*e.g.* executors) are entitled to be registered depends upon the articles of a company. One or two representative specimens of articles dealing with the subject may be taken as illustrations. Articles usually provide that the executors or administrators of a deceased sole holder of a share shall be the only persons recognised by the company as having any title to the share. (See also s. 117 of the Act.) The object of this clause is that the company shall not be concerned to go into questions as to who is, or is not, beneficially entitled. The company is to look to the legal personal representatives and to them alone. Table A, clause 30, provides that 'any person becoming entitled to a share in consequence of the death or bankruptcy of a member may, upon such evidence being produced as may from time to time be properly required by the directors and subject as hereinafter provided, elect either to be registered himself as holder of the share or to have some person nominated by him registered as the transferee thereof; but the directors shall, in either case, have the same right to decline or suspend registration as they would have had in the case of a transfer of the share by that member before his death or bankruptcy as the case may be.' Another very common form is that 'any person becoming entitled, etc., upon producing such evidence that he sustains the character in respect of which he proposes to act under this clause, or of his title, as the directors think sufficient, may, with the consent of the directors (which they shall not be under any obligation to give), be registered as a member in respect of such shares, or may, subject to the regulations as to transfer, transfer such shares.' The effect of Table A is to entitle any such person, upon production of such evidence as the company may properly require, to be registered as a member, or to elect to have a nominee registered as a transferee, after executing a transfer to the nominee. There is no very substantial variation between any of the above provisions, and the general result is that executors may, but need not, be registered as members.

When a member dies, his estate remains liable to the company. His name is on the register. In due course, probate or letters of administration or confirmation as executor are produced to the company as evidence of the representative capacity of the executors or administrators; and s. 82 of the Act provides that 'the production to a company of any document which is by law sufficient evidence of probate of the will, or letters of administration of the estate, or confirmation as executor, of a deceased person having been granted to some person shall be accepted by the company, notwithstanding anything in its articles, as sufficient evidence of the grant.' If nothing more is done, the proper course is to make a note in the register of the death and production of the probate with the full names and addresses of the executors; but it is not the proper course, in the circumstances, to enter the representatives in the register as holders of the shares. Section 76 of the Act makes this clear: 'A transfer of the share or other interest of a deceased member of a company, made by his personal representative, shall, *although the personal representative is not himself a member of the company,* be as valid as if he had been such a member at the time of the execution of the instrument of transfer.' So that executors may, by statute, transfer without being first registered as members; and if they do so, the transferee will in due course be registered in the ordinary way. If personal representatives propose to retain shares for any length of time before transferring them (which includes a transfer to themselves as trustees) it is preferable that they should be registered as members. This is so because many articles of association withhold payment of dividends to personal representatives unless registered. Such a restraint is perfectly valid (cf. Table A, clause 32). If they are registered they may also exercise rights of voting as members, but not otherwise (see p. 153). Pending a transfer, the estate of the deceased member remains liable to the company and his representative is not entitled to notices of meetings [*Allen* v. *Gold Reefs of West Africa* (1900), 1 Ch. 656], unless the articles provide that such representative is entitled to receive them. Clause 134 of Table A is an instance of such a provision.

On the death of a sole, or sole surviving, executor who has not been registered, the production of probate of his will by his executor entitles that executor to deal with the shares of the deceased shareholder. But the administrator of a deceased executor must not be recognised; the person entitled to deal with the unadministered estate of the deceased shareholder (who will generally be the residuary legatee or one of the next of kin) must take out letters of administration *de bonis non* and the secretary can then recognise that person. Similarly neither the executor of an administrator nor the administrator of an administrator can be recognised.

In practice, cases often arise when the next of kin writes to the company and explains that the value of the shares held does not warrant the taking out of letters of administration (or letters of administration *de bonis non*). As a general rule, letters of administration must always be taken out and a company is fully justified in refusing to hand over the shares to the next of kin unless they are produced. In the case of estates under £100* the Estate Duty Office will usually,

---

* This figure is likely to remain constant despite the fact that estates under £2,000 are not now liable to estate duty.

especially in the case of foreigners, issue a letter to the effect that estate duty is not payable. These letters are very indefinite but are usually accepted. In such cases, upon the production of a formal request to be registered and a statutory declaration by the person claiming title, setting out the facts and including an indemnity in respect of any losses, claims or demands which may be made against the company, the company should permit the next of kin to be registered as the holders of the shares. Where the next of kin is obviously not a man of substance, it is desirable that a banker or solicitor should join in such statutory declaration and indemnity and agree to be bound thereby. Most companies request that a letter from the Estate Duty Office to the effect that estate duty is not payable should also be produced. It is realised that in pursuing this course the following risks are run: (i) that if estate duty is payable the company may be liable, (ii) that if there are debts due by the deceased the company, by acting without a grant, intermeddles with the estate and may render itself liable, (iii) that the person who claims to be next of kin and entitled to deal with the estate may not be so entitled. It is considered that these risks are substantially covered by the said statutory declaration and indemnity.

Double Probate. A company can safely act on production of probate, notwithstanding that power is reserved to another person named as executor to prove (Administration of Estates Act, 1925, s. 8). The fact of this reservation should, however, be noted, although the reservation of the right to prove does not limit the powers of proving executors. If the proving executors require the company to register them as shareholders in their own right or to register a transfer by them of the shares, the company should, before complying with such request, give notice to the executor in whose favour the reservation was made in order to give him an opportunity of intervening. Again, if all the proving executors die, the company should, before recognising the title of the executors of the last survivor of them to act as executor of the original testator, enquire whether the person in whose favour power to prove had been reserved had renounced probate or had been cited and failed to appear.

If the executor in whose favour power was reserved afterwards takes out double probate and the shares had not been registered in the names of the first proving executors in their own right, the company should deal with the shares only on the authority of all the executors who have proved. If, however, the first proving executors have been registered as holders of the shares in their own right, a transfer will be necessary to perfect the title of the executor to whom double probate was granted; but if the company has notice of the grant of the double probate and the executors on the register attempt to transfer the shares, the directors should not register the transfer without giving notice to the executor to whom the double probate was granted and giving him an opportunity of intervening.

Dominion and colonial probates or letters of administration **Colonial** must be resealed in this country before the personal repre- **Probates, etc.** sentative can be recognised. Similarly Scottish and Northern Ireland probates and letters of administration must be resealed in England, English or Northern Irish in Scotland, and England or Scottish in Northern Ireland. In the case of Scottish probates (called 'confirmations') the actual production thereof is no longer essential as evidence of the grant, and in lieu thereof the executors may, if they so desire, now lodge extracts under the seal of the local commissariat and signed by the Clerk of the Court, which state that confirmation was issued on a certain date in favour of named persons as executors. (See Act of Sederunt, Scottish Court of Session, dated 3rd February, 1933). Under the Trusts (Scotland) Act, 1921, unless the contrary is expressed in the confirmation, a quorum is permitted to act. The section (*inter alia*) provides further that a majority of the trustees accepting and surviving is a quorum.

No machinery exists for re-sealing in England grants made in the Isle of Man or the Channel Islands, and the general rule is that company registration officers should call for production of an English grant before allowing the shares of a deceased holder to be dealt with. An English grant may be dispensed with in cases where the total value of the property in England does not exceed, say, £150. Where, however, an English grant is dispensed with, the company registration officer should insist on production of (*a*) a letter from the Estate Duty Office certifying that no claims for death duties arise, (*b*) a declaration that there are no assets in England other than the shares with which it is desired to deal, and (*c*) a document indemnifying the company against any claims for duties or otherwise which might arise in future.

The resealing of Scottish, Northern Irish and colonial grants is effected at the Principal Probate Registry, Somerset House, London, W.C., and the following fees are payable:—

(*a*) In the case of Scottish and Northern Irish grants:

    (i) On small estates under £500 .. 2s. 6d.

    (ii) On all other estates a composite fee of £1 5s. 0d.

(*b*) In the case of colonial grants the fee is £1 5s. 0d. in all cases and there is no allowance for small estates.

It may be noted that a 'certified copy of entry in the Register Book of Deaths' in the Irish Republic is the equivalent of the English death certificate.

Probate in the Irish Republic.

It is not now the practice to reseal probate or letters of administration granted in the Irish Republic; a fresh grant is required.

Foreign Probate.

As regards deceased foreign shareholders, it is necessary for a grant to be taken out in England by an attorney appointed for the purpose by the person entitled. The latter need not necessarily be the administrator in a foreign country, but as a rule the court will follow the foreign grant. (See Williams on 'Executors,' 12th ed., p. 292.) This procedure of obtaining a fresh grant is, in simple cases, followed in the case of colonial probates, as it is slightly less expensive than the process of resealing, and may be found more expeditious.

Letters of Request.

Upon production of probate a company should not, unless requested, enter the names of the executors upon the register as the holders of the shares. As long ago as 1879, in *Buchan's Case* (1879), 4 A.C. 549, in the House of Lords, the then Lord Chancellor, Lord Cairns, laid it down that the names of executors should not be entered on the register without 'a distinct and intelligent request' on the part of the executors. But when the articles, as they commonly do, provide for the executors being entitled to require the company to register them, it is then the duty of the company, upon request, to enter their names, unaccompanied by any mention of their representative capacity [*T. H. Saunders & Co.* (1908), 1 Ch. 415]. If this be done, the executors become personally liable on the shares, and the company has nothing to do with the deceased or his estate. Hence the frequent provision in articles that directors shall not be obliged to consent to the registration of executors; they may not desire, where the shares are not fully paid, to accept the liability of the executors, who may be men of straw, in lieu of the liability of the estate of the deceased, and may prefer to await a substantial transferee. When an executor is, upon a proper request, entered on the register, a fresh certificate should be issued, and the request should be recorded as a transfer. Where a sole executor or administrator is also beneficially entitled to shares he can, upon a proper request being made, be placed on the register without any transfer being executed. A form of request by executors or administrators to be placed on the register will be found in Appendix F (Form 104).

Evidence of Death.

As to the evidence which should be demanded on death, in the case of the death of a holder in sole account, the production of probate or letters of administration or confirmation as executor should be required; in the case of the death of one holder in joint account, a certificate of death is usually sufficient. A form of certificate of identity, where one is required, will be found in Appendix F, Form 42. Under s. 82 any document which is by law sufficient evidence of probate or letters of administration or confirmation as executor must be accepted by the company as sufficient evidence of the grant. A form of marking stamp (on share certificates) for the registration of death (or marriage) certificates will be found in Appendix F, Form 103.

Upon the death of a joint shareholder, the shares vest, by right of survivorship, in the survivors or survivor.

A company is sometimes appointed executor, and if, as is usually the case, it is a trust corporation, probate will be granted to the company together with the other executors, if any. If the company is not a trust corporation, it must appoint under its seal a representative, called a syndic, to whom letters of administration with the will annexed will be granted, and these will be produced to the company in which the deceased held shares. In the case of a company (not a trust corporation) being appointed co-executor with individuals, no grant can be made to the syndic unless the individuals have renounced probate, since probate and letters of administration cannot be granted in respect of the same estate.

Company Executor or Administrator.

In cases where executors are to be noted in the register in their representative capacity, probate should be exhibited, and the register of probates should give the names and addresses of the executors. The common practice of making a note in the register of members that probate has been exhibited, and giving the names of the executors, to whom the probate has been granted, is to be recommended. The same applies to administrators.

In the event of the sale by the executors of part of the holding—they being entitled to sell the holding under s. 76 of the Act—the balance certificates should be made out in the name of the deceased, the names of the executors being given in the margin of the certificate. Where executors have been noted in their representative capacity, dividend warrants should be made out to (say) 'John Brown, one of the executors of A. Smith, deceased.' John Brown would endorse the warrant. If sent to a bank, the warrant would be payable to (say) 'Coutts & Co. A/c A. Smith, deceased' (or as per instructions).

It is usually desirable, whenever possible, to compel the registration in their personal capacity of persons claiming by transmission. The best method of so doing is to withhold dividends, but this can only be done when the articles authorise it. An article in some such form as follows will serve the purpose: If within a year and a day from the death of a shareholder his executors or administrators have not [themselves been registered as the holders of his shares, or have not] transferred his shares, the directors may withhold payment of all dividends that may be payable in respect of such shares until such time as the executors or administrators shall [themselves have been so registered, or shall] have transferred the shares, when the said dividends shall be payable to the [executors or administrators, or the] transferee of the shares [as the case may be].

Photographic Copies of Documents. The general practice at present with regard to photographic copies of the undermentioned documents is briefly as follows:

(i) Probates and letters of administration, when bearing the modified seal of the probate office, are universally accepted. (Cf. s. 82 of the Act.)

(ii) Court orders bearing the seal of the appropriate court are accepted.

(iii) Powers of attorney can be accepted where the company is satisfied as to authenticity and continuing validity. Some protection is afforded by the Law of Property Act, 1925, s. 124. (See p. 76 and chapter XXII.)

(iv) Birth, marriage and death certificates are occasionally accepted.

For complete safety a secretary should insist on the production of original documents or copies which bear the seal of the appropriate court, and it is in each case a matter for his discretion whether he so insists or not. While it is proper for him to take a stand on correct procedure, he should not be obstructionist, and if he is in doubt as to the correct procedure he should be guided by the advice of the company's solicitors. It may be noted that the Judicature Act, 1925, s. 174 (1) provides that 'in the Principal Probate Registry there shall be used such seal as the President of the Probate Division may from time to time direct,' and s. 174 (2) that 'all probates, letters of administration, orders and other instruments *and copies thereof* and all exemplifications purporting to be sealed with any such seal as aforesaid shall be received in evidence in all parts of the United Kingdom without further proof.'

Destruction of Documents. It is acknowledged that the practice as regards the destruction of documents must vary widely in accordance with the size and needs of the company concerned. The following summary is intended as a guide:

(i) Transfers should be retained indefinitely; they are usually deeds and they record transactions which may be required at any time to be proved in court.

(ii) Share registers should be retained indefinitely, as s. 110 (1) (c) of the Companies Act, 1948, requires that a company shall keep a register of its members and enter therein, *inter alia*, the date at which any person ceased to be a member. For that reason, too, all sheets relating to 'dead' accounts removed from loose-leaf share registers also should be retained indefinitely.

(iii) Transfer registers. In the case of companies registered under the Companies Acts, transfer registers, if used, need not be kept for longer than each company considers it desirable, as they are not statutory books. Companies registered under the Companies Clauses Acts are, however, required to keep registers of transfers, and in the case of such companies they should be retained indefinitely.

(iv) Cancelled share certificates contain information endorsed on them which may be useful in case any documents relative to a particular transaction should become lost or mislaid, but it is not considered that their retention for more than, say, three years is necessary.

(v) Notifications of changes of address, if not filed on the general correspondence files, should be retained for at least two years, after which no enquiry in relation to them is likely to arise.

(vi) Paid dividend warrants need not be retained for more than 12 years, having regard to the Limitations Act, 1939.

(vii) Paid dividend sheets should, for the same reason, be retained for at least 12 years and for so long thereafter as they contain particulars relating to any unclaimed dividends.

(viii) Dividend mandates should be retained until they are cancelled by the shareholder.

(ix) Bearer scrip surrendered for registration should be retained long enough to be available for reference in case any enquiry arises, which in practice is not likely to occur after a lapse of three years.

A company should protect itself, by means of an insurance policy, from the consequences of accidental destruction of its documents by fire. Heavy liability can be incurred by a company which is not so covered. For instance, the destruction by fire of transfers waiting to be passed by the board of directors may, if the Inland Revenue authorities refuse to entertain an application for the allowance of duty on the destroyed transfers, involve the company in liability for stamp duty which might then have to be paid again on all such transfers. In such a case the Inland Revenue authorities, before allowing such an application, would require the full facts relative to the loss or destruction to be submitted, and in general would require evidence:

(i) as to the amount of stamp duty impressed on the deeds in question;

(ii) that the document was at the time of loss or destruction at least partly executed;

(iii) that a duplicate transfer had been stamped in lieu thereof.

Bankruptcy. In the case of the devolution of title to shares on the bankruptcy of a shareholder, the trustee in bankruptcy is the representative of the bankrupt, and the company should require as evidence either an office copy of his appointment or a copy of the *Gazette* containing notice thereof. If the shares are partly paid, the trustee may exercise the right of disclaimer conferred by s. 54 of the Bankruptcy Act, 1914; but, if the shares were charged, the disclaimer does not destroy the interest of the person entitled to the charge [*Wise* v. *Lansdell* (1921), 1 Ch. 420].

Registration of Court Orders. There are certain orders of the English court which a company is bound to note and act upon. When shares belong beneficially to a lunatic, the court appoints a committee or a receiver and may authorise him to transfer the shares. The order appointing a committee or receiver, and the scope of the authority given to him to transfer, should be noted, and a transfer in accordance with the authority should be registered as if it were a transfer by the shareholder himself. When shares are held by a lunatic as trustee, in many other cases when a transfer by an existing trustee cannot be obtained, and in certain other cases when a vesting order is desirable, the court makes an order vesting the right to transfer in some other person. Such an order must be noted, and a transfer by the other person in accordance with it must be registered as if it were a transfer by the shareholder himself. The company is also bound to act on an order of a Scottish court appointing a curator of a lunatic and to give effect to any powers of transfer which the order vests in the curator. The Scottish curator has by statute the same powers as an English committee. It is doubtful, however, whether an English company is entitled to act on vesting orders made by a Scottish court in connection with a trust; an English court has no power to make such orders which would bind a Scottish company, and the reverse is probably true. Of still more doubtful authority are orders of foreign courts: it may happen that there is some provision in the articles enabling the company either expressly or by implication to act on the order; and if that be so, and the shareholder concerned is domiciled in the country which makes the order, the company can act, otherwise it is not usually safe to give effect to a foreign order. In the commonest case, a foreign order vesting the property of a foreign lunatic, the proper course is for an English vesting order to be obtained under s. 134 of the Lunacy Act, 1890.

Liquidation. If a company holding shares in another company goes into liquidation, the latter company should require evidence of the appointment of the liquidator, *e.g.* a certified copy of the notice of appointment of liquidator filed with the Registrar of Companies. In compulsory liquidation, a copy of the *Gazette* containing notice of the appointment of the liquidator is sufficient.

In all the above cases the change of title should be noted in the register of members. Registers should be kept of proofs of death, marriage and other changes of title.

It is usual for companies to charge fees for the registra- **Registration** tion of various documents, and the issue of certificates in **Fees.** certain cases. But none of these fees is properly chargeable, unless authorised by the articles of association. Opportunity should be taken to alter the articles of association, where necessary, in order to justify the charges. The following fees are those usually charged:—

			s.	d.
For registration of transfer			2	6
		(some companies charge 5s.)		
"	"	probate	2	6
"	"	proof of death in joint holdings	2	6
"	"	request by executors to be placed on register	2	6
"	"	proof of marriage	2	6
"	"	power of attorney	2	6
"	"	change of name by deed-poll, or otherwise	2	6
"	"	lunacy orders	2	6
"	"	appointment of trustee in bankruptcy, etc.	2	6
For issue of duplicate certificates (each)			2	6*
" " split certificates (do.)			2	6*

No fee should be charged for registration of change of address, or for the issue of balance certificates, although in this latter case a fee of 1s. is charged by some companies.

* Table A, 1948, cl. 8 and 9.

CHAPTER IX

Calls. UNDER modern practice it is not unusual to call up the total amount payable on shares on application and allotment, and where this is done there will, of course, be no further calls. If, on the other hand, the shares are not fully paid after allotment, further calls will probably be made and therefore the machinery for securing due payment of the balance requires attention.

By the terms of the contract, *i.e.* the conditions of allotment, the unpaid balance may be payable at fixed dates. Thus, if 2s. 6d. for a £1 share is paid on application, and 2s. 6d. on allotment, the balance may be made payable by instalments as follows: 5s. on June 1st, 5s. on July 1st, and 5s. on October 1st. Or the unpaid balance may be payable by certain instalments at not less than certain fixed intervals. Thus, by the conditions of allotment, the balance of (say) 15s., due after the allotment money is paid, may be payable by three instalments of 5s. each at intervals of not less than (say) two months. Or again, there may be no conditions as to the payment of the balance, in which case one or more calls will be made as and when the money may be required.

Where the balance is by the terms of allotment payable at fixed dates, it is the duty of the shareholder to pay each instalment on the date fixed without a demand being made for it. In the other cases mentioned, the directors (if, as is usual, the power is vested in them) will resolve that the next instalment of a fixed sum be called up, or that a call be made of whatever amount is required, as the case may be.

As to the liability of infants, see the notes at the end of this chapter.

A form of resolution to make a call will be found in chapter XIV, and a form of call letter in Appendix F (Form 33).

Power to make calls may be vested in the company in general meeting, but, as stated above, it is more frequently vested in the directors (*e.g.* Table A, cl. 15). Since the articles of the company are the terms of the contract whereby a shareholder has agreed to take his shares, all the requirements of the articles must be strictly observed in making a call; otherwise the call may be invalid.

For instance, if a call be made by directors, the board meeting must be duly convened, and the directors must be properly appointed [*Garden Gully Co.* v. *McLister* (1875), 1 A.C. 39]. The prescribed quorum must be present [*Alma*

Spinning Co., Bottomley's Case (1880), 16 Ch. D. 681]; but a call made by less than a quorum, and afterwards confirmed when a quorum was present, has been held good [*Phosphate of Lime Co., Austin's Case* (1871), 24 L.T. 932].

Power to make calls is in the nature of a trust, and must be exercised by the directors for the good of the company [*Gilbert's Case* (1870), 5 Ch. App. 559]. Directors may not protect their own shares from a call and let the whole burden fall upon the other shareholders [*Alexander* v. *Automatic Telephone Co.* (1900), 2 Ch. 56].

A company may, if authorised by its articles, make arrangements on an issue of shares for a difference between the shareholders in the amount and times of payment of calls (s. 59). *Prima facie*, however, there is an implied equality between shareholders of the same class, and it is wrong to make a call on some members only of a class [*Galloway* v. *Hallé Concert Society* (1915), 2 Ch. 233].

The amount of the call and the time for payment must be fixed by the resolution [*Cawley & Co.* (1889), 42 Ch. D. 209]. A call is made when the resolution is passed, not when notice is given to the shareholder [*R.* v. *Londonderry Rly. Co.* (1849), 13 Q.B. 998], and the articles generally contain a provision to that effect. A call is owing from the day on which it is made, although it is payable on a subsequent day [*China Steamship Co.* (1869), 38 L.J. Ch. 512].

A call is in the nature of a specialty debt [*Cork and Bandon Railway* v. *Goode* (1853), 13 C.B. 827; s. 20], and is recoverable at any time within 12 years [Limitation Act, 1939, s. 2 (3)]. A company may prove in the administration of the estate of a deceased shareholder, whose estate is insolvent, for the estimated value of the liability to future calls in respect of the shares standing in his name [*Fuller* v. *McMahon* (1900), 1 Ch. 173].

Where the articles so provide (*e.g.* Table A, cl. 18), a shareholder will be liable for interest on overdue calls.

Where Table A, cl. 21, applies, or similar provision is made in special articles, calls may be paid in advance, and the company may pay interest on moneys so prepaid, even though it is earning no profits, and the payment has to be made out of capital [*Lock* v. *Queensland Mortgage Co.* (1896), A.C. 461]. Money paid in advance of calls is capital paid up, and not an ordinary loan, so that it cannot be repaid except on a legal reduction of capital [*London & Northern Steamship Co., Ltd.* v. *Farmer* (1914), 111 L.T. 204]. The power to accept from a member the whole or any part of the amount remaining unpaid on any shares held by him, although no part of that amount has been called up, is conferred by s. 59 of the Act upon companies which are so authorised by their articles— hence the above-mentioned provision in many articles.

Lien.

Under the articles of association of most companies a lien is given to the company on the shares (or more generally upon the shares not fully paid) of the members in respect of any debts for the time being due from them to the company, e.g. in the case of partly paid shares, for calls [cf. Table A, cl. 11–14]. The Council of the Stock Exchange, however, requires the articles to provide that fully paid shares shall not be subject to a lien. If the original articles do not provide for a lien they may be altered by special resolution, or if under the original articles the lien only applies to partly paid shares, it may be extended by special resolution to fully paid shares [*Allen* v. *Gold Reefs of West Africa* (1900), 1 Ch. 656]. If such a lien exists no transfer of the shares belonging to a member who is indebted to the company should be sanctioned by the directors until the debt is discharged.

Forfeiture.

The articles of most companies authorise the forfeiture of shares in the event of failure on the part of a member to pay any call or instalment on or before the day appointed for the payment thereof (see e.g. Table A, cl. 33–39). The provisions of the articles as to forfeiture must be very carefully studied and scrupulously observed, for the right of forfeiture is very strictly construed by the courts, and any irregularity in or deviation from the powers given to the directors by the articles will render the forfeiture bad. Where the articles give no power of forfeiture, the sanction of the court must be obtained to make it valid [*Clarke* v. *Hart* (1858), 6 H.L.C. 633].

A power to forfeit for non-payment of debts generally as distinct from calls or instalments is invalid, as the exercise of such a power would amount to an illegal reduction of capital [*Hopkinson* v. *Mortimer Harley & Co.* (1917), 1 Ch. 646]. Probably a power to forfeit on any ground except non-payment of calls or instalments, e.g. a power to forfeit shares of a deceased holder whose personal representatives do not apply for registration, is equally invalid.

A power of forfeiture must not be exercised in the interests of a shareholder to enable him to escape liability, but in the interests of the company [*Spackman* v. *Evans* (1868), L.R. 3 H.L. 171].

Notwithstanding forfeiture, a shareholder is liable to pay all calls owing at the time of the forfeiture, with interest, if the articles so provide [*Stocken's Case* (1868), 3 Ch. App. 412]. Where shares have been forfeited for non-payment of calls and re-sold, then (even if an article equivalent to Table A of 1862, cl. 22, applies) fresh calls may be made on the purchaser for the unpaid amount [*New Balkis Eersteling* v. *Randt Gold Mining Co.* (1904), A.C. 165]. He is, however, entitled, in the absence of agreement to the contrary, to be credited with sums paid by the original holder since forfeiture

[*Randt Gold Mining Co.* (1904), 2 Ch. 468]. It has been held that, where by the articles a member is not entitled to vote when calls are due from him, and is liable to pay the calls even after forfeiture, the purchaser of shares forfeited for non-payment of calls is not entitled to vote so long as the calls are unpaid by the original holder [*Randt Gold Mining Co.* v. *Wainwright* (1901), 1 Ch. 184].

The articles generally contain a power for the directors to annul a forfeiture, but such a power cannot be exercised adversely to the former shareholder, so as to make him liable for calls made subsequently [*Exchange Trust, Larkworthy's Case* (1903), 1 Ch. 711].

A form of resolution of the board to forfeit shares will be found in chapter XIV, but before using any such form the company should make sure that it complies with the requirements of the particular articles concerned.

A *bona fide* forfeiture made in accordance with the articles of the company will not be disturbed by the court [*Sparks* v. *Liverpool Waterworks Co.* (1807), 13 Ves. 428]. A shareholder may bring an action to set the forfeiture aside if he desires to test its validity [*Sweny* v. *Smith* (1869), L.R. 7 Eq. 324]. A slight irregularity, *e.g.* claiming interest from date of call instead of due date of payment, is sufficient for the court to annul a forfeiture [*Johnson* v. *Lyttle's Iron Agency* (1877), 5 Ch. D. 687].

When shares which have been forfeited are resold, the purchaser may require a statutory declaration to confirm that the necessary formalities have been complied with. Although such a declaration is only evidence and does not affect the validity of the forfeiture, the requirement is reasonable and should usually be met.

Dead Accounts and Unclaimed Dividends. It frequently occurs that a company has a number of 'dead accounts' and it is impossible to trace the shareholders in question. Such 'dead accounts' give rise to large balances of unclaimed dividends. There is no provision of law which enables such shares to be forfeited, except, like any other share, for non-payment of calls.

Unclaimed Dividends. Unless acknowledged, dividends due are in the nature of specialty debts and become barred by the Statute of Limitations if not claimed within 12 years of the date of the declaration, cf. *Jones* v. *Bellegrove Properties* (1949), 1 All E.R. 998; (1949), 2 All E.R. 198. It is usual to placed unclaimed dividends to an unclaimed dividend suspense account, and articles of companies sometimes provide that 'all dividends unclaimed for one year after having been declared, may be invested or otherwise made use of by the directors for the benefit of the company until claimed.' The Council of the Stock Exchange objects to articles which provide for the forfeiture of unclaimed dividends.

Surrender.   Surrender, like forfeiture, involves a reduction in capital, and is *prima facie* invalid, unless the sanction of the court is obtained. It has, however, been upheld in the following particular cases:

(i) when the surrender is in substance a forfeiture by agreement of shares for non-payment of calls [*Trevor* v. *Whitworth* (1887), 12 A.C. 409];

(ii) where existing fully paid shares are surrendered in exchange for new fully paid shares of the same nominal value [*Rowell* v. *John Rowell & Son* (1912), 2 Ch. 609];

(iii) when fully paid shares are gratuitously surrendered to trustees for the company [*Kirby* v. *Wilkins* (1929), 2 Ch. 444].

Schemes of arrangement under s. 206 sometimes provide for shares to be surrendered by the holders and immediately re-issued to other persons, and such schemes have been sanctioned by the court.

Underwriting Commissions.   The important subject of the payment of commissions on the issue of shares is dealt with in s. 53 of the Act, to which reference may be made. The interpretation of the section is in some respects difficult, but it is believed that the following is a correct summary of the present law as to the payment of underwriting commissions, both by the company and by vendors and promoters:

1. By the company—

(i) *Where there is a public issue.*

The following conditions must be complied with:

(*a*) The articles, either as originally framed, or as altered by special resolution, must authorise payment of the commission.

(*b*) The commission must not exceed 10 per cent. of the price at which the shares are issued or the amount or rate authorised by the articles, whichever is the less.

(*c*) The amount or rate must be disclosed in the prospectus.

(*d*) The number of shares which persons have agreed for a commission to subscribe absolutely must be disclosed in the prospectus. This requirement presumably includes 'firm' underwriting.

(ii) *Where there is no public issue.*

(*a*) The payment must be authorised by the articles.

(*b*) The commission must not exceed the amount or rate above mentioned.

(c)   The amount or rate must be disclosed (1) in the statement in lieu of prospectus, or (2) in a statement in
the prescribed form, signed in like manner as a
statement in lieu of prospectus, and delivered before
payment of the commission to the Registrar of
Companies for registration.

(d)   The amount or rate must be disclosed in any circular
or notice, not being a prospectus, inviting subscriptions, if any such circular or notice is issued.

(e)   The number of shares which persons have agreed for
a commission to subscribe absolutely must be
disclosed in the manner specified in (c) and (d).

It would seem that on a first issue, or on an issue made on
the conversion of a private company into a public company,
the disclosure must be made in the statement in lieu of prospectus, and on subsequent issues and in the case of a private
company it must be made in the statement in the prescribed
form.   Unless the statement in the prescribed form has been
duly filed before the shares are allotted, the commission
cannot be recovered from the company [*Andreae* v. *Zinc
Mines of Great Britain* (1918), 2 K.B. 454].   Section 53 also
applies to private companies [*Dominion of Canada General
Trading* v. *Brigstocke* (1911), 2 K.B. 648].

'Prescribed' means prescribed by Statutory Instrument
made by the Board of Trade (s. 455).

2.   By vendors or promoters—

Vendors or promoters, who wish to pay underwriting commissions out of money or shares received from a company,
must comply with the conditions under (i) (above), where
there is a public issue, and with the conditions under (ii)
(above), where there is not a public issue.

The following points are to be noted as to underwriting
generally:

The commission may be paid in consideration of (a) an
absolute subscription, *i.e.* in effect shares may be issued
firm at a discount (see below); or (b) a conditional subscription, *i.e.* underwriting; or (c) an agreement to procure either
form of subscription, *i.e.* an overriding commission.

Not only may shares not be applied, but the proceeds of
shares issued may not be used, in payment of commission,
unless the terms of the Act are complied with [*Shorto* v.
Colwill (1909), 101 L.T. 598].

Options to subscribe additional shares at par or at a premium
in consideration of subscribing part of the capital of a company
are not affected by the Act (except in so far as particulars of
options must be set out in a prospectus, Schedule IV, Part 1,
para. 7).   Such options are not an application of the shares

or capital money of the company within the prohibition [*Hilder* v. *Dexter* (1902), A.C. 474].

Issues at Discount.

Prior to the Act of 1929 shares could not be issued at a discount except in so far as the payment of a commission in consideration of an absolute subscription was authorised by the appropriate Companies Act [*Ooregum Gold Co.* v. *Roper* (1892), A.C. 125], and a colourable attempt to issue shares at a discount, purporting to be merely the payment of a commission as authorised by earlier Acts, was restrained [*Keatinge* v. *Paringa Consolidated Mines* (1902), W.N. 15].

Under the Act of 1948 (s. 57) shares can be issued at a discount subject to the following conditions:

   (i) The shares issued must be shares of a class already issued.

  (ii) No such issue can be made until one year has elapsed from the date on which the company was entitled to commence business.

 (iii) The issue must be authorised by resolution of the company in general meeting and the resolution must specify the maximum rate of discount.

 (iv) The issue must be sanctioned by the court.

  (v) The issue must be made within one month after the sanction of the court is obtained or within such extended time as the court may allow.

Where shares are not offered to the public for subscription, the amount or rate of the commission must be disclosed in a statement in lieu of prospectus or in a statement in the published form [s. 53 (1) (c) (ii)] (see Appendix F, Forms 5 and 6).

Where an issue of shares can be underwritten for a commission of 10 per cent. or less, it is unlikely that recourse will be had to this section, as the desired result can be achieved under s. 53 without recourse to the court.

Every prospectus relating to the issue of the shares and every balance sheet issued subsequently to the issue at a discount must contain particulars of the discount allowed, or so much thereof as has not been written off [s. 57 (3)], and every annual return subsequent to the issue must contain particulars of the discount so far as not written off [s. 124 (1) and Sixth Schedule, Part I (3) (g)].

Debentures may be issued at a discount, unless the provisions of the memorandum or articles of association prevent it [*Compagnie Générale, Campbell's Case* (1876), 4 Ch. D. 470; *Webb* v. *Shropshire Railways Co.* (1893), 3 Ch. 307], but where debentures issued at a discount are exchangeable for fully-paid shares this may involve the issue of shares at a discount and such an issue of debentures would be illegal [*Mosely* v. *Koffyfontein Mines* (1904), 2 Ch. 108].

Any discount or commission allowed or paid for placing debentures must be disclosed in a prospectus [s. 38 and the Fourth Schedule] or statement in lieu [s. 40 and the Fifth Schedule], and must appear in the annual return [s. 124 and Sixth Schedule, Part I, 3 (1) (b)], and particulars must be given on registration of the debenture [s. 95 (9)]. Moreover, any such discount not written off must be stated in the balance sheet (s. 149 and the Eighth Schedule). There is no limitation on the amount of rate of discount which may be allowed in the case of an issue of debentures.

The previously existing power of a company to pay brokerage is reserved by the Act [s. 53 (3)]. The power had been recognised in *Metropolitan Coal Association* v. *Scrimgeour* (1895), 2 Q.B. 604, where 2½ per cent. was paid. The basis of the decision in the case quoted was that 2½ per cent. was a reasonable remuneration for the work done by the brokers in placing shares. The decision is limited to work done by stockbrokers, but there appears to be no reason why similar brokerage should not be paid to any person or company who *bona fide* renders similar services.

Commissions may be paid to individuals on the issue of specific shares, subject, of course, to the provisions of s. 53; but more commonly they are paid upon a large number of shares being underwritten. 'An underwriting agreement' means an agreement, entered into before the shares are brought before the public, that in the event of the public not taking up the whole of them, or the number mentioned in the agreement, the underwriter will, for an agreed commission, take an allotment of such part of the shares as the public has not applied for' [per Cotton L.J., in *Licensed Victuallers' Association* (1889), 42 Ch. D. 1, at p. 6]. The object of underwriting is thus to insure the subscription of the issue.

The terms of underwriting are now usually embodied in a definite agreement, but sometimes the agreement takes the form of a letter from the underwriter addressed to the promoter of the company undertaking, in consideration of a commission to be paid in any event, to take up a certain number of shares, or a proportion of them, if not subscribed for by the public. Whether such letter amounts to a concluded contract, or whether it is merely an offer, the acceptance of which must be communicated to the underwriter, depends upon its terms [*Consort Deep Level Gold Mines* (1897), 1 Ch. 575].

In practice it is generally arranged to pay a broker or other person an underwriting commission of (say) 2 per cent., and an overriding commission of (say) ½ per cent. for his procuring others to sub-underwrite. The underwriter enters into sub-underwriting contracts with others to cover the liability undertaken on such terms as are thought fit. The prospectus in such a case usually states that 'sub-underwriting contracts have been entered into to which the company is not a party.' This statement avoids the necessity of disclosing particulars of the sub-underwriting contracts, which are often numerous; but, if it is made, care must be taken to see that the underwriting agreement is so framed that the statement is true, and any interest of the directors in the sub-underwriting must, of course, be disclosed. It might be held to be untrue if the underwriting agreement contained a clause releasing the underwriters on the acceptance by the company of sub-underwriters' applications and cheques. In any event such a clause is most undesirable. The underwriters should be in a position to know whether their sub-underwriters are substantial persons and ought to be made to guarantee their solvency, at any rate, unless the company has the right to reject applications by sub-underwriters. A form of sub-underwriting letter will be found in Appendix F, Form 29.

Register of Members. The register of members [s. 110], and the index thereto should be kept at the registered office of the company, but where the work of making up is done at another office of the company it may be kept there. Further, if the company arranges with some other person to make up the register it may be kept at the office of that person at which the work is done. But the register must not be kept outside England if the company is registered in England or outside Scotland if registered in Scotland [s. 110 (2)]. Every company must send notice to the Registrar of Companies of the place where the register is kept and must notify him of any change within 14 days unless the register has at all times been kept at the registered office (see Appendix F, Form 90). There are penalties for default [s. 110 (3) (4)]. If, owing to the default of an agent employed under s. 110 (2), the company fails to comply with the provisions of s. 110 (3), s. 111 (3) or s. 113 of the Act, the penalties extend to that agent and an order may be made by the court against him, his officers and servants, under s. 113 (4), for the immediate inspection of the register (s. 114). The register and index, except when closed pursuant to s. 115, must during business hours be open to inspection by any member without fee, or by any other person at a fee not exceeding one shilling. The hours for inspection may, however, be restricted by the company in general meeting, provided that not less than two hours daily be allowed [s. 113 (1)]. Any person, whether a member or not, may require a copy of the register, or of any part of it, on payment of a sum not exceeding sixpence for every hundred words or part of a hundred words required to be copied [s. 113 (2)]; but he is not entitled to take copies himself without payment [*Balaghat Gold Mining Co.* (1901), 2 K.B. 665]. The company must comply with any request under s.113 within ten days from the day on which the request is received by the company, and in the event of default the company and its officers are liable to penalties and the court may order immediate inspection. A person desiring to inspect need not give any reason for doing so [*Holland* v. *Dickson* (1888), 37 Ch. D. 669], and even if it be known that the object of inspecting the register or of requiring the copy thereof is antagonistic to the company, it is illegal to refuse such inspection or copy [*Davies* v. *Gas Light & Coke Co.* (1909), 1 Ch. 708]. The right to inspect and require copies ceases when the company is in liquidation. It may be observed that in the case of statutory companies there is a right to take copies of all material parts of the register [*Mutter* v. *Eastern and Midlands Railway* (1888), 38 Ch. D. 92].

The register may be closed for a period or periods not ex- **Closing Register.** ceeding in all thirty days in each year, but before so closing it the company must give notice by advertisement in some newspaper circulating in the district in which the registered office is situate [s. 115]. A form of directors' resolution to close the books will be found in chapter XIV.

The court has power to rectify the register in any case **Rectification.** where a name is improperly entered in or omitted from the register, or where there is default or unnecessary delay in entering on the register the fact of a person having ceased to be a member. The person aggrieved, or any member of the company, or the company itself, may apply to the court for rectification [s. 116 (1)], and if the application is granted the court may award damages to any party aggrieved [s. 116 (2)]. Where an order is made by the court under this section, the secretary's duty is to strike out the entry ordered to be struck out by drawing a line through it, or to make the entry ordered to be made, as the case may be. He should add some such words as 'This entry was deleted (*or* made) pursuant to order of the court, dated the   day of   19 .' An entry which has to be struck out should not be erased. An unauthorised alteration of the register by the secretary is a nullity [*Indo-China Steam Navigation Co.* (1917), 2 Ch. 100], since the power of rectification lies solely with the court.

The register of members is *prima facie* evidence of any matters directed or authorised by the Act to be inserted in it [s. 118], but the presumption thus raised may be displaced by evidence of the incorrectness of the entry.

A company authorised to transact business in any part **Dominion** of His Majesty's dominions outside Great Britain, the Channel **Register.** Islands or the Isle of Man, may keep in any such part of His Majesty's dominions where it transacts business a branch register of members resident in that part. This register is called a 'dominion register', and references to a colonial register occurring in any articles registered before the 1st November, 1929, are to be construed as references to a dominion register.

The Registrar must be notified of the situation of the office where any dominion register is kept, and of any change in its situation, and of its discontinuance [s. 119]. A duplicate of a dominion register must be kept, duly entered up, at the place where the company's principal register is kept, which duplicate is deemed to be part of the principal register and, in the event of default in this obligation or in transmitting to the registered office copies of entries in the dominion register, the company and its officers are liable to penalties [s. 120]. For further details as to dominion registers, reference may be made to ss. 119–123 of the Act. Under s. 122, sections 119-121 may be applied by order in Council to foreign countries in which His Majesty the King has jurisdiction, and by s. 123, if a branch register is lawfully kept in Great Britain by a company incorporated in any part of His Majesty's dominions outside Great Britain (including protectorates and British Trust Territories), s. 113 (as to inspection), and s. 116 (as to rectification of the register), may by order in Council be applied to such branch register. The usual objects of keeping a dominion register are: first, to facilitate local dealings in shares which are largely held in a dominion; and, secondly, to save the dominion shareholders from having to pay United Kingdom stamp duty on a transfer of their shares. A form of request to be placed on a dominion register will be found in Appendix F, Form 98. A form of receipt for certificate lodged on transfer from England to a dominion register will be found in Appendix F, Form 99.

Annual Return of Companies having a Share Capital. Sections 124–129 contain the statutory law on the subject, and the statutory form of the document applicable to a company having a share capital is contained in the Sixth Schedule to the Act. See Appendix F, Forms 54 and 55.

The annual return must be made once in each year and must contain the matters specified in Part I of the Sixth Schedule to the Act with regard to the registered office of the company, registers of members and debenture holders, shares and debentures, indebtedness, past and present members and directors and secretary. The actual return must be in the form set out in Part II thereof or as near thereto as circumstances admit [s. 124 (1)]. Under s. 124 (1), proviso (a), an annual return need not be made in the year of incorporation nor in the following year, unless the company is required by s. 131 of the Act to hold an annual general meeting in that year. The annual return must contain (inter alia) (i) a list of the names and addresses of all persons who, on the fourteenth day after the company's annual general meeting for the year, are members of the company, and of persons who have ceased to be members since the last return, or in the case of the first return, since the incorporation of the company; (ii) the number of shares held by each of the present members

at the date of the return (*i.e.* on the fourteenth day aforesaid);
(iii) particulars of shares transferred since the date of the last
return (or in the case of the first return since the incorporation
of the company) by (*a*) present members and (*b*) the above-
mentioned past members; and (iv) the dates of registration
of all such transfers.

If the names are not arranged in alphabetical order an index
must be annexed.   Under s. 124 (1), proviso (*c*), if the return
for either of the last two years has given full particulars as
required by para. 5 of the Sixth Schedule (regarding present
and past members and the shares and stock held and transferred by them), the annual return need only give such of the
particulars required by that paragraph as relate to persons
ceasing to be or becoming members since the date of the last
return, and to shares transferred since that date, or to changes
in the amount of shares or stock held by a member.   The
effect of this is that the annual return need only include a full
list of members once every three years.   In this connexion
the following practical points should be observed:—

(*a*)   Where a member has increased his holding since the
        date of filing the last return, the full present holding
        should be entered in the first column of the return
        showing the number of shares held.   A note of the
        increase and the date of the increase in the holding
        should be entered in the remarks column.   In cases
        where there are several transactions which during the
        period result in a net increased holding at the close of
        the period, the dates can be omitted.   It is not neces-
        sary to cross-reference the account of the shareholder
        acquiring the shares with that of the shareholder
        disposing of those shares, although in the case of small
        companies, the Registrar would appreciate such
        information, as it may be of interest to anyone inspect-
        ing the company's file.

(*b*)   It does not matter that the number of shares held at
        the date of the return cannot be added up throughout
        so as to make one total to agree with that stated in the
        summary to have been taken up, provided that secre-
        taries clearly mark the return as being one relating to
        changes only.   In this connexion secretaries should
        indicate on the returns whether they are full returns
        or returns of changes only.

(*c*)   Self-balancing totals of increased shareholdings and
        shares transferred are not required to be shown.

(*d*)   All names should be shown in alphabetical order, but
        it is understood that the Registrar will not object to a
        separate list of persons, who have ceased to be members
        during the year, being added at the end, provided, of

course, that this return is itself in alphabetical order. Where this is done there should be an indication at the head of the return that the index is in two sections. Many companies who concentrate on the dividend mandate system have their share register divided under banks. In such cases it is simpler to file the annual return with alphabetical sections for each bank than to amalgamate such accounts with one composite list. The limit to the number of split indices which the Registrar will allow is governed by whether the name can be readily found by anyone inspecting the file. In practice, however, the Registrar will accept a return comprising three or four self-contained lists, provided once again that there is sufficient indication at the head of the return that this has been done. This concession applies only to large companies where the fusion of the split lists would prove an onerous task. Smaller companies are expected to prepare one composite alphabetical list.

(e) There is no need to include the change of name of a female shareholder on marriage nor the splitting of an existing account into designated accounts, *e.g.* nominee companies. The Registrar will not object if this is done, but is of opinion that it is not essential.

(f) Where it is more convenient for a company to prepare a full return the Registrar will always accept it in lieu of a return showing changes only. For example, it will be appreciated that in cases where a company has made a bonus issue during the year to which the return relates, it is usually far simpler to prepare and run off a complete return than a return of changes only, but in that case the return must comply fully with the Sixth Schedule to the Act.

Where a company keeps a dominion register and particulars required for the annual return are not received at the registered office of the company before the date when the return is made, they are not to be included in the return. Where, however, the annual return is made between the date when any entries are made in the dominion register and the date when copies of these entries are received at the company's registered office, these entries (if relevant) shall be included in the next or a subsequent return as appropriate [s. 124 (2)]. It is thought that the names of members presumed to be dead should be included in the return unless official notification of death has been received.

If the company has converted any shares into stock the list must state the amount of stock held by each existing member instead of the amount of shares and the particulars relating to shares required by the section.

The annual return must be completed within forty-two days after the annual general meeting for the year, and should, therefore, in the case of large companies, be put in hand as early as possible, as it must be signed by a director and by the secretary and forwarded to the Registrar forthwith.

The work of preparing the return is very much reduced by addressing machines which are now in general use in company offices of any size. The Registrar will accept an annual return made up by an addressing machine even though the order of the christian names and surnames is reversed from that given in the Sixth Schedule to the Act. The loose-leaf register is also very useful in preparing a lengthy return.

The return must state the address of the registered office and where the register of members is kept, if not at the registered office. It must contain a summary, which, besides distinguishing between shares issued for cash and shares issued as fully or partly paid up otherwise than in cash, must specify a number of particulars, which may readily be ascertained from Part I to the Sixth Schedule of the Act, or from the statutory form of annual return set out in Part II thereof. Among the particulars required by the Sixth Schedule are the particulars required by s. 200 to be included in the register of directors and secretaries. This section is discussed on p. 174, but it may usefully be pointed out here that under sub-s. 9 of that section a person in accordance with whose directions or instructions the directors are accustomed to act is himself to be deemed a director and officer of the company. [See also s. 126 (2).]

Except in the case of an exempt* private company or an **Balance** assurance company which has complied with s. 7 (4) of the **Sheet.** Assurance Companies Act, 1909, there must be annexed to the annual return (i) a written† copy, certified both by a director and by the secretary of the company, to be a true copy, of every balance sheet laid before the company in general meeting during the period to which the return relates (including every document required by law to be annexed to the balance sheet); and (ii) a copy, certified in the same manner, of the report of the auditors on, and of the report of the directors accompanying, each such balance sheet. If any of these documents is in a foreign language, a certified translation must be attached [s. 127 (1)].

If any such balance sheet or document required by law to be annexed thereto did not comply with the requirements of the law in force at the date of the audit with respect to the

* See chapter XXIII on Private Companies.
† This includes printing, lithography or reproduction by mechanical means.

form of balance sheets or documents aforesaid, the requisite corrections must be made in the copy to bring it into conformity with such law, and the fact that the copy has been so amended must be stated thereon.

Annual Return of Companies not having Share Capital. An annual return is required of companies not having a share capital, but the particulars required to be included in the return or in the annexed statement are only as to (1) registered office, (2) the directors and the secretary, (3) certain indebtedness, (4) address where register of members is kept if not at the registered office, (5) address where register of debenture holders (if any) is kept [s. 125 (1) (2)]. Section 127, however, applies, and accordingly the return must include a certified copy of the balance sheet and other documents mentioned above. See Appendix F, Form 99.

Default in complying with the requirements of the Act as to the annual return renders the company and its officers liable to penalties.

Although the returns cannot be made up strictly in accordance with the statute if no general meeting has been held, yet directors, who are themselves in default as regards the holding of the meeting [s. 131], cannot rely upon the fact that no meeting has been held as a defence to proceedings for default in filing the annual return [*Park* v. *Lawton* (1911), 1 K.B. 588].

NOTE *re* INFANTS (TRANSFERS, DIVIDENDS, ETC.)

Infant Shareholders. In the administration of companies questions of difficulty sometimes arise as to the course to be pursued where an infant is sought to be registered as a member, or, where an infant has been so registered, whether or not with the knowledge of the company that he was an infant, as to the rights, duties and liabilities of the company and the infant respectively.

It is settled law that an infant may be a holder of shares in a company, whether incorporated by special Act of Parliament or registered under the Companies Acts. In the case of statutory companies, the possible infancy of a shareholder is expressly recognised by s. 79 of the Companies Clauses Act, 1845, which provides that, if any shareholder be a minor, he may vote by his guardian or any one of his guardians. An infant who subscribes the memorandum of association of a registered company is a 'person' within the meaning of s. 1 of the Companies Act, 1948, so that the company is duly incorporated by registration notwithstanding his infancy [*Laxon & Co.* (1892), 3 Ch. 555], and he becomes a member upon the registration. But although an infant may legally be a shareholder, he cannot compel a company to register him as a shareholder. In many cases the articles of association of a company expressly prohibit the transfer of shares to an infant. Even in the absence of such an article, a company could not be compelled to register an infant. There are not in general any such provisions applicable to a statutory company, but it has been held [*R.* v. *Midland Counties and Shannon Railway Co.* (1862), 15 Irish Common Law Reports 514; 9 L.T. 155] that a railway company cannot be compelled to register a transfer of partly paid shares to an infant. It was said (by O'Brien J. in that case) that the result of so doing would be to relieve the original shareholder from liability without giving the company a shareholder whom they could hold. If the company brought an action against the infant for future calls it would be open to him, during his infancy, to plead his infancy (and, it must be added, to repudiate his shares), and if the action were brought against him after he had attained his full age it would be open to him to plead that he had repudiated the transfer after coming of age.

This reasoning obviously does not apply to a transfer of fully paid shares to an infant, but it is submitted that the principle is the same, for a company ought not to be compelled to accept a transferee who might conceivably repudiate the transfer at some future time, leaving the company in a difficulty as to the true ownership of the shares in case the transferor could not then be discovered, and (before repudiation) in respect of payment of dividends and other matters, although, as O'Brien J. said in the case above cited, referring to fully paid shares, 'it is not likely that there would be any repudiation either during infancy or on majority; and the company might not raise any objection to the registering of the transfer.' There does not, however, appear to be any direct authority upon this point, all the decided cases, naturally enough, being cases in which there was a liability upon the shares.

Where a company has registered an infant as a shareholder in ignorance of his infancy, it may, upon discovering the fact, obtain an order of the court for rectification of the register by substituting the name of the transferor [*Symon's Case* (1870), 5 Ch. App. 298].

If, however, the company, after discovering the infancy of the shareholder, continues to treat him as such, it may be precluded by laches and delay from obtaining the substitution of the name of the transferor for that of the transferee [*National Bank of Wales, Massey and Giffin's Case* (1907), 1 Ch. 582; *Parson's Case* (1869), L.R. 8 Eq. 656]. *A fortiori*, if a company has allowed an infant to transfer shares of which he is the registered holder and has accepted and registered his transferee, who is an adult, it cannot go behind it and avoid the original transfer to the infant [*Gooch's Case* (1872), 8 Ch. App. 266].

So if a company registers an infant, knowing that he is such, it would seem that it cannot afterwards repudiate him. A transfer of shares to or by an infant is voidable, but not void. Where the company is a going concern, the court may determine whether an infant ought to retain the shares or not [*Reid's Case* (1857), 24 Beav. 318].

If an infant has been registered as a shareholder, and the company does not desire to have his name removed, or is precluded from doing so as above mentioned, to what extent can the infant insist upon exercising rights as a shareholder during his minority? This may be dealt with under the following heads:—

1. *Voting.*—In the case of companies regulated by the Companies Clauses Acts, express provision is made [s. 79 of the Act of 1845] enabling him to vote by his guardian or guardians. In the absence of any similar provision in the articles of association of a registered company, it is thought that an infant cannot vote by his guardian at a general meeting of such a company, but that, in the absence of any prohibition in the articles, he could vote personally. An authority to vote by his guardian might be construed as implying a prohibition against voting personally.

2. *Dividends.*—An infant shareholder is entitled, as a member, to the dividends declared on his shares; the difficulty is that, in general, an infant, except in the case of a married woman, is incapable of giving a legal discharge for money paid to him. When, however, an infant has in fact received money, he cannot demand it over again on attaining his majority [*Earl of Buckinghamshire* v. *Drury* (1761), 2 Eden. 60, at p. 72]. Although the receipt of dividends by him does not prevent him from repudiating his shares, yet, if he does so, he must repay the dividends which he has received [*Bentinck's Case* (1873), 18 Sol. J. 224]. Moreover, a dividend warrant in the ordinary form is a bill of exchange [*Thairlwall* v. *Great Northern Railway Co.* (1910), 2 K.B. 509] and the endorsement of it entitles the holder to receive payment, although the indorser is an infant [Bills of Exchange Act, 1882, s. 22 (2)]. It would seem, therefore, that there is no great risk in paying dividends to an infant by a warrant crossed 'not negotiable.' Finally, the court, in its general jurisdiction over infants, can make an order authorising a guardian to receive the dividends; that would enable any case of difficulty to be met.

3. *Transfers.*—A transfer of shares held by an infant cannot effectually be made except under an order of court. The company should, therefore, refuse to accept a transfer made by a shareholder known to be an infant.

4. *Calls.*—An infant is liable to pay calls upon partly paid shares held by him unless and until he repudiates his shares.

Taking shares is not merely a contract, but the purchase of an interest to which statutory obligations are attached [*North-Western Railway Co.* v. *McMichael* (1850), 5 Exch. 114]. This being so, it seems that the Infants' Relief Act, 1874, does not affect the matter [*Simpson on Infants*, 4th ed., p. 37].

The views set forth may be summarised as follows:—

1. An infant may be a holder of shares or stock in a company.

2. He cannot compel a company to register him as a holder of partly paid shares nor (probably) as a holder of fully paid shares or stock.

3. A company, upon discovering that a transferee of shares who has been registered as a member is an infant, may apply to have the name of the transferor registered in his stead unless precluded from doing so by laches.

4. If a company registers an infant, knowing him to be such, it cannot afterwards repudiate him.

5. An infant can vote by his guardian at a general meeting of the company if the company is governed by the Companies Clauses Act, 1845, or if there is express provision for that purpose in the articles of association of a registered company. He cannot vote personally if the company is governed by the Companies Clauses Act, 1845, but, if it is incorporated under the Companies Acts, he can vote personally in the absence of any prohibition, express or implied, in the articles.

6. A company does not run any substantial risk in issuing dividend warrants to a member, though he may be an infant.

7. A transfer of shares by a shareholder known to be an infant should not be accepted.

8. An infant holder of partly paid shares is liable for calls unless and until he repudiates the shares.

The allotment of shares to an infant is dealt with in chapter VI, p. 58.

CHAPTER X

SHARE WARRANTS

A share warrant is a document under the seal of the company to the effect that the bearer is entitled to the number of fully paid shares of the company stated therein, the distinguishing numbers, if any, being specified (Appendix F, Form 113). A share warrant is by mercantile usage and by virtue of s. 83 (3) of the Act, a negotiable instrument transferable by mere delivery, that is to say, it may be passed from hand to hand, and a *bona fide* holder for value for the time being is entitled to the benefit of it, notwithstanding some defect in title, *e.g.* theft by a previous holder. The statutory law relating to share warrants is contained in ss. 83, 112, 182 (2) of the Act.

Share warrants may be issued in respect of any fully paid up shares or stock by any public company limited by shares which is authorised so to do by its articles, and it may be noted that the issue of share warrants is not confined to ordinary shares. A private company must not take power by its articles to issue share warrants, as otherwise it cannot comply with the requirements of s. 28. A share warrant cannot be issued for partly paid shares.

Under the Exchange Control Act, 1947, s. 10, no person shall, without the permission of the Treasury, issue any bearer certificate or coupon in the United Kingdom and no person resident in the United Kingdom shall issue such certificate or coupon outside the United Kingdom. Further, ss. 15 and 16 of the same Act provide that bearer certificates must be deposited in the custody of an authorised depository, *e.g.* a bank.

Conditions of Issue. The conditions governing the issue of share warrants are settled either by the company's articles of association or by resolution of the board of directors, passed pursuant to some provision in the articles.

Sometimes the conditions are printed on the back of the warrant, but it is more usual to print them separately and to issue them on application. The holder can then keep his conditions of issue by him, but under the Exchange and Control Act, 1947, he must lodge his warrants with a bank or other authorised depositary. This course also enables the company more easily to vary the conditions subsequently, if it should become desirable to do so.

It is highly important to guard against forgery, and the warrants should therefore be printed on paper bearing a distinctive water mark. It is desirable that the printing should be done direct from a steel plate which cannot easily be imitated.

Upon making an issue of share warrants the following points require consideration:

(1) The power of the company and the directors to issue share warrants under the articles of association.

(2) The denominations to be issued, that is to say, the number of shares to be comprised in each class of warrant it is proposed to have printed, e.g. it may be decided to issue warrants in three classes representing 1, 5 and 25 shares per warrant respectively. Each warrant should be given a distinctive serial number, and the respective denominations should be denoted by an initial letter, so that, if the warrants are in denominations of 1, 5 and 25 shares respectively, warrants for 1 share would have the letter A before the warrant number, warrants for 5 shares would have the letter B, and warrants for 25 shares would have the letter C. In each denomination the numbers of the warrants printed could commence with the number one. It is usual to have each class of warrant printed on a distinctive coloured paper. The distinguishing numbers of the shares comprised in each warrant would be written in by hand when the warrant is being issued.

(3) The conditions of issue must in no way controvert the articles of association. A specimen set of conditions is given hereunder:

1. Share warrants shall be issued in denominations of 1, 5 and 25 shares.

2. No share warrant shall be issued, except upon a request in writing by the person for the time being upon the register of members as the holder of the share or shares in respect of which the share warrant is to be issued, or in exchange for other share warrants.

3. The request shall be in such form and authenticated by such statutory declaration or other evidence as to the identity of the person making the same, and of his right or title to the share or shares as the directors may from time to time require, and shall be lodged at the registered office of the company, or elsewhere, as the directors may from time to time determine.

4. Before the issue of a share warrant the share certificate (if any) then outstanding in respect of the shares intended to be included in it shall be delivered up to the company and retained by it, unless the directors dispense with this condition for special reasons.

5. Any member applying to have a share warrant issued shall, at the time of the application, pay to the company any stamp duty payable in respect thereof, and also such fee for each share warrant as the directors may from time to time determine.

6. Share warrants shall be issued under the common seal of the company and authenticated in such manner as the directors may from time to time determine.

7. Each share warrant shall be in such language and form as the directors may think fit. The number (if any) originally attached to each share shall be stated in the share warrant.

8. Coupons payable to bearer, of such number as the directors may think fit, shall be attached to the share warrants providing for the payment of the dividends in respect of the shares included therein, and there shall be attached to each share warrant a talon or voucher exchangable in due course for a fresh sheet of coupons and talon (comprising so many coupons as the directors may determine), providing for the payment of subsequent dividends upon or in respect of such shares, and upon production and surrender of the appropriate talon, a fresh sheet of coupons with appropriate talon, shall be issued to the person making such production and surrender.

9. Each coupon shall be distinguished by the number of the share warrant to which it belongs, and by a number showing the place it holds in the series of coupons belonging to the share warrant. The coupons shall not be expressed to be payable at any particular period, nor shall they contain any statement as to the amount which shall be payable.

10. Upon any dividend being declared to be payable upon the share or shares specified in any share warrant, the directors shall publish an advertisement in one daily newspaper published in London, and in such other newspapers, if any, as they may think fit, stating the amount per share or per cent. payable, the date and place or places of payment, and the serial number of the coupon to be presented, and thereupon any person presenting and delivering up a coupon of that serial number at the place or one of the places stated in such advertisement shall be entitled to receive at the expiration of such number of days (not exceeding five), after so delivering it up as the directors may from time to time direct, the dividend payable on the shares specified in the share warrant to which such coupon belongs, according to the notice which shall have been so given by advertisement.

11. The company shall be entitled to recognise an absolute right in the bearer for the time being of any coupon so advertised for payment to such amount of dividend on the shares specified in the share warrant to which such coupon belongs as shall have been declared payable upon presentation, and delivery of such coupon shall be a good discharge to the company accordingly.

12. If any share warrant or coupon be worn out or defaced, the directors may, upon surrender thereof for cancellation and upon payment by the applicant of the stamp duty imposed upon the issue of a new warrant and of such fee as the directors may determine, issue a new one in its stead.

13. No person shall as bearer of a share warrant be entitled (a) to sign a requisition for calling a meeting or to give notice of his intention to submit a resolution to a meeting, or (b) to attend or to exercise any privilege as a member at a meeting unless he shall in case (a) before or at the time of lodging such requisition or giving such notice of intention as aforesaid, or in case (b) three days at least before the day fixed for the meeting have deposited at the registered office of the company or at such other place as the directors may from time to time determine, the share warrant in respect of which he claims to act and vote as aforesaid, and unless the share warrant shall remain so deposited until the close of the meeting and any adjournment thereof. The names of more than one as joint holders of a share warrant shall not be received, and the board may, if it deem necessary, require from the depositor of a share warrant a statutory declaration to the effect that he is the owner of the share warrant so deposited, and may endorse on such share warrant a statement of the fact, date, purpose and consequence of its production.

14. The company shall deliver to the person so depositing a share warrant, a certificate stating his name and address and the number of shares represented by such share warrant, and the certificate shall entitle him to attend and vote at a meeting in respect of the shares specified therein in the same way as if he were a registered member. Upon delivery up of such certificate to the company the share warrant in respect whereof it shall have been given shall be returned.

The certificate may be as follows:—

THE 'A' COMPANY LIMITED.

No.........

' This is to certify that ...... of................
has in accordance with the regulations of the company deposited the undermentioned share warrants, in respect of which he is entitled to attend the general meeting of the company to be held at...........
on the...............day of..................
....

FOR THE 'A' COMPANY LTD. *Secretary.*

(Particulars of share warrants deposited.)

15. No holder of a share warrant shall be entitled to exercise any of the rights of a member (save as hereinbefore expressly provided in respect of meetings) without depositing such share warrant and stating his name and address, and (if and when the directors so require) making a declaration in writing in such form and authenticated in such manner as they may require, that he is the true owner of the share warrant so deposited, and permitting an endorsement to be made thereon of the fact, date, purpose and consequence of its deposit.

16. If the holder of a share warrant shall surrender it to be cancelled, together with all outstanding dividend coupons, and shall therewith lodge at the registered office of the company or at such other place as the directors may determine, a declaration in writing signed by him in such form and authenticated in such manner as the directors may require, requesting to be registered as a member in respect of the shares specified in such share warrant and stating in such declaration his name and address, then upon payment of such fee as the directors shall determine, he shall be entitled to have his name entered as a member in the register of members of the company and to receive the ordinary certificate for shares in respect of the shares specified in the share warrant so surrendered.

17. The directors may from time to time vary the above conditions, and the holder of a share warrant or warrants shall be subject to any conditions made by the directors in accordance with the provisions of article.....of the articles of association of the company, either before or after the issue of the share warrants.

18. In the above conditions 'share warrant' means a warrant in respect of a share or shares issued pursuant to the Companies Act, 1948, and the articles of association of the company.

Passed at a meeting of the directors held on the....................

Notes on Conditions. (For the purpose of illustration it is presumed that the company has shareholders in the United Kingdom.) It is required by condition 10 that notice of any dividend payable be advertised, and the following is a form of advertisement for this purpose:

THE 'A' CO. LTD.

DIVIDENDS ON ORDINARY SHARES.

Notice is hereby given that a dividend of four shillings per share (less United Kingdom income tax) has been declared payable upon the ordinary shares of the company as on the 1st July, 19 . Coupon No. 14 attached to share warrants will be payable on and after the 1st July, 19 , at the A. B. Bank Ltd., Lombard Street, London, E.C., at the rate of four shillings per share (less United Kingdom income tax) in payment of the aforesaid dividend.

Listing forms may be obtained from the said bank.

Coupons must be left three clear days for examination.

By order of the Board,

Secretary.

Address

Date

The following intimation may sometimes be added usefully to the notice:

'Holders of share warrants intending to submit a claim to the Inland Revenue for refund of income tax should apply for a certificate as to deduction of tax when presenting their coupons for payment.'

Lost Share Warrants. The above specimen conditions do not provide for the replacement of share warrants which are lost or destroyed. Sometimes a condition is added providing for such replacement upon proof of loss or destruction and on such indemnity being given as the directors deem adequate. In any event, in dealing with cases of a share warrant stated to have been lost or destroyed, it is necessary to act with the utmost caution. In no case should a duplicate share warrant be issued without the fullest possible indemnity from a bank or guarantee society, and only then after most exhaustive investigation and proof, confirmed by a statutory declaration, that it has been lost beyond recovery.

Condition 14 gives the form of the certificate to be delivered to anyone depositing warrants in accordance with condition 13, and forms of this certificate may, when printed, be bound in book form with a counterfoil to each (see Appendix F, Form 114). The issue of this certificate requires to be carefully controlled and each form should bear a separate folio number. As a safeguard in the use of this form the following words should always be added at the foot, viz.: 'Important—The warrants named herein will be delivered only in exchange for this certificate, which must be carefully preserved.'

Subject to the articles of association the fees referred to **Fees.** in Conditions 5, 12 and 16 may be fixed by the board.

A specimen form of application for share warrants is given in Appendix F, Form 115, and upon such a form being completed and handed in to the company's office together with the share certificates and fees payable, the company would issue a receipt (see Appendix F, Form 116).

In recording the issue of share warrants three types of register are usually required, as follows:

(1) particulars of share warrant applications received and details of the warrants issued in respect thereof (see Appendix F, Form 119);

(2) particulars of applications received for the exchange of warrants into registered shares, giving details of the warrants surrendered (see Appendix F, Form 120);

(3) the serial number of every warrant, printed with columns in which to enter the distinctive share numbers inserted on the warrants (see Appendix F, Form 121).

In addition to the foregoing a stock book should be kept **Stock Book.** recording all the warrants printed and a summary of all warrants issued, so that at any time it may be possible to ascertain full details of the warrants remaining in stock.

Before execution of a warrant, stamp duty thereon must **Stamp Duty.** be paid by means of an impressed stamp at three times the *ad valorem* duty payable upon transfers of shares, that is to say, at the rate of £6 per cent, on warrants issued on and after 1st August, 1947, the duty being calculated upon the nominal value of the shares or stock comprised in the warrant (Stamp Act, 1891, Sch. 1, s. 1; Finance Act, 1947, s. 52). The stamp duty must be impressed before the warrant is executed.

It is provided by the Stamp Act, 1891 (s. 107) that any person who, at the time when a share warrant is issued without being duly stamped, is the managing director, secretary or other principal officer of the company, shall be liable to a fine of £50.

The requirements of the articles of association with regard to the affixing of the seal should be strictly followed in the case of share warrants.

On issuing a share warrant, the name of the registered **Issue.** holder must be struck out of the register of members as if he had ceased to be a member, and the following particulars entered therein:

(a) the fact of the issue of the warrant;

(b) a statement of the shares [or stock] included in the warrant, distinguishing each share by its number (if any);

(c) the date of the issue of the warrant [s. 112 (1)].

These requirements may conveniently be carried out by using a rubber stamp, which may be impressed on the right-hand side of the accounts concerned in the register of members, the latter being posted from the entries in the share warrant issue register referred to above, the distinguishing numbers, if any, of the shares being entered in the proper columns of the register of members, as if the shares were being transferred out of the member's name.

In view of the importance of safeguarding issues of warrants, the applications and cancelled share certificates are sometimes examined by the company's auditors and the share warrants checked and initialled by them before submission to the board for issue and sealing, the auditors giving a certificate that the warrants are in order and duly stamped.

When ready for delivery the warrants should be issued in strict accordance with the instructions upon the application, and a form on the lines of Appendix F, Form 113, may be usefully employed for this purpose.

Exchange. The necessity may arise for dealing with applications for the exchange of share warrants of certain denominations for warrants of other denominations, and for this purpose a form similar to Form 123 in Appendix F may be used, and the receipt issued by the company upon the lodgment of such an application with the warrants for surrender may be on the lines of Form 118 in Appendix F.

Annual Return. The only direct information given to the Registrar of Companies regarding the issue of share warrants by a company is contained in the annual return. In the return the issue of share warrants in exchange for registered shares during the period covered should be treated as if the members had transferred the shares since the date of the last return. The information required to be stated in the summary is set out in the Sixth Schedule to the Act, Part I, para. 3 (*j*), and appears on the form of return.

Surrender. Subject to the articles of the company, the holder of a share warrant is entitled, in accordance with s. 112 (2), upon surrendering the warrant for cancellation, to have his name entered as a member in the register of members. The warrant must be actually surrendered and cancelled, as otherwise the company is responsible for any loss which may be involved [s. 112 (3)]. In dealing with such cases, an application form for exchanging share warrants for registered shares should be required (see Appendix F, Form 122). A form of receipt for this application and for the share warrants deposited in connection therewith should be issued by the company (see Appendix F, Form 114), and might, in practice, be treated as a transfer receipt in the event of the shares being sold before the share certificate is ready for delivery. The application for

registered shares should be entered in the share warrant
surrender register (Form 120, Appendix F), and the entry
posted in due course from there to the holder's account in the
register of members.

If by the conditions or articles the holder of a share warrant **Notices.**
is entitled to receive notice of meetings, it is generally provided
that this may be given by advertisement, the right to attend
being subject to the warrant having been previously deposited
at the company's office or bankers (see specimen condition
13 *supra*). When the annual report and accounts with notice
of general meeting are printed, a paragraph on the following
lines may be inserted after the usual notice of meeting:

> 'Holders of share warrants are reminded that if they
> wish to attend and vote at the meeting, either personally
> or by proxy, they must, three clear days before the day
> appointed for the meeting, deposit their warrants at the
> registered offices of the company at....................
>
> ....or at the......................Bank......
> ....London.'

The payment of dividends [see s. 83 (1)] is provided for
by means of a series of detachable coupons at the foot of
the warrant (see Appendix F, Form 113). These coupons
should be numbered consecutively, the numbers commencing
at the bottom right-hand corner in order to facilitate detach-
ment, and they must bear on each one the serial number of
the warrant to which they belong. A talon (see Appendix F,
Form 113) should be provided for the issue of fresh coupons
when the original series is exhausted. It is usual for the
secretary's facsimile signature to be printed on the coupons
and talon. A form of receipt for talons will be found in
Appendix F, Form 117.

When a dividend is about to be paid, arrangements should **Dividends.**
be made for the coupons to be received and paid, usually at
the company's bankers, or at the offices of the company.

The exact amount payable on the whole of the shares
represented by the share warrants in circulation should be
transferred from the general account to Coupon No.......
Account with the bankers.

It should be noted that shares represented by share warrants **Share War-**
cannot be reckoned in the qualification of a director or **rants not**
manager of the company, where such a qualification is **reckoned in**
required by the articles [s. 182 (2)]. **Director's**
Qualification.

A contract to sell registered shares will not be satisfied by **Share War-**
a delivery of share warrants [*Iredell* v. *General Securities* **rants not**
Corporation (1916), 33 T.L.R. 67]. **good delivery**
on Sale of
Under the provisions of the Exchange Control Act, 1947, **Registered**
however, coupons must be presented by the authorised **Shares.**

depositary (Exchange Control Act, 1947, s. 16).　See chapter XXX below.

Forgery.　Section 2 of the Forgery Act, 1913, details the penalties to which a person will become liable if he forges or otherwise alters any share warrant or coupon with intent to defraud, or falsely and deceitfully personates any owner of a share warrant or coupon.　(See also s. 84 of the Act, as to the penalties for personation and s. 85 as to the penalties for forgery and kindred offences in Scotland.)

Share Warrants in Foreign Circulation.　Share warrants are more popular on the continent than in England, the majority of companies issuing warrants being those whose shares are dealt in abroad, and it is not uncommon for the terms on the warrants to be printed in two or three languages in parallel columns for the convenience of the foreign holders.

Coupon Registers.　Coupon registers should be kept in which the payment of coupons can be recorded.　The coupon listing forms are numbered consecutively and the corresponding number written or stamped against the numbers of the warrants in the coupon registers.

CHAPTER XI

NOTICES

IT has already been seen (see p. 12) that, by s. 437 of the Act, a document (which includes a notice) may be served on a company by leaving it at or sending it by post to the registered office of the company, and that special provision is made for the service of the process of an English court on a company registered in Scotland, which carries on business in England. It is proposed in this chapter to deal generally with the notices which a company may require to give to its members.

A very important duty of the secretary of a company is to prepare, or supervise the preparation of, all notices, and to ensure their due despatch to the proper persons.

It will be remembered that by s. 108 every limited company must have its name, including, of course, the word 'Limited,' mentioned in legible characters in all notices of the company, and this will head the notice. The address of the registered office of the company, from which the notice will in general be sent, will follow, with the date, or the date may be placed at the foot of the notice on the left-hand side. As to the signature, or authentication, of the notice, s. 36 of the Act provides that a document (which by s. 455 includes notice) or proceeding requiring authentication by a company may be signed by a director, secretary, or other authorised officer of the company, and need not be under its common seal. The secretary will not, of course, send out any notice to the shareholders without the authority of the board, and the ordinary and proper method of authenticating a notice is for the words 'By order of the Board' to appear over the signature of the secretary. Thus the general form of the notice will be as follows:

The 'A' Company, Limited.

London Wall, London, E.C.

July, 19....

NOTICE is hereby given that, &c., &c.

By order of the Board,

Secretary.

Notices to individuals will in general take the form of letters, headed by the name of the company, with the address and date following, and commencing in some such form as follows:—'Dear Sir, I am directed to inform you that, &c.,' or 'Sir, I hereby give you notice that, &c.,' and concluding, 'Yours faithfully, John Smith, Secretary.'

The most important notices unquestionably are notices of **Notice of** general meetings. Others, such as notice of call, and notice to **Meetings.** holders of share warrants of declaration of dividend, although accuracy and clearness of expression are necessary, do not require special treatment. Ambiguity should be carefully avoided.

The general meetings of a company which will have to be convened are the statutory meeting, the annual and extraordinary general meetings. (See Appendix F, Forms 45, 46 and 47.) Sometimes, where special business is to be transacted, the board issues an explanatory circular with the notice convening the meeting. Further, special notice is necessary for passing certain resolutions (see p. 131). Such a circular need not contain the names of the directors, as it is not a trade circular or business letter within s. 201. Care must be taken to ensure that the circular is not misleading, as a misleading circular may vitiate the resolution.

Apart from the preliminary matter of ensuring that the meeting is convened by the proper authority (as to which see p. 145), the secretary's duties are threefold. He must take care (1) that the proper length of notice is given; (2) that it is duly given to all persons entitled to receive it; and (3) that it is properly framed. The salient point to remember is that the provisions of the articles must be strictly followed, whether the meeting be the statutory meeting, or the annual or an extraordinary general meeting. Attention is called to two provisions in the Act. (i) Section 136 (2) provides that, in every notice calling a meeting of a company having a share capital, there shall appear with reasonable prominence a statement that a member entitled to attend and vote is entitled to appoint a proxy or, where that is allowed, one or more proxies, to attend and vote instead of him. Further, it must be stated that the proxy need not also be a member. In the case of a public company it is thought that a member may appoint more than one proxy unless the articles otherwise provide, but in the case of a private company he may only do so if the articles so allow. (See Appendix H.) (ii) Section 162 (4) provides that the auditors of a company shall be entitled to attend any general meeting of the company and to receive all notices of, and other communications relating to, any general meeting which any member of the company is entitled to receive.

Length of Notice. As to the length of notice, the articles must be consulted. Also, especially when the articles have not been brought into line with the 1948 Act, the statutory requirements must be borne in mind; notwithstanding any provision of the articles, the Act requires at least the following notice:—

(a) for the annual general meeting, 21 days (s. 133) (Appendix F, Form 45);

(b) for any general meeting to pass a special resolution, 21 days (s. 141) (Appendix F, Form 47);

(c) in any other case, 14 days, or in the case of an unlimited company, 7 days (s. 133).

There are also special provisions for certain resolutions which require 'special notice,' as to which see below.

A meeting can be called at shorter notice than is required by the Act or the articles, if:—

(a) in the case of the annual general meeting, *all* members entitled to attend and vote so agree;

(b) in the case of any other meeting (even if a special resolution is to be passed), a majority in number of the members entitled to attend and vote, holding at least 95 per cent. of the shares giving the right to attend and vote, so agree. If the company has no share capital, the corresponding requirement is a majority in number of the members representing 95 per cent. of the votes.

To comply with the statutory requirements (and unless **Clear Days.** they otherwise provide, any additional length of notice required by the articles), the only safe view is that the period of days prescribed must be 'clear days,' that is, they must be exclusive of the day on which the notice is served and the day of the meeting [*Hector Whaling Ltd.* (1936), Ch. 208]. To illustrate: if 21-day notices are posted on the 1st August, they are (under the usual article, *e.g.* Table A, cl. 50) deemed to be served on the 2nd August; the 21 days begin on 3rd August and expire on 23rd August; the 24th August is therefore the earliest day for which the meeting may be summoned.

The Act provides that special notice must be given in **Special** the case of certain ordinary (not special or extraordinary) **Notice.** resolutions. The object of special notice appears to be that in certain cases, which do not warrant the majority requisite for a special resolution, (i) the members should be given adequate time to consider the proposals, and (ii) in the case of resolutions originating from a shareholder, the board of directors should be given the opportunity of communicating its views to the members. There are two elements in a special notice, namely, the notice which must be given *to* the company and the notice which must be given *by* the company. Section 142 of the Act provides that the resolution shall not be effective unless notice of the intention to move it has been given to the company not less than 28 days before the meeting at which it is moved. There is, however, an important proviso to this first element. If, after notice of the intention to move such a resolution has been given to the company, a meeting is called for a date 28 days or less after the notice has been given, the notice to the company shall be deemed to have been properly given. It is submitted that the effect of the proviso is to prevent the company from relying on the technicality of defective notice to prevent the passage of the resolution. In the case where the board of directors itself puts forward a resolution which requires special notice, the position is doubtful, but it would be safer for the board to go through the formality of giving notice to the company of its intention to move the resolution. Section 142 then goes on to provide that the company shall give its members notice of the resolution (the second element) at the same time and in the same manner as it gives notice of the meeting (21 days in the case of the annual general meeting or a meeting at which a special resolution is to be passed, and 14 days in any other case). If, however, this is for some reason impracticable, the company must give its members not less than 21 days' notice, 'either by advertising in a newspaper having an appropriate circulation, or in any other mode allowed by the articles.' The following resolutions require special notice:

(i) a resolution at a company's annual general meeting appointing as auditor a person other than a retiring auditor, or providing expressly that a retiring auditor shall not be re-appointed [s. 160 (1)];

(ii) a resolution for the removal of a director before the expiration of his term of office [s. 184 (2)];

(iii) a resolution for the appointment of a director over the age limit [s. 185 (5)].

It should be noted that in both (i) and (ii) the company must, on the receipt of notice, forthwith send a copy thereof to the auditor or director concerned. If the auditor or director makes written representations with respect thereto to the company (not exceeding a reasonable length) and requests their notification to the members of the company, the company must (unless the representations are received too late):

(i) state, in the notice of the resolution given to members, the fact that representations have been made; and

(ii) send a copy of the representations to every member of the company to whom notice of the meeting is sent (whether before or after receipt of the representations by the company).

To whom Notice sent.   In despatching the notices the secretary will have to consider whether all the shareholders are entitled to receive a notice, and this depends on the articles of the company. In the absence of articles to the contrary, all shareholders on the register are entitled to receive notices of meetings and to attend and record the votes to which they are entitled. Sometimes, however, particular classes of shareholders, *e.g.* preference shareholders, or shareholders the calls upon whose shares are in arrear, are excluded by the articles from receiving notices or attending general meetings. Moreover, it would appear that an article which merely excludes the right of particular shareholders to vote is to be read (in the absence of any other article dealing with the point) as also including by implication their right to attend or speak at meetings [*Mackenzie & Co.* (1916), 2 Ch. 450]. In some companies, while certain classes of shareholders are excluded from general meetings, they are specially empowered to attend meetings called for certain specified purposes, and more particularly meetings convened for the purpose of passing a resolution for winding up.

Notices need not be sent to shareholders who are not within reach [*Union Hill Silver Co.* (1870), 22 L.T. 400; *Warden and Hotchkiss Ltd.* (1945), Ch. 270; *Smyth* v. *Darley* (1849), 2 H.L.C. 789]. It is, however, doubtful whether mere absence abroad would disentitle a member to receive notices, and the articles usually provide that a member living abroad may supply an address within the United Kingdom at which notices may be given to him, and that if he does not do so he shall not be entitled to any notice of meetings. As an alternative to disenfranchising a member living abroad, who does not supply an address in the United Kingdom at which notices may be served on him, the articles sometimes provide for his being given notice by advertisement, or by posting up a copy at the registered office of the company.

Where the company has issued share warrants to bearer, the articles, or regulations made by the directors in pursuance of the articles, may provide for notices being given to the holders by advertisement, or, where they have furnished the company with an address, for the sending of notices to that address.

Sometimes non-members, *e.g.* debenture holders, are given the right of attending and voting at meetings, in which case notices should be sent to them. Their votes cannot, however, be taken into account for the purpose of a special or extra-ordinary resolution.

It is commonly provided that, in case of joint holders, notice to the joint holder first named in the register is notice to them all. There is a possible trap here when the first joint holder lives outside the United Kingdom, which can be illustrated from Table A. Suppose that three joint holders X, Y and Z are registered in that order and that X has an address outside the United Kingdom, while Y and Z have addresses in the United Kingdom. If X has given an address in the United Kingdom for service of notices, a single notice sent to that address is notice to all joint holders (Table A, cl. 131, 132). But if X has not given such an address, although Table A, cl. 134, provides that notice of meeting need not be sent to X, there is apparently no provision that it need not be sent to Y and Z, nor is there any provision that notice to Y, the second named on the register, is good notice to Z. Accordingly, it seems that in such a case either notice must be sent to X to his foreign registered address, or else notices must be sent to each of Y and Z.

Representatives of a deceased or bankrupt shareholder are not entitled to receive notices until they have become members by formal registration [*Allen* v. *Gold Reefs of West Africa* (1900), 1 Ch. 656] unless the articles otherwise provide.

Notice of Statutory Meeting.

With reference to the statutory meeting, doubts have been expressed whether all the members of the company are necessarily entitled to notice of it, although they may not all be entitled to notices of other general meetings. Section 130 (1) of the Act provides for 'a general meeting of the members of the company which shall be called the statutory meeting.' Section 130 (2) provides that the statutory report shall be sent 'to every member of the company.' If the notice of the statutory meeting is, as is common, endorsed on the statutory report, all the shareholders must necessarily receive it, but even if it is not, it would be unsafe to assume that certain members need not receive it. The words of s. 130 (1), 'a general meeting of the members of the company,' differ from those of s. 131 (1) (which makes provision for the annual general meeting) 'every company shall in each year hold a general meeting.' Although there can be no doubt that some members may be precluded from attending general meetings of the company, other than the statutory meeting, yet, having regard to the special wording of s. 130 (1) and to the object of the statutory meeting, it appears to be intended that no member is to be precluded from attending that meeting. If, however, a company has issued share warrants before the statutory meeting, it seems clear that, apart from special provisions in the articles, or regulations made by the board in pursuance thereof, a holder is not entitled to notice of the statutory meeting or to receive the report, since he is not a member unless the articles provide that he is to be deemed to be a member [s. 112 (5)]. The notice convening the statutory meeting should state that it is convened as such.

In addressing notices it is not necessary that they should be directed exactly in the same way as the member's address appears upon the register, but the member's place of abode must be given with substantial accuracy [*Liverpool Marine Insurance Co.* v. *Haughton* (1874), 23 W.R. 93]. In large offices addressing machines are used and the plates or stencils of the machines exactly comply with the registered addresses. If a shareholder gives instructions for notices to be sent to some other person or address, a careful note must be made thereof and the address plate or stencil altered accordingly. A separate plate or stencil should be used for notices and the annual return.

It is a matter of the utmost importance that proper notice should be given to every shareholder who is entitled to receive it, for the omission to serve even a single member will render a resolution invalid [*Smyth* v. *Darley* (1849), 2 H.L.C. 789; *Young* v. *Ladies Imperial Club* (1920), 2 K.B. 523; *The State* v. *O'Connell* (1945), I.R. 169], unless, as is commonly the case, there are provisions in the articles to the effect that the accidental omission to give notice to any member, or the non-receipt by any member of the notice, is not to invalidate the meeting. A record should be kept in the postage book of the despatch of the precise number of notices sent and a certificate of posting should be signed by the clerks responsible. It should be observed that, where by the articles notice may be given personally, or by sending it through the post to a member at his registered address, it is not properly given if it be left by hand at the registered address.

In framing the notice, the primary point to remember is **Contents of** that the meeting has no power to pass any resolution outside **Notice.** the scope of the notice [*Bridport Old Brewery Co.* (1867), 2 Ch. App. 191; *Vale of Neath Brewery Co.*, *Lawes' Case* (1852), 1 De G.M. and G. 421; *Isle of Wight Railway Co.* v. *Tahourdin* (1883), 25 Ch. D. 320]. The provisions of the articles also must be strictly followed.

The articles usually provide that the notice of a meeting shall state the place, day, and hour of meeting, and, in the case of special business, the general nature of such business. Special business is usually defined as all business transacted at an extraordinary general meeting, and all business transacted at an annual general meeting, except the sanctioning of a dividend, the consideration of the accounts, balance sheet and the reports of the directors and auditors, the election of directors, and appointment and remuneration of the auditors. [Table A, 1948, cl. 52.]

The principle of law, that a meeting has no power to pass **Examples.** any resolution outside the scope of the notice, must be considered in connection with the common provision of articles of association, just mentioned, to the effect that a notice of a meeting to transact what is commonly described as special business must state the general nature of the business. The sufficiency of notices has frequently been discussed before the court, and a few instances may be mentioned as affording some guidance. It is impossible to lay down any hard and fast rule as to what notice is or is not sufficient, since it has been held, in *Normandy* v. *Ind, Coope & Co.* [(1908), 1 Ch. 84], that the sufficiency of a notice must be determined by the special circumstances of each case. Here are five concrete examples: (1) A notice specified a resolution to the effect that directors' remuneration should be 40 per cent. of certain profits; the resolution was passed with the substitution of 30 per cent. for 40 per cent.: held, that the alteration did not invalidate the resolution [*Torbock* v. *Lord Westbury* (1902), 2 Ch. 871]. (2) Notice was given of an extraordinary meeting for the purpose of altering the company's articles; the notice did not indicate the nature of the alterations, which were important: held, that the notice was insufficient [*Normandy* v. *Ind, Coope & Co. (supra)*]. (3) The notice convening a general meeting stated that it would be held for the purpose of receiving the directors' report, and the election of directors and appointment of auditors. The directors' report which accompanied the notice, mentioned special business not referred to in the notice, namely, the ratification of the board's previous election of a director: held, that the notice and report together were sufficient notice of this special business [*Boschoek Proprietary Company* v. *Fuke* (1906), 1 Ch. 148]. (4) The notice of the annual general meeting stated that the meeting was for the purpose of considering and, if thought fit, of passing certain resolutions, 'with such amendments and alterations as shall be determined upon at such meeting.' One of the resolutions was for the appointment of three specified persons as directors. To this resolution an amendment was carried that two additional specified persons should also be appointed; the articles provided that the number of directors should not be more than seven nor less than three: held, that the business transacted was within the scope of the special business indicated in the notice [*Betts & Co.* v. *Macnaghten* (1910), 1 Ch. 430]. (5) The notice of a meeting to pass special resolutions, authorising directors to retain the remuneration they had received as directors of a subsidiary company, did not specify the amount of such remuneration, which was large; neither did an accompanying circular: held, that the resolutions were invalid [*Baillie* v. *Oriental Telephone* (1915), 1 Ch. 503].

The above cases illustrate two general principles which have been laid down with regard to notices, namely, (1) that the notice must fairly disclose the purpose for which the meeting is convened [*Kaye* v. *Croydon Tramways Co.* (1898), 1 Ch. 358; *Tiessen* v. *Henderson* (1899), 1 Ch. 861]; and (2) that at the same time it must not be construed with excessive strictness [see remarks of Selwyn, L.J., in *Wright's Case* (1868), reported in footnote 12 Eq. 334, *et seq.*].

The body of the notice convening the statutory meeting will be in the following or some similar form:

'Notice is hereby given that, pursuant to s. 130 of the Companies Act, 1948, the statutory meeting of the company will be held at   House,   Street, London, E.C., on   day, the   day of   19 , at   o'clock in the   noon.'

A member entitled to attend and vote at this meeting is entitled to appoint a proxy or proxies* to attend and vote on his behalf, and a proxy need not also be a member of the company.'

A number of forms of common resolutions will be found in chapter XIV. Great care must be taken in framing a notice of a meeting at which it is proposed to pass either a special or an extraordinary resolution. In this connection it is important to observe the precise words of s. 141 (1) and (2), where an extraordinary resolution and a special resolution are respectively defined. These two sub-sections run as follows:

'1. A resolution shall be an extraordinary resolution when **Extra-** it has been passed by a majority of not less than three- **ordinary** fourths of such members as, being entitled so to do, vote in **Resolution.** person or, where proxies are allowed, by proxy, at a general meeting of which notice specifying the intention to propose the resolution as an extraordinary resolution has been duly given.

'2. A resolution shall be a special resolution when it has **Special** been passed by such a majority as is required for the passing **Resolution.** of an extraordinary resolution, and at a general meeting of which not less than twenty-one days' notice, specifying the intention to propose the resolution as a special resolution, has been duly given: Provided that, if it is so agreed by a majority in number of the members having the right to attend and vote at any such meeting, being a majority together holding not less than 95 per cent. in nominal value of the shares giving that right . . . a resolution may be proposed and passed as a special resolution of which less than twenty-one days' notice has been given.' [For form of agreement see Appendix F, Form 52.]

It will be observed that, in the case of an extraordinary or **Extra-** special resolution, the notice must specify the intention to **ordinary and** propose the resolution as an extraordinary or special resolution, **Special** as the case may be. The body of the notice will accordingly **Resolutions.** be in the following or some similar form:

'Notice is hereby given that an extraordinary general meeting of the above-named company will be held at , on   day, the   day of   , 19   , at   o'clock in   the   noon, when the subjoined resolution will be proposed as an [extraordinary] [special] resolution; that, etc.'

'A member entitled to attend and vote at this meeting is entitled to appoint a proxy or proxies* to attend and vote on his behalf, and a proxy need not also be a member of the company.' See also Appendix F, Forms 46 and 47.

* Where this is allowed see pp. 130 and 154, and Appendix H.

The length of notice required for an extraordinary resolution is the usual length of notice for the general meeting at which the resolution is to be passed, *i.e.* twenty-one days if it is an annual general meeting, and fourteen days in other cases.

In the case of an extraordinary or special resolution, it is customary (and perhaps essential) for the notice of meeting to state the exact wording of the resolution which is proposed. It is doubtful whether any amendment of the terms of the resolution as set out in the notice of meeting can be permitted; on this point there is no clear authority. In practice one is probably safe in assuming that a quite minor amendment, not affecting the substance of the resolution, will not invalidate the resolution, but that no substantial amendment is permissible.

If the notice does not specify the intention to propose the resolution as an extraordinary resolution, or special resolution, as the case may be, the resolution will not be validly passed [*MacConnell* v. *E. Prill & Co.* (1916), 2 Ch. 57].

In computing the requisite three-fourths majority, members present but not voting are not taken into account.

The requirements of the statute and of articles of association regarding notices are intended for the protection of the shareholders, and it appears that if, in spite of non-compliance with these requirements, the entire body of shareholders passes the resolution and waives the irregularity of the notice, the court will declare the resolution valid [*Express Engineering Works* (1920), 1 Ch. 466; *Oxted Motor Company* (1921), 3 K.B. 32]. It is not essential to the validity of a resolution so passed that all the shareholders should have given their assent at the same time or in the same place [*Parker & Cooper Ltd.* v. *Reading* (1926), Ch. 975]. The resolution in that case was an ordinary resolution. Section 143 (4) (*c*) of the Act appears to assume that the same principle applies to special and extraordinary resolutions. This is, however, open to question, particularly as regards matters which the Act itself requires to be dealt with by special resolution, *e.g.* reduction of capital, and it would be inadvisable to rely on an agreement reached without a meeting being held.

It is frequently found that persons are confused by the different senses in which the expressions 'ordinary,' 'extraordinary' and 'special' are used in relation to meetings and resolutions, and it may therefore be useful to point out that. an extraordinary general meeting is not essential in order to pass extraordinary or special resolutions. Such resolutions can equally well be passed at the annual general meeting if proper notice is given. Similarly, ordinary resolutions can be passed at an extraordinary general meeting provided that notice is given of the intention to submit them to the meeting. Again, special business is not business which necessarily requires a special resolution, but is merely any business other than ordinary business, ordinary business being the routine business of the annual general meeting of which it is not necessary to give particular notice. As to 'special notice,' see p. 131.

Class resolutions usually require to be passed by a special majority of the class affected (see p. 291 *et seq.* below).

By s. 61 of the Law of Property Act, 1925, 'In all deeds, contracts, wills, orders and other instruments, executed, made or coming into operation after the commencement of this Act, unless the context otherwise requires:

(a) "Month" means calendar month.

(b) "Person" includes a corporation.

(c) The singular includes the plural and *vice versa*.

(d) The masculine includes the feminine and *vice versa*.'

A notice would appear to be clearly within the meaning of the word 'instrument.'

CHAPTER XII

MEETINGS OF SHAREHOLDERS

THE subject of this chapter is meetings of shareholders of a company, board meetings being dealt with in chapter XIII. Besides general meetings of shareholders, there may also be class meetings, *i.e.* meetings of a particular class of shareholders summoned for a specific purpose specially affecting the class; and these are also dealt with here so far as they appear to require special mention.

The provisions of the Act as to meetings of shareholders are, for the most part, contained in ss. 130–146, under the general title of 'Meetings and Proceedings.' Section 130 deals with the statutory meeting and statutory report. Section 131 provides for the holding of the annual general meeting. Section 132 treats of meetings convened on requisition. Section 134 contains a few general regulations as to meetings, which apply in the very rare instances where a company's articles contain no appropriate provisions, and s. 135 enables the court to give directions as to the convening, holding and conduct of a meeting in any case where it is impracticable to proceed under the articles or the Act. Section 139 provides for the representation of companies at meetings of other companies and of creditors. Section 141 defines extraordinary and special resolutions. Section 143 provides for the registration of certain resolutions and agreements. Section 144 provides that resolutions passed at adjourned meetings shall be treated as having been passed on the date on which they were in fact passed. Section 145 enjoins the keeping of minutes of proceedings at general meetings and meetings of directors and managers, if any. Section 146 provides for the inspection of the minute books of general meetings.

A meeting *prima facie* means a gathering of two or more persons, and the courts have consistently held that there cannot in general be a meeting of one person [*Sharp* v. *Dawes* (1876), 2 Q.B.D. 26; *Sanitary Carbon Co.* (1877), W.N. 223; *James Prain & Sons Ltd.* (1947), S.C. 325]. Lord Coleridge said in *Sharp* v. *Dawes*, 'It is, of course, possible to show that the word "meeting" has a meaning different from the ordinary meaning,' and this was shown in the case of *East* v. *Bennett Brothers* (1911), 1 Ch. 163. In that case, the memorandum provided that, no new shares could be issued so as to rank equally with or in priority to the existing preference shares, unless the issue was sanctioned by an extraordinary resolution of the holders of the preference shares at a separate meeting of the holders specially summoned for the purpose. The existing preference shares being all in the hands of one person, and there being nothing in the constitution of the company to prevent one person holding them all, the word 'meeting' was held to be applicable to the case of a single shareholder. It should be noted that, under the Act, in two exceptional cases, the court [s. 135 (1)] and the Board of Trade [s. 131 (2)] have power to convene a meeting of one member present in person or by proxy (see p. 143 and p. 146).

The general meetings of a company comprise the statutory meeting, annual general meetings and extraordinary general meetings. Requisitioned meetings are extraordinary general meetings summoned in a particular way. There are also class meetings of shareholders.

The statutory meeting is a general meeting of the members, **Statutory** which must be held by a company limited by shares, or limited **Meetings.** by guarantee and having a share capital, not less than one month nor more than three months from the date at which the company is entitled to commence business (s. 130). The notice convening the statutory meeting must clearly state that it is the statutory meeting and that all the requirements of the Act have been complied with [*Gardner* v. *Iredale* (1912), 1 Ch. 700]. The object of the meeting is to give shareholders the opportunity of making themselves acquainted with the promotion and flotation of the company, both by means of the statutory report (see below) which they receive before the meeting, and by means of discussion at the meeting, in case there are any points not included in the report upon which they desire information. The provisions as to the statutory meeting and statutory report do not apply to a private company [s. 130 (10)].

Fourteen (clear) days at least before the day on which the **Statutory** statutory meeting is held, the statutory report must be sent by **Report.** the directors to every member of the company [s. 130 (2)]. The statutory report may, however, be forwarded later than the prescribed 14 days if so agreed by all the members entitled to attend and vote at the meeting [s. 130 (2)].

The statements which the statutory report must contain are set out in s. 130 (3) of the Act. (See Appendix F, Form 43.)

The report must (*a*) be certified by not less than two directors of the company [s. 130 (3)]; and (*b*) so far as it related to the shares allotted by the company, and to the cash received in respect of such shares, and to the receipts and payments of the company on capital account, be certified as correct by the auditors (if any), of the company [s. 130 (4)].

Immediately after the report is despatched to the members, a copy, certified as above, must be delivered to the Registrar for registration [s. 130 (5)].

At the commencement of the meeting a list must be produced, showing the names and addresses of the members, with their respective holdings, and this must remain open and accessible to any member during the meeting [s. 130 (6)]. (See Appendix F, Form 44.)

At the statutory meeting, the members may discuss any matter relating to the formation of the company, or arising out of the statutory report, whether previous notice has been given or not. No resolution, however, may be passed, unless notice has been given in accordance with the articles [s. 130 (7)]; and if a resolution is submitted it is thought that only those members entitled to vote under the articles can vote on the resolution.

The Act provides that 'the meeting may adjourn from time to time.' This appears to continue a modification of the usual practice, for, generally speaking, the chairman of a meeting has a discretion as to adjournment, but it would seem that at a statutory meeting the majority can compel the chairman to adjourn. The adjourned meeting has the same powers as the original meeting and it may pass any resolution of which notice has been given in accordance with the articles, either before or subsequent to the original meeting [s. 130 (8)].

If default is made in complying with the provisions of s. 130 as to the statutory meeting [s. 130 (9)] or report, every director who is knowingly or wilfully guilty of the default or, in the case of default by the company, every officer of the company who is in default, is liable to a fine not exceeding £50.

Moreover, in case of default in holding the statutory meeting or delivering the statutory report to the Registrar, a shareholder may present a petition for winding up the company [s. 222 (b)], and in such case the court may, instead of making a winding up order, direct that the statutory report shall be delivered or a meeting held and order the costs to be paid by those responsible for the default [s. 225 (3) (b)].

The petition cannot be presented by any person except a shareholder, nor before the expiration of 14 days after the last day on which the meeting ought to have been held [s. 224 (1) (b)].

Annual General Meeting. The Act requires every company to hold a general meeting in every calendar year as its annual general meeting (s. 131). It must be held not more than 15 months after the previous annual general meeting. The first annual general meeting, however, if held within 18 months of the company's incorporation, need not be held in the year of incorporation or the following year. The notice of the annual general meeting must describe it as such [s. 131 (1)], and must give 21 days' notice in writing [s. 133 (1) (a)]. It is usual for the articles to provide how the meeting is to be held, the directors being usually empowered to fix the date, place and hour.

The Act requires that the register of directors' shareholdings shall be open to inspection 14 days prior to and three days after the annual general meeting [s. 195 (5)] and be produced thereat and be open to inspection [s. 195 (7)]. In addition, the balance sheet and other documents mentioned below, which have to be laid before some general meeting, are usually laid before the annual general meeting.

If default is made in holding the annual general meeting the Board of Trade may, on the application of any member, call or direct the calling of a general meeting, and in doing so may give directions modifying or supplementing the company's articles for the purpose of that meeting; and in particular, it may direct that one member present in person or by proxy shall constitute a meeting [s. 131 (2)]. Such a meeting, if held within the year in which default is made, will be treated as the annual general meeting; if not held within that year it will not be the annual general meeting for the year in which it is held, unless the meeting resolves that it shall be so [s. 131 (3)]. If the meeting so resolves, a copy of the resolution must be sent to the Registrar within 15 days from the date on which it is passed.

Heavy fines are prescribed for default in holding the meeting or in complying with any directions of the Board of Trade [s. 131 (5)].

The directors of every company must, not later than 18 months after the incorporation of the company and subsequently once at least in every calendar year, lay before the company in general meeting a balance sheet and a profit and loss account, or, in the case of a company not trading for profit, an income and expenditure account, for the period, in the case of the first account since the incorporation of the company, and, in any other case, since the preceding account, made up to a date not earlier than the date of the meeting by more than nine months, or, in the case of a company carrying on business or having interest abroad, by more than 12 months. These periods may, however, be extended at the discretion of the Board of Trade [s. 148 (1)]. A balance sheet made up to the date of the profit and loss account must be laid before the meeting [s. 148 (2)]. For details see chapter XVI, p. 205.

A copy of every balance sheet including every document required by law to be annexed thereto, which is to be laid before a company in general meeting, together with a copy of the auditors' report, must be sent to every member (whether entitled to receive notice of general meetings of the company or not), to every holder of debentures of the company (whether he is so entitled or not) and to all other persons so entitled not less than 21 days before the date of the meeting [s. 158 (1)].

The section applies to private companies as well as to public companies, but, in the case of a company not having a share capital, the sending of the documents required by s. 158 (1) does not apply to a member or debenture-holder of the company who is not entitled to receive notice of general meetings of the company [s. 158 (1) (a)]. See also chapter XVII, p. 204 et seq.

Auditors have a right to receive notice of and attend any general meeting of the company and to be heard thereat in respect of any matter which concerns them [s. 162 (4)].

Class Meetings. Articles often make provision for meetings of classes of shareholders, usually with a view to enabling a specified majority of a class to bind the minority to a variation of the rights of the class. Table A, clause 4, is typical of the kind of article which is often found in the articles of a company. It runs as follows: 'If at any time the share capital is divided into different classes of shares, the rights attached to any class (unless otherwise provided by the terms of issue of the shares of that class) may, whether or not the company is being wound up, be varied with the consent in writing of the holders of three-fourths of the issued shares of that class, or with the sanction of an extraordinary resolution passed at a separate general meeting of the holders of the shares of the class. To every such separate general meeting the provisions of these regulations relating to general meetings shall apply, but so that the necessary quorum shall be two persons at least holding or representing by proxy one-third of the issued shares of the class, and that any holder of shares of the class present in person or by proxy may demand a poll' [see *Carruth* v. *Imperial Chemical Industries Ltd.* (1937), A.C. 707].

The provisions of the particular article must be carefully observed in convening and holding a class meeting, special care being exercised in ensuring that the necessary quorum is present. It was held in *Hemans* v. *Hotchkiss Ordnance Co.* (1899), 1 Ch. 115, that where no quorum was present at a class meeting convened pursuant to an article similar to the above mentioned clause of Table A, and the meeting therefore stood adjourned in accordance with the provision in that behalf relating to general meetings, the quorum prescribed by the articles for the holding of a class meeting was still required at the adjourned meeting, and those members present who held less than one-third of the shares of the class were not a sufficient quorum (see p. 147). As to the right of members of the class who allege that they are unfairly prejudiced by a resolution passed under such an article to appeal to the court, see s. 72 and p. 35.

Requisitioned Meetings. Extraordinary general meetings may be convened by requisition. Section 132 of the Act entitles 'members of the company holding at the date of the deposit of the requisition not less than one-tenth of such of the paid-up capital of the company as at the date of the deposit carries the right of voting at general meetings of the company, or, in the case of a company not having a share capital, members of the company representing not less than one-tenth of the total voting rights of all the members having at the said date a right to vote at general meetings of the company, forthwith to requisition such a meeting [s. 132 (1)]. The requisition, which may consist of several documents in like form, each signed by one or more requisitionists, must be signed by the requisitionists and deposited at the registered office of the company, and it must state the objects of the meeting [s. 132 (2)]. See Appendix F, Form 53. Thereupon it becomes the duty of the directors, within 21 days, to cause a meeting to be convened, and this they will do, instructing the secretary to call the meeting. If the requisition is for the purpose of passing a special resolution and the directors do not give the notice required by s. 141, they will be deemed not to have duly convened the meeting [s. 132 (6)]. After the 21 days from the date of the deposit of the requisition, if no meeting has been duly convened by the directors, the requisitionists, or any of them representing more than one-half of the total voting rights of all of them, may themselves convene it [s. 132 (3)] in the same manner as nearly as possible as meetings are to be convened by the directors [s. 132 (4)]. It was decided in 1901 by Wright, J. [*State of Wyoming Syndicate* (1901), 2 Ch. 431], that the secretary cannot, within the 21 days, convene the meeting without the authority of the directors; but the further point was left open whether, after the expiration of the 21 days, the requisitionists could convene the meeting by notices signed by the secretary. It seems, however, they could do so, as a meeting convened by the directors would be convened in this way. In any event, no meeting convened by the requisitionists can be held more than three months from the date of deposit of the requisition [s. 132 (3)]. Under s. 132 (5) the company must reimburse the requisitionists any reasonable expenses incurred by them by reason of the default of the directors in convening the meeting, and any sum so repaid to the requisitionists must be charged against the remuneration of the directors in default.

The matter of notices is dealt with at length in chapter XI.

Before a meeting is convened it is necessary to be sure that it **Convening** is convened under proper authority, and the articles should **Meetings.** be consulted as to who may convene a meeting. In most cases (as, for instance, in clause 49 of Table A) the directors may convene an extraordinary general meeting whenever they think fit, and the secretary, acting on their instructions, will then prepare and send out notices. Unless the articles otherwise provide, directors cannot act without

meeting as a board. Accordingly, the secretary's first duty
will in general be to see that the board meeting, at which it was
resolved to call a general meeting, was itself duly convened
and that a quorum of the directors was present. If the
board meeting was in order, he may then prepare and despatch
the notices. Although a secretary cannot convene a meeting
without authority [*State of Wyoming Syndicate* (1901), 2 Ch.
431], yet, if under the authority of an irregularly constituted
board he has convened a meeting, the resolutions passed at
that meeting are not invalid [*Boschoek Proprietary Co.* v.
Fuke (1906), 1 Ch. 148]. The articles may possibly provide
that general meetings may be convened by persons other than
the directors. If no provision as to convening meetings is
contained in the articles, the Act supplies the deficiency by
providing that, in default of regulations, two more members
holding not less than one-tenth of the issued share capital, or,
if the company has not a share capital, not less than 5 per cent.
in number of the members of the company, may call a meeting
[s. 134 (*b*)].

Notices of the meeting must be served in the manner
required by the articles (cf. Table A, cl. 134).

Section 135 (1) provides for cases where for any reason it is
impracticable to call or conduct a meeting of a company in a
proper manner. In such cases the court is empowered, either
of its own motion or on the application of any director or
of any member who would be entitled to vote at the meeting,
to order a meeting to be called, held and conducted in such
manner as the court thinks fit.

The order may include a direction similar to that which may
be given by the Board of Trade and referred to on p. 143, to the
effect that one member present in person or by proxy shall be
deemed to constitute a meeting [s. 135 (1)].

Quorum.   The quorum is practically always determined by the articles
and needs little further comment. In the absence of any other
provision in the articles, three members (or, in the case of a
private company, two members) personally present constitute
a quorum [s. 134 (*c*)]. It was stated on p. 140 that except in
certain defined cases there cannot, in general, be a meeting of
one. This principle will also apply to the quorum, but there
are exceptions to the rule, *e.g.* where one person is a member
of a class of shares [*East* v. *Bennett Bros.* (1911), 1 Ch. 163],
or where there is a committee of one [*Taurine* (1884), 25
Ch. D. 118], and, in a winding up, where only one creditor has
lodged proof of debt. The articles usually provide that,
if at a general meeting a quorum is not present within a
specified time from the hour appointed for the meeting, the
meeting, if convened in pursuance of a requisition, shall be
dissolved, but in any other case shall stand adjourned for a
specified period, and at the adjourned meeting the members

present shall constitute a quorum. Where, however, special majorities are required under the articles, *e.g.* at class meetings, an adjourned meeting with less than the prescribed quorum would be invalid [*Hemans* v. *Hotchkiss Ordnance Co.* (1899), 1 Ch. 115]. The want of a quorum invalidates a meeting [*Cambrian Peat Co.* (1875), 31 L.T. 773]. The representative of a company, authorised under s. 139 of the Act to vote on its behalf, may be reckoned in the quorum [*Kelantan Coco Nut Estates* (1920), W.N. 274]. It may be noted that where there is a quorum at the beginning of the meeting, such meeting cannot transact any business after the members present have ceased to constitute a quorum [*Henderson* v. *Louttit* (1894), 21 Rettie (Ct. of Sess.); *Hennessy* v. *National Agricultural and Industrial Development Association* (1947), I.R. 195].

The articles usually provide that the chairman of the board **Duties of** shall be chairman at general meetings; failing this, the meeting **Chairman.** elects a chairman from among the directors, or, failing them, from among the members present. In default of any regulations in the articles, any person elected by the members present may take the chair [s. 134 (*d*)].

The duties of a chairman are to preserve order, to conduct proceedings regularly, and to take care that the sense of the meeting is properly ascertained with regard to any question before it [*National Dwelling Society* v. *Sykes* (1894), 3 Ch. 159]. Occasions arise when a group of individuals at the meeting may attempt obstruction by means which are apparently legitimate. Such individuals will probably be well versed in the technique of meetings, and they may endeavour to confuse the chairman by moving formal motions or amendments which may or may not be in order. If the chairman rules these motions out of order he may be accused of bias and prejudice; if he rules them in order he may be heading for trouble. This is particularly important in the exercise by the chairman of any discretion vested in him by the articles, *e.g.* where the chairman has the right to demand a poll [*Second Consolidated Trust* v. *Ceylon Amalgamated Tea and Rubber Estates*, per Uthwatt, J. (1943), W.N. 186]. In due course a motion will be put to the meeting, and any motion which is purely obstructive or dilatory should be ruled out of order.

It is not necessary for any motion to be seconded; and the chairman can put it without its having been proposed by a member, provided that the members clearly understand the matter on which they are voting. Two or more motions may be put to the meeting *en bloc* by the chairman if no member requires them to be put separately [*Jones* (*R.E.*) (1933), 50 T.L.R. 31]. A motion for the appointment of two or more persons as directors of a public company by a single resolution is not permissible under the Act, unless it has first been agreed to by the meeting without any vote being given against it [s. 183 (1)].

On a show of hands the principle of 'one man, one vote' obtains, but by the terms of s. 141, which apply to extraordinary and special resolutions, no one may vote who is not a member of the company (or the representative of a corporation which is a member or, of course, a proxy of a member), and no member may vote who is by the company's regulations not entitled to vote. Articles often extend the principle to ordinary resolutions, though in certain cases provisions are inserted enabling such persons as debenture holders to vote on ordinary resolutions or on specified questions. It would obviously be easy in many cases for a member not entitled to vote to attend and vote on a show of hands; hence the desirability of members signing their names on entering the room. Proxies are not counted on a show of hands [*Ernest* v. *Loma Gold Mines* (1897), 1 Ch. 1].

Should an amendment be moved, this should be disposed of before the original question is voted upon. The following points regarding amendments should be noted:—

(a) An amendment which is not strictly within the scope of the notice convening the meeting is out of order.

(b) Amendments substantially altering the motion or a new notion cannot be put without proper notice, *e.g.*
'That this meeting be adjourned' unless moved to facilitate business, *e.g.* to take a poll.
'That this meeting do proceed to the next business.' This is out of order if it prevents the consideration of the reports and accounts with a view of either adopting or rejecting them.
'That the report and accounts be received, but not adopted' (or any mere negative of an original motion) [but see *Clinch* v. *Financial Corporation* (1869), 4 Ch. App. 117; *Torbock* v. *Lord Westbury* (1902), 2 Ch. 871].

(c) Only one amendment at a time should be considered, and an amendment put when another amendment is under consideration should be ruled out of order.

It the chairman improperly refuses to put an amendment, the resolution carried will be invalidated [*Henderson* v. *Bank of Australasia* (1890), 45 Ch. D. 330].

When the views of the minority have been fairly heard, the chairman may move the closure; and, if the motion is carried by the meeting, he may declare the discussion closed and put the question to the vote.

Chitty, L.J., observed in *Wall* v. *London etc. Corporation* (1898), 2 Ch. 469, where a minority complained of the chairman stopping discussion, 'As to the closure, I think if we laid it down that the chairman, supported by the majority, could not put a termination to the speeches of those who were desirous of addressing the meeting, we should allow a small minority, or even a member or two, to tyrannise over the majority. If we accepted this proposition, we should put this weapon into the hands of the minority, which might involve the company in all-night sittings.'

A chairman has no casting vote unless it is conferred by the articles. Table A, cl. 60, confers such a right. A casting vote can only be used where there is an equality of valid votes, and it should be used sparingly if the chairman's reputation for impartiality is to be preserved. The motion is lost if he declines to exercise his casting vote in favour. The chairman may give a contingent or hypothetical casting vote to come into force if it should subsequently appear that there is an equality of valid votes [Bland v. Buchanan (1901), 2 K.B. 75].

Most articles provide that a declaration of the chairman that a resolution has been carried or lost is, unless a poll is demanded, to be deemed conclusive evidence of the fact and it is expressly provided by s. 141 (3) in the case of extraordinary and special resolutions that the declaration of the chairman that the resolution is carried shall, unless a poll is demanded, be conclusive. The question how many votes were in fact given cannot afterwards be discussed [Arnot v. United African Lands Co. (1901), 1 Ch. 518], but a declaration which is on the face of it erroneous in point of law is not conclusive [Caratal New Mines (1902), 2 Ch. 498].

A chairman cannot, without the consent of the shareholders, dissolve or adjourn a meeting while any business for which it was convened remains unfinished, unless the articles authorise him to do so. If he attempts to do so, the meeting may elect another chairman and proceed with the business [National Dwelling Society v. Sykes (1894), 3 Ch. 159].

If disorder makes it impossible to transact the business for which the meeting has been convened, the chairman should do one of two things: (a) he may adjourn the meeting for a short time to clear the meeting of disorderly elements, or (b) he may order the immediate removal of disorderly persons without adjourning. Recourse to the alternative procedure would, however, be extremely unlikely in the case of a company meeting.

Provided that the items required by statute to be transacted have been dealt with by a meeting (e.g. the presentation of accounts, etc., at the annual general meeting), there is no reason why a majority of members should not resolve to terminate a meeting before all the points on the agenda have been discussed or voted on.

The office of secretary was given statutory effect under **Duties of** s. 177 (1) of the Act. The statutory provisions relating to the **Secretary.** office of secretary are detailed in chapter XIII, p. 178.

The duties of a secretary, in so far as they relate to meetings of shareholders, are twofold:—

(1) those which relate to statutory requirements
  (i) prior to the meeting;
  (ii) at the meeting;
  (iii) subsequent to the meeting;

(2) those which relate to routine duties in connection with general, class, or requisitioned meetings.

The statutory requirements prior to the meeting comprise the following:—

(1) the issue of notices for the statutory meeting [s. 130, see p. 134]; the annual general meeting [s. 131, see p. 130]; class meetings [s. 291, see p. 206]; requisitioned meetings [s. 132, see p. 144];

(2) a statement of particulars relating to proxies in notices convening meetings of companies having a share capital [s. 136, see pp. 137, 154];

(3) the issue of notices dealing with meetings called for the purpose of passing extraordinary or special resolutions [s. 141, see p. 137];

(4) the circulation of resolutions [ss. 140 and 142, see pp. 131 and 191];

(5) notice to be given to the auditor of the annual general meeting [s. 162 (7)].

The statutory requirements governing the duties of the secretary at the meeting comprise the following:—

(1) the production at the commencement of the meeting of the register of directors' shareholdings [s. 195 (7), see p. 169];

(2) the reading of the auditor's report [s. 162 (2)].

Meetings are usually opened by the secretary reading the notice convening the meeting, and in the case of the annual general meeting, the auditors' report, which under s. 162 (2) of the Act must be read and not taken as read. Although there is no statutory requirement for the reading of notices, it provides a convenient opportunity of sensing the temper of a meeting and should not be omitted. In *Betts* v. *Macnaghten* (1910), 1 Ch. 435, Eve, J., stated that 'the mere fact that the shareholders dispensed with the actual reading of the document . . . does not in my opinion do away with the necessity of treating that document as having proved part of what was referred to and dealt with at the meeting.'

The statutory requirements after the meeting comprise the following:—

(1) filing of the annual return (ss. 124 to 129, see p. 112 *et seq.*);

(2) registration of extraordinary and special resolutions (s. 143, see p. 186).

The routine duties in connection with general meetings can also be divided into three categories:—

(1) those which relate to matters prior to the meeting;

(2) those which relate to matters at the meeting;

(3) those which relate to matters subsequent to the meeting.

The routine duties prior to the meeting consist of the following:—

1. *Notices.* The Act requires 21 (clear) days' notice for an annual general meeting and 14 (clear) days for meetings other than for the annual general meeting, except in the case of an unlimited company (s. 133), or in the case of meetings at which a special resolution is to be passed. In large companies the envelopes containing notices convening the annual general meeting are addressographed, and it is necessary to ensure that changes of address, dividend requests, and other instructions are noted on the plates well in advance of the last day for sending out the notices.

2. *Arrangements for room.* Where the meeting is to be held at a place other than the registered office of the company, adequate arrangements should be made beforehand.

3. *Preparation of directors' report and chairman's speech.* The secretary will most probably be deputed to prepare the directors' report for approval by the board. The report should deal briefly with the main events of the year reviewed, *cf.* s. 157 (2), leaving the matters affecting the particular trade, and national, international and political considerations in general, to be dealt with by the chairman in his speech. This speech will also probably be drafted by the secretary.

4. *Preparation of Agenda.* The agenda, in addition to covering the matters referred to in the notice of the meeting, should contain the names of proposers and seconders of motions, and copies should be distributed to the directors, the proposers and seconders and those who have a direct interest in the proceedings. (See chapter XV, p. 195.)

5. *Proxies.* The secretary will, before the meeting, have examined the proxies received at the company's office, rejecting all those not delivered in time, not in proper form, or sent in by members who for some reason, *e.g.* non-payment of calls, are not entitled to vote.

F

6. *Poll Scrutineers.* Adequate arrangements should be made beforehand for recording votes in the event of a poll being demanded and agreed to by the chairman. Admission and voting cards should be printed and lists of shareholders prepared in readiness for the meeting. The procedure in the conduct of a poll is described on p. 159.

7. *Stewards.* Arrangements should be made for persons to be present at the doors for the purpose of securing the signature of members on attendance sheets as they enter the room. These lists may be arranged in such a way that the names of members attending in person could be separated from those attending by proxy and those representing corporations. If admission cards are to be circulated, arrangements should be made for their collection and 'keying.'

The routine duties at the meeting consist of the following:—

1. to read the notice of the meeting and the auditor's report;

2. to ascertain the votes cast:—

   (i) Where a specified majority is required for the passing of any resolution a careful count should be made by the secretary.

   (ii) *On a poll.* Every voter when polling should be required to sign his name, and insert the number of shares held by him on the voting paper. When all the votes have been cast, it is the usual practice for the chairman, or for the meeting, to appoint scrutineers to examine the votes; sometimes the articles provide for the appointment of scrutineers. In the absence of scrutineers, the responsibility of rejecting any invalid votes will rest with the chairman, who will in most cases be guided by the information furnished him by the secretary.

Arrangements for the conduct of a poll when the number attending the meeting is considerable are detailed on p. 159.

There are several other matters on which, though the ultimate responsibility is the chairman's, the secretary's assistance and advice will often be required, for example: ensuring that the meeting is a valid meeting, that all necessary formalities have been complied with, that a quorum is present, and that a resolution passed has been validly passed.

The routine duties after the meeting consist of the following:—

1. *Minutes.* The minutes of the meeting should be recorded immediately after the meeting. These should express, as concisely as possible, the business transacted at the meeting, the names of the proposers and seconders of each motion, with a note to the effect that the motion was put to the meeting by

the chairman and duly carried. The minutes of general meetings of most large companies are now recorded in loose-leaf books by machines, and copies should be distributed to the directors. See chapter XV, p. 194.

2. *Press Notices.* If the board has agreed to send copies of the report and chairman's speech to the press, these should be prepared before the meeting so that they can be released immediately afterwards.

3. *Annual Return.* The procedure in connection with the completion and filing of the annual return is detailed in chapter XI, p. 112 *et seq.*

The *prima facie* rule regarding the right to vote is that **Voting.** every member of a company whose name is on the register of members is entitled to vote. The register is the only evidence by which that right can be ascertained. The fact that shares have been transferred to a member by other shareholders in order to increase their voting power, or with an object alleged to be adverse to the interests of the company, and that such member is not the beneficial owner of the shares, does not disentitle him to his vote [*Pender* v. *Lushington* (1877), 6 Ch. D. 70; *Stranton Iron Co.* (1873), 16 Eq. 559].

A prohibition in a company's articles against a director voting as a director in respect of any matter in which he has an interest does not preclude him from voting as a shareholder at a general meeting in respect of any such matter [*East Pant Du United Lead Mining Co.* v. *Merryweather* (1864), 13 W.R. 216], even though his interests in the subject matter are opposed to those of the company [*North West Transportation Co.* v. *Beatty* (1887), 12 A.C. 589].

Unless otherwise provided by the articles, a holder of any class of shares has the right to vote. Some articles restrict the right to ordinary shareholders, while some companies even allow debenture holders to vote. The votes of debenture holders cannot, however, be counted on an extraordinary or special resolution.

A transmission clause is usually inserted in articles, enabling any person who becomes entitled to shares, in consequence of the death or bankruptcy of any member, to be registered in respect of those shares, and to exercise the right of voting. Until he is so registered, a legal personal representative may not vote unless the articles make such a provision. Under Table A, cl. 134, a legal personal representative is entitled to receive notices of every general meeting, but by cl. 32 he cannot vote until he is registered as a member. Under the proviso to cl. 32, directors may by notice give any such person the option either to become registered or to transfer his shares and to withhold dividends, etc., if the notice is not complied with within 90 days. In the case of joint holders of shares, Table A provides that the vote of the senior who tenders his vote shall be accepted to the exclusion of the other joint holders. Seniority in such a case is determined by the order in which the names appear on the register. Should, therefore, the first named be absent, the second named person could vote. The bearers of share warrants are usually given power to vote, but on certain conditions, *e.g.* that the warrants are produced and lodged for a stated time for examination.

The articles usually forbid any member upon whose shares any calls are in arrear to vote. It has been held that, where an article provided that a member should not be entitled to vote while any call or other sum should be due and payable in respect of his shares, and the shares of a member were forfeited for non-payment of calls, the purchaser of the forfeited shares, which had been re-sold to him by the company with a certificate stating that he was to be deemed to be the holder of the shares discharged from all calls due, was not entitled to vote [*Randt Gold Mining Co.* v. *Wainwright* (1901), 1 Ch. 184]. The articles sometimes preclude from voting any member who has acquired his shares less than three months (or other specified period) before the date of the meeting.

Proxies. Prior to the passing of the Companies Act, 1948, there was no statutory right to vote by proxy, though such right was almost always given by the articles. The Act provides that any member of a company entitled to attend and vote at a meeting of the company is entitled to appoint another person, whether a member of the company or not, to vote instead of him at any meeting of a company (other than a company not having a share capital). A member of a private company may not appoint more than one proxy to attend on the same occasion [s. 136 (1) (*b*)]. A proxy appointed at a meeting of a private company may speak [s. 136 (1)], but this right does not apply to meetings of a public company. The purpose of this distinction is to protect the interests of persons in small companies who, but for the assistance of a professional advocate, might be incapable of stating their case and would thus be at a disadvantage. In a public company there is less likelihood of minority interests being sacrificed through inadequate proxy representation. In every notice calling a meeting of a company having a share capital there must appear with reasonable prominence a statement that a member entitled to attend and vote is entitled to appoint a proxy and that a proxy need not be a member. Where a member may appoint more than one proxy that fact should also be stated in the notice [s. 136 (2)]. See pp. 130, 158 and Appendix H. There is frequently a provision in articles requiring proxies to be lodged 48 hours or even longer before the meeting; but 48 hours is now the longest period allowed by statute and an article is void in so far as it requires a longer period [s. 136 (3)]. The issue at the company's expense to a limited number of members only of invitations to appoint as proxy a person or one of a number of persons specified in the invitations is prohibited by s. 136 (4), and any officer knowingly permitting such issue is liable to a fine not exceeding £100. It is provided, however, that no officer will be liable if, at a member's request in writing, he sends him a form of appointment naming the proxy or a list of proxies willing to act, but the form or list must be available on request in writing to every member entitled to vote at the meeting by proxy. Subject to the above mentioned statutory requirements, proxy voting depends upon the articles of association, and their provisions must be strictly followed.

The fact that one member holds a proxy for another does not entitle him to another vote on a show of hands, but it appears that if the articles allow voting by proxy on a show of hands (which is, however, unusual), every non-member who holds a proxy can give one vote [*Ernest* v. *Loma Gold Mines* (1897), 1 Ch. 1].

To comply with Stock Exchange regulations a proxy form must, if it is to apply to special business, be in a 'two-way' form. The form of such a proxy should provide not only for votes to be cast 'for' or 'against' a motion but also for any modification of it that may be submitted to a meeting. There is considerable variation in the form of proxies used by companies, and the adoption of a standard form is commended. See Appendix F, Forms 49 and 50. Reference should also be made to the form given in Table A, cl. 71, which is in accordance with Stock Exchange regulations.

The exercise of the right, subject to the aforementioned statutory requirements, depends on the regulations of the company. Where articles prescribe a form of proxy, the provisions and form must be strictly followed [*Harben* v. *Phillips* (1882), 23 Ch. D. 14], but where articles state that proxies must be in a specified form, 'or as near thereto as circumstances permit,' and the specified form is a proxy applicable to a single meeting, general proxies should not be excluded [*Isaacs* v. *Chapman* (1915), W.N. 413]. There is no need for a shareholder's signature on a proxy to be witnessed, unless the articles so require. If this is the case, the donee of a proxy should not act as witness, as this may invalidate the proxy. There is no authority directly in point, but in *re Parrott* (1891), 2 Q.B. 151, a creditor appointed her solicitor to represent her at a meeting of creditors and the solicitor witnessed her signature. The proxy was held invalid despite the fact that the official receiver accepted it at the meeting.

A proxy can be revoked (i) by the valid deposit of a subsequent proxy in favour of another person; or (ii) by the attendance and voting in person of the donor at the meeting; or (iii) by the death of the donor; or (iv) by the cancellation of the authority. A proxy may normally be revoked at any time, even between the last date for lodgment of proxies and the date of the meeting, or in the period between the date of a meeting and the date of an adjourned meeting. Doubt exists whether such revocation need be communicated to the company, and some articles, *e.g.* Table A, cl. 73, contain a provision that a proxy is valid notwithstanding the previous death of the principal or revocation of the proxy, provided that no notice in writing of the fact of death or revocation has been received by the company before the meeting [*Cousins* v. *International Brick Co.* (1931), 2 Ch. 90].

The proxy may be signed in blank so long as it is properly filled up by the time it is used [*Ernest* v. *Loma Gold Mines* (1897), 1 Ch. 1], even though at the time of the execution the date of the meeting has not been fixed [*Sadgrove* v. *Bryden* (1907), 1 Ch. 318]. It would appear that this applies to inserting the name of the proxy, provided the name is inserted by someone with express or implied authority to complete it [*Lancaster* (1877), 5 Ch.D. 911; *ex parte Duce*, 13 Ch.D. 429]. If a company sends out forms of proxy, it usually inserts the name of the intended proxy; but if no name is inserted and a shareholder signs the form of proxy and returns it to the company without inserting any name, it seems that the board of directors has implied authority to complete it by directing the secretary to insert the name of a proxy [*Ernest* v. *Loma Gold Mines, supra*]. The above cases do not apply to meetings held pursuant to s. 206 to confirm a scheme of arrangement, since the form approved by the court is framed with the object of compelling the shareholder to exercise his own discretion in the matter of how he shall vote [*Magadi Soda Company* (1925), 94 L.J.Ch. 217]; nor, apparently, do they apply to meetings of statutory companies (see p. 380). If an unqualified person is named in a proxy but if the qualification exists when the proxy is lodged and when it is used, no objection can be taken to it [*Bombay Burmah Corporation* v. *Shroff* (1905), A.C. 213]. If both the member and his proxy attend the meeting, the member is entitled to vote personally and a vote tendered by his proxy must be rejected, unless the articles otherwise provide [*Cousins* v. *International Brick Co., supra*].

The company's funds may be used by the directors in sending out proxies containing the names of the directors, provided that the directors in so doing are acting *bona fide* in the interests of the company, and that the proxies are sent to all members entitled to the notice of meeting [*Peel* v. *London and North Western Railway Co.* (1907), 1 Ch. 5; *Wilson* v. *L.M.S. Railway Co.* (1940), Ch. 398].

A company which is a member of another company may, **Company** under s. 139 of the Act, by resolution of the directors or **Representa-** other governing body, authorise such person as it thinks fit **tion.** to act as its representative at any meeting of the company or of any class of members. The chairman of the meeting is entitled to reasonable evidence of the representative's appointment. There is normally no need for a separate resolution of appointment for each meeting. The form of appointment need not bear the corporation seal. Although it is not strictly necessary, it is desirable for the representative to be armed with a copy of the resolution of appointment certified by a director and the secretary of the appointing corporation. In practice it is not unusual for the corporation shareholders to inform the secretary of the company that the appointment has been duly made, in addition to supplying the representative with the aforesaid copy. If the resolution of appointment names the representative impersonally, e.g. 'the secretary of the corporation for the time being,' the representative should be armed not only with a certified copy of the resolution, but also with means of establishing his identity. It is preferable to appoint individuals where possible, even if this involves the appointment of several alternate representatives. In this event the wording should follow the lines of a proxy: 'A should be appointed to attend and failing him B or failing him C, etc.' It has been held that the chairman of the meeting may properly admit the vote on the evidence afforded by a copy of the resolution [*Colonial Gold Reef* v. *Free State Rand* (1914), 1 Ch. 382]. Such a representative may be reckoned in the quorum. The power to appoint a representative is given to every corporation, whether a company within the meaning of the Act or not, and extends to class meetings of shareholders and to meetings of creditors as well as to general meetings (s. 139); a corporation registered abroad can exercise this power.

If the voting is taken by a poll, the number of votes to **Poll.** which each member is entitled depends on the articles. In default of regulations, every member, in the case of a company originally having a share capital, has one vote in respect of each share or each ten pounds of stock held by him, and in any other case one vote [s. 134 (*e*)].

Many articles provide that upon a poll every member present in person or by proxy shall have one vote for every share held by him. Various sliding scales are also sometimes adopted. It is occasionally provided that no member shall have more than a fixed number of votes; sometimes a member is not given a vote unless he holds a fixed number of shares. A sliding scale is necessary where a promoter takes a large block of fully paid shares, unless it is desired that he should control the company.

It is thought that a member of a public company may appoint more than one person, whether members or not, as proxies unless the articles otherwise provide (s. 136), but on a poll a member entitled to more than one vote need not use all his votes or cast all the votes he uses in the same way (s. 138). Under the provisions of the Act, a trustee, if he is present at a meeting in person, or a proxy acting on behalf of beneficiaries, or a director acting for various members, may cast one vote one way and another vote in another way, in accordance with the wishes of the beneficial owners of the shares. These provisions will be of value to nominee companies and trust corporations who may be called upon by the persons for whom they act to vote both for and against a resolution according to the interests of the persons whom they represent.

Prior to the 1948 Act, the only statutory right to demand a poll related to extraordinary and special resolutions, other cases being usually dealt with by the articles. The Act extends the right to any resolution (other than that of a company limited by guarantee and having no share capital).

Under s. 137 (1) of the Act any provision contained in a company's articles shall be void, in so far as it would have the effect either

(a) of excluding the right to demand a poll at a general meeting on any question other than the election of the chairman of the meeting or the adjournment of the meeting; or

(b) of making ineffective a demand for a poll on any such questions which is made either

    (i) by not less than five members having the right to vote at the meeting; or

    (ii) by a member or members representing not less than one-tenth of the total voting rights of all the members having the right to vote at the meeting; or

    (iii) by a member or members holding shares in the company conferring a right to vote at the meeting being shares on which an aggregate sum has been paid up equal to not less than one-tenth of the total sum paid up on all the shares conferring that right.

A proxy holder has the right to demand or join in demanding a poll [s. 137 (2)], and in fact one member holding four proxies can himself demand the poll.

The company's articles cannot limit the statutory right, but can, and often do, prescribe less stringent requirements for demanding a poll. In particular they usually allow the chairman himself to demand a poll.

If the members demanding a poll are duly qualified voters, which should not be lightly assumed, the chairman will grant the poll. Table A provides that the poll shall be taken in such manner as the chairman directs, unless it be demanded on the election of a chairman or on a question of adjournment, in which case it shall be taken forthwith (cls. 59 and 61). However, where articles provide in the ordinary way for votes being given either personally or by proxy, the chairman cannot direct that the poll shall be taken by means of polling papers signed by the members and delivered at the company's office; there must be a personal attendance by the voter or his duly appointed proxy [*McMillan* v. *Le Roi Mining Company* (1906), 1 Ch. 331].

Where a poll is demanded upon more than one resolution, the resolutions should, on the poll being taken, be separately voted upon [*Blair Open Hearth* v. *Reigart* (1913), 108 L.T. 665].

A poll is not a new meeting, but it is a mode of ascertaining the sense of the meeting, which is continued for that purpose [per Cotton, L.J., in *R.* v. *Wimbledon Local Board* (1882), 8 Q.B.D. 459, at p. 465]. It follows that the taking of a poll is not an adjournment of the meeting and therefore does not make proxies which have been obtained after the meeting, but before the poll, available in a case where the articles permit the use of proxies lodged a specified time before the meeting or adjourned meeting [*Shaw* v. *Tati Concessions* (1913), 1 Ch. 292]. Where the articles provide that proxies must be deposited not less than two clear days before the day for holding the meeting, proxies lodged after the meeting, but more than two clear days before the day fixed for an adjournment thereof, cannot be used [*McLaren* v. *Thompson* (1917), 2 Ch. 261].

The chairman may direct that the poll be taken forthwith. The following method for conducting a poll has been found satisfactory:—

(1) The chairman explains how members are to vote and gives instructions that no member is to leave or enter the room, other than those present during the progress of the poll.

(2) Members are advised to leave the hall by the doors leading into an ante-room, where they will find

    (i) separate tables each indicated by letters of the alphabet applicable to the group to which the members belongs, *viz*. A to G, H to M and so on,

    (ii) a separate table reserved for those voting by proxy and for corporation representatives,

    (iii) a separate table for members holding bearer shares,

    (iv) a separate table reserved for enquiries.

At each table a clerk should be in attendance, and should have for inspection a list of members, with numbers of votes of each member of the group over which he has control. A complete list should be available at the enquiry table.

(3) Each member should present himself at the table belonging to his alphabetical group. The clerk thereupon ascertains whether an admission card has been deposited, and, if satisfied on that point, he hands the member a voting card. A card will have been prepared before the meeting for each member and checked during the meeting with the admission cards. Each member completes and deposits the card in a box reserved for the purpose.

(4) The member then returns to the hall.

(5) At the conclusion of the poll the scrutineers collect the voting papers, count the number of votes (by calculating machines if the numbers are considerable) and arrange for them to be checked by the directors.

(6) The chairman then declares the result.

The above procedure can be modified according to the number of members expected to be present. Where the estimated number is less than 100 members, the retirement from the main hall and segregation into groups could possibly be eliminated.

Adjournment. The general rule is that a meeting, once convened, cannot be cancelled unless there is an express provision in the articles providing for such cancellation [*Smith* v. *Paringa Mines Ltd.* (1906), 2 Ch. 193]. In cases where, after the meeting has been convened, it is found impossible or impracticable to hold a meeting on the date originally fixed, notice should be sent to members to the following effect. The notice should relate the facts briefly, and state that, in order to comply with the law, the meeting must be held, but that it will be adjourned immediately to a time and place to be arranged, no business being transacted. At the same time the board responsible for the issue of the circular may issue fresh notices for the adjourned meeting, or alternatively, the first meeting may be adjourned *sine die* and notices of the adjourned meeting may be sent out subsequently.

The articles usually give power to a chairman to adjourn a meeting with the consent of the members present; he may do so, but is not bound to adjourn, although requested so to do by a majority of the meeting [*Salisbury Gold Mining Co.* v. *Hathorn* (1897), A.C. 268], except at the statutory meeting, where the right to adjourn is vested in the meeting [s. 130 (8)].

An adjourned meeting is legally a continuation of the original meeting even if there is no quorum at the original meeting [*Scadding* v. *Lorant* (1851), 3 H.L.C. 418], and therefore no business can be transacted at an adjourned meeting which was not within the scope of the original meeting, except in the case of the statutory meeting. If a member becomes registered on some date between the meeting and the adjourned meeting, there is no reason why he should not attend and vote at the adjourned meeting, even though he was precluded from attending and voting at the original meeting.

A resolution passed at an adjourned meeting must be treated as having been passed on the date on which it was actually passed and not on any earlier date (s. 144).

An important duty of the secretary is the recording of **Minutes.** minutes. These are required by s. 145 to be entered in books kept for the purpose, and minutes of proceedings at general meetings, as well as of proceedings at meetings of directors and of managers, if any, must be kept, and there are penalties for default [s. 145 (4)]. The minutes in each case should be signed by the chairman of the meeting at which the proceedings recorded took place, or by the chairman of the next succeeding meeting. They then become evidence of the proceedings. This does not mean that they are conclusive evidence, but, in the absence of any other evidence to show their incorrectness, they will be accepted by the courts as reliable. Neither are the minutes exclusive evidence of what took place at a meeting, and an unrecorded resolution may be proved by other evidence [*Fireproof Doors* (1916), 2 Ch. 142]. Detailed information in regard to minuting will be found in chapter XV.

The books containing the minutes of general meetings must be kept at the registered office, and the members have a statutory right to inspect them without charge [s. 146 (1)] and to be furnished with copies within seven days of request on payment of sixpence per hundred words [s. 146 (2)]. This right can be enforced by the court [s. 146 (4)]; but it does not extend to the minutes of board meetings. It is therefore desirable to keep in separate books the minutes of the general meetings and of the directors' and managers' meetings. The minute book may either be in the form of a bound book or may record the matters in question in any other manner, *e.g.* a loose-leaf book [s. 436 (1)]. Where the minute book is in a form other than that of a bound book adequate precautions must be taken for guarding against falsification [s. 436 (2)]. See chapter XV, p. 194.

CHAPTER XIII

DIRECTORS

Definitions. By s. 455 of the Act the expression 'director' includes 'any person occupying the position of director by whatever name called.' Moreover, for certain purposes, *e.g.* the register of directors and secretaries (s. 200), a person in accordance with whose directions or instructions the directors of a company are accustomed to act is to be deemed to be a director. A director is a person who guides or governs the policy of a company; he may be called a manager, or a governor, or, as in the case of some financial and trust companies, a trustee; so long, however, as he occupies a position which imposes on him the duty of guiding or governing the policy of a company, he is a director in law, with all the consequent liabilities and responsibilities.

A managing director is usually also an ordinary director, who, besides having as an ordinary director to guide and govern the policy of the company, has in his capacity of managing director to perform certain executive functions. In so far as he performs those functions, he is simply an officer of the company; in so far as he guides and governs the policy of the company, he is, with the other ordinary directors of the company, from some points of view a trustee and from others an agent or a managing partner.

A detailed consideration of the position of a director is beyond the scope of this work, but it may be pointed out that 'a director of a company is precluded from dealing on behalf of the company, with himself, and from entering into engagements in which he has a personal interest conflicting, or which possibly may conflict, with the interests of those whom he is bound by fiduciary duty to protect; and this rule is applicable to the case of one of several directors as to a managing or sole director' [*North-West Transportation Co.* v. *Beatty* (1887), 12 A.C. 587, at p. 593]. The above principle will not, however, prevent a director being interested in contracts with the company, provided the articles so allow, and he discloses his interest as required by s. 199 (see below); nor will it prevent him voting as a shareholder on the transaction if it comes before the company in general meeting (see above). If a director makes any profit from a transaction entered into in contravention of the above principle, he can be compelled to pay over such profit to the company.

Every company registered after the commencement of the 1929 Act and not being a private company must have at least

two directors (s. 176). Under the old law the control might
be vested in a single director or manager. It is clear from
s. 200 that a corporation can be a director of a company, and
there seems to be no reason why both or all the directors of a
company should not be corporations, except in the case of an
exempt private company. (See chapter XXIII.)

1 and 2 Vict, cap. 106, ss. 28 to 31, and 4 and 5 Vict. cap.
14, provide that it is not lawful for any spiritual person
holding any cathedral preferment, benefice, curacy, or
lectureship, or who shall be licensed or allowed to perform the
duties of any ecclesiastical office, to act as a director of any
trading company carrying on business for gain and profit,
except in a few specified cases such as schools and insurance
companies.

A director is usually appointed in one of the following **Appoint-
ways: ment.**

   1. by the articles;

   2. by the signatories to the memorandum and articles;

   3. by other directors to fill a vacancy;

   4. by the shareholders in general meeting.

1. As to appointment by the articles, the conditions laid
down by s. 181 as to signing and delivering to the Registrar
a consent to act, etc., must be complied with unless the
company is a private company or has not a share capital. The
signing and delivery to the Registrar of an undertaking to
take and pay for qualification shares is equivalent to signing
the memorandum [s. 181 (2)] and therefore under s. 26
constitutes an agreement to become a member. (See Appendix F, Form 9.)

2. The articles of association may provide that the signatories
shall appoint the first directors.

The appointment may be made at a meeting by a majority
of the subscribers [*London & Southern Counties Land Co.*
(1885), 31 Ch. D. 223], which must be held after, and not
before, the registration of the company [*Möller* v. *Maclean*
(1889), 1 Meg. 274]; but without a meeting an appointment
in writing is good if all the subscribers to the memorandum
of association concur [*Great Northern Salt & Chemical Works*
(1889), 44 Ch. D. 472], or, in case the articles give the power
to the majority, if signed by the majority.

3. It is commonly provided that any casual vacancy on
the board may be filled by the existing directors.

4. The articles usually provide that the directors are to be
appointed by the company in general meeting; and, even when
the existing directors have power to fill a casual vacancy, a
director appointed for that purpose will usually hold office
only until the next general meeting. If the articles do not

provide how directors are to be appointed, the company in general meeting has an implied power to appoint directors, which it can exercise by ordinary resolution. Subject to the articles, the company in general meeting may appoint any number of directors [*Choppington Collieries Ltd.* v. *Johnson* (1944), 1 All E.R. 762].

Section 183 of the Act provides that, in a public company, a single resolution to appoint two or more persons as directors is invalid, unless the meeting has first agreed without vote to the contrary that the appointment shall be so made. Except with such agreement there must be a separate resolution for each person to be appointed. Where a resolution passed is invalid under s. 183 a provision for the automatic re-election of retiring directors does not apply. If, however, the persons invalidly appointed act as directors in the belief that their appointment is valid, their acts will be valid notwithstanding that their appointment is bad (s. 180).

In all the cases (2), (3) and (4) above, no consent to act or contract to take qualification shares is required by the Act, but the articles must be complied with, and as pointed out below, s. 182 makes it incumbent upon a director to obtain his qualification within the time thereby limited, failure to do which renders his office vacant.

Section 187 of the Act makes it an offence for any person being an undischarged bankrupt to act as a director of, or directly or indirectly to take part in or be concerned in the management of, any company without leave of the court by which he was adjudged bankrupt, but this provision does not apply to a person who was so acting on the 3rd of August, 1928, and has continuously so acted since that date where the bankruptcy was prior to that date. In this section, 'company' includes unregistered companies and companies incorporated outside Great Britain which have an established place of business within Great Britain.

To avoid inconvenient consequences in cases where a director has inadvertently acted when his appointment or qualification was defective, s. 180 of the Act provides that 'the acts of a director or manager shall be valid notwithstanding any defect that may afterwards be discovered in his appointment or qualification.'

Improperly appointed directors, or directors acting after disqualification, may bind the company by their acts. Persons dealing with the company are not concerned with the indoor management thereof, and the company is bound by contracts entered into by such *de facto* directors on its behalf, unless it can show that the other party knew of the defective appointment [*Mahony* v. *East Holyford Co.* (1874), L.R. 7 H.L. 869; see also *Kanssen* v. *Rialto (Westend) Ltd.* (1944), Ch. 346; *Morris* v. *Kanssen* (1946), A.C. 460].

The articles of most companies require a director to be a **Qualification.** shareholder, although there is no enactment rendering it obligatory. Table A, 1948, provides that the shareholding qualification for directors may be fixed by the company in general meeting, and unless and until so fixed no qualification, shall be required.

The language of articles providing for the share qualification of directors must be carefully studied, as it varies considerably and is strictly construed. If, for example, the articles provide that no person shall be 'eligible as' or 'qualified to become' a director unless he holds so many shares, the election of any person not holding the prescribed qualification is void *[Barber's Case* (1877), 5 Ch.D. 963; *Jenner's Case* (1878), 7 Ch.D. 132]. Nor can the company ratify such an election without first altering the articles *[Boschoek Proprietary Co.* v. *Fuke* (1906), 1 Ch. 148]. Where the articles provide that the qualification of a director must be the holding of a certain number of shares 'in his own right,' he need not be the beneficial owner *[Pulbrook* v. *Richmond Consolidated* (1878), 9 Ch. D. 610], but he must hold the shares in such a way that the company can safely deal with him in respect of them *[Bainbridge* v. *Smith* (1889), 41 Ch. D. 462]; thus, a bankrupt director does not, after notice to the company by his trustee, hold in his own right *[Sutton* v. *English & Colonial Produce* (1902), 2 Ch. 502; see also *Boschoek Proprietary Co.* v. *Fuke, supra*]. Where the articles provide simply that a director must be the registered holder of a certain number of shares, the joint holding of shares is a sufficient qualification *[Grundy* v. *Briggs* (1910), 1 Ch. 444]. It is a breach of duty on the part of a director to accept his qualification shares as a gift from a promoter of the company or from any person having contacts with the company *[Eden* v. *Ridsdale's Railway Lamp and Lighting Co.* (1889), 23 Q.B.D. 368]. Such shares, however, although improperly received, will none the less suffice to form his qualifications *[Hercynia Co.* (1894), 2 Ch. 403; *Carling's Case* (1876), 1 Ch. D. 115]. It is possible for a director to lose his share qualification as the result of a reduction of capital. The share qualification laid down by the articles might, for instance, be 500 shares of £1 each. If the £1 shares are then written down to 10s. and subsequently consolidated into £1 shares, a director holding 500 shares prior to the reduction would be holding only 250 and would cease to be qualified. In such a case, where directors inadvertently continue to act as directors after ceasing to hold their qualification shares, the court may make an order under s. 448 of the Act granting relief from liability *[Gilt Edge Safety Glass Ltd.* (1940), Ch. 495]. It should be noted, however, that where the share qualification is increased, the directors concerned may be deemed to have contracted to obtain the necessary qualification within a reasonable time. In such case the director has not ceased to be qualified [*Molineaux* v. *London, Birmingham and Manchester Insurance Co.* (1902), 2 K.B. 589]. Under s. 182 a director must acquire his qualification (if any) within two months of his appointment or such shorter time as is fixed by the articles; if he does not do so his appointment is automatically vacated, and he is incapable of being re-appointed a director until he has actually obtained his qualification. An unqualified person, acting as a director after the date when he should have obtained his qualification, becomes liable to a fine of five pounds for every day while he so acts. Shares represented by share warrants cannot form any part of a director's qualification [s. 182 (2)]. Since a director cannot be said to hold his qualification shares until he is actually registered in respect of them, and since delays in delivery by the market frequently preclude his registration within the two month time limit, it is often the practice of the director to 'borrow' the shares. The 'borrowed' shares are transferred to the director for nominal consideration and are then transferred back again when he is registered in respect of his own shares. It may be noted in this connection that this action need not affect any entries to be made in the register of directors' shareholdings since, by virtue of s. 195 (3) of the Act, the nature and extent of a director's interest or right in any shares is only disclosed in the register if so required by the director. The point sometimes arises whether a director who is not bound by the articles to hold any share qualification, and who in fact is not a member of the company, is entitled to attend a general meeting of the company. The point has never come before the court and is not likely to do so. It is submitted, however, that the director has a duty to attend general meetings, in that a company is entitled to the services and to the advice of all its directors. A director holding no shares cannot, however, be counted in a quorum or vote, for the simple reason that he is not a member, *cf.* s. 26 of the Act.

Loans to Directors. Section 190 of the Act prohibits a company from making loans to its directors or to directors of its holding company. It is also unlawful for a company to enter into any guarantee or to provide any security in connection with such loan There are, however, four exceptions to this rule and accordingly the section does not apply:—(i) to exempt private companies; (ii) in the case of a subsidiary where the director is its holding company; (iii) in the case of a company whose ordinary business includes the lending of money or the giving of guarantees in connection with loans made by other persons; and (iv) where a loan is made to a director to meet expenditure incurred or to be incurred by him in order to enable him properly to perform his duties as an officer of the company. In the last-mentioned case the prior approval of the company in general meeting must be obtained, and the purposes of the expenditure and the amount of the loan (or the extent of the guarantee or security) must be disclosed to such meeting. Such a loan may, however, be made to a director conditional on such approval by the company, and, if the approval cannot be obtained, the money borrowed must be repaid (or the guarantee or security discharged) within six months from the conclusion of the meeting.

Full disclosure of all loans made to officers of the company must be made in the company's accounts in compliance with s. 197. The term 'officer' includes 'director, manager and secretary' (s. 455). The following particulars must be shown:— (a) the amount of any such loans made during the financial year to any officer even though he became an officer after the loan was made; (b) the amount of any such loan made before the current financial year and outstanding at its expiration. To qualify for inclusion, the loan must have been made (i) by the company; or (ii) by one of its subsidiaries; or (iii) by any person under a guarantee from, or on a security provided by, the company. Two categories of loans are excepted from the provisions of s. 197: (a) loans made in the ordinary course of a company's business of lending money; and (b) loans made, and certified by the directors as being made, to employees which do not exceed £2,000, provided that they are made in accordance with the company's usual practice with regard to loans to employees. It will be noted that a distinction is drawn in this section between 'officers' and 'officers who are employees.' The company's secretary, though an officer, will usually also be an employee; an ordinary director or managing director will not, it is thought, usually be an employee; in the case of a manager it will depend on the terms of his service whether or not he is also an employee [*Normandy* v. *Ind, Coope* (1908), 1 Ch. 84]. Under s. 198 it is the duty of the officer concerned to give notice to the company containing the information required by s. 197.

The remuneration of a director is not a matter of right **Remuneration.** unless it is so provided by the articles of association. Where no remuneration is specified in the articles of association, the company may vote it in general meeting, but in such a case the remuneration would be a mere gratuity and apparently the resolution would not give rise to a cause of action [*Dunstan* v. *Imperial Gas Co.* (1833), 3 B. & Ad. 125]. If, however, the remuneration is fixed by the articles and no power is given to the company in general meeting to vote additional remuneration, the articles must be altered by special resolution before such additional remuneration can be voted.

Unless otherwise provided, a director is not entitled to his expenses of attending board meetings in addition to his remuneration [*Young* v. *Naval & Military, etc., of South Africa* (1905), 1 K.B. 687].

A director may sue for his fees [*Nell* v. *Atlanta Gold Co.* (1895), 11 T.L.R. 407], or may prove for his fees with other creditors in the winding-up of a company [*Beckwith's Case* (1898), 1 Ch. 324].

When the articles of a company merely provide that directors' remuneration shall be a specified sum per annum, the directors are not entitled to an apportioned part of such remuneration for serving for part of a year [*Salton* v. *New Beeston Cycle Co.* (1899), 1 Ch. 775; *London & Northern Bank, McConnell's Case* (1901), 1 Ch. 728]. It has been suggested that the Apportionment Act, 1870, applies to such a case, and that a director is accordingly entitled to be remunerated in such circumstances for a broken period of a year; but the Court of Appeal has expressly left the point open [*Moriarty* v. *Regent's Garage & Engineering Co.* (1921), 2 K.B. 766]. Where the remuneration is a certain sum per annum to be paid at such time as the directors shall determine, it is a condition precedent to a director's right to sue that the directors shall have determined a time for payment [*Caridad Copper* v. *Swallow* (1902), 2 K.B. 44]. Similarly, if the remuneration is an aggregate sum, to be divided in such manner as the directors shall determine, a director cannot sue until the board has made a formal division [*Joseph* v. *Sonora (Mexico) Land* (1918), 34 T.L.R. 220]. It is now usually provided that their remuneration shall accrue due *de die in diem*, or shall be at the rate of so much per annum [cf. *Gilman* v. *Gulcher Electric Light & Power Co.* (1886), 3 T.L.R. 133].

Prohibition of tax-free payments to directors. Section 189 of the Act prohibits tax-free payments to directors except under a contract which was in force on the 18th July, 1945, and provides expressly, and not merely by reference to the articles, for tax-free remuneration. Any provision in a company's articles or in any contract (not in force on 18th July, 1945) or any resolution of a company or its directors for tax-free payment to directors shall have effect as if it provided for the payment, as a gross sum subject to income tax and surtax, of the net sum for which it actually provides. The operation of the section is not retrospective.

Directors as Receivers and Managers. Directors who are appointed by the court to be receivers and managers at a remuneration are entitled to their remuneration as directors in addition [*South Western of Venezuela Railway* (1902), 1 Ch. 701].

The provisions of the 1929 Act as to remuneration of directors (ss. 128 and 148) proved to be inadequate and were replaced by s. 196 of the 1948 Act. Disclosure of directors' emoluments must be made in any accounts of a company laid before it in general meeting. Full details of what must be disclosed relating to directors' emoluments, pensions and compensation for loss of office are given in chapter XVII, p. 231.

Full disclosure of sums paid as consideration for, or in connection with, a person's retirement from office must be made to the members of the company, and the proposal must be approved by the company in general meeting. Further details of what must be disclosed will be found in chapter XVII, p. 231. Compensation for loss of office under a reconstruction is dealt with in chapter XX, p. 303. *(margin: Compensation for loss of Office.)*

Section 195 of the Act provides for the keeping of a register of directors' shareholdings, and the following particulars must be entered on the register:—the number, description and amount of any shares in, or debentures of, (i) the company, (ii) any subsidiary of the company, (iii) the company's holding company, (iv) any subsidiary of the company's holding company, which are held by, or in trust for, a director, or of which he has any right to become the holder (whether on payment or not). For the purposes of s. 195 a director includes any person in accordance with whose instructions the directors of a company are accustomed to act. Moreover, a director of a company is deemed to hold, or to have an interest in any shares or debentures, if a body corporate other than the company either holds them or has an interest or right in or over them, and either (i) that body corporate or its directors are accustomed to act in accordance with his directions or instructions; or (ii) he is entitled to exercise or control the exercise of one-third or more of the voting power at any general meeting of that body corporate. This definition complicates the duties of the secretary and he must bear it closely in mind when compiling the register. It is true that the onus of providing the necessary information is on the director [see below s. 198 (1) and (2)], but it is also the duty of the company to see that the register is properly kept, and this duty will naturally devolve on the secretary. The register need not, however, include shares in any body corporate which is the wholly owned subsidiary of another body corporate. For the purposes of s. 195 a body corporate is deemed to be a wholly owned subsidiary of another, if it has no members but that other and that other's wholly owned subsidiaries and its or their nominees. The register must show any alteration in a director's holding made by reason of any transaction entered into after 1st July, 1948, while he is still a director, and the register must show the date of, and the price or other consideration for, the transaction [s. 195 (2)]. If a director so requests, the nature and extent of his interest or right in or over any shares or debentures recorded in the register shall be indicated in the register [s. 195 (3)]. (See Appendix F, Form 15.) *(margin: Register of Directors' Shareholdings.)*

The register must be kept at the company's registered

office and must be open to inspection by any member or
debenture holder of the company during the period beginning
14 days before the company's annual general meeting, and
ending three days after its conclusion (Saturdays, Sundays and
Bank Holidays are to be disregarded in reckoning the number
of days). The register is to be open at all times to any person
acting on behalf of the Board of Trade. In both cases,
however, the right of inspection is limited to business hours
and subject to such reasonable restrictions as the company
may impose by its articles or by general meeting, but so that
not less than two hours in each day is allowed for inspection
[s. 195 (5)]. The Board of Trade may at any time demand a
copy of the register or any part thereof [s. 195 (6)]. The
register must also be produced at the commencement of the
company's annual general meeting and must remain open and
accessible during the continuance of the meeting to any
person attending the meeting. It is thought that doubts
may arise as to the meaning of 'produce.' It is probable that
if the register is actually brought into the room where the
meeting is being held at or before the commencement of the
meeting, this is sufficient compliance with the section. On
the other hand, the court may at some future date hold that
some unequivocal act of production of the register is necessary.
In general there are heavy penalties for non-compliance with
the provisions of s. 195 and, in the case of inspection being
refused or of refusal to send a copy of the register or part of it
as required by the section, the court may order an immediate
inspection of the register. A form of the register of directors'
shareholdings will be found in Appendix F, Form 15.

With reference to ss. 195, 196 and 197, it should be noted
that in each case it is the duty of any director to give notice
to his company of the matters relating to himself required by
these sections (s. 198). In the case of s. 195, notice must be
given in writing, and if it is not given at a meeting of the
directors, the director giving it must take reasonable steps to
ensure that it is brought up and read at the next meeting of
directors. As regards s. 197, the duty to give notice applies to
other officers besides directors and, in the case of both ss. 196
and 197 it applies to all persons who are, or who have been,
directors at any time during the five preceding years.

Vacation of Office. The office of director may be vacated by disqualification,
removal, resignation, or rotation.

Disqualification. Disqualification depends upon the articles of the company;
but the majority of companies provide in their articles that
a director vacates office (a) when he becomes bankrupt or
makes any arrangement or composition with his creditors
generally, and even though under such an article a person
already bankrupt may be appointed director [*Dawson* v.
African Trading Co. (1898), 1 Ch. 6] he may not act in that

capacity without leave of the court (s. 187), or (b) when he becomes of unsound mind; or (c) when he fails to acquire, or ceases to hold, his qualification shares [s. 182 (3); or (d) becomes prohibited from being a director by reason of any order made under s. 188 of the Act; or (e) ceases to be a director by virtue of s. 185 of the Act; or (f) resigns his office by notice in writing to the company; or (g) shall for more than six months have been absent without permission of the directors from meetings of the directors held during that period. Where the articles so provide, a director automatically vacates his office on the happening of the event which disqualifies him, and the board cannot waive the event though the disqualification ceases, but the director is elegible for re-election on its cessation [*Bodega Co.* (1904), 1 Ch. 276]. 'Insolvent' in a disqualification article means commercially insolvent in the ordinary acceptance of the term [*James v. Rockwood Colliery Co.* (1912), 28 T.L.R. 215; *London & Counties Assets* v. *Brighton Grand Hall* (1915), 2 K.B. 493; see also, *Sissons & Co.* v. *Sissons* (1910), 54 Sol.J. 802]. An article providing that a director vacates office 'if he is concerned in or participates in the profits of any contract with the company,' means that he vacates office if he, or a firm of which he is a member, is concerned in any contract with the company, though he has not participated in the profits [*Star Steam Laundry* v. *Dukas* (1913), 108 L.T. 367].

The company may recover from a director any fees erroneously paid to him while disqualified [*Bodega Co., supra*].

Under s. 184, a company may by ordinary resolution **Removal** (notwithstanding anything in the articles or in any agreement **from Office.** with the directors) remove a director at any time before the expiration of his period of office. The only exception to this provision is in the case of life directors of private companies appointed for life before the 18th July, 1945. Special notice, however, is required before such resolution can be moved (see p. 131). The director is entitled to receive a copy of the notice as soon as possible after it is received by the company. He is entitled to make written representations to the company in his defence and to require them to be circulated to members. If these representations are of reasonable length and they are received by the company in time, the company must (i) state in the notice convening the meeting at which the resolution is to be passed, that representations have been received; and (ii) send a copy thereof to every member to whom notices of the meeting are to be, or have been sent. If these representations are received too late for circulation, the director may require them to be read out at the meeting without prejudice to his right to be heard orally [s. 184 (3)]. The rights given to a director under s. 184 must not, however, be abused to secure the needless publicity of defamatory matter, and accordingly, either the company or any other person who claims to be an aggrieved party may apply to the court for an order that the representation need not be circulated or read out at the meeting [s. 184 (3)]. A vacancy created by the removal of a director under this section may be filled as a casual vacancy; and the director appointed in his place shall (for the purpose of rotation and retirement) be deemed to have been appointed on the day on which the evicted director was last appointed a director [s. 184 (4), (5)]. Finally, the removal of a director under this section does not deprive him of any right to compensation or damages which he may have against the company as the result of his removal [s. 184 (6)]. It should be noted that in the following instances an order may be made under s. 188 of the Act prohibiting a person from being a director or from taking any part in the management of any company: (a) if a person is convicted on indictment of any offence in connection with the promotion, formation or management of a company; and (b) where a person is guilty of an offence under s. 332 of the Act and in certain other cases where evidence comes to light on a winding up (see chapter XXI, p. 335).

Resignation. The articles usually provide that a director may resign. A resignation, when given, cannot generally be withdrawn [*Glossop* v. *Glossop* (1907), 2 Ch. 370]. An oral resignation, if accepted by the company, is valid notwithstanding that the articles provide for resignation by notice in writing [*Latchford Premier Cinema* v. *Ennion* (1931), 2 Ch. 409].

Retirement by Rotation. It is very often provided in the regulations of a company that the directors shall retire year by year by rotation. This provision is a convenient one, for a director anxious to retire need not offer himself for re-election; and a company anxious to remove a director may refuse to re-elect him after his retirement by rotation. The articles often provide that, if the place of a director retiring by rotation be not filled, he shall be deemed to be re-elected unless the company resolve to reduce the number of directors. If it is desired that a director be not re-elected under such an article, a resolution should be passed similar to the following: 'that the director be not re-elected, that the vacancy created be not filled up and that the number of directors be reduced accordingly' [*Bennett Bros.* v. *Lewis* (1903), 48 Sol.J. 14; *Grundt* v. *Great Boulder Proprietory Mines Ltd.* (1948), 1 Ch. at p. 159]. Attention is also called to the wording of Table A, clause 92. It should also be noted that, where an article provides that one-third of the directors, or if their number is not a multiple of three, then the nearest number to, but not exceeding one-third, should retire from office, and there are in fact only two directors, neither is bound to resign [*David*

Moseley & Sons Limited (1939), Ch. 719]. It is, of course, otherwise if the words 'not exceeding one-third' are omitted.

The basic provision of s. 185 of the Act is that no person **Retirement** who has reached the age of 70 shall be capable of being **under** appointed a director of a company (other than a private **Age-limit.** company, see p. 372); and subsections (2) and (3) of s. 185 provide that a director of a company, which is subject to the section, shall vacate his office at the conclusion of the annual general meeting commencing next after he attains the age of 70, and that where a director has so vacated his office no provision for automatic reappointment shall apply. This basic provision is qualified to a considerable extent by the following important exceptions: (i) A director shall not have to retire on reaching the age of 70, so as to terminate his then appointment, before the conclusion of the third annual general meeting after the commencement of the Act (*viz.* 1st July, 1948). This is, of course, only a transitional provision [s. 185 (4)]. (ii) A director may be appointed at any age and he need not retire at any time, if this is approved by the company in general meeting. Special notice (see p. 131), however, is required for any resolution approving the appointment of a director over the age limit and must state the director's age (and so also must the notice given by the company to its members); if special notice is not given, the resolution is of no effect [s. 185 (5)]. (iii) In the case of a company first registered on or after 1st January, 1947, s. 185 is to have effect subject to the company's articles; and in the case of a company registered before 1st January, 1947, the section is to have effect subject to any alterations in the company's articles made after that date, and has no effect if, before 1st January, 1947, the company's articles contained a provision for the retirement of directors under an age limit or for preventing or restricting the appointment of directors over a given age [s. 185 (7)]. It may also be noted, for the purpose of determining the date of retirement by rotation of a director appointed in lieu of a director retiring under the age limit, that he shall be deemed to have become a director on the day on which the retiring director was last appointed before his retirement. Finally, a private company is not excepted from the provision of the section if it is the subsidiary of a body corporate which is neither a private company nor a Northern Ireland company analogous to a private company.

Section 186 of the Act provides that if a director is appointed, or to his knowledge is proposed to be appointed, a director of a company which is subject to s. 185, and he has attained the retiring age applicable either under s. 185 or under the articles of the company, he must give notice of his age to the company.

Assignment of Director-ships. Any provision making the office of director assignable will be inoperative except so far as any assignment made pursuant thereto may be confirmed by special resolution of the company (s. 204).

Register of Director and Secretaries. Among the books which the Act requires a company to keep at its registered office is a register of directors and secretaries (s. 200) (see Appendix F, Form 16). For the purposes of that section, a person in accordance with whose directions or instructions the directors of a company are accustomed to act is deemed to be a director and officer of the company; but if a person gives the directors advice in a professional capacity and they act on that advice, he will not thereby be deemed to be a director [s. 455 (2)]. The particulars with respect to each director required to be inserted in this register are, in the case of an individual his present christian name and surname, any former christian name or surname, his usual residential address, his nationality, his business occupation, if any, particulars of any other directorships held by him, and, in the case of a company wherein directors are liable to retire over the age limit (or would if the articles had not been amended be so liable) under s. 185, the date of his birth. It is not necessary, however, for the register to contain particulars of directorships held by a director in companies of which the company is the wholly owned subsidiary, nor in the companies which are the wholly owned subsidiaries either of the company or of another company of which the company is the wholly owned subsidiary. In the case of a corporation which is a director, the particulars required are its corporate name and registered or principal office. The register must also contain the following particulars with respect to the secretary or joint secretaries:—

(i) in the case of an individual, his present christian name and surname, any former christian name and surname and his usual residential address;

(ii) in the case of a corporation or a Scottish firm, its corporate or firm name and registered or principal office.

Where all the partners in a firm are joint secretaries, the name and principal office of the firm may be stated instead of the above named particulars.

The company must, within 14 days from the appointment of the first directors, send to the Registrar a return in the form prescribed by the Board of Trade containing the above particulars and must, within 14 days of any change among the directors or secretary or in any of the particulars, send to the Registrar a notification in the form prescribed by the Board of Trade of such change [s. 200 (4) (5)]. For the prescribed forms see Companies (Forms) Order, 1949, Forms 9

and 9A. A statutory right of inspecting the register of
directors and secretaries is given to the members without
charge and to any other person on payment of one shilling
[s. 200 (6)].

If a director of the company obtains or loses a directorship of some other company, the Act requires that change
to be entered on the register within 14 days, but it does not
expressly place on the director concerned an obligation to
inform the company's secretary of the change. No doubt
there is an implied obligation on him to do so. The secretary
should, however, in his own interests, take reasonable steps to
ensure that he is notified of such changes, lest he should become
liable to a default fine. It is suggested that he should, as a
matter of routine: (a) ensure that every new director is
informed on his appointment of his obligation to notify the
company of any changes; (b) enquire of the directors, at
reasonable intervals, say, every six months, whether there
have been any changes; and, (c) if it is found that changes
are not being promptly notified, remind the directors of their
obligation to do so at once. A secretary who did that would
hardly be considered to be in default.

In this connection it must be remembered that, unless **Publication**
exempted by order of the Board of Trade, companies registered **of Directors'**
after 22nd November, 1916, foreign companies establishing **Names in**
a place of business in the United Kingdom after that date, **Trade Circu-**
and all companies licensed under the Moneylenders Act, **lars, etc.**
1927, are required to publish in trade catalogues, trade
circulars, show cards and business letters, on or in which the
company's name appears, and which are issued or sent to any
part of His Majesty's dominions, the present christian names
(or initials) and surnames, any former christian names and
surnames and the nationality, if not British, of all directors
(s. 201). The question often arises whether the documents
specifically named in this section are exhaustive. In the
absence of judicial authority, the precise wording of the Act
is the only guide, and there should be no need to exceed its
scope. There is, however, no harm in giving the particulars
required by the section on other documents bearing the
company's name, and in practice this is frequently done.
Initials of existing christian names are sufficient, but former
christian names must be set out in full.

The business of a company is usually transacted by the **Board**
directors at board meetings and, unless the articles provide **Meetings.**
otherwise, the directors must act together as a board, and
cannot act without meeting [D'Arcy v. Tamar Ry. (1866),
L.R. 2 Ex. 158; Haycraft Gold Reduction Co. (1900), 2 Ch. 230].
Another question which sometimes arises is whether board
meetings can be carried on by telephone. It is thought that,
in the absence of a decision by the court, a telephone

conversation should not be regarded as a meeting. The difficulty may, however, be circumvented, if the articles so permit, by all the directors of the company signing a resolution confirming the telephone conversation. It is now quite usual for the articles of association to provide that a resolution in writing, signed by all the directors for the time being in the United Kingdom, shall be as valid as if it had been passed at a meeting of directors duly convened and held. Such signed resolution should be inserted in the directors' minute book.

Board meetings are usually regulated by the articles. Clauses 98 and 99 of Table A are, in substance, very frequently the governing regulations as to board meetings. Clause 98 is as follows: 'The directors may meet together for the dispatch of business, adjourn and otherwise regulate their meetings as they think fit. Questions arising at any meeting shall be decided by a majority of votes. In case of an equality of votes, the chairman shall have a second or casting vote. A director may, and the secretary on the requisition of a director shall, at any time summon a meeting of the directors. It shall not be necessary to give notice of a meeting of directors to any director for the time being absent from the United Kingdom.' By the first words of clause 98 a very wide discretion is left to directors as to regulating their meetings. It would, no doubt, be competent to them, under such a power, to frame an elaborate code of rules as to the convening of meetings and as to the procedure thereat, and to place these on the minutes, after which they would govern future proceedings until altered. In practice, however, few, if any, rules are definitely made and, apart from any practice which may grow up, matters are left very much at large.

Quorum. Clause 99 runs: 'The quorum necessary for the transaction of the business of the directors may be fixed by the directors, and unless so fixed shall be two.'

The articles usually prescribe the number of directors required to constitute a quorum, but, if not so prescribed, the number who usually act in conducting the business of the company will constitute a quorum [*Tavistock Ironworks Co., Lyster's Case* (1867), 4 Eq. 233; *Bank of Syria* (1901), 1 Ch. 115], or possibly a majority of the whole board [*York Tramways Co.* v. *Willows* (1882), 8 Q.B.D. 685]. Where the articles provided that the minimum number of directors should be four, that A and B should be the first directors, and that the first directors should have power to appoint others, it was held that there could be no valid board meeting until A and B had appointed two other directors [*Sly, Spink & Co.* (1911), 2 Ch. 430].

The articles usually contain also a clause enabling a director to contract with the company. A director interested in any contract or proposed contract with the company must

disclose his interest at the meeting of the directors at which
the contract is first taken into consideration or, if the director
was not then interested, or did not become interested until
after the contract was made, at the next meeting after he
became interested [s. 199]. This section is very wide, and
every secretary should take legal advice as to its operation
in the case of his own company. It should be noted, however,
that, when a director gives general notice under s. 199 (3),
such notice is of no effect under the 1948 Act, unless either
(i) it is given at a meeting of the directors; or (ii) the director
concerned takes reasonable steps to secure that it is brought up
and read at the next meeting of the directors after it is given.
The articles often expressly prohibit a director from voting
on contracts in which he is interested, and even in the absence
of express prohibition in the articles a director is by common
law precluded from so voting. It is sometimes, however,
found convenient to provide in the articles that a director may
vote, either generally or in particular cases, where it is impossible otherwise to get an independent quorum, *e.g.* in the
case of a contract between a company and its subsidiary
company. Where an independent quorum cannot be obtained
and interested directors cannot vote, a contract in which they
are interested can be valid only if previously sanctioned or
subsequently ratified by the company in general meeting. In
such cases full details of the transaction must be furnished to
the members before they are asked to vote thereon. The
interested director can, as mentioned above, vote as a member
at the general meeting [*North Western Transportation Co.* v.
Beatty (1887), 12 A.C. 589].

A board meeting of a number less than the quorum prescribed by the regulations is invalid [*Faure Electric Accumu-
lator Co.* (1888), 40 Ch. D. 141]; and, where a director may not
vote on any matter in which he is interested, he does not
count towards a quorum for such business [*Greymouth
Point Elizabeth Co.* (1904), 1 Ch. 32; *North Eastern Insurance
Co.* (1919), 1 Ch. 198], *e.g.* where the business is the allotment
of shares to himself [*Neal* v. *Quinn* (1916), W.N. 223]. Most
companies have a clause empowering directors to act in spite
of vacancies; but (unless the article expressly so provides)
this will not enable them to act unless they form a quorum
[*Newhaven Local Board* v. *Newhaven School Board* (1885),
30 Ch. D. 350]. A meeting of directors cannot transact
business if at any time the number of directors present ceases
to be a quorum, even though a quorum was present at the
beginning of the meeting [*Henderson* v. *Louttit* (1894), 21
Rettie (Ct. of Sessions) 390; *Hennessy* v. *National Agricultural
and Industrial Development Association* (1945), I.R. 195].

The invalidity of a meeting will not affect persons dealing
with the company without notice [*Royal British Bank* v.

Turquand (1856), 6 E. & B. 327; *County of Gloucester Bank* v. *Rudry Colliery Co.* (1895), 1 Ch. 629]. The transactions of an invalid meeting may be ratified at a subsequent board meeting, though such ratification may be ineffective if not made within a reasonable time [*Portuguese Copper Mines, Badman's and Bosanquet's Cases* (1890), 45 Ch. D. 16].

A director can, if qualified, sustain an action in his own name against the other directors, on the ground of individual injury to himself, for an injunction to restrain them from wrongfully excluding him from acting as a director [*Pulbrook* v. *Richmond Mining Co.* (1878), 9 Ch. D. 610].

A director does not make himself responsible for an act done at a meeting at which he was not present, and which is complete without further confirmation, merely by voting at a subsequent meeting for the verification of the minutes [*Burton* v. *Bevan* (1908), 2 Ch. 240].

Statutory Provisions as to the Secretary. Section 177 of the Act provides that every company must have a secretary. A corporation, the sole director of which is the sole director of the company, may not, however, be the secretary of that company, and a company may not have as its sole director a corporation the sole director of which is the secretary of the company (s. 178). If the office of secretary is vacant, or there is for any reason no secretary capable of acting, any act required to be done by the secretary may be done by the assistant or deputy secretary, or, failing them, by any officer of the company authorised by the director. As a matter of practice, the Registrar will accept the signature 'Acting secretary,' but will not usually accept the signature 'Assistant' or 'Deputy secretary' unless evidence is produced from the directors of the company that the assistant or deputy secretary was acting as the secretary. Where there is a provision requiring any act to be done by a director and the secretary, that provision will not be satisfied by the act being done by the same person as director and as, or in place of, the secretary.

Doubts have arisen whether a company can have joint secretaries, but in view of the wording of s. 200 it is thought that there can be no objection.

Duties of Secretary at Board Meetings. The secretary's duties in relation to board meetings can be summarised as follows:—

(1) matters arising prior to the meeting;

(2) procedure at the meeting;

(3) matters arising subsequent to the meeting.

(1) The routine duties prior to the meeting consist of the following:—

Convening of Meetings. Ordinary board meetings are usually held at fixed intervals (*e.g.* once a fortnight) at some fixed hour and place; special

board meetings are usually summoned by the secretary or
one or more of the directors (for form of notice see Appendix
F, Form 48). For a meeting to be valid, unless it is one of
the ordinary meetings held at fixed intervals, notice must
always be given to all the directors [*Portuguese Copper
Mines, Steele's Case* (1889), 42 Ch. D. 160]; but not if they
are so far as to be out of reach, though mere absence abroad,
e.g. residence in Calais, the company's office being in Dover,
would not dispense with the necessity for notice [*Halifax
Sugar Co.* v. *Francklyn* (1890), 59 L.J. Ch. 591]. Even
for meetings held at fixed intervals it is usually convenient
also to give notice to the directors. An accidental meeting
of directors cannot be treated as a board meeting against the
wish of one of them [*Barron* v. *Potter* (1914), 1 Ch. 895].
The notice need not state what business is to be transacted,
unless it is so provided in the articles [*Compagnie de Mayville*
v. *Whitley* (1896), 1 Ch. 788], or in the regulations made by
the directors themselves; but it is advisable to specify the
business in the case of a notice of a special board meeting.
Subject to any provisions in the articles or to any regulation
made by the directors, no special length of notice is required,
but the notice should be a reasonable one.

Under Table A, clause 98, a director may, and the secretary
on the requisition of a director shall, at any time summon a
meeting of the directors. It shall not be necessary to give
notice of a meeting of directors to any director for the time
being absent from the United Kingdom.

The preparation of the agenda is dealt with in chapter XV,
see p. 195.

(2) The secretary's duties at the board meeting.

The secretary's first duty is to secure the signature of the
directors present to the minutes of the last meeting. Where
there are several directors, the secretary should keep a
directors' attendance book. The secretary should always have
available at the meeting a copy of the company's memorandum
and articles of association.

The remaining duties of the secretary at the meeting will
depend largely upon the kind of company and the extent of
the duties delegated to him. In the case of a board consisting
of managing or executive directors, his duties will be closely
identified with the members of the board, and the extent of
his intervention will depend on the matters discussed. In
certain cases, where his duties are clearly demarcated, the
secretary's main functions at board meetings will be to record
any decisions taken or resolutions passed. Under s. 145
minutes of meetings of directors must be kept, and these
must be signed by the chairman of the meeting at which the
proceedings took place, or by the chairman at the next

succeeding meeting. The first business of the board is invariably the signing of the minutes of the preceding meeting.

It is not usual at board meetings to have movers and seconders of motions nor for decisions to be decided by formal voting, although cl. 98 (*supra*) provides that questions arising at any meeting shall be decided by a majority of votes. The more usual procedure is for the chairman to summarise the matters decided on any particular question, and the secretary concludes the minute with the words 'this was agreed' or merely the one word 'agreed.' Should there not be unanimity on any question, the chairman should put the question to the vote, but it should be noted that cl. 98 (*supra*) states that, in case of an equality of votes, the chairman shall have a second casting vote. Even though a formal vote is not taken, any member of the board may request the secretary to include his name in the minutes as voting against any particular question.

(3) The following matters arise subsequent to the meeting:

(a) *Circulation of minutes.* In companies of any magnitude and where the board is fairly large and meets regularly, it is a common practice to record the minutes in the form of loose-leaf books. This method can be adopted either by typing on to loose-leaf sheets, which are afterwards clasped in the form of a book, or by typing direct by machine in to a book. The great advantage of using loose-leaf sheets is that copies of the minutes can be circulated to a director (or members of a committee) after each meeting. It is most important that the minutes be carefully indexed.

(b) *Inspection of minutes.* The auditors, under s. 162 (3), have a statutory right to inspect the books of the company, and this right extends to the directors' minute book. Directors also have a right to inspect minutes of their meetings, but this right may be withheld in cases where the director is not acting in the interest of the company.

(c) *Executive duties.* In cases where matters arising out of the meetings come within the ambit of the secretary's duties, he should advise the executive officers of decisions affecting their office. It may be necessary, in certain cases, to send copies of the relevant minute to the officials concerned, including the managing directors, should they so desire them.

Seal. A company must have a common seal, upon which its name must be engraved [s. 108 (1)]. The custody and use of the seal are matters which should be strictly regulated. The regulations are usually prescribed by resolution of the board, duly entered upon the minutes. It is common for the seal of a company to be provided with two locks, and for the keys of those locks to be kept by the chairman and the secretary respectively, so that the seal cannot be used in any informal or improper manner. A useful provision is to have a duplicate set of the keys deposited with the company's bankers in case the seal has to be used in the absence of the chairman, although it is now a common practice to provide each director with a key to one of the locks of the seal.

Table A, clause 113, states that the directors must provide for the safe custody of the seal, which shall only be used by the authority of the directors or of a committee of directors so authorised by the board. Further, 'every instrument to which the seal shall be affixed shall be signed by a director and shall be counter-signed by the secretary or by a second director, or by some other person appointed by the directors for the purpose.' Special articles frequently vary these provisions, but strict formalities are almost invariably prescribed.

A company should not have two seals in existence but, if it transacts business in foreign countries and is authorised by its articles, it may then have a facsimile thereof, called an official seal, for use abroad (s. 35). The facsimile must contain on its face the name of the territory, district or place where it is to be used.

The Law of Property Act, 1925, s. 74 (see Appendix K), contains provisions as to the execution of instruments by or on behalf of corporations. A company can take advantage of these provisions, notwithstanding anything in its articles. Sub-section (1) operates only in favour of a purchaser as defined by s. 205 of the same Act.

A seal book should always be kept in which should be entered **Seal Book.** particulars of the documents to which the seal of the company is affixed. This should contain a description of the document, the date of the resolution authorising its sealing, and the names of those in whose presence the seal was affixed and who signed the document; these persons should also initial the entry in the seal book. See Appendix F, Form 108.

It is not advisable to affix the seal of the company un- **Sealing of** necessarily to contracts and agreements, since, if sealed, they **Contracts.** become liable to be stamped with a deed stamp of 10s. The making of contracts by a company, whether under seal, in writing, or by word of mouth, is expressly provided for by s. 32 of the Act. The effect of this provision is to place a company in the same position as an individual in regard to the formalities to be observed. As to bills of exchange and promissory notes, see s. 33.

If an officer or auditor of a company is sued for negligence, **Relief from** default, breach of duty or breach of trust, the court may **Liability.**

relieve him, wholly or in part, from liability therefor on such
terms as it thinks fit if it appears that the party charged has
acted honestly and reasonably, and that, having regard to all
the circumstances of the case, he ought fairly to be excused
(s. 448). The term 'officer' includes a director, manager or
secretary (s. 455). Under sub-s. (2) of s. 448 the officer
may himself apply to the court when he apprehends that
proceedings may be commenced against him even before
proceedings are actually commenced, and the court can grant
relief. It has been held that the sub-section gives power to the
court to grant relief from liability to fines and penalties as
well as from civil liability [*Barry & Staines Linoleum, Ltd.*
(1934), I Ch. 227].

Alternate Directors. It has been seen that s. 204 of the Act prohibits a director
from assigning his office (see p. 174). The appointment of
alternate directors is, however, on an entirely different footing,
since its effect is only a temporary delegation of duties.

The authority to appoint an alternate is derived from the
articles of association, and most modern articles give a director
power to appoint either any other director or some other
person to act in his place, either conditionally on the director's
absence abroad, or, as is now more usual, in any circumstances.
It is important for the articles to define clearly the position of
the alternate. Where the articles provide that a director
shall possess a share qualification, the article empowering the
appointment of an alternate should state whether the alternate
shall possess such qualification. The article should also define
whether the director's remuneration is to be paid to the
director himself or to his alternate; presumably, in the absence
of any specific authority in the articles or from the director,
the remuneration should be sent to the director himself, who
may have made his own arrangement with his alternate as to
payment for services. It is usual to make the appointment
of an alternate subject to the approval of the remaining
directors, and the phrasing should be either 'subject to the
approval of all the remaining directors of the company who
may for the time being be resident in Great Britain,' or
'subject to the approval of the majority of the other directors
of the company,' and the articles should provide that such
approval may be given either in writing or at a properly
convened meeting of the directors.

The minimum of two directors which s. 176 of the Act
requires for a public company would not be satisfied by one
director and his alternate, because the latter is a substitute
for the former. For the same reason it is considered that the
requirement in s. 181 as to filing with the Registrar of a consent
in writing to act as director does not apply to an alternate.

The question of the application of s. 182, which provides
for a share qualification of a director, will depend upon the

provisions of the clause in the articles of association governing his appointment. If a share qualification is required, it must be taken up irrespective of the period during which the alternate acts, and in default the alternate will be liable to the statutory penalty. The disqualification for the office of director imposed by s. 187 applies equally to an alternate, and the penalties under that section would appear to attach equally to a director and an alternate.

The protection to third parties afforded by s. 180 of the Act, providing for the validity of acts of directors notwithstanding any defect that may afterwards be discovered in the appointment or qualification, extends to the acts of alternate directors, notwithstanding that, as the director purporting to make the appointment was not in fact a director, the alternate director is not in law a director at all. The register of directors and secretaries required to be kept under s. 200 must contain an entry of the appointment of an alternate, and the same notice must be sent to the Registrar for filing in the case of an alternate as is required for a director. Likewise notice must be filed with the Registrar of a change of any particulars contained in the register [sub-s. (2)].

The question whether a director is responsible for the acts of his alternate will depend on the articles of association. As a rule, the articles are so framed that the alternate director is not the agent of the director who appointed him; but, if he is such an agent, the legal doctrine that a principal is responsible for the acts of his agent, which was dealt with at length by the House of Lords in *Lloyd* v. *Grace Smith* (1912), A.C. 716 (*The Secretary*, vol. ix, p. 378), would apply and then the appointing director would be responsible for the delinquencies of his alternate. A director and his alternate do not act simultaneously, but alternatively, so that, when a director resumes his directorial functions, his alternate ceases to act.

The requirement of s. 201 for the display of particulars in respect of directors in trade catalogues, circulars, etc., applies to alternates, and may be regarded in practice as a continuing requirement; that is to say, the name of the director and his alternate are displayed on these documents even though the alternate may be at any given time acting for his appointor, or *vice versa*.

An alternate director can resign if he desires to retire before the termination of his prescribed term (if any), unless precluded by the articles or by specific agreement on the point with his appointor.

The obligation as to disclosure by directors of their interest in contracts, for which provision is made in s. 199, attaches also to an alternate, because while so acting he has all the powers of a director, including voting on contracts made by the company.

G

Sections 193 and 194, which make provision as to payments received by directors for loss of office or on retirement, would apply to an alternate if (which is unlikely) the transaction involved payment to an alternate of compensation for loss of office, but the point is one depending on the particulars of each individual case.

A provision in the articles of association that a resolution signed by all the directors is as effective as a resolution duly passed at a properly convened board meeting, would include the signature of an alternate in lieu of the signature of the director, but not both.

Delegation of Powers and Duties. Directors can delegate their powers to a committee of their number, if authorised so to do by the articles, but not otherwise [*Howard's Case* (1866), 1 Ch. App. 561]. The committee need not consist of more than one director [*Taurine Co.* (1884), 25 Ch. D. 118; *Fireproof Doors* (1916), 2 Ch. 142]. The articles usually provide that the regulations as to meetings of directors, keeping minutes, etc., shall apply also to meetings of committees. A person dealing with an individual director, or servant of the company, to whom power to bind the company by the particular transaction could be delegated under the articles, may be entitled to presume that such power has in fact been delegated [*British Thomson-Houston Co.* v. *Federated European Bank* (1932), 2 K.B. 176]; but he cannot do so if he was in ignorance of the power of delegation and therefore was not relying on any ostensible authority, or if the circumstances were such as to put him on enquiry, *e.g.* if the director with whom he was dealing was managing director but the transaction was outside the ordinary powers of a managing director [*Houghton & Co.* v. *Nothard Lowe and Wills* (1927), 1 K.B. 246; (1928), A.C. 1; *Kreditbank Cassel* v. *Schenkers, Ltd.* (1927), 1 K.B. 828]. See also *Clay Hill Brick and Tile Co. Ltd.* v. *Rawlings* (1938), 4 All E.R. 100.

CHAPTER XIV

RESOLUTIONS

THE passing of a resolution is the manner in which a meeting formally acts; the resolution expresses the will of the meeting and, if it be a meeting of shareholders, the will of the company. Until a resolution is formally passed the proceedings at a meeting are no more than discussion and debate.

Accordingly, in keeping the minutes of a meeting, the most important duty of the secretary is to ensure that the resolutions passed are accurately recorded in the minutes. In small or informal meetings it sometimes happens that general agreement is signified without any resolution having been formally put to the meeting; it is then the duty of the secretary, by reminding the chairman, to be sure either that a resolution is formally put, or at least that what is being informally resolved is precise, so that a clear resolution can be recorded in the minutes.

The usual resolutions are those of either a directors' meeting or a meeting of shareholders (or of a class of shareholders). Resolutions of shareholders are of three kinds—ordinary, extraordinary and special. Ordinary resolutions are those passed by a simple majority of those voting at the meeting; extraordinary and special resolutions (which are discussed below) require a special majority and particular forms of notice. For certain types of motion the Act requires a special or extraordinary resolution and the company's articles sometimes require such resolutions for particular purposes. In the absence of such a requirement any power exercisable by 'the company in general meeting' requires only an ordinary resolution.

Articles sometimes provide that written agreement of all the directors shall be equivalent to a resolution passed at a directors' meeting, and such a provision is effective. A similar provision is occasionally found in the articles in regard to shareholders' meetings and would be effective; it seems also that, even without such provision in the articles, a resolution consented to by all shareholders without a meeting would be effective [*Express Engineering Works* (1920), 1 Ch. 466; *Oxted Motor Co.* (1921), 3 K.B. 32; and see s. 143 (4) (c) of the Act, p. 187]. A resolution agreed to without a meeting by part only of the shareholders, even a 99 per cent. majority of them, would not, it is thought, be effective as an extraordinary or special resolution; nor, in absence of special provision in the articles giving effect to it, would it even be a valid ordinary resolution.

When Invalid.

A resolution is invalid:—

1. if it contravenes any provision of the law, or is contrary to public policy;

2. if it proposes that something shall be done which is beyond the powers of the meeting or of the company as a whole;

3. if the meeting is not validly constituted according to the articles or the Act, or if any of the provisions of the articles or the Act as to the conduct of business are not observed; but a resolution duly passed by a meeting convened by a board irregularly constituted is valid [*Boschoek Proprietary Co.* v. *Fuke* (1906), 1 Ch. 148]; as also is a resolution passed at a meeting irregularly convened, but at which all the members were present and voted for the resolution.

Extraordinary Resolution.

The characteristics of extraordinary and special resolutions have already been dealt with to some extent in chapter XI. Both are defined in s. 141 of the Act, the effect of which is here summarised.

For a resolution to be an extraordinary resolution:

(1) It must be passed, at a general meeting, by a majority of not less than three-fourths of the members as are present voting in person or by proxy (where proxies are allowed);

(2) Only those members who are entitled to vote may be counted;

(3) Fourteen clear days' notice of the meeting must have been given in writing (seven clear days' notice in the case of an unlimited company);

(4) The notice must have specified the intention to propose the resolution as an extraordinary resolution.

Special Resolution.

For a resolution to be a special resolution:

(1) It must be passed at a general meeting by the same majority as is required for the passing of an extraordinary resolution. This involves the fulfilment of the first two of the conditions specified above as necessary in the case of an extraordinary resolution.

(2) Not less than twenty-one clear days' notice of the meeting must have been duly given (see chapter XI).

(3) The notice must have specified the intention to propose the resolution as a special resolution.

The requirement of twenty-one days' notice may be dispensed with only if it is so agreed by a majority in number of members, having the right to attend and vote at the meeting, being a majority together holding not less than 95 per cent. in nominal value of the shares giving that right.

The effect of the other provisions of s. 141, which are

applicable both to extraordinary and to special resolutions, may be thus summarised:

(1) At any of the meetings referred to above, a declaration of the chairman that the resolution is carried is, unless a poll is demanded, conclusive evidence of the fact, without proof of the number or proportion of votes recorded in favour of or against the resolution.

(2) On a poll, members may give the number of votes to which they are entitled by the Act or by the articles for or against the resolution.

(3) Notice of any of the meetings is duly given and the meeting duly held when the notice is given and the meeting held in accordance with the Act or the articles.

Section 143 of the Act provides that the following resolutions must be filed with the Registrar of Companies within fifteen days after they are passed or made:— **Filing of certain Resolutions.**

(a)   a special resolution;

(b)   an extraordinary resolution;

(c)   a resolution agreed to by all the members of the company which, if not so agreed to, would not have been effective for its purpose unless passed as a special or extraordinary resolution as the case may be;

(d)   a resolution or agreement agreed to by all the members of some class of shareholders which, if not so agreed to, would not have been effective for its purpose unless passed by a particular majority or in a particular manner, and all resolutions or agreements which effectively bind all the members of any class of shareholders, though not agreed to by all those members;

(e)   a resolution for voluntary winding up.

A printed copy of the resolution or agreement must be forwarded to the Registrar. In addition, copies of all such resolutions or agreements in force must be embodied in or annexed to every copy of the articles issued after the passing of the resolution, or making of the agreement. If no articles have been registered, a member is entitled to have a printed copy of every such resolution or agreement forwarded to him on payment of a sum not exceeding 1s. There are penalties for default in obeying these provisions. An exempt private company need not forward a printed copy of any such resolution or agreement, if instead it forwards to the Registrar a copy in some other form approved by him (e.g. written, typewritten).

A resolution should be clearly expressed and should deal definitely with the result intended to be attained, providing as may be necessary for the means by which the result is to be attained, and for the consequences that will follow. If a resolution required by the Act is to be passed, it should usually follow the wording of the Act.

Thus a resolution to increase the share capital should, as a rule, define the nature of the new shares; a resolution to pay a dividend should, besides stating the amount, state the date on, and the period in respect of which, it is to be paid, and the members to whom it is to be paid (*e.g.* those on the register on a fixed day).

Forms of Resolutions. A few common forms, both of directors' resolutions and of shareholders' resolutions, are given below, and may be adapted to meet the requirements of particular cases.

DIRECTORS' RESOLUTION TO ISSUE PROSPECTUS.

THAT the prospectus of the company which has been considered at this meeting be dated   and be signed by the directors now present, and sent to each other director named therein for signature by him or his authorised agent, and that the same when so signed by all the directors named therein it be delivered forthwith to the Registrar of Companies for registration and that immediately thereafter the prospectus be issued and advertised.

DIRECTORS' RESOLUTION TO ALLOT SHARES.

The minimum subscription £   being subscribed and the application moneys payable thereon being received   .
RESOLVED That the number of shares mentioned in the column set against the name of each applicant mentioned in the column of the application and allotment sheets (initialled for indentification by one of the directors) be, and the same are hereby, allotted to such applicant, making a total allotment of   shares.

DIRECTORS' RESOLUTION TO MAKE CALL.

THAT a call of   s. per share be made upon the members (*or*, upon shares Nos.   to   ), payable on the   day of   , 19   , to Messrs.   , the company's bankers, at

DIRECTORS' RESOLUTION TO FORFEIT SHARES.

THAT   , the registered holder of shares of £   each, numbered   to   inclusive in this company, having failed to pay the instalment of   per share due on the said shares on the   day of   , 19   , and having failed to comply with the notice served upon him, dated the   day of   , 19   , the said shares be and the same are hereby forfeited.

DIRECTORS' RESOLUTION AS TO INTERIM DIVIDEND.

THAT an interim dividend of   per cent., less tax, on the ordinary capital of the company, be and is hereby declared payable on the day of   to shareholders recorded in the register at the closing of the books on the   day of   .

DIRECTORS' RESOLUTION AS TO FINAL DIVIDEND.

THAT a recommendation be laid before the shareholders in general meeting that a final dividend of   per cent. on the ordinary capital, less tax, be paid, making, with the interim dividend of   per cent. paid on the   day of   , a total of   per cent. for the year.

THAT such final dividend be paid (subject to the approval of the company in general meeting) on the   day of   to shareholders recorded in the register at the closing of the books on the   day of .

NOTE.—Dividends on preference shares or stock are usually payable under the terms of issue at the half year and the end of the year, and not left until the annual meeting. Should the final preference dividend have to be submitted to the shareholders, the foregoing resolution should be used, substituting the word 'preference' for the word 'ordinary.'

DIRECTORS' RESOLUTION TO CLOSE BOOKS.

THAT the transfer books of the company be closed from the   day of   to the   day of   , 19 , both inclusive, and that they be closed also to dividend mandates during that period.

SPECIAL RESOLUTION TO ALTER ARTICLES.

THAT the articles of association of the company be altered as follows:

1. That in article 17 the words '   ,' be inserted after the words '   ,'
2. That in article 23 the words '   ,' be omitted.
3. That the following article be substituted for article 113:

SPECIAL RESOLUTION TO ADOPT NEW ARTICLES.

THAT the regulations contained in the printed form of articles submitted to the meeting and for the purpose of identification signed by the chairman thereof be adopted as the articles of association of the company in place of the existing articles.

RESOLUTION OF COMPANY TO INCREASE SHARE CAPITAL.

THAT the share capital of the company be increased to £   divided into   preference shares of   each and   ordinary shares of   each by the creation of   new preference shares of   each, to rank *pari passu* as regards dividend and in all other respects with the preference shares of the original capital of the company, and that such new shares be offered in the first instance at a premium of   per share to the members of the company in proportion, as nearly as may be, to their holdings, whether of preference or of ordinary shares, on such terms as to payment as the directors may determine, and that the directors be authorised to dispose of all such new shares as may not be taken up by the members of the company as aforesaid to such persons and upon such terms as they may deem expedient in the interests of the company.

RESOLUTION OF COMPANY TO ISSUE DEBENTURE STOCK.

THAT the directors be and they are hereby authorised to borrow the sum of £50,000, and to secure the same by the issue of £50,000 debenture stock bearing interest at the rate of   per cent. per annum payable half yearly on   and   and charged upon the undertaking of the company, and all its assets, present and future, including its uncalled capital, and that except as aforesaid the said stock be issued upon such terms and conditions in all respects as the directors think fit.

NOTE.—The foregoing resolution pre-supposes that the directors have no borrowing powers under the articles and, as it amounts to an alteration of the articles, it would have to be passed as a special resolution.

RESOLUTIONS FOR WINDING UP.

Special Resolution.

'THAT the company be wound up voluntarily, and that
of   be and he is hereby appointed liquidator for the purposes of
such winding up.'

Extraordinary Resolution.

'That it has been proved to the satisfaction of this meeting that the
company cannot, by reason of its liabilities, continue its business, and
that it is advisable to wind up the same and, accordingly, that the
company be wound up voluntarily, and that   of   be and
he is appointed liquidator for the purposes of such winding up.'

**Amend-
ments.**

As regards amendments to resolutions the following points
may be noted:—

Any amendment relevant to the motion may be moved,
provided that it does not go beyond the scope of the notice
convening the meeting, or of the business that may be transacted at a meeting without notice. Where it is desired to
alter a resolution, already passed, this should normally be
done in one stage, cancelling or amending the old resolution
and embodying the new proposal. If it is done in two stages,
i.e. first by rescinding the old resolution and, secondly,
embodying the new proposals, there is a risk of deadlock, as
the first resolution may be carried and the second defeated.

If an amendment is improperly withheld by the chairman
from the meeting, the court will declare the resolution invalid
[*Henderson* v. *Bank of Australasia* (1890), 45 Ch. D. 330]. If
such an amendment is passed, the chairman should put to
the meeting the resolution as amended. If there are more
amendments than one, they may be put to the meeting in
the order in which they are proposed, or, if this is inconvenient,
in the order which the chairman judges most convenient. If
an amendment is proposed to an amendment, the former
should be put first, and if it is passed, the amendment as
amended should then be put, followed by the resolution as
amended.

Unless the articles otherwise provide, directors' resolutions
are passed by a simple majority in all cases. If the voting is
equal, the chairman may, if so authorised by the articles,
give a second or casting vote. If he has no casting vote, and
the voting is equal, the resolution is not carried. The matter
of voting generally is dealt with in chapter XII.

Although a resolution of the company in general meeting
is a formal expression of the will of the majority of the shareholders, yet it does not follow that such a resolution is effective
to control the policy of the company, for by the articles the
control may be vested in the directors. Sometimes practically
the whole of a company's powers are vested in the directors,
and in that case, unless the articles otherwise provide, neither
an ordinary resolution, nor even an extraordinary resolution,

of the members can coerce the directors in the exercise of those powers, but the articles must be altered by special resolution, if the directors are to be controlled [*Automatic Self-Cleansing Filter Co.* v. *Cuninghame* (1906), 2 Ch. 34; *Marshall's Valve Gear Co.* v. *Manning, Wardle & Co.* (1909), 1 Ch. 267; *Quin & Axtens* v. *Salmon* (1909), A.C. 442; *Scott* v. *Scott* (1943), 1 All E.R. 582. It should, none the less, be borne in mind that under s. 184 a director may be removed by ordinary resolution of which special notice has been given. Section 140 of the Act provides facilities for giving notice of resolutions and the circulation of statements (not exceeding 1000 words) with respect to the matters referred to in any proposed resolution or the business to be dealt with at a meeting. Subject to the conditions set out below, the company is bound, on the requisition of the specified number of members, to give such notice and to circulate any such statement to members entitled to receive notice of the next annual general meeting. The number of members necessary for requisition under this section is:—

(a)   any number of members representing not less than one-twentieth of the total voting rights of all members having at the date of the requisition a right to vote at the meeting to which the requisition relates; or

(b)   not less than a hundred members holding shares in the company on which there has been paid up an *average* sum per member of not less than £100.

The company need not give notice of any resolution or circulate any statement unless

(a)   a copy of the requisition signed by the requisitionists (or several copies bearing the signature of all the requisitionists) has been deposited at the registered office of the company, in the case of a requisition requiring notice of a resolution, not less than six weeks before the meeting, and in the case of any other requisition not less than one week before the meeting; and

(b)   there has also been deposited or tendered with the requisition a sum reasonably sufficient to meet the company's expenses.

A company cannot evade the provisions of this section by giving short notice of a meeting after receiving a copy of the requisition, since under the proviso to sub-s. (4) the requisition will be deemed to have been deposited at the right time.

The company need not circulate any statement under s. 140 if the court is satisfied (on the application of the company or any aggrieved person) that the rights conferred by the section are being abused to secure needless publicity for defamatory matter.

CHAPTER XV

AGENDA AND MINUTES

ONE of the principal parts of a secretary's duties is the preparation of agenda for general meetings and board meetings, the attendance at such meetings, and the drafting of the minutes to record the decisions reached.

Minutes. Section 145 of the Act provides that every company shall cause minutes of all proceedings at general meetings and of its directors or managers to be entered in books kept for that purpose. If a company fails to comply with this provision, every officer in default is liable to a default fine. The same section provides that minutes, when signed by the chairman of the meeting at which they were passed, or by the chairman of the next succeeding meeting, shall be evidence of the proceedings (see s. 145).

The reading of the minutes of one meeting at the next meeting, where they are commonly signed, is not infrequently a matter which degenerates into a mere formality; and, accordingly, very great care should be taken to write them both accurately and with sufficient fullness. It is often found in legal proceedings that a company's minute book contains no record of matters which individual directors know to have occurred, and the difficulties of satisfying a court in these circumstances sometimes prove insuperable. What the secretary is really doing when he prepares the minutes is to make a permanent record of the transactions of the board, or of the general meeting, which in the future may very possibly be the only evidence of those transactions which it is possible to produce. It is quite impossible to forecast what will or what will not be required in future contingencies, and the only safe plan is to make the record both accurate and complete.

If, upon the reading of the minutes of one meeting at the succeeding meeting, inaccuracies are noticed and alterations made, the chairman, upon signing the minutes, should initial all the alterations; but no alterations should be made in the minutes except in these circumstances, and then only such alterations as are necessary to ensure an accurate record of the proceedings. Any alteration rendered necessary after signature of the minutes must be the subject of a separate amending minute of a subsequent meeting. Except as just mentioned, a secretary should never, whether acting under the express instructions of a director or directors, or on his own initiative, alter minutes of meetings, either by striking out anything or adding anything [*Cawley & Co.* (1889), 42 Ch.D. 209, at p. 226].

If the minutes are correctly recorded by the secretary, the **Minutes** appropriate minute should read: 'The minutes of the board **Read and** meeting held on the   day of   last were **Signed.** read and signed by the chairman.' The use of the word 'confirmed' should be avoided, as that may imply that the resolutions are not complete without 'confirmation,' whereas the resolution is binding directly it is passed. The secretary or other official is justified in acting upon any resolution directly it is agreed to. Confirmation of resolutions is, however, sometimes required in the case of the meetings of local authorities. The only reason for reading the minutes of the preceding meeting is to give all the directors an opportunity of seeing that the secretary has correctly recorded their proceedings.

If it be found on reading the minutes that any alteration is required, such alteration should be made, not by erasure, but by striking out in ink the incorrect words, and writing in the correct ones, and the alteration should be initialled by the chairman.

No alteration in a decision can be allowed on the reading of the minutes, the only permissible revision being those which affect the correctness of the record of those decisions.

The adoption of minutes at a subsequent meeting of directors does not make those taking part in such adoption necessarily responsible for the acts done at the earlier meeting if such acts were complete before the minutes came up for consideration.

Minutes signed by the chairman of the relevant meeting are *prima facie* evidence of the proceedings at the meeting, but as a general rule they are not the only admissible evidence of those proceedings. Where the company's articles provide that the minutes of meetings purporting to be signed by the chairman should be 'conclusive evidence' without 'any further proof of the facts therein stated,' the minutes are, as between the members and the company, conclusive and in the absence of fraud or bad faith no evidence will be admitted to contradict them. [*Kerr* v. *John Mottram, Ltd.* (1940), Ch. 657.]

In the case of municipal authorities and other public bodies the minutes are usually circulated among the members prior to the meeting, and are not therefore read at the following meeting. This course is sometimes followed in the case of board meetings of companies, but where this is not done the secretary should, on reading the minutes of the preceding meeting, hand the chairman the agenda of the preceding meeting, so that the latter may check the minutes as they are read by the secretary with his own notes on the agenda, and immediately the chairman has signed the minutes as a correct record, the agenda paper should be torn up. The objection to keeping it is that there then exist two records of the same transaction, one, the rough notes often made hurriedly and not always with exactness by the chairman on the agenda paper, and secondly, the more careful minutes written out in detail by the secretary and signed by the chairman with the approval of his colleagues. It is advisable to have only one record, and that record should, of course, be the minute signed by the chairman in the minute book.

The Taking and Keeping of Minutes.
The time honoured method of taking minutes is to write them by hand in a bound book provided with a lock, the key to which is jealously guarded by the secretary. This method is excellent and far from obsolete, but modern requirements demand greater speed and economy in staff. It is now common practice for the secretary to dictate minutes of board meetings in draft form to a stenographer, who types the original, with a carbon copy for retention by the secretary. The original is sent to the chairman for his consideration and, when he returns it approved or amended, sufficient copies are prepared for one to be sent to each director. Any amendments submitted by directors are referred to the chairman, who instructs the secretary whether in his opinion they should be incorporated in the final minutes or not; in the former event, the amendments are circulated to all directors. The retention of copies of minutes by individual directors should not be encouraged, and when the minutes have finally been approved and signed by the chairman, all copies of the minutes in possession of the secretary should be destroyed. Section 436 of the Act provides that minutes may be kept otherwise than in a bound book, but if this is done adequate steps must be taken to prevent falsification and to facilitate its discovery. If such precautions are not taken, the company and every officer of the company in default is liable to a fine not exceeding £50 and also to a default fine.

The following precautions against falsification should be observed where minutes are kept otherwise than in a bound book:—

(i) The minute book should be provided with a lock which, for preference, should be on the spine of the book rather than outside the covers, so as to permit reference to be made to the book without having to undo the lock.

(ii) The key to the lock should be kept by the secretary or other responsible official.

(iii) Loose leaves should be kept under lock and key and issued under the control of the secretary or other responsible official.

(iv) Loose leaves should be serially numbered as issued by the official in whose care they are kept.

(v) Minutes should be numbered serially throughout the book and not in a separate series for each meeting.

(vi) The last page relating to each meeting should be signed by the chairman and all other pages initialled (or signed) by him.

Where minutes are typed on paper which is subsequently pasted into a bound book, the chairman should sign and initial as in (vi) above so that his signature (or initials, as the case may be) appears half on the typed sheet and half on the guard sheet to which it is pasted.

Where the decision of a board meeting is not unanimous **Minuting Dissent.** it is not usual to record the fact that the decision is only that of a majority; but if, on the point being put by the secretary, the dissentient director or directors desire such dissent to be recorded, there is no objection to stating, after recording the resolution: 'Mr. A. B. and Mr. C. D. voting against the resolution,' or 'Messrs. A. B. and C. D. dissenting.'

If it be found on reading the minutes of a previous meeting that the dissent of a director who voted against a resolution has not been recorded, and such director desires his dissent to be inserted in the minutes, the words can be added, and the addition initialled by the chairman when signing the minutes. If the director did not actually vote against the resolution, but has, on reconsideration, decided against a particular resolution passed by the board, the minutes should not be altered, as they have been correctly recorded.

Formerly it was customary to keep an agenda book, **Agenda Paper.** but that course has disadvantages, and it is preferable to have the agenda prepared on separate sheets of paper, with the various items for consideration appearing on the left-hand side, leaving a large right-hand margin upon which the chairman may write any notes he desires of the decisions reached.

It is the secretary's duty to prepare the agenda paper, and he will keep a file in which he will put all letters and other documents coming into his possession between meetings which require the attention of the board.

There are various ways in which an agenda can be prepared and the particular method to be adopted will depend largely upon the nature of the company or institution concerned. For a board meeting of the average company, probably a very short summary of the various matters to be considered is sufficient, as the directors will be familiar with the details surrounding each particular item. In some cases, however, it may be desirable for the secretary, if he is in a position to forecast the decision to which the board is likely to come, to prepare suggested resolutions and to show them on the right-hand side of the agenda paper.

A second method is to show the items in considerable detail and to include or to attach any report from committees or departments which have to be considered before a decision can be made.

In either case, it is sometimes desirable to attach to the agenda copies of all essential correspondence which has not previously been sent to the members of the board.

In preparing an agenda the secretary should read through the minutes of the last meeting to see whether any matters which were then discussed were ordered to stand over until the next meeting. He should also read through the agenda paper of the last meeting to see whether any subject mentioned there was left over for further discussion, and therefore was not incorporated in the minutes.

The order of business is often prescribed by rules and it is often provided that all business left uncompleted at the preceding meeting be taken first, but in all cases (unless it is necessary to elect a chairman of the meeting) the first item on the agenda should be to read and sign the minutes of the previous meeting. It will generally be found advisable at a board meeting of a company to consider the cash position next. The company's cash book or a statement of the cash position should be produced, together with the pass book, and a certificate should be obtained from the bankers, made up to the close of business on the preceding day, showing the balances on the various accounts.

The secretary will, of course, in preparing his agenda, be careful to see that the various items for the consideration of the board are entered in logical sequence. For example, the cash position should be clearly shown, and a statement of future commitments set out, before the consideration of any new business involving an expenditure of money. This will avoid the necessity of taking items on the agenda out of their order, which is apt to be inconvenient, though quite permissible if the meeting so desires.

Continuing with the example of a board meeting, the routine business, such as the passing of share transfers (unless authority to pass transfers has been delegated to a committee), the consideration of departmental reports and other matters which are not likely to give rise to much discussion, should be taken as a rule at the beginning.

In large companies, committees are sometimes appointed by the board with power between board meetings to authorise payments and to register transfers. The proceedings should be summarised in a report, or their minutes read and embodied in the minutes of each board meeting as reports 'received and adopted.'

Secretary to take Notes. It is the secretary's duty to take the official notes of the proceedings, and therefore he should not rely upon the chairman's notes on the agenda paper. The secretary should take full and careful notes of all decisions, and it is wise to obtain the wording of any important resolution made out in the handwriting of the proposer; in any event, it should be initialled by the chairman unless it is in his handwriting on the agenda.

The minutes are only a record of the proceedings of, and decisions reached at, a board meeting and are not a narration of discussions or conversations between members of the board or governing body. It is inadvisable to give reasons in a minute for any resolution passed by the board unless, of course, the motion itself recites the reason. Indeed, it would often be impossible, as the reason for a particular decision which may operate in the mind of any one member may be quite different from that which influences his colleagues. When it is wished to record a reason, the proper course is for the reason to be recited as part of the resolution.

It is unusual and undesirable for the minute book of board **Inspection** meetings to be accessible to members generally. Members **of Minute** have, of course, a statutory right of inspecting minutes of **Books.** general meetings of the company, and, on payment, to a copy of such minutes; the book containing such minutes must be kept at the registered office of the company (s. 146).

An occasion might arise when refusal to inspect board minutes might be justified—without express instructions from the chairman—in the case of a director himself, if it appeared evident that he wished to utilise his privileged position for a purpose detrimental to the company and the board. A difficulty of this kind was the subject of judicial decision in *R.* v. *Hampstead Borough Council, ex p. Woodward* (1917) (116 L.T. 213), where the principle was affirmed that, while a member of a public body acting solely in the public interest has a right to inspect the documents of that body, yet if the inspection is sought for any other purpose, and the interest of the public is not his sole aim, he is deprived of his *prima facie* right, and will not be permitted to utilise his privilege for personal or other ulterior objects.

At a company's annual general meeting it used to be the **Minutes of** practice to read and sign the minutes of the previous general **General** meeting. The modern practice, however, is for the minutes **Meetings.** to be signed by the chairman as soon as they are written up, or at the latest at the board meeting following the general meeting. It is true that some companies still deal with the minutes of one general meeting at the succeeding one, but this practice is now considered to be out of date and should be discarded. In other respects the minutes of general meetings of companies usually follow certain stereotyped lines. The first resolution at the annual general meeting is for the adoption of the report and accounts, and generally takes the following form:—

> That the directors' report and statement of accounts as at the 31st December last, now submitted to this meeting, be received and adopted.

If the report recommends the payment of a dividend, a second resolution may be submitted to the following effect, or these words may be added at the end of the first resolution, namely:—'That a dividend of   per cent, for the year ended 31st December last, be declared on all the issued shares of the company payable, less income tax, to the shareholders appearing on the register as on the   day of   ' [the date on which the register of members was closed].

The wording must, of course, be altered to suit the circumstances, e.g. if there are two or more classes of shares the resolution must state exactly on which class of shares the dividend is payable. If an interim dividend has been paid it is desirable to add after the words 'dividend of per cent.' words in brackets to the following effect '(making with the interim dividend declared on the   last, a dividend of   per cent.).'

The next resolutions usually submitted are those for the election of directors, and the appointment of auditors (if this is necessary) and for fixing the remuneration of the latter. This resolution is usually proposed and seconded by some member other than a director. While this is usual and desirable, it is by no means necessary, and it is quite competent for the resolution to be proposed and seconded by directors or other officials, provided they are entitled to vote. The resolution should be in the following form:—

> That Messrs. 'A. B. & Co.,' chartered (certified or incorporated) accountants, be and they are hereby appointed auditors of the company to hold office until the next annual general meeting at a remuneration of £

A resolution to re-appoint auditors will not usually be required, though it will be necessary to fix their remuneration. Section 159 of the Act provides that at any annual general meeting a retiring auditor, however appointed, shall be re-appointed without any resolution being passed unless

(a) he is not qualified for re-appointment; or

(b) a resolution has been passed at that meeting appointing somebody instead of him or providing expressly that he shall not be re-appointed; or

(c) he has given the company notice in writing of his unwillingness to be re-appointed.

It should be noted that the appointment of auditors cannot be delegated to directors. The directors may, however, appoint the first auditors of a company at any time before the first annual general meeting and they may fill a casual vacancy in the office of auditor.

As to the remuneration of auditors see chapter XVII, p. 219.

As to resolutions for the election of directors, see chapter XIII, p. 164.

Next will follow any other business which is before the meeting.

If any amendment is proposed to a resolution, such amend-**Amend-** ment, after being seconded, is put to the meeting before **ments.** the original resolution is submitted. If the amendment is lost, the chairman will then proceed to put the original resolution. If the amendment is carried, it then takes the place of the original resolution, and, notwithstanding that it has already been voted upon by the meeting, the chairman will again put it in the form of a substantive motion.

In minuting a motion to which an amendment is proposed, it is desirable to give the names of the proposer and seconder of the original motion, and care must be taken to set out the exact words of the motion, then to record the names of the proposer and seconder of the amendment with the exact wording of the amendment. The secretary should be careful to state in his minute the declaration of the chairman upon the voting, first on the amendment, and then on the substantive motion. If two amendments are proposed to the same motion, the first amendment (after being seconded) should be disposed of before the chairman accepts a second amendment. It is not usual to allow the same person to move more than one amendment to any particular motion.

The minutes should record whether motions are carried or lost and may also record any remarks made by the chairman as to how they are carried or lost; *e.g.* 'unanimously,' '*nem. con.*,' 'by the requisite majority.' It usually, however, proves more satisfactory that the chairman should not make such remarks, and that the majority voting for or against the resolution should not be recorded; it is sufficient to state that the motion is carried or lost. The reason is that the chairman may easily make a mistake in thinking (for example) that a motion has been carried unanimously; and, unless there is special reason, it is unwise to record something which even if recorded has no effect and on which the chairman might be proved wrong.

Happily not of frequent occurrence in members' meetings, a proposal to move 'the previous question' is occasionally submitted by a member. This device is sometimes used when the meeting desires to close a discussion and it is not desired to take a vote on the particular question before the meeting.

By far the better way, when a member desires that a particular motion shall not be put to the vote, is for such member to move 'That the meeting do proceed to the next business.' These words convey the exact intention of the motion, and if seconded and carried, have the same effect as the moving of 'the previous question.' It is customary for a motion of this character to be put to the vote without debate.

The minute should read: 'Mr. A. B. moved, and Mr. C. D. seconded, that the meeting do proceed to the next business. This was put to the meeting and declared by the chairman to be carried. The meeting accordingly proceeded to the discussion of the next item on the agenda.'

Or: 'Mr. A. B. moved, and Mr. C. D. seconded, that the meeting do proceed to the next business. This was put to the meeting and declared by the chairman to be lost. The discussion of the subject under consideration was then continued.'

CHAPTER XVI

ACCOUNTS

In the organisation scheme of a business undertaking, secretarial responsibilities and accounting represent separate and distinct functions, which in the larger companies are generally controlled respectively by the secretary and the comptroller or chief accountant. In smaller businesses it is, however, not uncommon to find the control of these two functions combined and placed under the secretary, who thus becomes responsible for the whole of the secretarial and the accounting work of such a business. Accounting is, however, a technique of its own, and in such circumstances the secretary should possess a working knowledge of that technique.

In recent years great progress has been made in mechanisation of accounting and secretarial processes, and with these developments the secretary should also be familiar. Office machines are available in great variety, and are used for many different purposes, e.g. adding, calculating, ledger posting, analysing, addressing and stamping envelopes, giving change, sorting cash for wage payments, etc. By these means work is speeded up considerably and a much higher degree of accuracy is attained. In particular, great progress has been made in the development of 'punched card' systems, by means of which great flexibility is obtained. By this means a wide field of work can be covered with surprising speed and accuracy. There is no doubt that, in the future, an ever increasing proportion of both accounting and secretarial processes will be mechanised.

In the past, accounting was mainly upon an historical basis, but under the modern forms of organisation its boundaries are greatly extended and it becomes one of the main tools of management, by means of which the whole of the operations of a business undertaking are controlled. As one of the principal executive officers of a company, the secretary should have a working knowledge of this new technique, which has developed considerably in recent years, and, undoubtedly, is destined to make great advances in the future.

The difference between the old accounting methods and the new is a matter of viewpoint; the old-fashioned accountant looked backwards to the records of the past, whereas the modern comptroller is ever looking forward to the future and thus taking a direct part in the financial planning and control of the business enterprise with which he is concerned.

In the past the annual accounts of a company were regarded as essentially domestic documents, of concern solely to the members of the company. The view was also widely held by directors that it was inadvisable to give full information in published accounts, particularly in the profit and loss account. It was considered that the affairs of a company might be adversely affected if full information were made available to competitors, suppliers, consumers, employees and the general public; furthermore, directors contended that shareholders might press for increased dividends if the full profits were disclosed. For these reasons, and on the grounds of financial prudence, a widely adopted practice was developed in this country of understating the earnings and the financial position of companies. In the great majority of cases the reasons for the adoption and operation of this policy were strictly honest, but a series of cases, notably *Rex* v. *Kylsant* (1932), 1 K.B. 442, gravely disturbed the public conscience and shook confidence in the existing practices regarding published accounts.

Immediately after the Kylsant case this whole problem was reconsidered by many directors, secretaries and accountants, and the boards of an ever-increasing number of companies voluntarily commenced to redesign the form of presentation of their accounts, upon a basis that ultimately proved to be closely in line with the subsequent amendments to the Companies Act.

This movement represented a revolution in the basic thinking and approach to this problem. This is illustrated by two quotations from the report in 1945 of the Company Law Amendment Committee (known as the Cohen Committee). Regarding the profit and loss account the report states: 'We consider that the profit and loss account is as important as, if not more important than, the balance sheet, since the trend of profits is the best indication of the prosperity of the company and the value of the assets depends largely on the maintenance of the business as a going concern.' As to the possible effects of the publication of full information in accounts, the report adds: 'We do not believe that, if fully informed, shareholders would press for excessive dividends and we are in favour of as much disclosure as practicable. It is also important in our opinion to ensure that there should be adequate disclosure and publication of the results of companies so as to create confidence in the financial management of industry and to dissipate any suggestion that hidden profits are being accumulated by industrial concerns to the detriment of consumers and those who work for industry. We have framed recommendations with which we think most companies should comply.'

The report of the Cohen Committee made very clear the reasons upon which its recommendations were based, and further that the Committee discarded the old policy of understatement in the accounts of companies.

Within eighteen months after incorporation, and thereafter **Annual** once in every calendar year, the directors of a company must **Accounts.** lay before the company in general meeting (at the annual general meeting) a profit and loss account (or income and expenditure account where the company is not trading for profit) and balance sheet, drawn up in accordance with the provisions of the Eighth Schedule to the Act. The accounts must relate to a period ended not more than nine months prior to the date of the meeting, or twelve months in the case of a company carrying on business or having interests abroad, but the Board of Trade may in special cases extend this period (s. 148). The balance sheet which is submitted to the company in general meeting must have annexed to it the profit and loss account, group accounts (in so far as they are not incorporated in the balance sheet or profit and loss account) and any notes or statements upon or connected with any of them in accordance with the Eighth Schedule, clauses 7 (1), 11, 14, 15 (3), 15 (4), 15 (6), 21 and 22. There must also be attached the auditors' report and the directors' report.

The report of the directors, in addition to dealing with the **Directors'** state of the company's affairs, must set out the amount, if **Report.** any, which the directors recommend should be paid by way of dividend and the amount, if any, which they propose to carry to reserve. Unless the directors consider that disclosure would be harmful to the company's interests, the report must deal also with any material changes in the nature of the company's business or in its subsidiaries and changes in the class of business in which the company has an interest, whether as a member of another company or otherwise (s. 157). The report usually also mentions the directors who have retired during the year and those who retire at the annual general meeting, stating whether, if eligible, they offer themselves for re-election. Finally, the report will probably include a statement, if appropriate, to the effect that the auditors are eligible to continue in office and that it is intended to move at the annual general meeting that their remuneration be fixed at £.. for the ensuing year. The directors' report will generally be signed by the secretary upon the board's authority, which he should obtain. The report as a whole is not subject to audit, but where information in connection with the balance sheet and accounts which requires to be disclosed in statements annexed thereto if not shown in the balance sheet and accounts themselves, is shown in the directors' report, the report must be annexed, not merely attached, to the accounts, and the auditors must report upon the information so contained (s. 163).

Before circulation of the accounts to the members, the **Circulation** board is required to approve the documents annexed to the **of Accounts.** balance sheet (s. 156), *i.e.* the profit and loss account and group accounts (if any).   A resolution is then passed authorising the balance sheet to be signed on its behalf by two directors (or the sole director if a company has only one) (s. 155).

Every member of every company having a share capital, whether he is entitled to receive notices or not, and every debenture holder, has a right, under s. 158, to have sent to him at his registered address a copy of every balance sheet, together with the documents required to be annexed to it, and a copy of the auditors' report.   It is usually found convenient to attach the directors' report also, but in point of fact the Act does not stipulate that it shall be circulated, but merely that it shall be attached to every balance sheet laid before the company in general meeting (s. 157 (1)).   The document need not be sent to second and subsequent joint holders of shares or debentures who are not entitled to notice and members and debenture holders of whose address the company is unaware.   In the case of companies not having a share capital there is no obligation to send the documents to members or debenture holders who are not entitled to notice.   Any member or debenture holder, however, whether he is entitled to have the accounts sent to him or not, must be supplied without charge with a copy of the documents upon demand.

The balance sheet, documents annexed and auditors' report must be circulated not later than twenty-one days before the date of the meeting at which they are to be presented. Occasionally it may not be found convenient to circulate them so far in advance and it will then be necessary to obtain the agreement of all the members who are entitled to attend and vote at the meeting to the circulation of the accounts at shorter notice [s. 158 (1)].   An appropriate wording for such a waiver, for signature by those concerned, might be as follows:—

'We, the undersigned, being members of   Limited, hereby agree to accept as duly circulated all documents required by the Companies Act, 1948, to be circulated before the annual general meeting to be held on   19 , although circulated less than 21 days before the meeting.'

Balance Sheet, etc. in Annual Return.   Under s. 127 and 129 of the Act, it is necessary for every company other than an exempt private company to annex to its annual return a certified true copy of every balance sheet, together with documents required to be annexed and attached (including the directors' report) which have been presented to the company in general meeting during the period covered by the return.   Any document in a foreign language must be accompanied by an English version certified in the prescribed manner to be a correct translation.   It is not necessary for the documents annexed to the return to be signed by those who signed the original documents—their signature may be signed, printed, stamped, etc.—but each of the documents must be certified as being a true copy by a director and the secretary of the company.

An oversea company, that is a company incorporated **Oversea** abroad which establishes a place of business in Great Britain, **Companies.** is not exempt from the provisions of the Act in regard to the filing of accounts, but must each year prepare all those documents, including group accounts if it is a holding company, which it would be required to prepare and lay before the company in general meeting, had it been incorporated in Great Britain. (See chapter XXVI.)

Detailed provisions regarding both the profit and loss **Details of** account and the balance sheet are contained in the Eighth **Eighth** Schedule to the Act. By this means the Act is made flexible, **Schedule.** as the provisions of this Schedule can be modified by the Board of Trade both generally and as regards a particular company 'on the application or with the consent of a company's directors' [s. 149 (4)]. The detailed provisions contained in the Eighth Schedule require close study by all concerned with the preparation of the accounts of a company.

The provisions regarding the balance sheet and profit and loss account are contained in Part I of the Eighth Schedule.

In para. 4 (1) it is provided that 'reserves, provisions, liabilities and fixed and current assets shall be classified under headings appropriate to the company's business.'

The following are important items that must be separately **Balance** stated in the balance sheet:— **Sheet.**

(a) Share capital. Where redeemable preference shares have been issued, the balance sheet must show what part of the issued share capital consists of these shares and the earliest date on which the company has power to redeem [Eighth Schedule, para. 2 (a)]. Redemption of such shares shall not be taken as a reduction of authorised capital [s. 58 (3)].

(b) Capital reserves. These are defined as such reserves as do 'not include any amount regarded as free for distribution through the profit and loss account' [Eighth Schedule, para. 27 (i) (c)].

(c) Revenue reserves. These are defined as 'any reserve other than a capital reserve.'

(d) Capital redemption reserves. When redeemable preference shares are redeemed out of profits, an amount must be transferred to the capital redemption reserve fund equal to the nominal amount of the shares redeemed [s. 58 (i) (d)]. The fund may be applied in paying up unissued shares for distribution as fully-paid bonus shares [s. 58 (5)].

(*e*) Share premium account. This account may be applied in paying up unissued shares for distribution as fully-paid bonus shares, in writing off preliminary expenses, expenses of issue or commission or discount allowed on the issue of shares or debentures, or in providing premiums payable on the redemption of preference shares or debentures [s. 56 (2)].

(*f*) 'The aggregate amount of bank loans and overdrafts' [Eighth Schedule, para. 8 (1) (*d*)].

(*g*) 'The net aggregate amount (after deduction of income tax) which is recommended for distribution by way of dividend' [Eighth Schedule, para. 8 (1) (*e*)]. This settles a matter that had been disputed in accountancy circles for many years.

(*h*) The United Kingdom income tax liability. The basis on which this liability has been computed must be made clear in the accounts or by way of a note.

(*j*) The aggregate amounts respectively of capital reserves, revenue reserves and of 'provisions (other than provisions for depreciation, renewals or diminution in value of assets)' (Eighth Schedule, para. 6).

(*k*) Investments in and advances to and from subsidiary companies.

(*l*) Trade investments.

(*m*) Other investments (quoted).

(*n*) Other investments (not quoted),

(*o*) Goodwill, patents and trade marks. It is not necessary to separate the amount of goodwill from that of patents and trade marks [Eighth Schedule, para 8).

(*p*) Loans to directors and employees. (See chapter XIII, p. 166.)

With regard to disclosure of loans in the balance sheet, s. 197 (1) requires particulars to be shown of loans made during the financial year to 'officers' (this term is defined in s. 455 as including a director, manager or secretary, but the definition presumably extends to such officers as registrar, chief accountant, etc.) or to persons who afterwards became officers, whether the loans were made by the company or its subsidiary, or by another person on guarantee or security provided by either.

Particulars need not, however, be shown of a loan made in the ordinary course of business, or of a loan made by the company or its subsidiary to an employee of either, provided it does not exceed £2,000 and is certified by the directors as being made in accordance with normal practice regarding loans to employees.

(*q*) Preliminary, formation and issue expenses, etc.

(*r*) Where any liability of a company is secured on any assets of the company (otherwise than by operation of the law) this fact must be stated, although there is no need to specify the assets in which the liability is secured. Further, where any of the company's debentures were held by a nominee or trustee for the company, the nominal amount of the debentures and the amount at which they were stated in the books of the company shall be stated.

In paragraph 5 of the Eighth Schedule there are very important provisions regarding the 'method of arriving at the amount of any fixed asset.' In the past, a common practice was to show fixed assets at the net amount, that is, at the balance remaining after deducting all amounts written off the cost of such assets by way of depreciation, etc. It is now obligatory to show the aggregate cost or valuation of such assets and also 'the aggregate amount provided or written off since the date of acquisition or valuation, as the case may be, for depreciation or diminution in value.' These provisions regarding fixed assets do not apply:—

(*a*) to assets for which the necessary figures both prior to and after 1st July, 1948, 'cannot be obtained without unreasonable expense or delay' [Eighth Schedule, para. 5 (2) (*a*)];

(*b*) 'to assets the replacement of which is provided for wholly or partly—

(i) by making provision for renewals and charging the cost of replacement against the provision so made; or

(ii) by charging the cost of replacement direct to revenue' [para. 5 (2) (*b*)].

(*c*) 'to any investments of which the market value' or estimated value 'is shown either as the amount of the investments or by way of note' [para. 5 (2) (*c*)];

(*d*) 'to goodwill, patents or trade marks' [para. 5 (2) (*d*)].

In paragraph 11 of the Eighth Schedule particulars are given of a number of important matters which 'shall be stated by way of note, or in a statement or report annexed, if not otherwise shown,' for example, in the balance sheet itself. Thus it is necessary to show particulars of:—

(i) options to purchase the company's shares;

(ii) arrears of fixed cumulative dividends, shown gross before deduction of income tax;

(iii) general nature and estimated amount of contingent
       liabilities and contracts for capital expenditure for
       which no provision has been made in the accounts;

(iv)   market value of quoted investments other than trade
       investments if the value in the balance sheet differs
       from the market value. The stock exchange value
       should be shown also, if less than the market value;

(v)   basis for converting foreign currencies into sterling;

(vi)   basis for computing income tax provisions;

(vii) corresponding figures for the previous financial year
       of all items in the balance sheet;

(viii) 'if, in the opinion of the directors, any of the current
       assets have not a value, on realisation in the ordinary
       course of the company's business, at least equal to
       the amount at which they are stated, the fact that
       the directors are of that opinion' must be disclosed;

(ix)   particulars of any charge on the assets of a company
       to secure the liabilities of any other person, including,
       where practicable, the amount secured;

(x)   where practicable, the aggregate amount, or estima-
       ted amount, if it is material, of contracts for capital
       expenditures, so far as not provided for.

A further very important provision is contained in paragraph 27 (2) of the Eighth Schedule. This is that if, in the
opinion of the directors, excessive provision has been made
for depreciation and for known liabilities, then 'the excess
shall be treated for the purposes of this Schedule as a reserve
and not as a provision.'

The terms of the Act make it very clear that the balance
sheets of companies must give a full and fair view of the
financial position, and it is equally clear that the law will
not tolerate either a deliberate and material overstatement or
understatement of the financial position of the affairs of a
company.

Profit and Loss Account. Following the Kylsant case, many companies greatly improved the form of presentation of their profit and loss accounts
and increased the amount of information given therein. In
particular, following the lessons to be learned from that
case, the practice grew of showing separately in the profit and
loss account any items of an exceptional and non-recurring
nature, which, therefore, did not represent normal earnings
or charges directly connected with the ordinary revenue
transactions of the year. It was realised how extremely
important it was that the trend of the true results of a company
should be clearly revealed in its accounts. For this reason
the great importance of the profit and loss account emerged,

and this is made vividly clear in the report of the Cohen Committee. The amendments in the law regarding profit and loss accounts, brought about by the Companies Act, 1948, are clearly based upon the fundamental principle that a true and fair view must be given of the normal revenue results of a company. In order to achieve this, it is essential that the accounts shall be prepared from year to year upon the basis of accepted accounting principles consistently maintained and, if these basic principles are varied, then the effect on the results of such alterations must be disclosed.

The Act lays down the minimum of information that must be given in the profit and loss account of a company (Eighth Schedule, paras. 12–14). Here again, the provisions are closely in line with the standards of best practice that had been evolved in the two decades preceding the coming into force of the Act.

The main items that must be separately stated in the profit and loss account are as follows:—

(a) provisions for depreciation, renewals or diminution in value of fixed assets;

(b) interest on debentures and other fixed loans;

(c) United Kingdom income tax and other United Kingdom taxation on profits. The basis of the computation of the former must be made clear;

(d) amounts provided for redemption of share capital and loans;

(e) amounts, if material, set aside or proposed to be set aside to, or withdrawn from, reserves;

(f) income from trade investments;

(g) income from other investments;

(h) the aggregate amount of dividends paid and proposed;

(j) auditors' remuneration, including expenses reimbursed to them, if the remuneration has not been fixed by the company in general meeting;

(k) transactions of an exceptional or non-recurrent nature;

(l) the aggregate amount of directors' emoluments (s. 196);

The term 'emoluments' includes sums payable for services as a director of the company or its subsidiary—for example, fees, percentages, expense allowances in so far as they are chargeable to United Kingdom income tax in the hands of the directors, contributions made in respect of directors to a pension scheme, and estimated money value of benefits received other than in cash.

In determining the amount of emoluments, account must be taken of sums paid by or receivable from the company, its subsidiaries and any other person, but in the profit and loss account it is necessary only to distinguish between emoluments for services as a director, whether of the company or of its subsidiary, and other emoluments. Further details are given in chapter XVII, p. 231.

(m) the aggregate amount of directors' or past directors' pensions (s. 196);

The term 'pensions' as defined includes any super-annuation allowance, superannuation, gratuity or similar payment. As in the case of emoluments, account must be taken of sums paid by or receivable from the company, its subsidiaries and any other person, when determining the aggregate amount of pensions, but separate disclosure in the profit and loss account under each of these headings is not required. If the contributions by the company are substantially adequate to maintain a pension scheme—a scheme maintained wholly or partly by contributions—pensions paid by the scheme to a director need not be shown in the accounts. Further details are given in chapter XVII, p. 233.

(n) the aggregate amount of any compensation to directors or past directors in respect of loss of office (s. 196);

Compensation for loss of office includes sums paid in consideration of, or in connection with, retirement from office. All such payments require the approval of the company in general meeting. Disclosure of compensation must be made in the profit and loss account under three separate headings, namely compensation paid by or receivable from (1) the company, (2) subsidiaries, (3) any other person. Further details are given in chapter XVII, p. 234.

The Schedule also refers to certain matters which must be stated by way of note if not already shown in the profit and loss account:—

(1) the method of providing for depreciation or replacement of fixed assets if not by depreciation charge or provision for renewals; if no provision is made this should be stated;

(2) basis on which the United Kingdom income tax charge is computed;

(3) whether the dividends paid or proposed to be paid are subject to deduction of income tax or free of tax;

(4) if any item in the account is materially affected by unusual, exceptional or non-recurring transactions by the company, or if the basis of accounting has changed, disclosure must be made;

(5) corresponding figures for the preceding financial year of all items in the profit and loss account.

The term 'subsidiary' is defined in s. 154 of the Act. A company is a subsidiary:— **Holding and Subsidiary Companies.**

(1) if the shareholding company 'is a member of it and controls the composition of its board of directors.'

Power to appoint or remove a director must not depend on mere consent, but must depend upon the company's voting or other power, or be the consequence of the director concerned being also a director of the holding company, or arise from the fact that the directorship is held by the holding company or its subsidiary, or

(2) if the shareholding company 'holds more than half in nominal value of its equity share capital.'

Equity share capital is the issued share capital of a company 'excluding any part thereof which neither as respects dividends nor as respects capital, carries any right to participate beyond a specified amount in a distribution.'

In determining whether one company is a subsidiary of another there shall be disregarded shares held or power exercisable in a fiduciary capacity, or by virtue of the provisions of any debentures or debenture trust deed, or as security for loans made in the ordinary course of business. Shares held or power exercisable by the nominee of the holding company or of any of its subsidiaries are to be regarded as shares held or power exercisable by the holding company itself.

The Act makes it clear that the definition of a subsidiary embraces also sub-subsidiaries and sub-sub-subsidiaries and so on. A company is deemed to be another company's holding company if, but only if, that other company is its subsidiary.

Regarding holding and subsidiary companies, the Cohen Committee pointed out the defects in the Companies Act, 1929, and made clear the governing principles upon which it based its recommendations, as follows:—

'We consider that the accounting information published by the holding company to supplement the balance sheet which, as a separate legal entity, it publishes should, as far as is reasonably practicable, include information with regard to the financial position and results of the group similar to that which would be required by statute if the business were carried on by a single company operating through a number of branches.'

Prior to the coming into force of the Companies Act, 1948, there was no legal obligation requiring a holding company to publish consolidated or group accounts, but the Act of 1948 makes this compulsory except in the following circumstances:—

(a) where the holding company is 'the wholly-owned subsidiary of another body corporate incorporated in Great Britain' [s. 150 (2) (a)]. This is to avoid unnecessary consolidation, as in this case the principal holding company will be required to publish group accounts embracing the whole group of companies;

(b) if in the opinion of the directors:—

(1) 'it is impracticable or would be of no real value to members of the company, in view of the insignificant amounts involved';

(2) it would involve unnecessary expense or delay;

(3) 'the result would be misleading or harmful to the business of the company or any of its subsidiaries';

(4) the businesses 'are so different that they cannot reasonably be treated as a single undertaking.'

In the cases of (3) and (4) above, the approval of the Board of Trade is required.

The group accounts shall comprise 'a consolidated balance sheet dealing with the state of affairs of the company and all the subsidiaries dealt with in the group accounts' and 'a consolidated profit and loss account dealing with the profit and loss of the company and those subsidiaries' [s. 151 (1) (a) and (b)]. It should be borne in mind that group accounts must deal not only with subsidiaries incorporated in the United Kingdom, but with foreign subsidiaries also.

The consolidated balance sheet and profit and loss account shall comply so far as is practicable with the requirements of the Act as if they were the accounts of an actual company. but in the consolidated accounts it is not necessary to show the aggregate, for the whole group of companies, of (a) the directors' salaries, pensions, etc., or (b) particulars of loans to officers of the companies.

If the directors are of the opinion that it would be better to present 'the same or equivalent information' in a form other than by way of group accounts they are entitled to do so [s. 151 (2) (a)].

The Act lays it down that the group accounts 'shall give a true and fair view of the state of affairs and profit or loss of the company and the subsidiaries dealt with thereby as a whole, so far as concerns members of the company' [s. 152 (1)].

The Act provides that 'a holding company's directors shall secure that, except when in their opinion there are good reasons against it, the financial year of each of its subsidiaries shall coincide with the company's own financial year' [s. 153 (1)].

The preparation of group accounts is a highly technical matter and is one which is in the process of development. The detailed provisions in this regard are laid down in the Eighth Schedule, Part II. These provisions greatly increase the responsibilities of directors, accountants and auditors and, therefore, require close consideration by all concerned with the preparation of the group accounts of a company.

CHAPTER XVII

THE SECRETARIAL ASPECT OF ACCOUNTANCY

As has been explained in Chapter XVI, the primary functions of the secretary and the accountant are separate and distinct, but this does not mean that their work falls neatly into two watertight compartments. Many problems can confront a company secretary in which a knowledge of the technique of accounting and a general financial instinct are as necessary for the full appreciation and proper performance of his task as the knowledge of law and of company procedure, which is the secretary's primary contribution. The secretary and the accountant constitute a team—and a very strong one—upon which devolves the task of company administration and forward planning along the lines formulated by the board of directors.

In order that this team shall operate smoothly, it is important that a study be made of the common ground on which the secretary and the accountant meet. This chapter is therefore devoted to the study of various aspects of accountancy purely from the angle of the secretary. It does not aim to be an exhaustive treatise on the complicated technique of higher accounting, since there are many excellent books covering this subject, but no apologies need be made if it should trespass upon the accountant's preserves in order to present a clear picture.

Statutory Books of Account. Every company has a statutory obligation under s. 147 to keep proper books of account with respect to receipts and payments, sales and purchases and assets and liabilities, which together shall give a true and fair view of the company's affairs and explain its transactions. It is not necessary for the books to be in bound form, but if they are in any other form, for example, loose-leaf or card file, the company and every officer in default will be liable to a fine if adequate precautions are not taken to guard against falsification and to facilitate its discovery (s. 436). Thus, among other safeguards, it may be thought advisable to mark the sheets in some distinctive manner and to keep the spare sheets in the custody of a responsible official.

The books are required to be kept at the registered office or at such other place as the directors may think fit. If it is decided to keep them at a place other than the registered office there is no need to give notice to the Registrar as in the case of the register of members. A company is not prohibited from keeping its books of account outside Great Britain but, if it does so, periodical accounts and returns must be sent, at least every six months, to an office in Great Britain so that they will disclose with reasonable accuracy the financial position of the business dealt with in those books, and contain sufficient information to enable the statutory accounts to be prepared.

Any director who fails to take reasonable steps to secure **Penalties.** compliance with the Act in regard to the keeping of books of account is liable, under s. 147 (4), to a fine, or to imprisonment if the default is wilful, but he may escape liability if he can show that he had reasonable grounds to believe and did believe that a competent and reliable person had been employed to secure compliance. It is also provided, in s. 331, that, where proper books of account have not been kept during the two years preceding the commencement of winding up, every officer of the company in default is liable to imprisonment unless he acted honestly and the default was excusable.

The books of account, and also the accounts and returns sent **Inspection** to an office in Great Britain when the books are kept abroad, **of Books.** must at all times be open to the inspection of the directors (s. 147 (3)). The auditors also have right of access to the company's books, accounts and vouchers [s. 162 (3)], while the Commissioners of Inland Revenue and commissioners hearing appeals relating to income tax may, under s. 35 of the Finance Act, 1942, in certain circumstances, require the books to be produced to their representatives who may take copies or extracts. Where the court has made a winding up order, it may make an order for inspection of the books and papers of the company by creditors and contributories (s. 266). Under s. 441, if there is reasonable cause to believe that an officer of a company has committed an offence in connection with the management of the company's affairs and evidence of the commission of the offence is to be found in the company's books or papers, a court order for their inspection may be procured by the Director of Public Prosecutions, the Board of Trade or a chief officer of police. Finally, where an investigation of a company's affairs under s. 164 or s. 165 takes place, or where there is an investigation into the ownership of the company under s. 172, the inspector is entitled to inspect the books of the company under s. 167.

When a company has been wound up and is about to be **Disposal of** dissolved, the books and papers of the company may be dis- **Books.** posed of as may be directed by an extraordinary resolution of the company in a members' voluntary winding up, by the committee of inspection or creditors in a creditors' voluntary winding up, or by the court in a winding up by or under the supervision of the court, and the person into whose custody the books and papers are committed shall not be responsible for their production after five years from the dissolution of company (s. 341).

H

Auditors and Audit. The primary duty of auditors in relation to a company is laid down in s. 162 (1). 'The auditors shall make a report to the members on the accounts examined by them, and on every balance sheet, every profit and loss account and all group accounts laid before the company in general meeting during their tenure of office.' The documents and statements annexed to the balance sheet and accounts are also subject to audit, but not the directors' report, except in so far as it contains information which is required to be contained in a statement annexed to the balance sheet or accounts. The matters to be stated expressly in the auditors' report are given in the Ninth Schedule, but the report must also include particulars of directors' remuneration [s. 196 (8)] and of loans to officers [s. 197 (3)] to the extent that the information contained in the accounts falls short of statutory requirements.

Duties of Auditors. The headnote in *Republic of Bolivia Exploration Syndicate* (1914), 1 Ch. 139, usefully summarises some of the main duties and responsibilities of auditors: 'Auditors are bound to know or make themselves acquainted with their duties under the company's articles and under the Companies Acts for the time being in force, and if the audited balance sheets do not show the true financial condition of the company, and damage is thereby occasioned, the onus is on the auditors to show that this damage is not the result of any breach of duty on their part.' Under s. 205, any provision exempting an auditor from liability in respect of negligence, default, breach of duty or breach of trust is void, but the court has power to relieve an auditor, who has acted honestly and reasonably and ought fairly to be excused, from liability (s. 448).

Right of Access to Books. In order to enable auditors properly to perform their duties, it is provided in s. 162 (3) that they shall have a right of access at all times to the books (*i.e.* not merely books of account, but also minute books, etc.) and accounts and vouchers of the company, and shall be entitled to require from the officers of the company such information and explanations as they think necessary. Any regulations precluding auditors from availing themselves of all the information to which they are entitled under the Act are *ultra vires* and invalid [*Newton* v. *Birmingham Small Arms Co.* (1906), 2 Ch. 378]. The auditors are also entitled to attend any general meeting of the company and to receive all notices of and other communications relating to any general meeting which any member is entitled to receive, and to be heard at any general meeting, which they attend, on any part of the business of the meeting which concerns them as auditors [s. 162 (4)].

Duties of Secretary as to Audit. The audit of a company's accounts is mainly the concern of the accountant, but there are also practical matters connected therewith which, being dependent upon the organisation within the company, may to a greater or lesser extent require the attention of the secretary. For example, the secretary should ensure that sufficient notice, requesting the auditors to attend at the company's office for the purpose of the audit, is given in order that the audited accounts may be ready for circulation to members twenty-one clear days before the proposed date of the general meeting at which they are to be presented. If possible, a room should be set aside for the auditors' use. In addition to the books of account, vouchers, etc., there should be available for inspection the statutory books (including the minute books) and other registers normally maintained by the secretary. Documents of title to investments and property, leases and other agreements in consequence of which payments have been made or received by the company, will probably require to be produced, although where they have been inspected in previous years, the auditors may perhaps agree to accept a letter sent to them by the company's bankers stating that the documents are held in safe custody by them. The bank should also be instructed to supply the auditors with any other information they may require in connection with the audit; for example, the company's bank balances as at the close of business on the last day of the financial period under review. Such information is normally given to the auditors direct and not to the company. Every material transaction which does not come within the ordinary routine of the company's business should be covered by a minute of the board. Examples of such transactions include appropriations to or from reserve, the purchase or sale of investments and the writing off of bad debts. If the auditors feel that the minutes are deficient in this respect, as sometimes occurs, they may request the secretary to arrange for the board to pass certain resolutions with a view to making good the deficiency. The preparation of income and profits tax assessments for the purpose of calculating taxation provisions may in some cases call for highly specialised knowledge and on this subject the auditors are generally qualified to advise. The preparation of final accounts and balance sheet should also be carried out in close collaboration with the auditors. When the audit is complete, it will be necessary to hold a board meeting at which authority will be obtained for the signing of the balance sheet by two directors and it will usually be convenient at this meeting to pass any resolutions in connection with special payments, etc., which the auditors may require. When signed, the accounts are passed to the auditors for a report to be made thereon and they are then ready for circulation.

It has been held that a proper method for an auditor to **Auditor's** make his report to the shareholders is to send the report to the **Report.** company, and that it is the directors' duty to communicate that report to the members by causing it to be read, not merely taken as read, to the company in general meeting [as required by s. 162 (2)] and by circulating it prior to the meeting (as required by s. 158). Accordingly, the auditors are not deemed to have committed a breach of their duty if, having duly sent in their report to the company, the report is not communicated to the members owing to a breach of duty by the directors [*Allen Craig & Co., Ltd.* (1934), 1 Ch. 483].

Ancillary Duties of Auditors.

As stated above, the primary duty of the auditors is to report to the members upon the accounts of the company submitted to them in general meeting. They have, however, other duties in relation to a company, which, though equally important, do not recur so frequently. For example, the auditors are, under the Fourth Schedule, Part II, required to report in a prospectus upon the profits, losses, assets and liabilities of a company and its subsidiaries, and the name and address of the auditors must appear in every prospectus and statement in lieu of prospectus of the company. In the statutory report, the auditors are required to certify as correct the statements made with regard to the shares allotted by the company, the cash received in respect of such shares and receipts and payments on capital account, and their name, address and description must appear in the body of the report (s. 130). Finally, where an investigation of a company's affairs is being made in accordance with ss. 164–166, the auditors have, under s. 167 (5) a duty to assist the inspectors as prescribed in s. 167 (1). (See chapter XXVIII.)

Appointment of Auditor.

The first auditor of a company may be appointed by the directors at any time before the first annual general meeting and the auditor so appointed shall hold office until the conclusion of that meeting. If, however, the directors fail to appoint an auditor before the first annual general meeting, he shall be appointed by the meeting. Should no auditor be appointed or reappointed at this or any other annual general meeting, the Board of Trade must be given notice of the fact within a week and an auditor may then be appointed by the Board of Trade. An auditor who has been appointed at an annual general meeting holds office from the conclusion of the meeting until the conclusion of the next annual general meeting. However, if a casual vacancy in the office of auditor arises, the vacancy may be filled by the directors, although the surviving or continuing auditors, if any, may act while the vacancy continues. At any annual general meeting the retiring auditor, however appointed, is deemed to be re-appointed without the necessity of passing a resolution unless he is not qualified for re-appointment, or a resolution has been passed at that meeting appointing somebody instead of him or providing expressly that he shall not be re-appointed, or he has given the company notice in writing of his unwillingness to be re-appointed (s. 159).

In s. 161, there are set out the conditions which must be **Qualifica-** satisfied in order to qualify a person for appointment as an **tions of** auditor. These conditions may be summarised as follows:— **Auditor.**

(a) He must be qualified from the technical aspect in accordance with the provisions of s. 161 (1).

(b) He may not be an officer or servant, or the partner or employee of an officer or servant of the company.

(c) A body corporate may not be appointed as auditor. It is, however, provided that a Scottish firm is qualified for appointment, but only if all the individual partners are qualified.

(d) He must not have been disqualified from being appointed as auditor to the company's holding company, subsidiary company or fellow subsidiary of the same holding company.

The above conditions are modified in the case of an exempt private company in that the auditor need not be technically qualified, while a partner or employee of an officer or servant is not precluded from appointment as auditor.

In s. 159 (7) it is provided that the remuneration of an **Remunera-** auditor appointed by the directors or by the Board of Trade **tion of** shall be fixed by his appointor. In other cases the remunera- **Auditor.** tion is fixed either by the company in general meeting, or in such manner as it shall determine, for example, by delegation of its authority to fix remuneration to the board of directors. Any sums paid by the company in respect of auditors' expenses shall be deemed to be included in the expression 'remuneration.' It will be recalled that where the company in general meeting does not fix the auditors' remuneration for the ensuing year, the amount of remuneration, including expenses, must be disclosed in the profit and loss account (Eighth Schedule, para. 13).

Where it is desired that an auditor retiring at the conclusion **Non-Re-** of an annual general meeting, other than the first annual **appointment** general meeting, shall not be re-appointed or that another **and Removal** auditor be appointed in his place, notwithstanding the fact that **of Auditors.** the retiring auditor is qualified and willing to continue in office, it is necessary that the procedure contained in s. 160 shall be followed. Special notice (see p. 131) must be given to the **Special** company by a member of the intention to propose the neces- **Notice.** sary resolution. On receipt of this notice, the company is required to send a copy to the retiring auditor, who is then entitled to make representations in writing to the company (not exceeding a reasonable length) with a request that they shall be communicated to the members. The notice of the resolution which is given to the members must state that representations have been made, and a copy of them must be sent to each member entitled to notice. If, however, the representations are not circulated, whether because they are not received in time or for any other reason, the retiring auditor may require that they be read at the meeting and he may in any case address the meeting on the question of his removal. The auditor's right to have his representations circulated or read is subject to the proviso that the right shall not be abused by using the occasion as a means of securing needless publicity for defamatory matter. If the company or any other aggrieved person is of the opinion that the privilege has been abused, it is possible to obtain the court's permission to disregard the auditor's right, although the auditor may still address the meeting. The procedure given above applies also where it is desired to remove at the first annual general meeting an auditor previously appointed by the directors, with the exception that only 14 days' notice, instead of 'special notice,' need be given of the intention to propose the resolution in question. Moreover, it appears from s. 159 (5) (a) that the first auditors appointed by the directors may be removed and others appointed in their place at any general meeting prior to the first annual general meeting. Thus they could presumably be removed at the statutory meeting provided that 14 days' notice had been given to the company and the other requirements of s. 160 had been complied with.

Dividend and Interest Payments. The secretary should be acquainted with the essential accountancy points relating to the payment of dividends.

It is the general practice to debit dividends *less income tax* (*i.e.* the net amount payable) to the profit and loss appropriation account, as income tax liability is calculated upon the whole of a company's profits, and is therefore not affected by dividend payments. The total amount of income tax on the profits of the company is therefore shown in the profit and loss account, and the actual net payment to the shareholders in respect of dividend debited to profit and loss appropriation account.

The appropriate entries in the books of the company following the declaration of a dividend are as follows:—

(a) Profit and Loss Appropriation Account.   Dr.   £
    To Dividend Account—
      Amount of net dividend at......... per
        cent. on ....shares as per
        board/shareholders' resolution
        passed.............................19.........

(b) Bank—Dividend Account.   Dr.   £
    To Cash—
      Amount of net dividend transferred to
        'Ordinary/Preference' Share Divi-
        dend Account.

In the case of a dividend paid 'free of tax,' the actual amount of the dividend declared should be debited to profit and loss appropriation account.

For the purpose of dealing with the actual payment of dividends to shareholders, a separate banking account designated 'ordinary' or 'preference' dividend account, appropriately numbered, should be opened, and the net sum transferred from the company's current or deposit account to the credit of that account. Dividend warrants presented by shareholders for payment will be debited by the bank to this account, and the amount at credit will be absorbed in the event of all warrants being presented.

Payments to Shareholders.

If the cash required to meet the dividend is to be transferred from a deposit account, care should be taken to give prior notice of withdrawal, since most banks require 14 days' notice of a transfer from deposit account.

In practice, however, there is always a number of warrants unpresented for various reasons, and the amount remaining in the account is designated 'unclaimed' or 'outstanding' dividends. It is customary with some companies to transfer 'unclaimed' dividends at the end of the financial year to a separate account, or, alternatively, to transfer the 'unclaimed' balance to the 'general' or 'current' banking account. Many companies show the amount of 'unclaimed' dividends in the balance sheet as a separate liability, but this is not strictly necessary, as the item can be included under an omnibus heading.

In the event of there being arrears of dividend upon cumulative preference shares, the gross amount of such arrears and the period in respect of which the dividends are in arrear should be stated by way of a note in the balance sheet. They are not a debt or liability of the company, but no dividends can be paid on the ordinary or other inferior classes of shares until such arrears have been discharged.

Arrears of Dividend.

The attention of secretaries and registrars is particularly drawn to the instructions contained in E.C. (Securities) 7, in respect of interest, dividends and capital repayments on securities. The notice is one of an administrative series issued by the Bank of England in regard to the law contained in the Exchange Control Act, 1947, and Treasury Orders made thereunder. (See Appendix M.)

The appropriate entry when payment of interest on debentures for a period becomes due is:—

Interest on Debentures.

Profit and Loss Account.   Dr.   £

     To Debenture Interest Account—
         Net interest for the half-year ended
         ...., 19........., on
         £................ per cent. debentures

     To Income Tax Account—
         Tax deducted from above interest at
         ....in the £   ..   ..   ..

In other respects, the procedure relating to dividends should be followed, except that arrears of debenture interest, unlike arrears of preference dividend, are an actual liability of the company and must be entered in the balance sheet as such and not merely noted on it.

Salaries. In keeping with other aspects of secretarial practice, the payment of salaries has become, as a result of the legislation of recent years, a function of increasing complexity. The introduction of the Pay-As-You-Earn system of income tax collection, and the advent of compulsory national insurance for all, have both committed the employer to the task of collecting a State-imposed levy from his employees, the procedure of collection in both cases being governed by an extensive code of instructions and regulations, and requiring an intimate acquaintance with a large variety of forms and record cards. The collection of staff contributions to employer-sponsored superannuation schemes has also become a routine matter for the official dealing with salaries, who may be required, in addition, to collect the contribution of the national savings or hospital savings groups.

The Elements of a Salary Accounting System. When a salary accounting system is being installed, a survey of the mechanical and complementary systems devised for this purpose by the various accounting-machine manufacturers will prove a wise preliminary; it may even be possible to adapt a machine already in use in the office for the preparation of the pay-roll. The essential elements of a system of this kind are a ledger-posting machine incorporating automatic registers, a loose-card ledger housed in posting trolleys, and an electrically-operated typewriter for use in the preparation of cheques and traders' credit lists and the posting of subsidiary loose-leaf ledgers such as the national insurance register.

The ledger in this case will be made up of loose cards, one for each member of the staff, on which are detailed the monthly amounts of gross salary, the individual deductions therefrom— income tax, national insurance, superannuation, etc.—and the resultant net salary. In addition to these salary cards, tax deduction cards, specially designed for machine posting, record for each employee the cumulative figures of gross salary and tax deducted therefrom, these items forming the basis of assessment of the current weekly or monthly tax-deduction. These two cards are of different colour and size to facilitate rapid selection when posting is in progress. Alternatively, a single card system may be operated in which the two functions, the current tax computation and the net salary calculation, are combined. In both systems, however, the automatic compilation of control figures, an essential feature in all machine accounting systems, facilitates supervision and assists in rapid error location where the ledger is adequately sub-divided.

In devising a system of accounts and records for a salaries department it must furthermore be borne in mind that periodic statements of total salary payments and deductions therefrom must be presented in a form that can be easily assimilated in the general accounts. Where departmental costing is practised, or external charges based on salary costs are made for services rendered by the company, this consideration becomes of paramount importance, and applies with equal force to the presentation of figures of employer's contribution to national insurance and staff superannuation schemes. It is essential for each employee to receive with his pay cheque a clear statement of gross salary, the individual deductions therefrom, and the net figure he is to receive. Where, as a result of changed allowances, the basis of tax deduction has altered, a standard form of notice should be included with the salary statement advising the change in code number. This advice can be compared by the employee, for purposes of confirmation, with the notice of change of code number received direct from the tax office.

The cardinal requirement to be observed in the day-to-day administration of accounts, and in this the salary account is no exception, is the prior necessity for a valid authority in support of every change or variation. Whether it is a question of an increment to salary, a change in income tax allowances, or a revoked membership of the general national insurance scheme, an authority from the appropriate official source must first be obtained before effect can be given to the alteration. *General Administration.*

A close liaison should be established between the salaries department and the department in which personnel records and service agreements are filed, to ensure that arrangements with individual employees for agreed periodic increases in salary are automatically notified to the salaries department. From this department notice can be given to the secretary of current automatic salary increments with a request for his authority to implement these changes.

The official responsible for the payment of salaries must be well informed about the law relating to national insurance and P.A.Y.E., not only the law which imposes duties on the employer, but also the law which at first sight concerns only the employee; for the salaries officer is the first person to whom the employee turns when in doubt on, for example, his income tax allowances or the benefits he should receive under national insurance. While it is not usually within the officer's province or power to explain such matters in detail, it is useful to both himself and the employee if he can indicate the cause of the variation and direct the questioner to the appropriate Inland Revenue or National Insurance Office, where the query can be more adequately resolved. The paying officer should keep himself informed, furthermore, on all matters relating to the broader exercise of his duties. The legislation and restrictions on the employment of aliens, the necessity for Bank of England authority for payments to employees serving outside the sterling area, and the obligation to deduct income tax at the standard rate from interest payments by employees on housing and other interest-bearing loans granted by the employing company (the employee being responsible to the Inland Revenue for the declaration of the gross amount of such interest payments), are all matters with which he must be conversant.

Past Salary. Requests for details of an individual's past salary, his tax payments or insurance contributions in previous years and other such comparable queries often require considerable delving into correspondence and records of long standing. It is necessary therefore to keep reference and file records of this nature with a view to facilitating rapid location at a distant date.

Finally, the essentially confidential nature of the work undertaken in a salaries department is a feature that cannot be too strongly stressed when choosing and instructing the staff to operate the accounts, and in selecting from the accommodation available the space in which the staff will carry out its duties.

P.A.Y.E. The operation of the P.A.Y.E. system of income tax collection, which came into force on 6th April, 1944, is governed by the regulations made by the Board of Inland Revenue under the Income Tax (Employments) Act, 1943, and the Income Tax (Offices and Employments) Act, 1944. It applies to all income from offices or employments, including wages, salaries, bonuses, commissions, directors' fees, pensions and expense payments falling under ss. 38 to 46 of the Finance Act, 1948, where exemption has not been obtained under s. 42 of that Act.

General Administration. Before the 6th April, the commencement of the income tax year, each employer is provided with tax deduction cards, one for each employee known to be earning £3 a week or more or £12 10s. a month or more, tax tables and various forms, including an instructions card, which are required in the routine administration of the system. In addition to the general instructions which deal with the treatment of straightforward cases, the Board of Inland Revenue have issued an Employers' Guide to P.A.Y.E., which establishes the procedure to be followed where special problems arise. Should both the card and the guide fail to answer a particular problem, the employer should apply to the Inspector of Taxes for his advice. It should be noted that it is the employer's duty to deduct tax and pay it over to the Collector of Taxes, whether or not he has been directed to do so by the Inland Revenue.

If therefore at 6th April no tax deduction card has been **Tax** received for an employee who is liable to tax, the tax office **Deduction** must be notified at once on form P. 46 and an emergency card **Cards.** (form P. 13) started for the deduction of tax as instructed by the emergency card table. Tax deduction cards are of two types, weekly (P. 9) or monthly (P. 11), and they are completed by reference to the appropriate weekly or monthly tax tables as explained in the general instructions. Where it is desired to use a special form of tax deduction card, for example, in mechanised accounting, approval of the tax office must first be sought.

Each employee has a code number, determined by the tax office on the basis of his income tax allowances, and this is stated on the tax deduction card. Where the code is S.R., tax at the full standard rate must be deducted; code N.T., however, requires that no tax whatever is to be deducted. The code may only be amended on the explicit instruction of the tax office (form P. 6).

Separate tax tables are supplied for each week or month in **Tax Tables.** the year, each table consisting of two parts: Table.A, the free pay table, showing for each code number the total free pay to date; and Table B, the taxable pay table, which shows the total tax due on taxable pay to date. If the total free pay for a given code number (Table A) is deducted from the total gross pay to date, the resulting figure—the taxable pay to date—may be read off on Table B to give the total tax due to date. By simple deduction of the amount of tax already paid for this latter figure, the tax payable for the current period is readily determined. Where the amount of tax already paid is greater than the total tax due to date, as a result of either an increase in allowances giving a higher coding or a reduced current salary payment, then the difference should be refunded to the employee if he is leaving, but otherwise adjusted at the next ensuing pay-day. See Income Tax (Employments) Regulations, 1944, as amended (S.R. and O. 1944, No. 251), regulations 15 (3), 17 and 22 (2) and (3).

Tax must be deducted from all payments of emoluments irrespective of the period in which they were earned. Any adjustment in tax liability between the current and previous fiscal years, arising out of such retrospective payments, will be notified after the annual assessment.

When the pay of an employee reaches or exceeds £3 a week, or £12 10s. a month, the employer must notify the tax office immediately on form P. 46. Tax should not be deducted until a tax deduction card is received.

Form P. 45 must be prepared when an employee leaves; **Employee** part 1 is sent to the tax office, and parts 2 and 3 are handed to **Leaving.** the employee. The tax deduction card must be completed to the date of leaving and retained by the employer until the end of the fiscal year. On the death of an employee, or where the employee is joining H.M. Forces, all three parts of form P. 45 should be sent to the tax office. If an employee goes abroad in continuation of his employment, his remuneration nevertheless being payable in the United Kingdom, the employer must continue to deduct tax unless instructed by the tax office to the contrary.

Employee Joining. Where parts 2 and 3 of form P. 45 are produced by the new employee, a tax deduction card should be prepared in accordance with the general instructions; part 3 should then be completed and forwarded to the tax office. If there is no form P. 45, however, and the earnings equal or exceed £3 a week or £12 10s. a month, form P. 46 should be forwarded to the tax office, and an emergency card prepared for the deduction of tax on the emergency basis until further instructions are received. It should be noted that a refund of tax exceeding £5 may not be made to a new employee on his first pay day without the authority of the tax office.

Where a pension is paid to a pensioner resident overseas, the instructions of the Inspector of Taxes should always be obtained. This is because a pension paid to a pensioner resident overseas *may* suffer tax even where the same pension paid to a pensioner in the United Kingdom would be exempt.

Payment of Tax to the Collector. The amount of tax deducted, less any tax refunded, in any income tax month must be forwarded to the collector within 14 days of the end of that month.

The Annual Return. At the close of the fiscal year the employer must:—

(a) complete the tax deduction cards to show for each employee the pay and tax figures for the present employment, adding any details required of superannuation fund contributions, expenses paid, benefits in kind, etc.;

(b) prepare form P. 35 on which is listed the name of every employee for whom he has held a tax deduction or emergency card in the year, together with the amount of tax deducted or refunded in each case.

The completed cards together with form P. 35 are then sent to the collector. If the employer wishes to retain the tax deduction cards he may do so provided (i) he undertakes to hold them available for as long as the Inland Revenue may require, and (ii) he supplies the collector with a separate document for each employee, giving all the essential details borne by the original. In addition, the employer must give to every employee, from whose pay tax has been deducted, a certificate stating the total remuneration for the year and the total tax deducted therefrom. An official form of certificate (P. 60) is supplied to employers, but where mechanised accounting is practised by the employer it may be found convenient, with the prior authority of the tax office (which is not invariably given), for the employer to provide his own form of certificates. This will enable the form P. 35 and the certificates of pay and tax deduction to be prepared in one operation.

Specimens of the above-mentioned forms relating to P.A.Y.E. will be found in Appendix F, Forms 151 to 160.

Part 4 of the Finance Act, 1948, imposed liability to income tax in respect of expenses payments and benefits in kind made to directors of business concerns generally and those employees whose total emoluments amount to £2,000 per annum or more. Dispensation, under s. 42 of that Act, may in certain circumstances be granted on application to the Inspector of Taxes. The implementation of these provisions is fully explained, however, in a special supplement to the Employer's Guide to P.A.Y.E., and is dealt with in another section of this chapter (see p. 235).

On 5th July, 1948, the present National Insurance Scheme **National** came into operation, the administration of the benefits **Insurance.** and responsibilities that it confers being governed by the National Insurance Act, 1946, and the National Insurance (Industrial Injuries) Act, 1946. The scheme, which applies in general to all persons in Great Britain, irrespective of nationality, who are over school-leaving age, embraces three classes of insured persons:—

Class 1: employed persons: those who work for an employer under a contract of service or paid apprentices;

Class 2: self-employed persons: those in business on their own account, *i.e.* not under the control of an employer;

Class 3: non-employed persons: all insured persons not in Class 1 or Class 2.

The secretary, however, will only be concerned with persons in Class 1, that is, employed persons; the provisions of the Act relating to them, of which the following survey is but a brief outline, are dealt with in detail in the leaflet, 'Employer's Guide to National Insurance,' issued by the Ministry of National Insurance.

For the purpose of collecting the contributions payable in **Arrange-** respect of employed persons the general scheme of national **ments for** insurance is linked with the scheme for insurance against **Collection of** industrial injuries and diseases; the contributions due under **tions.** both schemes, for both the employer and the employee, are paid together, generally as a single stamp on a single contribution card.

The insurance card must be obtained, in the first instance, by **Types of** the employed person, but it is also incumbent on the employer **Cards.**

to see that a card is obtained and produced for stamping. The employer is responsible, furthermore, for the custody of the insurance card while the employment continues. The cards are of four main types, namely those for men aged 18 and over, women aged 18 and over, boys under 18, and girls under 18. There are, in addition, special cards for certain men aged 65 and over (women 60 and over) and certain married women.

If an employed person fails to produce a card for stamping, or if an insurance card is lost or destroyed, the employer must obtain an emergency card from a local National Insurance Office. This must be returned to the office of issue either at the end of its period of currency, or on the termination of the employment, or if the employed person subsequently produces an ordinary insurance card.

Employees' Contribution. The employer is responsible in the first instance for meeting the whole of the cost of the contributions, but he may recover from the employee the proportion of the contribution attributable to him. The contribution card must be stamped for each week for which remuneration is paid even though no services are rendered, with the exception that no contribution is payable for a complete week's absence through sickness. Normally the card must be stamped not later than the time of payment of the wages or salary; stamping should thus take place at weekly, fortnightly or monthly intervals according to **Cancellation of Stamps.** the period for which the remuneration is paid. Stamps must be date-cancelled immediately they have been affixed to a card, and it will probably be convenient to use a metallic die for the purpose. Alternatively, the date may be written in ink across the face of the stamp. Any person removing a stamp from an insurance card is liable to a penalty. Authority may be obtained by employers with regular staffs for the stamping of insurance cards by means of metallic dies—impressed stamping—instead of adhesive stamps. Where the number of regular employees exceeds fifty, permission may also be obtained to stamp at yearly, half-yearly or quarterly intervals.

Annual Exchange of Cards. It should be noted that in order to facilitate the annual exchange of cards, each person has allocated to him one of four different contribution years, A, B, C or D, the terminating dates of which are staggered at quarterly intervals. On the expiration of the period of currency of each category of cards, they must be signed by the employees concerned and forwarded collectively by the employer to the local National Insurance Office; new insurance cards will then be issued in their place.

Rates of Contribution Payable. The table on page 229 sets out the weekly contributions payable by the employer and the employed person in respect of the general scheme and the industrial injuries scheme.

Sex and Age.	National Insurance (General Scheme).			Industrial Injuries Insurance.			Total Joint Contribution.		
	Employer.	Employed Person.	Total.	Employer.	Employed Person.	Total.	Employer.	Employed Person.	Total.
	s. d.	s. d.	s. d.	s. d.	s. d.	s. d.	s. d.	s. d.	s. d.
1. Boys under 18	2 3	2 8	4 11	— 2½	— 2½	— 5	2 5½	2 10½	5 4
2. Girls under 18	1 9	2 2	3 11	— 2	— 2	— 4	1 11	2 4	4 3
3. Men between the ages of 18 and 65..	3 10	4 7	8 5	— 4	— 4	— 8	4 2	4 11	9 1
4. Women between the ages of 18 and 60	3 0	3 7	6 7	— 3	— 3	— 6	3 3	3 10	7 1
5. Men between the ages of 65 and 70 ..				See below					
6. Women between the ages of 60 and 65				(Special Contribution Provisons 1 and 2.)					
7. Men age 70 and over	3 10	—	3 10	— 4	— 4	— 8	4 2	— 4	4 6
8. Women age 65 and over	3 0	—	3 0	— 3	— 3	— 6	3 3	— 3	3 6

Special Contribution Provisions.

1. For persons over pensionable age (men 65, women 60) on 5th July, 1948, contributions are payable at rates shown in lines 7 and 8 of the table.

2. Persons attaining pensionable age after 5th July, 1948, continue to contribute at rates shown in lines 3 and 4 until they retire or reach age 70 in the case of men and 65 in the case of women, when contributions are payable as on lines 7 and 8. Where contributors have not, however, completed five (in some cases ten) years of insurance on attaining pensionable age, contributions then become payable at the rates shown in lines 7 and 8.

3. Married women and widows entitled to widow's benefit (other than the 10s. pension) may elect not to contribute to the general scheme, but they must contribute under the industrial injuries scheme. The employer remains liable, however, for the appropriate contributions to both schemes.

4. Where an employee proceeds abroad in continuation of employment in the United Kingdom, contributions under the industrial injuries scheme are not normally payable by either the employer or the employee; contributions under the general scheme, however, must be maintained by both for the first twelve months of the employment abroad.

5. The rates of contribution are varied in the case of certain apprentices and adult employees remunerated at the rate of 30s. per week or less.

Some Administrative Problems. Action required during Employee's Sickness Absence.

In order to implement the provision that no contribution is required for any week during the whole of which an employed person has been incapacitated for work through illness, the secretary must ensure that the system of reporting sickness absences and return is both comprehensive and subject to a minimum time-lag. This is even more important where the conditions of employment stipulate that at times of sickness absence the salary or wages paid will be reduced by an amount equivalent to the sickness benefit received. It is perhaps superfluous to add that where such a condition of employment obtains, it is essential that the adjustment should be effected by an absolute reduction of the gross salary payment; the practice of leaving the normal gross salary intact, making a subsequent deduction on account of sickness benefits received from the Ministry of National Insurance, involves the sick employee in income tax payments in excess of his true liability.

Company Directors— Employed or Self-Employed.

Difficulty is sometimes experienced by the secretary in determining whether for national insurance purposes a director should be considered as an employed or a self-employed person. The regulations require that directors and managing directors whose duties for the company are performed solely in that capacity, *i.e.* in whose appointment there is no element of a contract of service, must be regarded as self-employed persons, insurable under Class II. Where, however, such a person is also employed under a contract of service by the company of which he is a director, he must properly be regarded as an employed person, insurable under Class I. The question whether in any particular case a director is employed under a separate contract as a servant of the company should be determined by reference to all the conditions of his appointment.

In the event of loss or destruction of national insurance cards while in the possession of the employer, the Ministry will make an allowance in respect of the stamps affixed to the cards at the time of loss or destruction provided satisfactory evidence is offered that (1) adequate provision was made for the safe custody of the cards, and (2) that the cards had actually been stamped to the value of the contributions claimed, and provided furthermore that the loss or destruction is reported as soon as it becomes known to the employer. **Allowance in respect of Contribution Cards lost or destroyed.**

Allowance will not, however, be given in respect of loose stamps lost or destroyed in the interval between purchase and the stamping of the insurance cards. If, therefore, it is considered that the arrangements for the custody of the cards and the recording of individual contributions are sufficient to substantiate a potential claim for allowance in respect of cards either lost or destroyed, it would appear necessary to insure against the loss or destruction of loose stamps only. Insurance on this account might well be effected by incorporation in an existing cash-in-transit policy.

In chapter XVI, the provisions of the Companies Act, 1948, regarding disclosure of directors' remuneration in the statutory accounts have been conveniently summarised with a view to indicating briefly the various headings under which disclosure must be made. If, however, it should fall to the secretary to compute the actual amounts which require to be shown under those various headings, the following more detailed examination of the subject may be of assistance to him. **Directors' Remuneration.**

The provisions regarding disclosure of payments to directors are contained in s. 196, but reference must also be made to s. 198 and to paragraph 19 of the Eighth Schedule.

The amount disclosed must include all emoluments paid to or receivable by any person in respect of his services as director of the company or in respect of his services, while a director of the company, as director of any subsidiary of the company or otherwise in connection with the management of the affairs of the company or any subsidiary. 'Emoluments' is defined as including fees and percentages, any sums paid by way of expenses allowed in so far as those sums are charged to United Kingdom income tax, any contributions paid in respect of directors under any pension scheme and the estimated money value of any other benefits received by them otherwise than in cash. **Directors' Emoluments.**

The amount to be disclosed must include all relevant sums paid by or receivable from the company, the company's subsidiaries, and any other person, except sums to be accounted for to the company or any of its subsidiaries. Attention is drawn to the following points:—

(a) Salaries, such as those received by a director who also holds a managerial position, must be disclosed equally with directors' fees.

(b) Aggregates only are required (sub-divided as indicated below), not the individual amount paid to each director.

(c) Only the emoluments of directors of the parent company must be shown in its accounts, not the emoluments of directors of its subsidiary companies, who are not directors of the parent company itself. But a subsidiary company will, of course, have to show the emoluments of its own directors, and if a director of a company is also a director of its subsidiary, any salary or fees, etc., receivable by him from the subsidiary will have to be included with the amount receivable from the parent company and disclosed in the parent company's accounts. The term 'subsidiary company,' as defined in the Act, includes 'sub-subsidiaries,' and for the purposes of s. 196 'subsidiary company' includes a company of which a director of the company is a director by virtue of the company's nomination, whether or not such company is a subsidiary under the ordinary definition of that term.

(d) Sums to be accounted for to the company or any subsidiary need not be included. This will apply to fees paid by a subsidiary to a director which the director pays over to the parent company. Such sums will not, therefore, be included in the accounts of the parent company, but they will have to be shown in the accounts of the subsidiary which pays them.

(e) With reference to sums paid 'by any other person,' these have to be included only if they are in respect of the directors' services to the company or any subsidiary 'or otherwise in connection with the management of the affairs of the company or any subsidiary thereof.' Outside earnings would not, therefore, be included. The kind of payment intended to be caught by these words was indicated by Lord Chorley in the House of Lords, on the 24th February, 1947. He said (*inter alia*):—

'It is quite possible, and it may happen from time to time, that a director may receive payments in the nature of commissions from persons with whom he enters into business dealings on behalf of his company.

It may be that in some cases such emoluments ought not to be received, but in other cases they are perfectly legitimate and are sanctioned and, therefore, they certainly ought to appear.'

Other payments which answer the description of sums paid by 'any other person' are amounts paid to directors of the subsidiary by the parent company, so far as such sums are paid in connection with the management of the affairs of the subsidiary; such sums would therefore require to be disclosed in the subsidiary company's accounts, although not paid by it. Where it is necessary to do so, the directors may apportion payments between the matters in respect of which they have been paid in such manner as they think appropriate. If, to take an example, a director of a parent company who is also director of a subsidiary receives from the parent company remuneration of say, £5,000 p.a., of which one-half (*i.e.* £2,500 p.a.) is apportioned to his services in respect of the subsidiary, then not only would it be necessary to include £5,000 in the aggregate of directors' remuneration appearing in the parent company's accounts, but it would also be necessary to take the £2,500 into consideration when determining the aggregate to be disclosed in the accounts of the subsidiary company.

(*f*) With reference to expenses allowances, there is no need to include these unless the sums concerned are charged to United Kingdom income tax. The provision is designed to cover disguised remuneration. As the word used is 'charged' not 'chargeable,' the company need not include such amounts unless the director is actually charged thereon by the Inland Revenue and he notifies the company of that fact in accordance with the obligation imposed upon him by s. 198 of the Act.

(*g*) Contributions paid in respect of directors to a pension scheme must be included.

The responsibility for seeing that disclosure is made in accordance with the Act rests, of course, upon the board of directors but, if the requirements of the Act are not complied with, it is the duty of the auditors to include in their report on the accounts a statement giving the required particulars.

Directors' or Past-Directors' Pensions. The aggregate of directors' or past directors' pensions must be shown, whether paid by the company, the company's subsidiaries, or any other person. Pensions paid by persons other than the company and its subsidiaries need be included only if they are receivable in respect of services as director or of the management of the affairs of the company or its subsidiary. There should not be included any pension paid or receivable under a pension scheme if the scheme is such that the contributions are substantially adequate for the maintenance of the scheme. 'Pension' includes any superannuation allowance, superannuation gratuity or similar payment.

Compensation to Directors or Past-Directors in respect of loss of office. The aggregate to be disclosed under this heading must include any sums paid to or receivable by a director or past director by way of compensation for the loss of office as director of the company or for the loss, while director of the company, or on or in connection with his ceasing to be a director of the company, of any other office in connection with the management of the company's affairs or of any office as director or otherwise in connection with the management of the affairs of any subsidiary. 'Compensation for loss of office' includes sums paid as consideration for or in connection with a person's retirement from office. Payments made by other persons must be disclosed as well as those made by the company and its subsidiaries.

The Time Factor. The amounts of directors' emoluments, directors' and former directors' pensions, and directors' and former directors' compensation for loss of office to be shown for any financial year shall be the sums *receivable* in respect of that year, whenever they may be paid. If sums are not receivable in respect of any particular period, they must be included for the year in which they are paid. Expenses allowances which are charged to income tax after the end of the financial year in which they are receivable, must be disclosed in the first accounts in which it is practicable to show them or in a statement annexed thereto, and must be distinguished from the other amounts disclosed. The same rules apply to sums receivable in a year which are not disclosed because they are to be accounted for to the company or any of its subsidiaries and the liability to repay is wholly or partly released or is not enforced within two years.

How Disclosure is Made. The amounts required to be disclosed must be shown 'in any accounts of a company laid before it in general meeting, or in a statement annexed thereto' (which includes the directors' report). The amounts must be shown 'so far as the information is contained in the company's books and papers or the company has a right to obtain it from the persons concerned.' Section 198, however, imposes an obligation upon the directors to give any necessary information to the company in writing; this is important in connection with the expenses allowances charged to tax and payments by persons other than the company and its subsidiaries.

Separate aggregates must be given of emoluments, pensions and compensation for loss of office. Emoluments in respect of services as director must be distinguished from other emoluments; pensions in respect of services as director must be distinguished from other pensions—in other words, pensions for services as director must be shown separately from pensions for service as an employee, for example, general manager; and compensation in respect of the office of director must be distinguished from compensation in respect of other offices. In the case of compensation for loss of office, the two amounts must each be shown so as to distinguish between the sums respectively receivable from the company, the company's subsidiaries and other persons. Remuneration and pensions need not be so distinguished. In the case of consolidated accounts, no particulars of directors' remuneration, etc., need be given, as they will be disclosed in the holding company's own accounts, or directors' report. (Eighth Schedule, Part II, paragraph 19.)

Part IV of the Finance Act, 1948, is of importance to a company secretary, since it imposes upon the company an obligation to submit particulars to the income tax authorities of sums paid in respect of expenses and of the value of benefits in kind given by the company to the following:— **Company to Account for Directors' Expenses Allowances and Benefits in Kind for Income-tax Assessment.**

(a) all directors of a company; and

(b) employees of a company with total emoluments of £2,000 per annum or more, after taking into account any benefits taxable under the Finance Act, 1948, but without deductions under Rule 9, Schedule E, for expenses actually incurred. Where an employee of the company is a director of the company, or a director of any company controlled by the company, the £2,000 per annum limit does not apply. If any employee of the company has several employments with the company or companies controlled by it, the emoluments of all these employments must be aggregated for the purpose of determining whether the £2,000 per annum limit has been reached.

The reason for requiring the company to make a return of the relevant particulars is to provide the Inspector of Taxes with information which will enable him to take into account the value of expenses allowances and benefits in kind received by a director or employee when determining personal liability to income tax. The director or employee concerned* is, however, allowed to claim for a deduction, under Rule 9 of the Rules applicable to Schedule E, in respect of any part of his income which is applied 'wholly, exclusively and necessarily' in performing the duties of his office or employment. Thus, in many cases, the apparent increase in total income as a result of the Finance Act, 1948, is offset by a corresponding increase in the amount of the claim under Rule 9, leaving the amount of assessable income at the same figure as if that Act had not

---

* In this and the next four paragraphs the term 'employee' means an employee paid at the rate of £2,000 per annum or more.

been passed. Part IV is not designed to alter the legal liability of the class of taxpayer affected, but merely to provide machinery which will ensure collection of tax in respect of payments or benefits received which are in fact disguised remuneration.

This process of first raising an assessment in respect of the value of benefits in kind conferred and payments for expenses properly incurred, and subsequently allowing a deduction which cancels the liability to tax may, however, be 'short-circuited' as provided in s. 42. If the company furnishes the income tax authorities with a statement of the cases and the circumstances in which such payments are made, and the authorities are satisfied that no additional tax would fall to be paid thereon, they may notify the company accordingly; the payments will not then be chargeable, and the company will be relieved of its obligation to make the return. It is nevertheless necessary for companies enjoying this concession to keep accurate records of all those items which would otherwise be the subject of a return under the Act, since the income tax authorities have power to revoke their former notification as from the date on which it was originally made, if they think fit.

Benefits. In section 39 of the Finance Act, 1948, details are given of the benefits in kind enjoyed by directors and employees, to which the provisions of Part IV apply. These are:—living or other accommodation, entertainment, domestic or other services, or other benefits or facilities of whatsoever nature. The expense incurred by the company in providing these benefits (or so much of the expense as is not made good to the company by the director or employee concerned) is, for the purposes of the Act, to be regarded as expense incurred by the director or employee, which has been refunded by the company by means of a payment in respect of expenses. Section 39, however, provides that none of the benefits need be taken into account so far as they consist of accommodation, supplies or services provided for the director or employee himself and used by him solely in performing the duties of his office or employment, if they are supplied in the company's business premises. At first glance this relief would not appear to extend to meals, but sub-s. 4 makes it clear that expenses incurred in providing meals are chargeable to tax only if they are given otherwise than 'in any canteen in which meals are provided for the staff generally.' If, therefore, meals are not provided for the staff generally, any meals which are provided will be taxable. In this respect, the authorities may be able to exercise discretion under s. 42.

Living Accommoda-tion. Expense incurred in providing an employee with living accommodation in the company's business premises is not chargeable if the employee is required to live there by the terms of his employment, either in accordance with a practice not less than twenty years old when the Finance Act, 1948, was passed, or because it is necessary that employees of that class should reside on premises of the kind in question (sub-s. 3). This does not apply to directors of the company or of any company which it controls or which controls it; thus if living accommodation is provided for a director he will be charged to tax thereon. The amount upon which tax will be charged will be the rent paid by the company or the Schedule 'A' assessment as reduced for the purposes of collection, whichever is the greater [s. 40 (3)].

Benefits provided for the wife, family, servants, dependants or guests of a director or employee are treated as if provided for the director or employee concerned [s. 45 (2)].

Periodical Statements for Submission to the Board. It is the duty of the secretary to provide the directors with sufficient details of the financial operations of the company to enable them to maintain proper control and direction of its activities.

Financial Statements. The secretary should periodically submit financial statements for the consideration of the directors. The form of these statements will vary according to the nature of the company's business, but in all cases sufficient detail must be included in order to give a correct appraisal of the position, but too much detail should be avoided. If board meetings are held frequently, the financial statements should be submitted at the meetings or circulated shortly beforehand. On the other hand, where formal meetings of the directors are held at infrequent intervals, they should be submitted to the directors individually, and, if this method is adopted, a summary of the information thus provided should be prepared and laid before formal meetings of the board.

The financial statement should show the current cash position of the company, with comparative figures for the previous period, and should incorporate a summarised comparison between the cash book balances and the actual balances as shown by the bank pass books. The actual cash books and a certificate from the company's bankers should be available at the meeting so that the cash statement may be verified by the board of directors. The board may delegate this duty of verification to an individual director; in this event the verification may be made before the actual meeting, but the director concerned should formally report to the next ensuing board meeting that the statement produced has already been verified.

Loan and Deposit Accounts. All loan and deposit accounts, other than those with the company's banks, should be shown separately on the cash statement, and confirmatory certificates obtained from the other parties to these accounts.

Investments. It is the duty of the secretary to keep the board of directors fully informed of all movements and changes in the company's investments. In the case of a company holding relatively few investments a complete list of these investments should be submitted at each board meeting. Where the number of investments is too great to make this desirable, a statement setting out all variations which have occurred since the last meeting should be prepared. The market value of quoted investments should be given and compared with the value at which the respective investments stand in the company's books. The statement should group the various types of investments in categories such as gilt-edged holdings, trade investments, subsidiary companies, etc. A useful addition to the statement is an indication of the percentage of the company's holdings in trade and subsidiary company investments to the total issued capital of each company. Receipt of dividends and interest on share and debenture holdings should be reported to the directors. This information may well be incorporated in the list of investments.

Preparation of Estimated Profit and Loss Account. A statement of estimated profit or loss should be prepared for the directors from time to time as required. Generally, it will be found convenient for these estimated accounts to be prepared at monthly intervals, or, in the case of manufacturing concerns where wages are paid on a weekly basis, at four weekly periods. It is by means of this statement that the board is able to assess the progress of the company's business. The preparation of the profit and loss account is normally the duty of the accountant, but the secretary may have to prepare the periodic estimate. In any case, the secretary must be thoroughly familiar with the basis on which the account is prepared, and must be able properly to interpret it to the directors. In a work of this kind it is clearly impracticable to lay down any specific form in which the estimated profit and loss account should be prepared. It is possible, however, to consider in broad principle what information should be conveyed to the directors by the accountant.

The revenue of the business should be divided into appropriate departmental sections, and so far as practicable the expenses should be treated in the same manner. The general overhead expenses, that is those expenses which cannot be allocated departmentally, should be shown separately as a charge against the total departmental profits. In assessing the estimated profits or losses it is important to specify the basis on which stocks have been valued, and attention should be drawn to any stock lines of which it is proving difficult to dispose. It should be appreciated that generally the estimated profit and loss account is intended to convey trends rather than precise results, and therefore it may be necessary to spread particular items of revenue or expenditure over a period rather than include them in the account for the period in which they occur. Comparative figures for previous periods are a valuable addition to the estimated profit and loss account. The comparative figures shown should be those which give the most informative comparison; thus, in a business which is subject to wide seasonal variations in its activities, it is clearly more valuable to give the corresponding figures for the same period of trading in the previous year than those for, say, the preceding month. The value of comparative figures lies in the inferences that can be drawn from them as to the development of the business, and it is important, therefore, that great care should be exercised in the selection of appropriate sets of figures for comparative purposes.

The profit and loss account should be submitted to the directors relatively soon after each accounting date. In most cases this will necessarily introduce some measure of estimation, both on revenue and expenditure accounts, and, in the event of any of these estimates proving substantially inaccurate, an appropriate adjustment must be made in the following account. If the adjustment is substantial, an explanatory note should be incorporated in the accounts.

The board should also be kept informed of the current debtor position, and here too, comparative figures serve as a useful guide. In preparing this statement overdue accounts should be segregated. For a company with overseas debtors it is generally convenient for the list to be divided geographically, for by this means the board is able readily to consider the company's position in any particular country or area in relation to possible difficulties in collection arising from political or other disturbances.

When a company desires to engage a new employee, a valid **Service** contract of service, which is enforceable in a court of law, can, **Agreements.** as a general rule, be made orally. If, however, the contract is one which cannot in its nature be performed within a year, even if terminable by notice within that time, the company should obtain written evidence of it signed by the employee, for otherwise the contract may not be enforceable. If the contract is complicated, or is an important one, even though writing is not legally essential, it should be reduced to writing, so as to avoid dispute as to what was agreed. Moreover, if any of the terms agreed are to be recorded in writing, the whole agreement should be so recorded; a contract which is partly in writing and partly oral usually gives trouble if a dispute occurs.

The form which the written evidence of the contract should take is largely a matter of individual preference. A letter signed by the employee accepting the terms of employment as set out in a letter from the secretary is usually adequate, but many companies prefer to draw up a formal agreement, for execution both by the employee and by or on behalf of the company. The formal agreement may take the form of a deed, in which case the document would require to be executed under seal, but it would be no less valid if it were simply signed by the employee and by the secretary signing (over a 6*d*. stamp) for and on behalf of the company. In such a case, the secretary should obtain the authority of his board, unless the contract is of a type habitually entered into by him on behalf of the company and his authority in so contracting is acknowledged by the board.

The matters to be covered in a service agreement will vary according to the nature of service to be rendered and other factors, but the following items are mentioned with the purpose of providing a guide to what should be contained in an agreement. A secretary should, nevertheless, undertake the drafting only of simple and straightforward service agreements. Should he be in any doubt or should there be any complication, legal advice should be taken.

(1) Date;

(2) parties to an agreement, with their addresses;

(3) term of the agreement and the opening date;

(4) nature of service to be rendered by employee;

(5) locality in which services are to be rendered;

(6) whether the agreement is terminable by notice and, if so, the form and period of such notice;

(7) a condition that the employee shall not during employment carry on another business in competition with the company;

(8) a clause imposing secrecy in regard to the company's processes, etc.;

(9) provision for the payment of out-of-pocket expenses incurred in the course of duties;

(10) rate of remuneration, including a statement that the directors may increase the rate if they see fit;

(11) frequency of salary payments;

(12) provision for extra remuneration at agreed rate when employee is required to travel overseas for the company;

(13) provision for insurance while overseas;

(14) entitlement to holidays;

(15) termination if through ill-health or other cause the employee cannot perform his duties;

(16) termination by notice in the event of misconduct, breach of conditions, neglect or refusal to carry out duties, bankruptcy or composition with creditors;

(17) provision that the company's consent is required before employee undertakes work for the Government or a trade association;

(18) requirement that employee shall, if eligible, become a member of the staff superannuation scheme;

(19) arbitration clause;

(20) statement that inventions by employee shall belong to the company and that employee shall co-operate with the company in obtaining patents, but at the company's expense.

(21) provision for the payment of a reward at the directors' discretion in respect of any such invention;

(22) requirement that the employee shall deliver up all apparatus and papers relating to the company's affairs when the agreement terminates.

In addition, a contract of employment with an important employee frequently contains provisions to restrain the employee, after he has left the company's service, from entering new employment in competition with the company's business, or from doing various other acts prejudicial to the company, such as soliciting the company's customers. Such provisions, however, should be inserted only after legal advice. The law regards them as being in restraint of trade, and unless their scope is very strictly limited they will not be enforceable.

If the agreement is executed under the seal of the company, it is chargeable with the fixed stamp duty of 10s., counterparts of the agreement being stamped with a denoting fee of 5s. An agreement under the hand of an officer of the company is chargeable with a stamp duty of 6d. only.

CHAPTER XVIII

DIVIDENDS

THE payment of a dividend is a distribution (usually periodical) by a company among its shareholders, out of its profits. No interest can be paid to shareholders out of capital, except in the special circumstances mentioned in s. 65 of the Act, and subject to the provisions of that section.

Payment of Interest out of Capital. The section extends to companies incorporated under the Companies Acts the powers usually granted by private Acts of Parliament to statutory undertakings of paying out of capital interest on paid-up capital during the unprofitable period of construction of works. The section only permits interest to be paid on shares which are issued to provide money for the construction of works or buildings, or the provision of plant, 'which cannot be made profitable for a lengthened period.' The payment must be sanctioned by the company's articles and by the Board of Trade. The rate of interest cannot exceed 4 per cent. (or such other maximum rate as the Treasury may prescribe) and the period for which it is to continue is fixed by the Board of Trade. The capital on which it is paid and the rate of interest must be shown in the company's accounts.

Payment of Dividends. The power to declare a dividend can be vested by the articles in the directors absolutely, but is usually vested either in the directors with the sanction of a general meeting, or in the general meeting of shareholders. Where the power is vested in a general meeting, it is commonly provided that no dividend shall be declared exceeding in amount that recommended by the directors. The directors are generally authorised by the articles to pay to the members such interim dividends as the profits of the company appear to them to justify, but no interim dividend can be paid unless there is such authority in the articles.

All dividends must be paid in cash, unless the articles authorise some other form of payment [*Wood* v. *Odessa Waterworks Co.* (1888), 42 Ch. D. 636].

Unless the regulations otherwise provide, dividends are payable in proportion to the nominal amount of share capital held by each shareholder, irrespective of the amount paid up. For example, A has ten £1 shares with 5s. paid up on each, B has ten £1 shares with 10s. paid up on each; a 10 per cent. dividend is declared; both A and B receive £1 [*Oakbank Oil Co.* v. *Crum* (1883), 8 A.C. 65; *Bridgewater Navigation Co.* (1889), 14 A.C. 525]. The regulations of a company

242

usually, however, provide for the payment of dividends in proportion to the amount of capital paid by each shareholder, as permitted by s. 59 of the Act.

Dividends must be paid in accordance with the rights of the shareholders as fixed by the company's regulations, *i.e.* its memorandum or articles or, frequently, the resolution defining the terms on which the particular shares were issued. Thus the capital of a company may be divided into shares of different classes, *e.g.* preference and ordinary shares, and dividends must be paid accordingly. As to cumulative dividends see chapter V. As to the payment of arrears of dividend on a winding up see chapter XXI, p. 342.

All dividends become due immediately they are declared, but may not be payable until a later date if it is so provided by the resolution declaring the same. They are treated for all purposes as a debt due from the company to the shareholders [*Severn Railway Co.* (1896), 1 Ch. 559], except that under most articles they do not bear interest against the company and that in a winding up they do not rank as debts in case of competition between a member and a creditor who is not a member [s. 212 (1) (*g*)]. Even if a dividend is declared payable in instalments, the right to receive the whole dividend vests in the members immediately and a transfer of shares after such declaration does not pass the right to instalments subsequently payable [*Kidner's Agreement* (1929), 2 Ch. 121]. Once a dividend has been declared it cannot be rescinded by a subsequent resolution either of the board of directors or of the company in general meeting, as the matter is then out of the hands of the directors and also of the company as a whole. The only way in which a dividend may be rescinded is by an approach to each and every shareholder affected by the dividend.

A dividend due is a specialty debt and will become barred **Unclaimed** by the Statute of Limitations if not claimed within twelve **Dividends.** years from the date of declaration [*Artisans' Land Corporation* (1904), 1 Ch. 796]. Where, however, an item 'unclaimed dividends' appears on a company's balance sheet, that will usually constitute an acknowledgment of any unclaimed dividend which is not already statute barred and will permit the dividend so acknowledged from becoming barred for a further period of twelve years from the date of acknowledgment. Oral evidence is admissible to link any individual unclaimed dividend with the aforesaid item in the balance sheet, but each case must depend on its own merits [*Jones* v. *Bellegrove Properties* (1949), 1 All E.R. 498 (1949), 2 All E.R. 198]. In any case, even if a dividend is in fact statute barred, the company is quite entitled to pay it is it chooses. The length of time within which a dividend can be claimed is often provided for in the regulations of the company, the number of years varying in different companies. It is thought that there is no illegality in providing in articles that dividends unclaimed for a specified time will be forfeited, though one learned text-writer (see Palmer's *Company Precedents*, Vol. I, 15th edition, p. 726) suggests that such a provision is of doubtful validity. In any event the Council of the Stock Exchange objects to any such provision (see Appendix D), and consequently, if an official quotation is desired, it should not be inserted. If shares are forfeited it does not mean that unclaimed dividends declared on those shares are forfeited unless there is an express provision to this effect, but where a clause in the articles gives the company a lien on the shares of a member for sums due by him to the company, it usually extends that lien to dividends which are due but have not been encashed (see Table A, clause 11).

Whether or not unclaimed dividends lying to the company's credit may be used by the company in its business depends on the articles of the company. Unclaimed dividends are specialty debts and are not held in trust for the shareholders. It would seem, then, that in the absence of an express provision to the contrary unclaimed dividends may be so used. To be on the safe side an article such as the following is frequently adopted: 'All dividends unclaimed for one year after having been declared may be invested or otherwise made use of by the directors for the benefit of the company until claimed.'

A form of resolution to pay a dividend is given in chapter XIV.

Out of what Moneys Payable. As stated above, the fundamental rule with regard to the payment of dividends is that no dividends shall be paid out of capital; such a payment, being an *ultra vires* act on the part of the company, constitutes a breach of trust by the directors, and renders them liable to make good to the company any amount so paid [*Oxford Building Society* (1886), 35 Ch. D. 502; *Flitcroft's Case* (1882), 21 Ch. D. 519; *Masonic Assurance Co. v. Sharpe* (1892), 1 Ch. 154]. No such payment can be made, even though the memorandum [*Verner v. General and Commercial Trust* (1894), 2 Ch. 239], or articles [*Trevor v. Whitworth* (1887), 12 A.C. 409; *Masonic Assurance Co. v. Sharpe* (*supra*)], or a general meeting [*Flitcroft's Case* (*supra*)] purport to authorise it. As to the meaning of profits, see *Spanish Prospecting Co.* (1911), 1 Ch. 92; *L.C. Ltd.* (in voluntary liquidation) v. *G. B. Ollivant Ltd. and others* (1944), 60 T.L.R. at p. 338.

The question then arises whether dividends can be paid out of the revenue, or only out of the net profits after taking from revenue such amount as may be necessary to keep the capital intact. The answer depends upon the constitution and objects of each company [*Davison v. Gillies* (1879), 16 Ch. D. 347 (n); *Lambert v. Neuchatel Asphalte Co.* (1882),

51 L.J. Ch. 882] and varies with the class of business carried on. The question whether a company has profits available for distribution must be answered according to the circumstances of each particular case, the nature of the company, and the evidence of competent witnesses [*Bond* v. *Barrow Hæmatite Co.* (1902), 1 Ch. 353; *Hoare & Co. Ltd.* and reduced (1904), (1904), 2 Ch. 206; *Brown* v. *Gaumount-British Picture Corporation Ltd.* (1932), 2 All E.R. 609].

The following are some general principles extracted from the more important cases on the subject:—

1. The "fixed capital" of a company need not be maintained out of revenue, but the "circulating capital" must be made good before dividends are paid. **Fixed and Circulating Capital.**

Fixed capital is used to denote that portion of the company's assets which consists of investments of a more or less permanent form, such as land, buildings, plant, or securities purchased for the sake of the income they produce.

Circulating capital, on the other hand, consists of that portion of the company's assets which is used for "turnover" purposes. 'Fixed capital may be sunk or lost and yet current receipts over current payments may be divided, but the floating or circulating capital must be kept up as otherwise it will enter into and form part of such excess, in which case to divide such excess without deducting the capital which forms part of it will be contrary to law.' [Per Lindley L.J., *Verner* v. *General and Commercial Trust* (1894), 2 Ch. 239.] For a judicial explanation of the nature of fixed and circulating capital, see *Ammonia Soda Co.* v. *Chamberlain* (1918), 1 Ch. 266, per Swinfen Eady, L.J., at pp. 286 and 287.

2. If the objects of a company include the investment of capital in wasting property, depreciation by waste need not necessarily appear in the revenue account [*Lee* v. *Neuchatel Asphalte Co.* (1889), 41 Ch. D. 1]. It is for the shareholders to decide whether they will have a sinking fund to meet the waste (*Verner* v. *General and Commercial Trust, supra*).

3. A company may set off an appreciation in the value of its capital assets, as ascertained by *bona fide* valuation, against losses on revenue account [*Ammonia Soda Co.* v. *Chamberlain* (*supra*)]. The greatest caution should be exercised in distributing dividends on the basis of a valuation showing an appreciation, however great. There is no legal authority against pursuing such a course in a proper case, but it is a practice obviously open to abuse, and in many cases would lead the auditors to give a qualified report.

4. The position is different where assets have appreciated and have been realised. Thus, if the capital account is in credit, the credit balance, when realised, may, if the constitution of the company allows it, be distributed by way of

dividend. In such a case the dividend is usually discribed as a 'capital bonus.' There is nothing in the Act to prevent this, and there is no obligation to retain realised appreciation of the capital [*Lubbock* v. *British Bank of South America* (1892), 2 Ch. 198]. See Buckley, 12th Edn., p. 905.

5. If the capital account is in credit, the credit balance, when realised, may be used for the payment of dividends or a capital bonus free of tax, if the constitution of the company allows it, since there is nothing in the statute to prevent it, and there is no obligation to retain realised appreciation of the capital [*Lubbock* v. *British Bank of South America* (1892), 2 Ch. 198].

Reserve. The articles of a company usually contain a clause empowering the directors, before recommending any dividend, to set aside out of the profits of the company such sum as they think proper as a reserve fund which is to be applicable, at the discretion of the directors, for any purpose to which the profits of the company may be properly applied (see *e.g.* Table A, cl. 117). Even without such provision, a reserve fund may be formed, if the shareholders approve, and may be invested in such securities as the directors may select, subject to the control of a general meeting [*Burland* v. *Earle* (1902), A.C. 83]. Power is usually given to use the reserve fund in the business of the company. In practice, a general reserve fund is usually treated as employed in the company's business and appears in the accounts simply as a book-entry on the liabilities side of the balance sheet; there are in such a case no separate assets representing the reserve, which is constituted simply as an undivided part of the whole of the company's assets. A special reserve, set up for a particular purpose, *e.g.* to pay pensions, is more frequently represented by particular assets, usually Government securities.

Where the memorandum of a company provides that the profits available for dividend shall be distributed as directed, and the articles contain a clause similar to the above, a reserve fund may be created, if the directors think fit, before any distribution of dividend [*Fisher* v. *Black and White* (1901), 1 Ch. 174]. But if the memorandum is so framed as to give the holders of any particular class of shares a right to insist on the application of profits in paying dividends on such shares before any part of such profits is carried to reserve, that right will be enforced [*Evling* v. *Israel & Oppenheimer, Ltd.* (1918), 1 Ch. 102; *Buenos Ayres Great Southern Railway Co. Ltd.* v. *Preston* (1947), Ch. 384.]

If the fund is accumulated out of profits, it can be treated as undivided profits, and dividends can be paid thereout. It retains its character of undivided profits until effective steps are taken to capitalise it.

If a company issues redeemable preference shares and **Capital** redeems them out of profits, a special capital redemption **Redemption** reserve fund must be created (see s. 58 and *supra*, p. 36). **Reserve.** A company must also set up a special capital reserve, to be called 'share premium account,' when it issues shares at a premium (s. 56). The share premium account is treated as part of the share capital of the company and cannot be paid away in dividends.

It is often desired to distribute a bonus out of reserve, **Capitalisa-** satisfying it by the issue of fully paid shares. In such a **tion of** case it becomes necessary to capitalise such portion of the **Profits.** reserve as is required for the purpose, thereby divesting it of its character of undivided profits. In order that a company may properly carry out a scheme of this kind, it may be necessary to make certain alterations in its articles of association. The reserve fund article must authorise the payment out of the reserve fund of a special dividend or bonus; and, further, there must be a power to satisfy a dividend or bonus by the issue of fully or partly paid shares; for, as has been stated above, dividends can only be paid in cash, unless some other form of satisfaction is authorised by the articles. The article which enables the company to satisfy the bonus by the allotment of fully paid shares or debentures will authorise the company, by resolution in general meeting, to capitalise any part of the undivided profits and to distribute the same as a bonus, power being given to the directors to make provision as to fractions. Bonus shares so issued are issued for a consideration other than cash, and therefore, on making the return as to allotments (see s. 52), a contract or contracts constituting the title of the allottees to the shares must be filed. The contract is in the form of an agreement made between the company of the one part and, usually, the secretary of the company on behalf of the shareholders specified in a schedule to the agreement of the other part. It is stamped with 10s. impressed stamp duty.

The capital redemption reserve fund may be used for paying up and issuing fully paid bonus shares in the event and to the extent specified in s. 58 (5) (see *supra*, p. 37).

The articles having been altered if and so far as is necessary, and the capital of the company, if necessary, increased, the resolution to capitalise the profits will be passed, and the matter in due course carried out. If the article is so framed that it is necessary expressly to declare a bonus, the bonus will be made payable free of income tax. This can be done as the company will have already paid income tax on the profits used for the purpose of the bonus if they are taxable, while, if they represent capital appreciation, they will not be liable for income tax in the hands of the recipient [*Inland Revenue* v. *Reid's Trustees*

I

(1947), S. C. 700; Tax Leaflet No. 1429]; and they will not be liable to income tax even though the distribution may, as between tenant for life and remainderman, be regarded as income [re *Doughty* (1947), Ch. 263]. The article is, however, often framed in such terms that the resolution need not expressly declare a bonus. For an example of such an article, see Palmer's *Company Precedents*, Vol 1, 15th Ed., p. 722.

In cases where the issued shares of a company are not fully paid, a dividend can be declared out of the undivided profits and applied in paying a call made on the shares. The shares thus become fully paid and profits to the extent of the unpaid liability capitalised. It would, however, be better, in order to avoid any claim for income tax, to proceed under an appropriate article authorising the application of reserve fund or other undistributed profits in paying up partly paid shares.

Dividend Warrants. On the declaration of a dividend, warrants must be prepared. In practice it is usually possible to prepare and fill in all warrants and have them ready for despatch before the general meeting at which the dividend is formally declared. They can then be posted after the meeting. A form of dividend list is found in Appendix F, Form 66. In the case of large companies the use of machines greatly facilitates the work of preparing the warrants. If there is any likelihood of the company in general meeting declaring a dividend less in amount than that recommended by the directors, the warrants should not be prepared in advance. The resolution of the meeting is, however, in almost all cases merely a formal sanctioning of the previous recommendation of the board.

Facsimile Signatures. The following precautions should be adopted when facsimile signatures are used in dividend warrants:—

(i) The number of warrants printed with fascimile signatures is limited to approximately the actual number to be issued, leaving only a few spares in case any new ones are required in respect of errors. The warrants are numbered consecutively, and are kept in the company's office under the control of a responsible member of the staff, who issues only the exact number required according to the dividend sheets. If any warrant is spoilt in writing it has to be produced to the responsible clerk and cancelled before another warrant is issued in its place.

(ii) When written, the warrants are checked by the company's auditors or by responsible members of the company's own staff, who initial each warrant in a space provided for the purpose.

(iii) Immediately all warrants have been written and checked, the bank is informed of the total number of warrants which will be issued and the serial numbers of such warrants. They are also given the date which appears on the impressed revenue stamp on the warrants, and are informed that the warrants have been initialled by certain persons, with specimens of whose initials they are supplied.

(iv) When the warrants have been issued, all those in excess of the number used are immediately cancelled and the blocks for the fascimile signatures are obtained from the printers and carefully preserved.

(v) The printers furnish the company with a certificate of the number of warrants that they have printed and include a statement that they have broken up the type and have destroyed or cancelled all prints, other than those supplied to the company.

(vi) If any warrants have to be replaced after issue when no warrants with facsimile signatures are available, an ordinary form of dividend warrant, a supply of which would be printed with the others, would be used and signed by hand.

A form of dividend warrant and debenture stock warrant will be found in Appendix F, Forms 61 and 64, and also a form of dividend request by a shareholder requiring the company to pay dividends in a particular way (Form 62). A similar form, attached to a request by the company for a specimen signature, which is often sent out with share or stock certificates in the case of new holdings, is also given (Form 63). When forms of dividend request are received by the company, they must be carefully preserved. At the same time as the dividend warrants are sent out, a cheque should be sent to the company's bankers to cover the total amount to be disbursed by the bank. On the death of a joint holder, it is advisable, in order to avoid difficulty, for the company to ask the survivors to complete a new form of mandate for payment of dividends, or to write to the survivors or their solicitors stating that existing dividend mandates will be continued in force unless advice is received to the contrary. When a dividend mandate from a corporation is given under hand only, the company should insist upon the mandate containing at least two signatures on behalf of the corporation or upon being furnished with satisfactory evidence of the authority of the person signing. If these precautions were not taken, the company might be successfully sued for negligence, and be liable to repay dividends to the corporation if they were misappropriated.

In the case of coupons on share warrants to bearer, arrangements may be made for their presentation and payment at the company's bank, or, if thought fit, at the registered office of the company.

The articles of a company commonly provide that dividends may be sent through the post. As to joint holders, it is usually provided that the warrants shall, unless otherwise directed (*i.e.* by a dividend request), be sent to the registered address of the one whose name stands first on the register in respect of the joint holding, and that any one joint holder may give effectual receipts for dividends.

In the event of a dividend warrant being lost or mislaid, a fresh one should not be issued without a satisfactory indemnity. A form of indemnity and request for a duplicate dividend warrant is given in Appendix F, Form 65, and a form of stop notice in Form 67. Except in cases where the amount of the dividend is very large, this indemnity will probably be considered sufficient, but the guarantee of a third party in addition may occasionally be required.

The payment of dividends to a shareholder may be prevented by notice in lieu of distringas.

As to the payment of dividends to infants, see p. 116.

CHAPTER XIX

MORTGAGES, DEBENTURES AND RECEIVERS

PRACTICALLY all companies have an express power to borrow, **Borrowing** which is conferred by the memorandum of association, and **Powers.** in almost all cases this express power to borrow is coupled with a power to give security for the loan upon the company's property.

A trading company, however, has in general an implied power to borrow [*General Auction Co.* v. *Smith* (1891), 3 Ch. 432], and where a company has power to borrow, it can, unless forbidden by its memorandum or articles, give security, *e.g.* by mortgaging its property [*Patent File Co.* (1870), 6 Ch. App. 83].

The express power to borrow, which most companies possess, generally includes the power to "raise" money. The use of the word "raise" is not meaningless, since a power to borrow money merely, without power also to raise money, does not enable a company to issue irredeemable debentures, which are really a perpetual annuity [*Southern Brazilian Railway Co.* (1905), 2 Ch. 78].

The power to borrow may be exercised by the directors, if the articles expressly or impliedly authorise them to exercise it. Sometimes the exercise of the power is placed in the hands of the company in general meeting, but this is frequently inconvenient. It may be, for example, that a temporary overdraft is required, and if the power to borrow were exerciseable only by the company, it would be necessary to convene a general meeting before the transaction could be carried out.

The usual plan, however, is for the directors to be authorised to exercise the borrowing powers of the company up to a certain limit which must not be exceeded without the sanction of the company in general meeting. If permission to deal is to be obtained from the Stock Exchange, the articles must limit the borrowing powers of the board (see Appendix D). The limit may be the amount of the nominal capital of the company, or the amount of the issued capital of the company for the time being, or any other reasonable sum.

It has already been seen that, by s. 109 of the Act, a company may not exercise its borrowing powers until it has received a certificate entitling it to commence business, but that a company may nevertheless, before it obtains the certificate, offer shares and debentures simultaneously for public subscription, may allot shares and debentures, and may receive money payable on application for debentures.

Where a company has power to borrow and wishes to raise money more permanently than by a mere bank overdraft, the method usually employed is to issue debentures or debenture stock. There is, of course, nothing to prevent a company securing a loan from an individual by a specific mortgage of some or all of its freehold or leasehold property, or securing an overdraft by the guarantee of its directors or others, or securing any loan by any method available to an individual, but the common practice is for a company to secure its loans by the issue of debentures.

The following is an illustration of a directors' resolution for the creation of debentures. It should not, however, be used as a precedent, as each resolution must be carefully drafted in accordance with the circumstances of the case.

1. THAT the company do create £   per cent. first mortgage debenture stock 19   (hereinafter referred to as 'the stock') in accordance with the following terms:—

(a) The stock to be limited in the first instance to £   , but power to be reserved to the company to create and issue further debenture stock ranking *pari passu* in point of security with the stock, provided that the principal amount of the stock then outstanding including all such additional stock shall not exceed £   .

(b) Interest to be payable half yearly on   and   .

(c) The stock to be subject to redemption by the operation of an annual cumulative sinking fund of   per cent. commencing in the year ending the   , 19 , the sinking fund to be applied in the purchase of stock in the market at or under par (exclusive of accrued interest but inclusive of expenses) or, failing such purchases, by drawings at par.

(d) Power to be reserved to the company to redeem the whole or any part (to be selected by drawings) of the stock then outstanding as follows:—

On the   , 19 , and thereafter up to and including the   , 19 , at   per cent.
On the   , 19 , and thereafter up to and including the   , 19 , at   per cent.
After the   , 19 , at par,

together in each case with accrued interest.

(e) Any stock outstanding on the   , 19 , to be repaid at par on that date.

(*f*) The stock to be constituted by a trust deed in favour of   as trustees and to be secured by a first specific charge by way of legal mortgage on the freehold and leasehold properties of the company and a first floating charge on its undertaking and all its other assets for the time being both present and future (including its uncalled capital).

2. THAT the said trust deed be in the form of the draft (subject to any modifications approved by the company's solicitors and trustees) now produced to the board and approved and that the common seal of the company be affixed to an engrossment or engrossments thereof in due course.

3. THAT the offer of to underwrite the issue of the stock for a commission of   per cent. on the nominal amount of the stock on the terms of the underwriting letter now produced to the board be and is hereby approved and accepted and that the chairman be authorised to sign an acceptance of such offer on behalf of the company.

4. THAT the stock be offered for public subscription and the print of the prospectus to be issued by the company and the forms of application to accompany the same now produced to the board be and they are hereby approved and that the secretary be authorised to arrange for their despatch.

5. THAT the secretary be authorised to instruct   Bank Limited to take in application moneys; to receive on behalf of the company all moneys payable by subscribers and underwriters; and generally to do all such acts and things as may be necessary or incidental to the issue of the stock.

6. THAT the company shall comply with all formalities necessary to ensure that permission to deal in and quotation for the stock be obtained from The Stock Exchange, London, and that   as brokers to the company be authorised to make application for such quotation on behalf of the company.

"In my opinion a debenture means a document which **Nature of** either creates a debt or acknowledges it, and any document **Debentures.** which fulfils either of these conditions is a debenture. I cannot find any precise legal definition of the term; it is not either in law or commerce a strictly technical term, or what is called a term of art" [per Chitty, J., in *Levy* v. *Abercorris Slate Co.* (1887), 37 Ch. D. at p. 264; see also *Knightsbridge Estate Trust Ltd.* v. *Byrne* (1940), A.C. at p. 621].

A debenture is a document, not necessarily under the seal of the company [*Lemon* v. *Austin Friars Investment Trust* (1926), Ch. 1], acknowledging or creating a liability to pay a sum of money with or without interest thereon at a specified rate. The money may be payable at a fixed date, or on notice, or the debt may be irredeemable or redeemable only on the happening of a contingency, however remote [s. 89]. The debenture may be payable to bearer, in which case it is a negotiable instrument passing by delivery, or it may be registered in the name of the proprietor, the registered holder. The payment of principal and interest need not be secured at all, in which case the debenture amounts to a mere promise to pay; but more commonly the payment is secured by a mortgage or charge on the property of the company. The charge may be created (a) by a trust deed, to the benefit of which the debenture holders are by the words of the debentures declared to be *pari passu* entitled; or (b) by the language of the debenture itself. In either case the charge may be: (1) a fixed charge on the property of the company; (2) a floating charge on the property of the company; (3) a fixed charge on some and a floating charge on other parts of the property of the company.

Debentures secured by Trust Deed. In the case of debentures secured by trust deed the specific property which is to be secured is mortgaged to trustees upon trusts for the benefit of the debenture holders, and the deed prescribes the terms and conditions on which the security is to be held, and, if need be, enforced, by the trustees. In most cases the deed also contains a floating charge on the undertaking and the assets of the company. The debentures themselves, by one of the conditions endorsed thereon, declare the holders to be entitled *pari passu* to the benefit of, and subject to the provisions in, the trust deed, the terms of which are thus incorporated in the debentures. The debentures, even though a specific charge is created by the trust deed, often contain a general charge on the undertaking of the company.

The advantages of a trust deed are that a legal mortgage can be created in favour of the trustees, and that they, as representing the whole body of debenture holders, can act more conveniently on their behalf.

The trust deed also usually contains provisions for the calling of meetings of the debenture holders at which a specified majority (usually three-fourths) is able by resolution to bind the minority, and such provisions are valid [*Follit* v. *Eddystone Granite Quarries* (1892), 3 Ch. 75], but a majority will not be allowed to exercise its voting power in such a way as to defraud a minority [*New York Taxicab Co.* (1913), 1 Ch. 1].

The powers given to the majority should be strictly defined, as the court will refuse to allow the will of the majority to override that of the minority except in regard to matters definitely provided for in the trust deed, *e.g.* a power to release the mortgaged premises does not include a power to release the company; a power to modify the rights of the debenture holders does not include a power to relinquish their rights; a power to compromise their rights pre-supposes some dispute about them, or difficulty in enforcing them, and cannot be exercised where there is no such dispute or difficulty [*Mercantile Investment Trust Co.* v. *International Co. of Mexico* (1891), reported in footnote to *Sneath* v. *Valley Gold* (1893), I Ch. 477]. Moreover, even if the modification is within the express provision of the deed, the resolution effecting the modification may not be upheld if it is contrary to the interest of the class and is only carried by the vote of a debenture holder with a special interest in securing the modification [*British America Nickel Corporation* v. *M. J. O'Brien, Ltd.* (1927), A.C. 369; approving, but distinguishing, *Goodfellow* v. *Nelson Line* (1912), 2 Ch. 324].

For the Stock Exchange regulations as to trust deeds, see Appendix D.

The fact that the articles of association empower the directors to borrow does not restrict the company's general power to borrow which may be exercised through its properly authorised agents [*Mercantile Bank of India Ltd.* v. *Chartered Bank of India, Australia and China and Strauss & Co.* (1937), I All E.R. 231]. A lender dealing with such agent need not enquire as to the agent's authority, which is a matter of the internal management of the company, unless there is some provision in the memorandum or articles restricting the company's power to borrow through agents.

Section 88 of the Act has considerably curtailed the right of **Liability of** trustees under a trust deed (or under a contract with the **Trustees for** holders of debentures secured by a trust deed) to be indemni- **Debenture** fied against liability for breach of trust in cases where, having **holders.** regard to the provisions of the trust deed, they have failed to show the degree of care and diligence required of trustees. Section 88 lays down the general rule that any provisions containing such indemnity shall be void, but there are exceptions to this rule as follows:—

(i) A trustee is not deprived of any exemption or right to be indemnified in respect of anything done or omitted to be done by him while such provisions are in force.

(ii) No provision in force on 1st July, 1948, is invalidated so long as any person then entitled to or afterwards given the benefit of the provision remains a trustee of the deed. It should be noted that, while any trustee remains entitled to this benefit, the benefit of the provision may be given to all trustees present or future, or to any named trustees or proposed trustees, by a resolution passed by a majority of not less than three-fourths in value of the debenture holders present in person (or by proxy where permitted) at a meeting summoned for the purpose [s. 88 (4)].

(iii) A release, otherwise valid, may be given in respect of anything done or omitted to be done by a trustee before the release is given.

(iv) Section 88 does not invalidate a provision enabling such release to be given (a) if it is agreed to by a majority of three-fourths in value of the debenture holders present in person (or by proxy where permitted) at a meeting summoned for the purpose; (b) either with respect to specific acts or omissions or in the case of a trustee dying or ceasing to act.

The remedies of the debenture holder depend for the most part on the provisions of the trust deed. The deed generally provides that on default by the company the trustees may enter, sell the property charged, and distribute the proceeds amongst the debenture holders. The trustees may be plaintiffs in an action to enforce the charge, or one debenture holder may generally sue on behalf of the class, in which case the trustees as well as the company are defendants. A receiver can be appointed by the court in a proper case, or by the trustees under the power in the trust deed; a manager can also be appointed where necessary. As to receivers and managers, see p. 265 *et seq.*

Debentures secured without a Trust Deed. In the case of debentures secured without a trust deed the security is created solely by a charge contained in the debenture itself, charging the property which is to be the security with the payment of the mortgage debt. The debenture usually contains conditions providing for the enforcement of the security.

It seems doubtful whether the holder of debentures of this class has the remedies of a mortgagee under the Law of Property Act, 1925 [cf. *Blaker* v. *Herts & Essex Waterworks Co.* (1889), 41 C.D. 399, a case of a statutory company]. Accordingly the debenture usually provides that, if the security becomes enforceable, a majority of the debenture holders may exercise the power of sale and of appointing a receiver (see below) conferred by the Law of Property Act, 1925, s. 101, and that they may enter into possession. A debenture holder may bring an action on behalf of himself and other debenture holders to enforce the security, and the court may make a declaration of the charge, appoint a receiver and sometimes a manager (see below), direct necessary accounts and inquiries and order a foreclosure or sale of the mortgaged property. A debenture holder may also bring an action in his own name upon the covenant by the company contained in the debenture to pay the principal and interest. He may also petition the court to wind up the company. When the principal and interest are in arrear, the debenture holder is entitled as between himself and the company to a winding up order *ex debito justitiae*, but the court has discretion to refuse such an order in certain circumstances, *e.g.* if the petition is opposed by the majority of creditors and the petitioner would derive no substantial benefit from the order [*Western of Canada Oil Co.* (1873), L.R. 17 Eq. 1; *Chapel House Colliery Co.*, 24 C.D. 259].

A fixed charge is usually given upon the immovable property **Fixed and** of the company, while a floating charge as a rule covers the **Floating** whole of the undertaking and property, including stock- **Charges.** in-trade, book debts and cash of the company and all other property not subject to the fixed charge and including also as a rule the uncalled capital of the company.

A floating charge leaves the company free to use the property the subject of the charge as it pleases until the charge attaches; thus it is a charge on the company as a going concern, which will not attach until the company ceases to be a going concern [*Governments Stock Co.* v. *Manila Railway Co.* (1879), A.C. 81; *Borax Co.* (1901), 1 Ch. 326; *Illingworth* v. *Houldsworth* (1904), A.C. 355], or until, by the conditions (if any) of the debenture, the floating charge attaches. The usual conditions are if execution or distress is levied against the company, or if the company goes into liquidation or ceases to carry on business. (See Appendix F, Form 69.)

A floating charge does not prevent the company from creating mortgages on the property charged, unless there is a declaration that the company shall not have power to mortgage in priority to the floating charge [*Wheatley* v. *Silkstone Coal Co.* (1885), 29 Ch. D. 715; and see *Cox-Moore* v. *Peruvian Corporation* (1908), 1 Ch. 604]. Even if there is a declaration that the company has not power to make a mortgage in priority to, or *pari passu* with, a floating charge, this may be defeated by a legal mortgagee of any property subject to the charge other than land who can show that he had no knowledge of any clause in the floating charge preventing him from having the full benefit of his legal mortgage [*English and Scottish Investment Co.* v. *Brunton* (1892), 2 Q.B. 700]. As regards land, it is thought that the debenture holder will be protected by registration under s. 95; for such registration is equivalent to registration under the Land Charges Act, 1925 [see s. 10 (5) of that Act], and, under s. 198 of the Law of Property Act, 1925, a subsequent mortgagee will be deemed to have actual notice of the instrument creating the charge for all purposes. The company has complete power to deal with the property subject to the floating charge, until the company is wound up or a receiver put in [*Government Stock Co.* v,

Manila Railway, supra; Florence Land Co. (1878), 10 Ch. D. 530]. When a floating charge attaches, the rights of the debenture holders are good as against an execution creditor or general creditors of the company [*Davey* v. *Williamson* (1898), 2 Q.B. 194].

By s. 322 of the Act, a floating charge created within twelve months* of the commencement of a winding up is only good to the extent of the amount then or subsequently actually advanced to the company, with interest at 5 per cent., unless the company was solvent at the date when the floating charge was given. A company is not solvent within the meaning of the section if it is unable to pay its debts as they become due [*Patrick & Lyon* (1933), Ch. 786]. A floating charge may also, by s. 94, be postponed to preferential creditors.

Unsecured Debentures. The term "naked debentures" is frequently used to describe debentures which are not secured by any charge. They are simply promises to pay a certain sum. If the document is under seal, the debt is a speciality debt, but the holder is merely an unsecured creditor of the company, and he cannot prevent the company, unless it is so provided by the conditions of the debenture, from issuing mortgage debentures which will rank in priority to his claim.

The holder may bring an action against the company for the principal and interest due, and, if necessary, issue execution on his judgment; or he may present a petition for winding up the company, either before or after obtaining judgment; or, if a winding up is in progress, he may prove for the debt as an ordinary unsecured creditor.

Bearer Debentures. Debentures, whether secured by a trust deed, or by a charge, or unsecured, may be payable to the registered holder or to bearer. A debenture to bearer is a negotiable instrument and transferable by delivery, and is so treated by the law merchant [*Bechuanaland Exploration Co.* v. *London Trading Bank* (1898), 2 Q.B. 658]. Restrictions are imposed upon the issue and transfer of bearer debentures by the Exchange Control Act, 1947 (see p. 439, below). Details of the procedure as to deposit with authorised depositaries and collection of dividends through such depositaries are given in Appendix M.

Since a debenture to bearer is a negotiable instrument the property therein will pass on delivery free from all equities between the company and the original or intermediate holders, and the delivery by the holder to the company of the debenture and the interest coupons will be a good discharge to the company for the principal and interest respectively.

Debenture Stock. Debenture stock is a term used to denote the consolidated mass of capital sums lent to a company, which is usually

---

* Six months if the charge was created before 1st January, 1948.

secured by a trust deed creating a mortgage or charge in favour of the trustees upon the property forming the security. The trust deed usually provides that each stockholder shall be entitled to a certificate stating the amount of the stock to which he is entitled. The trust deed further provides for a register of holders being kept, and for transfers of the stock in certain fractions, and usually contains provisions for repayment of the stock and for enforcing the charge. The incidents of debenture stock are for practical purposes the same as those of debentures, and the holders of the stock occupy a position very similar to that of the holders of debentures. The term 'debenture' when used in the Act 'includes debenture stock, bonds and any other securities of the company, whether constituting a charge on the assets of the company or not' (s. 455).

Provisional scrip to bearer is often issued to applicants for **Scrip.** debentures and debenture stock, before the instalments are finally paid up and the debenture itself or the stock certificates issued. The scrip is a negotiable instrument, with the consequence that any person taking it in good faith and for value obtains a title to it, independent of the title of the person from whom he takes it [*Goodwin* v. *Robarts* (1876), 1 A.C. 476]. Transfer may be made by delivery. Stamp duty on scrip to bearer was abolished by the Finance Act, 1949.

Debentures giving a charge on the company's property **Registration.** need not be registered under the Bills of Sale Acts, 1878, and 1882 [*Standard Manufacturing Co.* (1891), 1 Ch. 627]; nor need trust deeds be registered under those Acts [*Richards* v. *Kidderminster Overseers* (1896), 2 Ch. 212].

There is, however, an elaborate system of registration of charges (which expression includes mortgages) prescribed by the Act, with which companies must comply. The object of the system is the protection of creditors and persons dealing with the company by compelling publicity of secured loans. The existing system is a double system, for not only must charges be registered with the Registrar, but the company must also itself keep a register of charges. It is unnecessary here to give in detail the relevant provisions of the Act, but the more important features of each of the two branches of registration are summarised.

1. The register kept by the Companies Registration **'Bush** Department at Bush House must contain the following:— **House' Register.**

(A) As regards companies registered in England,

    (i) a statement of the total amount of all the other secured indebtedness of the company created after July 1st, 1908, in respect of mortgages and charges of the first six classes set out in (ii);

    (ii) the statutory particulars of all mortgages and charges created after the fixed date mentioned below being either:

        (a) a charge for the purpose of securing any issue of debentures; or

        (b) a charge on uncalled share capital of the company; or

        (c) a charge created or evidenced by an instrument which, if executed by an individual, would require registration as a bill of sale; or

        (d) a charge on any land, wherever situate, or any interest therein, but not including a charge for any rent or other periodical sum issuing out of land; or

        (e) a charge on book debts of the company; or

        (f) a floating charge on the undertaking or property of the company; or

        (g) a charge on calls made but not paid; or

        (h) a charge on a ship or any share of a ship; or

        (i) a charge on goodwill, on a patent or a license under a patent, on a trademark or on a copyright or a license under a copyright [s. 95 (2)].

        The fixed date in relation to charges of the classes (a) to (f) is 1st July, 1908, and in relation to charges of the classes (g), (h) and (i) 1st November, 1929;

    (iii) the statutory particulars of charges on property acquired by a company after 31st October, 1929, subject to a subsisting charge which, if created by the company, would have required registration under s. 95 (s. 97).

(B) As regards companies incorporated outside England, but having a place of business in England:—

    (i) the statutory particulars of charges on property in England created by such companies since 31st October, 1929, which, if created by English companies, would have required registration under s. 95 (s. 106);

    (ii) the statutory particulars of charges on property acquired by such companies after 31st October, 1929, subject to a subsisting charge which, if created by an English company, would have required registration under s. 95 (s. 106).

These provisions apply to all companies registered outside England which have an established place of business in England (s. 106). They apply therefore (*inter alia*) to Scottish companies having a place of business in England.

It will be observed that loans secured by a deposit of **Loans by** shares are not included, nor are loans secured by the deposit **Deposit of** of acceptances, warrants, or other negotiable instruments. **Securities.** The list of mortgages and charges requiring registration at Bush House is thus still not complete.

Registration under s. 95 must be effected within 21 days **Time and** after the creation of the charge. To do so, the instrument **Mode of** (if any) by which the mortgage or charge is created or evidenced **Registration.** or in certain cases a copy thereof [see sub-ss. (3) and (5)], verified as required by Rule 4 of the Companies (Forms) Order, 1949, must be delivered to the Registrar, and in addition certain particulars are required to be furnished as set out in Companies (Forms) Order, 1949, Form 47 (see Appendix F, Form 72). These include the date and description of the instrument creating or evidencing the mortgage or charge, the amount secured, short particulars of the property charged, and the names, addresses and descriptions of the mortgagees or persons entitled to the charge. Further, the amount or rate of any discount or commission to subscribers for debentures must be given [s. 95 (9)]. In the case of a series of debentures, the particulars are in many respects different [s. 95 (8) and Companies (Forms) Order, 1949, Forms 47A and 48]. (See Appendix F, Forms 73 and 76; see also Form 75, being a certificate of registration in Scotland or Northern Ireland of a charge comprising property situate there.)

Where a company registered in England acquires any property which is subject to a charge which would, if it had been created by the company after the acquisition of the property, have been required to be registered under the Act, the company must cause the prescribed particulars of the charge [see Companies (Forms) Order, 1949, Form 47B] (see Appendix F, Form 74), together with a certified copy of the instrument, if any, by which the charge was created or evidenced, to be delivered to the Registrar of Companies within 21 days after completion of the acquisition. In the case of a charge created outside Great Britain on property situated outside Great Britain, the period of 21 days runs from the date on which the copy of the instrument could in due course of post, and if posted with due diligence, have been received in the United Kingdom [cf. s. 95 (3)].

Moreover, by s. 106, the provisions as to registration extend also to charges on property in England created, and to charges on property in England acquired, after the commencement of the Act by any company incorporated in Scotland or in any other place outside England if such company has an established place of business in England.

On registration the Registrar must give a certificate of registration [s. 98 (2)], and a copy of the certificate must be endorsed on every debenture, or certificate of debenture stock, issued after the creation of the charge [s. 99 (1)].

This register is open to the inspection of any person whatsoever on payment of a fee of one shilling for each inspection [s. 98 (3)].

It should be observed that the appointment of a receiver and the fact of his ceasing to act, must also be registered (s. 102).

Effect of Non-Registration. The effect of non-registration of a charge created by a company registered in England is that the mortgage or charge is void against the liquidator and any creditor of the company, and on its so becoming void (*i.e.* at the expiration of the twenty-one days allowed for registration) the money secured is immediately to become payable [s. 95 (1)]. The effect would apparently be the same if the charge were created by a company registered outside England, but having a place of business in England (s. 106). Charges which only require registration under s. 97, or under s. 106 if the charge subsisted before the property was acquired by the company, would not be void for want of registration, but penalties are imposed for any default in the obligations as to registration [see ss. 96, 97 (2) and 106]. The court may in certain cases extend the time for registration or direct the correction of mistakes (s. 101).

Company's Register. 2. *The Company's Register.*—By s. 104 of the Act every limited company must keep a register of charges at its registered office (see Appendix F, Form 82). This register should furnish a complete record of all the secured indebtedness of the company, since there must be entered therein 'all charges specifically affecting property of the company and all floating charges on the undertaking or any property of the company, giving in each case a short description of the property charged, the amount of the charge and, except in the case of securities to bearer, the names of the persons entitled thereto.'

In the case of the company's register, however, the registration of a mortgage or charge is not a condition precedent to its validity [*Wright* v. *Horton* (1887), 12 A.C. 371], but the officers of the company are liable to penalties for knowingly authorising the omission of a necessary entry [s. 104 (2)].

Copies of the instruments creating any charge requiring registration at Bush House must be kept at the registered office of the company although, in the case of a uniform series of debentures, a copy of one debenture will suffice (s. 103). These copies and the register itself must be open to the inspection of creditors and shareholders *gratis*, and the register must be open to the inspection of any other person on payment of a fee not exceeding one shilling for each inspection [s. 105 (1)]. The right to inspect includes the right to take copies [*Nelson* v. *Anglo-American Land Co.* (1897), 1 Ch. 130]. This decision appears to be based upon the fact that the section contains no provision as to a person being entitled to require copies on payment, and is therefore not in conflict with the decision as to taking copies of the register of members mentioned on p. 110. The company may impose reasonable restrictions as to the time during which inspection will be permitted, but at least two hours a day during business hours must be allowed for inspection. Penalties are imposed for unlawful refusal of inspection, and the court may compel immediate inspection [s. 105 (2), (3)].

In addition to the above register of charges, a company may keep a register of debenture holders. The Act does not compel a company to keep such a register, but unless the debentures are all payable to bearer a register is in practice necessary. By s. 87 of the Act, the register (if any) must be open to the inspection both of the debenture holders themselves and of shareholders of the company, except when closed in accordance with the provisions contained in the articles of the company or in the debentures or debenture stock certificates, or in the trust deed or other document securing the debentures or debenture stock for a period or periods not exceeding thirty days in any year. Inspection must be permitted for at least two hours in every day. A debenture holder or shareholder may require a copy of the register or any part of it on payment of sixpence for every hundred words required to be copied. He may also require a copy of a trust deed which has not been printed on payment at the same rate, or a copy of a printed trust deed on payment of a sum not exceeding one shilling. If inspection or copies are refused the company and its officers are liable to penalties, and the court may by order compel the company to comply. *Register of Debenture Holders.*

If a register of debenture holders is kept, it must be kept in accordance with the provisions of s. 86 of the Act, which apply both where the register (or its duplicate) is kept in Great Britain and where a duplicate is kept in Great Britain of any register kept outside Great Britain. The provisions may be summarised as follows: (1) In the case of a company registered in England, both register and duplicate must be kept in England, and, where a company is registered in Scotland, they must be kept in Scotland. (2) Whether the company is registered in England or in Scotland, the register must be kept either (a) at the company's registered office; or (b) at some other office of the company where the register is made up; or (c) at the office of any firm or any other company engaged to make up the register. (3) Where both a register and a duplicate are kept they must be kept at the same place. (4) Where part of a register is kept inside Great Britain and part outside, the part kept in Great Britain will be the principal register. (5) The Registrar of Companies must be informed of the place where the register and duplicate (if any) are kept and of any change in that place, unless register and duplicate are and have at all material times been kept at the company's registered office (see Appendix F, Form 78). A register of debenture holders should be kept substantially in the same manner as a share register (see Appendix F, Form 85). It may be noted that there is no statutory provision against the notice of trusts in the register of debenture holders (cf. s. 117), although it is uncommon to find a trust deed which does not give the directors power to refuse to register trusts. The trust deed or the debentures usually also contain provisions dealing with transfer of a debenture, death of a debenture holder and like matters.

Specimens of a mortgage debenture stock certificate and of a debenture stock certificate will be found in Appendix F, Forms 70 and 71.

Redemption of Debentures. When a debenture is paid off by the company, a formal receipt should be taken from the debenture holder, releasing the company from all claims in respect of the debenture, which should be surrendered to the company for cancellation. A certificate for debenture stock should similarly be surrendered. A form of redemption receipt is given in Appendix F, Form 84. Where only some of a series of debentures is to be redeemed at any one time, the selection of the debentures to be redeemed is often made by drawing lots. A form of letter giving notice of redemption will be found in Appendix F, Form 83.

Although there is no statutory obligation to lodge with the Registrar a memorandum of satisfaction of a mortgage or charge, the Registrar may, on evidence being given to his satisfaction that the debt for which the charge was given has been paid or satisfied, in whole or in part, direct the entry on the register of a memorandum of satisfaction (s. 100), and it is clearly to the interest of a company that this should be done. For the appropriate forms, see Companies (Forms) Order, 1949, Forms 49, 49A and 49B (see Appendix F, Forms 79, 80 and 81). The court has ordered an incorrect entry of satisfaction to be cancelled [*Light & Co.* (1917), W.N. 77].

Transfers. Transfers of registered debentures are effected in the manner provided by the conditions of the debenture, and on registration of the transfer the name and address of the new holder is endorsed on the debenture or the trust deed. The personal representative of a deceased holder is entitled, without the execution of any transfer, to have his own name placed on the register without any reference to his representative capacity [*Edwards* v. *Ransomes & Rapier, Ltd.* (1930), W.N. 180]. A specimen debenture transfer form, which is the usual form in current use, is given in Appendix F, Form 77.

It has already been pointed out that among the remedies **Receivers.**
of a debenture holder, when entitled to enforce his security,
is the right to appoint, or to apply to the court to appoint,
a receiver. It is common for the conditions of a debenture
to provide that, upon the security becoming enforceable, the
holder, or, in the case of a series of debentures, the holders of
a certain proportion of the debentures, may, by writing
under his or their hands, appoint a receiver with specified
powers. Whether or not this right exists, a debenture holder,
when entitled to enforce his security, can always commence
a debenture holder's action, and immediately after doing so
can apply to the court to appoint a receiver. A body
corporate cannot be appointed receiver (s. 366). An undischarged bankrupt may not act as receiver or manager
unless (a) the appointment under which he acts and the
bankruptcy were both prior to 1st July, 1948; or (b) he is
appointed by the court (s. 367).

The position of a receiver appointed by the court differs
considerably from that of a receiver appointed by debenture
holders themselves by virtue of a power contained in their
debentures. If the appointment is made by the court and the
company is being wound up by the court in England, the
Official Receiver can be appointed (s. 368).

Under the 1929 Act a receiver appointed by the debenture **Appointed by**
holders was usually agent of the company and incurred no **Debenture**
personal liability for his acts, but, if the power appointing him **Holders.**
so provided, he might be the agent for the debenture holders
or the trustees. It is provided by s. 369 of the 1948 Act
that a receiver appointed out of court shall be personally
liable on contracts entered into by him in the performance of
his functions (unless the contract otherwise provides) to the
same extent as if he had been appointed by the court. He is,
however, entitled to an indemnity out of the assets of the
company unless he entered into such contracts without
authority. Section 369 does not affect any right of indemnity
which he may have apart from the section, and the provision
does not apply to contracts entered into before 1st July, 1948.
A receiver or manager appointed out of court is now given
power to apply to the court for directions in relation to any
matter arising in connection with the performance of his
functions [s. 369 (1)]. On such an application the court has
wide powers to give directions, and to make such order as it
thinks just, declaring the rights of persons 'before the court
or otherwise.'

It was held in *Northern Garage Ltd.* (1946), Ch. 188, that, if
the court has made an order in the presence of the liquidator
under the Courts Emergency Powers Acts authorising a
debenture holder to exercise any remedy available to him
by way of the appointment of a receiver, such order implies

authorisation for the debenture holder to appoint a receiver who may then sell without further leave under the Courts Emergency Powers Acts.

Where a receiver has been appointed he 'entirely supersedes the company in the conduct of its business, deprives it of all power to enter into contracts in relation to that business or to sell, pledge or otherwise dispose of the property put into the possession or under the control of the receiver and manager.' It should be borne in mind, however, that the company still continues to exist, and the directors will be liable if the company fails to make the proper returns to the Registrar of Companies. This is so even if there are no funds out of which to pay the directors' fees, the whole of the company's assets having been taken over by the receiver. In such a case it may prove the wisest course to allow the company to be dissolved under s. 353 of the Act (see chapter XXI, p. 348). If it is intended to pursue this course, the directors should hold a meeting at which the resignation of the secretary and other officers should be accepted. The directors should then formally hand in their resignations addressed to the company. Notice of the resignation of the directors should then be filed with the Registrar. For this course to be pursued, the articles must provide for the resignation of directors in writing and must not require formal acceptance by the board of directors.

Duties. By s. 102 of the Companies Act, 1948, any person who appoints a receiver or manager under the powers contained in any instrument must within seven days of the appointment give notice to the Registrar. There are penalties for default. A receiver, although this notification to the Registrar is not his own duty, should nevertheless satisfy himself that it is being, or has been, done.

The statutory duties of a receiver appointed by debenture holders or their trustees are:—

In the case where a receiver or manager of the whole or substantially the whole of the company's property is appointed on behalf of the holders of any debentures of the company secured by a floating charge:—

(1) The receiver or manager shall forthwith inform the company of his appointment; the company must then within fourteen days of receiving the notice (unless the time is extended by the court or the receiver) furnish a statement as to the company's affairs in the form prescribed by the Board of Trade (s. 372). This statement should show (as at the date of the receiver's appointment) the particulars of the company's assets, debts and liabilities, the names, residences and occupations of its creditors, the securities held

by them and when they were given respectively, and such further information as the receiver may demand (s. 373). The statement should be verified by one or more directors of the company and by the secretary, and this verification should be by affidavit. Section 373 of the Act also provides that the receiver (subject to the directions of the court) may require certain other persons to submit and verify the statement.

(2) The receiver should then, within two months of receiving this statement, send the following documents:—(a) To the Registrar and to the court, a copy of this statement with his comments on it (if any). The Registrar should also receive a summary of the statement and any comments. (b) To the company, a copy of his comments or, if there are no comments, a notice to that effect. (c) To the trustees for the debenture holders on whose behalf he was appointed and to all debenture holders of whose addresses he is aware, a copy of the summary of the statement.

(3) Section 372 (2) provides that, within two months after the end of every twelve months' period of service (which period may be extended by the court, or by the Board of Trade if the receiver is appointed out of court) the receiver must send an abstract of his receipts and payments covering the relevant period to the following persons: (a) the Registrar, (b) the company, (c) the trustees for the debenture holders of the company on whose behalf he was appointed, and (d) all debenture holders whose addresses are known to him. A similar abstract must also be sent when a receiver ceases to act, and in this case the abstract must also show the aggregate total of his receipts and payments since his appointment.

(4) Where s. 374 applies (viz. in any case where a receiver is appointed under the powers contained in any instrument and he is not appointed on behalf of the holders of any debentures of the company secured by a floating charge as is the case under s. 372) the receiver must within one month (or such longer period as the Registrar allows) after the end of every six months' period of appointment send the Registrar an abstract similar to that required under s. 372 (2) above.

(5) On ceasing to act, the receiver must give the Registrar notice to that effect (s. 102).

(6) In the case of debentures secured by a floating charge (unless a winding up is in progress), the receiver must pay out of any assets coming to his hands, in priority to any principal or interest due on the debentures, the debts which in a winding up are entitled to preferential payment (s. 94).

The expression 'assets coming to his hands' in s. 94 includes assets which are subject to any floating charge, but not assets subject to a fixed charge created by the debentures [*Lewis Merthyr Consolidated Collieries* (1929), 1 Ch. 498].

The date as at which these debts are to be reckoned is the date of the appointment of the receiver, or of his taking possession.

His general duties depend to a great extent upon the terms of his appointment, and are closely analogous to those of a liquidator, so far as the collection and realisation of assets is concerned. As a rule, a receiver has express power given him to take possession of all or any of the property subject to the charge, to carry on the company's business, to sell, and to compromise, but he cannot carry on the business unless he is expressly empowered to do so.

He will accordingly enter into possession, and, if so authorised, carry on the business, collect the assets, and, if necessary, sell all or any of them. Out of the proceeds he will pay the expenses of the business, interest on prior charges, preferential debts and his own remuneration, after which he will pay to the debenture holders the interest due to them.

Under the 1929 Act the court had power to fix the remuneration of a receiver or manager on the application of the liquidator, if the company was in liquidation. Section 371 of the Act of 1948 extends this power in the following manner: the power of the court is made retrospective and may be exercisable even if the receiver or manager has died before the application is made. Further, in special circumstances, the court may require the receiver or his personal representatives to repay any amount in excess of that fixed by the court for the period.

Appointed by the Court. A motion to the court to appoint a receiver and manager is ordinarily the next step after the issue of a writ in a debenture holder's action. A receiver, and, if the business is a going concern, a manager, will be appointed in the following circumstances: (i) if either principal or interest is in arrear; or (ii) if the security is in jeopardy, *e.g.* by a threatened winding up, or by execution having been issued on a judgment against the company; or (iii) if the assets are in danger owing to disputes between the directors [*Stanfield* v. *Gibbons* (1925), W.N. 11].

When the court appoints a receiver it assumes the protection of the property which constitutes the security of the debenture holders, and holds it for their benefit. A receiver appointed by the court, and a manager appointed by the court, are officers of the court, and any interference with their possession or acts is contempt of court. They are agents neither of the company nor of the debenture holders. They are under the direction of the court; and, since the court cannot be liable as their principal, it follows that they are *prima facie* personally liable, although they have a right of indemnity against the assets [*Burt* v. *Bull* (1895), 1 Q.B. 276; *Strapp* v. *Bull* (1895), 2 Ch. 1].

A receiver appointed by the court must give security to account for what he receives. He is entitled to a proper salary or allowance for the performance of his duties.

His appointment must be notified to the Registrar by the person at whose instance it was obtained within seven days from the date of the order appointing him [s. 102 (1)]. The usual order directs an enquiry as to the preferential payments to be made under s. 94 of the Act and provides for the receiver passing his accounts at intervals, generally of six months.

His duties are to take possession, to collect rents and debts, and generally to act as owner of the property charged. He may obtain the directions of the court as to taking any contemplated step, and he should always do so where it is proposed to incur expenses, *e.g.* by borrowing money. As manager, when a favourable opportunity for a sale arises, and a sale is necessary in order to pay off the principal due on the debentures, he will invariably apply for the consent of the court to the proposed sale before attempting to carry it out.

If a receiver or manager is appointed by the court, or the debenture holders, any letters, etc., invoices, orders for goods or business letters on which the name of the company appears, must contain a statement that a receiver or manager has been appointed [s. 370], and if the company is being wound up, that fact must also be stated on each such document [s. 338].

If (*a*) a receiver makes default for more than 14 days after written notice has been served on him to make good the default in filing, delivering or making any return, account or other document, or in giving any notice required by law, or (*b*) a receiver or manager appointed by the debenture holders or trustees for them fails, after demand by the liquidator therefor, to render proper accounts and pay the amount due to the liquidator, the court may order the default to be made good and direct the costs of the application to be borne by the receiver (s. 375).

CHAPTER XX

RECONSTRUCTION, AMALGAMATION AND SCHEMES OF ARRANGEMENT

It is proposed in this chapter to give some account of the reconstruction of companies, indicating briefly the methods by which such reconstructions can be carried out. 'Reconstruction' is a word which is often used loosely, but inaccurately, to include amalgamations, absorptions, reorganisations, and arrangements of all kinds, and any such transaction is commonly described as a reconstruction scheme. It is in that sense that the word is used as the title of this chapter.

There are many reasons why reconstruction may be desirable; the following in particular may be mentioned. Often it is the result of a company having passed through a period of financial stress. The company may have been unable to pay its debts, but it may suit the creditors better to acquire an interest in the 'equity' of the company rather than to wind it up. The reconstruction will then give the creditors shares in exchange for their debts and cut down drastically the interests of the original shareholders. Or the company may, without becoming commercially insolvent, have been unable to pay its preference dividends for some years; it may then benefit all classes of shareholders that the arrears of preference dividend should be cancelled, the preference shareholders being compensated by a transfer of part of the ordinary shares. To take another example, it may be necessary to cut down the rights of the existing shareholders in order to raise new money essential to the company's business. Reconstruction, on the other hand, may be required for other reasons than financial stress. Amalgamation, for example, where two existing companies are to be combined, involves the reorganisation of the companies' share capitals, and often their replacement by shares in a new company. Again, it sometimes happens that a company's capital structure becomes in course of time unsuited to its needs; it may, for example, have founders' shares carrying exceptional rights to dividend which embarrass the directors in considering what reserves to set up, what new money to raise, and so forth. Generally, it is inconvenient for a large public company to have a highly unusual capital structure, and a reconstruction to rearrange the capital on more usual lines is likely to be an advantage. Finally, there may be special reasons for desiring to replace the existing company by an entirely new company; for example, to replace an English company by a foreign company or by another English company having much more extended objects.

This chapter indicates how such reconstruction can be carried out. The terms of the reconstruction will depend on the circumstances of the particular company. Generally reconstruction is a matter of altering shareholders' rights, giving new shares, either in the same or a new company in exchange for existing shares, or giving shares to creditors in satisfaction of their debts. Where the reconstruction is occasioned by financial stress, it will often be accompanied by a reduction of capital, existing shares being to some extent written off.

Articles of association frequently contain an article enabling the rights of a particular class of shareholders to be altered with the sanction of a resolution of a separate meeting of that class, *e.g.* clause 4 of Table A, Part I. A simple reorganisation of capital, which involves only an alteration in the rights attached to the different classes of shares, can be carried through by means of such an article, and requires only the necessary resolution of class meetings, and, as a rule, a special resolution of the company in general meeting to alter the articles which define the rights of the shares. Where, however, the articles do not contain such a provision for class meetings, or where the reorganisation is more complicated—for example, if creditors are involved or a new company is to be formed or a compulsory transfer of shares from one person to another is contemplated—it is necessary to make use of one of the following methods of reconstruction:—

(i) a sale under s. 287 of the Companies Act, 1948;

(ii) a sale under the powers in the memorandum of association;

(iii) a scheme of arrangement under s. 206 of the Act;

(iv) a scheme of arrangement with creditors alone under s. 306 of the Act; or

(v) the acquisition of a complete or controlling interest in a company.

In addition reconstruction may be effected by special Act of Parliament; but this method is rarely needed except by statutory companies, to which the provisions for reconstruction under the Act do not apply.

Method (iv) is little used, since a scheme of arrangement with creditors alone under s. 306 is unsatisfactory in all but the simplest cases. An arrangement between a company about to be, or in the course of being, wound up voluntarily, and its creditors, is binding on the company if sanctioned by an extraordinary resolution, and on the creditors if acceded to by three-fourths in number and value of the creditors, subject to an appeal to the court within three weeks by any creditor or contributory. A composition with creditors intending to make the company solvent and therefore to prevent a winding up is not within the section [*Contal Radio* (1932), 2 Ch. 66]. Since the required majority of creditors is more difficult to obtain than that required in the case of an arrangement under s. 206, and, further, since there is no power to bind classes of creditors, it is almost always better to proceed under s. 206 (see p. 283).

Of the remaining methods of reconstruction mentioned above, (i), (iii) and (v) are by far the most important, but it will be necessary later to deal shortly with (ii). It may be stated at the outset, that though the basis of most reconstructions is either s. 287 or s. 206 of the Act, yet in a very large number of cases the scheme is complicated by various other elements, *e.g.* subdivision of shares, or reduction of capital. If a reduction of capital is included in a scheme, the provisions of the Act relating to reduction must be strictly complied with, and the reduction cannot be effected merely by obtaining the sanction of the court to the reduction as part of the scheme [*Cooper, Cooper and Johnson* (1902), 51 W.R. 314]. It is not possible here to deal in detail with complex schemes of the nature just indicated.

Reconstruction under Section 287. Reconstruction under s. 287, involving the formation of a new company, is frequently resorted to when it is desired to obtain further working capital and the ordinary means of so doing are impracticable. It may also be utilised for various other purposes, *e.g.* as an alternative to a petition for reduction, or in some cases for alteration of objects, or to effect an alteration in the respective rights of more than one class of shareholders when these are fixed by the memorandum. Briefly, what happens is that a new company is formed, the existing company is put into liquidation and the undertaking of the existing company is sold to the new company in exchange for fully-paid shares of the new company; these new shares are either issued to the liquidator of the old company and divided by him among its shareholders, or else issued direct to the shareholders in the old company. As part of the consideration for the sale the new company will usually take over the debts of the old company.

The expense involved in registering a new company and transferring to it the old company's assets at one time discouraged reconstructions of this class when other means were available, but this objection has largely disappeared since the Finance Act, 1927, s. 55, came into force. By that section relief from capital and transfer stamp duty is given in case of reconstructions or amalgamations of companies where not less than 90 per cent. of the shares of the transferee company is acquired. Section 55 has been amended by the Finance

Act, 1928, s. 31, and the Finance Act, 1930, s. 42, which has in turn been amended by the Finance Act, 1938, s. 50 (see Appendix J). If it is desired to take advantage of s. 55 of the Finance Act, 1929, care must be taken to see that the requisite conditions are complied with, not only in the scheme as formulated [sub-s. (1)], but also in the scheme as carried out [s. 55 (6)]. The shares in the new company must be issued to and registered in the names of holders of shares in the old company. The issue of letters of allotment with a form of renunciation has been held not to amount to an issue of shares within the meaning of the Finance Act, 1927, and may therefore result in the exemption from capital duty not being obtained. [*Tillotson* v. *I.R. Commissioners* (1933), 1 K.B. 134; cf. also *Murex* v. *I.R. Commissioners* (1933), 1 K.B. 173; *Brotex Cellulose Fibres* v. *I.R. Commissioners* (1933), 1 K.B. 158]. The draftsmen of the necessary documents must also bear in mind the provisions of s. 55 (3) as to the form of the documents.

Relief from stamp duty in the case of transfers as between associated companies is granted by the Finance Act, 1930, s. 42, where one of the companies is the beneficial owner of ninety per cent. of the issued share capital of the other company or not less than ninety per cent. of the issued share capital of each of the companies is in the beneficial ownership of a third company (see Appendix J). This exemption may be useful where a holding company wishes to reconstruct one of its subsidiaries.

The effect of s. 287 is to enable the liquidator of a company in a members' voluntary liquidation (see p. 313) with the sanction of a special resolution (which may be passed either before or concurrently with or after the resolution for winding up), to sell the whole or any part of its business or property to another company (whether a company within the meaning of the Act or not). In such a case the consideration for the sale is either wholly or in part shares, policies or other like interests in the purchasing company for distribution among the members of the selling company, or the right for the shareholders of the old company to participate in the profits of, or receive any other benefit from, the new company. The power is, however, subject to the right of a dissentient shareholder to require the liquidator to purchase his interest. Accordingly, a three-fourths majority may effectively resolve upon this form of reconstruction, subject only to the liability to purchase the rights of a dissentient minority.

By s. 298 the provisions of s. 287 are made applicable also in the case of a creditors' voluntary winding up (see p. 313), with the modification that any powers conferred on the liquidator under that section can be exercised only with the sanction either of the court or of the committee of inspection. **Procedure under Section 287.**

The general procedure in this kind of reconstruction is shortly as follows. The agreement for sale to the new company, which will embody the particulars of the proposed scheme, must first be prepared. If the circumstances of the case permit, a meeting of directors will then be held and a statutory declaration of solvency made and filed under s. 283 of the Act (see p. 310) before the notices of the general meeting of the company are sent out. A meeting of the old company will then be convened for the purpose of passing a special resolution for winding up and appointing a liquidator, and a special resolution authorising the liquidator to enter into the proposed agreement. The meeting is held and the special resolutions passed, after which notice of the winding up resolutions must be inserted in the *Gazette*, and a printed copy of the special resolution forwarded to the Registrar. The new company will then be registered and the sale agreement duly entered into; in due course the shares in the new company will be distributed among the shareholders of the old company. The winding up of the old company will be completed, the final meeting held, and the return of the final meeting will be filed with the Registrar, the company becoming automatically dissolved three months thereafter. Section 287 will mainly be used in the case of a members' voluntary winding up. If, however, the liquidation is a creditors' voluntary winding up, the creditors' meeting must be held in accordance with s. 293, and, by virtue of s. 298, the liquidator will be unable to act on the resolution under s. 287 authorising the agreement for sale without the sanction of the court or the committee of inspection if one has been appointed under s. 295. If the requisite sanction is obtained, the subsequent proceedings will be similar to those in a members' voluntary winding up, though the completion of the winding up will be governed by different sections of the Act.

The new company is frequently registered with a name identical with that of the old. This is permissible under s. 17 unless the Board of Trade considers it undesirable. Unless the objects of the company are being enlarged, it is often advisable to retain the old name. As regards the distribution of the consideration, *i.e.* of the shares of the new company, among the shareholders of the old, it is always better to provide for their allotment direct to the persons entitled, in order to avoid the expense of transfer stamps and fees; but if the shares are partly paid it is especially desirable, in the liquidator's interest, that this should be done, since he might incur serious liabilities by taking partly paid shares into his own name.

A reconstruction of this kind is simple, unless more working capital is wanted. If the sole object of the reconstruction is to enable the company to carry on a class of business which it has no power to carry on, and objection to alteration of the memorandum has been successfully made under s. 5 of the Act, then the memorandum of the new company will be drawn to contain the necessary power, and after the sale is complete a share of the new company will (subject to adjustment in respect of undivided profits, or accumulated loss, valuation of assets, goodwill and similar consideration augmenting or diminishing the equity of the shareholders) be allotted for each share of the old company of the same value and denomination. Apart from the matter of dissentients, the result will be that a new company, exactly the same as the old, with the same board, the same capital, the same shareholders, and the same articles, and, perhaps, the same name, will continue to trade with enlarged powers. If, on the other hand, the object of the reconstruction is to write off 50 per cent. of the capital of the company which has been lost, or is unrepresented by available assets, each shareholder in the old company will receive, say, for every fully-paid £1 share held by him a fully-paid 10s. share in the new company; and, irrespective of this reduction, the same undertaking will be carried on by substantially the same people.

On a reconstruction of this kind, under s. 287 of the Act, **Alteration** the shares in the new company will be divided among the **of Rights.** shareholders in the old company in accordance with their rights on a winding up under the regulations of the old company, unless those regulations authorise a division in some other way [*Griffith* v. *Paget* (1877), 5 Ch. D. 894]. Thus, it may, for example, be impossible to give preference shares in the new company to the preference shareholders of the old company and ordinary shares in the new company to ordinary shareholders of the old company. For this reason articles often contain an express power to the liquidator to divide up the shares in the new company otherwise than in accordance with the shareholders' rights. Or again, if the articles contain provision for altering the rights of classes with the sanction of a class meeting, the necessary alteration of right can be made before the reconstruction is carried through. In other cases it is necessary to resort to a scheme of arrangement under s. 206 of the Act [method (iii), above]; under that section the court can sanction a distribution otherwise than in accordance with the rights of shareholders, but usually requires that the scheme shall give the same protection to dissentient members as would be given by s. 287 [*Anglo-Continental Supply Co.* (1922), 2 Ch. 723].

In a reconstruction under s. 287 the matter of dissentients **Dissentients.** is important. The number of dissentients might be more than a quarter of the shareholders, since the meeting at which the special resolution was passed might not be representative. Where there is likely to be any considerable amount of

dissent, the precaution will, in general, be taken of circularis-
ing the shareholders in advance to ascertain their views on
the proposed reconstruction, and, if there appears to be a
preponderance of dissent, the scheme will, of course, be
abandoned. The position of a shareholder in the old company is this: he may either (1) assent to the reconstruction and
claim the shares to which he is entitled; or (2) dissent as
provided by the section; or (3) he may do neither. To be entitled to dissent he must not have voted in favour of the resolution at the meeting, and within seven days after the passing of
the resolution he must leave at the registered office of the
company a written notice expressing his dissent and requiring
the liquidator either to abstain from carrying the resolution
into effect, or to purchase his interest as provided by the Act.
Two decisions as to the notice of dissent should be observed.
One is to the effect that the liquidator may waive a failure of a
dissentient to comply with a condition of the section which
was inserted solely for the benefit of the dissentient: thus, a
notice, even if not left at the registered office, may be accepted
by the liquidator [*Brailey* v. *Rhodesia Consolidated* (1910), 2 Ch.
95]. The other (following an earlier decision) lays down that
the notice must state both the alternatives, the option being
the liquidator's and not the dissentient's. It is not for the dissentient to require the liquidator to take one and only one
of the two alternative courses and frame his notice accordingly
[*Demerara Rubber Co.* (1913), 1 Ch. 331]. Since the notice
of dissent must be given within seven days after the passing
of the resolution, it obviously should not be given before
the passing, especially as no liquidator may then have been
appointed.

If a shareholder in the old company neither assents nor
dissents, and does not claim the shares to which he is entitled
under the scheme, he then loses his rights in the company,
unless any have been reserved to him by the particular
scheme: frequently, for example, the scheme provides that
he is to be entitled to the proceeds of sale of the shares which
he might have claimed. Buckley L.J., in his judgment in
the case of *Bisgood* v. *Henderson's Transvaal Estates* (1908),
1 Ch. 743 at p. 760, thus conveniently summarises the provisions in a reconstruction under s. 287 which may properly
be made without the dissentient being entitled to complain:
'There is no hardship upon him in any of the following
arrangements within reasonable limits: (1) that the shares for
distribution be partly-paid shares, or (2) that if he wants the
shares he must apply for them within a limited time, or (3) that
shares unapplied for are to be at the disposal of the new company, or (4) that shares unapplied for may be sold and the
member who does not assent shall take the proceeds (for this
is giving him something more than that to which he would be

otherwise entitled), or (5) that the shares shall not go to the company and be assets of the company, but shall go direct to the members.' Although there is no illegality in a provision that a shareholder loses the right to shares if he does not apply for them within a limited time, there seems to be no reason for requiring an application where the shares to be issued are fully paid shares except, perhaps, in a case where there are numerous shareholders on the register who cannot be traced.

If a shareholder effectually dissents, as provided by s. 287, the price at which his shares are to be purchased must be ascertained in accordance with the provisions of the section, that is to say, the parties may agree, or, failing agreement, the price is settled by arbitration, pursuant to the Companies Clauses Consolidation Act, 1845. That Act provides for a single arbitrator to be agreed upon, or for an arbitrator to be nominated by each party and an umpire to be agreed upon. The Arbitration Acts, 1889–1934, also apply where they are not inconsistent with the Companies Clauses Consolidation Act, 1845. But where the company's articles make other provisions for arbitration, they may be followed, to the exclusion of the Act [*De Rosaz* v. *Anglo-Italian Bank* (1869), L.R. 4 Q.B. 462]. The value must be determined by the arbitrator, who will often rely on the evidence of experts. He should not assume that the shares which form the purchase consideration are worth par, nor should he assume that the market price of the shares represents their true value. The value of the selling company's business as a going concern, taking all the circumstances into consideration, will be an important element in enabling him to come to a conclusion.

In framing the scheme care should be taken to provide a fund sufficient to purchase the interests of dissentients. This may be done by the exclusion from the sale of a sufficient portion of the assets of the old company, but it is more usual for the whole of the assets to be sold and the new company to undertake to provide the necessary money. This it may do by borrowing, or, if its shares are partly paid, out of the funds obtained by making a call thereon. If the interests of the dissentients are not adequately protected by the scheme, by the provision of adequate funds, the liquidator may be restrained from parting with the assets. The rights of dissentients are statutory rights, and members cannot be deprived of them by provisions in the articles; any such provisions are wholly invalid [*Baring-Gould* v. *Sharpington Syndicate* (1899), 2 Ch. 90; *Payne* v. *The Cork Co.* (1900), 1 Ch. 308].

A reconstruction under s. 287 is, as has been stated, binding **Creditors.** on the shareholders, but the rights of creditors are protected; for sub-s. (5) provides as follows: 'If an order is made within a year for winding up the company by or subject to the supervision of the court, the special resolution shall not be valid unless sanctioned by the court.' There is, accordingly, for the space of a year, a danger of the reconstruction becoming inoperative; but at the expiration of a year, if no winding-up order or supervision order is made, the reconstruction is binding upon creditors as well as shareholders. There is a method of ensuring that the reconstruction does not become inoperative which has sometimes been adopted; this is to procure a friendly creditor to petition for a supervision order, and afterwards to obtain the sanction of the court to the scheme. However, it is usual for the matter of the creditors to be dealt with when the scheme is first mooted. Debenture holders are asked to agree to accept debentures in the new company to be underwritten to pay off those who object. Unsecured creditors may be asked to accept the liability of the new company instead of that of the old company; but this is not usually necessary unless there are large creditors who cannot be paid off. As a rule the scheme will provide for the new company taking over the liabilities of the old company, and any creditors who do not accept the new company as their debtor will be paid.

In a reconstruction under s. 287 a practical difficulty arises where the shares, or some of them, upon which it is desired to make an assessment, are represented by warrants to bearer. In a case of this kind, extensive advertisement is necessary, and a much longer period must be allowed, during which a shareholder is to be entitled to claim his allotment, than where the shares are all registered.

Since a reconstruction of this kind almost invariably involves the allotment of shares, either wholly or partly paid, the provisions of s. 52 of the Act must be complied with, and within one month after the allotment the written contract constituting the title of the allottee to the allotment must be delivered to the Registrar, and the other returns prescribed by the section must be made. This appears to necessitate the execution of a contract between the new company and a trustee for the allottees, which, together with the reconstruction agreement, will have to be filed. If, however, the reconstruction agreement provides for the allotment to the liquidator of the shares in the new company, no supplementary contract will be necessary.

Underwriting on Reconstruction. Where the object of the reconstruction is to obtain fresh capital it is frequently necessary to resort to underwriting. The usual practice is for a preliminary underwriting agreement to be entered into between the board of the old company and the underwriters, and for that agreement to have scheduled to it the detailed agreement which the old company and its liquidator will enter into with the new company, when the former has gone into liquidation and the latter is registered. The shareholders of the old company approve the preliminary agreement and schedule at the liquidation meeting. This preliminary agreement usually provides that, if a certain percentage of shareholders effectively dissent, the underwriters shall be allowed to cancel the agreement. It is therefore usual to take no further steps until after the seven days allowed for dissent, but immediately that period has expired the new company will be registered, and the board will enter into the contract scheduled to the preliminary agreement and also an agreement for sale. The liquidator will then send out his circular to the shareholders of the old company and tell them how many shares they are entitled to apply for in the new company, giving particulars as to payment of the balance, names of the directors of the new company, their interest in the company, and the amount of commission payable to the underwriters, etc., and will state that the applications for shares must be accompanied by certificates for shares in the old company. The bankers of the company, to whom applications are sent, should be instructed to receive no applications unless accompanied by relative share certificates. It should be noted that underwriters must be, or become, holders of shares, even though of only a small number, before the offer is made in order to keep within the provisions for the saving of stamp duty.

The agreement usually provides that the shareholders of the old company shall be entitled, on the nomination of the liquidator, to a *pro rata* number of shares in the new company, credited with so much per share paid up. A method of avoiding considerable work is for the liquidator to write out the allotment sheets as applications for shares in the new company are received, and to sign those allotment sheets for the purpose of nominating the shareholders of the old company for allotment of shares in the new company. This saves the new company writing out fresh allotment sheets. Then, when the new company has allotted, and proposes to deliver the return as to allotments to the Registrar, the contract, which in ordinary circumstances would have to set out the names and particulars of the allottees, can be made with a trustee, and can state that the shares were allotted to the parties and in the proportions set out on the return as to allotments 'presented for registration herewith.' This course results in a considerable saving in labour.

If, as is usual, the liquidator has to sell all the shares not taken up by shareholders in the old company, he will, when sending out his circular, send out also a combined form of tender and application for such shares as are not taken up, and it is desirable to have this form printed on a different coloured paper, so as to avoid confusion. He should also advertise

K

the fact that such shares are for sale, and that forms of tender
can be obtained at his office. Having regard to s. 38 (3) of
the Act it appears to be necessary that the application form
should be accompanied also by a prospectus complying with
s. 38 (1). It will be necessary to fix a time within which
shareholders can claim their shares in the new company, but
it will also be found desirable considerably to extend this time
in the case of shareholders resident abroad.

After expiration of the time limit within which application
for shares may be made, the new company will allot the shares
on the nomination of the liquidator, but the liquidator should
not definitely accept tenders for excess shares until after the
expiry of the time allowed within which foreign applications
can be received. The agreement will usually provide that the
proceeds received on sale of shares not taken up by shareholders shall be divided among the shareholders (other than
dissentients) who do not come into the scheme, but the expenses of advertising the shares for sale will first be deducted.
If the liquidator has to sell a substantial number of shares he
may be confronted with the same difficulty in satisfying the
Commissioners of Inland Revenue that the conditions of s.
55 (1) of the Finance Act, 1927, have been fulfilled as in the
case of letters of renunciation in connection with a scheme of
reconstruction.

Reconstruc-
tion under
powers in
Memoran-
dum.
Reconstruction under the powers in the memorandum of
association, which was formerly common, is often impossible,
owing to the decision of the Court of Appeal in *Bisgood* v.
Henderson's Transvaal Estate (1908), 1 Ch. 743. The effect
of that decision, as stated in the head-note in the *Law Reports*,
is this: 'The sale of all a company's assets, and all its undertaking, and the distribution of the proceeds, cannot be a
corporate object, so that, under a clause for that purpose
introduced into the memorandum of association, such a sale
and distribution can be made without regard to the provisions
of s. 161 of the Companies Act, 1862' (now s. 287 of the 1948
Act). 'A company limited by shares cannot by its memorandum and articles of association provide as part of its constitution that in an event the corporator shall either submit
to a liability in excess of the limit of liability on his shares,
or shall be dispossessed of his status as corporator.'

The practical result is that sales under a power in the
memorandum appear to be legal, if liquidation is neither
contemplated nor in progress, but inasmuch as a scheme of
reconstruction by sale to a new company generally involves
liquidation and distribution in specie, it is not often practicable
to proceed under a power contained in the memorandum.
To use such a power the only possible procedure appears
to be to effect an out-and-out sale for shares, and, subsequently, as a wholly independent transaction, to resolve

upon liquidation with the object of distributing the proceeds. This would mean that the selling company would for a time become simply an investment-holding company. This course is sometimes adopted, especially when the shares of the selling company are held by a small number of persons who can by separate agreement bind themselves to put the company in liquidation and authorise the distribution of the assets in specie. The legality of this course was recognised in *Mason* v. *Motor Traction Co.* (1905), 1 Ch. 419, which, though mentioned in argument in *Bisgood's* case (*supra*) was not overruled, but apparently approved by Buckley L.J., himself. It is thought that *Etheridge* v. *Central Uruguay Railway* (1913), 1 Ch. 425, is not inconsistent with this view, as the resolutions submitted to the meeting in that case provided for liquidation and distribution of the shares forming the purchase consideration in specie among the members and the transaction was therefore clearly within s. 192 of the Act of 1908. It must, however, be pointed out that any attempt to evade the effect of *Bisgood's* case (*supra*) by these means would be very carefully scrutinised, and very slight evidence indeed of an ultimate intention to go into liquidation for the purpose of distributing the proceeds of sale would probably be sufficient to wreck the scheme. The conclusion is that for most purposes, at all events, schemes of reconstruction by means of a sale under the powers in the memorandum have become impracticable and are best left alone. This, however, is subject to the important proviso that, in cases where there is complete unanimity among the shareholders, there is nothing to prevent such a scheme going through, and plenty of such schemes have been carried out even since *Bisgood's* case (*supra*).

Amalgamations are in general effected either by means of **Amalgamations.** proceedings under s. 287 or by a purchase of shares. Where the amalgamation is effected under s. 287, the process where company A is absorbed by company B will be a simple sale; company A will sell its undertaking to company B in exchange for shares in company B, which will be distributed among the original shareholders of company A. Where a new company acquires the undertakings of both company A and company B, there will, of course, be an independent sale by each. The law is the same, and the difficulties are the same, as in simple reconstructions, and no further comment is necessary.

Amalgamation by a purchase of shares amounts simply to **Amalgamation by share purchase.** the acquisition by one company of all, or a majority, of the shares in the other company, the price paid being either cash or shares in the purchasing company. Sometimes, however, the acquisition is limited to those classes of shares which carry full voting rights.

This method of amalgamation has become increasingly popular, because it preserves the names and thus the goodwill of the original companies. A common method of procedure is for an agreement to be entered into with the directors of the company, the shares of which it is desired to acquire, on behalf of themselves and all other members of that company who ratify the agreement, the agreement being made conditional on ratification within a fixed period by an agreed majority. The directors then circularise the shareholders and, if the requisite majority ratify within the time limited, the agreement becomes absolute, subject to the rights of dissenting shareholders. This form of amalgamation is recognised by s. 209 of the Act, which enables a company which has acquired 90 per cent. of the shares in another company under a scheme to acquire the remaining 10 per cent. compulsorily. Under that section, if a scheme or contract involving the transfer of shares or any class of shares in a company (called 'the transferor company') to another company, whether a company within the meaning of the Act or not (called 'the transferee company'), has, within four months of the offer being made, been approved by the holders of at least nine-tenths in value of the shares affected, the transferee company may, on notice given in the prescribed manner to any dissenting shareholder within two months after the expiration of the above period of four months, purchase the shares held by any dissenting shareholder upon the terms specified in the scheme or contract. The expression 'dissenting shareholder' includes any shareholder who has not assented to or has failed to carry out the scheme. The dissenting shareholder has a right of appeal to the court exercisable at any time within one month after the notice was given to him; if a notice is given and no order is made by the court to the contrary, the purchase of the interest of the dissentient shareholder will be carried out through the transferor company as provided by sub-sections (2) and (3) of s. 209, and the transferee company is bound to purchase the shares. Forms of notice to dissenting and non-assenting shareholders and a form of notice by non-assenting shareholders to the transferee company will be found in Appendix F, Form 109, 110 and 111.

If the transferor company (or its nominee or subsidiary) already holds shares in the transferee company, the offer is made only to the outside shareholders; and in that case the majority required to put s. 209 into operation is 90 per cent. in value of the outside shares and 75 per cent. in number of the outside shareholders.

It should be observed that, where all the shares are being acquired, it is necessary to take care not to transfer the qualifying shares of the directors until by the machinery of the articles a fresh board of properly qualified persons has been appointed, after which the old qualifying shares can be transferred, thus completing the matter. Further, care should be taken that the shares acquired are, in the case of a public company, put into the names of not less than seven persons or, in the case of a private company, two persons.

If one or more dissentient shareholders appeal to the court under this section, the onus will be on him or them to establish that the scheme is unfair. Thus, it was held in re *Hoare & Co. Ltd.* (1934), 150 L.T. 374, that where not less than nine-tenths of the shareholders approved the scheme, *prima facie* the offer must be taken to be a fair one and the court will not 'order otherwise unless it is affirmatively established that notwithstanding the views of a very large number of shareholders the scheme is unfair.' [Cf. *Evertite Locknuts* (1945), Ch. 220, and *Press Caps Limited* (1949), Ch. 434.]

The third common type of reconstruction [number (iii) above], more properly described as a scheme of arrangement under s. 206 of the Act, is the most widely used of all. Section 206 provides (*inter alia*) that when a compromise or arrangement is proposed between a company and its creditors, or any class of creditors, or between the company and its members, or any class of members, the court may, on the application of the company, or of any creditor or member, or, in the case of winding up, of the liquidator, direct that a meeting of the creditors or class of creditors, or of the members or class of members, as the case may be, be convened. If a majority in number representing three-fourths in value of those present and voting at the meeting agree to the compromise, it is, when sanctioned by the court, binding on the creditors or class of creditors, or the members or class of members, as well as on the company; if the company is in liquidation the compromise is binding on the liquidator and the contributories, or, if there is a liquidation, then on the liquidator and the contributories. The chief advantages of a scheme of arrangement are that a majority of creditors may bind the minority, for example, to accept debentures or shares in lieu of cash, or to forgo arrears of interest; and that (unless as part of the scheme a new company is formed to purchase the undertaking and is not in a position to take advantage of s. 55 of the Finance Act, 1927), the expense of registration and the stamp duty on the transfer of assets is avoided. It will be remembered that under s. 287 creditors are not bound until a year has elapsed from the passing of the special resolution.

It should be noted that under the Act persons present, but not voting, are excluded in calculating whether the requisite majority has been obtained.

Schemes involving the consolidation of shares of different classes or the division of shares into shares of different classes are brought expressly within the section by sub-s. 6.

Schemes of Arrangements under Section 206.

The section is applicable not only to companies within the meaning of the Act, but to all companies liable to be wound up under the Act [s. 206 (6)]. It applies, therefore, not only to companies registered under the Act in England and Scotland, and to existing companies as defined by s. 455, but also to unregistered companies as defined by s. 398, unless within the exception referred to in s. 399 (2).

Forms of Schemes.
The court has jurisdiction to sanction any form of scheme which is within the ambit of the section and is not within s. 287. In general, if the provisions of the Act have been complied with and the scheme is reasonable, and no injustice has been done to any class, and if satisfied that the majority supporting the scheme are acting *bona fide*, the court will not withhold its sanction. If there have been irregularities in the conduct of the class meetings, or if explanatory circulars are found to have been misleading, the court may, instead of dismissing the petition to sanction the scheme, if requested to do so, order fresh meetings to be summoned on the understanding that another explanatory circular is issued [*Dorman Long & Co. Ltd.* (1934), Ch. 635]. The court may require modifications of the scheme as approved by the classes interested, or may attach conditions; and, in order to avoid the necessity for summoning fresh meetings to approve the scheme as modified by the court, it is usual to insert a clause in the scheme authorising the applicant to assent to any modifications or conditions in the scheme which the court may think fit to approve or impose. In one case, for instance, the court attached the condition that a minority of shareholders who disapproved the scheme should have the rights of dissentients under s. 287, *i.e.* should be entitled to require the liquidator to purchase their interests in the company [*Canning Jarrah Timber Company* (1900), 1 Ch. 708].

Kinds of Scheme sanctioned.
The schemes which have from time to time been sanctioned by the court are of the most varied description. Thus, debenture holders and creditors have accepted shares for their debts; existing debenture holders have been postponed to new debentures to be created; creditors have received part cash and part debentures, or part cash and part shares, in satisfaction of their debts; one creditor has taken over all the assets, and paid the costs of the winding up and a composition to the other creditors; shares or debentures have been accepted in lieu of arrears of debenture interest; debenture interest has been reduced, future profits being devoted to the redemption of the debentures. The scheme may, and often does, involve the formation of a new company to acquire all or part of the assets; or, if a liquidation is in progress, it may provide for a stay of the liquidation and the continuance of the old business.

Where a compromise or arrangement is proposed in

connection with a scheme of reconstruction or amalgamation involving the transfer of the whole or any part of the undertaking or property of one company to another company, the court is empowered to facilitate the scheme by making provision for such matters as the transfer of property, the allotment of shares, etc., pending legal proceedings and the dissolution of the transferor company without a winding up and provision for dissentients (s. 208). Notwithstanding this section, it would seem advisable for the scheme itself to contain provisions at least as to transfer of property, allotment, and, if it is intended to confer rights on dissentients, as to dissentients. The powers conferred on the court by the section are particularly valuable if any unforeseen difficulty arises in carrying out the scheme, as they can be exercised not only under the order sanctioning the scheme but at any subsequent time.

It should, however, be noted that when an order is made under s. 208, e.g. for the amalgamation of two companies, a contract of service existing at the date of such amalgamation between an employee and the transferor company does not automatically become a contract of service between the employee and the transferee company. The position is the same in relation to other non-transferable contracts [*Nokes* v. *Doncaster Amalgamated Collieries Ltd.* (1940), A.C. 1014].

In carrying out any scheme of reconstruction, whether under s. 287 or under s. 206 or otherwise, legal advice is almost invariably necessary.

An outline is given below of the procedure necessary to carry through a scheme of arrangement under s. 206 of the Act, directed to reorganising the company's capital, including modification of shareholders' rights. **Procedure under Section 206.**

Reconstruction of capital is usually found to be necessary where a company has encountered a number of successive difficult financial periods, the outcome of such difficult trading conditions having resulted in the company being burdened by excessive values for fixed assets following deflation, by excessive issued capital not required in view of changed conditions, by large quantities of obsolete plant and buildings or alternatively by a considerable debit on profit and loss account. In addition, a company may find itself burdened by high fixed interest charges, by arrears of cumulative preference dividends and similar fixed cumulative periodical payments, resulting in the possibility of the payment of an ordinary dividend or equity payment being extremely remote.

A company faced with difficulties similar to those outlined above usually finds it advantageous to reconstruct its capital structure, provided the necessary three-fourths majority of each class of shareholders or of creditors (if involved) is forthcoming.

The directors, having considered reconstruction necessary, are now faced with the task of drawing up the scheme of arrangement in terms which are acceptable to all the various parties interested. In doing this it will be apparent that the complexities of affording a fair and equitable settlement to all parties increase in proportion to the number of classes of holders and creditors. The scheme will embrace full details of how the members, debenture holders, creditors, etc., are affected and will state the effect of the scheme upon asset values, the opportunity being taken to eliminate from the balance sheet intangible assets, such as goodwill and preliminary expenses, and to reduce the values of buildings, machinery, etc. It is usual when drawing up the scheme to consult leading financial experts upon the question of interest or dividend rates which would be acceptable, based on the estimated rates ruling when the scheme will be approved by the holders. It is also useful, where an adjustment is to be made in the balance sheet values of fixed assets, for a revaluation to be made by an eminent firm of valuers, whose certificate will afford useful support for the scheme, but the directors themselves will have to decide whether a reasonable return can be expected from the capital as written down.

Variation of Debenture Holders' Rights. If debentures have been issued by the company and their rights are to be modified in any way, the debenture holders or the trustees for the debenture holders should be consulted in order that the scheme may be one which the debenture holders are likely to approve. It is not unusual for the scheme to embrace an adjustment of the debenture holders' rights as well as those of the members of the company. The following are some of the numerous instances of variations in debenture holders' rights:—

(1) the repayment of existing debentures (sometimes at a premium) and the issue of a new series of debentures bearing a lower rate of interest, the existing debenture holders being paid in cash or being given the right to exchange into the new stock, usually on advantageous terms;

(2) the reduction of interest rate on existing debentures, in conjunction with reduction of members' interests in the company;

(3) the issue of (say) ordinary or preference shares in satisfaction of reduction in interest rates on debenture stock;

(4) the right to convert the new debenture into ordinary shares for a period of years in satisfaction of waiving arrears of interest.

Scheme Documents. When the scheme has been finally settled by the board of directors, after consultation with all the interested parties, it is usual for a circular to be prepared explaining the history of the events leading up to the proposed scheme to be laid before the meetings for approval. Accompanying this circular will normally be the following documents, these also being approved at this stage: (1) the scheme of arrangement; (2) the notice convening the scheme meetings; (3) forms of proxy relative to the scheme meetings; (4) voting slips for use at the scheme meetings. In addition to the above documents relative to the scheme meetings there will be included:— (5) the notices convening the extraordinary general meeting of members for the purposes of passing special resolutions reducing the capital of the company and altering the memorandum and articles of association; (6) the form of proxy for use at the extraordinary general meeting; (7) a voting slip for use at the extraordinary general meeting.

These documents may now be considered separately:—

(1) *The Form of Scheme of Arrangement.* The form of scheme of arrangement sets forth the proposals to be placed before the creditors and shareholders whose interest in the company is affected. Details will be given of any proposed variation of rights, reduction of capital, etc., and reference will be made to any alterations required to the articles of association.

(2) *The Notice Convening the Scheme Meetings.* The only comment necessary is that although it is essential to hold separate meetings of each class of creditors and shareholders interested, the details of the dates and times of all the meetings may be embodied in the same notice.

(3) *Forms of Proxy Relative to the Scheme Meetings.* The forms of proxy relative to the scheme meetings will follow a standard form approved by the court, and must enable the creditor or shareholder to indicate whether he votes for or against the scheme. (See Appendix F, Form 51.) It will be found useful to print the forms for each separate class on paper of a different colour, in order to enable them to be readily distinguished.

(4) *Voting Slips for use at the Scheme Meetings.* The voting slips for use by those who attend the scheme meetings in person can be conveniently drafted to serve also as admission tickets. Similar arrangements for printing on differently coloured paper, as in the case of the proxy forms, should be made.

(5) *Notice Convening the Extraordinary General Meeting to Pass the Special Resolutions to Reduce the Capital, etc.* It may be wondered why an extraordinary general meeting is required in addition to the scheme meetings. The explanation is that, as the scheme will involve a reduction of capital, and may also vary the rights of one or more classes of shareholders, the

requisite special resolutions will have to be passed, and the scheme meetings are not appropriate for this purpose.

Fractions arising on Reduction of Capital. When the reduction of capital will result in inconvenient fractions, it is sometimes preferable to convert the unclaimed capital into stock. If this is contemplated a special resolution should be included providing that, on the scheme being sanctioned by the court, the issued capital, as reduced, shall automatically be consolidated and converted to stock in units of £1.

Should this course be adopted, it may subsequently be found necessary to issue, for cash, a small number of shares to bring up the aggregate of the fractional balances to an even £1. To avoid the inconvenience of calling another extraordinary general meeting to convert this small issue to stock, a further special resolution should also be included to the effect that, in respect of any shares issued subsequent to the sanction of the scheme, notice of the extraordinary general meeting necessary for the purpose of converting such shares to stock may be given by advertisement only, and that the articles be altered accordingly.

Where a reduction in the nominal value of the capital of the company takes place, it is the usual practice, in order to save stamp duty, for the reduced nominal capital to be increased to its original figure, *i.e.* as it was before reduction. If the articles do not require a special or extraordinary resolution, an ordinary resolution is all that is necessary for this purpose.

As all the special resolutions to be proposed at the extraordinary general meeting are conditional upon the scheme being sanctioned, it should be clearly stated in the notice convening the meeting that such resolutions will have effect only if the scheme is sanctioned, and a special resolution confirming this should be passed at the meeting.

(6) *Form of Proxy Relative to the Extraordinary General Meeting.* The only comment necessary is that, as this is not a scheme meeting, the regulations as to proxies contained in the articles of association will apply. It is, however, necessary, if the shares are quoted on the Stock Exchange, that the proxies should be two-way proxies, *i.e.* should permit the shareholder to vote either for or against the scheme. A person appointed as a proxy need not be a member of the company [s. 136 (5)].

(7) *Voting Slip for use at the Extraordinary General Meeting.* No special comment is required, any convenient form being suitable. It is often convenient to have different columns for different classes with provision for stating the holding thereon.

Explanatory Letter. A circular letter should be prepared to accompany the scheme documents, in which the board, in general terms, should explain the scheme proposals and recommend their acceptance. As this circular is often the subject of attack by shareholders when opposing the scheme, it is particularly important that it should state the position accurately, fully and fairly [*Dorman Long & Co.* (1934), Ch. 635].

The scheme documents, having been settled by counsel, should be formally approved by resolution of the board, and the preliminary work may then be regarded as completed.

Under s. 207 of the Act the circular referred to must, in **Circular** addition to explaining the effect of the compromise or arrange- **under** ment, state any material interests of the directors of the **Section 207.** company, whether as directors or as members or as creditors of the company or otherwise, and the effect thereon of the compromise or arrangement, in so far as it is different from the effect on the like interests of other persons. If the notice summoning the meeting is given by advertisement, the information required to be given above dealing with the effect of the scheme and the interests of directors must be included in the advertisement, or more usually, notification of the place at which, and the manner in which, creditors or members entitled to attend the meeting may obtain copies of such a statement free of charge must be stated.

Where the compromise or arrangement affects the rights of debenture holders of the company, the said statement must give the like explanation regarding the trustees of any deed for securing the issue of the debentures as it is required to give concerning the company's directors.

Consequent upon the writing down or variations of existing holdings under the terms of the scheme, there may arise fractions of shares or very small holdings which, although of minor importance in themselves, may present some difficulty, and, wrongly handled, may be a source of continual trouble to the company, and particularly the secretary, in the future.

When a severe reduction has to be made in the nominal value of shares, it is possible that certain holdings will be reduced to a total nominal value of less than £1. This is most likely to occur when the existing shares are already of a low nominal value (for example, when shares of 1s. each are reduced to 2d. each, any holding of less than 120 shares will result in a holding with a total nominal value of less than £1). From every angle such a holding is a nuisance to all concerned, and holders of such small amounts will probably have so little interest in them that they will neglect to notify changes of address, etc., and, in course of time, the accounts will become 'dead.' It is suggested, therefore, that some method should be adopted to eliminate holdings of this type from the register. Similarly, where preference shareholders agree to accept, in place of the existing holdings, a holding partly in ordinary shares and partly in deferred shares, fractions are almost certain to result.

Elimination of Fractions. The difficulties which arise from fractional holdings may be overcome in a number of ways, depending on the extent of the problem, but where a large number of holdings is affected, perhaps the most convenient method of eliminating at the same time both holdings under £1 and fractions, is to provide in the scheme that the shareholdings, as reduced or varied under the terms of the scheme, be consolidated and converted at once to stock in units of £1, and that the board be empowered to make such arrangements as will avoid any person holding a fraction of £1 of stock. In practice, the aggregate of all fractions of stock under £1, which would include all holdings under £1 and fractions in respect of any larger holdings not evenly divisible, would be entered upon the new register in the names of nominees, and the amount of stock thereby represented would be sold and the proceeds distributed *pro rata* to the holders entitled thereto.

The next stage is an application to the court for directions as to the holding of the scheme meetings. The procedure is by way of an originating summons in the Chancery Division taken out by the company's solicitor, when a date will be fixed by the registrar of the court for the hearing of the application. An affidavit by the secretary will be filed setting forth briefly the history of the company; the circumstances which have induced the directors to propose the scheme of arrangement; and all matters relevant to the scheme which it is appropriate to bring to the notice of the court. To this affidavit will be exhibited such documents as the company's certificate of incorporation, memorandum and articles of association, a copy of the last balance sheet, and a copy of the scheme of arrangement. Drafts of the notice convening the meetings, forms of proxy, and any form of notice relative to the scheme meetings which it is proposed to advertise in the press, will be submitted for approval, together with the names of the persons who it is proposed shall act as chairmen at the respective meetings.

Scheme Meetings. On the hearing of the application, counsel will ask the court to make an order directing the meetings to be held. The court will give such directions as it considers appropriate, to which the company must adhere rigidly.

It should be mentioned that the extraordinary general meeting at which the special resolutions relative to the reduction of capital, etc., will be proposed, not being a scheme meeting, will not be subject to the directions of the court.

The board should now pass a resolution authorising the secretary to convene the scheme and extraordinary meetings, and to issue the relative documents.

As to the secretary's duties in connection with the convening of meetings, it will be sufficient to mention only a number of points of practical interest which have a particular bearing on these special meetings.

(1) It is of the greatest importance that the secretary satisfies himself that the scheme documents which are sent out are in the exact form approved by the court.

(2) The secretary will have to decide whether to issue the proxy forms and voting slips in blank, or to fill in the names, addresses and holdings before despatch. Where the register is a large one, the task of filling in the forms before despatch, even with the aid of addressing machines, may be formidable. If, however, the forms can conveniently be filled in, the handling of the proxy forms, when returned, and the voting papers at the meeting will be greatly facilitated, especially as the difficulty of dealing with illegible signatures is overcome. If they cannot be filled in, it is an advantage to instruct holders to fill in their names in block capitals, as well as signing, so as to avoid the difficulty of illegibility.

(3) When the result of the scheme meetings is reported to the court, an affidavit will be required as to the posting of the notices convening the meetings, and it is advisable to obtain a certificate of posting from the post office.

With regard to the holding of the scheme meetings, again it is proposed to mention only a few points of practical interest.

(1) The scheme meetings being called under the direction of the court, the provisions in the company's articles of association relative to a quorum do not apply.

(2) It will be remembered that the majority required to pass the resolutions at the scheme meetings is a majority in numbers, representing three-fourths in value, of those present and voting either in person or by proxy. There is no point, therefore, in taking a show of hands, the result of the voting being shown by the signed voting slips and proxy forms.

(3) The chairman of each meeting should be provided with a statement of the number and value of votes cast for or against the scheme by holders voting by proxy, and it is suggested that, if possible, the accuracy of the figures should be verified beforehand by the company's auditors. The completed proxy forms should, of course, be available at the meetings for reference if required.

The proceedings at the extraordinary general meeting being regulated by the company's articles of association, the quorum stipulated in the articles must be present, and the majority **Extra-ordinary General Meeting.**

required to pass the special resolutions will be three-fourths of the number voting in person or by proxy as laid down by s. 141 of the Act, and not the majority which is required in the case of the scheme meetings.

Petition for Sanction by Court. If the scheme of arrangement is approved by the requisite majorities at the scheme meetings, and the special resolutions are duly passed, a petition will be presented to the court to sanction the scheme and confirm the reduction of capital. The petition will set forth the terms of the scheme; will give a brief history of the company and the circumstances which have given rise to the necessity for the scheme and the reduction of capital; and the result of the voting at the meetings. It will be supported by an affidavit by the chairman of the company verifying the petition; affidavits by the chairmen of the respective scheme meetings reporting the result thereof; an affidavit by the secretary or other officer of the company as to the posting of the notices of the meetings; the minutes of the extraordinary general meeting held to pass the special resolutions relative to the reduction of capital, etc.; and any other relevant document (for example, an affidavit by the valuer if a valuation of the fixed assets has been made for the purpose of the scheme).

The court will fix a day on which the hearing of the petition will be held, and will make such directions as it considers necessary as to the advertisement in the press of the presentation of the petition and the date appointed for the hearing.

If, after the hearing of the petition, the scheme is sanctioned and the reduction of capital confirmed, the court will direct that the order sanctioning the scheme be produced to the Registrar of Companies and an office copy delivered for registration, together with the minute of the reduction of capital, and will make such directions as it thinks expedient for the advertisement in the *London Gazette* and other papers of the order and minutes after registration. It is important to note that the scheme does not take effect until the office copy of the order has been registered. A printed copy of the special resolutions passed must, of course, be filed in the usual manner with the Registrar.

A copy of the order of the court, as registered with the Registrar, must be included in every copy of the memorandum and articles of association subsequently issued by the company.

Filing of Court Order. When the order of the court has been registered with the Registrar, the company will then proceed to put the approved scheme into operation. The complexities of the procedure will, of course, depend upon the classes affected by the scheme, and it is proposed to set out in general outline certain eventualities which may occur when carrying through the scheme.

Where debenture stockholders have agreed to accept a reduced rate of interest on the existing stock, other conditions remaining unchanged, it will be necessary only to call in the debenture stock certificates for endorsement. The endorsement may be conveniently effected by means of a suitably worded rubber stamp, and it is suggested that a note should be made on each account in the register as and when the certificate relative to that account is endorsed. **Stock Certificates.**

The point will arise as to the position with regard to stock certificates which, for any reason, holders fail to return for endorsement. In order to protect the company against the possibility of a claim by a third party who may act in good faith upon a certificate which has not been endorsed, it is advisable to make a suitable announcement in a number of daily papers, drawing attention to the alteration in the rate of interest on the stock and the fact that certificates should be returned for endorsement.

A memorandum of the reduction in the rate of interest should be made in the company's register of mortgages and charges, and a memorandum should also be endorsed on the trust deed securing the debenture stock.

Where debenture stockholders have agreed to surrender the existing security, and to accept in its place a proportion of the amount of the old debenture stock in the form of a new debenture stock, with the balance in shares, the procedure is more complicated, and it may be useful, therefore, to consider the procedure in detail. **Procedure after Sanction of Scheme.**

(1) Resolutions creating, issuing, and allotting the new debenture stock, and a resolution allotting the new shares, will need to be passed by the board.

(2) Allotment sheets should be prepared on which, against each debenture stockholder's name, should be shown the original holding, the amount of new debenture stock allotted, and the number of shares allotted, columns being provided for fractional balances and new certificate numbers, etc.

(3) Letters of allotment should be issued in exchange for the surrender of the original debenture stock certificates.

(4) Where it is intended to convert the new shares to stock to overcome the difficulty with regard to fractional balances, an extraordinary general meeting of members must be called to pass the requisite resolution. If the suggestion previously made when dealing with the alteration of the articles has been adopted, notice of this meeting may be given by advertisement only.

(5) The new certificates when ready will be exchanged for the allotment letters; and where the suggested method of dealing with the fractions has been followed, cheques will be issued for the fractional balances.

(6) The new registers of debenture stocks and shares (or stock when the shares have been converted) must be written up.

(7) A release of the charge secured by the old trust deed should, in the meantime, have been obtained from the trustees of the old debenture stock, and a new trust deed executed securing the new debenture stock.

(8) The requisite entries must be made in the company's own register of mortgages and charges to record the release of the old debenture stock and the creation of the new debenture stock.

(9) At the appropriate times, it will be necessary to file the following documents with the Registrar of Companies:—

(a) a return of allotment of the shares;

(b) particulars of the contract, namely the scheme of arrangement, under which the shares have been allotted, in view of the fact that the shares have not been allotted for cash;

(c) notice of the conversion of the shares to stock, where this has been done;

(d) a memorandum of satisfaction relative to the release of the charge secured by the old trust deed;

(e) particulars of the charge created by the new trust deed.

Unsecured Creditors. As the form of capital reconstruction which is now being considered relates to a continuing company, it is unlikely that the unsecured creditors, whose claims will probably represent ordinary trading debts, will be affected. It is possible that a scheme of this character might, for example, include provision for a moratorium in respect of unsecured debts, but it does not seem that the question of unsecured creditors is sufficiently important to require anything more than this passing reference.

Rights of Shareholders. The provisions of the scheme as regards the shareholders will probably fall into either one or a combination of the following four categories:—

A. a reduction in the rate of dividend on cumulative preference shares;

B. the writing down of the amount paid up on the shares held;

C. the acceptance of shares of a different class in exchange
    for the existing holding;

D. the cancellation of arrears of dividend on cumulative
    preference shares.

A. The procedure following a reduction in the rate of
dividend on preference shares is similar to that in the case of
a reduction in the rate of interest on debenture stock [see
(a) above].

B. A probable effect of the scheme is the writing down of
the amount paid up on the shares held.

In a simple case, for example where £1 shares are written
down to 10s. each, and the question of fractional balances
does not arise, share certificates may be called in for endorsement.   It is a wise course to consult the Stock Exchange
because, although it may not be incumbent on the company
to call in share certificates for endorsement, it will be a
convenience to the member and the broker to do so.

Where the circumstances are complicated, and to overcome
the difficulty of fractional balances, the shares as written
down have been consolidated and converted to £1 units of
stock, the following procedure is suggested:—

(1) Sheets should be prepared on which, against each
    shareholder's name should be shown the original
    holding, the new holding of stock, the fractional
    balance, if any, with columns for the new certificate
    number, etc.

(2) The fractional balances will be aggregated, and will be
    dealt with as previously described, an allotment of
    additional shares for cash and the conversion of such
    shares to stock being made, when the aggregate of the
    fractional balances results in a fraction of £1.

(3) The new certificates and cheques for fractional balances
    will be issued against the surrender of the old certifi-
    cates.

(4) A new register will be written up.

Where it has been necessary to allot shares for cash to make
up the aggregate of fractional balances to an even £1, a return
of allotment and notice of the conversion of such shares to
stock must be made to the Registrar of Companies in the usual
manner under s. 52 of the Act.

C. If shareholders of any particular class have agreed to
accept in place of their holdings shares of another class, for
example, ordinary shares for preference shares, it is interesting
to note that this does not require a new allotment by the
board, the order sanctioning the scheme being sufficient
authority for the change in the character of the holding.   In

such circumstances, although no reduction in the amount paid up may be involved, it is essential that new certificates should be issued against the surrender of the old certificates. If, in addition to a change in the class of holding, a reduction in the amount paid up is also involved, the procedure already mentioned in this respect will be appropriate.

D.   Cancellation of arrears of cumulative dividend does not, of course, call for any adjustment in the share register or in the share certificate. It is usual, however, for such cancellation of rights to cumulative dividends to be satisfied by the issue of (say) ordinary or preference shares, or sometimes, in suitable circumstances, by the issue of what are called 'funding certificates.'

Funding Certificates.   Funding certificates are certificates giving a right to payment of interest and of the redemption of capital out of profits only. They are not part of the issued capital of the company and, being payable only out of profits, are not included as a liability in the company's balance sheet, though it is usual and proper to note on the balance sheet the amount of funding certificates outstanding. They are only offered when the directors are convinced that prosperous times are ahead. If the effect of the scheme is to introduce holdings of funding certificates represented by fractions of a £, it is usual to provide in the scheme for settlement of fractions by a cash payment or for transfer of the fractions to trustees for sale.

The terms of the issue of funding certificates are endorsed on the certificates, and usually cover the points mentioned below:—

(1)   the amount and the priority of the issue;

(2)   the dates for the payment of interest;

(3)   that redemption of the certificates be effected out of available profits, and that the decision of the directors as to what are available profits is conclusive;

(4)   the following detailed provisions as to redemption:—

    (i)   that the interest (usually cumulative) on the funding certificates be a first charge on the available profits;

    (ii)   that after the payment of the interest, provision be made for the actual redemption of the certificates by allotting an initial sum, together with such further sums as the directors may determine. It is usual for funding certificates to be repaid by the company over a period of ten years, and, in this case, the initial sum would probably amount to the equivalent of one-tenth of the total issue to be redeemed;

REDEMPTION RECORD SHEET

REDEMPTION OF ___ % FUNDING CERTIFICATES

NAME	Holding	Amount Re-deemed	Ref. No.	INTEREST ACCRUED			Total Payment	Date Cert. Retd.	NEW CERT. ISSUED		
				Gross	Tax at 9s. in £	Nett			Date	No.	Amount
	£	£		£ s. d.	£ s. d.	£ s. d.	£ s. d.				£
	250	100		2 6 11	1 1 1	1 5 10	101 5 10	1/7/50	28/10/50	7836	150
	9	9		4 3	1 11	2 4	9 2 4	3/7/50			
	226	100		2 6 11	1 1 1	1 5 10	101 5 10	9/9/50	28/10/50	7837	126
	18	18		8 5	3 9	4 8	18 4 8	8/8/50			
	18	18		8 5	3 9	4 8	18 4 8	2/8/50			
	18	18		8 5	3 9	4 8	18 4 8	29/9/50			
	9	9		4 3	1 11	2 4	9 2 4	28/9/50			
	9	9		4 3	1 11	2 4	9 2 4	8/8/50			
	18	18		8 5	3 9	4 8	18 4 8	27/8/50			
	9	9		4 3	1 11	2 4	9 2 4	23/7/50			
	4	4		1 11	10	1 1	4 1 1	4/10/50			

    (iii) that the certificate to be redeemed be selected by lot;

    (iv) that interest cease from the date of redemption;

    (v) that all redeemed certificates be cancelled and not be re-issued;

(5) if the sum available for redemption cannot conveniently be distributed, the board shall have power to carry the amount to a separate expense account where the money may be held for the time being;

(6) the procedure to be adopted in the event of a winding up;

(7) particulars as to the keeping of registers;

(8) regulations as to the transfer of stock;

(9) fees chargeable on transfers;

(10) a stipulation that, in the case of joint registered holders, only the survivor shall have any title to the certificate;

(11) a provision that all moneys becoming payable in respect of certificates shall be paid to the registered holder, whose receipt therefor shall be a good discharge to the company;

(12) provisions for the convening of meetings of certificate-holders, and that a clear majority in value of the certificates shall be the quorum for the purpose of such meetings;

(13) provisions as to the voting rights of certificate holders, *e.g.* on a poll one vote per £1 (nominal amount) of the certificate registered;

(14) a provision that the company's articles of association shall apply *mutatis mutandis,* to the convening of, and proceedings and voting at, meetings of certificate-holders;

(15) a provision whereby the rights of certificate-holders may be varied by the sanction of an extraordinary resolution of the certificate-holders; and that an extraordinary resolution duly passed by the certificate-holders shall be binding upon all certificate-holders whether or not present at the meeting.

It is interesting to note that the Board of Inland Revenue has ruled in certain cases that stockholders are not liable to income tax or sur-tax on cash payments or funding certificates issued in satisfaction of arrears of cumulative preference dividends; in this connection, however, it must be borne in mind that each scheme will differ and should, therefore, be submitted to the Inland Revenue for a ruling regarding the liability to taxation of members on funding cash payments and certificates received.

Directly the scheme has been approved and registered in accordance with the procedure outlined earlier, the despatch of allotment letters covering the issue of the funding certificates can be proceeded with. Under the Finance Act, 1949, letters of allotment are exempt from stamp duty, as also are letters of renunciation and scrip certificates. If permission is being sought for the certificates to be dealt with on the stock exchange there are certain attendant conditions regarding procedure and forms with which the company must comply. Certain of these matters are now referred to, but it is recommended that for fuller information reference should be made to 'Quotation Rules and Procedure of the Council of the Stock Exchange regarding New Issues.' Attention should be drawn to the Stock Exchange regulations regarding redemption, which reads as follows:—'Where stock is subject to redemption by drawings, the amount (or unit) into which the issue is to be divided for the purpose of the drawing shall not exceed £100' (see Appendix D, p. 540). It is usual for a form of renunciation to be attached to the letter of allotment, the form containing a date up to which the holding will be capable of being renounced (maximum six weeks) after which time the holding is only capable of transfer by lodgment of form of transfer. The allotment letter must be serially numbered, and must be examined and autographically initialled by a responsible official of the company. In addition, renounceable allotment letters must contain a provision for splitting, and split letters must be certified by an official of the company. Allotment letters must also state how the next payment of interest on the holding will be calculated. Under the Exchange Control Act, 1947, the allotment letter will bear Declarations D.1 and D.2, which must be completed where renunciation (including splits) takes place (cf. Appendix F, Form 20). The Stock Exchange will call for the following undertakings:—(a) to issue the definitive certificates within one month of the date of the expiration of any right to renunciation or the lodgment of a transfer, and to issue balance certificates without charge if required within the same period; (b) to certify transfers against allotment letters, definitive certificates and balance receipts. The allotment letter will bear the date when the document should be lodged with the company for exchange for the relative definitive certificate and the certificate will be issued only against lodgment of this document. The normal procedure is for the company (which is usually pledged to redeem a minimum amount of certificates per annum) to consider when drawing up its annual account the amount which shall be set aside to provide

Allotment Letters for Issue of Funding Certificates.

Drawings.

for redemption of certificates. When the proposed appropriation has been approved by the shareholders of the company
in general meeting the board will fix a date for the drawing to
take place in accordance with the conditions of issue of the
funding certificates. A specimen clause dealing with the
drawing of funding certificates reads as follows:—

Whenever any drawing of certificates for redemption is
required under the provisions of the preceding paragraphs
the company shall cause such drawing to be made by one of
its officers at its registered office in the presence of a notary
public or a solicitor of the Supreme Court. Every such
drawing shall be made in such manner as the company
shall (subject to the reasonable approval of the notary
public or solicitor in whose presence it is made) determine
as convenient for selecting by lot the amount of certificates
required to be drawn.

An outline of a procedure for drawing which is in force in
respect of funding certificates (equally applicable to debenture
stock or redeemable preference shares) is set out below:—

Allot a number for each multiple to be drawn, usually
£100. Thus, on stock where the multiple is £100, a holding
of £1,000 would be given ten numbers. Broken amounts
of stock are amalgamated to form a unit of £100, one
number to cover this unit.

The mechanism employed is then as follows:—

All the holdings are listed from the registers, keeping the
broken holdings on one side to be dealt with at the end of
the list. The total of the list must of course agree with the
amount of stock outstanding at the time of the drawing.
In a separate column the numbers allotted to each holding
or part holdings are marked. A specimen list is printed
at the end of this chapter showing the procedure, and in
particular how holdings which are not multiples of £100 are
dealt with at the end of the list. This procedure is carried
out before each drawing.

The drawing box (or drum) contains cards numbered
from 1 upwards, each representing £100 stock. The required number of cards are then drawn in the presence of a
notary or solicitor and arranged in numerical order. They
are listed, and against each number is placed the name of
the stockholder to whom that number was allotted, and a
note is made of the amount of stock drawn. From this list
the notary or solicitor prepares his certificate and in due
course returns the drawn numbers to the box.

The stockholders affected are then advised of the result
of the drawing and given the required notice (say, three

months if that is stated in the conditions of issue) that redemption will take place at the end of the period of notice, with interest to that date.

RECORD OF DRAWINGS

X COMPANY LIMITED.

FUNDING CERTIFICATES.

SHEET No..........

Account	Amount of Stock	Denoting Numbers	Account	Amount of Stock	Denoting Numbers
	£		Fwd.	£	
	300	1– 3		40 ⎫	1134
	1,900	4–22		60 ⎭	
	700	23–29		52 ⎫	1135
				48 ⎭	
	100	1120			
	300	1121–1123			
	100	1124			
	300	1125–1127			
	400	1128–1131			
	50 ⎫	1132			
	50 ⎭				
	87 ⎫	1133			
	13 ⎭				
Fwd.			Total		

Details of a drawing where both the amount of stock outstanding and that to be drawn are odd, are now given.

£150,035 certificates outstanding.

Amount available for drawing £50,050.

Drawing box contains discs numbered 1 to 1501 inclusive, each representing £100 certificates with the exception of no. 1501 which represents £35 certificates only.

Draw 501 numbers, each of the numbers up to the 500th so drawn to represent £100, the final number representing £50 = £50,050, the amount required.

If no. 1501 (the odd £35) is drawn, one further number to be drawn representing £15, making a total of 502 numbers drawn.

When the drawing has been finally completed the amounts drawn for each holder will be transferred to a redemption record sheet (see specimen at p. 297). The total of the redemption column will agree with the approved appropriation and the redemption cheque to be sent on the due date will be equal to the amount drawn for redemption with an addition of the net interest payment. A notification to each holder whose holding will be wholly or partially redeemed must be sent to the registered address with an intimation as to the date of payment of redemption moneys and an outline of the procedure to be followed for surrender of certificate. The circular notifying the holder usually encloses a receipt form for use when the holder is despatching his certificate to the company. The redemption moneys are payable only against surrender of the certificate, indemnities being obtained where the certificate has been lost. When a holding has been drawn for redemption (or that part, where only partially redeemed) the holding (or part) will not be available for sale, the effect of the drawing being to prohibit the registration of transfers against the amount drawn.

When carrying through a re-organisation scheme such as has been outlined, there are certain practical difficulties of procedure which will usually arise. It will be found that patience is necessary to deal with the demands for information made by holders who have no knowledge of financial matters; there will be the residual group of holdings where the holder has died and probate or letters of administration are not available for exhibition at the company's offices; there will be the holders who have changed their addresses without advice and the holders who are dilatory in such matters; there will be delay while indemnities are signed and approved for such documents as allotment letters, warrants and certificates which have been lost. The secretary will find that throughout the period of carrying through the scheme he must be prepared to issue numerous circulars hastening the action of shareholders at each stage, and he must make arrangements for all the diverse reasons for delay to be suitably noted in order that duplicate requests shall not be sent.

At each stage, the Stock Exchange and daily and financial newspapers should be notified in order that full publicity is given to the actions of the company.

Filing, etc.　　No order sanctioning a scheme will take effect until an office copy thereof has been delivered to the Registrar for registration, and a copy of every such order must be annexed to every copy of the memorandum issued after the order has been made [s. 206 (3)]. Any order made under s. 208 must be delivered to the Registrar for registration within seven days after it is made.

It is frequently desired in connection with a scheme, especially an amalgamation, to pay compensation to directors for loss of office. Section 150 of the Act of 1929 restricted the payment of such compensation by preventing any such payment in connection with (1) the transfer of the whole or any part of the undertaking or property of a company, or (2) the transfer of all or any of its shares as the result of any offer to the general body of the shareholders, unless proper disclosure had been made to the shareholders and, in the former case, the proposal had been approved by the company in general meeting. The section also contained provisions preventing an evasion of the section and making any director receiving an illegal payment trustee of the amount received for the company or for the shareholders who sold their shares as the result of the offer, as the case might be. *Compensation for loss of office.*

Sections 192 and 193 of the 1948 Act have extended and tightened up the provisions of s. 150 of the 1929 Act which dealt with compensation for loss of office. Section 192 renders illegal the payment of any such compensation to directors unless it has been disclosed to and approved by the company in general meeting. It further provides that, if any such illegal payment is made, the director concerned is deemed to hold the amount received by him in trust for the company. Moreover, where such payment is made in connection with the transfer of all or any of the shares in a company, it is the duty of the director concerned to take reasonable steps to secure that particulars of the proposed payment are included in or sent with any notice of the offer made for their shares which is given to any shareholders. This applies whether the offer is made : (i) to the general body of shareholders, (ii) by another company with a view to the company becoming its subsidiary or a subsidiary of its holding company, (iii) by an individual with a view to his obtaining at least one-third of the voting control of the company, (iv) conditional on acceptance to a given extent, *e.g.* by the holders of a particular percentage of the shares.

A difficulty may arise, if the proposed payment by way of compensation is not approved before the transfer of the shares at a meeting summoned for the purpose of the holders of shares to which the offer relates and of other holders of shares of the same class. Thus, if these shareholders are not all members of the company, and no provision is made by the articles for summoning or regulating such a meeting, then the provisions of the Act and of the company's articles relating to general meetings shall apply either without modification or with such modification as the Board of Trade may on the application of any person concerned direct. Finally, if the above-mentioned meeting is held and no quorum is present and at the adjourned meeting there is once again no quorum present, the payment shall be deemed to have been approved. As to disclosure in the accounts of compensation paid to directors, see p. 234 above.

CHAPTER XXI

WINDING UP

COMPANIES may be wound up by three distinct methods. The winding up may be (1) compulsory, *i.e.* by the court; (2) subject to the supervision of the court; (3) voluntary. Of these, by far the commonest is voluntary winding up, and it is proposed in this chapter to deal mainly with that method, only mentioning a few salient features of the others.

Compulsory liquidation is brought about by order of the **By the Court.** court on petition, and is carried out under the direction of the court, the sections of the Act exclusively applicable being ss. 218 to 277. The circumstances in which a company may be wound up by the court are enumerated in s. 222 of the Act as follows:—

- (i) if the company has by special resolution resolved that the company be wound up by the court;
- (ii) if default is made in delivering the statutory report to the Registrar or in holding the statutory meeting;
- (iii) if the company does not commence its business within a year from its incorporation, or suspends its business for a whole year;
- (iv) if the number of members is reduced, in the case of a private company, below two, or, in the case of any other company, below seven;
- (v) if the company is unable to pay its debts;
- (vi) if the court is of opinion that it is just and equitable that the company should be wound up.

Section 223 provides that a company shall be deemed to be unable to pay its debts:—

- (i) if a creditor, by assignment or otherwise, to whom the company is indebted in a sum exceeding fifty pounds then due, has served on the company, by leaving it at the registered office of the company, a demand under his hand requiring the company to pay the sum so due, and the company has for three weeks thereafter neglected to pay the sum, or to secure or compound for it to the reasonable satisfaction of the creditor; or
- (ii) if, in England or Northern Ireland, execution or other process issued on a judgment, decree or order of any court in favour of a creditor of the company is returned unsatisfied in whole or in part; or

(iii) if, in Scotland, the induciæ of a charge for payment on an extract decree, or an extract registered bond, or an extract registered protest have expired without payment being made; or

(iv) if it is proved to the satisfaction of the court that the company is unable to pay its debts, and, in determining whether a company is unable to pay its debts, the court shall take into account the contingent and prospective liabilities of the company.

Presentation of Petition. A petition may, subject to certain restrictions (see s. 224), be presented by the company itself or by a creditor or shareholder or, if the company is already being wound up voluntarily, by the Official Receiver or, in certain cases, by the Board of Trade. Most petitions are presented by creditors on the ground of insolvency. There are, however, from time to time, petitions by shareholders, usually on the ground that it is 'just and equitable.' Before 1948, if a company, owned by a few shareholders, had reached a state of deadlock because the shareholders could not agree, it would be considered just and equitable to wind it up. Minority shareholders who were being oppressed also at times sought for a winding up on this ground, though rarely with success. The 1948 Act contains provisions to meet this class of case. Under s. 210 minority shareholders who are being oppressed may, without seeking a winding up, petition for an order to bring to an end the matters complained of; the court can then make an order regulating the future conduct of the company's affairs or providing for the purchase by the company or the majority shareholders of the shares of the minority or otherwise as it thinks fit. Section 225 (2) also provides that when a winding-up petition is presented by shareholders on the ground that it is just and equitable, and in the court's opinion the petitioners are entitled to some relief, a winding up shall be ordered unless, in the opinion of the court, some other remedy is available to the petitioners and they are acting unreasonably in seeking a winding up instead of the other remedy. These sections should make it easier in future for an oppressed minority to obtain relief, though in most cases they will probably be expected to proceed under s. 210 in preference to asking for a winding up.

Commencement of Winding up. The commencement of the winding up (a date of considerable importance) is deemed to be (1) if the company is not already in voluntary liquidation, the date of the presentation of the petition [s. 229 (2)], or (2) if it is already in voluntary liquidation, the date of the passing of the resolution for winding up, the order being thus retrospective [s. 229 (1)].

If a compulsory winding up supersedes a voluntary winding up, all proceedings in the voluntary winding up will be deemed to be valid, unless on proof of fraud or mistake, the court directs otherwise [s. 229 (1)].

After the winding up order is made, the court appoints a liquidator; pending his appointment the Official Receiver acts as provisional liquidator [s. 239 (a)]. The court has power, in any case where a voluntary winding up is superseded by a compulsory order, to review the remuneration which the members or committee of inspection (whichever is applicable) have fixed as payable to the liquidator [*Mortimers London Limited* (1937), 2 All, E. R. 364].

The liquidator, who is generally assisted and partly controlled by a committee of inspection composed of creditors and contributories, takes the necessary steps to collect and realise the assets, to settle the lists of creditors and contributories (unless the court dispenses with a list under s. 257), and to pay the debts, and then to adjust the rights of the contributories, distributing among them any surplus. Upon the completion of the winding up, he obtains his release from the Board of Trade (s. 251), and the court, on the application of the liquidator, makes an order for the dissolution of the company (s. 274). The liquidator must report the making of the order to the Registrar within 14 days of its being made [s. 274 (2)].

Since an order for a compulsory winding up is nearly always **Compulsory** made on the petition of a creditor when the company is **Order.** insolvent, the secretary of a company is unlikely to be appointed liquidator in a compulsory winding up. It is not, therefore, proposed to consider in any detail the other provisions of the Act applicable in a compulsory liquidation. Attention may, however, be called to the following points:—

(1) If a petition is presented, the court may, even before an order is made for winding up, stay any legal proceedings pending against the company (s. 226) or appoint a provisional liquidator (s. 238); and, after an order has been made or a provisional liquidator appointed, no proceeding may be commenced or proceeded with except by leave of the court (s. 231).

(2) A copy of the winding up order must be forwarded forthwith by the company to the Registrar of Companies (s. 230).

(3) If an order is made, any disposition of the property of the company or transfer of its shares after the commencement of the winding up (see p. 306 above), will be void unless the court otherwise orders (s. 227), and any execution put into force against its assets after the same date will be altogether void (s. 228).

(4) If an order is made or a provisional liquidator is appointed, the liquidator or provisional liquidator (if one is appointed) takes into custody or under his control all the company's property (s. 243), but the property does not vest in the liquidator unless an order is made under s. 244.

(5) If an order is made, a statement of affairs must, unless the court otherwise orders, be made out, verified by affidavit and delivered to the Official Receiver. The Official Receiver, subject to the direction of the court, will decide who is to submit and verify the statement; but, as a rule, he will direct this to be done by one or more directors and the secretary (s. 235). As soon as practicable after the statement is delivered, or if it is dispensed with by the court, after the order for winding up is made, the Official Receiver will submit a preliminary report to the court in the manner prescribed by s. 236 (see also Rules 52–57 of the Companies (Winding-up) Rules, 1949).

(6) The court may at any time after a winding up order is made, make an order on certain persons, including the secretary or any other officer of the company, for delivery to the liquidator of any property and books and papers in his hands to which the company is *prima facie* entitled (s. 258).

(7) At any time after the provisional liquidator is appointed or a winding up order is made, the court may order the private examination on oath before the court of any officer of the company or other person known to have or suspected of having in his possession any property of the company or believed to be capable of giving information as to its promotion, formation, trade dealings, affairs or property (s. 268).

(8) If an order is made for winding up by the court and the Official Receiver reports that in his opinion a fraud has been committed in connection with the company by any promoter, director or officer, the court may direct a public examination of the person alleged to have been fraudulent (s. 270), or may, on the application of the Official Receiver, order that that person shall not without the leave of the court be concerned or take part in the management of any company for such period, not exceeding five years from the date of the report, as may be specified in the order (s. 188).

(9) The court may, at any time after an order has been made, stay the winding up on the application of the liquidator, the Official Receiver, or any creditor or contributory on such terms as it thinks fit (s. 256).

The jurisdiction of the court to make an order for the winding up of a company extends not only to companies as defined by s. 455 but also to unregistered companies as defined by s. 398, unless within the exception mentioned in s. 399 (2). An order for winding up an unregistered company can, however, only be made on the occurrence of one or other of the events mentioned in s. 399 (5). No unregistered company can be wound up voluntarily or subject to the supervision of the court.

Winding up, subject to the supervision of the court, is **Winding up** brought about by order of the court (s. 311) on petition pre- **Subject to** sented when a voluntary winding up is already in progress, **Supervision.** by one or more of the parties who may petition for compulsory order (see above). The presentation of a petition for a winding up under supervision gives the court the same jurisdiction over proceedings against the company as the presentation of a petition for winding up by the court (s. 312), and, if an order is made, the provisions of s. 227 avoiding dispositions of property and s. 228 avoiding executions apply as if an order for winding up by the court had been made (s. 313). The date which was the commencement of the voluntary winding up which it supersedes (*i.e.* the date of the passing of the winding up resolution) is not altered, and becomes the date of the commencement of the winding up under supervision. By the supervision order the court may appoint liquidators either in substitution for or in addition to those already appointed by the company (s. 314).

The liquidator's powers, unless restricted by the court, are identical with those possessed by a liquidator in voluntary winding up, except that he cannot pay any class of creditors in full or make any compromise within s. 245 (1) (*d*), (*e*) and (*f*) without the sanction of the court [s. 315 (1)]. By s. 315 (2) it is provided that an order for winding up under supervision is to be deemed a winding up by the court except for the provisions of the Act set out in the Eleventh Schedule thereto. In view, however, of s. 315 (1) the liquidation will proceed generally as in a voluntary winding up. The company will ultimately be dissolved in the same way as in a voluntary winding up.

Having regard to the practically unlimited powers of application to the court under s. 307 of the Act, there is seldom any great advantage in obtaining a supervision order, and such orders are rare.

Voluntary winding up and the position of the liquidator **Voluntary** therein require much more detailed treatment, since the office **Winding up.** of liquidator is frequently undertaken by a company's secretary.

Section 278 of the Act enumerates the circumstances in

which a company may be wound up voluntarily. These are as follows:—

(a) when the period, if any, fixed for the duration of the company by the articles expires, or the event, if any, occurs, on the occurrence of which the articles provide that the company is to be dissolved, and the company in general meeting has passed a resolution requiring the company to be wound up voluntarily;

(b) if the company resolves by special resolution that the company be wound up voluntarily;

(c) if the company resolves by extraordinary resolution to the effect that it cannot by reason of its liabilities continue its business, and that it is advisable to wind up.

Of the above, (a), which, it will be observed, requires only an ordinary resolution, is seldom met in practice. In the case of an insolvent company, (c) is appropriate, and an extraordinary resolution will suffice. In any other case, e.g. if the winding up is for the purpose of reconstruction, (b) is applicable, and a special resolution is necessary. It need hardly be pointed out that, if a valid voluntary winding up is to be commenced, extreme care must be taken in every detail connected with the convening and holding of the meeting.

Members' and Creditors' Voluntary. Winding up.

Declaration of Solvency.

A distinction is drawn between a solvent and an insolvent winding up, the former being called 'a members' voluntary winding up,' and the latter 'a creditors' voluntary winding up.' The winding up is a members' voluntary winding up if, not more than five weeks before the passing of the resolution to wind up the company, (1) the directors, or, if there are more than two directors, the majority of the directors at a board meeting, make a statutory declaration to the effect that they have made a full enquiry into the affairs of the company, and that having so done, they have formed the opinion that the company will be able to pay its debts in full within such period not exceeding twelve months from the commencement of the winding up as may be specified in the declaration; and (2) such declaration is delivered to the Registrar for registration (s. 283). The declaration is of no effect if it is not made within the five weeks, and it is also of no effect unless it contains a statement of the company's assets and liabilities as at the latest practicable date before the declaration is made [s. 283 (2)]. There are heavy penalties under the Act for declaring without reasonable grounds that the company will be able to pay its debts (see Appendix B), and if the company is wound up in pursuance of a resolution passed within the five weeks, but its debts are not paid or provided for in full within the period stated in the declaration, the onus is on the directors to show that they had reasonable grounds for their opinion. A form of declaration of solvency will be found in Form 108 annexed to the Companies (Winding-up) Rules, 1949. See Appendix F, Form 126. If no such declaration is made and delivered to the Registrar for registration before the notices are sent out, the winding up is a creditors' voluntary winding up, even though the company may in fact be solvent.

It is provided by s. 288 of the Act that, if after the commencement of a winding up, the liquidator is at any time of opinion that the company will not be able to pay its debts in full within the period specified in the statutory declaration, he must immediately summon a creditors' meeting and lay before such meeting a statement of the assets and liabilities of the company. Thereafter, in effect, the liquidation is a creditors' winding up and the liquidator is bound to hold annual meetings of creditors under s. 299 and a final meeting of creditors [as well as of the company under s. 300 of the Act (s. 291)]. It should however be noted that a liquidator need not summon a meeting of creditors at the end of the first year from the commencement of winding up, unless the above-mentioned meeting, held under s. 288, is held more than three months before the end of that year.

The secretary of a company is more likely to be appointed liquidator in a members' voluntary winding up than in a creditors' voluntary winding up; but it is proposed to deal with the provisions applicable to both classes of voluntary winding up. Before this is done, however, it should be observed that under s. 211 the provisions of the Act with respect to winding up apply, unless the contrary appears, alike to winding up by the court, winding up under supervision and voluntary winding up. In addition, therefore, to the provisions expressly made applicable to voluntary winding up the following portions of Part V of the Act apply:—ss. 212–217 (which deal with contributories and their liability) and such of the sections contained in the group headed 'Provisions applicable to every mode of winding up,' which include ss. 316–365, as are not expressly made applicable exclusively to either or both of the other kinds of winding up. Moreover, under s. 307 the liquidator may apply to the court to exercise, as respects the enforcing of calls, or any other matter, all or any of the powers which the court might exercise if the company were being wound up by the court. This section, in effect, makes applicable in a voluntary winding up the group of sections headed 'General Powers of Court in case of Winding up by the Court,' which comprises ss. 256 to 274. Sections 263 and 270, however, will not apply, s. 263 because

L

the Official Receiver will never be liquidator in a voluntary winding up, and s. 270 because the Official Receiver does not report to the court in a voluntary winding up.

Practice. The practice rules as to voluntary winding up are to be found in the Companies (Winding-up) Rules, 1949, but a detailed examination of these rules is beyond the scope of this work, and a liquidator would always be well advised to consult a solicitor before making any application to the court. Certain of the Rules, however, affect liquidators in matters other than applications to the court, and such rules are dealt with hereafter. Rule 2 in effect provides that the Rules are to be applicable to every form of winding up, including all proceedings under s. 210 of the Act, unless, from their nature or subject matter, or by the headlines above the group in which they are contained, or by their terms, they are or are made applicable only to a particular form or particular forms of winding up. There is thus no serious difficulty in discovering what rules are and what are not appropriate. The more important rules affecting a liquidator in a voluntary liquidation are set out in Appendix N.

Commencement and Effect of Voluntary Winding up. Before considering further any of the sections of the Act which are of general application, it will be convenient to refer to the sections which are applicable only in a voluntary winding up. The first point to be observed is that the commencement of a voluntary winding up is the time of the passing of the resolution for winding up (s. 280). This date is of great importance, e.g. as to the liability of past members (s. 212), as to matters of fraudulent preference (s. 320) and as to the validity of floating charges (s. 322). On the commencement of the winding up the company must cease to trade, except for the purpose of beneficial winding up (s. 281). A transfer can be sanctioned by the liquidator, but any other alteration in the status of a member after commencement of a winding up is void (s. 282). None the less—and it is important to remember this point—the corporate existence of the company and its corporate powers continue until its dissolution, notwithstanding anything in its articles (s. 281). A resolution for voluntary winding up may in some cases operate as a dismissal of the company's servants, but whether or not it has this effect depends on the facts in each particular case [*Reigate* v. *Union Manufacturing Co.* (1918), 1 K.B. 592 and particularly per Scrutton L.J., at p. 606; *Midland Counties Bank* v. *Attwood* (1905), 1 Ch. 357; *Nokes* v. *Doncaster Amalgamated Collieries* (1940), A.C. at p. 1040].

Advertisement. The resolution for voluntary winding up must be advertised in the *London Gazette* within fourteen days after the passing thereof, and in the event of default in doing so, the company and every officer of the company in default (including the liquidator) will be liable to a penalty (s. 279).

In a members' voluntary winding up the liquidator will be **Members'** appointed by the company in general meeting [s. 285 (1)]. **Voluntary** The appointment will usually be made at the meeting which **Winding up.** resolves on the winding up. The appointment need not be made by special resolution, and the notice need not name the liquidator, though it must give notice of the intention to appoint a liquidator. Although more than one liquidator may be appointed in the case of a members' voluntary winding up, this is unnecessary as extra expense is involved and difficulties arise if one liquidator dies [see s. 303 (3)]. Accordingly the usual course will be to appoint a sole liquidator. On the appointment of a liquidator the powers of the directors cease except so far as the exercise thereof is sanctioned by the company in general meeting or by the liquidator [s. 285 (2)]. Any vacancy in the office of liquidator will, subject to any arrangement with creditors, be filled by the company in general meeting at a meeting convened by any contributory or by the continuing liquidator if such there be (s. 286). No creditors' meeting will be called in a members' voluntary liquidation.

In a creditors' voluntary winding up, *i.e.* if no declaration of **Creditors'** solvency has been made and lodged with the Registrar **Voluntary** pursuant to s. 283, the company must summon a meeting of **Winding up.** creditors to be held at the place most convenient to the majority of the creditors [Rule 131 of the Companies (Winding-up) Rules, 1949], on the same day as or on the day after the day on which the meeting of the company to pass the resolution for winding up is to be held (s. 293). The provisions of s. 293 may be summarised as follows:—

(1) the notices to the creditors must be posted simultaneously with the notices to the members. General and special forms of proxy must be sent with the notices [Rule 148 of the Companies (Winding-up) Rules, 1949];

(2) the notice of the creditors' meeting should be sent to the last known address of each creditor and must be advertised once in the *Gazette*, and at least once in two local newspapers circulating in the district where either the registered office or the principal place of business is situate. The Act does not state when the advertisements must be inserted, but it is thought that they must be inserted not later than the date when the notices are posted;

(3) the directors must appoint one of their number to preside at the creditors' meeting, and the director so appointed must preside at the meeting;

(4) the directors must prepare and lay before the meeting a full statement of the position of the company's affairs and a list of creditors and the estimated amount of their claims.

The business of the creditors' meeting is to be gathered from ss. 294 and 295. Under s. 294 the creditors may nominate a liquidator, and under s. 295 they may appoint a committee of inspection consisting of not more than five persons. If a resolution is passed at the creditors' meeting and the general meeting of the company is adjourned, but at the adjourned meeting a resolution for winding up is passed, any resolution passed at the creditors' meeting will take effect as if passed immediately after the resolution for winding up [s. 293 (5)]. For the rules as to the convening and conduct of and as to proxies at such meetings see Rules 127–156 of the Companies (Winding-up) Rules, 1949.

Liquidator in Creditors' Winding up. It will be noted that s. 294 gives the creditors power to nominate, not to appoint, a liquidator. The reason for this is that the section confers a like power of nomination on the company exercisable at the meeting at which the resolution for winding up is passed. If both meetings nominate the same person or, subject as below mentioned, if they nominate different persons, the person nominated by the creditors will be liquidator. If, however, the creditors nominate no one, the person nominated by the company will be liquidator. If different persons are nominated by the company and the creditors, any director, member or creditor may, within seven days after the date on which the creditors' nomination was made, apply to the court for an order directing that the company's nominee be liquidator instead of or jointly with the creditors' nominee, or that some third person be appointed liquidator in place of the creditors' nominee. It will be noted that this application cannot be made by the company. In a creditors' liquidation, unlike a members' liquidation, only one person can be appointed liquidator unless a joint liquidator is appointed by the court. Any vacancy in the office of the liquidator may be filled by the creditors unless the liquidator was appointed or nominated by the court (s. 297). As in a members' voluntary winding up, after the appointment of a liquidator, the powers of the directors can be exercised only with the express sanction of the committee of inspection, or if there be no committee, of the creditors [s. 296 (2)].

Committee of Inspection in Creditors' Winding up. A committee of inspection can be appointed either at the creditors' meeting convened pursuant to s. 293, or at any subsequent meeting of the creditors. If the creditors appoint a committee of inspection, the company may appoint not more than five persons to act as members of such committee, either at the meeting at which the resolution for winding up is passed, or at any subsequent general meeting; but the creditors may resolve that all or any of the members of the committee appointed by the company ought not to be members thereof, and if the creditors do so resolve, the persons mentioned in the resolution will, unless the court otherwise directs, be disqualified from acting as members of the committee (s. 295). Subject as above and subject to the Winding-up Rules, the provisions of ss. 253 (except sub-s. (1)) and 255 of the Act (which sections deal with committees of inspection in a winding up by the court) apply to a committee of inspection appointed in a voluntary winding up. Under these sections the committee will meet at such times as it from time to time appoints, and, failing such appointment, must meet at least once a month. The liquidator, or any member of the committee, can at any time call a meeting when he thinks it necessary. The committee acts by a majority of those present, but a majority of its members must be present to constitute a quorum. Any member of the committee may resign, and he will automatically vacate office if he becomes bankrupt, makes an arrangement with his creditors or is absent from five consecutive meetings without the leave of those members of the committee, who, together with himself, represent the creditors or contributories as the case may be. A creditors' representative may be removed by a meeting of the creditors and a contributories' representative by an ordinary resolution of the company in general meeting. Any vacancy among the creditors' representatives can be filled by the creditors, and any vacancy among the contributories' representatives can be filled by the company in general meeting; and it is the duty of the liquidator forthwith to convene the necessary meeting on a vacancy occurring. It is, however, provided that if, in the liquidator's opinion, it is unnecessary to fill the vacancy, the liquidator may apply to the court and the court may make an order accordingly. If the committee falls below two in number, it cannot function. Rule 161 of the Companies (Winding-up) Rules, 1949, forbids a purchase of any of the company's assets by or on behalf of a member of the committee without leave of the court, and Rule 163 forbids a member of the committee directly or indirectly to make any profit out of his office, except with the sanction of the court.

Joint Liquidators. If several liquidators are appointed, the powers conferred on a liquidator by s. 303 may be exercised by such one or more of them as may be determined at the time of their appointment or in default of such determination by any number not less than two [s. 303 (3)].

Remuneration of a Liquidator. The remuneration of a liquidator in a members' voluntary winding up may be fixed by the company in general meeting either when the liquidator is appointed or subsequently [s. 285 (1)]; in a creditors' voluntary winding up the committee of inspection, or, if there be none, the creditors, may fix the remuneration [s. 296 (1)]. In either case the court can be asked to fix the remuneration under the joint effect of ss. 307 and 242 (2), e.g. where the creditors think the committee has allowed too much. The remuneration may be a lump sum, or a percentage of the assets, or may be at the rate of so much per day or per hour spent exclusively on the liquidation; or other methods of remuneration may be adopted. It is generally inadvisable to fix the liquidator's remuneration at the time of his appointment, as the amount of work involved cannot be known: but this objection does not apply so strongly in the case of a members' voluntary liquidation for the purpose of reconstruction, where the work involved can be fairly estimated and the liquidator will probably be an officer of the old company and become an officer of the new company and will often be remunerated by the payment of a moderate lump sum. If application is made to the court, it will in general adopt the scale applicable to trustees in bankruptcy [*Carton* (1923), 39 T.L.R. 194]. A course sometimes adopted is for the liquidator to take what he considers reasonable remuneration, and then, when his final accounts are passed at the final meeting (see below), that sum, if approved, is by the vote of the company appropriated to him. Rule 160 forbids a liquidator to accept any gift, remuneration, consideration or benefit from any solicitor, auctioneer or any other person connected with the company or employed in connection with the winding up, beyond the remuneration to which he is entitled, or to make any arrangement for giving any of his remuneration to any such solicitor, auctioneer or other person. Rule 161 forbids him to purchase any of the company's assets without leave of the court, and Rule 162 forbids him, when carrying on the company's business, without the express sanction of the court to purchase goods for carrying on the business from any person whose connection with him is such as to result in his obtaining any part of the profit arising from the transactions.

Service of Notices, etc. By Rule 23, all notices, summonses and other documents, other than those of which personal service is required, may be sent by prepaid post letter to the last-known address of the person to be served therewith; and the notice, summons or document is to be considered as served at the time when the same ought to be delivered in the due course of post by the post office, and notwithstanding that the same may be returned by the post office.

Although in a compulsory liquidation the books of a company close at once, it may be, and often is, otherwise in a voluntary liquidation.

A negative effect of a voluntary winding up is that it does not operate to stay actions, as a compulsory order or a supervision order does, nor does it prevent actions being brought against the company after the commencement of the voluntary liquidation. It is, however, always open to the liquidator to apply to the court for a stay. In *Currie* v. *Consolidated*

Kent Collieries (1906), 1 K.B. 134, it was held that the onus is upon the liquidator applying for a stay to show that an order should be made that in case of a real dispute a stay should not be granted, and that, so far from a stay being a convenience, it would in such cases be an unnecessary waste of time and money. In a case where liability is substantially admitted, and the question is really one of amount, the matter is one which may properly be dealt with by the creditor proving in the liquidation, and accordingly a stay should be granted. The matter is in each case one for the discretion of the court.

It should be noticed that by s. 310, a voluntary winding up is not to bar the right of any creditor or contributory to have the company wound up by the court, but in the case of an application by a contributory the court must be satisfied that the rights of the contributories will be prejudiced by a voluntary winding up.

It is not easy to define accurately the status of the liquidator. It is to be gathered from the following statutory provisions (some of which have already been mentioned): that liquidators are appointed for the purpose of winding up the affairs of the company and distributing its property [ss. 285 (1), 294]; that they shall pay the debts of the company and adjust the rights of the contributories amongst themselves (s. 302); that upon their appointment all the powers of the directors cease, except so far as the continuance thereof may be sanctioned in accordance with s. 285 (2) or s. 296 (2); and that until the winding up is complete the corporate state and all the corporate powers of the company continue (s. 281). The company, then, continues to exist, but the directors (subject to the exceptions mentioned) cannot act, and the liquidator has the duty of winding up the company's affairs. The liquidator steps into the shoes of the directors, not for carrying the company's business on, but for winding it up, although he may carry it on so far as is necessary for the beneficial winding up (s. 281); and his status resembles in many ways the former position of the board. Directors, as is well known, have a dual capacity—they are both agents and trustees. The liquidator is in a certain sense a trustee. He may be said to hold the assets of the company in trust for the creditors and then for the contributories; but his primary duty being to realise and distribute, he is, perhaps rather the company's agent for certain specified purposes [*Knowles* v. *Scott* (1891), 1 Ch. 717]. A contract, for example, made by him for the purpose of realising some of the company's assets is made by the company through him, the common form of the statement of parties being: 'Between the——Company, Limited, by J—— S——, of——, etc., the liquidator thereof, of the one part, and A—— B——, of——, etc., of the other

Position of a Liquidator.

part.' It may, further, be observed that the liquidator in a voluntary winding up, being appointed by the shareholders, is not an officer of the court, although he has certain duties imposed on him by statute, and if he neglects those duties the parties injured, whether creditors or contributories, may be able, if the winding up is still in progress, to compel the liquidator to make good to the assets of the company the damage he has done, by a misfeasance summons under s. 333 [*Windsor Steam Coal Co.* (1929), 1 Ch. 151; *Home & Colonial Insurance Co.* (1930), 1 Ch. 102], or if the company has been dissolved to make him personally liable in an action for damages [*Pulsford* v. *Devenish* (1903), 2 Ch. 625; *Armstrong Whitworth Securities Ltd.* (1947), Ch. 673 at p. 692].

His Powers. The powers of the liquidator in a voluntary winding up are, in general, so inextricably involved with his duties that comment on them may be reserved until his duties are more fully dealt with. By s. 303 the liquidator has power, without any sanction, to exercise all the powers given to a liquidator in compulsory winding up, except (1) the power to pay any class of creditors in full and (2) the power to make such compromises and arrangements as are mentioned in paragraphs (*d*), (*e*) and (*f*) of s. 245 (1). He may accordingly under s. 243 take all the property of the company into his custody; under s. 245 appoint a solicitor and bring or defend any action in the name of the company; carry on the business of the company, so far as may be necessary for its beneficial winding up; sell the whole of its real and personal property; execute deeds and other documents, and use the company's seal; prove as creditor in the bankruptcy of any contributory; draw bills and raise money upon the security of the assets of the company; take out letters of administration to any deceased contributory; appoint an agent to do any business which he is unable to do himself; and do all such other things as may be necessary for winding up the affairs of the company and distributing its assets. Under s. 303 he may summon general meetings, settle the list of contributories, make calls, pay debts, and adjust the rights of the contributories among themselves; under s. 307 apply to the court, and under s. 333 institute misfeasance proceedings. He may exercise the above-mentioned powers of paying any class of creditors in full and making compromises and arrangements, in the case of a members' voluntary winding up with the sanction of an extraordinary resolution of the company, and in the case of a creditors' voluntary winding up with the sanction of (*a*) the court, (*b*) the committee of inspection, or (*c*) a meeting of creditors if there is no committee of inspection [s. 303 (1) (*a*)]. Under the corresponding section of the Act of 1908 (s. 214) it was held that a compromise with a creditor

under that section, unless set aside, was binding even though
the sanction of an extraordinary resolution had not been
obtained [*Cycle-makers Company* v. *Sims* (1903), 1 K.B. 477],
and *semble* this decision will apply to a compromise made
without the sanction required by s. 303; but if a liquidator
makes a compromise without the sanction required by the
Act, he does so at his own risk and, if the compromise is held
to have been improper, will be liable to misfeasance proceedings under s. 333 [*Windsor Steam Coal Co.* (1929), 1 Ch.
151].

The above are the principal powers expressly conferred by
statute upon the liquidator, but it will be found that incident-
ally the wide powers expressly specified by the legislature
include numerous minor auxiliary powers.

A liquidator should enter upon his duties at the earliest **His Duties.**
possible moment after his appointment. His primary duties
are realisation and distribution of assets, and all that he
does will be directed towards these two ends.

One of his earliest duties is prescribed by s. 305 of the Act.
By s. 305 he is bound, under a penalty of £5 per day, within
fourteen days of his appointment, to publish in the *Gazette*
and to deliver to the Registrar a note of his appointment in
the form prescribed by the Board of Trade; and, as already
mentioned, he must see that the winding up resolution has
been duly advertised in accordance with s. 279. (See Appendix
F, Forms 127, 128 and 129.)

The liquidator, after his appointment, will immediately **Taking**
proceed to take possession of the company's books and **Possession**
documents. If he is the secretary, he will, probably, have **of Property.**
no difficulty in doing this, as the books kept at the registered
office of the company will be ready to hand, while, if the
company is a trading company, the ordinary business books
will be available at the place where the company's business
has actually been carried on. If the liquidator is unconnected
with the company, *e.g.* a chartered accountant, his labour in
ascertaining that he has control of all the books and documents of the company, whether at the registered office or
elsewhere, will usually be greater. It is the duty of the
liquidator, if he finds any book or document missing, to
ascertain its whereabouts, or, if he fails to discover books or
documents that he would expect to find, to make inquiries
and satisfy himself as to their existence or non-existence.
Practically all the company's books will be of assistance to
the liquidator in the discharge of his duties. For example,
the seal book, if one be kept, should contain particulars of
documents to which the common seal has been attached, and
will be of use in enabling the liquidator to ascertain what
documents of importance are in existence.

In taking possession of the books and documents of the

company, the liquidator may find that some are in the possession of a solicitor or other person who claims a lien upon them for money due. The liquidator will then proceed to inquire whether this lien is valid. If it is obviously invalid, *e.g.* if it is upon certain books which are, by statute, required to be kept at the registered office of the company—the register of members, for instance—the liquidator must insist upon the delivery to him of the books or documents in question. If the validity of the lien be doubtful, and no reasonable compromise can be reached, the question will have to be decided, the obvious course being for the liquidator to apply to the court, under s. 307 of the Act, for an order for the delivery to him of the documents, whereupon the court will adjudicate upon the matter. In the meantime, if the possession of the document is necessary for the purposes of the winding up, it is advisable for the liquidator to pay the amount claimed to an independent third party, or to a joint account, pending the decision of the question, and thus to obtain delivery. If the lien appears, on due examination, to be valid, and the documents are necessary, the liquidator should if possible pay the amount due, or undertake to do so, out of the first available assets. If the lien is claimed by a solicitor, it may be desirable to have the bill taxed, delivery being generally obtained by paying the money claimed into court pending the taxation.

After taking possession, or taking all needful and possible steps towards taking possession, of the company's books and documents, the liquidator will then obtain possession, so far as he can, of the other property of the company. This does not mean, of course, that he is to have the land and buildings (if any) of the company conveyed to him, or any of the chattels of the company formally made over to him. He will take possession by assuming the control over them. For example, he will assume the control of the company's business, and of its stock-in-trade and other assets, thus putting himself into the position formerly occupied by the directors. It must not be forgotten that the corporate status and all the corporate powers of the company still continue, the liquidator being, as observed before, the company's agent for the purpose of winding up its affairs.

The liquidator, however, cannot assume the control or physical possession of all the company's property. He can, for instance, have no physical control over the book debts of the company, or any property of the company which has been taken possession of, as is frequently the case, by mortgagees, or by a receiver on their behalf. His duty in these cases is to give notice to the debtors, or the mortgagees, or receiver, as the case may be, of the fact that the company is in voluntary liquidation, and that he is the liquidator.

In taking possession, special care is necessary in the case of **Disclaimer** leasehold property. If the company is insolvent, it is neces- **of Onerous** sary to inquire whether the retention of the leaseholds is **Property.** for the benefit of the winding up. This will depend very largely upon the nature of the covenants in the lease. If the rent is high and the covenants onerous, the value may be small, and on the property being retained the landlord will be entitled to be paid rent in full during the liquidation.

Section 323 of the Act gives the liquidator the power of disclaimer of leaseholds and other onerous property analagous to that which a trustee in bankruptcy has under the Bankruptcy Act, 1914. That section provides that where any part of the property of a company which is being wound up consists of land of any tenure burdened with onerous covenants, of shares or stock in companies, of unprofitable contracts or of any other property that is unsaleable, or not readily saleable, by reason of its binding the possessor thereof to the performance of any onerous act, or to the payment of any sum of money, the liquidator, notwithstanding that he has endeavoured to sell or has taken possession of the property or exercised any act of ownership in relation thereto, may, with the leave of the court, but subject to the provisions of the section, by writing signed by him disclaim the property. It will be noted that the leave of the court is essential prior to the disclaimer and notice of disclaimer must be in writing signed by the liquidator. The court in exercising its discretion when an application for leave to disclaim is made will take into consideration the effect of a disclaimer on interested parties, and will balance the advantages and disadvantages of a disclaimer to be gained by the liquidator in the liquidation of the assets and the persons affected by the disclaimer. [*Katherine et Cie* (1932), 1 Ch. 70]. Moreover, notice of disclaimer must be given within 12 months after the commencement of the winding up, or such extended period as the court may allow, unless the properties which it is desired to disclaim do not come to the knowledge of the liquidator within one month after the commencement of the winding up, in which case the period within which the notice of disclaimer must be given is calculated from the date on which the liquidator became aware of the property. By sub-s. (2) the disclaimer operates to determine as from the date of disclaimer the ownership rights, interests, and liabilities of the company in or in respect of the property disclaimed, but does not, except so far as is necessary for the purpose of releasing the company and the property of the company from liability, affect the rights or liabilities of any other person. In order that persons interested may not be left in doubt as to the intentions of the liquidator, sub-s. (4) provides that any interested person may make application to the liquidator in writing requiring him to decide whether he will or will not disclaim, and that if he has not within 28 days after receipt of such application or within such further period as the court may allow given notice to the applicant that he intends to apply to the court for leave to disclaim, and in the case of a contract, if the liquidator, after such an application, does not within the said period or further period disclaim the contract, the company shall be deemed to have adopted it. It would appear that if the liquidator desires an extension of time within which to give notice of disclaimer he must apply to the court for such extension within the period of 28 days [*ex parte Lovering*, 9 Ch. App. 586, *Richardson*, 16 Ch. D. 613]. Accordingly in any application to the court for leave to disclaim a contract, it is advisable, if such an application as mentioned above has been received from a party interested, to ask also for an extension of the period in which notice of disclaimer may be given. It is not clear what is the effect of the words 'The company shall be deemed to have adopted' the contract. In the analogous section of the Bankruptcy Act the trustee is made expressly liable. No personal liability is, however, imposed on the liquidator. [*Stead Hazel & Co.* v. *Cooper* (1933), 1 K.B. 840.] There appear to be two alternatives:— (*a*) that the interested party is to have a mere right of proof, or (*b*) that the contract is to be treated as if it had been made by the liquidator on behalf of the company in the course of carrying on its business, in which case the interested party would be entitled to be paid in full. Probably the latter is the correct interpretation. A liquidator who has to consider the question would be well advised to obtain the decision of the court and not act on his own interpretation of s. 323. The section contains other provisions enabling the court, either before or on granting leave to disclaim, to require notices to be given to interested parties, and enabling any interested person to apply to the court to make an order rescinding the contract on terms or vesting the property in the applicant or directing the delivery to him of any disclaimed property. The consideration of this section is, however, beyond the scope of this book. The decisions on s. 54 of the Bankruptcy Act, 1914, afford some guide to the application of this section, but the sections are not identical and, since different considerations arise in a liquidation from those in a bankruptcy, cases decided under the Bankruptcy Acts are not necessarily applicable to a disclaimer under the Act [*Katherine et Cie* (1932), 1 Ch. 70]. Section 323 (7) provides that any person injured by the operation of a disclaimer shall be deemed a creditor of the company to the amount of the injury and may prove the amount as a debt in the winding up. The section does not apply in the case of a winding up in Scotland [s. 323 (8)].

An important duty of the liquidator is the keeping of **Keeping** proper accounts. It is nowhere laid down that a liquidator **Accounts.** in a voluntary winding up must keep accounts, but Rule 172 (3) of the Companies (Winding-up) Rules, 1949, provides that in a creditors' voluntary winding up the liquidator shall keep such books as the committee of inspection or, if there is no such committee, as the creditors direct, and that all books kept by the liquidator shall be submitted to the committee or the creditors with any other books, documents, papers and accounts in his possession, relating to his office as liquidator or to the company, as and when the committee or the creditors direct. Moreover, under s. 342, if the winding up is not concluded within one year, the liquidator must send to the Registrar at the prescribed intervals a statement in the prescribed form containing the prescribed particulars with respect to the proceedings in and the position of the liquidation. As to intervals, forms and particulars see Rules 196 and 197 of the Companies (Winding-up) Rules, 1949, and see Appendix F, Forms 130, 131 and 132. It is, therefore, perfectly obvious that a liquidator cannot comply with this section or adequately perform his other duties without keeping accounts. Further, on the completion of the winding up, it is the duty of the liquidator to lay before the final meeting of the company, or in the case of a creditors' voluntary winding up the final meeting of the company and the creditors, an account showing how the winding up has been conducted, and how the property of the company has been disposed of (ss. 290, 300). This would be impossible, had the liquidator not kept complete and systematic accounts throughout the liquidation. It is also desirable for the liquidator, in order that he may be able to give an account of his stewardship, to keep the record book which is prescribed by Rule 171 of the Companies (Winding-up) Rules, 1949, in the case of compulsory winding up. In this he will enter notes of all his transactions in conducting the winding up. The book may conveniently take the form of a diary. A cash book should be kept in the form found in Appendix F, Form 139.

It may be noted that the bankruptcy rules relating to the doctrine of reputed ownership are not imported into the winding up of companies [*Gorringe* v. *Irwell Rubber Works* (1887), 34 Ch. D. 128].

In realising the assets the liquidator should act with all **Carrying on** convenient speed, remembering that the longer the liquida- **Business.** tion is protracted the greater is the expense of the mere administration likely to be. However, in the case of a trading company with outstanding trade contracts, it will frequently be of advantage to the assets to carry out the contracts and receive the agreed payments for them. This will be a legitimate carrying on of the business. In all cases where, for whatever reason, the liquidator considers it desirable to carry on the business of the company for anything more than a very short time, it is advisable for application to be made to the court, under s. 307, for liberty to do so, or at all events for the sanction of the committee of inspection, if one has been appointed, to be obtained. The court, in granting leave to carry on the business, usually imposes a limit to the time during which this may be done, *e.g.* three months. In the event of an extension being required, a further application must be made to the court.

The right to carry on the business involves the right to do everything incidental thereto: contracts may be made, the trade generally may be continued, bills of exchange may be drawn or accepted, and even, in a proper case, money may be borrowed for the purposes of the company, upon such security as the company is able to offer. It is generally advisable to obtain the sanction of the court before borrowing money. It is hardly necessary to point out that any security given by the liquidator for loans ranks after all existing securities. The liquidator will, of course, make it clear to all persons with whom business is done that the company is in voluntary liquidation.

In carrying on the business, the liquidator must bear in mind that every invoice, order for goods, or business letter issued by or on behalf of the company, or of the liquidator himself, must contain a statement that the company is being wound up (s. 338).

Debts incurred by the liquidator in the course of carrying on the business of the company must be paid in priority to debts and liabilities incurred before the commencement of the liquidation. They are, in reality, provided they are properly incurred, part of the costs of the administration of the company's affairs, which, as will be seen hereafter, have a priority over the ordinary liabilities.

Collecting Debts. In collecting the debts due to the company, the liquidator will make written demands upon the debtors, and if all other means fail he will, if he considers it desirable, take proceedings for recovering debts outstanding. It is necessary, however, to consider carefully whether the proceedings are likely to be productive of any adequate result. A liquidator would not be justified in suing a debtor when he knew the debtor could in no circumstances pay. Proceedings would, in such a case, be merely a waste of the company's money. The liquidator has also, as has been stated, power to compromise with the sanctions indicated on p. 318.

It has been seen that a liquidator can sell all or any of the company's property, taking care to do so to the best of advantage. Thus, he may, if he thinks it advantageous, sell the book debts instead of realising them himself. It may here be remarked that, speaking generally, the liquidator may employ agents to act for him in cases where the skill and experience of a professional man is desirable in the interests of the company. Perhaps a fair statement is that in all cases where an ordinarily capable and reasonable individual would employ an agent, *e.g.* an auctioneer, or a broker, or a solicitor, the liquidator may do the same. And he may pay them reasonable remuneration for their services. It is in the case of sales of the company's more important assets that professional services are most likely to be required; but the advice of a solicitor may often be properly sought in almost every phase of a winding up. When dealing with the company's property and when employing agents to act for him, the liquidator should bear in mind the provisions of Rules 160 to 162, cf. *Gertzenstein* (1937), Ch. 45 (see p. 316).

In connection with the realisation of the company's assets, **Private** the important powers conferred upon the liquidator by the **Examina-** combined effect of ss. 268 and 307 of the Act must be noticed. **tions.** Section 268 empowers the court to 'summon before it any officer of the company or person known or suspected to have in his possession any of the property of the company, or supposed to be indebted to the company, or any person whom the court deems capable of giving information concerning the trade, dealings, affairs, or property of the company,' and any person so summoned may be required to produce books, etc. In a proper case, therefore, if the liquidator suspects that any of the company's property is being kept back, whether by the company's officials or other persons, or if he has reason to suppose that there has been fraud in the promotion of the company, and that certain persons have received moneys which really belong to the company, he will make application to the court, under s. 268, for an order for the examination (called private examination, in contradistinction to the public examination which can only take place in winding up by the court) of any one who will voluntarily give, or from whom can be extracted, information as to the existence of assets, or information on which to ground misfeasance proceedings.

Misfeasance proceedings are provided for by s. 333, their object being to compel any delinquent promoter or officer of a company to make restitution of any money or property of the company improperly applied or retained, or to make good any default. If misfeasance proceedings require to be taken, the liquidator will invariably employ a solicitor, as indeed he will generally do in case of any application under s. 307.

Section 320 of the Act provides that where a company is **Fraudulent** being wound up, any act which would have been a fraudulent **Preference.** preference in bankruptcy had the company been an individual trader is an undue or fraudulent preference of the creditors of the company and is invalid. In bancruptcy, by virtue of s. 44 of the Bankruptcy Act, 1914, any conveyance or transfer of property, or any payment made to any creditor by a person unable to pay his debts, with a view to preferring that creditor to other creditors, is void if made within six months before the bankruptcy. In the case of voluntary winding up, the period of six months dates backwards from the resolution for winding up. It is incumbent upon the liquidator if, on examination of the company's affairs, it appears that any such fraudulent preference has taken place, to take steps, by application to the court under s. 307 if necessary, to have the transaction set aside and recover the money or property.

It may be observed that the term 'fraudulent preference' is a misnomer. In re *Patrick and Lyon* (1933), Ch. at p. 790, Maugham J. (as he then was) said that 'a fraudulent preference within the meaning of the Companies Act, 1929, or the Bankruptcy Act, 1914, whether in the case of a company or an individual, possibly may not involve moral blame at all. For example, there may be discrimination between creditors, irrespective of pressure, on grounds with which most people would sympathise' (see Williams on *Bankruptcy*, 16th Edition, p. 361). It is often difficult to determine whether a particular transaction does or does not constitute a fraudulent preference. There must not only be a preference, but also the intention to prefer. It has been held that the preferring of the creditor must be the dominant view with which the preference was made, but not necessarily the sole view. A payment made *bona fide* under pressure will not be a fraudulent preference. The burden is on the liquidator, who seeks to set aside a transaction as being a fraudulent preference, of showing the insolvency of the company—not as a rule a difficult task—as well as of showing the intention to prefer. The court will not, however, infer the intention to make a preference where there is no direct evidence of such intention, and where it is clear that there is more than one explanation of the transaction [*Peat* v. *Gresham Trust Ltd.* (1934), A.C. 252. This does not, however, mean that the court is precluded from drawing an inference in the absence of evidence by the debtor himself or of admission by him. The court should form its judgment as to whether or not to confer a preference upon review of all the circumstances [*M. Kushler Ltd.* (1943), Ch. 248 at p. 253].

It is provided by s. 321 of the Act that where anything made or done (after 1st July, 1948) is avoided as a fraudulent preference 'of a person interested in property, mortgaged or charged, to secure the company's debt,' the person who is preferred shall be subject to the same liabilities and shall have the same rights as if he had undertaken to be personally liable as a surety for the debt, to the extent of the charge on the property or the value of his interest, whichever is the less. The method of valuation of the preferred person's interest is governed by s. 321 (2). It is further provided by s. 321 (3) that, in the case of an application to the court on the ground that a payment was a fraudulent preference of a surety or guarantor, the court has power to determine questions as between the person to whom payment has been made and the surety or guarantor, e.g. in the case where a director has deposited securities with a bank to secure a company's overdraft and payment is made to the bank in fraudulent preference. The bank must repay, but has a right of action against the director.

Section 320 also makes void to all intents and purposes any conveyance by a company of all its property to trustees for the benefit of all its creditors. It will be noted that this provision, unlike the provision as to fraudulent preference, applies only where the conveyance is of all the property and all the creditors benefit.

Another matter affecting the getting-in of the assets of the company must be noticed. Under s. 325 an execution **Execution Creditors.** creditor who has not completed execution before the commencement of the winding up or, if he had notice of a meeting having been called to pass a resolution for voluntary winding up, before the date on which he had such notice, will not be entitled to retain the benefit of the execution against the liquidator, and if the liquidator finds that there has been any execution shortly before his appointment, he should inquire into the circumstances to see if the section applies. Moreover, under s. 326, the liquidator can, in certain cases, obtain delivery from the sheriff of goods seized or the proceeds of sale thereof, and accordingly should inquire whether the circumstances require the giving of any notice or the service of any demand under the section. It is provided that, in the case of both s. 325 and s. 326 above, the rights conferred on the liquidator may be set aside by the court to such extent and subject to such terms as the court thinks fit.

The liquidator will take steps, as soon as possible, to **Proof of Debts.** ascertain the extent of the company's liabilities. In most cases the books of the company, assuming them to have been properly kept, will disclose the bulk of these and, if the liabilities have been incurred in the ordinary course of the company's business, probably most of them can be admitted without demur. In a voluntary winding up only those creditors need prove their debts whose claims have not been admitted. The liquidator will accordingly make out a list of the claims he admits, i.e. of all the known and undisputed liabilities of the company, whether they be trade liabilities,

or office expenses, or directors' fees, or anything else. His
duty is then laid down by Rule 106 of the Winding-up Rules
of 1949, which requires him to fix a day, not less than fourteen
days after the date of the notice on or before which creditors
(*i.e.* in a voluntary winding up, creditors whose claims have not
been admitted) are to prove their debts or claims and to
establish any title they may have to priority under s. 319 of
the Act, or be excluded from the benefit of any distribution
of assets made before their debts are proved; he is to give
notice of the day fixed by advertisement in a newspaper, and,
further, by sending notice in writing to each person who
to his knowledge claims to be a creditor or preferential creditor
and whose claim has not been admitted. The notice is
ordinarily inserted in the *Gazette*, and in one or more newspapers circulating in the district where the registered office
of the company is. One or more repetitions of the newspaper
advertisement is often advisable. In dealing with proofs
the liquidator must bear in mind that (subject in the case of
insolvent companies to the application of s. 317 of the Law of
Bankruptcy), all debts payable on a contingency and claims
present or future, certain or contingent, ascertained or
sounding only in damages are admissible to proof (s. 316).
(See Bankruptcy Act, 1914, s. 30, as to the debts which are
provable in bankruptcy and therefore in the winding up of
an insolvent company.) It should be borne in mind that
only debts which are legally recoverable can be proved for
in a winding up, and if a liquidator admits and pays a claim
which is merely a moral obligation, however strong, on the
company, he commits a misfeasance and may be compelled
to make good the amount so paid, at any rate so far as the
creditors have been damaged thereby [*Home & Colonial
Insurance Co.* (1930), 1 Ch. 102].

Rule 92, Companies (Winding-up) Rules, 1949, provides
for the proof of debts by affidavit, and by Rule 95 the affidavit
is required to state whether the creditor is or is not a secured
creditor. Most of the Rules from 92 to 110 contain further
regulations as to the proof of debts which are applicable to
voluntary winding up. When the proofs have all been lodged
the liquidator must examine them, and in writing admit or
reject each, either in whole or in part, or he may require
further evidence in support of it. If he rejects a proof he
must notify to the creditor in writing the grounds of his
rejection (Rule 107). Any creditor dissatisfied with the
decision of the liquidator may apply to the court within
twenty-one days, and the court may reverse or vary the
decision (Rule 108). Sould the liquidator himself, after
admitting a proof, consider that it has been improperly
admitted, he may apply to the court, after notice to the
creditor, to expunge the proof or reduce its amount (Rule 109).

A similar application may be made by any creditor or contributory (Rule 110).

In due course the liquidator will have a complete list of claims, of which some may be disputed. Disputed claims may be dealt with by the liquidator in various ways. He may compromise any claim with the sanction required by s. 303 (1), or he may apply to the court, under s. 307, to adjudicate upon any disputed claim. Or he may leave the creditor to apply to the court to adjudicate, or to bring an action to enforce the claim. The usual practice now is for the liquidator to reject so much of the claim as he disputes, leaving it to the creditor to apply to the court to reverse or vary his decision. The position of the liquidator in the matter of applying for a stay of any such action has already been dealt with above (see p. 316). In exceptional cases, where the disputed claims are likely to be numerous, the method of procedure is open to the liquidator of applying to the court, under s. 307, for an order for an inquiry as to who are the creditors of the company. The effect of such an order is that all claims are formally proved in chambers, and disputed claims adjudicated upon where necessary by the court. If the liquidator is in doubt whether he has a complete list of claims and desires to make a distribution, he can exercise the powers given him by Rule 106 or apply to the court under s. 307 to exercise the power conferred by s. 264 to fix a time within which creditors must prove their debts or be excluded from any distribution made before their debts are proved.

The position of secured creditors requires some explanation. **Secured** By s. 317 of the Act, the provisions of the bankruptcy law **Creditors.** as to secured creditors are applied to insolvent companies in winding up. The result is that a secured creditor of an insolvent company in liquidation may adopt one of four courses: (1) he may rely on his security and not prove at all—although, of course, should his security on realisation prove to exceed the amount of his debt, he must hand over the surplus to the liquidator; (2) he may realise his security, and if it shows a deficit, he may prove for the balance; (3) he may give up his security to the liquidator and prove for the whole debt; (4) he may assess the value of his security, and, after deducting the assessed value, prove for the balance of his debt. If the creditor adopts the last course, the liquidator can redeem at the assessed value; or if he is dissatisfied with the assessed value, require the property to be sold (Bankruptcy Act, 1914, 2nd schedule, para. 13). A creditor can, however, amend his valuation and proof under para. 13 of that schedule on showing to the satisfaction of the liquidator, or the court, that the valuation and proof were made *bona fide* on a mistaken estimate, or that the security has increased or diminished in value since its previous valuation.

An important duty of the liquidator arises in connection with secured creditors. Most of the secured creditors of a company are ordinarily debenture holders, that is to say, creditors of the company whose debts are secured in most instances by a mortgage or charge upon the whole undertaking of the company, including, generally, its uncalled capital. There may also be creditors having a specific charge on particular property, e.g. a bank with security for an overdraft. The liquidator must ascertain whether the debentures, or other charges, were validly issued, and whether they are duly registered in cases where registration is required, remembering that, should the security turn out to be invalid, the debenture holders will rank merely as unsecured creditors. The question of what is the best policy for the liquidator to adopt where the whole of the company's assets are mortgaged to debenture holders is often one of extreme difficulty, and sometimes it happens that a scheme of arrangement under s. 206 (see p. 283) is the best solution. In this connection, s. 320 as to fraudulent preference (see p. 325), and s. 322 must not be overlooked. By the latter section a floating charge, given within twelve* months before the commencement of the winding up, is invalid except to the amount of any cash paid to the company at the time of, or subsequently to the creation of, and in consideration for, the charge, with interest at 5 per cent. on that amount, unless it be proved that the company was solvent immediately after the creation of the charge [*Matthew Ellis Ltd.* (1933), Ch. 458; *Destone Fabrics Ltd.* (1941), Ch. 319]. The onus of proof lies on the person claiming under the charge.

When the liquidator has ascertained the company's liabilities and assets, he will be able to determine what further steps are necessary in the winding up. If the assets exceed the liabilities and the costs of winding up, he will be able to pay the debts and the expenses of winding up, and will then distribute any surplus assets among the shareholders in accordance with their rights. If, however, the company is insolvent, or if the liabilities, including the cost of the liquidation, exceed the assets, it will be his duty to increase the assets, if possible, by calling up the whole or part of the unpaid capital. If the whole of the capital is fully paid, no further sum can be raised from the shareholders, except in cases where the articles of association of a company provide for such further payments, e.g. in companies limited by guarantee. If the capital is not fully paid the liquidator proceeds to settle lists of contributories and to make calls.

Lists of Con-   It must not, however, be assumed that the liquidator will
tributories.   take no steps towards settling the lists of contributories until

---

* Six months if the charge was created before January 1st, 1949.

he has accurately ascertained the amount of both assets and liabilities. In many cases he will be able to determine whether or not calls upon the contributories will be required long before he knows the precise financial position of the company, although he will generally not proceed actually to make calls until he knows approximately how much is required to be called up. It may in some cases be obvious at the outset that every farthing of unpaid capital will be wanted, and in these cases the work of settling the list of contributories and making calls can be taken in hand at once.

Section 303 gives the liquidator in voluntary winding up the same powers as the court in the matter, and provides that 'any list so settled shall be *prima facie* evidence of the liability of the persons named therein to be contributories.' A contributory is defined by s. 213 of the Act, and means in effect any member of the company or any past member who is liable to contribute. It does not include an ordinary debtor to the company.

There are two lists of contributories, commonly called the 'A List' and 'B List.' The 'A' list contains the names of existing members of the company who are liable to contribute, and the 'B' list the names of such past members as are liable to contribute. The liabilities of both classes are regulated by s. 212 of the Act, the effect of which may be summarised as follows: existing members are primarily liable to contribute to the extent of the amount unpaid on their shares, or if the company is limited by guarantee, to the extent of their guarantee; if the amount collected from existing members is insufficient, then, and only then, are past members liable to contribute, and contributions by past members are subject to the further restrictions that a member who has ceased to be a member for a year or more before the commencement of the winding up cannot be made liable, that no past member is liable to contribute in respect of debts incurred after he ceased to be a member, and that his liability is limited to the amount unpaid on the shares he held. The contributions of the 'B' contributories become part of the general assets of the company, and cannot be exclusively appropriated to the payment of the debts incurred before they ceased to be members (*Webb* v. *Whiffin* (1872), L.R. 5 H.L. 711) but if the proceeds of a call made on them exceed the amount of such debts the surplus must be returned to them [*City of London Insurance Co.* (1932), 1 Ch. 226]. It often happens that it is unnecessary to settle the 'B' list at all. The liquidator is not bound by Rules 80–85 of the Companies (Winding-up) Rules, 1949, since they apply only to compulsory winding up, but in practice he will generally follow the procedure there indicated. His 'A' list will be in two parts, the first part containing contributories in their own right, *i.e.* the beneficial holders of shares in the company, and the second part containing contributories other than in their own right, *e.g.* as executors or administrators of deceased shareholders, or as trustees of bankrupt shareholders. The 'B' list, if any, will similarly be in two parts.

After making out the lists, the liquidator will fix a day for settling them, giving notice to each person whose name has been inserted therein of the time and place and of the particulars in the list referring to such person, and stating that, if no sufficient cause is shown to the contrary, the list will be settled to include him therein. At the time fixed the liquidator will hear objections and either decide them on the spot or hold them over for further consideration; he will of course usually require legal advice. He may either, after due consideration of the case, place the name of the objector on the list as settled, and leave him to apply to the court under s. 307 as a contributory for rectification of the list or of the register, or himself apply to the court for a declaration of liability. The usual course is for the liquidator to place the name on the list and leave the contributory to his remedy. Having settled the lists, the liquidator will proceed to make such calls as may be necessary.

Here may conveniently be noticed the power which the liquidator has of enforcing the payment by contributories of sums due from them before the winding up, whether in respect of calls or other matters. By the combined effect of s. 259 and s. 307 of the Act, he may apply to the court for an order upon contributories already settled on the list to pay any such sums due from them. Orders of this kind are called balance orders. Balance orders may be enforced by writ of execution by virtue of s. 449 of the Act. A balance order is, however, not a judgment, and accordingly does not extinguish the right of action for calls. Nor can an action be brought upon the order, as upon a judgment, nor a bankruptcy notice be issued in respect of it. In practice, orders are sometimes made for payment, not only of calls made before the winding up, but also of calls made during the winding up. The court will not order a holder of fully-paid shares to be put on the list of contributories merely in order to enable this jurisdiction to be exercised against him, but if he is already on the list as a shareholder entitled to receive a share of the surplus assets, the court may exercise the jurisdiction against him [*Aidall, Ltd.* (1933), 1 Ch. 323].

Set-off. The doctrine of set-off in winding up must be briefly dealt with at this point. A set-off is the placing of a debt against a credit, and striking a balance, the payment of which will settle both transactions. It is an ordinary reasonable business transaction to simplify the adjustment of mutual accounts. Thus, if A owes B £15, and B owes A £10, obviously both debts can be adjusted by A paying B £5. So, in the case of a company not being wound up, if there is due from a shareholder to the company £100 in respect of calls, while the company owes the shareholder £75 for goods supplied, both transactlons may properly be closed by the shareholder paying £25 to the company. But in winding up the rule is different. A contributory cannot set off a debt due to him from the company against money due from him to the company in his capacity of contributory, *e.g.* for calls. He must first pay what, as a contributory, he owes the company, and then claim as a creditor of the company entitled to be paid with the other creditors, and if the company's assets are less than its liabilities he will only receive a dividend on his claim. Any other rule would give preferential treatment to the contributory who, by the accident of circumstances, is also a creditor of the company. However, when the contributory is a bankrupt, set-off is allowed. Thus, the liquidator, seeking to prove in the bankruptcy for calls due, must first deduct from the amount of the calls the amount owing from the company, and prove for the balance. Conversely, where the debt due from the company exceeds the amount of the calls, set-off is allowed and the balance due to the bankrupt's estate may be proved for in the winding up. When all the creditors of a company are paid in full, any sum due to a contributory from the company on any account whatever may be allowed to him by way of set-off against any subsequent calls [s. 259 (3)]. A joint debt cannot be set off against a separate debt [*Pennington and Owen, Ltd.* (1925), 41 T.L.R. 657].

Some of the incidental duties which the liquidator may **Meetings in** have been called upon to perform before all the assets have **Liquidation.** been realised require a passing notice. It may be necessary or desirable for him to summon general meetings of the company from time to time. Section 303 (1) of the Act empowers him to do so for the purpose of obtaining the sanction of the company by extraordinary resolution, or for any other purpose he may think fit. There may often be important steps in the winding up upon which the liquidator may deem it advisable to take the opinion of the company before acting. When a meeting is to be called, the liquidator will summon it in the usual way by notices in writing stating the objects of the meeting. Sections 289 and 299 make it incumbent upon the liquidator, in all cases where the winding up continues for more than a year, to summon a general meeting of the company at the end of the first and of every subsequent year from the commencement of the winding up; and at every such meeting he must lay before the shareholders 'an account of his acts and dealings, and of the conduct of the winding up during the preceding year.' In the case of a creditors' winding up an annual meeting of creditors must also be called for the same purpose (s. 299). Under ss. 289 and 299 the meeting must be called within three months of the expiration of the year unless the Board of Trade extends the period. Under Rule 127 (2) the liquidator in a creditors' voluntary winding up may from time to time summon, hold and conduct meetings of creditors for the purpose of ascertaining their wishes in all matters relating to the winding up. In addition to the meetings already mentioned, which are summoned by the liquidator, the court may, by virtue of ss. 307 and 346 of the Act, direct meetings of creditors or contributories to be summoned, with the object of ascertaining their wishes in any matter. Any resolution passed at any adjourned meeting is to be treated as having been passed on the date on which it was actually passed and not on the date of the original meeting (s. 345, and see p. 160). The rules regulating the summoning and conduct of the above-mentioned creditors' meetings are contained in Rules 127 to 145 of the Companies (Winding-up) Rules, 1949, and provisions in regard to proxies at meetings of creditors in a creditors' voluntary winding up are contained in Rules 146 to 156.

Periodical Returns. The liquidator is bound, by s. 342, in all cases where the liquidation is not concluded within a year, to send periodical statements to the Registrar of Companies in the form prescribed by the Board of Trade. If it appears from any such statement or otherwise that the liquidator has in his hands or under his control any unclaimed or undistributed assets, which have remained unclaimed or undistributed for more than six months, he must pay the same forthwith into the companies liquidation account (s. 343). These unclaimed assets include amounts held by the company in respect of unclaimed dividends or other sums due to any person as a member of the company. Directions as to the dates on which, and the method in which, that payment is to be made are contained in Rule 199 of the Companies (Winding-up) Rules, 1949. By Rule 200 a liquidator is bound to furnish to the Board of Trade particulars of any money in his hands, or under his control, representing unclaimed or undistributed assets, and any other particulars which the Board of Trade may require for the purpose of ascertaining and getting in any money payable into the companies liquidation account. This Rule applies whether the liquidation has been concluded or not. By Rule 201, the Board of Trade may order an account of the sums received and paid by the liquidator and may enforce an audit of the account. As to the investment at the request of the committee of inspection or liquidator of funds standing to the credit of a company with the Board of Trade, see s. 362 and Rule 173 of the Companies (Winding-up) Rules, 1949.

Under the Act [s. 334 (2)], it is the duty of the liquidator in a voluntary winding up, if he considers that any past or present officer, or any member of the company, has been guilty of any offence in relation to the company for which he is criminally liable, to report the matter at once to the Director of Public Prosecutions and give him all information in his power relating to the matter. The Director of Public Prosecutions may refer the matter to the Board of Trade for further enquiry; but he is under no obligation to do so. If it appears to the court in the course of a voluntary winding up that any past or present officer or any member has been guilty as above and no report has been made to the Director of Public Prosecutions or the Lord Advocate, the court may direct the liquidator to make such a report. If the Director of Public Prosecutions or the Lord Advocate institutes a prosecution, it is then the duty of the liquidator and of every officer and agent of the company, past and present, to give him all assistance which they can reasonably give [s. 334 (5)].

It may here be noted that the category of criminal offences in relation to a company was greatly extended by ss. 271–275 of the 1929 Act, now ss. 328–332 of the 1948 Act. It is not considered necessary to set out these sections in detail, but it may be mentioned that the list of offences includes such matters as the following:—

Failure to disclose to the liquidator any property of the company;

failure to deliver to the liquidator property, books or papers;

concealment or fraudulent removal of any property of the value of £10 or upwards;

making any material omission in any statement of affairs;

concealment of falsification in any book or paper;

making false entries in any book or paper;

obtaining property on credit by fraud within twelve months before commencement of winding up;

making any transfer of property with intent to defraud creditors;

omitting to keep proper books of account throughout the period of two years immediately preceding commencement of the winding up;

carrying on any business of the company with intent to defraud creditors or for any fraudulent purpose.

If it appears that any business of the company has been carried on fraudulently within the section, the court may, under s. 332, declare that any persons who were knowingly parties to the fraud shall be personally responsible, without any limitation of liability for all or any of the debts or other liabilities of the company as the court may direct. The words 'intent to defraud' and 'fraudulent purpose' in this section, unlike the words 'fraudulent preference' in s. 320, connote actual dishonesty [*Patrick and Lyon* (1933) Ch. 786]. It has been held that a company carrying on business and incurring debts, when to the knowledge of the directors there is no reasonable prospect of the debts being paid may, in general, be properly inferred to be carrying on business with intent to defraud creditors within the meaning of s. 332 [*Leitch Brothers* (1932), 2 Ch. 71]. It was also held in that case that the declaration must state the amount for which the director is liable and must not be expressed in general terms. The amount recovered under such a declaration forms part of the general assets of the company, and is not payable exclusively to the particular creditors defrauded. [*Leitch Brothers* No. (2) (1933), Ch. 261.]

By s. 188 of the Act a person may be suspended, by order of the court, from the office of director or from taking any part in the management of any company, without the leave of the court, for a period not exceeding five years. This applies if, in the course of winding up, it appears that any person has been guilty of any offence for which he is liable under s. 332 (whether he has been convicted or not) or has been guilty (while an officer of the company) of any fraud or breach of duty in relation to the company. Application for such an order may be made by the official receiver, the liquidator, or any past or present member or creditor of the company, and at least ten days' notice of such application must be given to the person against whom the order is sought. There are very heavy penalties for the infringement of an order under this section, and an order may be made notwithstanding criminal liability on the ground on which the order is made. For the purposes of the section the word 'officer' includes any person in accordance with whose instructions the directors of the company have been accustomed to act.

Distribution of Assets. The duty of the liquidator in distributing the assets may now be considered. Where the assets are insufficient to pay in full the liabilities of the company and the costs of the liquidation, the liquidator must be careful to observe the legal priorities. The first payments to be made are payments of the expenses of the liquidation, for s. 309 of the Act enacts that 'all costs, charges, and expenses properly incurred in the winding up, including the remuneration of the liquidator, shall be payable out of the assets of the company in priority to all other claims.' The expenses will, of course, include legal expenses properly incurred. Whether or not a solicitor's bill should be taxed is, in a voluntary winding up, a matter for the liquidator to consider; if he requires it to be taxed he must apply to the court under s. 307. In a compulsory winding up the matter must be referred to the Registrar, pursuant to Rule 195 of the Companies (Winding-up) Rules, 1949. It will be noticed that the liquidator's own remuneration is expressly included amongst the expenses. Payments on account of expenses may be made by the liquidator from time to time out of any funds in his hands.

After the expenses, the company's debts must be paid **Preferential** in the order of priority given by s. 319, which reads as follows: **Payments.**

'319.—(1) In a winding up there shall be paid in priority to all other debts—

   (a) (i) all local rates due from the company at the relevant date and having become due and payable within twelve months next before that date;

       (ii) all land tax, income tax, profits tax, excess profits tax or other assessed taxes assessed on the company up to the fifth day of April next before that date, and not exceeding in the whole one year's assessment;

      (iii) the amount of any purchase tax due from the company at the relevant date and having become due within twelve months next before that date;

   (b) all wages or salaries (whether or not earned wholly or in part by way of commission) of any clerk or servant in respect of services rendered to the company during four months next before the relevant date, and all wages (whether payable for time or for piece work) of any workman or labourer in respect of services so rendered;

   (c) any sum ordered under the Reinstatement in Civil Employment Act, 1944, to be paid by way of compensation where the default, by reason of which the order for compensation was made, occurred before the relevant date, whether or not the order was made before that date;

   (d) all accrued holiday remuneration becoming payable to any clerk, servant, workman or labourer (or in the case of his death to any other person in his right) on the termination of his employment before or by the effect of the winding up order or resolution;

   (e) unless the company is wound up voluntarily merely for the purposes of reconstruction or of amalgamation with another company, all amounts due in respect of contributions payable during the twelve months next before the relevant date by the company as the employer of any persons under the Unemployment Insurance Act, 1935, the National Health Insurance Act, 1936, the Widows', Orphans' and Old Age Contributory Pensions Act, 1936, the National Insurance (Industrial Injuries) Act, 1946, or the National Insurance Act, 1946;

(f) unless the company is being wound up voluntarily merely for the purposes of reconstruction or of amalgamation with another company or unless the company has, at the commencement of the winding up under such a contract with insurers as is mentioned in section seven of the Workmen's Compensation Act, 1925, rights capable of being transferred to and vested in the workman, all amounts due in respect of any compensation or liability for compensation under the said Act, being amounts which have accrued before the relevant date in satisfaction of a right which arises or has arisen in respect of employment before the fifth day of July, nineteen hundred and forty eight (that is to say the day appointed for the purpose of the National Insurance (Industrial Injuries) Act, 1946);

(g) the amount of any debt which, by virtue of sub-section (5) of section three of the Workmen's Compensation (Coal Mines) Act, 1934, is due from the company to an insurer in respect of a liability in respect of the satisfaction of a right falling within the last foregoing paragraph.

(2) Notwithstanding anything in paragraphs (b) and (c) of the foregoing sub-section, the sum to which priority is to be given shall not, in the case of any one claimant, exceed two hundred pounds.

Provided that where a claimant under the said paragraph (b) is a labourer in husbandry who has entered into a contract for the payment of a portion of his wages in a lump sum at the end of the year of hiring, he shall have priority in respect of the whole of such sums, or a part thereof, as the court may decide to be due under the contract, proportionate to the time of service up to the relevant date.

(3) Where any compensation under the Workmen's Compensation Act, 1925, is a weekly payment, the amount due in respect thereof shall, for the purposes of paragraph (f) of sub-s. (1) of this section, be taken to be the amount of the lump sum for which the weekly payment could, if redeemable, be redeemed if the employer made an application for that purpose under the said Act.

(4) Where any payment has been made:—

(a) to any clerk, servant, workman or labourer in the employment of a company on account of wages or salary; or

(b) to any such clerk, servant, workman, or labourer, or in the case of his death to any other person in his right, on account of accrued holiday remuneration;

out of money advanced by some person for that purpose, the person by whom the money was advanced shall in a winding up have a right of priority in respect of the money so advanced and paid up to the amount by which the sum in respect of which the clerk, servant, workman or labourer or other person in his right would have been entitled to priority in the winding up has been diminished by reason of the payment having been made.

(5) The foregoing debts shall—

(a) rank equally among themselves and be paid in full, unless the assets are insufficient to meet them, in which case they shall abate in equal proportions; and

(b) in the case of a company registered in England so far as the assets of the company available for payment of general creditors are insufficient to meet them, have priority over the claims of holders of debentures under any floating charge created by the company, and be paid accordingly out of any property comprised in or subject to that charge.

(6) Subject to the retention of such sums as may be necessary for the costs and expenses of the winding up, the foregoing debts shall be discharged forthwith so far as the assets are sufficient to meet them, and in the case of the debts to which priority is given by paragraph (e) of sub-s. (1) of this section formal proof thereof shall not be required, except in so far as is otherwise provided by general rules.

(7) In the event of a landlord or other person distraining or having distrained on any goods or effects of the company within three months next before the date of a winding up order, the debts to which priority is given by this section shall be a first charge on the goods or effects so distrained on, or the proceeds of the sale thereof:

Provided that in respect of any money paid under any such charge the landlord or other person shall have the same rights of priority as the person to whom the payment is made.

(8) For the purposes of this section—

    (a) any remuneration in respect of a period of holiday or absence from work through sickness or other good cause, shall be deemed to be wages in respect of services rendered to the company during that period;

    (b) the expression "accrued holiday remuneration" includes in relation to any person, all sums which by virtue either of his contract of employment or of any enactment (including any order made or direction given under any Act) are payable on account of the remuneration which would, in the ordinary course, have become payable to him in respect of a period of holiday had his employment with the company continued until he became entitled to be allowed the holiday;

    (c) references to remuneration in respect of a period of holiday include any sums which, if they had been paid, would have been treated for the purposes of the National Insurance Act, 1946, or any enactment repealed by that Act as remuneration in respect of that period; and

    (d) the expression "the relevant date" means—

        (i) in the case of a company ordered to be wound up compulsorily, the date of the appointment (or first appointment) of a provisional liquidator, or, if no such appointment was made, the date of the winding up order, unless in either case the company had commenced to be wound up voluntarily before that date; and

        (ii) in any case where the foregoing sub-paragraph does not apply, means the date of the passing of the resolution for the winding up of the company.

(9) This section shall not apply in the case of a winding up where the relevant date as defined in sub-section (7) of section two hundred and sixty four of the Companies Act, 1929, as originally enacted, occurred before the commencement of this Act, and in such a case the provisions relating to preferential payments which would have applied if this Act had not passed shall be deemed to remain in full force.'

It may be noted that there are special provisions for preferential payments in Stannaries cases (s. 358).

If a debenture contains a fixed as well as a floating charge, the priority conferred by the section as read with s. 94, applies only in respect of the assets subject to the floating charge [*Lewis Merthyr Consolidated Collieries* (1929), 1 Ch. 498; *Griffin Hotel Co.* (1941), Ch. 129].

With reference to the priority of salaries and wages of clerks and servants, it has been held that a managing director is not a clerk or servant within the meaning of the section [*Newspaper Proprietary Syndicate* (1900), 2 Ch. 349]. It has been held that a company's secretary who does not give the whole of his time to the service of the company, but pays a clerk to do the bulk of the work, is not a servant so as to be entitled to priority, although in other cases he may be [*Cairney* v. *Back* (1906), 2 K.B. 746]. There have been other decisions on particular facts. It would seem that a person cannot claim preferential payment as a 'workman or labourer,' unless he can prove a contract of service [*General Radio Company* (1929), W.N. 172].

After the above debts have been paid, the liquidator will **Surplus** then proceed to pay the other creditors as far as possible, by **Assets.** means of one or more dividends (see Appendix F, Form 134). Subject as provided by s. 212 (1) (*g*) as regards debts due to a member in his character of a member, *e.g.* for dividends declared, all creditors must be treated alike and receive a proportionate amount of their respective debts. If all creditors have been paid in full and assets still remain, then it is the duty of the liquidator, under s. 302, unless it is otherwise provided by the articles of the company, to distribute the money in hand among the members (see Appendix F, Form 133) according to their rights and interests in the company. Section 303 provides that the liquidator shall adjust the rights of the contributories among themselves, and empowers him to make calls for the purpose. The rights of the members must be ascertained from the memorandum and articles, and the available assets distributed in accordance therewith. Very difficult questions frequently arise as to how, in the particular circumstances, having regard to the provisions of the memorandum and articles, the assets should be distributed, and legal advice is often sought by the liquidator as to how he should proceed, or application is made to the court under s. 307.

A few general principles may, however, be noticed. If the memorandum and articles are wholly silent as to the rights of members on a winding up, the liquidator's first duty is to pay off the paid-up capital. If the assets do not allow the whole of the paid-up capital to be paid off, the liquidator must first repay those shareholders who have paid up a larger amount than others, in proportion to the number of shares held by them, the excess which they have so paid, and, if necessary, he must make a call upon those who have paid the lesser amount, so as to equalise matters. To take a simple concrete instance, suppose that in a company with an issued capital of 3,000 shares of £1 each, of which 2,000 are paid up to the extent of 10s. and 1,000 to the extent of 5s., the liquidator, after paying all expenses and all creditors, has a sum of £50 in hand. If this were returned to the holders of the 2,000 shares, 10s. paid up, the result would be merely to return 6d. per share, and these shareholders would be at a disadvantage. The liquidator's duty, accordingly, is to make on the holders of the 1,000 shares, 5s. paid, a call of 3s. per share, which will enable him to return an additional 1s. 6d. per share to the holders of the 2,000 shares, thus leaving every share 8s. paid. If, after all the paid-up capital has been returned, there is still a surplus, it is, in the absence of special provision to the contrary, returnable to all the shareholders alike in proportion to the number of shares held by each [*Bridgewater Navigation Company* (1889), 14 A.C. 525].

The memorandum or articles of a company commonly make some provision as to the distribution of what are called 'surplus assets' in a winding up, *e.g.* preference shareholders with priority as to capital are entitled to be repaid in full before ordinary shareholders receive anything. The term 'surplus assets' in articles of association often gives rise to difficulty. It may have one of two distinct meanings, according to the context, and according to the interpretation of the memorandum and articles as a whole. Sometimes it means the assets remaining after paying the expenses of the liquidation and the creditors, and sometimes the assets remaining after also returning the paid-up capital. The remaining assets must be distributed in accordance with the true construction of the relevant memorandum and articles. It is to be observed that the holders of preference shares have no priority in the matter of the return of capital unless it is so provided, but of course in modern articles there nearly always is such a provision. Their preference is a preference as regards dividends alone. It is impossible here to go into the widely varying clauses in articles of association as to the distribution of surplus assets.

Application to the Court. It seems advisable, however, to deal more systematically with a subject which has already several times been mentioned. This is the matter of applications to the court. Section 307 of the Act enables the liquidator, or any contributory, or any creditor, to make application to the court in practically any matter of difficulty or dispute. It will be observed, on a perusal of the section, that its wording is very wide; application may be made to the court to determine *any* question arising in the winding up, or to exercise *any* of the powers exercisable in compulsory winding up; and, further, the court may, upon application, make *any* order—even an order totally different from what is asked for.

A number of cases in which application to the court is sometimes made have already been noticed. Applications by the liquidator may be of almost any kind, but they may be roughly divided into three classes, namely, applications made with the object of obtaining a decision on a disputed point, applications to the court to exercise its statutory powers to permit acts which may not be done except with the leave of the court, and applications made with the object of obtaining the sanction of the court to a proposed step or arrangement.   In the third class of case, the liquidator may generally, if he thinks fit, take the proposed step without any application to the court, and his object in applying is to protect himself.   Just as trustees are empowered to apply to the court for direction in cases of doubt or difficulty, so the liquidator may, in order to safeguard himself, apply under s. 307.   In case of any matter involving a large amount of money, or any specially important or unusual act, he may properly take steps to protect himself, and if he acts without doing so, the omission may tell against him if the propriety of the transaction is subsequently impeached.   It would be prudent, for example, to apply to the court for its sanction before taking proceedings in a matter of magnitude, or before borrowing more than a small amount of money.   Applications by contributories are generally made when they are dissatisfied with the decision of the liquidator on their rights or liabilities, *e.g.* when they consider themselves improperly settled on a list of contributories.   Creditors' applications are generally of one of two kinds, that is to say, applications made in consequence of decisions of the liquidator adverse to their interests in individual cases, and applications made when they are dissatisfied with any matter in the liquidation as being disadvantageous to them generally, as, for example, if they consider the liquidator's remuneration too high; or, if in their opinion, a proposed compromise is not sufficiently in the interests of the company.

With reference to the liability of the liquidator in volun- **Liability of** tary winding up, it seems unnecessary to deal with his criminal **Liquidator.** liability, or with his liability to penalties in case of certain defaults.   As to his civil liability, he is the agent of the company, and while not strictly a trustee, he is liable for any misfeasance or breach of his duty as liquidator.   The negligence, which consists in a mere error of judgment, is not a sufficient ground upon which to charge a liquidator, but, of course, personal misconduct, *e.g.* by failure to perform his statutory duties, or by negligence amounting to a failure to exercise proper care [see *e.g. Windsor Steam Coal Co.* (1929), 1 Ch. 151, *Home & Colonial Insurance Co.* (1930), 1 Ch. 102], will always render him liable.   When he employs a solicitor in the course of the liquidation, he is not, in the absence of an

M

express bargain, personally liable for the solicitor's costs. When he contracts he should, of course, be careful to make it clear that he contracts on behalf of the company and not personally; otherwise, it is possible that he might, as between himself and the other party to the contract, inadvertently assume a personal liability.

A few matters in which it behoves the liquidator to be specially careful may be noticed. In carrying on the business of the company for the purposes of its beneficial winding up, he will do well to consider carefully the precise effect of any proposed step, for a new contract might, in many instances, be made in excess of his duties; in case of doubt, application to the court may often be desirable. Again, he should hesitate before embarking on costly litigation; for although in general an unsuccessful liquidator will be allowed his costs out of the assets of the company, yet it has been held that the court has jurisdiction to order him to pay them personally, and, in case of an action being improperly or recklessly brought, he may find himself ordered to pay the costs out of his own pocket. Too much care cannot be exercised by the liquidator in avoiding all payments from or dealings with the company's assets which are not expressly or obviously authorised. For instance, it is permissible, on a liquidation, for the liquidator to recognise a request made by a shareholder that the distribution in respect of his holding should be paid to a third party. The liquidator should, however, satisfy himself that the mandate received authorises him to accept the receipt of the third party in full discharge of his liability. On the payment of the final dividend to shareholders, the liquidator should obtain the surrender of the relevant share certificates. There is no statutory provision on the point, but it is clear that, after the payment of the final dividend, the shareholder has no right to retain his certificate, whereas it ought to be held by the liquidator as evidence that the final dividend has been paid on the shares concerned.

Removal of Liquidator. In certain circumstances a liquidator may be removed from his position. It is not open to the shareholders themselves to remove a liquidator; the power of removal lies in the court alone. Section 304 of the Act provides that 'the court may, on cause shown, remove a liquidator, and appoint another liquidator.' Contributories or creditors may apply for the removal of a liquidator, and the matter is one for the discretion of the court, which, however, can only act 'on cause shown.' It is impossible to predicate with certainty what circumstances will, or will not, amount to 'cause.' It may, however, be safely assumed that gross misconduct, such as wrongful dealing with the company's assets, will constitute sufficient cause; and although pecuniary interest in the winding up, apart from the liquidator's remuneration, might not be sufficient unless it is calculated to interfere with the proper performance of his duties, flagrant breaches of Rules 161 and 162 of the Companies (Winding-up) Rules, 1949, might afford a ground for removal. The dominant principle on which the court acts in this, as in all matters connected with the winding up, is that the benefit of the company and the wishes of the shareholders are to be first considered; and, unless the facts proved upon the application are sufficient to show that the continuance of the liquidator in office will be prejudical to the company's welfare, that is, to the creditors and the contributories, or is for adequate reasons distasteful to the shareholders or creditors, the liquidator will not be removed. By Rule 168 of the Companies (Winding-up) Rules, 1949, 'if a receiving order in bankruptcy is made against a liquidator he shall thereby vacate his office, and for the purposes of the application of the Act and Rules shall be deemed to have been removed.'

Sections 286, 297 and 304 provide for filling vacancies in **Vacancy in** the office of liquidator. Under s. 304, when no liquidator is **Office of** acting, the court may appoint a liquidator; and, as has already **Liquidator.** been seen, the court may, on the removal of a liquidator, appoint another. Further, it has been held that the court may, if an additional liquidator is required, appoint him, and that an application to the court for the appointment of an additional liquidator may be made by an existing liquidator [*Sunlight Incandescent Gas Lamp Company* (1900), 2 Ch. 728]. Under s. 286, on the occurrence in a members' voluntary winding up of a vacancy in the office of liquidator appointed by the company, by death, resignation, or otherwise, the company may in general meeting, subject to any arrangement the members may have entered into with their creditors, fill the vacancy; and any contributory or the continuing liquidators (if any), may convene the meeting; it must be convened and held according to the provisions of the articles, or as the court upon application may direct. Under s. 297, if in a creditors' voluntary winding up a vacancy occurs by death, resignation, or otherwise in the office of a liquidator other than one appointed by or by the direction of the court, the creditors may fill the vacancy. Rules 127 to 156 apply to the convening and conduct of the meeting and to proxies to be used thereat.

The duties of the liquidator upon the conclusion of the **The Final** winding up may now be considered. These are laid down **Meeting.** by ss. 290 and 300 of the Act. The first step in the final proceedings is for the liquidator to make up an account, showing how the winding up has been conducted and how the property of the company has been disposed of. The forms in which this account is to be prepared is prescribed by Rule 182 and Form 110 annexed to the Companies (Winding-up) Rules, 1949 (see Appendix F, Forms 135, 136 and 137).

The account having been prepared, the next step is to convene a general meeting of the company, and also, in the case of
a creditors' voluntary winding up, a meeting of creditors.
Sections 290 and 300 require the meetings to be summoned by
advertisement. The advertisement is to be published in the
Gazette one month, *i.e.* one calendar month, at least, before
the day fixed for the meeting. Even although no extraordinary resolution of the kind to be mentioned presently is
required to be passed, few liquidators will be content merely
with the notice by advertisement in the *Gazette*, but will send
notices to the shareholders in the manner prescribed by the
articles, and also, in the case of a creditors' winding up, to
the creditors known to him at their last-known addresses.
An advertisement in the *Gazette* only, might result in no one
being present at the meeting except the liquidator, or at all
events, no quorum of shareholders or creditors. However, if
the sole business of the meeting is that specified in ss. 290 or
300, as the case may be, there is no legal obligation to give any
notices other than the advertisement, and the lack of a quorum
at the final meeting will not interfere with the dissolution.
In the great majority of cases, however, unless there is a committee of inspection, advantage will be taken by the liquidator
of the provisions of s. 341 of the Act as to disposing of the
company's books. The section empowers a company which
has been wound up voluntarily, and is about to be dissolved, to
dispose of the books in the case of a members' voluntary
winding up in such way as the company by extraordinary
resolution directs, and in the case of a creditors' voluntary
winding up in such a way as the committee of inspection, or if
there is none, as the creditors may direct. Since in the case of
a members' voluntary winding up an extraordinary resolution
is necessary for the purpose, notice of the intention to propose
such resolution must, by s. 141, be duly given to all the
members. A single notice will suffice for both purposes: it
will intimate to the shareholders that the meeting is to be held
for the purpose of having the liquidator's account laid before
them, showing the manner in which the winding up has been
conducted and the property of the company disposed of, and
of hearing any explanation that may be given by the liquidator,
and also for the purpose of determining by extraordinary
resolution how the books and papers of the company and of
the liquidator are to be disposed of.

At the meeting or meetings the liquidator will lay his
account before the shareholders or the shareholders and the
creditors as the case may be, and should have ready for
inspection, if required, the books and other documents from
which it is compiled. His record book, or diary, should also
be before him for reference if necessary. He will, in general,
explain the steps which have been taken in the liquidation,

drawing attention to any matters of more than ordinary importance, and will answer such questions or give such explanations as the shareholders or creditors may ask or require. It is not necessary for the meeting to pass any resolution adopting the liquidator's account, although this is sometimes done, but the question of the disposal of the books must be dealt with by resolution. Frequently it is resolved to destroy the books, but, seeing that the dissolution of the company does not take place for three months from the registration of the liquidator's return as to the holding of the meeting, it is obviously inadvisable, and even improper, to authorise immediate destruction. Indeed, in view of s. 352, they should be preserved for two years. Where destruction is resolved upon, the resolution should authorise the liquidator to retain the books until two years from the dissolution of the company and then to destroy them. If it is inadvisable for any reason to destroy the books, the liquidator, or any one else, may be required to keep them for a stated period. Or, if the business of the company has been sold as a going concern, the meeting may resolve that the trading books of the company be handed over to the purchaser, and the remainder destroyed or retained for a time. It lies entirely with the meeting to determine the fate of the books and papers of the company and the liquidator in connection with the liquidation, but in most cases it will be guided by the liquidator in deciding upon the desirability or otherwise of retaining them. There is no responsibility on any one for the custody of the books after five years from dissolution [s. 341 (2)].

Dissolution. Within one week after the meeting or meetings, or if the meetings of members and creditors respectively are held on different dates, within one week after the later of such meetings, the liquidator must send to the Registrar a copy of the account laid before the meeting and make a return to the Registrar of the holding of the meeting and of the date on which it was held or, if a quorum was not present at either meeting, a return that such meeting was duly summoned and that no quorum was present. (See Appendix F, Form 137.) The quorum at the meetings of contributories and creditors is three, unless there shall be less than three contributories or creditors, as the case may be. In that event all the contributories or creditors constitute the quorum. [See Rule 138 of the Companies (Winding-up) Rules, 1949, p. 851.] If the liquidator fails to send the copy of the account or make the requisite return, he is liable to a penalty of £5 per day during default. The company is deemed to be dissolved at the expiration of three months from the registration of the return. The dissolution may, however, be deferred by order of the court for any length of time, on the application of the liquidator or any person appearing to the court to be interested (ss. 290, 300); or it may, on a similar application within two years from dissolution, be set aside (s. 352). In the latter case the dissolution is avoided *ab initio* and all consequences which flowed from the dissolution are also avoided [*C. W. Dixon Limited* (1947), Ch. 251]. Any order deferring the dissolution or declaring it void must be filed with the Registrar within seven days after it is made, but in the case of an order declaring the dissolution void the court may extend the time for filing the order.

Until dissolution the company continues to exist, and the result of this is that proceedings may still be taken, or claims made against the company; or assets may be discovered which it would be the duty of the liquidator to distribute. Should a liability be discovered, which the creditor was not by his own default precluded from pursuing, an order might be obtained from the court that a call be made to meet it. The existence of the company is revived, with similar results, if the dissolution is set aside.

A company may also be dissolved if it is struck off the register under s. 353, and notice of this being done is published in the *Gazette*. The Registrar may act under this section, even though there is no winding up. If there is no winding up, he may act if he has reasonable cause to believe that the company is not carrying on business or in operation. If it is being wound up, he may act if he has reasonable cause to believe that no liquidator is acting or that the liquidation is complete, and if the returns require to be made by the liquidator have not been made for six consecutive months. Before actually striking the company off the register he must give notices and issue advertisements in the *Gazette* as provided by the section. If a company is struck off the register under this section, and the company or any member or creditor feels aggrieved by its being struck off, the court may, on the application of the company or such member or creditor made within twenty years of the publication in the *Gazette* of the notice that the company had been struck off the register, order the company to be restored to the register; and on an office copy of the order being filed with the Registrar, the company will be deemed to have continued in existence as if it had never been struck off.

A company may also be dissolved without any winding up if the court makes an order to that effect upon an application under s. 208 in connection with a reconstruction under s. 206 (see p. 285).

After dissolution a company ceases to exist. It cannot sue or be sued. Any property which it may still have will vest in the Crown as *bona vacantia* (s. 354). Generally, no further step of any sort can be taken in relation to the company unless the dissolution has first been set aside.

CHAPTER XXII

POWERS OF ATTORNEY*

THE capacity to appoint an attorney (and it should be **Capacity.** remembered that capacity primarily depends upon domicile) is practically co-extensive with the capacity to contract. Thus a power of attorney given by an infant is void [*Zouch* v. *(a)* **Infants.** *Parsons* (1765), 3 Burr], except for doing acts by which the infant himself could be legally bound. On the other hand, 'an infant may be an agent, an infant may be the donee of a power of attorney' [per James, L.J. in re *D'Angibau* (1880), 15 C.D. 228]; for the acts of an agent as such are not his own but those of his principal, of whom he is merely an instrument. As to married women, s. 129 *(b)* **Married** of the Law of Property Act, 1925, provides that 'a married **Women.** woman, whether an infant or not, has power, as if she were unmarried and of full age, by deed to appoint an attorney on her behalf for the purpose of executing any deed or doing any other act which she might herself execute or do, and the provisions of this Act relating to instruments creating powers of attorney apply thereto.' If a woman marries a foreigner, it may be that by the law of her new nationality and domicile she loses the capacity to appoint an attorney, and thereby becomes subject to 'disability' within the meaning of ss. 124, 126 and 127, set out below.

The capacity of trustees to appoint attorneys is regulated *(c)* **Trustees.** by ss. 23 and 25 of the Trustee Act, 1925. Section 23 gives an unqualified right of delegation where the trust property is out of the United Kingdom (which by s. 68 is defined to mean Great Britain and Northern Ireland). Section 25 provides that in other cases a trustee who intends to remain out of the United Kingdom for more than one month may, by power of attorney, delegate the execution of trusts, subject to the following qualifications: if he has only one co-trustee, the latter, if not a trust corporation, cannot be appointed as attorney; the instrument must be filed at the Central Office within ten days after execution or, if executed abroad, within ten days after its receipt in the United Kingdom; and it is operative only during the donor's absence and is revoked by his return. The third party, however, is not affected by the last restriction if he has no notice that the donor never left the country or has returned, and he may accept

* For fuller discussion of this subject, and forms and precedents, see the Institute's manual on *Powers of Attorney*, prepared by the late Mr. H. M. Cohen, Solicitor for the Council of the Institute.

as conclusive a statutory declaration by the attorney that the power is in force; and companies are further protected by sub-section (10) which provides that 'the fact that it appears from any power of attorney given under this section, or from any evidence required for the purposes of any such power of attorney or otherwise, that in dealing with any stock the donee of the power is acting in the execution of a trust shall not be deemed for any purpose to affect any person in whose books the stock is inscribed or registered with any notice of the trust.' ['Stock' includes fully paid shares (Trustee Act, 1925, s. 68).]

(d) Executors and Administrators. The expression 'trustee' in the Trustee Act, 1925, also includes a personal representative [s. 68 (17)]; but an executor or administrator, like a trustee, can delegate purely ministerial powers, including power to collect debts due to the deceased [*Vane* v. *Rigden* (1870), 5 Ch. App. 663].

(e) Companies and their Liquidators. The Companies Act, 1948, confers the following powers:

(i) A company may, by writing under its common seal empower any person, either generally or in respect of any specified matters, as its attorney, to execute deeds on its behalf in any place not situate in the United Kingdom; and every deed signed by such attorney on behalf of the company, and under his seal, shall bind the company, and have the same effect as if it were under its common seal (s. 34).

(ii) A company whose objects require or comprise the transaction of business in foreign countries may, if authorised by its articles, have for use in any territory, district, or place not situate in the United Kingdom, an official seal, and may by writing under its common seal, delegate power to affix such official seal to any deed or document to which the company is a party in that locality (s. 35).

(iii) The liquidator of a company may appoint an agent to do any business which he is unable to do himself [s. 245 (2) (g)].

(f) Bankrupts and their Trustees. By s. 22 of the Bankruptcy Act, 1914, a bankrupt is bound to execute such powers of attorney as may be reasonably required by the Official Receiver, special manager, or trustee, or as may be prescribed by the Bankruptcy Rules or directed by the court, for the due administration of his estate; and by s. 55 (4) a trustee in bankruptcy may execute any power of attorney for the purposes of carrying into effect the provisions of the Act.

(g) Persons of unsound mind. If a power of attorney is granted by a person who at the time is of such unsound mind that he has no knowledge of what he is doing and only signs his name as a mere mechanical act, the instrument is void. Thus where a company transferred shares, acting on a deed of transfer executed under a power of attorney which was signed by the shareholder while of unsound mind, it was held that the power was void and the deed of transfer a nullity [*Daily Telegraph Newspaper Co., Ltd.* v. *M'Laughlin* (1904), A.C. 776; see also the decision of the Privy Council in *Molyneux* v. *Natal Land, & Co., Ltd.* (1905), A.C. 555]. The position arising if the principal was sane at the time of execution, but subsequently becomes insane, will be dealt with later.

The instrument appointing the attorney should always be **Sealing.** executed under seal, for a power of attorney, which, as is nearly always the case, confers authority to execute a deed, must itself be in the form of a deed [*Powell* v. *London & Provincial Bank* (1893), 2 Ch. 555, at p. 563]. In *Colonial Gold Reef, Ltd.* v. *Free State Rand, Ltd.* (1914), 1 Ch. 382, the articles of association of an English company provided that 'the instrument appointing a proxy shall be in writing under the hand of the appointor or his attorney duly authorised in that behalf, or, if such appointor is a corporation, under its common seal.' A South African company having no common seal and not required to have one was a shareholder, and by writing under the hands of two directors appointed an attorney in England to vote on its behalf, with power of substitution; it was held that the requirement of a common seal in the article only applied to corporations having a common seal according to English law, and that the instrument in question could be recognised as valid and effective.

Next, as evidence that the signature is that of the alleged **Attestation.** donor, the instrument should be attested, and it is desirable that there should be two witnesses, since this is required for the transfer of certain stocks.*

Moreover, powers for use abroad should always be attested by two witnesses; if for use in the dominions or colonies they should be notarially certified, and if for use in foreign countries they should also be legalized by the consul of the country to which they are to be sent. The advice of a notary should be obtained in such cases, and the notary will see to the necessary legalisation.

Conversely, powers from the dominions and colonies should be notarially certified, and those from foreign countries should also be legalised by the local British consul [see Order 61 (*a*) of the Rules of the Supreme Court].

A power of attorney should be stamped in the country **Stamp.** in which it is to be used with the appropriate duty imposed

---

* So long as the Evidence and Powers of Attorney Act, 1940, remains in force, there should be included in all powers of attorney, where such is the case, the statement that 'This is not an instrument to which section 3 of the Evidence and Powers of Attorney Act, 1940, applies.'

by the laws of that country. The English stamp duty is ten shillings.

Apparent Authority the real Authority.

In ascertaining the scope of the document it should be remembered that the third party is entitled to act upon the principle of law that the apparent authority is the real authority. The following statement of this principle, taken from an American case, was approved by the Privy Council in *Bryant* v. *La Banque du Peuple* (1893), A.C. 170: 'Whenever the very act of the agent is authorised by the terms of the power, that is, whenever, by comparing the act done by the agent with the words of the power, the act is in itself warranted by the terms used, such act is binding on the constituent as to all persons dealing in good faith with the agent. Such persons are not bound to inquire into facts *aliunde*.'

Limitation of above doctrine.

Where, however, the act is on the face of it one which is being done by the attorney otherwise than for the purposes and on behalf of his principal, and either this is known to the third party or the circumstances are such that he was put upon enquiry and could have ascertained the fact, then the third party cannot retain the benefit of the act so done to the detriment of the donor of the power. The principle was finally established by the House of Lords in *Reckitt* v. *Barnett, Pembroke & Slater, Ltd.* (1929), A.C. 176.*

Powers strictly construed.

Apart, however, from this question of the third party's knowledge that the attorney is abusing his authority, to say that the apparent authority is the real authority is not to say that the third party must not be on his guard. If a person is acting *ex mandato*, those who have dealings with him must look to his authority and assure themselves of its genuineness, its legal form, and its limitations. The important point to remember is that on the one hand specific powers are construed with great strictness, and that on the other hand where, after the enumeration of specific powers, there is added (as is often the case) a general clause, the latter does not give the attorney powers at large, but it confers on him the authority to do any unspecified acts which may become necessary for the proper fulfilment of the purposes for which the instrument was primarily granted [*Attwood* v. *Munnings* (1827), 7 B. & C. 278; *Withington* v. *Herring* (1829), 5 Bing. 422; *Harper* v. *Godsell* (1870), L.R. 5 Q.B. 422; *Hawksley* v. *Outram* (1892), 3 Ch. 359; *Dowson and Jenkins* (1904), 2 Ch. 219; *Bryant* v. *La Banque du Peuple, supra*].

Recitals.

If the instrument contains recitals showing the general object for which the power is given, these must be regarded as controlling the operative part of the deed. Thus, in *Danby* v. *Coutts & Co.* (1885), 2 Ch.D. 500, there was a recital that the plaintiff was going abroad and was desirous of

* See also below, under the heading of fraud of the attorney.

appointing an attorney to act in his absence; it was held that the recital limited the exercise of the powers to the plaintiff's absence from this country.

Power to borrow must be found indisputably expressed in the instrument if a third party wishes to lend to the attorney without risk [*Jonmenjoy Coondos* v. *Watson* (1884), 9 A.C. 561; *Bryant* v. *La Banque du Peuple, supra; Jacobs* v. *Morris* (1902), 1 Ch. 816]. **Power to Borrow.**

'In every case where an act requires a signature, it is a pure question of construction on the terms of the particular act whether its words are satisfied by signature of an agent ......we ought not to restrict the common law rule, *qui facit per alium facit per se*, unless the statute makes a personal signature indispensable' [*Whitley Partners, Ltd.* (1886), 32 C.D. 337]. This case decided that a company's memorandum and articles may be signed on behalf of a subscriber by a duly authorised agent; and similarly, it has been held that a bill of sale may be executed by an attorney [*Furnivall* v. *Hudson* (1893), 1 Ch. 335]. **Power to sign pursuant to Statute.**

An attorney cannot delegate his powers to a substitute, unless there is an express provision to this effect; and, similarly, a power of substitution does not, in the absence of a special provision, include a power of sub-delegation by the substitute. The rule, however, unless the power of attorney contains an express provision to the contrary, does not prevent the employment of brokers or agents such as are necessarily or customarily required for carrying out any particular transaction. **'Delegatus non Potest Delegare.'**

External circumstances, such as a custom of trade, may be used for the interpretation of the powers granted by the principal, but a usage or custom—if it was unknown to the principal—must be shown to be reasonable [*Hay* v. *Goldsmidt* (1804), 1 Taunt. 349]. For example when a man, unaware of the usages of a market, engages a broker on that market, he authorises that broker to contract on the footing of such usages as are reasonable and do not alter the nature of the contract [*Perry* v. *Barnett* (1885), 15 Q.B.D. 388]. **Custom.**

If a power of attorney is granted abroad, and even though it is written in a foreign language and drafted in a foreign form, then, when once it is ascertained from the evidence of competent translators and experts that it is the intention of the grantor that it should be acted upon in England, the extent of the authority, so far as transactions in England are concerned, must be determined by English law [*Chatenay* v. *Brazilian Telegraph Company* (1891), 1 Q.B. 79]. **Application of Local Laws.**

Where a power admits of two different interpretations, the attorney is within his right to adopt consistently the interpretation which to him seems best; 'if a principal gives an order to an agent in such uncertain terms as to be susceptible **Alternative Interpretations.**

of two different meanings, and the agent *bona fide* adopts one of them and acts upon it, it is not competent for the principal to repudiate the act as unauthorised because he meant the order to be read in the other sense of which it is equally capable' [*Ireland* v. *Livingstone* (1872), 5 H.L. 395, at p. 416]. Where, however, there is a choice between a definite and an indefinite construction of the instrument, the attorney is bound to act upon the definite construction [*Bertram* v. *Godfray* (1830), 1 Knapp 381].

Attorney's Signature. The attorney should sign all documents in the name of the principal, lest he may make himself a party to any covenant. The form of words is immaterial; it does not make any difference whether the name of the attorney appears before or after that of the principal, provided it is made clear that the attorney is acting solely as the agent of the principal. The generally accepted form of signature is A.B., by his attorney C.D.

When property is to be conveyed under a power of attorney of which the grantor or grantee is a corporate body, a special mode of execution is provided by s. 74 (sub-ss. 3 to 5) of the Law of Property Act, 1925, which will be found in Appendix K.

Custody of the Power. It has been held that 'the power of attorney is the deed of the attorney to whom it was given, and he is to keep it and under it to show that he has authority for what he has done' [*Hibberd* v. *Knight* (1848), 2 Exch. 11, per Baron Parke]. This dictum, however, having regard to the facts in that case can only apply as between the attorney and the third party; and on revocation the principal should always demand the return of the power, and if this is refused, should claim production for the purpose of endorsing a note of the revocation, or insist on its being filed at the Central Office, and then himself file a deed of revocation.

Filing. The Supreme Court of Judicature (Consolidation) Act, 1925, s. 219, made the following provisions as to filing:—

(1) An instrument creating a power of attorney, the execution of which has been verified by affidavit, statutory declaration, or other sufficient evidence, may, with the affidavit or declaration, if any, be deposited in the Central Office.

(2) A separate file of instruments so deposited shall be kept, and any person may search that file and inspect every instrument so deposited, and an office copy thereof shall be delivered out to him on request.

(3) A copy of an instrument so deposited may be presented at the office, and may be stamped or marked as, and when so stamped or marked shall become, an office copy.

(4) An office copy of an instrument so deposited shall, without further proof, be sufficient evidence of the contents* of the instrument and of the deposit thereof in the Central Office.

(5) Rules of Court may be made for the purposes of this section, regulating the practice† of the Central Office and prescribing, with the concurrence of the Treasury, the fees to be taken therein.

Such filing, however, is optional except in the case of powers executed by trustees under s. 25 of the Trustee Act, 1925, and powers relating to the disposition of land, the latter of which are governed by the following provision of s. 125 of the Law of Property Act, 1925:

> 'Where an instrument creating a power of attorney confers a power to dispose of or deal with any interest in or charge upon land, the instrument or a certified copy thereof or of such portions thereof as refer to or are necessary to the interpretation of such power shall be filed at the Central Office pursuant to the statutory enactment in that behalf, unless the instrument only relates to one transaction and is to be handed over on the completion of that transaction; Provided that if the instrument relates to land or a charge registered under the Land Registration Act, 1925, the instrument or a certified copy thereof or of such portions thereof as aforesaid shall be filed at the Land Registry, and it shall not be necessary to file it at the Central Office unless it also relates to land or a charge not so registered, in which case the instrument or a certified copy thereof or of such portions thereof as aforesaid shall be filed at the Central Office and an office copy shall be filed at the Land Registry.'

Registration is effected by presenting:—

(1) the original power of attorney marked as exhibit to the affidavit of witness of execution,

(2) a certified copy, and

(3) an affidavit of execution.

The filing fee is 2s. 6d. on the power of attorney and 2s. 6d. on the affidavit. The original power is retained by the Central Office and the copy, marked 'office copy,' is returned.

---

* *I.e.* of the existence of the contents, not of the truth thereof or of the identity of the parties [*O'Kane* v. *Mullan* (1925), Northern Ireland L.R.I., at p. 5].

† In practice, deeds of revocation may also be filed, if similarly verified, and the original power will then be marked 'revoked.'

It should be noted that a power under the Trustee Act must be filed within the time limit thereby prescribed, whereas a power covering the disposition of land need not be filed until it is needed for effecting the disposition.

In all other cases a third party has, therefore, no power to insist upon registration; and, while the law remains as it is, the only alternative would seem to be the possession by the third party of a copy of the power carefully collated by him. Such a copy, however, would not strictly be admissible in evidence.

Statutory Protection.
Certain safeguards are, however, afforded by statute. Section 124 of the Law of Property Act, 1925, provides as follows:—

(1) Any person making any payment or doing any act, in good faith, in pursuance of a power of attorney, shall not be liable in respect of the payment or act by reason that before the payment or act the donor of the power had died or become subject to disability* or bankrupt,† or had revoked the power, if the fact of death, disability, bankruptcy,† or revocation, was not at the time of the payment or act known to the person making or doing the same.

(2) A statutory declaration by an attorney that he has not received any notice or information of the revocation of such power of attorney by death or otherwise, shall, if made immediately before or within three months after any such payment or act as aforesaid, be taken to be conclusive proof of such non-revocation at the time when such payment or act was made or done.

Where the donee of the power of attorney is a corporation aggregate, the officer appointed to act for the corporation in the execution of the power may make the statutory declaration in like manner as if that officer had been the donee of the power.

Where probate or letters of administration have been granted to any person as attorney for some other person,‡ this section applies as if the payment made or acts done under the grant had been made or done under a power of attorney.

---

* *E.g.* unsoundness of mind.
† Includes liquidation (s. 205).
‡ Where administration is granted to the attorney of an executor or next of kin, the grant is made to the attorney for the use and benefit of his principal and determines on the latter's death. This clause protects third parties who have no notice of such death and deal in good faith with the attorney.

(3) This section shall not affect any right against the payee of any person interested in any money so paid; and that person shall have the like remedy against the payee as he would have had against the payer if the payment had not been made by him.

(4) This section applies to payments and acts made and done before or after the commencement of this Act, and in this section 'power of attorney' includes a power of attorney implied by statute.

A power of attorney, even though executed under seal, **Express** may be revoked by spoken words without even a document of **Revocation.** revocation [*R.* v. *Wait* (1823), 1 Bing. 121]. In practice, however, express revocation by the donor should be effected by deed. It is also open to the donee to effect revocation by giving notice to the donor that he renounces the power.

The common law was thus laid down by Lord Blackburn in **Implied** *Debenham* v. *Mellon* (1880), 6 A.C., at p. 36: 'Where an **Revocation.** agent is clothed with an authority and afterwards that authority is revoked, unless the revocation has been made known to those who have dealt with him, they would be entitled to say: "The principal is precluded from denying that the authority continued to exist, which he had led us to believe, as reasonable people, did formerly exist." '

There is left, however, the problem which dwells in those words in Lord Blackburn's judgment (above)—'as reasonable people.' The expression suggests at once that there is such a thing as implied revocation, and that the third party may be deemed to have constructive, as distinct from actual, notice of revocation. There are many circumstances which would be held to amount to such an implication, *e.g.* the appointment by the principal of another attorney—especially if the second attorney were invested with powers, the exercise of which would clash with the authority of the first; a lapse of time since the creation of the power, such as would lead any ordinary man to doubt the probability of its continued currency; the intervention of the principal himself in the conduct of the business for which the power had been originally granted. Similarly, if a donor says that the attorney is to act only when he is himself prevented from acting, a third party may be at his wits' end to know what to do. In all such cases the third party would be justified in requiring proof of the continuing validity of the power of attorney. The first paragraph of s. 124 (2), set out above, enables the third party to obtain the necessary protection by requiring the attorney to make a statutory declaration as therein provided. Such a declaration, however, will not protect a third party who is in fact aware, of his own knowledge, that the power has been revoked [*Mutual Provident Land* v. *Macmillan* (1889), A.C. 596].

Powers given for valuable consideration or made irrevocable for not exceeding one year. Still greater security is afforded under the powers covered by ss. 126–127 (1) of the Law of Property Act, 1925, which provides as follows:

A. If a power of attorney is given for valuable consideration and is in the instrument creating the power expressed to be irrevocable [s. 126], or

B. If a power of attorney, whether given for valuable consideration or not, is in the instrument creating the power expressed to be irrevocable for a fixed period therein specified not exceeding one year from the date of the instrument [s. 127], then in favour of a purchaser*

(i) the power shall not be revoked, at any time (or in case B during the fixed time) either by anything done by the donor of the power without the concurrence of the donee of the power, or by the death, disability, or bankruptcy of the donor of the power; and—

(ii) any act done at any time (or in case B within the fixed time) by the donee of the power, in pursuance of the power, shall be as valid as if anything done by the donor of the power without the concurrence of the donee of the power, or the death, disability, or bankruptcy of the donor of the power had not been done or happened; and—

(iii) neither the donee of the power, nor the purchaser, shall at any time be prejudicially affected by notice of anything done by the donor of the power without the concurrence of the donee of the power, or of the death, disability, or bankruptcy of the donor of the power at any time (or in case B within the fixed time).

If a power has been made irrevocable under s. 127, then (unless the context otherwise requires) it does not lapse on the expiration of the fixed period, but continues to operate in the same way as if it had not been made irrevocable for any fixed period.

---

* 'Purchaser' means a purchaser in good faith for valuable consideration, and includes a lessee, mortgagee or other person who for valuable consideration acquires an interest in property, and, where the context so requires, includes an intending purchaser; 'valuable consideration' includes marriage, but does not include a nominal consideration in money; and 'property' includes any thing in action and any interest in real or personal property (s. 205).

According to the common law, the death of the grantor of **Death of** a power was a revocation of the authority, but it has been **Principal or** pointed out how this principle has been modified by statute. **Attorney.** The representatives of a dead principal, it is true, could ratify, at their discretion, a contract made by the attorney in the name of the principal after his death, but in the absence of ratification they were not bound by it [*Foster* v. *Bates* (1843), 12 M. & W. 226]. On the death of the attorney, the latter's representatives have no authority to exercise the power, and the death of the attorney, unless the power of attorney otherwise provides, revokes the appointment of a substitute made by him under a power authorising delegation.

For the same reason, where two attorneys are appointed **Joint** to act jointly and one of them dies, the survivor cannot act **Attorneys.** alone.

Where there are two or more joint principals, the death **Joint** of one of them will generally revoke the power as to the **Principals.** other or others [*Gee* v. *Lane* (1812), 15 East 592]. Although the courts nowadays might not insist upon observing the old strictness as regards this rule, the third party would be well advised not to place faith in speculation, but to assume that the old rule was still valid.

As has already been shown, if the principal was insane at **Insanity of** the time when he executed the power, the instrument is abso- **the Donor.** lutely void. If, however, he was sane at the time of execution, but subsequently becomes insane, the rule of common law is that the power is determined as between the principal and the attorney, but that the revocation is not operative as against a third party who deals with the attorney in good faith and without knowledge of the insanity [*Drew* v. *Nunn* (1879), 4 Q.B.D. 661]. The sections of the Law of Property Act, 1925, set out in this chapter, show how this principle of protecting third parties is recognised by statute.

Insanity of the attorney revokes his authority, since he **Insanity of** loses the capacity to exercise the will of his principal; and **the Attorney.** third parties who deal with him are in a better position than the principal himself to ascertain the fact of his insanity.

In the case of bankruptcy of the principal, as in the case **Bankruptcy** of his insanity, the position of third parties is protected by **of the** the Law of Property Act, 1925. According to the common **Principal.** law, bankruptcy of the principal revokes the power, except in respect of a purely formal act necessary to complete a transaction already binding on the principal and not involving the passing of any interest vested in the trustee in bankruptcy [*Markwick* v. *Hardingham* (1880), 15 Ch. D. 339]; and this rule is also without prejudice to the rights conferred on third parties by ss. 40 to 47 of the Bankruptcy Act, 1914, in respect of transactions entered into *bona fide* and without notice of an act of bankruptcy. As already stated, by s. 22 of the Act a bankrupt is bound to execute such powers of attorney as may be reasonably required by the Official Receiver or the trustee in bankruptcy, or as may be prescribed by the Bankruptcy Rules or directed by the court, in order to effect the due administration of his estate.

Liquidation of Donor Company.
Where a company has given a power of attorney, liquidation and also dissolution revoke the power, but without prejudice to the validity of acts done before the attorneys have notice of the liquidation [*Oriental Bank* (1885), 28 C.D. 634; *Salton* v. *New Beeston Cycle Co.* (1900), 1 Ch. 43]. There is the same statutory protection as in the case of bankruptcy; for by s. 205 of the Law of Property Act, 1925, the expression 'bankruptcy' in ss. 124, 126 and 127 includes liquidation.

A liquidator has power to appoint an agent to do any business which he is unable to do himself [Companies Act, 1948, s. 245 (2) (g)].

Bankruptcy of the Attorney.
It is probably still an open question whether bankruptcy of the attorney automatically revokes the power. There are dicta to this effect, as in the old case of *Hudson* v. *Granger* (1821), 5 B. & A. 27, relating to a factor. On the other hand, it was held in *McCall* v. *Australian Meat Co.* (1870), 19 W.R. 188, in relation to an agency contract, that it was a question of fact in each case whether the circumstances of the bankruptcy, having regard to the nature of the agent's duties and the terms of his employment, were such as to render the agent unfit to carry out his agency.

Possibly the only safe course for the principal to take on hearing of his attorney's bankruptcy is to execute an express revocation of the power, without prejudice to any prior revocation which may have arisen by operation of law.

Ratification.
Ratification of an unauthorised act may be given expressly in writing or orally, or may be implied either by some adoptive act or by silent acquiescence after knowledge of the irregularity. The effect of ratification is thrown back to the date of the act done, and the agent is put in the same position as if he had had authority to do the act at the time the act was done by him. The act must, therefore, be one which at that date was both lawful in itself and within the capacity of the principal. It must also be an act which is done by the agent on behalf of his principal and not on his own behalf [*Keighley Maxsted & Co.* v. *Durant* (1901), A.C. 240].

Powers Coupled with Interest.
Where the power, though not expressed to be irrevocable, is coupled with an interest, it cannot be recalled until that interest has been satisfied or abandoned. But it must be clear that the interest—if it is to keep alive a power which would otherwise be revocable—must be in the subject matter of the power itself; the power and the interest must be united in the same person. The power must be given to secure some

claims of the attorney [*Frith* v. *Frith* (1906), A.C. 254]; a power would not be irrevocable under this doctrine merely because the attorney happened to have some lien upon the estate in respect of which the power was granted [*Taplin* v. *Florence* (1851), 10 C.B. 744]. For example, a commission payable to an agent for collecting debts is not such an interest in the power as to make the appointment of the agent irrevocable [*Doward Dickson & Co.* v. *Williams & Co.* (1890), 6 T.L.R. 316]. On the other hand, an underwriting letter given for valuable consideration and authorising an application for shares to be made in the name of the signatory, is an authority coupled with an interest within the meaning of the rule [*Carmichael* (1896), 2 Ch. 643, and *Olympic Reinsurance Co.* (1920), 2 Ch. 341].

Should the authority be but partly exercised when revocation takes place, the position is that the revocation will be effective as to the part of the authority which has not been executed, but not as to the part already executed, if the authority permits such a distinction. Performance can, therefore, be enforced of a transaction in respect of which the attorney and the third party have entered into a binding contract before the death of the principal. But a third party must not allow an attorney, after notice of the donor's death, to continue to carry out transactions of a nature similar to those already carried out under the power, on the plea that the transactions after the donor's death are but part of a continuous series, constituting in reality the execution of but one uniform commission. Where, for instance, a stockbroker, having a continuation account with a client, instead of closing the account on the death of the client, enters at once on his own authority into a fresh continuation and ultimately makes a sale of the securities at a loss, he has been held liable for the loss incurred [*Overweg, Haas* v. *Durant* (1900), 1 Ch. 209]. **Powers Partly Exercised.**

Where an attorney acting within the scope of his authority commits a fraud, the person who has been defrauded may hold the principal responsible, even in cases where the principal has not derived any benefit from the fraudulent activities of his attorney [*Lloyd* v. *Grace Smith* (1912), A.C. 716]. **Fraud.**

If, however, the third party is aware that the attorney is using his powers for his own benefit in fraud of the donor of the power, he will be accountable to the donor for any property so transferred to him by the attorney. For where the act is on the face of it done for the private purposes of the attorney himself or otherwise than for the purposes and on behalf of his principal, or where, even if the third party has not express notice, the circumstances are such that he was put upon enquiry and could have ascertained that this was the fact, the third party cannot rely on the doctrine of 'apparent authority' or claim protection as an innocent party:

knowledge or notice, actual or constructive, affects the whole position [*Reckitt* v. *Barnett, Pembroke & Slater, Ltd.* (1929), A.C. 176; *Reckitt* v. *Nunburnholme* (1929), 45 T.L.R. 629].

Thus, where a cheque is drawn by an attorney on his principal's account and paid by the attorney into his or his firm's overdrawn account, the collecting bank is put upon enquiry as to whether the money is being applied for the attorney's own benefit in fraud of his principal [*Reckitt* v. *Midland Bank, Ltd.* (1932), 48 T.L.R. 271; (1933), A.C. 1].

Forgery.

Where a forged instrument induces contractual relations between parties ignorant of the forgery, and acting in an honest belief as to the genuineness of the document, it is the person that set the negotiations in motion by the introduction of the forged instrument who must bear the loss. Thus, where it became necessary to decide whether a bank or a stockbroker was to lose the value of stock improperly transferred through a forged power of attorney presented by the stockbroker, when both parties had acted in ignorance of any defect in the instrument, it was held that the professed attorney, *i.e.* the stockbroker, was liable to indemnify the bank [*Oliver* v. *Bank of England* (1902), 18 T.L.R. 341; *Starkey* v. *Bank of England* (1903), A.C. 114; *Sheffield Corporation* v. *Barclay* (1905), A.C. 392, where Lord Davey said: 'I dissent from the proposition that a person who brings a transfer to the registering authority and requests him to register it makes no representation that it is a genuine document'].

The Forged Transfers Act, 1891, provides that local authorities and companies (including companies incorporated by statute or by royal charter) may 'impose such reasonable restrictions on the transfer of their shares, stock, or securities, or with respect to powers of attorney for the transfer thereof, as they may consider requisite for guarding against losses by forgery,' and may make compensation out of their funds for any loss arising from a forged transfer or a transfer under a forged power of attorney. In the case of any stock to which the Colonial Stock Acts apply, the Government of the colony issuing the stock may apply the Act to the stock so issued.

Specially prescribed forms.

Finally, it must be remembered that companies and other bodies or authorities (*e.g.* the Bank of England and the Pay Office) prescribe special forms for use in certain cases. Their right to do so cannot be questioned where it is made one of the terms on which the property to be dealt with is created or retained under their control, whether by virtue of a statute, rules of the Supreme Court, or articles of association; and as such forms are presumably prescribed as a reasonable measure of protection against forgery, it is open to doubt whether in any event the right to insist on their use could successfully be challenged [*Prosser* v. *Bank of England* (1872), L.R. 13 Eq. 611].

The following, therefore, are some practical questions for consideration when a company is asked to act upon a power of attorney:

  (i) Is there any reason to doubt the genuineness of the instrument or the capacity of the donor?

  (ii) Is there satisfactory evidence of the identity of the donee?

  (iii) Is the form of the instrument—*e.g.* as to stamp duty and authentication—correct?

  (iv) If there is more than one attorney, is the grant in favour of the donees joint or joint and several?

  (v) Are there any recitals affecting the interpretation of the operative clauses?

  (vi) (*a*) Is the intended act within the apparent scope of the power?

     (*b*) Has the company notice of anything indicating that the act is being done otherwise than for the purposes and on behalf of the donor?

  (vii) At the date of the act is the power irrevocable under s. 126 or s. 127 of the Law of Property Act, 1925? [N.B.—These sections apply only in favour of a purchaser: a company in registering a transfer of shares to or from the donor of the power or a banker in paying cheques on the donor's account is not a purchaser.]

  (viii) Is there any circumstance, *e.g.* lapse of time since the date of the instrument, which renders it advisable to call for a statutory declaration by the attorney as to non-revocation under s. 124?

  (ix) If the transaction in question is a disposition of or charge upon land or premises or any interest therein, have the provisions of s. 125 been complied with?

  (x) If the instrument includes a delegation by the donor in the capacity of trustee, have the provisions of s. 25 of the Trustee Act, 1925, been complied with? [N.B.— Paragraph (10) of the section provides that a company in whose books stocks or shares are inscribed or registered shall not be affected with notice of the trust to which the stocks or shares are subject; but this does not entitle the company to ignore the statutory requirement as to filing.]

The office scrutiny of the power of attorney should result in the following summary being recorded in the appropriate power of attorney, etc., journal or register, a specimen of which is given below:—

(i) Name and address of donor;
(ii) Name and address of attorney;
(iii) Is it a general power?
(iv) If not, are powers given to:—
    (a) buy shares/stock;
    (b) sell shares/stock;
    (c) vote (including proxy);
    (d) sign transfers;
    (e) receive dividends.
(v) Duration;
(vi) Special powers;
(vii) Any condition as to determination.

Special regard should be given to the following points:—

(i) Stamp duty 10s. (official copy stamped 1s.);
(ii) If notarially certified—extra 1s. stamp;
(iii) Note journal folio in register;
(iv) By whom presented;
(v) Note if power of attorney is enrolled at Central Office;
(vi) Company's registration stamp to be endorsed on power of attorney, and endorsement signed and dated.

The particulars having been recorded in the power of attorney journal or register, only the folio thereof need be noted for reference in the register of members, thus avoiding the publicity which might be objected to if full particulars of the power were recorded in the register of members.

It is not necessary to demand the deposit of a copy if the above extracts are fully made. If any doubt should arise in the absence of a copy, the company is entitled to demand the exhibit of the power on every occasion an attorney seeks to act upon it.

There is nothing to compel the principal to give notice of the revocation of a power of attorney to any third party who may have acted upon it, and it is therefore a wise precaution to obtain confirmation that it is still in force on any occasion when the attorney seeks to act thereunder after, say, five years' interval.

Powers of attorney from the dominions and colonies should be notarially certified, and those from foreign countries should also be legalised by the local British consul. Where they are not so certified and legalised, a notary should be asked to advise whether the instruments are sufficiently authenticated

JOURNAL OF PROBATES, POWERS OF ATTORNEY, ETC.

Shareholder	Document to be Registered			Details	Date Document Registered	By Whom Exhibited	Noted in Register of Members	Fee Paid
	Date	Description	In Favour of					
		★						

★ Use abbreviations such as:—

P/W for probate of will
L/A " Letters of administration
T/T " Testament testamentar
D/C " Death certificate
M/C " Marriage certificate
P/A " Power of attorney
D/P " Deed poll

as having been executed in accordance with local law. In this connection it must be observed that a notarial declaration attracts an extra 1s. stamp duty if the seal of the notary or consul is affixed.

When powers of attorney given under hand are presented for registration, it is necessary to consult the articles of association. If these provide that a transfer may be in writing or shall be *signed* by the transferor and transferee, there is no occasion for the transfer to be a deed, and therefore the signature of the attorney appointed by an instrument under hand could be accepted. Some companies will act upon a Scottish power of attorney under hand, but stipulate that a copy of the instrument should be registered in the Books of Council and Session and an official extract presented to the company.

When an attorney seeks registration of a deed transferring the holding of the principal to the attorney, it is customary to ask the principal to confirm such a transaction.

CHAPTER XXIII

PRIVATE COMPANIES

BESIDES large companies, raising their money from the public and having many shareholders, companies are often found convenient for regulating what is in substance a partnership, for running a family business, or even for managing the property of an individual. Again, it is nowadays common for the large industrial companies to operate by means of subsidiary companies in which it may be that no one but the parent company holds shares. For purposes such as these the law recognises a special class of companies, known as private companies, which are relieved from some of the obligations that apply to public companies. By the 1948 Act this class has been further subdivided into exempt and non-exempt private companies, the former being, as will be seen later, under fewer statutory obligations than the latter.

By s. 28 of the Companies Act, 1948, a private company **Definition.** is defined as 'a company which by its articles:

'(a) restricts the right to transfer its shares; and

'(b) limits the number of its members to fifty, not including persons who are in the employment of the company and persons who, having been formerly in the employment of the company, were while in that employment, and have continued after determination of that employment to be, members of the company; and

'(c) prohibits any invitation to the public to subscribe for any shares or debentures of the company.'

Section 55 enlarges upon this sub-paragraph.

On the registration of a private company the memorandum and the articles need only be subscribed by two persons (s.1), although there is no objection to a larger number of signatories, subject, of course, to the limit of fifty members. A private company may register as a company limited by shares, or a company limited by guarantee with a share capital, or an unlimited company with a share capital, and it is also the practice of the Registrar to permit a company limited by guarantee without a share capital to register as a private company.*

Part II of Table A of the First Schedule of the Act introduces modifications of the ordinary Table A regulations, applicable

---

* There is, however, some doubt as to the true construction of the Act on this point, since, despite s. 1 of the Act, it is arguable that a company without a share capital cannot comply with the provisions of s. 28.

to every private company in so far as they are not excluded by
the articles of the company. The more important modifications are as follows:—

(1) They contain the three essential provisions set out
above, and they exclude the power to issue share
warrants to bearer (cl. 2); but of course the articles
must themselves expressly apply Part II of Table A to
the company, or must expressly declare the three
provisions; for otherwise by the definition in s. 28 the
company will not be a private company at all and
Part II of Table A will not apply. The issue of share
warrants to bearer has to be excluded, since the transfer
of the shares specified in warrants could not be restricted
as the Act requires.

(2) They give a wide discretion to directors to refuse to
register shares (cl. 3). This paragraph contains a
sufficient restriction on the transfer of shares for the
purposes of s. 28 (1); but it is wise to add words in the
articles requiring them to refuse any transfers the
registration of which would cause the number of
members to exceed fifty. The restrictions must
apply to the transfer of all classes of shares. Alternatively to giving the directors a discretion to refuse to
register shares, s. 28 (1) would be complied with by an
article, or set of articles, giving to existing members the
right of pre-emption; such provisions were common in
the articles of old private companies.

(3) Clause 5 validates (subject to the provisions of the Act)
a resolution in writing signed by all the members
entitled to vote at general meetings as if it had been
passed at a general meeting duly convened and held.

The article limiting the number of members to fifty
usually follows the wording of the Act (as in Table A, Pt. II)
and thus excludes employees and ex-employees from the
fifty; but an article simply limiting the number to fifty
without mentioning employees is sufficient, in which case
employees holding shares will count in the fifty. Joint
holders rank as a single member [s. 28 (2)].

As to persons who are in the employment of the company,
the ordinary subordinates, e.g. clerks and workmen of all
kinds, are clearly included, and it is equally clear that directors
who are not otherwise employees are not. A director may,
however, be employed in a particular capacity or as a managing
director in such circumstances that he will be an employee of
the company [Anderson v. James Sutherland (Peterhead)
(1941), S.C. 203]. It cannot safely be assumed that even a
managing director is an employee, though he may be [News-
paper Proprietary Syndicate (1900), 2 Ch. 349, and Normandy

v. *Ind, Coope & Co.* (1908), 1 Ch. 84]. An ordinary whole-time secretary will be an employee, but a part-time secretary acting under special contract and using his own staff is not [*Cairney* v. *Back* (1906), 2 K.B. 746].

The provision prohibiting public issues, whether of shares or debentures, presents no difficulty. As to public issues, see chapter VI.

The Act of 1948 provides that while certain privileges shall **Exempt** continue to relate to every private company, others shall only **Private** relate to exempt private companies, that is to say, private **Companies.** companies which fulfil certain further conditions, set out in s. 129 and Schedule VII of the Act.

An exempt private company is one which (*a*) at the date of its annual return satisfies and has at all times since 1st July, 1948, or since the date of incorporation, if later, satisfied the conditions set out below, or (*b*) at the date of its annual return satisfies those conditions and has obtained the direction of the Board of Trade in respect of its subsequent returns that it shall not be necessary to have satisfied those conditions before that date. The conditions are:—

(1) That the number of debenture holders is not more than 50 (joint holders being treated as a single person) [s. 129 (2) (*b*)].

(2) That no body corporate is a director of the company and neither the company nor any of its directors is party to any arrangement whereby the policy of the company is capable of being determined by persons other than the directors, members and debenture holders or trustees for debenture holders [s. 129 (2) (*c*)].

(3) That no body corporate is the holder of any share or debenture (Schedule VII, para. 1).

(4) That no person other than the holder has any interest in any share or debenture (Schedule VII, para. 1).

The last two conditions are referred to in the Schedule as the basic conditions of exemption; nevertheless they are subject to certain exceptions which are set out in the paragraphs of the Schedule. Therefore, to qualify for exemption, a company must conform with s. 129 (2) (*b*) and (*c*), and either it must wholly comply with the two basic conditions, or any share or debenture in respect of which it does not so comply must be within a class covered by these exceptions.

Exceptions from the basic conditions are allowed for by the Schedule under the following headings:—

(*a*) Normal dealings of a business nature (para. 2).

(*b*) Cases of death and family settlements (para. 3).

(*c*) Cases of disability (para. 4).

(*d*) Trusts for employees (para. 5).

(*e*) Shares held by exempt private companies (para. 6)

(*f*) Banking or finance companies providing capital (para. 7).

(*g*) Bankruptcies, liquidations, etc. (para. 8).

Under these general headings, the exceptions from the basic conditions (some of which are set out below) are particularised:—

Under (*a*) Shares or debentures charged in favour of a banking or finance company.

Under (*b*) (1) Shares or debentures forming part of the estate of a deceased holder up to the completion of the administration of his estate, and
(2) Shares or debentures held by trustees on the trusts of a will or family settlement disposing thereof, so long as no body corporate has for the time being any immediate interest under the trusts other than (*a*) a charitable corporation with no voting power, or (*b*) a corporation which is a trustee of the said trusts and whose only interest therein is by way of remuneration therefor. By para 3 (2) trusts arising under an intestacy are put on a par with trusts arising under a will; but the shares or debentures must have formed part of the intestate's estate at the time of his death.

Under (*e*) This exception does not apply if the total of the shareholders in (1) the 'relevant company' (*i.e.* the company whose exemption is in question) and (2) any company to which this exception is to be applied in determining the 'relevant company's' right to exemption and (3) any further company taken into account to determine the right to exemption of a company in (2) *supra*, together number more than 50 persons.
Where the 'relevant company' (being an exempt private company) and another company hold shares in each other, that other company shall be treated as an exempt private company if the shares in it held by the 'relevant company' would be excepted under the provisions of the above paragraph and in all other respects it is entitled so to be treated.

Under (*f*) This exception does not apply if the banking or finance company (or companies, if more than one) can between them exercise one-fifth or more of the total voting power at a general meeting of the 'relevant company.'

Where shares are excepted from condition 3 under heading (e) or (f), condition 4 is subject to an exception for any interest in those shares which a person has as a debenture holder of the company holding those shares [paras. 6 (3) and 7 (2)].

Under (g) Shares or debentures (1) forming part of the assets in a bankruptcy or liquidation of a holder thereof or (2) held on trust for the benefit of his creditors or otherwise for the purpose of any composition or scheme made under any Act by a court or officer thereof are excepted.

Paragraph 9 of Schedule VII defines a banking or finance company for the purposes of the Schedule.

Clause 6 of Part II of Table A authorises the directors to demand of shareholders any information which may assist them in proving the company's right to exemption. Plainly a private company which wishes to be exempt should not exclude this clause of Table A.

The Cohen Committee in its report issued in 1945 described the private company's privileges of not having to file its accounts etc. with its annual return as 'the most highly prized of the privileges enjoyed by private companies.' It was the intention of the Committee that this privilege should continue to be available to the genuine small private company so that it might not be prejudiced in competition with large public companies or with partnerships or individuals, but that it should not be available to the private company which was the subsidiary of a public company or which did not fit into the category of a small family business incorporated as a company. It was with this intention in view that these involved provisions relating to 'exemption' were drafted (pp. 26–29 of the Report).

It is as yet too early to estimate to what extent this part of the Act relating to exemption will prove workable in practice. But it may be surmised that every private company which intends to establish and maintain its right to exemption will insert provisions in its articles binding its shareholders and debenture holders to take no action which will offend against the 'basic conditions' of exemption and that the company will need to watch vigilantly to see that such conditions are not infringed. This duty of vigilance will fall primarily upon the secretary.

The privileges to which all private companies are entitled **Privileges.** under the Act are as follows:—

(1) They may register with a minimum of two members (s. 1). This also involves the right to trade with a minimum of two members. By s. 31 of the Act, if the number of

members of a private company is reduced below two, or the number of members of any other company below seven, and it carries on business for more than six months while the number is so reduced, every person who is a member of the company during the time that it so carries on business after those six months, and is cognisant of the fact that it is so carrying on business, is severally liable for the payment of the whole debts of the company contracted during that time, and may be sued for the same. This leads to the curious result, in the case of a private company, that an individual may in effect carry on business for six months with limited liability, although after that time his liability becomes unlimited.

(2) They need not hold a statutory meeting or deliver to the Registrar or forward to their members, a statutory report [s. 130 (10)].

(3) Persons may be appointed directors by the articles of a private company, without first signing or delivering to the Registrar consents to act or signing the memorandum for qualification shares, etc., and no list of persons who have consented to be directors need be delivered with the application for registration [s. 181 (5)].

(4) They need not file a statement in lieu of prospectus before allotting shares or debentures [s. 48 (3)]. They need not, indeed, file any statement in lieu of prospectus at all.

(5) They need have no regard to a minimum subscription, but may make their first allotment of shares irrespective of it [s. 109 (7) (a)].

(6) They may commence business without any restriction and require no certificate entitling them to do so [s. 109 (7) (a)].

(7) A private company may have a sole director (s. 176), but a sole director may not also be the secretary [s. 177 (1)].

(8) A private company may appoint two or more persons as directors by a single resolution without the necessity of passing a prior resolution to authorise such an act [s. 183 (1)].

(9) A director of a private company who on 18th July, 1945, held office for life is not liable to removal under the provisions of s. 184.

(10) A private company is not subject to the provisions of s. 185 concerning the age of retirement of directors, unless it is the subsidiary of a company incorporated in the United Kingdom which is neither a private company nor a company incorporated under the laws of Northern Ireland such as would, if it were registered in Great Britain, entitle it to rank as a private company [s. 185 (8)].

The following privileges are those to which only exempt private companies are entitled:—

(1) They are not required to include in their annual returns copies of the balance sheet, auditors' report and other documents mentioned in s. 127 [s. 129 (1)].

(2) They may appoint auditors who are not members of an established body of accountants or otherwise qualified under s. 161.

(3) Partners or employees of officers or servants of the company, may be appointed auditors [s. 161 (2)].

(4) They may make loans to their directors or enter into guarantees or provide security in connection with loans to directors [s. 190 (1)].

(5) They need not send to the Registrar a *printed* copy of the resolutions or agreements specified in s. 143, but may send a copy in such form as the Registrar shall approve [s. 143 (1)].

By s. 30 (1) of the Act, if a private company alters its articles in such manner that they no longer include the provisions required to be contained in its articles (see above), it ceases to be a private company, and must within fourteen days of the alteration either deliver to the Registrar for registration a statement in lieu of prospectus or issue and deliver to the Registrar a prospectus relating to the company. The form of the statement in lieu of prospectus is set out in Schedule III.

By s. 29 of the Act, if default is made by a private company in complying with any of the provisions required to be contained in its articles (see above), it ceases to be entitled to the privileges and exemptions mentioned in that section, and accordingly:—

(a) Its numbers must not fall below seven; otherwise, after six months, all its members aware of the facts are faced with unlimited liability;

(b) An exempt private company forfeits the exemption granted by s. 129 (1) and so must include in its annual return the copy of the last balance sheet, auditor's report and other documents mentioned in s. 127;

(c) If its numbers fall below seven, it is liable to be wound up by the court. Moreover a contributory may present a petition for winding up by the court when the numbers have fallen below seven [ss. 222 (d) and 224 (1) (a) (i)].

The other privileges of a private company are not taken away. It would appear that the company is still entitled to the remaining privileges, for the section does not state that the company shall cease to be a private company, but that certain provisions shall apply to the company as if it were not a private company.

Relief from the consequences of default may be granted by the court upon grounds set out in the proviso to s. 29 of the Act.

Accounts. As from 1st July, 1948, a private company is under the same liability to send to its members a copy of the balance sheet and annexed documents as a public company (s. 158).

Annual Return. By s. 128 of the Act a private company is required to send with the annual return:—(a) a certificate signed by a director and by the secretary that the company has not, since the date of the last return, or in the case of a first return since the incorporation of the company, issued any invitation to the public to subscribe for shares or debentures of the company; and (b) if the list of members exceeds fifty, a certificate that the excess consists wholly of employees or ex-employees; and, in the case of an exempt private company, (c) a further certificate that the conditions of s. 129 (2) have been complied with. The form in which these certificates are to be drafted is set out in Part II of Schedule VI. The object of this provision is that the authorities may be satisfied that the company is still entitled to the privileges of a private company or exempt private company as the case may be.

The reduction of the number of members of a private company below two is a ground for the company being wound up by the court (s. 222).

Proxies. Section 136 (1) confers the right to speak at a meeting upon a proxy appointed to attend and vote instead of a member of a private company. Sub-paragraph (6) of this sub-section enacts that, unless the articles otherwise provide, a member of a private company may not appoint more than one proxy to attend on the same occasion, however many shares he may hold. (By implication it would seem that a member of a public company is not thus restricted, but see p. 154.)

Quorum. Unless the articles otherwise provide, two members personally present form a quorum [s. 134 (c) and see para. 4 of Part II of Table A].

Commissions. It has been expressly decided that a private company, like any other company, may pay commissions for subscriptions, or procuring subscriptions for its capital, subject to the provisions of s. 53 of the Act [*Dominion of Canada Trading Syndicate* v. *Brigstocke* (1911), 2 K.B. 648]. The conditions to be complied with are set out in chapter IX.

Duties of Secretary. The secretary of a private company will (apart from the duties from which he is relieved by reason of a private company's privileges, to which reference has already been made in this chapter) have the same duties to perform as the secretary of any other company; for, apart from these matters, a private company may do whatever any other company may, and must do whatever any other company must do. The only additional duty which is imposed on him by the Act is the signing of the certificates relating to a private company required to accompany the annual return: to these certificates both a director and the secretary are necessary signatories. In practice, the private company's secretary may have other additional duties: for instance, where by reason of a right of pre-emption granted by the articles the members of a private company have a right to purchase the shares or debentures of a deceased member or of a member who wishes to dispose of his shares, the duty of informing the members of their right falls upon the secretary, but the onus of exercising the option of purchase falls upon the members, and it is for them to inform the secretary of their intention to take up the shares rather than for the secretary to obtain the acceptance or renunciation of each individual member. So also it is the secretary's duty to see, so far as it lies within his control, that 'exemption' as a private company is not forfeited by infringement of conditions. His work may be lighter in some respects, *e.g.* in keeping the register posted, in making out the annual return, and in the matter of transfers.

Public Company becoming Private. There is nothing in the Act to prevent a company, which is not a private company, making in its articles such alterations as are necessary to constitute itself a private company, *i.e.* by deleting inappropriate provisions, such as those relating to share warrants and public issues, and unsuitable provisions relating to transfers, and inserting the provisions required by s. 28, and thereafter claiming the privileges of a private company.

Private Company becoming Public. The converse case of the transformation of a private company into a public company is provided for by s. 30 (1) of the Act of 1948, under which a private company automatically becomes a public company if it alters its articles in such manner that they no longer contain the provisions necessary to a private company. Under the Act of 1908 the power of a private company to convert itself into a public company by altering its articles was expressed to be 'subject to anything contained in the memorandum or articles.' These words were omitted from the Acts of 1929 and 1948, but, *semble*, are implied: for if there is in the memorandum an express provision that the company shall always be a private company, that provision would be alterable only in accordance with the process provided by the Act (s. 4); while if there was such a provision in the articles, it would bind the company until the articles had been amended by deleting the provision in accordance with s. 10.

The procedure to enable a private company to become a public company is accordingly:—

(1) If the memorandum provides for or prohibits the transformation of a private company into a public company, the company is bound by such provision or prohibition (s. 20),

but the memorandum may itself be altered by special resolution so as to enable the transformation to be achieved, unless the memorandum itself prohibits such alteration or unless the court refuses to confirm such alteration (s. 23).

(2) If the articles forbid the conversion into a public company, to pass a special resolution deleting this provision; and, in any case,

(3) to pass and file a special resolution in accordance with s. 30;

(4) to file a statement in lieu of prospectus in the form set out in the Third Schedule within fourteen days after the last-mentioned special resolution has been passed, or to issue and file a prospectus within the like period (s. 39 and Third Schedule). (See Appendix F, Form 5.)

The special resolutions referred to in (1) and (2) above can be passed at the same meeting.

CHAPTER XXIV

STATUTORY COMPANIES

A company can be incorporated in Great Britain only by Royal Charter or by or under an Act of Parliament. Historically, a Royal Charter was the earliest method of incorporation; but the practice grew of passing a special Act of Parliament to form a company for a particular purpose; and, finally, the general Companies Acts were passed under which companies could be formed without requiring a special Act. While, in recent times, the great majority of companies are formed under the general Companies Acts, incorporation by special Act has continued to be used for public utility companies, such as railway, gas, water, electricity, dock and harbour companies. Such companies usually require for their business special statutory powers and rights, such as the power to acquire land by compulsion and the exclusive right to supply a particular district; and they are often subject to special statutory limitations as to prices charged and such matters. It is no doubt for these reasons that incorporation by special Act continues to be used.

Strictly, any company formed by or under an Act of Parliament, including any company formed under the Companies Acts, could properly be described as a statutory company as distinct from a chartered company. Nevertheless the term 'statutory company' has come to be used to describe a company incorporated by special Act as distinct from both a chartered company and a company formed under the Companies Act; and it is so used in this chapter.

The Transport Act, 1947, the Electicity Act, 1947, and the Gas Act, 1948, which nationalised the railway, electricity and gas industries and transferred the undertakings of the companies to public authorities, have greatly reduced the importance of statutory companies. Some however still remain, for example water, dock and harbour companies. It may be noted that such public authorities as the Transport Commission or British Electricity Authority are corporations formed by Act of Parliament and could properly be described as statutory corporations. They are not however statutory companies, for the word 'company' implies a body controlled by private individuals and carrying on business for their profit.

A statutory company owes its existence to its special Act, which contains its powers and regulates its procedure. The Companies Acts do not (except as mentioned below) apply to it; it has no memorandum or articles of association; and the whole of its regulations are to be found either expressly or by reference in its special Act. Action by the company beyond the powers conferred by the special Act is *ultra vires*.

An important exception to the general rule that the Companies Acts do not apply to a statutory company should, however, be noted. By s. 435 and Schedule XIV of the Companies Act, 1948, the main provisions of that Act relating to prospectuses and allotments, annual returns, accounts and audits, investigations, the register of directors and secretaries, and ancillary matters, can by Statutory Instrument be made applicable with or without modification to statutory companies incorporated by private Act of Parliament. The provisions in question have been made applicable to all such companies without modification by the Companies (Unregistered Companies) Regulations, 1948 (S.I., 1948, No. 1398).

A further regulation made under this section provides that all relevant references in the Companies Act, 1948, to the registered office of a company shall be taken to mean the principal office of an unregistered company [the Companies (Unregistered Companies) Regulations, 1949 (S.I., 1949, No. 1137)].

In order to avoid repeating in every special Act regulations which had become common form, certain general Acts were passed containing provisions which to a greater or less extent the special Act will usually incorporate. These will now be mentioned.

Companies Clauses Act, 1845. As long ago as 1845 the Companies Clauses Consolidation Act (8 & 9 Vict. c. 16) was passed, the object of which is well expressed in its preamble (repealed by the Statute Law Revision Act, 1891): 'Whereas it is expedient to comprise in one General Act sundry provisions relating to the constitution and management of Joint Stock Companies, usually introduced into Acts of Parliament authorising the execution of undertakings of a public nature by such companies, and that as well for the purpose of avoiding the necessity of repeating such provisions in each of the several Acts relating to such undertakings as for securing greater uniformity in the provisions themselves.' This Act has been added to in subsequent years, the principal addition being the Companies Clauses Act, 1863 (26 & 27 Vict. c. 118), but no substantial amendment has taken place in the original great piece of legislation relating to statutory companies. The Act of 1845 and Part III of the Act of 1863 apply to all statutory companies except so far as modified by the special Act. The remainder of the Act of 1863 only applies in so far as incorporated by the Special Act.

(See also the Companies Clauses Act, 1869, and the Companies Clauses Consolidation Acts of 1888 and 1889.)

The advantages of these Acts, which are always incorporated in special Acts, occasionally with slight alterations, additions or omissions, are obvious. They secure practical uniformity in the internal management of statutory companies. The enormous differences in matters of detailed management, which constantly appear when the articles of association of companies incorporated under the Companies Acts are compared, are thus almost entirely eliminated. One important result of this uniformity is the diminution of litigation.

Applications for special Acts, whether in the case of new companies, or in the case of existing companies seeking extended powers, involve many formalities. Besides the preliminary advertisements in the *London Gazette* and local newspapers, the deposit of the Bill in Parliament, the appearance by counsel with witnesses before Committees of both Houses of Parliament, to meet and deal with the opposition of local authorities and other more or less interested persons or bodies, there are numerous other matters to be dealt with. In the case of applications by existing companies as well as new companies, close attention to the standing orders of Parliament relating to private Bills is essential. These matters are generally attended to by Parliamentary agents, but the secretary of an existing company is required to give notice calling a special meeting (sometimes called a Wharncliffe Meeting), at which the shareholders consider the Bill deposited, and he will be required to prove by affidavit the due and proper summoning of the meeting and the result of the voting thereat.

All applications for special Acts are most carefully scrutinised in Committee. Involving, as they may do, the compulsory acquisition of land, and interference with existing rights of all kinds, they will not be granted without adequate examination and consideration, and without the insertion in the Bills of clauses of all kinds ensuring the due protection of the rights of others and adequate benefit to the public.

Besides the Companies Clauses Acts, the special Act usually incorporates the Land Clauses Consolidation Acts, and the appropriate general Acts relating to particular undertakings, *e.g.* the Waterworks Clauses Act. Furthermore, the clauses from time to time appearing in the model Bills will in general be incorporated.

The Statutory Companies (Redeemable Stock) Act, 1915, gives authority, which was not previously available, to companies having power to carry on a public undertaking to create and issue preference shares or stock and debentures or debenture stock, so as to be redeemable. **Statutory Companies (Redeemable Stock) Act, 1915.**

The secretary of a statutory company will necessarily be fully acquainted with the provisions of his company's special Act or Acts, and the incorporated Acts.

Provisions of Companies Clauses Acts. The matters which are provided for in the Companies Clauses Acts for the most part cover the same ground as the articles of association of a company incorporated under the Companies Acts. They include detailed provisions for the general management of the company.

The resemblance between the requirements of these Acts and of the Companies Act, 1948, is in many cases so strongly marked as to indicate that the framers of the Companies Acts borrowed largely from the law already existing and applicable to statutory companies. This was a well tried foundation upon which to build, but clearly the needs and development of ordinary trading companies have led to many additions to and to many divergencies from the Companies Clauses Acts. Great care is necessary in seeking to apply to statutory companies decisions of the courts given in regard to companies under the Companies Acts. They may or may not be applicable, according as the wording of one section, or of an article, sufficiently resembles or materially differs from the wording of another section. Very many of the decisions are in point and of value; others are irrelevant and useless, and misleading to the secretary of a statutory company.

In considering in any particular case the provisions of the Companies Clauses Acts, the special Act must always be consulted, as the application of some of the clauses in the general Acts is often excluded or limited.

General Meetings. Only such business shall be transacted at an ordinary meeting as the 1845 Act or the company's special Act provides, unless special notice has been given in the advertisement convening it. Every general meeting of shareholders, other than an ordinary meeting, is an extraordinary meeting (s. 68 of the 1845 Act). Fourteen clear days' notice must be given of all meetings, and the quorum is, if not prescribed, an aggregate holding of not less than one-twentieth of the capital, and being in number not less than twenty members or one member for every £500 of such required proportion of capital, whichever be the smaller figure (s. 72). When the shareholder is a body corporate a voting proxy may be any member of the body, though not personally a shareholder in the company (s. 2 of the Companies Clauses Consolidation Act, 1888, as amended by the Companies Clauses Consolidation Act, 1889).

Proxies. It would appear that in the case of a statutory company, having regard to para. 62 of the standing orders of Parliament, all blanks in the form of proxy for use at general meetings, or at any rate the name of the proxy, must be inserted by the shareholder, and that neither the company nor its secretary has implied authority to fill in any blanks.

Statutory companies are not required to use the word 'Limited' as part of their name, nor are they registered.

A point of considerable interest to the secretary of a statutory company is that unless otherwise provided in the special Act, his remuneration is fixed by a general meeting of the company (s. 91 of the Act of 1845).

The duties of a secretary of a statutory company are necessarily of the same kind as fall to the lot of secretaries of other companies, and need not be detailed here. In the case of statutory undertakings, however, such matters as assessments, and the continuous growth of legislative enactments (*e.g.* those dealing with workmen's compensation and national insurance) and departmental regulations, are probably in general more before his notice than in the case of many registered companies. **Duties of Secretary.**

There are numerous differences between a statutory company and a company under the Companies Acts, and the more important of these are noticed below.

Section 9 of the Companies Clauses Consolidation Act, 1845, requires a statutory company to keep a register of shareholders. The section is as follows:— **Register of Shareholders.**

> The company shall keep a book to be called the 'register of shareholders'; and in such book shall be fairly and distinctly entered, from time to time, the names of the several corporations, and the names and addresses of the several persons entitled to shares in the company, together with the number of shares to which such shareholders shall be respectively entitled, distinguishing each share by its number, and the amount of the subscriptions paid on such shares, and the surnames or corporate names of the said shareholders shall be placed in alphabetical order; and such book shall be authenticated by the common seal of the company being affixed thereto; and such authentication shall take place at the first ordinary meeting, or at the next subsequent meeting of the company, and so from time to time at each ordinary meeting of the company.

It will be noticed that there is no right of inspection given of the register of shareholders; there is, however, a right to require a copy [*Mutter* v. *Eastern and Midland Railway* (1888), 38 Ch. D. 92].

In addition, by s. 10, a 'shareholders' address book' is required to be kept. This must contain the names in alphabetical order, places of abode and descriptions of the shareholders, so far as known to the company, but particulars of their holdings are not required to be stated. It is open to the inspection of shareholders gratis, and copies may be required on payment. **Shareholders' Address Book.**

Further, when shares have been consolidated into stock, pursuant to s. 61 of the Act, the company shall, by s. 63, **Consolidation.**

'from time to time cause the names of the several parties who may be interested in any such stock as aforesaid, with the amount of the interest therein possessed by them respectively to be entered in a book to be kept for the purpose, and to be called "The Register of Holders of Consolidated Stock"; and such book shall be accessible at all reasonable times to the several holders of shares or stock in the undertaking.'

Trusts. Trusts should not be recognised by a statutory company, whether by any entry in the register or in any other manner (s. 20).

Transfers. Shareholders have an absolute right of transfer (s. 14), subject to the restriction that when a call has been made the shares cannot be transferred until it has been paid (s. 16), and, of course, to any provisions contained in the special Act.

Transfers must be by deed; the deed must be duly stamped and the consideration truly stated (s. 14). Although a statutory form of transfer is scheduled to the Act, the common form of transfer (Appendix F, Form No. 92) is generally used and invariably accepted. There is thus practical uniformity in the form of transfers, whether a company be a statutory company or not.

Bonds. The Companies Clauses Act, 1845, authorises the borrowing of money on mortgage or bond (s. 38), and the succeeding clauses define the form of the bond and register and also define the form of transfer, which differs from the common form used for stocks and shares.

I, A.B., of   in consideration of the sum of
            paid by G. H., of   do hereby
    transfer to the said G. H. his executors administrators
    and assigns a certain bond number   made by
    the   Company to   bearing
    date the   day of   for securing the
    sum of   and   interest (or if such
    transfer be by endorsement 'the within security') and
    all my right estate and interest in and to the money
    thereby secured. In witness whereof I have hereunto
    set my hand and seal, etc., etc.

The creation of debenture stock in place of the borrowing by mortgage or bond was allowed by the Companies Clauses Act, 1863 (Part III).

A good many companies still exercise their borrowing powers by the issue of debenture bonds, and it should be particularly noted that the common form of transfer does not apply to these.

Transfers. The duties of the secretary, upon a duly executed deed of transfer being delivered to him, are prescribed by s. 15, and are as follows:—

1. he must keep the transfer;

2. he must enter a memorial thereof in a book to be called the 'register of transfers';

3. he must endorse such entry on the deed of transfer;

4. he must, on demand, deliver a new certificate to the purchaser;

5. he may, for every such entry, together with the endorsement and certificate, demand a sum not exceeding the prescribed amount, or if no amount be prescribed (*i.e.* by the company's special Act) a sum not exceeding 2s. 6d.;

6. he must, if the purchaser requires it, instead of giving a new certificate, make and sign an endorsement of the transfer on the old certificate; the old certificate with the signed endorsement is equivalent to a new certificate.

The duty of endorsing the deed of transfer seems hardly necessary in the days of certificates, and it has been suggested that it was inserted inadvertently in the Act of 1845. A private Act of 1801, authorising the construction of a railway from Wandsworth to Croydon (41 Geo. III. c. xxxiii.) required the endorsement on 'deeds of conveyance' of shares in the undertaking, which deed was to be kept by the purchaser 'as his security,' certificates not having then been introduced. It is the modern practice to issue a new certificate and not to endorse the old certificate. However, the requirement of endorsement is statutory and must be complied with.

The legal interest in the shares transferred passes to the purchaser upon the delivery of the transfer, duly executed, to the secretary. The duties of the secretary as regards certification and scrutiny of the transfer, and scrutiny of any power of attorney lodged, will be substantially the same as in the case of a company under the Companies Acts. He must, in short, satisfy himself that the deed of transfer is 'duly executed' and in order in every detail. If he returns the transfer because of some failure to comply with the provisions of the Act, the deed is deemed not to have been delivered and therefore not to pass the legal interest [*Nanney* v. *Morgan* (1888), 37 C.D. 346].

Trans-mission.

There are, however, some special points in which, owing to the provisions of the Companies Clauses Act, 1845, the secretary of a statutory company cannot follow the practice of the secretary of a registered company. Thus if a transfer be lodged for registration after the death of the transferor and after probate or letters of administration have been exhibited, it cannot be acted on, since (as appears below) the names of the personal representatives of the deceased transferor would already be on the register in their individual capacities, and they alone would be entitled to deal with the shares. If the personal representatives of a deceased proprietor have been duly registered, a transfer by them should not be accepted if they are described as executors or administrators, although in the case of fully paid shares or of stock the fact that they are so described seems immaterial.

While there is no express provision permitting a statutory company to make regulations as to such matters as allowing more than one account on the same transfer form, or limiting the number of holders in a joint account, or permitting more than one account in the same name or names, or allowing transfers of more than one class of stock on the same deed, there seems to be no reason why a statutory company should not have its own practice in such respects, and adhere to it until forced in individual cases to abandon it.

There is an important difference in the matter of transmission between statutory companies and companies under the Companies Acts. By s. 18 of the Companies Clauses Consolidation Act, 1845, it is the duty of a secretary, upon proof of the transmission of interest of a proprietor, to enter the name of his representative on the register. Such representative therefore becomes a shareholder in his personal capacity, with all the consequent rights and liabilities. It appears that it is not necessary for the secretary to obtain the consent of his board before performing this statutory duty, but that he ought to perform it at once.

There is thus a *prima facie* right in the company to register the representative in his personal capacity, upon the necessary formalities being complied with. But if the representative does not desire to have the shares registered in his name, he ought to be allowed a reasonable time to sell the shares and to produce a purchaser who will take a transfer of them, [*Buchan's Case* (1879), 4 A.C. 549], and it is doubtful whether he will be compelled to become personally liable by becoming registered without any request, express or implied, by him.

Section 18 provides for transmission 'in consequence of the death or bankruptcy or insolvency of any shareholder, or by any other lawful means than by a transfer according to the provisions of this or the special Act.' The transmission is to be authenticated by a declaration in writing of a formal character, 'or in such other manner as the directors shall require.' Section 19 requires the declaration, in the case of transmission by will or on intestacy, to be produced to the secretary, together with probate or letters of administration, or an official extract therefrom. Upon the declaration being left with the secretary, he is to enter the name of the person entitled by transmission on the register of shareholders

(s. 18). It is incorrect and contrary to the Act for any mention of a representative capacity to appear on the register of a statutory company, or for the company to recognise the representative capacity in any way. Upon production of probate or letters of administration, the secretary is to make an entry of the declaration in the register of transfers. In the absence of a declaration, it appears that a form of request by the executors or administrators to be entered on the register should be required [*Buchan's Case, supra;* and see Appendix F, Form 104]. The declaration itself, if produced, is probably sufficient evidence of a request.

The practical result of the words, 'or in such other manner as the directors shall require,' seems to be that the secretary of a statutory company, in satisfying himself as to the right of a representative, shall require the same evidence as is required by the secretary of a company under the Companies Acts.

If probate be granted to the attorney of an executor, he should be registered as the holder of the stock in his personal capacity, without any reference to his capacity as an attorney or executor.

It follows from the fact that a person entitled by transmission is, upon proper evidence being furnished, entitled to be registered, that, if an executor or administrator is also the beneficiary, he can be registered without a transfer being executed.

Since executors, when entered upon the register pursuant to s. 18, become joint shareholders in their individual capacities, a transfer by them must be executed by all the executors [*Barton* v. *London & North Western Railway* (1889), 24 Q.B.D. 77].

Should the register of a statutory company require to be altered in consequence of a change of name, whether by marriage, acquisition of title or otherwise, similar evidence should be required as in the case of an ordinary limited company.

The fee which a statutory company may demand upon transmission is, in the absence of any prescribed amount, a sum not exceeding 5s. (s. 18). As already stated, a fee of 2s. 6d. may be demanded on every transfer. Apart from these two fees, it does not appear that a statutory company has any power to charge any other fees in respect of matters connected with transfers and transmission; but it is usual for a similar fee to be charged on registration of probate or letters of administration, on proof of marriage or death, and on registration of powers of attorney; and until the right to demand these fees is challenged there seems no reason why the practice should not be continued.

CHAPTER XXV

SCOTTISH COMPANIES

THE Companies Act, 1948, applies generally only to England (including Wales) and Scotland. Certain parts of the Act are expressly limited to companies registered in England, while some provisions apply only to companies registered in Scotland. It is proposed in this chapter to point out and consider the principal portions of the Act relating to companies before liquidation which are confined to Scottish companies, and those from the operation of which Scottish companies are excluded, and to indicate the principal points of difference between Scottish and English business practice in connection with these statutory provisions.

Trusts. The most important differences appear in the matter of the recognition of trusts and the practice as to transfers, etc., and in the law as to debentures. Section 117 of the Act prohibits the recognition of trusts on the registers of companies registered in England. The existence of a trust is commonly recognised by Scottish companies, and persons may be registered in any representative capacity, *e.g.* as executors, or trustees, of a deceased person; 'curator bonis for . . .'; 'factor loco tutoris to . . .'; 'in trust for . . .'; 'for behoof of . . .'; 'for and on behalf of . . .'; or as office-bearers. Registration as trustees does not limit the holders' liability for calls to the amount of the trust estate in their hands; they are as completely liable as if the trust were not disclosed. The notice of trust on the register is for the benefit of the beneficiaries. It demonstrates the trust. A majority of the accepting and acting trustees or executors usually form a quorum and can act so as to bind the estate under their charge, and a transfer signed by such quorum is therefore quite in order unless the deed of trust otherwise provides [see the Trusts (Scotland) Act, 1921, s. 3]. When changes take place in the personnel of the trustees or executors by death, resignation, or the assumption of new trustees, effect is given in the register to such changes on production to the company of an extract from the register of deaths, the minute of resignation, or the deed of assumption, as the case may be.

Where buyers are described in a transfer as office-bearers, *e.g.* president, secretary, or treasurer, it is usual to add the words 'and their successors in office' after the words 'do hereby bargain, sell, assign, and transfer to the said transferees.' When that is done, all that is usually required, before substituting in the register the name of any new office-bearer for that of an office-bearer who may have died or demitted office, is the production of a certified extract from the minutes of the meeting of the company, institution, or society at which such new appointment is made, in some cases supported by a statutory declaration by a responsible person conversant with the facts.

Where it is intended to register shares or stock of a Scottish **Joint** company in the names of two or more persons with a desti- **Holders.** nation to the survivor, words to that effect must ordinarily be inserted in the transfer, as survivorship is not implied under Scots law. The words necessary are 'and the survivor of them,' or 'and the survivors or survivor of them' placed after the words 'do hereby bargain, sell, assign, and transfer to the said *A.B.*,' although some companies pass transfers with the words written immediately after the names and addresses of the buyers. Failing the inclusion of such words, and in the absence of any special provision to the contrary in the company's articles of association, the transferees would be held to have an equal and separate interest in the shares or stock, and, on the death of one of them, his confirmation or probate would require to be exhibited and his executors' names would be noted in the register in respect of his share; and, in the event of a sale, the transfer would require to be executed by the survivor and by the executors of the deceased. Where the survivorship clause is registered, and one of the holders dies, production of evidence of death is all that is necessary to enable a company to remove his name. In any subsequent transfer by the survivor he should be described as 'survivor in a joint account with   deceased.' It is, however, now customary in the case of Scottish companies to make special provision in the articles of association that where shares are registered in joint names without qualification the survivors or survivor are alone to be recognised as holding the title following upon a death, thereby bringing the practice more into line with that prevailing in England.

Shares of Scottish companies may also be registered in joint names so that a quorum only of the holders require to sign. This method of registration has been adopted by the nominees of some of the banks in Scotland who are described in transfers as, say, '*A.B.*, *C.D.*, and *E.F.*, all of the Bank, Limited, Glasgow, and the survivors or survivor of them, any two being a quorum.'

Shares in a company are moveable property and upon the decease of a member pass according to the law of succession to moveables. It is the deceased's executor who obtains a title to the shares, and this, in Scotland, is evidenced by a grant of confirmation from the appropriate court. The confirmation should specifically mention the shares by name and description. If shares have been omitted from the confirmation the omission can be remedied by an eik or a confirmation *ad omissa*. The confirmation is the authority to the company to recognise the executor as the person having right to deal with the shares, and no company should pay dividends or transfer shares of a deceased member without production of confirmation or of probate or letters of administration. In the absence of such title a company renders itself liable to estate duty and penalties by transfering shares or paying dividends. Probate or letters of administration must be resealed in the Commissary Court of Edinburgh in terms of the Confirmation and Probate Acts, 1858 and 1859, before the title is validly completed. Foreign executors must obtain a title from the court before a company is bound to recognise them. In Scotland this means a grant of confirmation from the Commissary Court, Edinburgh.

The photostatic copy of the act of sealing of a confirmation in England is of no validity for Scottish estates but applies only to estates in England.

Where, as is usual in the case of Scottish companies, the articles of association do not prohibit the registration of trusts, trustees are entered in the register as such. If, having been registered as trustees, they subsequently wish to be registered as individuals, a transfer will be required which may be liable to 10s. stamp duty. If the trustees are continuing to hold as such, though wishing to be registered as individuals, no stamp duty is claimed by the Inland Revenue, but the secretary of a company is entitled to ask that the transfer, or letter of request where acceptable, be adjudicated, as he cannot tell whether the trustees have a beneficial interest or not.

The law of Scotland, unlike that of England, does not permit of the delegation of power by a trustee, and therefore a power of attorney by a trustee in a Scottish trust is not acceptable.

Under Scottish law a lien cannot be constituted except by transfer or diligence. A distringas is not valid in Scotland.

Partnerships. Although under the law of Scotland partnerships may own property and may quite competently be registered as shareholders and act as transferors or transferees, there are obvious objections to registering a firm as such, and the practice should be discouraged.

Persons unable to Write. The execution of a deed by a mark is not valid in Scotland. Where in consequence of illness or blindness or other cause the granter of a deed is unable to write, the deed must be executed for him by a Scottish solicitor, or a notary public, or a justice of the peace, in the presence of the granter and by his authority, all before two witnesses who have heard the deed read over to the granter and heard or seen such authority given. The execution consists of a docquet in the following terms added by the solicitor (or other person acting) in his own handwriting at the end of the deed, and signed by him and the witnesses:—

> Read over to, and signed by me for, and by authority of the above-named A.B. (without designation) who declares that he is blind (or is unable to write) all in his presence, and in presence of the witnesses hereto subscribing.
>
> C.D., solicitor (or notary public) adding address, or
>
> E.F., justice of the peace for the county of...........
>
> G.H. (designation and address) witness.
>
> J.K. (designation and address) witness.

If the deed consists of more than one page, the solicitor (or other person acting) adhibits his signature at the foot of each of the previous pages.

It may be mentioned that, in the case of a will, a parish minister, acting in his own parish, may also competently sign for the granter, the same procedure being followed.

Powers of attorney and other Scottish legal documents may be registered in the Books of Council and Session in Edinburgh, where the originals are preserved. The production of an 'extract registered' copy from the books mentioned of a power of attorney, a deed of assumption, or a minute of resignation, or other legal instrument, is equivalent to the exhibition of the deed itself. It is now the practice for the Keeper of the Register to issue photographic copies of the original deeds (instead of manuscript or typewritten copies) under authority recently granted by the court. **Registration of Documents.**

The Scottish law as to debentures requires special attention in view of the great differences which exist between the laws of England and Scotland in this respect. **Debentures**

According to the common law of Scotland no security can be effectively created over moveables or personal property so long as remaining in the possession of the debtor. This general rule has been to some extent modified by statute, but broadly speaking the law remains as stated. In order, therefore, to create an effective charge or security over such property, delivery, either express or constructive, must have been given to the creditor and retained by him. In the case of moveables, such as stock-in-trade, etc., actual delivery or transfer to the creditor—an operation, however, which, consistently with the proper carrying on of business, is usually found to be more or less impracticable—leaves no room for doubt, but the same result may be achieved constructively, e.g. by the transfer of goods in store from the name of the owner and borrower into that of the lender. Similarly, if obligations are assigned, the assignment must be intimated to the obligant; e.g. the assignment of uncalled capital by intimation to the shareholders who are liable.

Floating Charge.

One result of the rule referred to is to render the existence of the floating charge known to English law impossible in the case of a company registered in Scotland over Scottish assets [*Clark* v. *West Calder Oil Company* (1882), 9 R. 1017; *Ballachulish Slate Quarries* v. *Menzies* (1908), 45 S.L.R. 667].

Accordingly, in Scotland, debentures issued under the Companies Acts are confined to three classes: (1) naked debentures, which are no more than a personal obligation by the company for repayment of money advanced on loan; (2) debentures secured over moveable or personal rights or property by actual or constructive delivery or transfer to the lenders or trustees for lenders; and (3) mortgage debentures secured over heritable or real property.

Naked Debentures.

As to (1), naked debentures, the lender is, subject to the variations in procedure in the matter of enforcing recovery, practically in the same position as a lender under a naked debenture of an English company. The rights of debentures of this class are now not infrequently regulated by the terms of a separate deed of trust, under which trustees are appointed, instead of being expressed in the debenture itself. The advantages of such an arrangement in case of default lie chiefly in the convenience by which the claims of the debenture holders in case of liquidation are advanced and controlled by the trustees in the general interest in terms of the provisions of the trust deed. The existence of such trusts, of which there are now many, does not, however, carry the actual rights of the debenture holders as regards security any further than is the case with the holders of ordinary naked debentures.

Security over Moveable Property.

As to (2), debentures secured over moveable or personal property, either by delivery or transfer to the actual lenders or trustees for their behoof, may be illustrated by the case of shipping property. Many debentures are effectively charged over ships by mortgage, or by transfer of the vessels themselves, or in some cases, of the shares of the limited companies owning them, to the lenders or trustees on their account. In the former case the mortgage or bill of sale must be recorded on the ship's register, and in the latter a transfer of the shares must be registered by the company. In such cases the trust deed usually makes provision for the changing of the security according to the exigencies of business, but so that the value will always be maintained. There are other cases (becoming more frequent under modern practice) of debentures in which shares or stocks of ordinary limited companies are impledged in security.

Security over Heritage.

As to (3), debentures secured over heritage, the system of land registration in Scotland lends itself very readily to the creation of effective securities over land and buildings by mortgage debentures, the registration of the necessary deed in the Register of Sasines, assuming its validity on other grounds, creating a preference in favour of the grantees. This security is usually created by an *ex facie* absolute conveyance to trustees for the debenture holders on registration of which these trustees, subject to the provisions of the separate deed of trust, become vested in the property as if they were absolute owners. Under the deed of trust, provision is made for the administration of the trust, the use by the company of the subjects conveyed so long as there is no default, the enforcement of the debenture holders' rights in case of default, etc., and as a rule the trustees are entitled, though not bound, to satisfy themselves that the security subjects are being duly maintained and kept insured against loss by fire. The deed of trust, as a matter of fact, runs largely on the lines of similar deeds by English companies securing mortgage debentures over property there. (See chapter XIX.)

It may be worth noticing that certain leases which, in the **Long Leases.** ordinary case, could not be effectively charged, may be made the subject of a good security. By the Registration of Long Leases Act, 1857, it was made lawful to record in the Register of Sasines any lease of heritage in Scotland for a period of thirty-one years or upwards, and any assignations of such leases, the effect of which was to make such leases and assignations during their subsistence as effective against singular successors as if they were ordinary feudal conveyances of land. Accordingly, it is not uncommon, particularly in the case of mineral companies, to have leases answering the requirements of the Act as to duration, such leases then becoming susceptible to being charged or mortgaged by the company, if it desires to borrow, as security for debenture holders or other lenders, without the necessity of actual possession by the security holders.

The question has been raised whether a floating charge of **Registration** a company registered in England would be effective over **of** moveables in Scotland, and, on the other hand, whether **Mortgages.** a floating charge purporting to be given by a company registered in Scotland over moveables in England would be valid. It is now generally agreed that a company registered in England cannot create by a floating charge a security over moveables situated in Scotland which would be a valid security according to the law of Scotland. Accordingly any party having a security or rights by diligence valid by Scots law would be preferred to the holder of the floating charge. In the case of a Scottish company having property in England, a floating charge would be a competent method of creating a security over English assets, provided the company had a place of business in England. Such security would be void unless registered with the Registrar of Companies in England in view of s. 106 of the Act. Section 95 of the Act affects companies registered in Scotland to the extent that if a Scottish company having an established place of business in England creates a charge on property in England or acquires property in England subject to a charge which would, if the charge were created or the property were acquired by an English company, require to be registered in England, such charge must be registered in England, notwithstanding that the company is a Scottish company (s. 106). (See also s. 91.) Under s. 95 (5), where a charge comprises property situate in Scotland and registration in Scotland is necessary to make the charge valid or effectual according to the law of that country, it is sufficient to deliver to the Registrar in England a copy, verified in the prescribed manner, of the instrument creating or evidencing the charge, together with a certificate in the prescribed form stating that the charge was presented for registration in Scotland on the date on which it was so presented.

In order to prevent the possibility of misapprehension, it may be added that the provisions of s. 104 of the Act as to the keeping by the company itself of a register of charges, in which are to be entered all charges specifically affecting property of the company, are applicable to companies registered in Scotland as well as to those registered in England. Further, the annual return which a company must file under ss. 124–129 of the Act must include, in the case of companies registered in Scotland as well as those registered in England, a statement of the total amount due by the company in respect of all mortgages and charges.

Statutory Companies. Bonds and debenture stock may also be issued under the Companies Clauses Acts of 1845 and 1863, which, together with certain other Acts, regulated the share and loan capital of railway companies and other similar public undertakings (see chapter XXIV). The bonds contemplated by the first Act are naked debentures, though the word 'debenture' does not itself appear, but if a mortgage deed be also granted, the assignment of the company's undertaking, etc., to the creditor in security of his debt is declared to have the full effect of an assignation duly completed. This, it will be seen, is an exception to the common law rule already mentioned, and its effect is to create a valid statutory security on the property assigned, very much in the nature of a floating charge in England. It must be noted, however, that this is inapplicable to companies operating under the Companies Act, 1948.

In the same way debenture stock issued under the Companies Clauses Act, 1863, is a statutory charge in the nature of a perpetual annuity upon the undertaking preferable in character to all stocks or shares, and it may in case of default be enforced by application for the appointment of a judicial factor. Again, that is a provision peculiarly applicable to companies incorporated under these special Acts and not to ordinary limited liability companies.

A few other points as to companies registered in Scotland **Other Points** may be noticed. By ss. 3 and 9 of the Act it is expressly **under 1948** provided that the attestation of the signatures to the memor- **Act.** andum and articles is sufficient in Scotland, as well as in England, if made by one witness.

Section 32 (4) of the Act provides that any deed to which a company is a party shall be held to be validly executed on behalf of the company according to the law of Scotland if it is executed in accordance with the provisions of the Act or is sealed with the common seal of the company and subscribed on behalf of the company by two of the directors or by a director and the secretary of the company, and such subscription on behalf of the company shall be binding whether attested by witnesses or not. It is customary for the signatures of the directors and secretary to be attested by witnesses, but as indicated above this is unnecessary.

Section 437 of the Act provides that where a company registered in Scotland carries on business in England, the process of any court in England may be served on the company by leaving it at or sending it by post to the principal place of business of the company in England addressed to the manager or other head officer in England of the company. The person issuing out the process must also send a copy thereof by post to the registered office of the company.

An agreement executed under the seal of a company, which is not otherwise charged with stamp duty, is chargeable in England with a fixed duty of 10s., but in Scotland is chargeable with the duty of 6d., unless it contains a clause of registration.

CHAPTER XXVI

OVERSEA COMPANIES

Oversea Companies with places of business in Great Britain. OVERSEA COMPANIES (that is, companies incorporated outside Great Britain) may be divided into two classes according to whether or not they have established their place of business in Great Britain. Sections 406 to 416 of the Act contain special provisions which apply (s. 406) to all companies having an established place of business within Great Britain In this connection it must be remembered that a 'place of business' is defined by s. 415 to include a share transfer or share registration office. This means that a company which establishes a share registration office in Great Britain is within the jurisdiction for the purpose of serving process and notices [*The Madrid* (1937), p. 40]. By s. 407 (1) any oversea company establishing a place of business within Great Britain must within one month from the establishment of the place of business deliver to the Registrar for registration the following documents:—

1. A certified copy of the documents constituting or defining the constitution of the company and, if such documents are not in the English language, a certified translation thereof.

2. A list of the directors and secretary of the company containing similar particulars to those which would be required in the case of the directors and secretary of an English company. [See s. 407 (2)].

3. The names and addresses of some one or more persons resident in Great Britain authorised to accept on behalf of the company service of process and any notices required to be served on the company.

As to the proper method of certification of the above-mentioned documents, see Rules 2 and 5 of the Companies (Forms) Order, 1949. The forms prescribed by the Board of Trade for use under s. 407 (1) are scheduled to this order. (See Forms 1F. to 3F.) (See Appendix F, Forms 140, 141 and 142.)

Particulars of any alteration in any of the documents, or particulars delivered for registration pursuant to s. 407 (1), must be delivered to the Registrar for registration within twenty-one days of the date of the alterations being made, or within twenty-one days after the date on which notice thereof could in due course of post have been received in Great Britain [s. 409 and Rule 3 of the Companies (Forms) Order, 1949].

The return should be in the form set forth in Nos. 4F to 6F of the forms scheduled to this order. Penalties for default in compliance are laid down by s. 414.

Every oversea company with an established place of **Balance** business in Great Britain is under similar obligations as to **Sheet and** making out a balance sheet and profit and loss account and, **Loss** if the company is a holding company, group accounts, in such **Account.** form, containing such particulars, and including such documents as (subject to any prescribed exceptions) are imposed on an English company by ss. 147 to 163. It must deliver to the Registrar for registration a copy of such balance sheet and profit and loss account, and, where applicable, group accounts (including the above-mentioned particulars and documents) together with a certified translation if the balance sheet or other documents are not in the English language (s. 410). The requirements of ss. 147 to 163 are considered in chapters XVI and XVII.

Every oversea company with an established place of **Particulars** business in Great Britain must also:— **to be included in various documents.**

(i) state the country in which the company is incorporated in every prospectus issued by it which invites subscriptions for its shares or debentures in Great Britain;

(ii) conspicuously exhibit on every place where it carries on business in Great Britain the name of the company and the country in which it is incorporated;

(iii) cause the name of the company and of the country in which it is incorporated to be stated in legible characters in all billheads and letter paper, and in all notices and other official publications;

(iv) if the liability of the members of the company is limited, cause notice of that fact to be stated in legible characters in every such prospectus as above-mentioned and in all billheads, letter paper, notices, advertisements, and other official publications of the company in Great Britain and to be affixed on every place where it carries on business (s. 411).

Having regard to s. 201, all trade catalogues, trade circulars, show cards and business letters on or in which the name of any such oversea company appears, which are issued or sent by the company to any person in any part of His Majesty's dominions, must also state in legible characters the particulars as to directors required by s. 201, unless the company established its business in Great Britain before 23rd November, 1916. (See p. 175.)

Any process or notice requiring to be served on an oversea **Service of** company with an established place of business in Great **Documents.** Britain will be sufficiently served if addressed to any person whose name has been filed with the Registrar under s. 407 and

left at or sent by post to the address so filed. If the company
has made default in filing the name and address of a person
authorised to accept service on its behalf, or if all the persons
whose names and addresses have been so filed are dead, or
have ceased to reside at the addresses so filed, or refuse to
accept service, or for any reason cannot be served [*e.g.* as in
The Madrid (1937), P. 40], service may be effected by leaving
the process or notice at or sending it by post to any place of
business established by the company in Great Britain (s. 412).

Companies Incorporated in the Channel Islands and Isle of Man. If a company incorporated in the Channel Islands or the
Isle of Man has a place of business in England or Scotland
it must comply with all provisions of the Act requiring
documents to be forwarded to or filed with the Registrar
(other than provisions requiring the payment of the fee in
respect of the registration of a company) in the same manner
as if it had been actually registered in England or Scotland
as the case might be (s. 416).

Carrying on business in England and Scotland. If any oversea company establishes a place of business in
both England and Scotland the requisite documents and par-
ticulars must be filed at the Registration Office in each
country [s. 413 (1)].

Ceasing to carry on business. If any oversea company ceases to have a place of business
in either England or Scotland, it must forthwith give notice of
the fact to the Registrar of Companies for England or Scotland
as the case may be, and as from the date on which such notice
is given the obligation of the company to file a document with
such Registrar will cease [s. 413 (2)].

Holding Land. Oversea companies which have complied with the provisions
of s. 407 by delivering to the Registrar the documents and
particulars therein stated have the same power of holding
land in the United Kingdom (s. 14) as a company incorporated
under the Act (s. 408). Section 408 is without prejudice to
the power of a company registered in Northern Ireland to
hold land. Other oversea companies which have failed to
comply with s. 407 are subject to the provisions of the Mortmain Acts.

Registration of Charges. Under s. 106, particulars of certain charges on property in
England created, or subsisting on property in England
acquired, by an oversea company having an established place
of business in England must be duly registered. The effect
of these sections has been considered on p. 259 *et seq.*

The provisions summarised above apply only to companies
establishing a place of business in Great Britain; but those set
out below (which consist principally of the provisions relating
to prospectuses enacted in ss. 417–423 inclusive) apply to all
oversea companies whether or not they have established a
place of business in Great Britain.

Prospectuses. Under ss. 417–423 it is illegal to issue, circulate or distribute
in Great Britain any prospectus offering for subscription

shares or debentures of a company incorporated or to be incorporated outside Great Britain (whether or not such company has, or when formed will have, a place of business in Great Britain) unless before the issue, circulation or distribution the following conditions have been complied with:—

1. The prospectus is dated [s. 417 (1)].

2. A copy of the prospectus, certified by the chairman and two other directors of the company as having been approved by a resolution of the managing body of the company, has been delivered to the Registrar for registration [s. 420 (1)].

3. The prospectus states on the face of it that the copy has been so delivered [s. 420 (1)].

4. The prospectus otherwise conforms with ss. 417–423 of the Act.

The first three conditions speak for themselves. To comply with the fourth condition the prospectus must contain the particulars and matters specified in sub-s. (1) of s. 417, unless in accordance with s. 418 a certificate of exemption is given by a prescribed stock exchange. The effect of sub-s. (b) of s. 417 is substantially that the prospectus must contain all the information and statements which would be required in the case of the prospectus of an English company and in addition must contain the particulars specified in s. 417 (1) (a). Section 418 extends the provisions of s. 39 to oversea companies. See chapter VI, p. 44 et seq.

By analogy with s. 38 (5) (a) it is provided by s. 417 (5) that the section shall not apply to the issue of a prospectus to existing members or debenture holders of the company; nor does it apply to an offer of shares or debentures for subscription to any person whose ordinary business or part of whose ordinary business it is to buy or sell shares or debentures, whether as principal or agent, for s. 423 (2) provides that such an offer shall not be deemed an offer to the public for the purpose of Part X of the Act.

By analogy with s. 38 (3) it is provided by s. 417 (3) that it is illegal to issue to any person in Great Britain a form of application for shares in or debentures of an oversea company or intended oversea company unless the form is issued with a prospectus which complies with Part X of the Act and does not contravene s. 419 (see chapter VI, p. 44 et seq.). As in the case of an English company, this provision does not apply where the form of application is issued to existing members or debenture holders of the company or in connection with a bona fide invitation to a person to enter into an underwriting agreement with respect to the shares or debentures. In the case of an English company there is a further exception where the form of application is issued in relation to shares or debentures which are not offered to the public. This exception does not apply to oversea companies and accordingly in the case of oversea companies it is illegal, except in the two cases mentioned above, to issue an application form for the purpose of getting capital privately subscribed unless it is accompanied by a prospectus.

Sections 419 and 420 extend to oversea companies the provisions of ss. 40 and 41 (1) and (2) whereby there must be endorsed upon the copy of the prospectus delivered to the Registrar the following:—

1. any such written consent of any expert to the issue of the prospectus as is required by s. 419 (1);

2. a copy, or a memorandum, or a translation if the original is in a foreign language, of any such contract as is specified by para. 14 of Schedule IV;

3. a written statement setting out any such adjustments as are mentioned in para. 29 of Schedule IV and giving the reasons therefor, signed by the auditors.

(As to ss. 40 and 41 see chapter VI, p. 44 *et seq.*)

The provisions of s. 43 as to the liability of directors and other persons for statements contained in the prospectus are extended to prospectuses of oversea companies by s. 422. Moreover, any person knowingly responsible for contravention of ss. 417 to 420, whether as regards the issue, circulation or distribution of a prospectus or the issue of an application form, is liable to a fine of £500 (s. 421).

Offer of Shares for Sale. By sub-s. (1) of s. 423 the provisions of s. 45 of the Act as to offers for sale where the shares or debentures have been allotted with a view to their being offered for sale to the public are extended to the like offers for sale of shares or debentures of an oversea company. (As to ss. 43 and 45 see chapter VI, p. 45.)

Having regard to the definition of an unregistered company in s. 398, any oversea company can be wound up by the court unless it was incorporated in Northern Ireland and had a principal place of business there and did not have a principal place of business in either England or Scotland [see ss. 398 and 399 (1) and (2)]. Moreover, under s. 400, every oversea company which has been carrying on business in Great Britain, but ceases to do so, may be wound up by the court as an unregistered company, notwithstanding that it has been dissolved or otherwise ceased to exist as a company under or by virtue of the laws of the country in which it was incorporated.

Winding Up. The Act provides only for the compulsory winding up of oversea companies [s. 398 (4)]; voluntary winding up is left to the law of the country in which the company is incorporated.

CHAPTER XXVII

TAXATION OF TRADING COMPANIES

THE Income Tax Act, 1918, places responsibility upon the secretary of a joint stock company. By s. 106 of that Act the secretary of a company, or other officer performing the duties of secretary, shall be answerable for doing all such acts as are required to be done under the Act for the purpose of assessment of the company and payment of the tax, and for the purpose of assessment of the officers and persons in the employment of the company. A knowledge of the general principles of income tax is therefore essential to a secretary in order that he may draw up the necessary returns and make claims for such relief as the Acts, the practice of Commissioners, and decisions in the courts, afford him the opportunity of pursuing.

Scope. The Income Tax Acts, as amended and extended by annual Finance Acts, charge with tax all income derived from sources within the United Kingdom, whether the person to whom the income accrues is resident in the United Kingdom or abroad. The Acts also charge income derived by United Kingdom residents from foreign and commonwealth sources, the charge applying in some cases to the whole income and in other cases to the amounts received in this country.

Schedules. For the purpose of income tax, incomes are classified under five main headings as defined in Schedules A, B, C, D and E of the Income Tax Act, 1918. Schedule A charges the owners of land and buildings situated in the United Kingdom. Schedule B charges occupiers of lands which are not occupied for the purpose of trade and woodlands managed for profit. Schedule C charges annuities, dividends and interest payable in the United Kingdom out of the public revenue of the United Kingdom, or of any foreign state, dominion or colony. Schedule D charges all other annual profits not charged under any other Schedule which accrue to United Kingdom residents from any source wherever situate, annual profits arising to non-residents from property situate in the United Kingdom, and interest of money, annuities, and other annual profits and gains; in particular, trading profits fall under Schedule D. Schedule E charges income from offices and employments, and pensions.

Collection at Source. So far as possible, income tax is collected at the source of the income, irrespective of the circumstances of the ultimate beneficiary, though without prejudicing the latter's right to claim repayment if allowances or reliefs are available to him. The tax charged under Schedule A is usually collected from the occupier, who is authorised, on payment of rent, to deduct tax therefrom; the owner in his turn deducts a proportion of the tax from any ground rent, annuity, rent charge, interest or other annual sum charged on the property. Similarly, profits arising from a trade or business are assessed in one sum, under Schedule D, on the company, firm, or individual carrying on the business, and then the burden is apportioned among all persons who are entitled to share in the profits or receive dividends, or are entitled to interest or other annual payments, by deduction of tax from each such payment. When dividends and interest are paid by agents in the United Kingdom of foreign or colonial governments or companies, tax is deducted and paid over to the Inland Revenue. Similarly, when interest or other annual payments are paid out of funds which have not been taxed, the interest or other payment is taxed on the payer and he is authorised to deduct tax when he makes the payment.

It is not possible within the scope of this chapter to deal with all the problems arising out of the liabilities imposed by the Acts on individuals, partnerships, and companies. This chapter is therefore confined to the practical issues confronting the secretary of a company engaged in trading. They comprise the computation and settlement of liability under Schedules A and D, practical problems involved in the deduction of tax at the source from dividends, interest, and other annual payments, the liability of a company to profits tax, possible liability to surtax, and the responsibilities of a company as employer under Schedule E and the Pay-As-You-Earn scheme.

SCHEDULE A

Gross Annual Value. The assessments under Schedule A are based on valuations, which are normally made quinquennially. The gross annual value of a property is the rental value, that is, the rent which would be obtained by the year if the landlord paid for repairs and insurance (and in Scotland owners' rates), and the tenant paid tenant's rates. Once a value has been fixed it cannot be altered in England and Wales until the next valuation, unless there is a discovery of new facts, or unless structural alterations, additions, or improvements are made, but in Scotland land and buildings are revalued annually.

Net Annual Value. Tax is charged on the net annual value, which is arrived at by deducting from the gross annual value an allowance for repairs, namely for lands, one-eighth of the gross value, and for buildings the following scale:—

Gross annual value up to £40 .. One-fourth.
" " " £40 to £50 .. £10.
" " " £50 to £100 One-fifth.
" " " Over £100 .. £20, plus one-sixth of the excess over £100.

Deductions are also allowed for land tax, tithe rent charge, and (in Scotland) owners' rates.

Although the statutory deduction is fixed irrespective of actual repairs expenditure, a maintenance claim may be made if the average actual expenditure during the five preceding years exceeds the statutory allowance. The maintenance claim should take into account repairs, and costs of maintenance, insurance, and management of the property, but the cost of alterations and improvements may not be included. *Maintenance Claim.*

Formerly a company letting its property on long or short leases escaped tax on the excess of the rent received over the net annual value. The Finance Act, 1940, removed this anomaly. In the case of long leases, *i.e.* those which the lessor cannot determine within fifty years, the lessee is authorised to deduct tax at the standard rate on the whole rent, whereas formerly the lessee deducted the tax paid under Schedule A. For short leases, the lessor suffers the additional tax by a separate assessment under Case VI of Schedule D. The measure of the assessment is the excess of rent received less the statutory repairs allowance appropriate to a gross annual value of that amount over the net annual value of the property, or over the rent paid by the lessor himself under a short lease if that rent exceeds the net annual value. *Excess Rents.*

SCHEDULE D

Trading profits in the United Kingdom are assessed under Case I of Schedule D. The procedure usually followed is for the secretary, or other officer, to send to H.M. Inspector copies of the balance sheet and profit and loss account together with supporting statements showing how the amount which the company proposes to return has been computed. Correspondence and interviews with the inspector then follow until the liability is agreed. The secretary must then complete a formal return of income on the appropriate statutory form. The Revenue looks to the completion of this statutory return as the formal act of responsibility by the company, notwithstanding all the antecedent or auxiliary correspondence that may have taken place. *Procedure.*

The basis of assessment of profits arising from trades or businesses is normally the profit of the accounts year ending in the preceding year of assessment. *Normal Basis of Assessment.*

The basis for the year of assessment in which a trade or business commences is the actual profit arising during that year of assessment. In the following year of assessment the profits of one year from the date of commencing business are taxed, and in the third year of assessment the normal preceding year basis applies. The taxpayer may claim reduction of the assessments for the second and third years to the actual *New Trades.*

profits of those years, but a claim will not be admitted for one year only. It is necessary to note that the above rules are applied not only to completely new trades or businesses, but also on the conversion of an existing firm into a limited company.

Cessation. For the year of assessment in which a business is permanently discontinued, the assessment is adjusted to the actual profits from 6th April to the date of cessation. If the actual profits arising in the penultimate year of assessment are greater than those already taxed in that year of assessment the Commissioners will raise an additional assessment on the excess.

Change of Accounting Date. In the case of a change of accounting date, it is for the Commissioners to decide what period of twelve months ending on a date within the year preceding the year of assessment is to be used as the basis of assessment. Having made this decision, the Commissioners may (subject to the taxpayer's right of appeal) also adjust the assessment for the previous year to the profits of the twelve months corresponding to the twelve months adopted for the year of change. Where the Commissioners make an adjustment under the latter provision (or omit to make an adjustment) to the taxpayer's detriment, the General or Special Commissioners may, on appeal, grant such relief as is just. The customary adjustment in such cases (where the amount is material) is calculated by comparing the average annual profits of three accounting periods ending with the changed period with the average profits charged by three assessments ending with the assessment based on the new accounting date.

Profits to be Excluded. One of the first steps in drawing up a computation under Case I of Schedule D is to exclude from the profit included in the accounts all dividends, annuities, patent royalties, interest, ground rents, etc., which have already borne tax by deduction at the source.

(a) Income Taxed at Source.

(b) Income Taxed under other Schedules. Similarly, any income assessable under another Schedule, or another Case of Schedule D, must be excluded. Rents received will be deducted, since for long leases the full tax has been deducted at the source, and for short leases any excess rent over and above the net annual value, on which the tenant has paid Schedule A tax, falls under Case VI. Bank or other untaxed interest should be assessed separately under Case III, but in practice is often left in the Case I computation. Dividends received from oversea companies will be separately assessed under Case V, and mortgage or debenture interest from overseas under Case IV.

(c) Capital Profits. Capital profits and proceeds of sales of capital assets are generally exempt from tax. The profit on sales of land, buildings, plant, investments, and goodwill will normally be deducted in arriving at assessable profits, but, as will be seen later, balancing charges may arise on disposal of industrial buildings and plant and machinery. It must not be forgotten, however, that it is the nature of the transaction which determines exemption. If the company is one which deals in property or investments, profits arising from sales will be ordinary trading profits and liable to tax. Liquidators realising current or fixed assets in the process of winding up a company (as distinct from carrying on the trade) are deemed to make only capital profits, which are not assessable.

EXPENSES ALLOWED

All expenditure wholly and exclusively laid out for the purposes of the trade may remain as a charge against profits. **Expenses Allowed.** 'It is not enough that the disbursement is made in the course of or arises out of or is connected with the trade. It must be made for the purpose of earning the profits.' [Ld. Davey: *Strong & Co. of Romsey* v. *Woodifield* (1906), A.C. 448.]

The application of the general rule to particular items of expenditure has given rise to many differences of opinion between taxpayers and the Inland Revenue, but decisions of the Commissioners and the courts have resulted in established practice on many important points. Subscriptions to trade or professional associations are allowed to the extent to which such associations apply their revenue for the benefit of the trade. In order that the members shall be spared the inconvenience of proving this point each year, most associations have agreed with the Inland Revenue to suffer tax on the excess of receipts over expenditure, in which case subscriptions will be allowed as deductions to members without investigation. **(a) Trade Subscriptions.** Donations given for the purposes of the business may be deducted, including, in particular, donations to the general funds of a charity or hospital to which the company's employees may be admitted or from which they may derive benefits. **(b) Donations.** Legal expenses incurred in the defence of existing rights are allowed, and such expenses as the collection of trade debts, renewal of leases, and expenses connected with the renewal of patents, and the registration of trade marks. Although the cost of removing a factory or office to a new location is not generally allowable, it is usual in practice for the expense to be allowed as a deduction if the removal is compulsory. The cost of removing trade stocks is always allowed. Debts proved to the satisfaction of the Commissioners to be bad are allowed, and also specific provisions for doubtful debts to the extent they are estimated to be bad. **(c) Legal Expenses.** **(d) Removal Expenses.** **(e) Bad Debts.**

The law in regard to retirement provisions for employees is extremely complicated, but the position of the employer is broadly as follows: ordinary annual contributions to pension funds approved under the Finance Act, 1921, s. 32, are allowed. **Retirement Provisions.** Lump sum payments to cover an employee's service with the company before joining the fund are usually allowed to be spread forward in annual amounts which are approximately equal to the ordinary annual contribution. Contributions to unapproved pension and provident funds are deductible when the contributions are paid away irrevocably to independent trustees. Some further information on these points is given in chapter XXXI, p. 445 *et seq.*

Premiums on life policies or deferred annuity contracts taken out by employers for the benefit of employees are deductible as expenses of the employer, regardless of whether or not the employee may be taxable on the premium under the Finance Act, 1947, s. 19. Voluntary and contractual pensions to former employees may be deducted, and also lump sum retirement gratuities.

U.K. Taxes. There is statutory authority for the deduction of profits tax (Finance Act, 1937, s. 25), but income tax itself is not an allowable deduction.

Foreign Taxes. Foreign and dominion taxes are allowed as a deduction from profits only to the extent that relief is not available against United Kingdom income tax. Thus deduction of taxes levied by foreign, commonwealth, and colonial governments arises in three circumstances:—

    (i) where no arrangement exists for granting double tax relief against United Kingdom income tax;

    (ii) where the overseas taxes exceed the relief available against United Kingdom income tax. The excess is wholly deductible under the new type of double tax arrangement, but, in the absence of such an arrangement, relief is limited to a special allowance under the Finance Act, 1920, s. 27 (4) (*b*), which relates to taxes paid to non-reciprocating dominions and colonies only;

    (iii) where partial relief is given against profits tax. In this case, the taxes so relieved may be deducted from profits for income tax purposes.

Other Deductions. Certain sums are allowed to be deducted which do not necessarily figure at all in the company's trading and profit and loss accounts.

Net Annual Value. One such item is the net annual value of any property owned and occupied for the purposes of the business, since tax on this amount has already been paid under Schedule A. When property is similarly occupied under a short lease, the rent or net annual value is deductible, whichever is the greater. The net annual value only may be deducted if the property is held under a long lease in respect of which the tax deducted from the rent is not restricted to tax paid under Schedule A.

Mills and Factories Allowance. For mills, factories, and other similar premises, s. 15 of the Finance Act, 1947, authorised a special deduction in the nature of a depreciation allowance for the comparatively heavy wear and tear suffered by such premises.   In general, the allowance was the lower of the statutory repairs allowance for Schedule A or one-fifth of the net rating value (one-sixth of the gross rating value in London and Scotland).   For electricity and brick works, and properties not assessable under Schedule A (such as overseas properties), the allowance was 1 per cent. of cost. To qualify for the deduction, the taxpayer must be the owner of the premises or be liable under a lease for the whole burden of wear and tear.   The deduction continues to be available until 1950/51 to any taxpayer who has not elected its cessation in favour of the industrial buildings allowances provided by the Income Tax Act, 1945.

Up to and including 1945/46 an obsolescence allowance was **Obsoles-**given when obsolete machinery was replaced.   The allowance **cence** was computed by deducting from original cost any wear and **Allowance.** tear allowances received and any proceeds of sale, but was limited in all cases to the cost of the new machinery.   The Income Tax Act, 1945, substituted balancing allowances for obsolescence allowances for replacements after 5th April, 1946, but gave the taxpayer a right to claim obsolescence allowance if the replaced machinery were acquired on or before that date.   Such an election may be advantageous in two ways.   In the first place, if the machinery were provided partly out of public grant or subsidy, an allowance for obsolescence would be calculated by reference to the full cost, whereas a balancing allowance would be calculated by reference to net cost to the taxpayer.   Secondly, an obsolescence allowance is a deduction from profits, whereas a balancing allowance is allowed in charging the profits.   Therefore, in the event of an adjusted loss for the year being the subject of a s. 34 claim, an obsolescence allowance would form part of the loss and be enjoyed immediately, whereas a balancing allowance would have to be carried forward.

A special basis is sometimes adopted for plant and machinery **Renewals.** whereby normal wear and tear allowances are not claimed on the initial expenditure, additions and improvements.   In their place, the taxpayer is allowed to deduct the net cost of replacement.

EXPENSES NOT ALLOWED

Expenses which may not be deducted in computing profits **Expenses** fall into three main classes: (a) items from which tax has been **not allowed.** deducted at the time of payment; (b) expenses of a capital nature; and (c) payments not made wholly and exclusively for the purpose of earning the profits, being mainly distributions of profit.

In the first class are rents paid by the company on long **Annual** leases, and rents paid on short leases if the net annual value **Payments.**

(being the greater) has been allowed. Debenture and other annual interest payments are similarly disallowed, together with patent royalties, annuities, and other annual payments such as payments to charities under covenants for a period of more than six years. The deduction and retention of tax under Rule 19 has given the taxpayer the full tax benefit of these payments.

Capital Expenditure. Expenditure on providing or improving capital assets may not be deducted, allowances being available under other provisions of the law for many items such as plant and machinery, industrial buildings, patents, and capital expenditure on mineral and other deposits. Expenditure on such premises as retail shops, showrooms, hotels and offices does not qualify for any writing-off allowance, and no allowances are available for lump sum premiums paid for leases, whatever the purpose for which the premises are used. Provisions for depreciation of capital assets and for leasehold redemption are also disallowed, together with any losses on disposal of such assets. **Depreciation.** When considering this general class of expenditure, it is important to remember that the taxpayer's own description and classification of the expenditure is not conclusive. In **Capital in Repairs.** particular, the Inspector will scrutinise all items described as repairs and maintenance to ensure that nothing in the nature of capital additions or improvements is included.

Formation and Raising Capital. The preliminary expenses of a company, and costs of conversion, may not be deducted; nor expenditure in connection with new share or debenture issues; nor reserves for redemption of debentures or redeemable preference shares.

Income Tax Fines. Expenses not wholly and exclusively laid out for the purposes of the trade include income tax and the cost of appeals in connection therewith; and fines and costs in **Donations.** connection with breaches of the law. Charitable donations, other than those conferring some benefit on employees, are disallowed, but it should be remembered that this hardship may be overcome by entering into covenants, not revocable within six years, to make annual payments to the charitable institutions concerned. Tax is then deducted from each payment under Rule 19 and retained by the company.

Dividends. Reserves. Dividends paid or provided for in the accounts are not deductible, being distributions of profit. Similarly, amounts placed to general reserve or to contingencies reserves are disallowed. In particular, the practice of creating a bad debts reserve on the basis of a percentage of good debts is not recognised as giving rise to admissible deductions for income tax purposes.

ALLOWANCES

After all the adjustments referred to have been made, the resulting figure is the assessable profit for the year of

assessment, or the adjusted loss, as the case may be. When
the result is a profit, certain allowances are available and
these are given for the year of assessment in charging the
profit.

Under Rule 6 of Cases I and II, Schedule D, the Commis- **Wear and**
sioners were authorised to grant such allowance as they con- **Tear.**
sidered reasonable for wear and tear of plant and machinery
used for the purposes of the trade. In 1932 and 1938 additional allowances were granted, but the Income Tax Act,
1945, substituted for these additional allowances a general
increase of one-quarter of the basic rates granted by the
Commissioners. Basic rates of wear and tear have been
agreed between the Inland Revenue and representatives of
industry for most classes of plant and machinery, and the
rates (as now increased) are commonly applied to the original
cost on the reducing balance method. In addition to the
increased annual allowance, the 1945 Act provided for an
initial allowance of 20 per cent. for expenditure on new or
secondhand machinery or plant. For expenditure after
5th April, 1949, the rate of initial allowance was increased
to 40 per cent. by the Finance Act, 1949. The full initial
allowance is granted for expenditure incurred during the basic
period for the year of assessment, and the full annual allowance
is given for machinery and plant in use for the purposes of the
business on the last day of the basic period. If machinery or
plant is sold, scrapped or destroyed before cessation of the
business, a balancing allowance is given for the amount by
which cost less proceeds exceeds allowances already received.
If the allowances received exceed cost less proceeds, a balancing
charge is made on the excess or on the sum of allowances
received, whichever is the less. Alternatively, when the
machinery or plant is replaced, the taxpayer may have the
amount of the balancing charge deducted from the new expenditure for allowance purposes, in which case immediate
payment of tax on the charge is avoided.

The Income Tax Act, 1945, also introduced a new system **Industrial**
of allowances in respect of capital expenditure incurred after **Buildings.**
5th April, 1946, by a trader or his landlord on the construction
of industrial buildings or structures, as defined in s. 8 of the
Act. An initial allowance of 10 per cent. is granted in the
first year of assessment and annual allowances, normally at
the rate of 2 per cent. for each year in which the building
continues in industrial use. For new buildings, therefore, the
whole expenditure is allowed over 45 years. There are
provisions extending the annual allowance to expenditure
incurred less than 50 years before 6th April, 1946, whereby
2 per cent. is granted for each year up to and including the
fiftieth. These provisions apply equally to second-hand
buildings purchased after 5th April, 1946, which have not

o

previously been used as industrial buildings, but the allowance of 2 per cent. is calculated by reference to the original cost of construction. In the case of second-hand industrial buildings purchased after 5th April, 1946, no initial allowance is given, but an annual allowance is granted at such a rate as will amortise the purchase price (or the original cost of construction, if lower) by the fiftieth year of life. When an industrial building is sold or destroyed before the fiftieth year of life, a balancing allowance or balancing charge may be made according as the proceeds fall short of, or exceed, the residue of unallowed expenditure.

Mines, Oil Wells, etc. An initial allowance of 10 per cent. is given for expenditure incurred on constructional or development work in connection with mines, oil wells, quarries, or other mineral deposits. Annual allowances are also granted, calculated on the reducing balance method, the rate applied being one-twentieth or (if greater) the fraction represented by the year's output over the remaining potential output. The allowances are also given for expenditure on the acquisition of such deposits outside the United Kingdom. There are provisions for balancing allowances and charges on sale of the deposits or cessation of working.

Agricultural Buildings. Expenditure by owners or tenants of agricultural lands on erection of farm houses, buildings, cottages, fences, etc., attracts a flat rate of allowance of 10 per cent. for ten years. Not more than one-third of expenditure on farm houses is admitted for allowance, the balance being attributed to the use of the building as a residence.

Patents. Capital expenditure incurred on the acquisition of patent rights, after 5th April, 1946, is allowed over 17 years, or over the remaining life of the patent, but no allowance is available for any patent rights which were the subject of a sale on or before that date. On the sale of a patent for which an allowance has been received, balancing allowances or charges are made but there are provisions whereby a charge may be spread forward over six years of assessment.

Scientific Research. Under the provisions of the Finance Act, 1944, s. 28, when a company undertakes capital expenditure for the purpose of scientific research related to the trade, an allowance of one-fifth is given in each of the following five years of assessment, provided the buildings or plant concerned remain in use for scientific research during that period. In respect of expenditure after 5th April, 1949, the Finance Act, 1949, provides that three-fifths be allowed in the first year, and one-tenth in each of the next four years. When the building or plant ceases to be used for scientific research, a balancing allowance or charge is made, based on the proceeds if the asset is sold, or on market value if the asset is retained for normal use in the business.

RELIEF FOR LOSSES

The income tax law provides for relief when the computation results in an adjusted loss, and when, owing to such a loss or to inadequacy of the profit, the full wear and tear and other allowances for the year of assessment cannot be taken.

The only immediate relief available to a company is a claim for repayment under s. 34, Income Tax Act, 1918, but this provides relief only for the adjusted loss, not for the allowances which would have been enjoyed if the result had been a profit. It has already been mentioned that the profits assessed in any year of assessment are normally those of a preceding year. Section 34 provides that if the actual trading result of the year of assessment is an adjusted loss, repayment of tax thereon may be claimed, but not so as to exceed the tax already paid on the aggregate income. The aggregate income against which relief is obtainable includes not only income assessed under Case I, Schedule D, but also income assessed under any other Case or Schedule in the year of assessment, or income which has suffered tax by deduction at the source. *Section 34 Claim.*

Although s. 34 clearly requires the claim to be made by reference to the actual loss in the year of assessment (normally involving an apportionment of accounting results), the rule is strictly followed only in the opening and closing years of a business. In the normal course, claims based on a loss in the accounts period ending in the year of assessment are admitted. When the assessment under Case I for the year of claim was nil by reason of a loss in the basic period, or insufficiency of the profit to absorb all allowances due, the balance of allowances for that year of assessment may, by concession, be added to the loss claimed. A claim under s. 34 must normally be made within twelve months of the end of the year of assessment in which the loss arises.

When adjusted losses have not been the subject of repayment under s. 34 they may be carried forward and set off against Case I profits in the six following years of assessment. By virtue of the Finance Act (No. 2), 1945, s. 22, the time limit has been extended, and this extension affects cases in which any of the six following years of assessment are within the period 1939/40 to 1945/46 inclusive, the concession being that the assessment years 1939/40 to 1945/46 shall not be taken into account in calculating the six years' time limit. *Losses Carried Forward.*

Wear and tear allowances not taken in consequence of adjusted losses or inadequate profits may be carried forward indefinitely (except in so far as allowed by concession under s. 34). In the first year after a loss or series of losses, or after years in which wear and tear allowances have not been fully absorbed, the order of deduction from the adjusted profit is:

(1) allowances for the current year of assessment, (2) accumulated allowances unabsorbed in previous years, (3) accumulated losses not yet out of time. The Finance Act, 1932, s. 19, provided that where the deduction of accumulated allowances impedes the deduction of accumulated losses, so much of the losses may be carried forward indefinitely.

When annual payments are made out of profits brought into charge, tax is deducted and retained by the company under Rule 19, but if such payments are made in a year of assessment in which a loss arises, the payments cannot be regarded as made out of profits brought into charge, and the tax deducted will be taken from the company by means of a separate assessment under Rule 21. In that event, the loss carried forward may be increased by the amount of the Rule 21 assessment.

DOUBLE TAXATION RELIEF

Until 1945/46, the only special provisions for double taxation relief were those contained in the Finance Act, 1920, concerning income taxed in both the United Kingdom and in the colonies and dominions, and a special agreement with Eire. An agreement was then entered into with the United States providing for the avoidance of double taxation in many circumstances, and introducing a form of relief new to this country in cases where double taxation persists. Similar arrangements have followed with Australia, Canada, New Zealand, South Africa, most of the colonies and Sweden. Agreements are under negotiation with several other foreign countries.

From the viewpoint of a United Kingdom company, the arrangements are briefly as follows: such a company trading overseas is exempt from the foreign or dominion tax on transactions in the overseas territory, unless a permanent establishment is maintained therein. Dividends received from investments in the overseas territory are usually exempt from dividend or withholding taxes, or, alternatively, the overseas country concedes a reduction in the normal rate of tax. Special provisions are included dealing with such matters as shipping and aircraft profits, interest, royalties, remuneration and pensions received from the overseas territory. Each of the agreements is embodied in a Statutory Instrument (formerly Statutory Rules and Orders), copies of which may be obtained from H.M. Stationery Office.

Tax Credits. When income is taxable in both the United Kingdom and the overseas territory, relief under the agreements is given in the United Kingdom by means of a tax credit against United Kingdom taxes for the overseas taxes paid on the same income. To the extent that relief is given in the form of a tax credit, the overseas taxes must not be deducted from the overseas income forming the basis of the United Kingdom assessment. Thus trading profits from abroad are assessed in this country on the gross amount arising before overseas taxes, and from the United Kingdom tax liability so calculated the overseas taxes may then be deducted. The tax credit may be taken first against profits tax and the balance against income tax.

For preference dividends, debenture interest, and other annual payments received from overseas, the tax credit is limited to the dividend or withholding taxes directly levied on such payments, but, in the case of ordinary dividends, the overseas taxes imposed on the profits out of which the dividends are paid may be taken into account as well as the dividend taxes, the dividends being correspondingly grossed for United Kingdom tax purposes.

The dominion income tax relief provisions of the Finance **Dominion** Act, 1920, now apply in an ever-narrowing field, arrangements **Income Tax** of the modern type being expected in the near future, with the **Relief.** remaining commonwealth and Empire countries. Broadly the dominion income tax relief provisions as applied to companies are as follows: relief is allowed on the doubly-taxed income at half the United Kingdom rate or the dominion rate, whichever is the lower.   When the dominion granted reciprocal relief, the result was that the taxpayer suffered in aggregate the United Kingdom rate or the dominion rate, whichever was the greater. When the dominion was non-reciprocating, s. 27 (4) (b) permitted a deduction from the assessable income to the extent that dominion taxes paid for the basic period exceeded the dominion income tax relief received.

Under an agreement made between the British Government **Eire.** and the Government of Eire in respect of doubly-taxed income (Finance Act, 1926, s. 23, and Finance Act, 1928, s. 21) a person resident in Eire and not resident in Great Britain or Northern Ireland is entitled to exemption from United Kingdom income tax in respect of income arising in Great Britain or Northern Ireland, and a person resident in Great Britain or Northern Ireland and not resident in Eire is entitled to exemption from Eire income tax in respect of income arising in Eire. Special provision is made in the agreement for relief in cases of persons resident both in Eire and in Great Britain or Northern Ireland. A company is deemed to be resident in the country in which its business is managed and controlled. The above agreement does not extend to Eire corporation profits tax and United Kingdom profits tax, concerning which a separate arrangement was entered into in 1949 (1949, S.I. No. 1439).

PAYMENT

Payment of tax under Schedules A and D is due on 1st **Due Date.** January in the year of assessment in the case of companies, or, if the assessment should be made after 1st January, the tax is due on the day following the assessment. In practice, provisional assessments, against which formal notice of appeal should be lodged, are usually made before 1st January when final agreement seems likely to be delayed.

Tax Reserve Certificates. Tax reserve certificates may be purchased in advance of the due date, and when such certificates are surrendered in settlement of tax liabilities, interest is credited at ¾ per cent. per annum from the date of purchase to the due date of the tax up to a maximum period of two years. The interest so credited is exempt from income tax and profits tax.

Interest. The Finance Act (No. 2), 1947, s. 8, requires interest at the rate of 3 per cent. per annum to be paid on settlement of taxes more than three months overdue. The interest runs from the due date until the date of payment, but is remitted when the total tax charged by the assessment is £1,000 or less, and when the interest involved is £1 or less. In the event of overpayment of tax subject to interest, involving subsequent repayment or discharge of tax, the interest appropriate to the overpayment is refunded. The taxpayer is not allowed to deduct tax from the interest payments, nor is the interest a permissible deduction for income tax and profits tax purposes.

DEDUCTION OF TAX AT THE SOURCE

Reference has already been made on several occasions to the collection of tax by deduction at the source. This branch of British tax law gives rise to a number of practical problems, and some of those most frequently encountered will now be considered.

Rent. The occupier of a property under a short lease, having borne tax under Schedule A, may deduct tax from rent paid to his landlord. Under Rule 1 of No. VIII of Schedule A, tax should be deducted from the next instalment of rent at the rate or rates in force (applied to the full annual rent) during the period through which the rent was accruing due. When the annual rent is greater than the net annual value the deduction is limited to the tax paid under Schedule A, but when the net annual value exceeds the rent, tax on the latter only may be deducted, the tenant being required to bear the balance of the Schedule A tax. The tenant who fails to deduct from the next rent payment has no remedy unless the Schedule A tax in question has been levied on him as occupier for the time being through default by a previous tenant or by the landlord. In the latter cases, tax may be deducted from any subsequent payments of rent. The landlord may in turn deduct tax from payments of ground rent, interest, etc. The deduction from rents under short term leases may not exceed the tax suffered, but in the case of mortgage interest there is no such limitation, Rule 19 or Rule 21 (considered below) being applicable to such payments.

Taxation by deduction at the source is also applicable to rents under long leases, charges on property which is the subject of a long lease, royalties, annual interest, annuities or other annual payments. Such payments are now all subject to Rules 19 and 21 of the General Rules applicable to all Schedules (Income Tax Act, 1918). Rule 19 is merely **Rule 19.** machinery for collection of tax, whereby a person making such payments wholly out of profits brought into charge to tax must deduct and retain tax thereon at the rate in force when the amount payable becomes due. In consequence of this procedure, no deduction from profits is allowed to the person making the payment, and no assessment is raised on the person entitled to it.

When any payments of the type mentioned in the preceding **Rule 21.** paragraph are made, and the payments are not payable, or are not wholly payable, out of profits brought into charge, Rule 21 applies. Under this rule the payer must deduct tax at the rate in force on the date of payment, but an assessment is raised on him for the amount not brought into charge. Thus a company paying patent royalties or debenture interest under deduction of tax during a year of assessment may have a loss under Case I for that year of assessment, or may have a Case I profit less than the annual payments. The company will then have deducted from the annual payments more tax than it has itself paid under Case I. A Rule 21 assessment takes this excess from the company. Reference to Case I profits in this example does not imply that these are the only profits by reference to which the need for a Rule 21 assessment is established. Such an assessment is made only when the annual payments exceed the total taxed income of the company whether taxed under the Schedules or by deduction.

Whether or not particular classes of interest are annual, and **Interest.** consequently subject to Rules 19 and 21, has not always been an easy matter to determine. For the Rules to apply, the interest should be yearly interest on loans which are in the nature of investments with some degree of permanence, *i.e.* not repayable on demand. Thus the rules are clearly applicable to mortgage and debenture interest, while interest paid to banks, trade interest, and interest on bills is usually paid gross and allowed to the payer as a deduction from profits.

Rule 20 of the General Rules provides that a company **Deduction** shall be charged to tax on the full amount of its profits before **from** deducting any dividend, but on payment of a dividend the **Dividends.** company may deduct the tax applicable thereto. The rate of tax to be deducted is the standard rate for the year in which the amount payable becomes due, *i.e.* the year in which the dividend is declared (Finance Act, 1927, s. 39). When the dividend is not paid out of assessable profits, *e.g.* a dividend of capital profits, the rule regarding deduction of tax does not apply, nor would the recipient be under obligation to declare the dividend for income tax and surtax.

Change of Rate. When a change of tax rate is introduced by the annual Finance Act, it is unavoidable that some dividends should already have been declared and paid under deduction of tax at the old rate. Section 12, Finance Act, 1930, contains rules for adjusting this matter. In the case of ordinary dividends, the net amount paid remains unadjusted, but for the purpose of the shareholder's tax returns the dividend is grossed up by reference to the new rate of tax. In the case of preference dividends (and also royalties and other annual payments) the under- or over-deduction must be adjusted on the next payment. If there is no subsequent payment, an under-deduction is recoverable from the recipient; on the other hand an over-deduction must not be retained by the company more than one year from the introduction of the new rate.

Explanation of Tax Deduction on Warrants. Every company is required by the Finance Act, 1929, s. 33, whenever it issues 'a warrant or cheque or other order, in payment of any dividend or interest,' to annex thereto or to accompany it by a statement in writing shewing:—

(*a*) the gross amount which, after deduction of the income tax appropriate thereto, corresponds to the net amount actually paid; and

(*b*) the rate and the amount of income tax appropriate to such gross amount; and

(*c*) the net amount actually paid.

The rule applies even when a dividend is paid 'free of tax,' or 'without deduction of tax' (Finance Act, 1940, s. 20), so that such dividends are always grossed up for the purpose of the shareholders' income tax returns, and the statutory statement evidences the amount of the income and the tax already suffered. Failure to comply with s. 33 makes the company liable to a penalty of £10 for each offence, but the aggregate amount of penalties under any one distribution of dividends or interest will not exceed £100.

Dividends out of Profits Affected by Double Tax Relief. The Finance (No. 2) Act, 1945, s. 52, changed the law regarding the deduction of tax from dividends under Rule 20 in cases affected by double taxation relief, whether the relief is dominion income tax relief under the Finance Act, 1920, or a tax credit under the modern type of double tax agreement. The section applies to all dividends, whether preference or ordinary payable after 20th February, 1946, and has the following effects:—

(i) Tax is to be deducted from the dividends at the full standard rate in force on the due date;

(ii) The relief or repayment available to a shareholder is limited to the 'net United Kingdom rate' payable by the company after taking into account double taxation relief enjoyed. The 'net United Kingdom rate' is computed by deducting from the full standard rate a rate representing the relief enjoyed by the company in the period for which the dividend is paid. Thus, in the case of a dividend paid out of the profits of the accounts year to 31st March, 1948, the rate deducted would be total 1947/48 relief divided by 1947/48 statutory income. For other accounting dates, the rate deducted is a combination of the company's double tax relief rates for two years of assessment.

(iii) In addition to the requirements of the Finance Act, 1924, s. 33, the dividend counterfoil must shew the net United Kingdom rate. The Board of Inland Revenue, have recommended that the following memorandum be printed on the front or back of the counterfoil:

> By reason of double taxation relief, the net United Kingdom rate of tax payable by the company is........s.........d in the £. Under s. 52 of the Finance (No. 2) Act, 1945, tax is deductible by the company from this dividend at the full standard rate of ....s.........d. in the £, but the rate at which any relief or repayment due may be allowed to a shareholder is limited to the net United Kingdom rate.

If this appears on the back of the counterfoil, it is further recommended that the secretary's certificate should be amplified by a reference to the amount of the company's net United Kingdom rate.

In the case of dividends paid 'free of tax' or 'without deduction of tax,' the gross amount equivalent to the dividend paid is computed by reference to the full standard rate, the second sentence of the memorandum mentioned above being suitably re-worded in such circumstances.

SURTAX LIABILITY OF COMPANIES

The Finance Act, 1922, s. 21, is designed to prevent evasion **Companies** of surtax by individuals accumulating undistributed profits **Liable.** in companies under their control. The provisions apply to any company which is controlled by not more than five persons, and which is not an exempt subsidiary company, or a company in which the public is substantially interested. An exempt subsidiary is one controlled by a company which is itself exempt. The public is regarded as substantially interested in a company when it holds shares (other than those with a fixed rate of dividend) carrying at least 25 per cent. of the voting power, and the shares have been dealt in on the Stock Exchange during the period, and quoted in the Official List. A company is deemed to be controlled by five persons or less when they are able to exercise or acquire control over the company's affairs, or possess or are entitled to acquire the greater part of the issued share capital, or so much as would entitle them to receive the greater part of any income distributed. Special provisions prevent avoidance of liability by separate holdings of shares in the names of relatives, nominees, partners, and beneficiaries under trust, etc.

Section 21 is applied unless the company, within a reasonable time after the end of its accounts period, has distributed a reasonable part of its actual income in such a way as to render it chargeable to surtax. In determining whether or not a reasonable part of the income has been distributed, the Commissioners have regard not only to the current requirements of the business but also to such other requirements as may be necessary and advisable for the maintenance and development of the business.

When the Commissioners decide that the section should be applied, the whole of the undistributed profits for the period is deemed to be income of the members, and is apportioned among them. Surtax is then charged in respect of each member according to his particular circumstances. The assessments are made in the name of the company, and if the members do not elect to pay within 28 days, or do not in fact pay, payment must be made by the company. Subsequent distributions of profits so charged to surtax are exempt from surtax when they are distributed.

PROFITS TAX

The profits tax was first imposed for a period of five years by the Finance Act, 1937, under the name of national defence contribution, but in 1942 powers were taken to continue the tax indefinitely. The contribution was levied on the profits of trades or businesses carried on in the United Kingdom or carried on at home or abroad by persons ordinarily resident in the United Kingdom. From 1st April, 1939, to the end of 1946, national defence contribution was an alternative to excess profits tax, the taxpayer being required to pay the greater of the two over the whole period. The Finance Act, 1947, introduced many important modifications which were effective from 1st January, 1947. From this date, sole traders and partnerships were exempt, so that the profits tax is now imposed only on limited companies, other corporate bodies, and unincorporated societies. A limited company is also exempt if its income for the year has been apportioned among the members for surtax purposes under the Finance

Act, 1922, s. 21 (see above), and the members to whom the income is so apportioned are all individuals.

For profits tax purposes profits are computed on income tax principles subject to the following modifications:—

(1) *Annual payments.* Rent, debenture interest, and other annual payments are deductible from profits.

(2) *Income from property.* Rents received must be included in profits, and no deduction is allowed for the net annual value taxed under Schedule A.

(3) *Income from investments.* Debenture interest, royalties, and other annual sums are not included in Case I profits for income tax, being taxable under other Cases or subject to tax by deduction at the source. For profits tax they must be brought into account.

Preference and ordinary dividends received are primarily taxable, but exemption is granted to dividends received from companies which are themselves liable to profits tax. Such exempt dividends are termed 'franked investment income.'

(4) *Expenses related to other accounting periods for excess profits tax purposes.* By the Finance Act, 1946, s. 37 (as later amended) deferred repairs and renewals carried out before 31st March, 1952, may be related back so as to reduce profits for excess profits tax purposes. Such expenditure may not then be deducted for profits tax.

Similarly, amounts expended in 1947 but attributable to earlier accounting periods for excess profits tax under the Finance Act, 1940, s. 33 (2), may not be deducted from profits for profits tax.

Funding payments to superannuation funds in respect of the back service of employees are normally spread forward in the same way as for income tax, but if the payment was made before or during the excess profits tax period, the deduction allowed will be that which would have been given for excess profits tax (if it had continued) under a proviso of s. 23 of the Finance Act, 1943, *i.e.* 5 per cent. per annum.

(5) *Allowances.* The income tax allowances for wear and tear of plant and machinery, industrial buildings, scientific research, etc., apply equally to profits tax. The allowances for income tax years of assessment are apportioned to the corresponding chargeable accounting periods for profits tax. Thus, a chargeable accounting period ending 31st December, 1948, attracts one-quarter of the 1947/48 allowances and three-quarters of 1948/49 allowances. Balancing allowances and charges are similarly apportioned.

From 1st January, 1947, to 30th September, 1949, the chargeable profits were liable to profits tax at 25 per cent., but non-distribution relief at the rate of 15 per cent. was granted for the part of the profits not distributed. If distributions for a chargeable period exceeded the profits, the excess was subject to a distribution charge of 15 per cent., but only to the extent of profits in earlier periods which had enjoyed non-distribution relief. The Profits Tax Act, 1949, increased the rate of profits tax to 30 per cent., with non-distribution relief at the rate of 20 per cent., in respect of profits attributable to periods after 30th September, 1949. The rate for distribution charges was correspondingly increased from 15 per cent. to 20 per cent., but a charge at the higher rate is made only on distributions out of profits subsequent to 30th September, 1949—that is, profits which have enjoyed non-distribution relief at the rate of 20 per cent.

The practical result is that the company pays tax at 10 per cent. on any profits which it does not distribute and at 25 per cent. or 30 per cent. on any profits which it does distribute. If having accumulated profits in one year, it distributes these accumulations later, the distribution charge ensures that the tax originally charged at 10 per cent. is raised on the later distribution to 25 per cent. or 30 per cent., according as to whether the profits relate to periods before or after the end of September, 1949.

If the taxable profits of a period plus franked investment income do not exceed £2,000, complete exemption is given. When taxable profits (T.P.) and franked investment income (F.I.I.) are more than £2,000, but not more than £12,000. an abatement is deductible from the taxable profits as follows:

$$\text{Abatement} = £\frac{\text{T.P.}}{(\text{T.P.} + \text{F.I.I.})} \times \frac{12,000 - (\text{T.P.} + \text{F.I.I.})}{5}$$

The distributions taken into account in computing non-distribution relief or a distribution charge are known as 'net relevant distributions' and, when gross relevant distributions (*i.e.* normally gross preference and ordinary dividends expressly declared out of the period's profits) are less than taxable profits (before abatement) plus franked investment income, they are computed as follows:—

Net relevant distributions =

$$\text{Gross relevant distributions} \times \frac{\text{T.P. after abatement}}{\text{T.P. before abatement} + \text{F.I.I.}}$$

When gross relevant distributions exceed taxable profits (before abatement) plus franked investment income, net relevant distributions are taxable profits (after abatement) plus the amount of the excess.

Although the dividends to be related to any chargeable accounting period are those which a company declares or announces to be paid out of the profits of that period, such a declaration or announcement must, to be effective, be made within six months of the end of the period. The company may elect an extension of this time to nine months, or twelve months if it has overseas interests. If a dividend is declared outside the time limits, it is related to the period in which it is declared.

On liquidation of a company, distributions of assets, in excess of the total nominal amount of paid-up share capital and any cash premium paid on issue, are treated as gross relevant distributions of the last chargeable accounting period, and are liable to a distribution charge up to a maximum of the profits after 1st January, 1947, in respect of which non-distribution relief has been granted. This may become a point of considerable importance in considering whether a company should go into liquidation. The practical effect of putting into liquidation a prosperous company which has accumulated reserves will be to attract tax at 15 per cent. on undistributed profits accumulated between 1st January, 1947, and 30th September, 1949, and 20 per cent. on un-distributed profits accumulated after 30th September, 1949.

There are special provisions to prevent avoidance of the additional tax on distributions in the case of director-controlled companies. Interest paid to the members of such companies is not an allowable deduction and must be included in gross relevant distributions. Remuneration to directors, other than whole-time service directors, in excess of certain limits, is similarly treated. The allowable limits of such remuneration are £2,500 or 15 per cent. of profits, whichever is the greater, with an overall ceiling of £15,000. Loans to director-members are also included in gross relevant distributions, but in a subsequent year when a loan is repaid corresponding relief is granted by means of a reduction of that year's distributions.

SCHEDULE E—EMPLOYEES

Although s. 105 (1) of the Income Tax Act, 1918, gave the surveyor a right to require from employers returns of persons employed and payments made to those persons, this responsibility has been greatly extended by the administrative requirements of the Pay-As-You-Earn system of collection. Under this system, the employer is required to calculate and deduct tax when paying wages, salaries, or other emoluments, and the tax so collected must be paid over to the Revenue monthly.

The system was introduced by the Income Tax (Employ- **P.A.Y.E.** ments) Act, 1943, and was extended to all employments in 1944. Subsequent regulations governing the detailed working of the scheme have been laid down in Statutory Instruments. Briefly, the scheme operates as follows: just before the beginning of the fiscal year, the employer receives from the Inspector a tax deduction card for each employee, shewing the employee's code number. Official tax tables are also issued, and each week (or month) the tax due by each employee is calculated from the tables by reference to his code number and the amount of accumulated pay and tax deducted to date. At the end of the fiscal year, the tax deduction cards must be sent to the collector together with the employer's annual return. It would be out of place in this chapter to give details of the procedure in the case of new employees or when employees leave. For information on these and other special points, the secretary is referred to the 'Employer's Guide' issued by the Board of Inland Revenue. See also p. 224.

Definition of Income for P.A.Y.E. Pay-As-You-Earn applies to all income from offices or employments, and therefore embraces not only weekly wages but also monthly salaries, annual salaries, bonuses, commissions, directors' fees, pensions, and any other income from an office or employment. The emoluments to be taken into account are gross pay before any deduction such as national insurance or superannuation fund contributions. Any relief due for such items is given in the employee's coding. Items which are not generally regarded as income for the purpose of Pay-As-You-Earn include benefits in kind, *e.g.* free board and lodging, allowances in lieu of uniform, rent-free residence which the employee is required to occupy, benefits under the Workmen's Compensation Acts, and allowances for travelling and entertaining expenses actually incurred in carrying out the duties of the employment.

Retirement Gratuities. Lump sum payments to employees on retirement or discharge are liable to tax in their hands only in certain circumstances. Thus, if the payment is due under the terms of the contract of service, or even under a gentleman's agreement made at the beginning of, or during, the service, it is regarded as deferred pay and tax is payable thereon. Agreements of this description are frequently made with temporary employees who, being denied the benefits of membership of established pension funds, are promised retiring gratuities varying directly with the length of their service. On the other hand, wholly gratuitous payments made on cessation of the employee's service, and compensation payments for loss of office or for premature termination of the service contract, are exempt in the hands of the employee. In practice, this exemption is usually extended also to payments in lieu of notice.

Expense Allowances to Directors, etc. The Finance Act, 1948, introduced measures to counter the growing practice of granting tax-free expense allowances to senior officials. Such expense allowances are now assessable emoluments under Schedule E when paid to a director of a company or to an employee whose gross emoluments are £2,000 per annum or more. It is then for the employee to provide proof in support of a claim for deduction of any amounts wholly, exclusively, and necessarily expended in performing the duties of the office or employment. The provisions apply not only to allowances paid in cash, but also to the expense of living or other accommodation, entertainment, domestic and other services provided by the employer without recovery from the employee. By s. 41 of that Act the surveyor is authorised to relieve the company from making declarations of expenses paid on behalf of or to employees, if he is satisfied that the arrangements do not include any expenses other than those deductible under the rules of Schedule E.

CHAPTER XXVIII

INVESTIGATIONS BY THE BOARD OF TRADE

THE Companies Act, 1948, has extended the power of the Board of Trade to investigate the affairs of companies. The provisions of the 1929 Act had proved to be ineffective, partly because of the comparatively high proportion of shareholders' votes required to put the necessary machinery into action, and partly because those provisions put an onus on the applicants to establish that they were not actuated by malicious motives.

General Investigation of a Company's Affairs.

Investigations under the 1948 Act are of two kinds:—

A. The general investigation of a company's affairs; and

B. the investigation of the ownership of a company.

A. The provisions of the Act enabling a general investigation to be made are briefly as follow:—

(1) The Board of Trade *must* appoint an inspector if either the company by special resolution, or the court by order, declares that the company's affairs ought to be investigated by an inspector appointed by the Board (s. 165).

(2) The Board of Trade *may* appoint an inspector in any of the following circumstances:—

(a) when the company has a share capital, on an application by not less than 200 members of the company or by members holding not less than one-tenth of the shares issued [s. 164 (1) (a)];

(b) when the company has no share capital, on an application by not less than one-fifth of the members [s. 164 (1) (b)];

(c) if it appears to the Board of Trade that there are circumstances suggesting either:

(i) that the company's business is being conducted with intent to defraud its creditors or the creditors of any other person, or otherwise for a fraudulent or unlawful purpose, or in a manner oppressive of any part of its members, or that it was formed for any fraudulent or unlawful purpose; or

(ii) that persons concerned with a company's formation or management have in connection therewith been guilty of fraud, misfeasance or other misconduct towards it or towards its members; or

(iii) that the company's members have not been given all the information which they might reasonably expect. For further reference see s. 165 (*b*) (i), (ii), (iii) of the Act.

It is no longer necessary for applicants for an investigation to show that they are not inspired by malicious motives.

An inspector, when appointed, has power to carry his **Powers of** investigation into the affairs of any other company which is, **Inspectors** or has been at any relevant time, the company's subsidiary **and the** or holding company, or a subsidiary of its holding company or **Court.** a holding company of its subsidiary (s. 166). Where the inspector does so investigate the affairs of another company the various powers and provisions mentioned below in relation to the principal company apply equally to the other company investigated. The inspector also has power to demand the production of all books and documents relating to the company, and it is the duty of all officers and agents of the company to produce such books and documents as are in their custody and power, and generally to give the inspectors reasonable assistance. An inspector may examine on oath the officers and agents of the company [s. 167 (2)].

The court will, when necessary, enforce the inspector's powers by punishing the offender as though he had committed a contempt of court [s. 167 (3)]. The court also has power to order the examination on oath of any person whom the inspector would not otherwise be entitled to examine on oath [s. 167 (4)]. In these provisions the expression 'officers' or 'agents' includes past as well as present officers or agents; and the company's bankers, solicitors and auditors are included in the word agents [s. 167 (5)]. Bankers are not, however, obliged to disclose information as to the affairs of customers other than the company, nor are solicitors obliged to disclose privileged communications, except the name and address of their client [s. 175].

A copy of the inspector's report (or interim reports) must **Inspectors'** be forwarded (*a*) to the registered office of the company, **Report.** (*b*) on request to the members concerned when the inspectors are appointed by an application of members, (*c*) to the court when the investigation is ordered by the court. The Board of Trade may also furnish a copy of the report (or interim reports) on payment of the prescribed fee to any member of the company or to any person whose interest as a creditor appears to the Board to be affected. The Board may also print and publish the report (s. 168).

Prosecutions. If it appears from an inspector's report that any person has been guilty of a criminal offence, the Board shall (in a suitable case) refer the matter to the Director of Public Prosecutions, or in Scotland to the Lord Advocate [s. 169 (1)]. If the Director of Public Prosecutions institutes proceedings, it is the statutory duty [under s. 169 (2)] of all officers and agents of the company to give him all reasonable assistance.

Power of Board to Petition for Winding up or to institute Civil Proceedings. If the company is not already being wound up by the court, the Board of Trade may present a petition for its winding up or a petition for an order under s. 210 of the Act (see p. 306) or both [s. 169 (3)]. The Board may also take proceedings in the company's name for the recovery of damages for any fraud, misfeasance or any other misconduct in connection with the promotion, formation or management of the company, or for the recovery of its property which has been misapplied or wrongfully detained [s. 169 (4)].

Expenses of General Investigation. The expenses of and incidental to a general investigation of a company's affairs will in the first instance be defrayed by the Board of Trade. In certain cases, however, details of which are given in s. 170, these expenses may have to be repaid to the Board by the company, the persons who applied for investigation, or a person found to be at fault. Where the investigation is made on the application of the company or its shareholders under s. 164, the Board of Trade may require them to forward security for costs up to £100 before it appoints an inspector [s. 164 (2)].

Investigation of Ownership. B. The power to investigate the ownership of the company is exercisable whenever it appears to the Board of Trade that there is good reason to do so (s. 172). Moreover, if not less than 200 members, or members holding one-tenth of the issued shares, ask for an investigation, the Board of Trade is bound to appoint an inspector unless it considers the application vexatious [s. 172 (3)].

The inspector is appointed to investigate and report on the membership of the company and otherwise with respect to the company for the purpose of determining the true persons who are or have been financially interested in the success or failure (real or apparent) of the company or able to control or materially to influence its policy. The scope of the investigation may, however, be limited, *e.g.* to the ownership of particular shares. The inspector has power under this section to investigate any circumstances suggesting the existence of an arrangement or understanding which, although not legally binding, is or was observed, or is likely to be observed, in practice. An inspector appointed under s. 172 has substantially the same powers as regards the investigation of associated companies, the production of documents, examination of witnesses and like matters as an inspector appointed under s. 164 on a general investigation of the company's affairs.   Moreover, the powers extend not only to officers and agents of the company but to any person whom the inspector has reasonable cause to believe to be, or to have been, financially interested in the success or failure (apparent or real) of the company or able to control the company or influence its policy [s. 172 (5)].   The publication of the inspector's report is more restricted than that of a report under s. 164.

If the Board of Trade considers that there is a good reason **Enquiries** to investigate ownership, but that it is unnecessary to appoint **without** an inspector, it has an alternative procedure of making **ment of an** enquiries under s. 173.   It can require any person whom it **Inspector.** has reasonable cause to believe to be or to have been interested in the shares or debentures of a company to give any information which he has, or can reasonably be expected to obtain as to present and past interests in the shares or debentures, the names and addresses of persons interested and of persons who have acted on their behalf.   Similar information can be required from the solicitors and agents of persons interested in the shares.

If the Board of Trade encounters difficulties in the course **Restrictions** of its investigation and is of the opinion that such difficulties **in Transfer,** are due wholly or mainly to the unwillingness of the persons **Voting** concerned to assist the investigation, it has power under s. 174 **Rights, etc.** to order that the shares or debentures shall be subject to statutory restrictions; such an order has the following effect as regards the shares or debentures concerned:—

(a)   Any transfer of them (or in the case of unissued shares any transfer of the right to be issued therewith and any issue thereof) is void.

(b)   No voting rights are exercisable in respect of them.

(c)   No further shares may be issued in the right of the shares or debentures concerned or in pursuance of any offer made to the holder thereof.

(d)   Except in a liquidation, no payment may be made of any sums due from the company on the shares or debentures whether in respect of capital or otherwise.

Section 174 gives any person aggrieved by the imposition of these restrictions a right of appeal to the court, but imposes very heavy penalties for contravention.

It is obvious that an investigation by the Board of Trade **The** may place the secretary of the company in a position of **Secretary's** some personal embarrassment.   Such an investigation will **Position on** usually concern the conduct of one or more of the directors, **gation.** under whose orders the secretary has been accustomed to act.   It is, however, the duty of the secretary, as a principal officer of the company, to put freely at the disposal of the inspector all material information in his possession; and the performance of that public duty must plainly override all personal considerations.

CHAPTER XXIX

THE CONTROL OF BORROWING AND ISSUES OF CAPITAL

THE control of internal finance and investment is one of the essentials of a planned economy. In order that such control might be set up on a permanent basis, the Borrowing (Control and Guarantees) Act, 1946, was passed whereby the Treasury is enabled to regulate all borrowing beyond £10,000 in any one year by any one person (extended to £50,000 by the Control of Borrowing Order, 1947, S.R. & O. 1947, No. 945). Before the provisions of the above-named Act and Order are examined, it may be useful to quote from the Government memorandum, which briefly sets out the objects of this legislation and was published at the time of its introduction into Parliament. (Cmd. 6726.) 'It is the policy of His Majesty's Government to establish and maintain a proper balance between the economic resources of the community and the demand upon them. This means that priority must always be assured for those projects of capital development which are of the greatest importance in the national interest. . . . It will therefore be essential to plan both public and private investment, not merely in the narrow financial sense of controlling borrowing, but also in the wider sense of planning real capital development of all kinds. . . . The planning of the investment programme as a whole must, therefore, be continuously guarded by the Government and must be related to other Government plans for the use of the country's economic resources.'

It should, however, be emphasised that the position of the law is bound to be fluid and is liable to be changed at very short notice; consequently secretaries should always watch for the publication of new Orders under the Act.

Effect of Contravention. Attention is, however, drawn to two provisions of the Act itself:—

(1) Section 1 (3) (which deals with the enforcement of the Act and penalties) lays down that the rights of persons concerned in any transaction shall not be affected by the fact that the transaction was in contravention of any Orders made by the Treasury under the Act. Thus the effect of contravention is that the persons in default may incur very heavy penalties, but the rights of persons concerned in any transaction will not be affected.

426

(2) Where an offence has been committed under the Act **Onus on** by a body corporate (other than a local authority), every **Officers of** person who at the time of the commission of the offence **Companies** was a director, general manager, secretary or other **to prove** similar officer of the body corporate is deemed to be **innocence.** guilty of an offence, unless he proves that the offence was committed without his consent or connivance and that he exercised all such diligence to prevent the commission of the offence as ought to have been exercised, having regard to the nature of his functions and to all the circumstances.

The Borrowing (Control and Guarantees) Act, 1946, is an **Borrowing.** enabling Act. The actual scheme of control is contained in the Control of Borrowing Order, 1947 (S.R. & O. 1947, No. 945), made under the Act. This Order is a complicated document, many of the details of which lie outside the scope of this chapter, which endeavours to give to the secretary a short outline of its provisions, so that he may be aware of the pitfalls and dangers which he may expect to encounter. If any transaction is contemplated which may conceivably involve borrowing (within the meaning of the Order) or other restricted transaction beyond the permitted limit of £50,000 in any one period of twelve months, legal advice should be sought, or the permission of the Treasury obtained, through the Capital Issues Committee.

The general effect of the Order in relation to a British company is that, subject to important exceptions, the company is prohibited from raising money by borrowing or the issue of shares, except with Treasury consent (ss. 1 and 3). The company is also prohibited, subject to exemption and except with Treasury consent, from issuing partly-paid shares, issuing securities in exchange for other redeemable securities, issuing securities for the purpose of capitalising reserves or issuing securities in exchange for the securities of another company unless one of the companies is to be wound up. Borrowing in the ordinary course of business from a bank and certain other short-term borrowings are not, however, prohibited by the Order; on the other hand, various arrangements equivalent to borrowing are treated as borrowing (see below).

There is a general exemption for transactions not exceeding in the aggregate £50,000 in a single year (Article 8). If during the preceding twelve months a company has not (whether with or without Treasury consent) borrowed any money, raised any money by issuing shares, issued partly-paid shares or generally done any of the other matters which the Order restricts, it may without Treasury consent borrow up to £50,000 or raise up to £50,000 by the issue of shares or generally do any of the other restricted transactions up to that limit. If, on the other hand, the company has already during the preceding twelve months, borrowed money or engaged in any other restricted transaction, the amount involved in all its restricted transactions during the twelve months is added together and the limit of £50,000 is applied to the aggregate of all the transactions. So, for example, if a company has in March, 1950, borrowed £10,000 and in June, 1950, raised £20,000 by the issue of shares, it could without Treasury consent raise another £20,000, but not more, before March, 1951. Rules are prescribed as to how the amount involved in any transaction is to be calculated for the purpose of seeing whether the £50,000 limit has been reached [Article 8 (5)]. There are also special provisions for calculating how the £50,000 limit applies where money borrowed has been repaid or applied in discharging a capital liability other than a short-term liability such as a bank overdraft [s. 8 (2)].

There is a further exemption of £10,000 which applies to borrowing only (Article 1). A company may without Treasury consent borrow in the aggregate up to £10,000. So, for example, if a company in January raises £45,000 by the issue of shares and in June borrows £5,000, it could still borrow another £5,000 in December, for although that would not be brought within the £50,000 exemption on all transactions, it would fall within the £10,000 exemption applicable to borrowing alone.

The Order, in addition to restricting British companies, also applies, as regards most of the prohibited matters, to transactions carried out in Great Britain by foreign companies, but for the details of its application to foreign companies, reference must be made to the Order itself. There is a special restriction on the issue of prospectuses in Britain offering for subscription, sale or exchange, the securities of a foreign company, except, of course, with Treasury consent (Article 6).

What Constitutes Borrowing. 'Borrowing' under the Order includes the following transactions (Article 2):—

(1) The making of any arrangement by which the repayment of any money borrowed or any money due under a security, which would otherwise be repayable at any particular date, is postponed. This includes an arrangement to give any guarantee to or to mortgage or charge any property to secure the payment of a sum which is already due when the arrangement is made, or is payable not later than six months after the arrangement is made. In the case of payment by instalments, the postponement of any instalment other than the last does not constitute a borrowing.

(2) The making of any arrangement by which the price of any property is allowed to remain unpaid either for a fixed period or indefinitely, but is charged upon the

property. It will be noted that this does not include the following:—

(i) the price of goods sold by a person in the ordinary course of business;

(ii) the price of any undertaking under a sale thereof to a private company;

(iii) any other arrangement by which a sum which would otherwise be payable at a specified date is made payable at a later date.

It should further be noted that a sum which at the time of (or by virtue of) the making of any arrangement is payable on demand (or on the expiration of a fixed period after demand) is deemed to be payable at the time of the making of the arrangement (or on the expiration of the fixed period after the making of the arrangement). This is the case whether or not a demand has in fact been made. [Article 2 (3).]

Borrowing does not include and the Order does not restrict (Article 1):—

(i) borrowing from a bank in the ordinary course of business;

(ii) borrowing, when the money borrowed is repayable on demand or not more than six months after demand and the loan is unsecured and not guaranteed or is secured only by a bill of exchange payable on demand or at a fixed period not exceeding nine months after the date of borrowing or after sight, or by a promissory note payable not more than six months after the date of borrowing;

(iii) borrowing from a Government department.

The Order expressly prohibits (except with Treasury **Raising** consent) the raising of money in Great Britain by the issue of **Money by** shares or perpetual debentures, subject to the exemption of **the Issue of** issues up to £50,000 (Article 3). There are two exceptions to **Shares.** this prohibition:—

(1) money raised by the issue of shares to the subscribers of a memorandum of association where the total consideration for the issue to the subscribers does not exceed £500;

(2) money raised by the issue by a private company of shares to the vendors (or nominees of the vendors) of any undertaking sold to the company. For this exception to apply, however, the shares must be fully paid; and the money raised must be cash forming part of the assets of the undertaking or cash which has been paid to the vendors, as the purchase price (or part thereof) of the undertaking.

This provision apparently restricts only the raising of *money* by the issue of shares (or perpetual debentures). To issue shares for a consideration other than money is not apparently restricted by this provision. If the consideration is securities of another company, then the provision of the Order just discussed imposes a restriction, but there does not appear to be any restriction on the issue of shares for a consideration which is neither money nor securities, *e.g.* the issue of shares in exchange for land.

Issues of Partly-paid Shares. Article 4 (1) of the Order prohibits (subject to Treasury consent and the £50,000 exemption limit) the issue of partly-paid shares. It is not, however, thought that Article 4 prevents the issue of shares payable by instalments, *e.g.* 10s. on allotment and 10s. eighteen months thereafter. For the purposes of the Order such an issue of shares would probably be treated as the raising of £1 each by the actual issue, *cf.* Article 8 (5) (*b*).

Issues of Securities where Consideration is shown in another Body Corporate. Article 4 (2) prohibits (subject to Treasury consent and the £50,000 exemption limit) the issue of *any securities* where the whole or part of the consideration for the issue is the issue or transfer of securities of another body corporate, unless one or other of the bodies corporate in question is to be wound up. Article 4 (2) involves the necessity of obtaining Treasury consent for the execution of many single types of reconstruction, *e.g.* where a reconstruction is effected by a sale of the assets of company X to company Y for shares in company Y if the assets of company X consist in part of securities. Article 4 (2) must, then, be borne in mind whenever a reconstruction is contemplated. It should be noted that the expression 'securities' means and includes 'shares, bonds, notes, debentures and debenture stock.'

Miscellaneous Restrictions in the Issue of Securities. The Order prohibits (subject to Treasury consent and the £50,000 exemption limit) the issue by a body incorporated under the law of England or Scotland of securities for any of the following purposes:—

Capitalisation of Profits.   (*a*) the capitalisation of profits and reserves (see S.I. 1949, No. 755);

Raising of Money outside the U.K.   (*b*) the raising or borrowing of money outside Great Britain;

Exchange of Securities.   (*c*) the exchanging or substituting of new securities for redeemable securities already issued.

Unit Trusts. Further Exemptions. Unit trusts are brought within the framework of the Control of Borrowing by Article 7 of the Order. The following further exemptions may be noted:—

Building and other Societies.   (1) the borrowing or raising of money or any issue of securities by building societies and industrial and provident societies;

(2) the issue of shares under a profit-sharing scheme as **Profit-sharing Schemes.** defined by Article 10 of the Order.

Article 8 (4) provides that the Treasury may at any time **Power of the Treasury to make Directions.** direct that the £50,000 exemption shall not apply to any person specified in that direction.

Treasury consent may be obtained by application to the **Application for Treasury Consent.** Capital Issues Committee, Treasury Chambers, Whitehall, S.W.1. Application should be made in the form of a letter which should be headed 'Reference form Q.1, Q.2, Q.3, Q.4, Q.5 or P.O.S.Q.,' whichever the case may be. The appropriate forms for use are obtainable from any Bank.

All letters of application and documents forwarded to the Capital Issues Committee should be in triplicate. Legal documents or copies thereof should not, however, be forwarded at all unless specifically requested.

Treasury consent is usually granted by letter, and is subject **Grant of Treasury Consent.** to certain conditions. These are generally:—

(1) if the authority given is not exercised within a certain period (generally six or twelve months) it will lapse;

(2) if any prospectus or other invitation for subscription is issued, a paragraph is to be inserted in the form referred to under Regulation 6 except that, instead of the reference to 'Regulations, 1939,' there is substituted a reference to 'the Order made under s. 1 of the Borrowing (Control and Guarantees) Act, 1946';

(3) no bearer documents are to be issued, including renounceable allotment letters, although, if permission to issue the latter is sought with a limited period of validity, it will generally be granted in the case of public issues;

(4) in the case of public issues the consent of the Bank of England must be obtained with regard to the time for making the issue: the Stock Exchange normally settles this.

The letter of consent has to be produced to the Registrar of Companies when registering returns of allotments, trust deeds or mortgages or other documents relating to transactions affected by the restrictions, and has also to be produced when any such document is submitted for stamping. Where the transaction falls within one of the exemptions and therefore there is no Treasury consent to be produced, a certificate signed by the solicitors submitting the document that the transaction falls within a specific exemption by reference to the Order is usually accepted.

When consent is given to an issue, the applicants will be required, in appropriate cases, to include in any published document connected with the issue a statement to the effect that consent does not imply any responsibility on the part of the Treasury for the financial soundness of the proposals involved, or for the correctness of any statements made or opinions expressed with regard to them.

Application should be made at the same time for permission to issue renounceable allotment letters in connection with the issue, such application being addressed either to the Bank of England (Exchange Control Office) if the consent of the Capital Issues Committee is not required, or to the Capital Issues Committee in those cases where its consent is necessary.

CHAPTER XXX

EXCHANGE CONTROL

(Unless otherwise stated, all references in this chapter are to the Exchange Control Act, 1947.)

THE Exchange Control Act, 1947, replaced the Defence (Finance) Regulations and set up exchange control on a permanent basis designed to suit conditions prevailing in times of peace. The object of the 1947 Act is to exercise Treasury control over all dealings which may affect foreign exchange, and it is therefore necessary that this Act should restrict not only direct payments across the exchanges, but also all kinds of transactions which might involve the transfer of assets abroad (*e.g.* payments in sterling to non-residents, or the transfer of assets outside the sterling area). The provisions of the Act are necessarily complicated, and it is outside the scope of this chapter to deal exhaustively with the intricate machinery provided to enforce this Treasury control.

The Act is framed to allow considerable freedom for trans- **The** actions within the 'scheduled territories,' the statutory phrase **Scheduled** for what is ordinarily known as the sterling area. The most **Territories.** recent definition of the scheduled territories is printed in E.C. (Securities) 7*, but it is, of course, liable to variation by Treasury order. Transactions with persons outside the scheduled territories are much more strictly controlled.

The principal types of transaction with which the Act is **General** concerned are the following:— **Scope of the Act.**

(*a*) all dealings in foreign currency or the equivalent of foreign currency, *e.g.* gold or travellers' cheques;

(*b*) the import or export of British treasury notes, bills of exchange, certificates of title and various similar documents;

(*c*) all payments to non-residents, that is to say, persons not resident in scheduled territories, and arrangements which would indirectly have the effect of payments to non-residents;

(*d*) the issue of securities to non-residents, or the transfer of securities to or by non-residents;

(*e*) many matters connected with bearer securities, these being, of course, convenient instruments whereby exchange control might be avoided.

As a broad general principle it may be assumed that a transaction which falls directly or indirectly under any of the above heads will probably require Treasury consent, either specific consent to the particular transaction or a general

* Obtainable from the Bank of England or any other Bank.

warrant given under proper safeguards to certain common classes of transaction as a whole. In most cases the statutory instructions apply to transactions of the relevant classes in the United Kingdom, whether effected by a United Kingdom resident or not, and also to transactions outside the United Kingdom if effected by a United Kingdom resident. Transactions completed outside the United Kingdom by a person resident outside the United Kingdom are not usually affected by the Act, though, if the person concerned is resident in some other part of the scheduled territories, they may well be prohibited by the exchange control law of the place where he resides.

The Secretary's Concern with the Act. The secretary is concerned with the Act in two ways. If his company trades with non-residents he will have to ensure that the provisions of the Act are complied with. Even, however, if the trade is wholly with residents, he will be concerned if any shareholder is a non-resident, and, as registrar, he is required to comply with the statutory procedure for ensuring that shares and other securities are not, without the proper consent, transferred to or by non-residents.

Residence. Residence is a point of cardinal importance in the administration of exchange control. It is not defined by the Act, but has a meaning much wider than residence in the normal commercial sense [*Swiss Bank Corporation* v. *Boehmische Industrial Bank* (1923), 1 K.B. 673] or for the purposes of income tax [*Egyptian Delta Land and Investment Co., Ltd.* v. *Todd* (1929), A.C. 1]. Two references only are made to residence in the Act, and both of them are important.

Residence of Corporation and Business Branches. Section 39 empowers the Treasury to make orders or directions to the following effect:—

(a) in order to provide that any transaction with or by a branch of any business, whether carried on by a corporate body or otherwise, shall be treated in all respects as if the branch were a body corporate resident where the branch is situated;

(b) in order to provide that the making of any book entry or other statement recording a debit against a branch of any business in favour of another branch of that business shall be treated as a payment to that other branch;

(c) in order to provide that any property held by or on behalf of the person carrying on the business shall be deemed to be held by such of the branches of the business as may be determined in accordance with the order or direction made by the Treasury. Further, any reference to a branch of a business is deemed to include a reference to its head office. The Treasury has, in fact, made a general order under s. 39 directing that branches of businesses in different countries are to be treated as if they were separate corporations (S.R. & O. 1947, No. 2039).

The other important section relating to residence is s. 41. **Direction of** Under this section, the Treasury is enabled to give directions **Treasury as** as to the country of which a person is to be treated as a **to Residence.** resident. This section, in fact, empowers the Treasury to determine the residence of a person for any particular purpose, even when it is abundantly clear that for other purposes his residence is elsewhere. In cases of doubt as to residence, a ruling from the Treasury should, if possible, be obtained under s. 41 (2).

Unless the permission of the Treasury is obtained, no person **Dealings in** may, in the United Kingdom, and no person resident in the **Gold and** United Kingdom may, outside the United Kingdom, buy or **Foreign** borrow any gold or foreign currency from, or sell or lend any **Currency.** gold or foreign currency to, any person (s. 1). Authorised dealers are, however, excepted from this prohibition. The Treasury has power under s. 1 (2) to impose conditions as to the use to which any gold or foreign currency bought or borrowed with its consent may be put and also as to the length of time for which it may be retained.

The Act treats payments under two headings, namely, those **Payments.** made in the United Kingdom and those made outside the United Kingdom. These two types of payment are mainly governed by ss. 5 and 6 of the Act, which may be said to be the kernel around which the exchange control system is built.

(1) As to payments in the United Kingdom, s. 5 of the Act **Payments in** provides as follows:— **the United** **Kingdom.**

'Except with the permission of the Treasury, no person shall do any of the following things in the United Kingdom, that is to say:—

(a) make any payment to or for the credit of a person resident outside the scheduled territories; or

(b) make any payment to or for the credit of a person or resident in the scheduled territories by order or on behalf of a person resident outside the scheduled territories; or

(c) place any sum to the credit of any person resident outside the scheduled territories.

Provided that where a person resident outside the scheduled territories has paid a sum in or towards the satisfaction of a debt due from him, paragraph (c) of this section shall not prohibit the acknowledgment or recording of the payment.'

Certain payments are exempted from control under this **Exemptions.** section by the Exchange Control (Payments) Order, 1950

(S.I. 1950, No. 1072), see Appendix M. The following payments, *inter alia*, are exempted:—

    (i) the transfer of the whole or any part of an amount standing to the credit of an account of a person resident outside the scheduled territories to, or to the account of, a person resident in the scheduled territories;

   (ii) any payment made in cash in the United Kingdom or in the Channel Islands to a person resident outside the scheduled territories by a person resident in the scheduled territories, if that payment:—

       (i) does not exceed £10 sterling in value;

      (ii) does not form part of a transaction or series of transactions wherein the aggregate value of the payments exceeds £10 in value.

Permission. Permission to pay money to the credit of a non-resident is obtained by means of a Sterling Transfer Form and permission to open a credit by means of Form E.2. This form is obtainable from any Bank.

Payments Outside the United Kingdom. (2) As to payments outside the United Kingdom, s. 6 of the Act provides as follows:—

  '(1) Except with the permission of the Treasury, no person resident in the United Kingdom shall, subject to the provisions of this section, make any payment outside the United Kingdom to or for the credit of a person resident outside the scheduled territories.

   (2) Nothing in this section shall prohibit the doing of anything otherwise lawful by any person with any foreign currency obtained by him in accordance with the provisions of Part I of this Act or retained by him in pursuance of a consent by the Treasury.'

It will be noticed that this section is confined to payment made outside *the United Kingdom* (not outside the scheduled territories) by residents of the United Kingdom.

Compensation Deals. Compensation deals are prohibited by s. 7 of the Act without the permission of the Treasury. Thus no person shall, in the United Kingdom, and no person resident in the United Kingdom shall, outside the United Kingdom, make any payment to or for the credit of a person resident in the scheduled territories as consideration for or in association with:—

   (*a*) the receipt by any person of a payment made outside the scheduled territories, or the acquisition by any person of property which is outside the scheduled territories; or

   (*b*) the transfer to any person, or the creation in favour of any person of a right to receive a payment outside the scheduled territories, or to acquire property which is outside the scheduled territories.

A *payment* is essential to bring any transaction within this section. This section gives rise to unexpected difficulty. Thus, for example, let it be supposed that X. transfers his business to the X. Company, Ltd., for cash, which he then uses to subscribe for shares in the X. Company, Ltd. If in such a case the assets include property situate outside the scheduled territories (*e.g.* patents registered outside the scheduled territories), the permission of the Treasury is necessary. Even if the consideration for the sale is a direct allotment of shares with no cash payment, if any payment is made to X. in association with the transaction, the permission of the Treasury is still necessary. If a secretary is in any doubt as to the implications of this section in relation to any particular problem, he would do well to take legal advice.

Part III of the Exchange Control Act (ss. 8–20 inclusive) **The Issue** controls the issue and transfer of securities, both bearer and **of Securities.** otherwise; it controls also the export of capital arising from the sale of securities, and prohibits the export of capital by means of dealings in securities. Unless the permission of the Treasury is obtained, the issue of securities in the United Kingdom or of securities which are or are to be registered in the United Kingdom is prohibited (s. 8). Such issue is not, however, prohibited if neither the person to whom the security is to be issued nor his nominee (if any) is resident outside the scheduled territories, but in all cases evidence of residence must be produced in the prescribed manner to the person issuing the security. (See Appendix M.)

The subscription of a memorandum, without the permission **Subscription** of the Treasury, by a person resident outside the scheduled **of Memor-** territories (or his nominee), is invalid in so far as it would make **andum.** that person a member of the company concerned, but it does not invalidate the incorporation of the company (s. 8). If, on the other hand, as a result, the company has less than the legal minimum number of members (seven in the case of a public company and two in the case of a private company), the Companies Act, 1948, s. 31, applies, and the members become liable for its debts in accordance with this section.

The transfer of securities registered in the United Kingdom **Transfer of** and the transfer in the United Kingdom of securities not so **Securities.** registered are both prohibited by s. 9 of the Act, unless the permission of the Treasury is obtained or unless certain requirements have been fulfilled. These requirements, and also the instances in which transfers are permitted, are set out fully in the Bank of England publication *E.C.* (*Securities*) 6 (see Appendix M). The object of these provisions is to ensure that the transfer of securities in the United Kingdom between residents in the scheduled territories may take place with as little formality as possible, but that the control is sufficiently rigid to prevent transfers across the exchanges.

It may, however, be noted that declarations as to residence are not required in relation to a letter of request signed by the personal representatives of a deceased shareholder (where they are already registered in a representative capacity) that the shares be registered in their individual capacity.

Validation of Transfer. A transfer of securities executed in contravention of the Act by reason of the residence of any person concerned is valid in the hands of an innocent transferee for value [s. 18 (1)]. Even where a transferee had notice of the facts by reason of which the transfer was prohibited, the Treasury has power under s. 18 (2) to validate the transfer. The validation of a transfer does not affect the liability to prosecution of any person for an offence against the Act.

The Duty of Persons Keeping Registers. The procedure to be adopted by registrars and company secretaries as to the issue and transfer of securities is fully dealt with in Appendix M. Section 13 of the Act further lays down the duty of persons keeping registers as follows:—

'Except with the permission of the Treasury, no person concerned with the keeping of any register in the United Kingdom shall:—

(*a*) enter in the register the name of any person in relation to any security, unless there has been produced to him the prescribed evidence that the entry does not form part of a transaction which involves the doing of anything prohibited by this Act; or

(*b*) enter in the register, in respect of any security, an address outside the scheduled territories, except for the purpose of any transaction for which the permission of the Treasury has been granted with the knowledge that it involved the entry of that address; or

(*c*) do any act in relation to the register which recognises or gives effect to any act appearing to him to have been done with such intent as is mentioned in the two last preceding sections [*i.e.* ss. 11 and 12, see below], whether done by a person in or resident in the United Kingdom or not.'

Penalties for contravention of this section (and any provision of the Act) are laid down by the Fifth Schedule to the Act.

Nominee Holdings. The evasion of the exchange control by means of nominee holdings (in so far as it is not prevented by other provisions of the Act) is covered by s. 14. In this connection, it should be noted that where the transferor or the transferee of a security is a nominee of a person resident outside the scheduled territories, neither the transferee or his agent, nor the transferor or his agent (as the case may be) shall be deemed to have committed an offence under s. 9 of the Act unless he knew or had reason to believe that the requirements of s. 9 as to nominees had not been fulfilled.

Unless the permission of the Treasury is obtained, no bearer certificate or coupon may be issued or any document altered so that it becomes a bearer certificate or coupon, by any person in the United Kingdom, or outside the United Kingdom by any person resident in the United Kingdom. The term 'bearer certificate' has a very wide meaning and includes (*inter alia*) bearer bonds, share warrants, scrip certificates to bearer, renounceable allotment letters, and deposit receipts to bearer. Letters of allotment or rights issued with permission may be split without further authority, and declarations are not required for this purpose. **Issue of Bearer Certificates and Coupons.**

Securities registered in the United Kingdom and bearer certificates in the United Kingdom may not be replaced by securities registered outside the United Kingdom or by bearer certificates outside the United Kingdom. Nor may any certificate of title to a security be issued outside the United Kingdom in substitution for, or in addition to, a certificate of title which is in, or which has been lost or destroyed in, the United Kingdom. An offence is committed under the Act by any person who does any act with intent to secure any such replacement or substitution (s. 11). **Substitution of Registered and Bearer Certificates Forbidden.**

Except with the permisssion of the Treasury no resident in the United Kingdom may procure the payment outside the United Kingdom of any capital moneys payable on a security registered in the United Kingdom (s. 12). **Payment of Capital Moneys outside the United Kingdom.**

All certificates of title to bearer securities, securities registered in the United Kingdom in a subsidiary register and any other securities which may be prescribed by the Treasury, must, except with Treasury permission, be kept at all times in the custody of an authorised depositary. This restriction applies to certificates of title which are in the United Kingdom, or which are held outside the United Kingdom by, or to the order of, a resident in the United Kingdom. An authorised depositary may part with the deposited certificates in any one of the following cases:—(*a*) for the purpose of their transfer from one authorised depositary to another, where there is no change of beneficial interest; (*b*) for the purpose of obtaining the payment of capital moneys. The certificates of title are then handed over to the person entrusted with making the payment; (*c*) for the purpose of collecting coupons (s. 15). [See Bank of England publication *E.C.* (*Securities*) 7, Appendix M.] Section 16 of the Act provides (*inter alia*) that the Treasury may obtain information as to the real owner of a deposited certificate. The effect of this section is that until the prescribed declarations have been made, and until any coupons which are missing from the certificate of title (which **Deposit of Certificates of Title.**

would not have been detached in the ordinary course of events for the collection of dividends) have been replaced, the securities and all moneys received on them are frozen in the name of the original depositor.

Import and Export. The Exchange Control Act does not deal with the general control of import and export, apart from the control of payment for exports. The Act does, however, control the import and export of currency and of valuables which can easily be converted into currency. In order that the secretary may be on his guard against accidental infringements of the Act in this connection, it may be useful to quote ss. 21 and 22 of the Act in full.

Import of Currency and Valuables. Section 21 (1) of the Act lays down as follows:—'The importation into the United Kingdom of:—

(a) any notes of a class which are or have at any time been legal tender in the United Kingdom or any part of the United Kingdom; and

(b) any such other notes as may be specified by order of the Treasury, being notes issued by a bank or notes of a class which are or have at any time been legal tender in any territory; and

(c) Treasury bills; and

(d) any certificate of title to any security, including any such certificate which has been cancelled, and any document certifying the destruction, loss or cancellation of any certificate of title to a security,

is hereby prohibited except with the permission of the Treasury.'

Section 21 (2) provides, in addition, that the expression 'note' includes part of a note, and the expression 'security' includes a secondary security.

Export of Currency and Valuables. Section 22 (1) of the Act lays down as follows:—'The exportation from the United Kingdom of:—

(a) any notes of a class which are or have at any time been legal tender in the United Kingdom or any part of the United Kingdom or in any other territory; and

(b) any Treasury bills; and

(c) any postal orders; and

(d) any gold; and

(e) any of the following documents (including any such document which has been cancelled), that is to say:—

(i) any certificate of title to a security and any coupon; and

(ii) any policy of assurance; and

(iii) any bill of exchange or promissory note expressed in terms of a currency other than sterling; and

(iv) any document to which s. 4 of this Act applies not issued by an authorised dealer or in pursuance of a permission granted by the Treasury;

and any document certifying the destruction, loss or cancellation of any of the documents aforesaid; and

(f) any such articles exported on the person of a traveller or in a traveller's baggage as may be prescribed,

is hereby prohibited except with the permission of the Treasury.'

Section 22 (2) provides, in addition, that the expression 'note' includes part of a note, the expression 'security' includes a secondary security, and the expression 'coupon' shall be construed in accordance with the meaning of 'security.'

The export of goods to any prescribed territory outside the United Kingdom, without the permission of the Treasury, is prohibited, unless the Commissioners of Customs and Excise are satisfied: (a) that payment for the goods has been made to a person resident in the United Kingdom in the manner prescribed for the relevant type of transaction, or that such payment will be made not later than six months* after the date of exportation; and (b) that the amount of the payment is such as to represent a return for the goods which is in all the circumstances satisfactory in the national interest. The exporter should complete a form, No. C.D.3 (obtainable at any Bank). One copy of this, with copies of the invoices, should be handed to the Commissioners and the other surrendered to the bank when payment is received. In practice the Commissioners will raise queries if they are not satisfied that the transaction is in order. **Payment for Exports.**

Attention is called to the following provisions of the Act, which are summarised shortly. Should any practical question arise on them, reference should be made to the relevant section of the Act, and legal advice taken where necessary. **Miscellaneous Provisions of the Act.**

(1) Where a person resident in the United Kingdom has any right to receive any specified† currency, or to receive from a person resident outside the scheduled territories a payment in sterling, he must not delay the receipt of that currency or payment, and he must not do anything whereby that currency or payment ceases to be receivable by him (s. 24). On a contravention of s. 24, the Treasury has wide powers to obtain and to expedite the receipt of the currency or payment in question. The Treasury has power also in such cases to make directions, and may direct that the right to receive the currency or payment be assigned to the Treasury or its nominee. **Duty to Collect Certain Debts.**

* Subject to variation by the Treasury (see s. 23).
† Specified by the Treasury.

Duty not to Delay Sale or Importations. (2) Section 25 imposes a duty not to delay the sale or importation of goods where Treasury permission has been granted or currency obtained on the faith that any goods should be sold outside the scheduled territories, or on the faith or subject to a condition that any goods should be imported from outside the scheduled territories into any part of the scheduled territories. If it appears to the Treasury, either **Power of the Treasury to make Directions.** that the goods have not been sold or imported within the time stipulated (or within a reasonable time if no time was stipulated), or that the goods cannot be sold or imported, then the Treasury has wide powers to give directions as to how the goods should be dealt with, including a direction that the goods shall be assigned to the Treasury or to its nominee.

Foreign Companies. (3) Section 30 and the Second Schedule to the Act extend the exchange control to foreign companies which are controlled, or to some degree controlled, by persons resident in the United Kingdom. One of the main objects of the section is to bring within the control family companies which have been formed for the purpose of avoidance of taxation and death duties. The control is, of course, much wider than this and includes foreign subsidiaries of United Kingdom companies.

The Treasury may serve a notice on any person in the United Kingdom requiring that person (a) to cause a foreign company to comply with any of the under-mentioned requirements; (b) to remove any obstacle to the foreign company complying with any of the requirements; or (c) render it in any respect more probable that the foreign company will comply with any of the requirements. The requirements in respect of which such notice may be served are that the foreign company shall:—

(i) furnish to the Treasury such particulars as to its assets and business as may be mentioned in the notice;

(ii) sell or procure the sale to an authorised dealer of any gold or specified currency mentioned in the notice (being gold or specified currency which it is entitled to sell or of which it is entitled to procure the sale);

(iii) declare and pay such dividend as may be mentioned in the notice;

(iv) realise any of its assets mentioned in the notice in such manner as may be so mentioned;

(v) refrain from selling, transferring or doing anything which affects its rights or powers in relation to, any such Treasury bills or securities as may be mentioned in the notice.

Alienation of Control Prohibited. Except with the permission of the Treasury, no person resident in the United Kingdom shall do any act whereby a body corporate which is by any means controlled (whether directly or indirectly) by persons resident in the United Kingdom ceases to be controlled by persons resident in the United Kingdom. This does not, however, include the sale of any securities authorised to be dealt in on any recognised stock exchange in the United Kingdom if the sale takes place in pursuance of an agreement entered into in the ordinary course of business on that exchange.

Except with the permission of the Treasury, no person resident in the United Kingdom may lend any money, Treasury bills or securities to any body corporate resident in the scheduled territories which is by any means controlled (whether directly or indirectly) by persons resident outside the scheduled territories. **Loans to Corporations controlled by Persons outside the Scheduled Territories.**

(4) Section 31 gives the Treasury power to make exemptions in relation to any obligation or prohibition imposed by the Act; any exemption so made may be absolute or conditional. **Exemptions.**

(5) A term in all contracts is implied to the effect that where, by virtue of the Act, the permission or consent of the Treasury is at the time of the contract required for the performance of any term thereof, that term shall not be performed except in so far as the permission or consent is given or is not required. This provision applies only where there is no contrary intention in the contract (s. 33). **The Effect of the Act upon Contracts.**

Particulars as to legal proceedings, contributions, bankruptcy proceedings, the administration of the estates of deceased persons, the winding up of companies and proceedings under deeds of arrangements or trust deeds for behoof of creditors are given in the Fourth Schedule to the Act [s. 33 (3)]. **Legal Proceedings.**

Detailed provisions for the enforcement and the administration of the Act are made by the Fifth Schedule to the Act. Particular attention is drawn to the requirement of s. 34 that certain classes of people, among whom are included those concerned with the keeping of any register in the United Kingdom, must comply with certain directions from the Treasury. Such directions extend to the exercise of any functions exercisable by them by virtue of, or by virtue of any thing done under, the Act. **Enforcement and Administration.**

Any permission, consent or authority granted by the Treasury under the Act may be:— **Treasury Permission.**

(a) general or special; (b) revoked by the Treasury; (c) absolute or conditional; (d) limited so as to expire on a specified date unless renewed; and (e) shall be published in such a way as, in the opinion of the Treasury, to give any person entitled to the benefit of it an adequate opportunity of getting to know of it, unless, in their opinion, publication is not necessary for the purpose [s. 37 (1)].

Any directions given by the Treasury may be:— **Treasury Directions.**

(a) general or special; (b) revoked or varied by subsequent directions; and (c) shall be given to such persons and in such manner as the Treasury thinks appropriate, and, if so given, shall be valid for all purposes [s. 37 (2)].

CHAPTER XXXI

SUPERANNUATION

I have done all that I came into this world to do.
I have worked task work and have the rest of the day
to myself. (*The Superannuated Man*—Chas. Lamb.)

BUT one can well imagine that the 'ecstasies of delight'
with which 'The Superannuated Man' welcomed his new
conditions were inspired in great measure by the fact that
his employers had, of their own volition, awarded him a
pension of an amount equal to two-thirds of his salary. It is
a safe deduction that the delight was a reaction from a condition of worry and unrest engendered by the absence of any
provision for his retirement—a condition all too common still
and one which contributes directly and forcefully to the
inefficiency of the individual and, in aggregate, to that of the
business in which he is engaged. A sound provision for
superannuation is as much a necessity from the point of view
of the employer as of the employee. A company which
employs too many old men will itself suffer from senility, and in
every business the situation gets worse with every year that its
solution is delayed. There is, of course, nothing new about
superannuation, but in former days it was given very largely
from motives of benevolence, rather than as a recognition of
service and as a sound economic principle. Organised
systems for the provision of pensions, however, are a growth
of the last hundred years or so, and more particularly of the
last quarter of a century.

The first Superannuation Act, that for civil servants, was
passed in 1834, and was followed by further legislation in
1859 and 1909. The railway companies were among the
earliest private employers to institute funds—the London
and North Western Railway Fund for Salaried Staff was
established in 1853; the Railway Clearing System Fund
(which ultimately covered the staffs of some 45 of the minor
railways) was founded in 1873; and subsequently most of the
staffs of the railway companies—both salaried and wages—
were covered by pension schemes of a more or less adequate
character.

The legislation of 1921, providing relief from income tax
on properly constituted funds, materially stimulated the
movement, and, contrary to anticipation, the passing of the
National Insurance Act, 1946, has resulted in a further
considerable development.

Prior to the passing of the Finance Act of 1921, properly **Legislation.** constituted pension funds enjoyed, by arrangement with the Inland Revenue, a certain amount of relief from income tax upon their investment income—such relief being equivalent to the amount of tax which would accrue upon the pension payments. It was felt, however, that logically such investment income should be entirely free from tax, a pension fund being merely a channel into which contributions were paid, to be poured out again at some later date in the shape of pensions, and that, accordingly, it should not be subjected to tax until the individual pensions were paid, as otherwise taxation would be duplicated. A case was, therefore, submitted to the Royal Commission on the Income Tax in 1920; the Commission reported favourably, and legislation was embodied in s. 32 of the Finance Act, 1921.

This section provides relief from tax to funds approved by the Commissioners of Inland Revenue, who require, before they will approve a fund, to be satisfied:—

(a) that a fund is really what it purports to be—a superannuation fund; therefore they require that the fund be *bona fide* established under irrevocable trusts in connection with some undertaking carried on in the United Kingdom.

In this connection 'irrevocable' is used in the sense that money contributed to a fund by an employer cannot go back to him;

(b) that it has for its sole purpose the provision of annuities for persons employed in the undertaking;

(c) that the employer is a contributor, and

(d) that the fund is recognised by the employer and employed persons in the undertaking.

Subject to these main conditions, the privileges enjoyed by an approved fund may be summarised as follows:—

(1) Income from investments or deposits is exempt from tax.

(2) Tax in respect of pensions paid is assessed and chargeable on the annuitant instead of on the fund. The fund has only to make a return of annuitants to the Inland Revenue Department.

(3) Tax in respect of contributions refunded to members is payable by the fund at a reduced rate (at present one-fourth the standard rate) but the fund may recover the amount from the member if its rules so provide.

(4) Employers' contributions are allowed as an expense in calculating their liability for tax.

(5) Members' contributions are allowed as an expense for the purpose of their personal assessments to tax.

Thus for the first time employers' superannuation funds received statutory recognition in a public Act of Parliament, but their legal status as private voluntary schemes remained practically unchanged. Parliament looked to the object of the funds rather than to their constitution.

Regulations have been issued by the Board of Inland Revenue under the Act of 1921 and may be obtained from H.M. Stationery Office—Statutory Rules and Orders 1921, No. 1699. They comprise *inter alia* directions for the application for approval of a fund, notification of any subsequent alteration in the rules, constitution, objects or conditions of a fund, definition of contributions and as to relief from taxation in respect of contributions, directions as to claims for relief in respect of tax on contributions and as to claims for relief in respect of tax on income from investments and deposits, and for the payment of tax on any contributions repaid to a contributor, or on a lump sum paid in commutation of an annuity.

Subsequently the Finance Act of 1930 included provisions which extended the legislation of 1921, in all material respects, to those funds which furnish pensions for widows and dependents of deceased employees. The only point of difference is that, in these funds, members' contributions are allowed, for income tax purposes, as life assurance premiums and not as expenses.

Reference must be made also to another Act of general application, viz. the Superannuation and other Trust Funds (Validation) Act of 1927. Briefly, if a fund is registered under the Act with the Chief Registrar of Friendly Societies, it is exempt from the legal rule known as the rule against perpetuities. Under this rule, land and money and property generally cannot be tied up for all time, and the Inland Revenue authorities, therefore, claim that the trust deed of a fund must have a time limit. The usual limitation employed for the purpose of the rule is 'twenty years after the death of the survivor of all the lineal descendants of His Majesty . . . now living.' The 1927 Act mentioned above exempts from the rule against perpetuities funds registered under the Act, which can therefore continue for an indefinite time. It should be noted that the rule against perpetuities has no application to Scottish trusts or to funds established under statute. For a fund to be registered under the 1927 Act it must comply with the regulations made by the Inland Revenue under the Finance Act, 1921; and there are also certain regulations under the 1927 Act which need to be observed, *e.g.* a copy of the annual statement of accounts and balance sheet of the fund duly audited, and a copy of the quinquennial investigation and report as to the financial condition of the fund must be sent to the above-named Registrar, copies of the rules of the fund and of the names and addresses of the trustees of the fund must be submitted with the application for registration and any amendment of the rules or of a change of the trustees or their addresses must be registered. A schedule to the 1927 Act indicates certain requirements as to rules of funds to be registered.

Further provision was made in regard to income tax by the Finance Act, 1947, ss. 19 to 23, designed to defeat devices which in recent years have been increasingly adopted with the object of avoiding tax liability without setting up a genuine pension fund.

Subject to the exemptions mentioned below, s. 19 of the Finance Act, 1947, imposes liability to income tax on directors or employees of corporate bodies in respect of the actual or assumed cost of the provision of future retirement or other benefits. Where the provision for the benefits is made by payment to a third person (*e.g.* to an insurance company or trustees) tax is to be charged on the amount paid in respect of the individual director or employee, but where future benefits are payable under agreement or conditions of service, and provision for them is not made by payment to a third person, the tax is to be charged on the amount which would have to be paid year by year to a third person to secure the provision of the benefits. Where the payments in respect of which the director or employee is charged to tax are insurance premiums, he is entitled to the life insurance relief which would have been due if he had himself made the payment on an insurance contract taken out by him.

Section 20 exempts from charge to tax provision for retirement benefits made under:—

(*a*) a statutory superannuation scheme;

(*b*) a superannuation fund approved under s. 32 of the Finance Act, 1921;

(*c*) an 'excepted' provident fund or staff assurance scheme as defined in s. 23 of the Act of 1947;

(*d*) certain insurance schemes in operation before 6th April, 1947, which are not confined to directors and employees with remuneration exceeding £2,000 a year;

(*e*) a scheme which was in operation before 6th April, 1944, providing a life pension or annuity as the main benefit;

(*f*) a scheme approved by the Commissioners of Inland Revenue which satisfies the conditions laid down under s. 21 of the Act of 1947.

These Acts constitute virtually all the general legislation affecting pension funds, though funds may be established under the Friendly Societies' Acts and secure freedom from tax.

Such funds, however, are limited to a maximum pension of £2 a week and a lump sum payment not exceeding £500.

There are, of course, many Acts of limited application, such as:—

    (1) those governing the civil service, fire brigades, etc.;

    (2) the Local Government and other Officers' Superannuation Acts of 1922 and 1937;

    (3) the various Acts under which statutory companies' schemes have been established.

Forms of Securing Retirement Benefits. There are several forms of securing retirement benefits to suit the varying circumstances of particular groups of employers and employees:—

    (1) old age and dependent pensions payable under a service contract for which no provision is made during the service;

    (2) old age and dependent pensions payable at the discretion of the employer for which no provision is made during the service;

    (3) old age or dependent pensions payable under a contract of service for which provision is made during the service by means of a trustee fund:—

        (a) approved under s. 32, Finance Act, 1921;

        (b) approved under s. 21, Finance Act, 1947;

        (c) not approved under either section;

        (d) joint contributory statutory superannuation schemes;

    (4) old age or dependent pensions payable under contract of service and provided by arrangements similar to 3 (a), (b) and (c), but by means of deferred annuity policies.

All of these may include lump sum benefits.

Lump Sums. Some funds include a provision for the payment of a lump sum at the date of retirement, but such funds are only 'approved' in so far as they are devoted to the provision of pensions. It is claimed that the provision of a lump sum at the time of retirement is useful in that there is often need of capital for the purchase of a house and to defray the cost of moving; that it provides a temporary cushion for the period immediately following the loss of income, on the change from salary to pension; that it is often beneficial for health reasons for a pensioner to take an extended vacation immediately on retirement; and that it may be used towards the provision of a widow's pension. On the other hand, the payment of a lump sum seriously reduces the amount of pension which would otherwise be available, and there is often the danger that the money so available may be used improvidently. The present tendency, at any rate of employers, is to consider that for these reasons the provision of large lump sum payments as the commutation of pensions (except small pensions) is not desirable.

Moreover, the contributor should realise that when the fund is not fully 'approved' he is not entitled to relief from income tax on the whole of his contribution, and that on commuting voluntarily in the case of a fully 'approved' fund he may be called upon to suffer tax under the Commissioners' regulations—at present at one-fourth of the current standard rate—which is a serious loss.

It is proposed to outline the steps to be taken in forming a **Promotion of** scheme to be worked jointly by employer and employees by **a Scheme.** means of a fund established by trust deed or by contract with a reputable insurance company.

The first step is for the employer to arrange a conference of the employer or his representatives with representatives of the employees, preferably selected by the employees themselves. The more important questions for consideration are:—

(1) whether an internal fund should be constituted or the pensions arranged with an insurance company;

(2) the age of retirement;

(3) the form or method of constituting the pensions, and whether or not a lump sum payment should be made on retirement;

(4) the method of assessing contributions;

and last, but by no means least in importance or in the difficulty of consideration, is the need

(5) for some provision to enable members of the staff who have already rendered long service to obtain a pension adequate to their need and equitable as compared with the pensions of their younger colleagues, whose pensions will mainly accrue as the result of the payment of contributions.

The scheme should be optional for existing staff up to (say) ten years below the ultimate compulsory retiring age which may be fixed. Every endeavour should be made to induce all existing members of the staff under that age to join the fund and they should be given to understand that if they do not do so the employer will not consider any appeal from them on or after their retirement. Membership should be compulsory for all future appointments.

No definite line can be laid down as to whether a fund **The Pros and** should be established and managed internally or a contract **Cons of** entered into with an insurance company, and the actuary's **Private and** advice on the point is useful. Provided that the expected mem- **Companies'** bership is large enough for the risks of mortality and longevity **Schemes.**

to average out, and the requisite knowledge and experience of investment and fund management are available, the maximum advantages are secured through the private fund approved by the Inland Revenue. Such a fund secures the largest possible exemption from tax, and normally the cost of administration is very low. There are many substantial funds, the work connected with which is a part-time job for one man on the employer's staff, while, frequently, such service as office accommodation and incidental expenses are met by the employer. A less tangible advantage, but a real one, is the value which attaches to the periodical meetings of the fund committee, usually composed of representatives of the employer and his employees. Such contact should be of great use in fostering good relations, and has a substantial, if not a cash, value. Again, an internal scheme can more easily be modified, if, as the result of actuarial examination, this is deemed desirable. A surplus can be used to provide larger benefits or reduced contributions—a deficiency similarly can be dealt with appropriately.

If the fund is to be internal it is essential that the number of members should be large enough to ensure that the various actuarial risks will average out. If the members are too few, the fact that certain pensioners live an exceptionally long time, or some other like risk, may endanger the stability of the fund. It is impossible to lay down any lower limit for the number of members which would justify an internal fund; it depends on a number of factors, such as the rate of retirement before pension age, the pension age chosen and the range of salaries of the employees concerned. Only an actuary can advise whether a private scheme can be considered safe.

Apart from the need to average out actuarial risks, the main arguments in favour of arranging the scheme with an insurance company are:—

(1) that the latter can invest to better advantage than the private investor or fund;

(2) that in handling a number of schemes the cost of administration is low and compares not unfavourably with the expense of running the private fund; and

(3) that the insurance company relieves the employer and those concerned in managing a fund of all responsibility of administration, and of the necessity for actuarial valuation.

Doubtless many employers, particularly small employers, would welcome this freedom from responsibility by passing the money to an insurance company, but it will, of course, be realised that the latter must look, for reimbursement of its expenses of management, for a profit on its transactions, and beyond this must necessarily, in any pension contract, have a margin of safety in its premiums. The suggestion that the insurance company can invest to better advantage is not necessarily true. In very many cases there will be directors or employees of the company who will have the experience and sound judgment necessary to direct the investment of the moneys available.

The age of retirement for men is usually 65, with provision **The Age of** for voluntary retirement on or after attaining the age of 60, **Retirement.** and provision for extension beyond the age of 65 with the concurrence of the employer and of the trustees and managing committee. For an employee who remains in service after 65, contributions may either cease when he attains 65 or continue until his actual retirement.

There are various ways of arranging the scale of pensions, **The Form or** *e.g.* in funds providing pension benefits only:— **Method of Constituting**

(a) one-sixtieth (or some other proportion) of the retiring **the Pension.** salary or of the average of the last five or seven years' salary for each year of membership of the fund (or for each year of employment, providing that an initial payment is made to cover the period of employment before membership began) with a maximum of (say) forty-sixtieths, or

(b) an average of the salary throughout the period of employment, most conveniently calculated at the rate of (say) 2 per cent. of the total salary on which contributions have been paid.

The first method provides a pension which is adequate to the circumstances of the retiring employee and, as between different employees, gives effect to the reasonable principle that a higher paid employee should get a larger pension. The amounts are not, however, entirely equitable as between different employees if one considers how much each has contributed. Contributions are usually reckoned either as a fixed percentage of the employee's salary or as a percentage of salary appropriate to the employee's age of entry into the scheme. In either case, but particularly in the latter, the employee who retires with a high salary gets, proportionally, a better pension for what he has contributed than the employee whose salary never attains a high level. This may be seen if one compares two employees who have had the same salaries during most of their service, rising towards the end of their service to salaries of £2000 and £1000 a year respectively; although the former gets twice the pension of the latter he will not have made twice the contributions, since in early years they would have been contributing the same. The second method is not free from this fault, but the difference in the relative incidence of total contribution is much less, inasmuch as the averaging of the salary often results in the lower-paid employee attaining a pension exceeding, occasionally considerably exceeding, the two-thirds level of final salary, whereas the pension attained by the highly-paid officer usually falls short of the two-thirds level. This is, of course, compensated for by the fact that he has had greater opportunity of making some additional provision for his old age in other ways. In either case, if a lump sum payment is provided on retirement, the ratio of pension to salary will be lower as the actuary may advise.

The Method of Assessing Contributions. The methods of assessing contributions are commonly either a flat rate percentage of salary payable by all contributors throughout their membership of the fund, without regard to the age of entry, or a progressive scale depending on the age of entry, and again payable throughout membership. The actuary will need to settle these rates after consideration of all the circumstances of the employment of those proposed to be included in the undertaking and of the proposed scale of pensions. If the rate varies with age of entry, it is customary to limit the rate of contribution by the employee to that appropriate to the age of forty or thereabouts, the balance, if any, for those entering above that age being dealt with in an initial solvency payment (see below).

The proportion of the contribution to be paid respectively by employer and employee is, of course, a matter of arrangement, but is usually on a fifty-fifty basis, except in the case of the older employees on the existing staff, whose contributions, as indicated above, may be limited, the balance being found by the employer in the initial solvency payment.

The Initial Solvency Payment. This is a difficult matter, indeed often the stumbling block to the establishment of a fund. All the existing employees will have periods of employment to their credit, which it will be desired should count for the computation of pension, and, if they are already over 40 years of age or thereabouts, even a half of the necessary contribution is of too burdensome an amount for the individual to pay. The actuary will need to calculate the capital value of these factors and, if the fund is to start successfully, the employer will need to provide this amount, which may be spread over several years if necessary, an appropriate rate of interest being paid on the outstanding balance. Such payments will be admitted by the Inland Revenue as a charge against profits spread over a term of years.

Special Payments. Occasionally it may happen that the employer will desire to appoint a person to the staff who has some special or technical qualification and who will generally be of a more mature age than is usual in the case of new appointments. In such cases the employer may need to arrange terms of superannuation as well as of remuneration. This is commonly done by adding a notional term of years to the term of his engagement and this will call for a special payment to the fund, the amount of which will be determined by the actuary.

The fund may comprise both men and women, but the **Admission of** terms for the latter will differ in some respects from those **Women.** indicated for men, *e.g.* it is usual to provide for the retirement of women five years earlier than men, *i.e.* compulsorily at 60 and optionally at 55. Moreover, women have a greater expectation of life than men, and this longer period of super-annuation will be taken into account in settling the terms of contribution. This greater cost, however, is to some extent offset by the larger number of withdrawals among women consequent upon marriage.

It will have to be decided whether the fund is to provide **Widows and** benefits for widows and children as well as the employees **Dependents.** themselves. This point is discussed further below. One solution frequently adopted is to give the employee a right on retirement to surrender a portion of his pension in exchange for a pension payable during his life and after his death to his widow for life.

A trust deed and rules will need to be drafted and, after **Trust Deed** careful consideration and agreement by the interested parties, **and Rules.** committed to a competent lawyer, preferably one who has had experience of such matters. There is no standard trust deed or set of rules available and there are many variations and differences rendered necessary by the differing require-ments of the various industries. It is to be emphasised that the drafting of a trust deed and rules, in a case of any complica-tion, is a difficult matter requiring great care, and that any attempt to do it cursorily will lead to difficulties later when pensions have to be paid.

The trust deed and rules must cover not only the matters previously discussed and relative subsidiary matters such as resignation, retirement due to ill-health, death before super-annuation, commutation of pension, etc., but also the appoint-ment of the trustees and managing committee and, if the employer is willing, a guarantee of the solvency of the fund or perhaps of a certain level of interest on the investments so as to eliminate one of the more uncertain elements of the calcu-lations of the actuary.

The trustees should include persons in the employ of the company who have experience in investment. It is well that the trustees should be incorporated or, if not, have the facility of holding their investments in the name of a corporate nominee, so as to avoid the trouble and expense of transferring the securities upon any change of trustees.

The committee of management should be constituted of repre-sentatives of the employer and of the employed contributors and should be subject to re-election from time to time.

If the employing company finds the initial solvency payments and assists in other ways, *e.g.* by guaranteeing the solvency of the fund or the level of interest, or by collecting the contributions and providing clerical labour and accommodation, it is usual that the company should have a majority of one on the managing committee and that the chairman of the fund and of the committee should be a representative of the company.

Funds for Operatives. The considerations so far expressed refer to funds for administrative staffs. It is equally necessary that pension funds should be provided for operatives, since there is less experience and less opportunity among the people concerned to provide for their old age. It needs a great deal of moral courage for an individual to put aside half-a-crown a week for 40 years, even if a suitable method of investment is found, but when the contribution is common to a body of men in a common employment and is deducted through the pay roll, the matter takes on a very different aspect.

Generally the same considerations apply with regard to the organisation of a fund, but with the important exception that it is better to provide a definite contribution per week for a definite amount of pension in due course, rather than that the scale of contribution and pension should be expressed in percentages of wages. Actuarial niceties are very suspect by the average operative and it has become usual to provide one or two, or even three, grades of pension for which the man may subscribe, the first one compulsory* as a condition of service, and the others voluntary and available to be taken up at a later date should the contributor receive promotion, become a charge-hand or foreman, and consequently be in a better position to afford another shilling or two a week.

For example, a first grade of pension which should be a condition of service might be 10s. per week with an appropriate weekly contribution, one-half to be provided by the employer and the other by the contributor. There would also, as stated in the last paragraph, be second and third grades of pension for which employees could have the option of subscribing; the rates of contribution for these would probably have to depend upon the age of the contributor when he started subscribing.

Trust deed and rules should be agreed upon by both the employer and the employees, and schedules should be set out at the end of the rules indicating precisely what pension a man may expect, having regard to the age at which he commenced contribution on the one hand and the age at which he retires on the other, the relative contribution being set out likewise.

When pensions have been arranged on these lines it becomes

---

* NOTE.—Care should be taken that this does not offend against the Shop Clubs Act, 1902.

necessary that the employer should take measures to ensure that they are receivable in due course. From time to time, when money values alter, it may be necessary to establish an increase in the rate of contribution for new entrants, but any change either in contribution or pension once the rate has been established should, so far as possible, be avoided.

Notwithstanding the enhanced provisions of recent Government legislation, some employers have recently instituted elaborate schemes, covering not only pensions for the men themselves, but also allowances for widows, children and dependents. An interesting provision in some of such schemes is that a member who retires unmarried shall be entitled to have his retirement pension increased as a consideration for the portion of the contributions paid by him to provide benefits for his widow and dependents.

As already indicated, it is common to provide in the rules of **Widows' and** a superannuation fund that a contributor entitled to receive a **Dependents'** pension may elect on retirement to surrender a portion of his **Funds.** pension, in exchange for a pension to be payable to the member during his life and after his death to his widow for life. Experience shows, however, that advantage is seldom taken of this provision. Indeed, there is too often neglect by a contributor to make the necessary provision for his widow and dependents, and the sum which is receivable from a fund upon his premature death is not sufficient to make any such adequate provision, being, at the most, the total of the contributions of the employer and himself during his membership. Of recent years, therefore, there has been a growing tendency to create a separate widows' and dependents' fund. Such funds are more difficult to establish than a pension fund, inasmuch as employees of middle age or beyond are perhaps not in a position to start making adequate contributions, while experience shows that the younger employees are generally not enthusiastic about such a scheme. Many, indeed, grudge the contribution towards their own pension, to say nothing of an annuity for a hypothetical—and far distant—widow. The arguments adduced in the opening paragraphs of this chapter in regard to the provision for superannuation are, however, equally applicable to the provision of means for the sustenance of widows and dependents, and the enlightened employer would do well to consider the setting up of a fund for such provision.

Now that so much progress has been made with pension **Group or** schemes, some advance in practice is desirable in the direction **Central** of group or central schemes. The ideal pension scheme, **Schemes.** particularly where the operative or factory staff is included, would be that which covered an industry and thus permitted fluidity of labour. We are far from that ideal. In most cases, if a man moves from the service of one employer to that

of another, he has to withdraw his contributions from one
fund, losing tax on the amount withdrawn, and start as a new
member in another fund.   Moreover, this is most unsatisfactory, since he can withdraw only his own contributions.

The Local Government and other Officers' Superannuation
Act, 1922, provides that when a contributor leaves one
authority to enter the service of another, the transfer value of
his contributions can be paid over to the new employer, in order
that he may not need to start again as a new entrant into a
fund.   Some similar development in industrial schemes is
desirable, and might be achieved if funds would include in
their rules provision for transfers from one fund to another.

An example of a 'group' or central scheme within an
industry is that of the National Joint Council of the Flour
Milling Industry.   The scheme covers clerical and administrative staffs of many firms in the industry, each firm agreeing
to subscribe for a minimum period of five years, with the
option of renewing the arrangements for successive periods of
three years.   Other schemes of a similar character have been
organised, *inter alia*, for stock exchange clerks, solicitors'
clerks and the Baltic Exchange clerks.

The advantage of such schemes can be illustrated by
reference to those connected with the co-operative movement.
In the retail and productive undertakings of the co-operative
movement, there are now established upwards of 500 funds
catering for more than 300,000 employees.   These separate
funds are almost entirely operated under separate trust
instruments within the particular societies concerned, and are
separately managed by joint committees elected by the
respective parties.   There were, however, a number of units
of distribution or production which employed only a small
number of workers and these, on actuarial grounds, were
insufficient to provide a sound basis as individual funds.
Many of these have been grouped into federal schemes and a
scheme has been adopted covering the majority of the undertakings, under which the value of pension rights is recognised
as between the various societies, and a rule on the following
lines is now included in the trust deeds of these schemes:—

'Should any employee who is a member of the fund leave
the society to enter the employment of another society
which has a superannuation fund approved under s. 32 of
the Finance Act, 1921, to the membership of which such
other society is prepared to admit the member leaving this
society, this society shall pay to the superannuation fund
of such other society out of the superannuation fund such
transfer value, being the contributions of the member of the
fund and interest thereon at 2½ per cent. compound interest,
and such other sum, if any, as the actuary shall certify
to be proper having regard to all the circumstances of the

case in respect of such member as may be ascertained by the actuary, on the other society undertaking to give to the member such benefits in respect of the transfer payment as may be advised by the actuary.

'Similarly, should a member leave the service of such other society to enter the service of the society, the aforesaid rules of transfer shall be applicable in such case also.'

In such cases as these, if the Inland Revenue authorities are satisfied that all the moneys paid out from one society are vested in another of like constitution, and both societies are 'approved' under s. 32 of the Finance Act, 1921, no claim is made for payment of tax on the sum so withdrawn as provided in Regulation 8 of the Statutory Rules and Orders, 1921, No. 1699 (see page 446).

Mention should be made of the Association of Super-annuation and Pension Funds, which was organised immediately after the passing of the Finance Act, 1921. It has now attained an authoritative position and is recognised as such by Government departments in all matters pertaining to superannuation and pension funds. It is a body from which useful advice and assistance can be obtained by a company wishing to start a pension scheme.

CHAPTER XXXII

STAMP DUTIES

THE Stamp Act, 1891, as amended by various subsequent Acts, requires many documents to bear stamp duty, the amount of which depends on the transaction effected by the particular document. If a document is not stamped, no offence is in general committed, but the document cannot be produced in evidence except in criminal proceedings. It will therefore be the concern of the secretary to see that the documents of the company which pass through his hands are properly stamped, in order that they may be available for evidence in any future civil legal proceedings.

The secretary is also even more closely concerned with stamp duties in connection with the transfer of shares or debentures of the company, which it is his business to register. By s. 17 of the Stamp Act, 1891, if any person whose office it is to enrol, register, or enter into or upon any books or records, any instrument chargeable with duty, enrols, registers, or enters any such instrument not duly stamped, he incurs a fine of £10. If, further, he is a party to a fraud on the Revenue he incurs larger penalties. The secretary is thus made personally responsible for seeing that any transfer of shares or debentures which he registers is duly stamped. If a transfer is presented which is not duly stamped, he must decline to register it or he will incur a penalty.

It is only documents which require to be stamped. If a transaction is carried through without there being a document capable of being stamped, no duty is payable; for example, an oral contract will, in many cases, be perfectly valid and will not attract any duty, although, if the same contract had been in writing, a sixpenny stamp would have been required.

A document which relates to several different matters, each of which attracts duty under the Act, will usually require to be stamped in respect of each of the matters attracting duty.

Fixed and *ad valorem* Duties. The stamp duty on a particular transaction may be a fixed duty or an *ad valorem* duty. A fixed duty is the same, whatever the amount concerned in the transaction; for example, the stamp on an ordinary cheque is a fixed duty of twopence, whether the cheque is for £1 or £1,000,000. *Ad valorem* duty is duty the amount of which is calculated by reference to the amount involved in the transaction. For example, on a sale of shares the duty is 2 per cent. of the purchase price. In practice, while the fixed duties are reasonably small, the *ad valorem* duties may, on a large transaction, be very substantial sums.

Stamps may be impressed or adhesive. If an impressed **Types of** stamp is required, the document has to be taken to the Inland **Stamps.** Revenue with the necessary money, and the stamp is impressed on it by them. An adhesive stamp may be stuck on by the person executing the document, but when fixed must be cancelled so that it cannot be used again. The commonest example of an adhesive stamp is the ordinary twopenny stamp on a receipt; the other common cases when adhesive stamps are permitted are given in Appendix A. In almost all other cases the stamp must be impressed. Generally speaking, where an adhesive stamp is permissible and the duty does not exceed 2s. 6d., an ordinary postage stamp may be used (Stamp Act, 1891, s. 7). In the case of contract notes and foreign bills of exchange, while adhesive stamps may be used even though the appropriate amount exceeds 2s. 6d., postage stamps are not permitted; the special adhesive stamp appropriate for the purpose must be obtained from the Revenue.

Impressed stamps state the amount which they represent, **Types of** but there are in addition certain particular impressed stamps **Impressed** called denoting stamps, penalty stamps, and adjudication **Stamp.** stamps. A denoting stamp is impressed when there are several documents relating to the same transaction, only one of which requires to be stamped with the duty; for example, a lease and duplicate lease, one of which will be kept by the landlord and the other by the tenant. One will be stamped in the ordinary way with the appropriate amount; the duplicate will be stamped with a denoting stamp to show that it does not require any other stamp. Penalty stamps are impressed to show that a penalty has been paid on a document which has been stamped late. An adjudication stamp shows that the document has been adjudicated as stated in the next paragraph.

If there is doubt whether a document requires a stamp, or **Adjudica-** what is the proper amount of duty, it should be submitted to **tion.** the Commissioners of Inland Revenue for adjudication. The Commissioners will decide what stamp, if any, it ought to bear, and the document must then be stamped with that sum within 14 days after the adjudication. It will also have impressed on it an adjudication stamp, and when so stamped it is a duly stamped document admissible in evidence even though it may subsequently appear that the Commissioners were wrong. There is provision for appeal to the court against the Commissioners' adjudication if it is considered that they have required too large an assessment (s. 13).

Certain documents require to be stamped on execution (*i.e.* **Date for** when the document is signed or sealed) and cannot generally **Stamping** be stamped afterwards except under penalty. The more **and** important of these will be mentioned later. Generally, how- **Penalties.** ever, a document need not be stamped until 30 days after execution, if it be submitted for adjudication, or 14 days after adjudication. After the period of 30 (or 14) days has expired it can still be stamped, but only on the terms of paying a penalty in addition to the stamp duty (s. 15). Where the original stamp duty was less than £10 the penalty will be a further £10 and also interest at 5 per cent. on the original duty. In the case of most instruments chargeable with *ad valorem* duty there is, in addition to the £10 penalty, a further penalty equal to the original amount of the *ad valorem* duty. The Commissioners have a general right to remit the penalty, which they would probably exercise if there were a good reason for not having the document stamped, *e.g.* if it had got lost in the post.

Foreign Documents. The documents which require stamping are all documents executed in the United Kingdom, and any document executed abroad which relates to any property situate in the United Kingdom or to any matter or thing done or to be done in the United Kingdom. So, for example, a document transferring property situate out of the United Kingdom will require stamping if it is executed in the United Kingdom, but will not require stamping if it is executed out of the United Kingdom. A document transfering property situate in the United Kingdom will require stamping even it it is executed abroad. A document executed abroad, however, which does require stamping, because it relates to property in the United Kingdom, or requires things to be done in the United Kingdom, need not be stamped until 30 days after it is brought to the United Kingdom (ss. 14 and 15). Documents stamped in Northern Ireland or the Irish Republic do not require additional stamps in Great Britain unless the duty chargeable in Great Britain is higher than the Irish duty. Similarly, documents stamped in Great Britain are available in Northern Ireland without further stamps, unless the Northern Ireland duty is higher.

Transfers of Shares and Debentures. As already stated, a secretary is particularly concerned with the stamp duty on transfers of shares and debentures of the company, for he commits an offence if he registers a transfer not duly stamped. This duty is an example of the general *ad valorem* duty at 2 per cent., which applies to transfers of almost all types of property on a sale or gift. Accordingly, on a sale of shares or debentures, duty is payable, calculated at 2 per cent. (in round figures) on the purchase price. The precise duty for various prices is given in Appendix A, which shows how the 2 per cent. figure is rounded off. In an ordinary case the price will be stated in the transfer and the secretary, before registering the transfer, will have to see that the stamp appropriate to the price has been impressed. It often happens, especially with stock exchange securities, that the original purchaser resells to a third person before the actual transfer, and there may be a succession of resales, with only one transfer from the original vendor to the final purchaser. In such a case the stamp duty is properly calculated on the price paid by the final purchaser, and this price should appear in the transfer.

There is not, on a transfer of shares or debentures, as would be the case with most transfers on sale, any reduction in the rate for small transactions. There is, however, an exemption under s. 54 (1) of the Finance Act, 1947, on a transfer to a body of persons established for charitable purposes only or to the trustees of a trust so established, the rate in such case being half only of the ordinary rate; since, however, a transfer, to come within the exemption, must have been adjudicated and bear an adjudication stamp, the secretary will not be concerned to see whether a particular transfer does or does not fall within this exemption. There is a further exemption under the Finance Act, 1920, s. 42, where shares or debentures are transferred on a sale to a dealer, that is to say, a member of a stock exchange in the United Kingdom who is recognised by the committee of that exchange as carrying on business as a dealer (Finance Act, 1931, s. 42). A transfer within this exemption will bear a supplemental stamp denoting that it has been stamped under the provisions of the section, so that again the secretary will not be concerned to see that the transferee is a dealer. Where the transfer falls within the section, the maximum duty chargeable is ten shillings, though of course the stamp will fall below ten shillings if the sale price is £25 or less. Finally, there are exemptions on transfers between associated companies or on reconstruction which are discussed later, but here again the transfer must be adjudicated, and the secretary will not be concerned to see that the case falls within the exemption.

Any voluntary transfer of shares or debentures *inter vivos*, **Voluntary** for example, a transfer effecting a gift of shares, requires to be **Transfer** stamped at the same *ad valorem* rate as a transfer on sale, *inter vivos.* except that the amount is calculated on the value of the shares or debentures and not by reference to the price paid [Finance (1909–10) Act, 1910, s. 74]. Subject to the exceptions mentioned below, any transfer of shares or debentures other than a transfer on sale falls within this section; and the stamp duty will be calculated on the value of the shares or debentures in any case where the Commissioners consider that the actual consideration is inadequate, so that the transfer conveys a substantial benefit on the transferee. So, for example, if a transfer is made for a nominal consideration or for something substantially less than the market price, and thereby results in a partial gift, it will require to be stamped *ad valorem* under this section on the actual value of the shares or debentures transferred. A transfer required to be stamped under this section is not, however, deemed duly stamped unless it has been adjudicated and bears an adjudication stamp. Theoretically, therefore, the secretary should require adjudication in any case where a transfer of shares is made as a gift. In practice, as stated in the Inland Revenue Circular in Appendix A, if a transfer by way of a gift is stamped with the full *ad valorem* duty calculated on the current market price of the shares or debentures, the secretary is permitted to accept it, since he could obtain adjudication later if it were necessary. He should, of course, only do so when the shares are quoted on a stock exchange, so that there is no doubt about the market price; a transfer by way of gift of shares which are not quoted should always be adjudicated. There are important exceptions to this section as mentioned in the next paragraph, but meanwhile the effect of the foregoing provisions may be noted so far as concerns the secretary's duty as registrar. A transfer will ordinarily state the price or else will state a nominal consideration. If it states a nominal consideration, then, unless it falls within one of the exceptions mentioned below, it requires to be adjudicated, and if this has not been done when the secretary sees it, he should return it for adjudication, unless, as stated above, it is in fact stamped on the full and recognised market price. If it states a substantial price and is stamped with the duty appropriate to that price, it can be accepted by the secretary as a transfer on sale, unless he has reason to think that it is not in fact a transfer on sale for full consideration. He may, for example, have personal information which leads him to think this, or the amount of the price may be so much below the ordinary market price of the shares that the transfer can hardly be part of a *bona fide* sale. In such a case he should ask for the transfer to be adjudicated.

The exceptions are stated in sub-s. (6) of s. 74 of the Finance (1909–10) Act, 1910, which reads as follows:—

'(6) A conveyance or transfer made for nominal consideration for the purpose of securing the repayment of an advance or loan or made for effectuating the appointment of a new trustee or the retirement of a trustee, whether the trust is expressed or implied, or under which no beneficial interest passes in the property conveyed or transferred, or made to a beneficiary by a trustee or other person in a fiduciary capacity under any trust, whether expressed or implied, or a disentailing assurance not limiting any new estate other than an estate in fee simple in the person disentailing the property, shall not be charged with duty under this section, and this sub-section shall have effect notwithstanding that the circumstances exempting the conveyance or transfer from charge under this section are not set forth in the conveyance or transfer.'

A transfer falling within this sub-section does not attract *ad valorem* duty, but must be stamped with a fixed duty of ten shillings. The procedure under this sub-section is explained in an Inland Revenue Circular (see Appendix A). The transfer will, in general, have been presented to the Revenue for stamping with the ten shillings duty, together with evidence that it falls within the exemption, the usual evidence being a certificate of the facts by a member of the stock exchange, a solicitor or a banker. On such presentation the marking officer of the Revenue will, if satisfied, mark the transfer or the certificate with the words 'transfer passed for 10s.' and his signature and stamp. The secretary can then safely register the transfer; if the certificate and not the transfer itself has been so marked, the secretary should retain it as evidence. In a case where a marking officer has not so certified, the onus is on the secretary to satisfy himself that the case falls within the exemption; if he is in doubt he should request the marking officer's certificate. If a secretary has special information leading him to think that the ten shilling stamp is not correct, he should require that the transfer be adjudicated, even if it has been passed by a marking officer.

It should be noted that by s. 54 of the Stamp Act, 1891, the expression 'conveyance on sale' includes every instrument and every decree or order of any court or the Commissioners whereby any property or any estate or interest in any property on the sale thereof is transferred to or vested in a purchaser or any other person on his behalf or on his direction. It is not, therefore, confined to a transfer of shares in the common form, but would include (for example) an order of the court vesting the shares in a purchaser; though in practice this particular example is unlikely to arise, since the ordinary vesting order of the court does not purport to transfer the shares, but only to vest a right to execute the transfer, so that there will normally be a further transfer which will be stamped.

There are provisions in the Stamp Act for calculating the appropriate stamp duty on a sale where, instead of a lump sum price, there is a consideration in the form of an annuity or in the form of transfer of stock, but these are unlikely to arise, since on a transfer of shares the consideration is nearly always stated as a lump sum.

There is provision in s. 115 of the Stamp Act, 1891, which **Composition** enables a company, by agreement with the Commissioners of **for Duty.** Inland Revenue, to compound for the duty on transfer of the stock of the company by paying a half-yearly or yearly composition fee. In practice, however, it is thought that the Commissioners do not now enter into such agreements and that the section is virtually a dead letter.

Statutory declarations, as for example, a declaration **Statutory** required as evidence before the issue of a duplicate share **Declarations.**

Allotment Letters, etc. certificate, formerly required a stamp. Allotment letters and letters of renunciation, proxies and scrip certificates also formerly required stamping. All these duties were, among others, abolished by the Finance Act, 1949.

Stamp Duty on other Documents. The Inland Revenue Circular printed in Appendix A sets out the rates of stamp duty on other documents with which the secretary is most likely to be concerned. It will be realised, however, that this book can deal with only a small part of the law of stamp duty. Most commercial documents attract some stamp duty, and on a large transaction it is advisable to obtain legal advice on what duty is payable; such advice is best obtained before the transaction is carried through, since there are sometimes several ways of effecting a transaction and one way may attract less stamp duty than another. Equally it is advisable for a secretary whose company habitually deals in certain types of documents to obtain legal advice on the duty which these particular documents attract. Some points arising on some common documents may now be noted.

Agreements. Agreements not otherwise chargeable with duty require a ten shilling stamp if under the company's seal and a sixpenny stamp (which may be a postage stamp) if not under seal. An agreement made informally by correspondence requires a sixpenny stamp, as much as a more formal agreement, and unless care is taken the stamping of such an informal agreement is apt to be forgotten.

Some of the commoner cases may be noted in which an agreement is chargeable under some other head with a duty greater than ten shillings or sixpence:

(i) An agreement which operates as a mortgage or charge on property will usually bear *ad valorem* duty either at the rates shown in Appendix A for 'Bonds, Debentures, Mortgages' or, in the case of an equitable mortgage, at a lower rate.

(ii) An agreement under seal to secure payment of a sum of money will usually be a bond or covenant and will be chargeable under the same head as is mentioned above.

(iii) An agreement, whether or not under seal, for the payment of an annuity or other periodical payments is chargeable with *ad valorem* duty under a special head 'Bond, Covenant, etc.' This head includes some rather unexpected cases, *e.g.* an agreement to pay yearly rent for hire of a telephone wire [*National Telephone Co.* v. *Commissioners* (1900), A.C. 1].

(iv) An agreement for a lease of land is usually chargeable with *ad valorem* duty as a lease.

(v) Agreements for the sale of property (other than chattels): if the agreement is to be followed by an actual transfer of the property, *e.g.* by a written conveyance or transfer, the agreement will for practical purposes be sufficiently stamped with the fixed duty of 10s. or 6d. If, however, it is proposed to rely on the agreement alone as transfering ownership, *ad valorem* duty at 2 per cent. will often be required.

The definition in the Stamp Act, 1891, of bills of exchange includes not only bills of exchange in the usual sense but also: **Bills of Exchange and Orders for Payment.**

(i) an order for the payment of money out of a particular fund which may or may not be available or upon any condition or contingency which may or may not happen; and

(ii) an order for the payment of money at stated periods; and

(iii) an order for payment of money which is sent to the person who is to pay and not to the person to be paid.

So, for example, an order directing regular subscriptions to be paid and an order to another person to make a payment out of any balance which may be due from him to the company (*Parsons* v. *Middleton*, 6 Hare 261), are bills of exchange payable on demand and require a twopenny stamp. It will be noted that an order by a creditor to his debtor to pay the debt to a third party, if sent to the third party, is regarded not as a bill of exchange but as an assignment; as such, it will usually be chargeable with *ad valorem* duty at 2 per cent.

The ordinary twopenny stamp on a receipt for £2 or more is familiar. The person who gives the receipt is liable to stamp it, and there are penalties for giving a receipt unstamped. There are certain exemptions, of which the most important is a receipt for any salary, pay or wages or like payment, paid to the holder of an office or employee in respect of his office or employment, or for money paid in respect of pension, superannuation allowance, compassionate allowance or like allowance (Finance Act, 1924, s. 36). This would cover, for example, a receipt for directors' fees or any wages or salary of a member of the company's staff. When such a receipt is given by cheque it is a convenient practice to mark the cheque: 'Receipt exempt from stamp duty under Finance Act, 1924, s. 36.' The remaining exemptions relate mainly to certain receipts given by banks and Government officials and receipts for purchase money or certain other payments contained in documents otherwise liable to stamp duty and duly stamped (Stamp Act, 1891, Schedule). A receipt for a gift to charity is in practice allowed exemption from duty. **Receipts.**

A receipt includes: 'any note, memorandum or writing whereby any money amounting to two pounds or upwards or any bill of exchange or promissory note for money amounting to two pounds or upwards is acknowledged or expressed to have been deposited, received or paid, or whereby any debt or demand, or any part of a debt or demand, of the amount of two pounds or upwards is acknowledged to have been settled, satisfied or discharged, or which signifies or imports any such acknowledgment, and whether the same is or is not signed by any person' (Stamp Act, 1891, s. 101). In particular it will be noted that the following are receipts requiring a stamp: an unsigned receipt; a letter acknowledging a cheque (since a cheque is a bill of exchange); an entry in a book against a figure on column of figures intended to acknowledge receipt, even if nothing more than initials are used (*A.G.* v. *Carlton Bank, Ltd.* (1899), 2 Q.B. 158]; or indeed any document given to the debtor with the intention of acknowledging receipt. An entry in a record of the creditor not given to the debtor does not require a stamp; under this principle an entry by a collector on an electricity prepayment card of the amount collected was held not to require a stamp, because the card, though kept on the consumer's premises, remained the company's property and was not therefore given to the debtor [*A.G.* v. *Northwood Electric Light & Power Co.* (1947), K.B. 511]. It is a penal offence, when a sum of £2 or more is paid, to avoid duty by giving more than one receipt each for less than £2 (Stamp Act, 1891, s. 103).

Capital Duty. Of the stamp duties more particularly connected with the company as a corporate body, the most important are duties on share capital at 10s. per cent. and on loan capital at 5s. per cent.

Share Capital. The duty on share capital is charged on the authorised capital of a limited liability company, regardless of whether the capital has been issued. It is payable when the company is formed, on its original capital, and subsequently, if the capital is increased, on the amount of the increase. The duty on increase of capital is, in the case of an ordinary company registered under the Companies Acts, payable fifteen days after the passing of the resolution which increases the capital. In a new chartered or statutory corporation the duty is normally payable one month after the company is formed or the increase of capital is authorised (Stamp Act, 1891, s. 113, and Finance Act, 1896, s. 12); but for such companies, so long as capital issues are controlled, the date for payment of duty, as regards any capital authorised by an Act or other instrument, is postponed until one month after the end of the year in which the capital is issued or the period of control ends, whichever first occurs (Finance Act, 1947, s. 59).

Where the capital of a company is reduced by cancelling

shares issued or unissued, and is simultaneously increased by
the creation of new shares, the practice of the Revenue is not
to charge capital duty on the increase of capital except in
so far as it exceeds the reduction. It is for this reason that
companies which reduce their capital usually create new
shares up to the original amount. There is a further important exemption from capital duty on the reconstruction or
amalgamation of companies, which is discussed later.

The duty at 5s. per cent. on loan capital is charged under **Loan**
the Finance Act, 1899, s. 8; as amended by the Finance Act, **Capital.**
1907, s. 10; the Finance Act, 1934, s. 29; and the Finance
Act, 1947, s. 52. It is payable by all companies and also by
a number of other bodies such as municipal authorities. It
applies not only to debenture stock but to any capital which
is borrowed, or has the nature of borrowed money, but only
if the capital is of such a description as to be capable of being
dealt with on a stock exchange in the United Kingdom.
Moreover, it is not chargeable where stamp duty in respect of
a mortgage or marketable security has been paid on a trust
deed or other document securing the loan capital. It is the
duty of the company to deliver a statement to the Commissioners, before the capital is issued, and to stamp that statement.

When loan capital is applied for the purpose of converting or
consolidating existing loan capital, repayment to the company
is made at the rate of 4s. per cent. (Finance Act, 1907, s. 10;
Finance Act, 1947, s. 52).

The rates of duty on debentures and share warrants to **Debentures**
bearer are stated in Appendix A.   **and Share**
                                                         Warrants
                                                         to Bearer.

Important exemptions from stamp duty on the reconstruc- **Reconstruc-**
tion or amalgamation of companies are given by the Finance **tion and**
Act, 1927, s. 55, as amended by the Finance Act, 1928, s. 31. **Amalga-**
The statutory provisions are printed in Appendix J, to which **mation.**
reference should be made. It will be seen that the exemption,
when it applies, covers both the *ad valorem* duty (which would
normally be 2 per cent.) on the transfer of shares and assets
involved, and also capital duty on the share capital of the
company to which transfer is made, to the extent to which
duty has been paid on the capital of the existing company.
When the transaction involves the issue of new shares to
existing shareholders, it is necessary, in order to comply with
the Finance Act, 1927, s. 55 (1) (c), that the issue should be
made to the existing shareholders themselves; issue to nominees of existing shareholders, by means of renounceable
allotment letters or otherwise, does not suffice [*Brotex Cellulose
Fibres Ltd.* v. *Commissioners* (1933), 1 K.B. 158; *Oswald
Tillotson* v. *Commissioners* (1933), 1 K.B. 134].

Transfers between Associated Companies. There is a further important exemption under the Finance Act, 1930, s. 42, as amended by the Finance Act, 1938, s. 50. It exempts from duty transfers of property between a parent company and its subsidiary or between two subsidiaries of the same parent company. To be within the exemption, the parent company must hold at least 90 per cent. of the issued share capital of the subsidiary, or both subsidiaries, as the case may be. The exemption does not apply if a third person (not being another associated company) has provided the consideration. A document for which the exemption is claimed must be adjudicated. The exemption only applies to the duty on transfers; it does not, for example, exempt from the ordinary fixed duties a receipt given by one associated company to another or a contract between two associated companies.

Liquidation. There is an exemption regarding various documents in a compulsory winding up or creditors' voluntary winding up under the Companies Act, 1948, s. 339, to which reference should be made.

When, in a liquidation, assets are distributed among shareholders in specie, the question arises whether the transfer of the assets to the shareholders requires the usual *ad valorem* duty at 2 per cent. The answer, it is thought, depends on whether the shareholder's right under the articles is to receive a particular sum of money or a proportion of the company's assets. A preference shareholder, for example, is usually entitled to repayment of his capital, that is, a sum of money; if he agrees to accept specific assets in satisfaction of this, there will usually be a notional sale and the transfer of the assets will attract *ad valorem* duty. An ordinary shareholder will usually be entitled simply to a share in the company's assets and not a particular sum of money; a transfer of specific assets to him will therefore usually be a transfer from a trustee to a beneficiary attracting only the fixed duty of ten shillings.

APPENDIX A

Table of Stamp Duties and Fees

Companies Act, 1948, Twelfth Schedule

FEES TO BE PAID TO THE REGISTRAR OF COMPANIES.

PART I.

TABLE OF FEES.

Matter in respect of which Fee is payable.	Amount of Fee.
For registration of a company limited by shares.	If the nominal capital does not exceed £2,000, the sum of £2.
	If the nominal capital exceeds £2,000 but does not exceed £5,000, the sum of £2 with the addition of £1 for each £1,000 or part of £1,000 of nominal capital in excess of £2,000.
	If the nominal capital exceeds £5,000 but does not exceed £100,000, the sum of £5 with the addition of 5s. for each £1,000 or part of £1,000 of nominal capital in excess of £5,000.
	If the nominal capital exceeds £100,000, the sum of £28 15s. 0d. with the addition of 1s. for each £1,000 or part of £1,000 of nominal capital in excess of £100,000.
For registration of a company not having a share capital.	If the number of members stated in the articles does not exceed 25, the sum of £2.
	If the number of members stated in the articles exceeds 25, but does not exceed 100, the sum of £2 with the addition of £1 for each 25 members or fraction of 25 members in excess of the first 25.
	If the number of members stated in the articles exceeds 100 but is not stated to be unlimited, the sum of £5 with the addition of 5s. for each 50 members or fraction of 50 members after the first 100.
	If the number of members is stated in the articles to be unlimited, the sum of £20.

Matter in respect of which Fee is payable.	*Amount of Fee.*
For registration of a company limited by guarantee and having a share capital or an unlimited company having a share capital.	The same amount as would be charged for registration if the company were limited by shares or the same amount as would be so charged if the company had not a share capital, whichever is the higher.
For registration of an increase in the share capital of any company.	An amount equal to the difference (if any) between the amount which would have been payable on first registration by reference to its capital as increased and the amount which would have been so payable by reference to its capital immediately before the increase.
For registration of an increase in the membership of a company limited by guarantee or an unlimited company.	An amount equal to the difference (if any) between the amount which would have been payable on first registration by reference to its membership as increased and the amount which would have been so payable by reference to its membership immediately before the increase.
For registration of any existing company except such companies as are by this Act exempted from payment of fees in respect of registration under this Act.	The same amount as is charged for registering a new company.
For registering any document by this Act required or authorised to be registered or required to be delivered, sent or forwarded to the Registrar other than the memorandum or the abstract required to be delivered to the Registrar by a receiver or manager, the statement required to be sent to the Registrar by the liquidator in a winding up in England or a document required to be delivered under section four hundred and sixteen of this Act.	Five shillings.

*Matter in respect of
which Fee is payable.*   *Amount of Fee.*

For making a record of any   Five shillings.
fact by this Act required
or authorised to be re-
corded by the Registrar.

PART II.
LIMITATIONS ON OPERATION OF PART I.

1.   Where in the case of a company limited by guarantee and
having a share capital or an unlimited company having a share
capital, an increase of share capital is made at the same time as
an increase of membership, the company shall pay whichever fee
is the higher, but not both.

2.   The total of the fees payable by any company by reference
to its membership shall in no case exceed twenty pounds.

3.   The total of the fees payable by any company by reference
to its share capital or of the fees payable by it by reference to its
membership and the fees payable by it by reference to its share
capital, shall in no case exceed fifty pounds.

The following table sets out the stamp duties and fees payable
on registration of a company having a share capital.

Nominal share capital.	Ad valorem duty on statement of capital. (10/- per cent.)			Fee stamps on memorandum of association.			Total, including 10s. deed stamp on memorandum, 15s. deed and fee stamps on articles, and 5s. each on the following:— (1) Declaration of compliance. (2) List of persons who have consented to be directors (b). (3) Directors' consent to act (b). (4) Contract to qualify, if there is any qualification (a), (b), (c).		
£	£	s.	d.	£	s.	d.	£	s.	d.
100		10	0	2	0	0	4	15	0
500	2	10	0	2	0	0	6	15	0
1,000	5	0	0	2	0	0	9	5	0
1,500	7	10	0	2	0	0	11	15	0
2,000	10	0	0	2	0	0	14	5	0
3,000	15	0	0	3	0	0	20	5	0
4,000	20	0	0	4	0	0	26	5	0
5,000	25	0	0	5	0	0	32	5	0
6,000	30	0	0	5	5	0	37	10	0
7,000	35	0	0	5	10	0	42	15	0
8,000	40	0	0	5	15	0	48	0	0
9,000	45	0	0	6	0	0	53	5	0
10,000	50	0	0	6	5	0	58	10	0
11,000	55	0	0	6	10	0	63	15	0

(a), (b), (c)—See footnote to next page.

Q

Nominal share capital.	Ad valorem duty on statement of capital. (10/- per cent.)			Fee stamps on memorandum of association.			Total, including 10s. deed stamp on memorandum, 15s. deed and fee stamps on articles, and 5s. each on the following:— (1) Declaration of compliance. (2) List of persons who have consented to be directors (b). (3) Directors' consent to act (b). (4) Contract to qualify, if there is any qualification (a), (b), (c).		
£	£	s.	d.	£	s.	d.	£	s.	d.
12,000	60	0	0	6	15	0	69	0	0
13,000	65	0	0	7	0	0	74	5	0
14,000	70	0	0	7	5	0	79	10	0
15,000	75	0	0	7	10	0	84	15	0
16,000	80	0	0	7	15	0	90	0	0
17,000	85	0	0	8	0	0	95	5	0
18,000	90	0	0	8	5	0	100	10	0
19,000	95	0	0	8	10	0	105	15	0
20,000	100	0	0	8	15	0	111	0	0
25,000	125	0	0	10	0	0	137	5	0
30,000	150	0	0	11	5	0	163	10	0
35,000	175	0	0	12	10	0	189	15	0
40,000	200	0	0	13	15	0	216	0	0
45,000	225	0	0	15	0	0	242	5	0
50,000	250	0	0	16	5	0	268	10	0
60,000	300	0	0	18	15	0	321	0	0
70,000	350	0	0	21	5	0	373	10	0
80,000	400	0	0	23	15	0	426	0	0
90,000	450	0	0	26	5	0	478	10	0
100,000	500	0	0	28	15	0	531	0	0
125,000	625	0	0	30	0	0	657	5	0
150,000	750	0	0	31	5	0	783	10	0
175,000	875	0	0	32	10	0	909	5	0
200,000	1,000	0	0	33	15	0	1,036	0	0
250,000	1,250	0	0	36	5	0	1,288	10	0
300,000	1,500	0	0	38	15	0	1,541	0	0
400,000	2,000	0	0	43	15	0	2,046	0	0
500,000	2,500	0	0	48	15	0	2,551	0	0
600,000	3,000	0	0	50	0	0	3,052	5	0
700,000	3,500	0	0	50	0	0	3,552	5	0
800,000	4,000	0	0	50	0	0	4,052	5	0
900,000	4,500	0	0	50	0	0	4,552	5	0
1,000,000	5,000	0	0	50	0	0	5,052	5	0

(a) Required only when not signed for in memorandum.
(b) Not required in the case of a private company.
(c) Stamp duty of 6d. on each contract if qualification is £5 or upwards in value.

And so on at the rate of ten shillings further capital duty on every £100 or fraction of £100.

In addition to the documents mentioned in the last column, the following, if not filed on registration, must be filed prior to commencing business: copy register of directors, notice of registered office, and prospectus or statement in lieu of prospectus (*b*) (see previous page). Fee 5*s*. each.

Before a company which files a prospectus or statement in lieu (*i.e.* not a private company) can commence business, it must comply with s. 109 by filing the declaration therein mentioned and obtain the Registrar's certificate.

It may be noted that the fee for registering a mortgage or charge not exceeding £200 is 10/- and exceeding £200 is £1.

NOTES.

1. *Colonial and foreign companies.*—All transfers of shares executed in the United Kingdom are liable to stamp duty [*Wright* v. *Commissioners of Inland Revenue*, 11 Exch. 48].

2. *Stamping after execution.*—The instrument, unless it is written upon duly stamped material, is to be duly stamped with the proper *ad valorem* duty before the expiration of thirty days after it is first executed, or after it has been first received in the United Kingdom, in case it is first executed at any place out of the United Kingdom.

In view of the risk of loss in transit of a stamped document, the Board of Inland Revenue allow transfers and other documents first executed in this country, and then sent to the colonies or abroad for completion and return, to be stamped on due proof to the satisfaction of the Board's Officer that they are presented for stamping within thirty days of their return to the United Kingdom.

3. *Renewal of Bonds, etc.*—Where bonds, debentures, or other similar securities maturing at a fixed date are renewed during the currency thereof, the memorandum or instrument of renewal is chargeable, if under hand only, with the duty of sixpence, or if under seal, with the duty of ten shillings, or with the duty of sixpence for every £100 of the amount secured, if such duty would not amount to so much as ten shillings.

4. *Contract Notes.*—The following stamp duty is levied on contract notes.

Where the value of the stock or marketable security—

						£	s.	d.
Is	£5 and does not exceed	£100	..	0	1	0
Exceeds	£100	"	"	£500	..	0	2	0
"	£500	"	"	£1,000	..	0	4	0
"	£1,000	"	"	£1,500	..	0	6	0
"	£1,500	"	"	£2,500	..	0	8	0
"	£2,500	"	"	£5,000	..	0	12	0
"	£5,000	"	"	£7,500	..	0	16	0
"	£7,500	"	"	£10,000	..	1	0	0
"	£10,000	"	"	£12,500	..	1	4	0
"	£12,500	"	"	£15,000	..	1	8	0
"	£15,000	"	"	£17,500	..	1	12	0
"	£17,500	"	"	£20,000	..	1	16	0
"	£20,000	..	..	..	..	2	0	0

INLAND REVENUE CIRCULARS RELATING TO
STAMP DUTIES

I

INLAND REVENUE,
SOMERSET HOUSE,
LONDON, W.C.2.
August, 1949.

The Board of Inland Revenue furnish the following information regarding the Stamp Duties with which Secretaries, Registrars and other Officers of Companies are most usually concerned.

Secretaries of Companies and others whose office it is to register or enter any instrument chargeable with Stamp Duty are required to see that such instrument is properly stamped before registration or entry. In any case of doubt the Commissioners of Inland Revenue may be asked to adjudicate upon and assess the Duty under the provisions contained in s. 12 of the Stamp Act, 1891, and officers responsible for registering instruments should suggest that applicants have recourse to this step whenever it appears to be in any way desirable.

Any person, being the proper officer to enrol, register, or enter in or upon any rolls, books, or records any instrument chargeable with any Duty, who enrols, registers, or enters any such instrument not being duly stamped, is liable to a fine of £10.

Persons executing instruments in which all the facts and circumstances affecting their liability to Duty, or the amount of such Duty, are not fully stated, or who, being employed or concerned in the preparation of any instrument, neglect to set forth such facts and circumstances, are liable to a fine of £10.

The duties are required to be denoted by impressed stamps, except in the following cases:—

Foreign Bills .:	Adhesive 'Bill' stamps must be affixed and cancelled before payment, endorsement or negotiation.
Agreements under hand (6*d.*) .. .. Bill of Exchange on demand (2*d.*) .. Fire, Accident, etc., Insurance Policy (6*d.*) Receipts (2*d.*)	Adhesive postage stamps may be used. Such stamps must be effectively cancelled by the person first executing the instrument.

Stamps of other countries are not recognised except the stamps of Northern Ireland and The Irish Republic. Instruments executed and stamped in either of these countries are deemed to be duly stamped in this country provided the amount of the stamp is not less than the amount chargeable on the instrument in this country.

	£	s.	d.
ACCIDENT INSURANCE POLICY	0	0	6
AGREEMENT not otherwise charged with Duty, under hand only or without clause of registration ..	0	0	6

	£	s.	d.
AGREEMENT not otherwise charged with Duty, under Company's seal or with clause of registration ..	0	10	0
BILL OF EXCHANGE (CHEQUE), payable on demand or at sight or on presentation or within three days after date or sight	0	0	2

BILL OF EXCHANGE and PROMISSORY NOTE, drawn or expressed to be payable in Great Britain and Northern Ireland—

	£	s.	d.
Not exceeding £10	0	0	2
Exceeding £10 but not exceeding £25	0	0	3
„ £25 „ „ £50	0	0	6
„ £50 „ „ £75	0	0	9
„ £75 „ „ £100	0	1	0
„ £100, for every £100 or part ..	0	1	0

BILL OF EXCHANGE, drawn and expressed to be payable out of Great Britain and Northern Ireland and actually paid, endorsed or negotiated in Great Britain and Northern Ireland—

	£	s.	d.
Not exceeding £10	0	0	2
Exceeding £10 but not exceeding £25	0	0	3
„ £25 „ „ £100	0	0	6
„ £100, for every £100 or part ..	0	0	6

BONDS, DEBENTURES, MORTGAGES AND OTHER SECURITIES.*

I.—Registered and transferable only by instrument of transfer—

	£	s.	d.
Where the amount secured does not exceed £10 ..	0	0	6
Exceeds £10 and does not exceed £25.. ..	0	1	4
„ £25 „ „ £50.. ..	0	2	6
„ £50 „ „ £100.. ..	0	5	0
„ £100 „ „ £150.. ..	0	7	6
„ £150 „ „ £200.. ..	0	10	0
„ £200 „ „ £250.. ..	0	12	6
„ £250 „ „ £300.. ..	0	15	0
„ £300, for every £100, and also for any fractional part of £100 of such amount	0	5	0
If given in substitution for a duly stamped security, whether registered or to bearer, for every £100, or part .. .. (Maximum duty 10s.)	0	1	0

II.—Transferable by delivery (Bearer Securities) :—

	£	s.	d.
(a) Repayable within not more than one year, for every £10, or part, of amount secured	0	1	0
(b) Repayable within not more than three years, for every £10, or part, of amount secured	0	2	0
(c) Repayable at a time exceeding three years, for every £10, or part, of amount secured	0	8	0
(d) If given in substitution for one duly stamped under (c), for every £20, or part	0	4	0

* The duty on a collateral security (other than an equitable mortgage) is 6d. for every £100 or part thereof of the amount secured.

A bearer security given in substitution for a registered security requires the full duty of eight shillings for every £10, or part.

The term 'amount secured' includes in certain circumstances any bonus or premium covenanted to be paid when the bonds or debentures are redeemed. For instance, a bond of £100 which secures the payment of the £100 with a premium of £5 must be stamped for £105, unless such premium is payable only in consequence of some voluntary act of the Company. This rule applies alike to original and substituted securities.

Where Debentures are re-issued under the provisions of s. 90 of the Companies Act, 1948, either by the re-issue of the same Debentures or by the issue of other Debentures in their place, such re-issued Debentures fall to be treated as new Debentures for the purposes of Stamp Duty, and the full *ad valorem* Duty is payable thereon. Similarly, if Debenture Stock is re-issued, further duty is payable either on the trust deed or by way of Loan Capital Duty.

In the case of substituted Securities of any description chargeable with a reduced rate of Duty, the Duty can only be impressed thereon upon presentation of both the original and substituted Securities at a date prior to the expiration of the original Securities. When registered Securities have changed hands, the transfers must be produced for inspection.

	£	s.	d.
CAPITAL (SHARE), per £100 or part of £100 nominal..	0	10	0

A stamped statement of the amount which is to form the nominal share capital of any Company to be registered with limited liability under the Companies Act, 1948, is to be delivered to the Registrar of Companies before the Company is registered. In the case of any increase of nominal share capital a statement must be delivered, duly stamped, within 15 days of the resolution of the Company authorising the increase.

	£	s.	d.
FIRE INSURANCE POLICY	0	0	6
LOAN CAPITAL, per £100 or part of £100	0	5	0

(Subject to deduction of 4s. for each £100 which is applied in conversion or consolidation of existing Loan Capital.)

	£	s.	d.
MARINE INSURANCE POLICY.			

I.—Where the premium or consideration does not exceed the rate of 2s. 6d. per centum of the sum insured

	£	s.	d.
insured	0	0	1

Where the premium or consideration is expressed to be a sum not exceeding the rate of half-a-crown per cent., and is subject to an increase (whether defined or not in the policy) in the event of the occurrence of a specified contingency, it shall be treated as one not exceeding the rate of half-a-crown per cent. But if, owing to the occurrence of the contingency, the premium or consideration is increased so as to exceed the rate of half-a-crown per cent., the policy or a new policy to be thereupon issued shall be stamped with the additional duty payable and may be so stamped without penalty at any time not exceeding thirty days after the date on which the increased premium or consideration becomes ascertained.

II.—In any other case:—

	£	s.	d.
(a) For or upon any voyage:—			
Where the sum insured does not exceed £250	0	0	3
Where the sum exceeds £250 but does not exceed £500	0	0	6
Where the sum exceeds £500 but does not exceed £750	0	0	9
Where the sum exceeds £750 but does not exceed £1,000	0	1	0
Where the sum exceeds £1,000, for every £500 or fractional part of £500 ..	0	0	6

(b) For time:—

Where the insurance is made for any time not exceeding six months a duty equivalent to three times the above amounts.

Where the insurance is made for any time exceeding six months but not exceeding twelve months a duty equivalent to six times the above amounts.

A policy of insurance on baggage or personal and household effects only, if made or executed out of Great Britain, is exempt from stamp duty.

	£	s.	d.
POWER OF ATTORNEY, or other instrument in the nature thereof:—			
For the receipt of the Dividends or Interest of any Stock:—			
Where made for the receipt of *one* payment only	0	1	0
In any other case connected with the receipt of Dividends or Interest	0	5	0
General	0	10	0

An order, request, or direction under hand only from the proprietor of any stocks or shares to any Company or to any officer of any Company or to any banker to pay the dividends or interest arising therefrom to any person therein named is not chargeable with duty.

	£	s.	d.
RECEIPT given for or upon payment of £2 or more ..	0	0	2
SHARE WARRANT AND STOCK CERTIFICATE TO BEARER—			
Issued under the provisions of the Companies Acts—three times the *ad valorem* Duty chargeable on a Transfer for a consideration equal to the nominal value of the Shares or Stock.			
Issued by colonial and foreign companies, per £10	0	8	0

TRANSFER on sale or operating as a Voluntary Disposition *inter vivos* of Stock, Shares or Marketable Securities where the amount or value of the consideration for the sale (or, in the case of Voluntary Disposition *inter vivos*, the value of the property) does not exceed £5 .. ..   0 2 0

Exceeds		and does not exceed			£	s	d
£5			£10	..	0	4	0
" £10	"	"	£15	..	0	6	0
" £15	"	"	£20	..	0	8	0
" £20	"	"	£25	..	0	10	0
" £25	"	"	£50	..	1	0	0
" £50	"	"	£75	..	1	10	0
" £75	"	"	£100	..	2	0	0
" £100	"	"	£125	..	2	10	0
" £125	"	"	£150	..	3	0	0
" £150	"	"	£175	..	3	10	0
" £175	"	"	£200	..	4	0	0
" £200	"	"	£225	..	4	10	0
" £225	"	"	£250	..	5	0	0
" £250	"	"	£275	..	5	10	0
" £275	"	"	£300	..	6	0	0

" £300, for every £50, and also for any fractional part of £50 of such amount or value 1 0 0

'Marketable Security' includes the registered Bonds and Debentures, generally, of Companies, Corporations and Public Bodies.

A transfer of any Stock, Shares or Marketable Security operating as a Voluntary Disposition *inter vivos*, is chargeable with *ad valorem* stamp duty at the above rates on the value of the property transferred. No such transfer is duly stamped unless it bears the Adjudication Stamp of the Commissioners of Inland Revenue. Registering Officers should therefore decline to register any transfers *inter vivos* by way of gift, unless they bear the Adjudication Stamp. An exception may, however, be made where the transfers are stamped with *ad valorem* duty upon the market value of the Stock or Securities at the date of the instrument, it being open to the Registering Officer to obtain the Adjudication Stamp at any time subsequently, should necessity arise.

By s. 42 of the Finance Act, 1920, special provision is made for the case of transfers to a dealer on a Stock Exchange, as therein defined, or his nominee, when the transaction to which the transfer relates has been carried out by the dealer in the ordinary course of his business. Such transfers are sufficiently stamped with 10s., if, in addition to that duty, they bear the special supplementary stamp under the terms of the Section, and should in no circumstances be registered unless they bear this stamp.

A transfer made in liquidation of a debt or in exchange for other Securities attracts *ad valorem* Duty.

Transfers executed under seal, by way of Mortgage, of any Stock, Shares or Marketable Security, are chargeable, if the loan be disclosed in the Instrument of Transfer, according to

the scale set forth under the head 'Bonds and Debentures.'
If the loan be not disclosed in the Transfer, and the transaction is disclosed by a further instrument, the further
instrument, if under hand only, is chargeable with the duty
of 6*d.* or if under seal is chargeable according to the said
scale, and in either case the Transfer is chargeable with a
duty of 10*s.*

A transfer made to a body of persons established for
charitable purposes only, or to the trustees of a trust so
established, is excepted from the increased *ad valorem* duty
imposed by the Finance Act, 1947, and remains liable at the
rate in force immediately before 1st August, 1947. A
transfer stamped at that rate is not, however, duly stamped
unless it bears the Adjudication Stamp of the Commissioners
of Inland Revenue. Registering Officers should decline to
register such a transfer stamped at the lower rate unless it
bears the Adjudication Stamp.

	£	s.	d.
TRANSFER of any other kind .. .. fixed duty	0	10	0

Included under this head are Transfers for nominal consideration within any of the following categories:—

(a) Transfers vesting the property in trustees on the appointment of a new trustee of a pre-existing trust, or on the
retirement of a trustee.

(b) Transfers, where no beneficial interest in the property
passes, (i) to a mere nominee of the transferor, (ii) from
a mere nominee of the transferee, (iii) from one nominee
to another nominee of the same beneficial owner.

(c) Transfers by way of security for a loan or re-transfer to
the original transferor on repayment of a loan.

(d) Transfer to a residuary legatee of stock, etc., forming
part of the residue divisible under a will.

(e) Transfers to a beneficiary under a will of a specific legacy
of stock, etc. (*Note.*—Transfers by executors in discharge, or partial discharge, of a pecuniary legacy are
chargeable with *ad valorem* duty on the amount of the
legacy so discharged.)

(f) Transfers of stock, etc., forming part of an intestate's
estate to the person entitled to it.

(g) Transfers to a beneficiary under a settlement on distribution of the trust funds of stock, etc., forming the share or
part of the share of those funds to which the beneficiary
is entitled in accordance with the terms of the settlement.

(h) Transfers on the occasion of a marriage to trustees of
stocks, etc., to be held on the terms of a settlement made
in consideration of marriage.

(i) Transfers by the liquidator of a company of stocks, etc.,
forming part of the assets of the company to the persons
who were shareholders, in satisfaction of their rights on
a winding up.

The evidence necessary to establish that a transfer is liable
to the fixed duty of 10*s.* should take the form of a certificate

setting forth the facts of the transaction. In cases falling within (b) or (c) such a certificate should be signed by (1) both transferor and transferee or (2) a member of a Stock Exchange or a solicitor acting for one or other of the parties or (3) an accredited representative of a bank; in the last case when the bank or its official nominee is a party to the transfer, the certificate, instead of setting out the facts, may be to the effect that 'the transfer is excepted from s. 74 of the Finance (1909–10) Act, 1910.' A certificate in other cases should be signed by a solicitor or other person (e.g. a bank acting as trustee or executor) having a full knowledge of the facts.

Registering Officers will in any case in which a Marking Officer's certificate has not been given require such evidence in order to satisfy themselves that a transfer stamped with the 10s. fixed duty is duly stamped.

The Board's arrangements at a Stamp Office for the stamping of transfers provide for their Marking Officer requiring similar evidence when an executed transfer is presented to him for stamping with 10s. On his being satisfied with the evidence produced to him he will mark the transfer or the certificate containing the evidence with the words 'Transfer passed for 10s.' and his signature and office stamp. When such marking is made on the certificate the certificate will be returned to the person presenting the transfer in order that it may be available for production to the Registering Officer.

The Board will not hold a Registering Officer liable to any penalty under s. 17 of the Stamp Act, 1891, if he accepts a transfer for registration without questioning the sufficiency of the stamp when the transfer is thus certified by a Marking Officer or is accompanied by the evidence accepted and certified to be sufficient by the Marking Officer. In the latter case the Registering Officer should retain the evidence.

A Registering Officer may thus satisfy himself by requiring and examining the evidence on his own responsibility or he may require that the Marking Officer's official certificate be obtained.

It is possible that cases may arise in which the Registering Officer, in consequence of special information in his possession, or for some other good reason, is not satisfied that 10s. is the correct stamp notwithstanding that it has been passed by a Marking Officer. In such cases he may require that the transfer be formally presented for adjudication.

II

INLAND REVENUE,
SOMERSET HOUSE,
LONDON, W.C.2.
January, 1947.

ADJUDICATION OF STAMP DUTY—STAMP ACT, 1891, S. 12.

1. Executed instruments, the adjudication of which is desired, may be presented personally either at the office of the Controller of Stamps (Room 205, Bush House, South West Wing) or at the Stamp Office, 61, Moorgate, E.C.2, or at any of the following

Provincial Stamping Centres:—Birmingham, Richmond House, 84, Newhall Street; Bristol, 26, Baldwin Street; Cardiff, 96/97, St. Mary Street; Leeds, Carlton Chambers, 84, Albion Street; Liverpool, Cotton Exchange Buildings, Edmund Street; Manchester, 184, Deansgate; Newcastle-on-Tyne, 63, Westgate Road; Nottingham, Queen Street; and Sheffield, Revenue Buildings, 123, West Street. They may also be forwarded by post, addressed to:—

THE CONTROLLER OF STAMPS
(Adjudication Section),
INLAND REVENUE,
Bush House
(South West Wing),
London, W.C.2.

If documents are transmitted through the registered post, postage and registration fees are required to be paid by the applicant.

In all cases a plain copy or an accurate and complete abstract in usual conveyancing form must accompany the original instrument. Where a number of transfers of stocks, shares or marketable securities between the same parties are presented for adjudication, it will be sufficient to furnish a copy of one transfer and a list of the others, showing for each the consideration and the number and description of the shares or securities or the amount and description of the stock.

2. Instruments presented for adjudication will be kept with due care but the Commissioners give notice that they do not assume any responsibility with reference to any loss or damage which may be occasioned, either in transit or during detention. Original instruments will be returned after the adjudication has been completed. Copies and abstracts will not be returned.

3. With a view to the avoidance of the delay which must be caused by requisitions for further information, full and sufficient information to enable an assessment to be made should be furnished in the first instance, when the instrument is presented for adjudication.

The nature of the information usually necessary in the case of certain specified classes of instruments is indicated at the end of this Notice. It must, however, be understood that, in requesting this information, no ruling is intended as to how a particular case will be adjudicated.

If there is a particular matter in doubt upon which the opinion of the Commissioners is desired, and which is not apparent on the face of the instrument, special attention should be drawn to it when the instrument is presented for adjudication.

4. When the duty has been assessed, a notice of provisional assessment will be sent to the applicant, who if he agrees the amount should pay the duty in the manner directed by the Notice. The instrument will then be stamped with the duty assessed and with the Adjudication Stamp, and will be returned to the applicant, either personally, at Bush House in the case of deeds presented there, at the Stamp Office, Moorgate, or the appropriate Provincial Office in the case of deeds presented through these

Offices, or through the post, as may be arranged. It should be added that, if a remittance is by uncertified cheque, the usual period of clearance must elapse before the instrument can be stamped.

If the Commissioners consider that the instrument is already duly stamped, or is not liable to any duty, they will cause the Adjudication Stamp to be impressed and will return the instrument to the applicant.

5. If the applicant dissents from the proposed assessment he should submit a statement of his reasons for dissenting, and his view of the basis upon which the instrument should be stamped. He may, if he so desires, have an interview with the Adjudicating Officer by appointment.

If dissatisfied with the final assessment, the applicant may, within twenty-one days after the date of the assessment and on payment of duty in conformity therewith, appeal against the assessment to the High Court and may for that purpose require the Commissioners to state and sign a case.

By Order of the Board,

J. H. EVANS,

Secretary.

I.—AGREEMENT FOR SALE.

Where it is claimed that any part of the subject matter of the Agreement is exempt from *ad valorem* duty as falling within one or other of the exceptions contained in s. 59 of the Stamp Act, 1891 (*i.e.* as being a legal estate or interest in lands, tenements, hereditaments or heritages, or as being property locally situate out of the United Kingdom, or goods, wares or merchandise, or stock, or marketable securities, or any ship or vessel, or part interest, share, or property of or in any ship or vessel).

Furnish an apportionment of the consideration, giving separate values of the property coming within each of the heads in respect of which exemption is claimed. Where a Balance Sheet or Valuation is in existence, which shows the value of the several items of any of them to be as stated, this should accompany the Abstract.

Where the purchaser takes over or indemnifies the Vendor against debts and liabilities.

The amount of these should be stated, and included in the apportionment.

NOTE.—The value of all fixed plant and tenant's or trade fixtures should be separately stated from those articles which were, at the date of sale, in an actual state of severance.

II.—CONVEYANCE ON SALE.

Where the property is sold subject to a mortgage.

State the amount owing for principal (and interest, if any, if the purchaser undertakes payment thereof) at the date of the Conveyance.

Generally, if property is sold subject to, or in consideration of, the taking over or release of any debt or pecuniary liability.

State the amount thereof.

III.—CONVEYANCE OR TRANSFER (INCLUDING SETTLEMENT, DECLARATION OF TRUST, ETC.) OPERATING AS A VOLUNTARY DISPOSITION *inter vivos.*

Where the subject matter is land.

Furnish a full description of the property. The question of value will be referred to the Valuation Office.

Where the subject matter is stocks, shares or marketable securities.

Furnish a valuation as indicated below under the heading 'Settlement.' With a voluntary settlement, produce duly stamped transfers of any securities transferable by deed subject to stamp duty executed by the settlor in favour of the trustees. Where the securities have been vested in the trustees otherwise than by direct transfer from the settlor particulars should be given.

Where the subject matter is property of any other description, *e.g.* reversions, life policies, furniture.

Furnish details and reasonable evidence of value, and give the ages of the parties concerned where the subject matter is a reversion or a life interest.

IV.—CONVEYANCE OR TRANSFER ON ANY OCCASION EXCEPT SALE, MORTGAGE OR VOLUNTARY DISPOSITION.

If the Conveyance or Transfer is made on the occasion of the appointment of a New Trustee of an existing Trust.

Produce the Deed of Appointment.

If the Conveyance or Transfer is made for effectuating a settlement.

Produce the settlement.

V.—INSTRUMENT OF DISSOLUTION OF PARTNERSHIP, WHETHER AGREEMENT OR CONVEYANCE.

In all cases.

Produce a copy of the Balance Sheet or statement of account between the partners, showing—

(a) The amount of the liabilities (separating mortgages from current trade liabilities);

(b) The liquid assets (stock-in-trade, cash and book debts); and

(c) (If the fact is not disclosed by the instrument) the share of the outgoing partner in the partnership assets.

VI.—MORTGAGE, ETC.

NOTE.—A security for advances without limit cannot be adjudicated.

Where a Trust Deed secures payment of Debentures.

Produce the Debentures executed and duly stamped.

Where it is claimed that collateral, auxiliary, additional or substituted security duty only is payable.

Produce the principal or primary security, or other evidence that it is stamped with full duty.

VII.—TRANSFER OF MORTGAGE.

If the transfer is made on the occasion of the appointment of a New Trustee of an existing Trust.

Produce the Deed of Appointment.

In all cases.

State the amount of interest in arrear (if any) at the date of transfer.

VIII.—SETTLEMENT (IF NOT WITHIN HEADING III).

Where Stocks $\frac{and}{or}$ Securities are settled, whether in possession or reversion, and whether the interest settled is contingent or vested.

Furnish particulars of the Stocks and Securities if not specified in the Settlement and in any case produce a statement of the value of each of the several items as at date of Settlement—

(a) From prices quoted in any authorised Stock and Share List; or

(b) Where there is no quotation, based on the average of the latest private transactions, which can generally be obtained from the Secretary of the Company.

Where a share only in a reversionary interest in a Trust fund is settled.

In addition to the above particulars of the investments of the fund at the date of Settlement, state the Settlor's interest therein.

Where a Settlor covenants to settle other property which he may then have, but which is not specifically mentioned.

State whether the Settlor was at the date of the Settlement entitled in possession or reversion, or in default of the exercise of a power of appointment, to any money, stocks or shares not specified in the deed, and give as above particulars and value of such property.

Where the settled fund comprises a policy of life insurance:

(a) If the Settlement (or any other instrument) contains provision for keeping the policy on foot.

(a) State the amount of any bonuses added.

(b) If there is no such provision.

(b) Produce a certificate of the surrender value from the Insurance Company.

NOTE.—Particulars of the value of unsold landed property brought into Settlement, whether subject to a trust for sale or not, need not be furnished.

SPECIAL EXEMPTIONS.

Where it is claimed that an instrument is not chargeable with duty by reason of an exemption not arising under any Revenue Act.

State the section of the Act conferring the exemption, and give an explanation of the grounds for claiming that the instrument falls within it.

APPENDIX B

Documents to be Delivered to the Registrar of Companies under the Companies Act, 1948

Section.	Nature of Return.	When to be filed.
5 (7) (a)	Printed copy of altered memorandum.	Within 15 days from end of period for making application to court.
(7) (b) (i)	Notice of application to court to cancel alteration to memorandum.	Forthwith.
(ii)	Office copy of order cancelling or confirming alteration.	Within 15 days from date of order (subject to extension by court).
6	Articles of association, if company is limited by guarantee, or unlimited.	On application for registration.
7	Particulars of increase of members (unlimited company or company limited by guarantee).	Within 15 days after increase was resolved or took place.
12	Memorandum of association and articles, if any.	On application for registration.
30	Prospectus or statement in lieu of prospectus where company by alteration of articles ceases to be a private company.	Within 14 days after alteration.
41	Copy of prospectus (duly dated and signed) and accompanying documents.	On or before date of publication.
48	Statement in lieu of prospectus in certain cases.	At least three days before first allotment.
52	Return as to allotments and contract when shares allotted for consideration other than cash, or prescribed particulars of contract.	Within one month after allotment.

Section.	Nature of Return.	When to be filed.
53	Particulars of payment of commissions in the case of shares not offered to the public for subscription.	Before payment of commission.
62	Particulars of consolidation of share capital, conversion of shares into stock, reconversion of stock into shares, subdivision of shares, redemption of preference shares or cancellation of shares.	Within one month.
63	Notice of increase in share capital, prescribed particulars concerning classes of shares affected, and printed copy of resolution authorising increase.	Within 15 days of passing of resolution authorising increase.
69	Copy of order of court and of minute as to reduction of capital.	Before reduction can take effect.
72	Copy of order of court as to variation of shareholders' rights.	Within 15 days after making of order.
86	Notice of place where register (or duplicate) of holders of debentures is kept, and of change in place.	No time stated.
95 (1)	Particulars of charges together with instrument.	Within 21 days after date of creation.
(3)	Copy of instrument by which charge is created, if charge is created out of U.K. on property outside U.K.	Within 21 days after date on which instrument or copy could reasonably have been received in U.K.
(5)	If charge is on property in Scotland or N. Ireland, verified copy of instrument, together with certificate stating that charge was presented for registration in Scotland or N. Ireland.	On date of registration in Scotland or N. Ireland.
(8)	Particulars of amounts, dates of resolutions, description of property and names of trustees, on issue of series of debentures creating charge.	Within 21 days after execution of deed, or of any debentures of the series.

Section.	Nature of Return.	When to be filed.
97 (1)	Particulars of acquisition of land subject to a charge and copy of instrument by which charge was created.	Within 21 days of acquisition being completed.
	Particulars of acquisition of land outside Great Britain and of charge created outside Great Britain.	Within 21 days after date of copy of instrument could reasonably have been received in U.K.
102 (1)	Notice of appointment of receiver or manager.	Within 7 days from date of order or appointment.
(2)	Notice of ceasing to act as receiver or manager.	On so ceasing.
107	Notice of situation and changes of registered office.	Within 14 days of incorporation or of change.
109 (1)	Statutory declaration as to shares held for cash and directors' holdings.	Prior to commencing business or exercising borrowing powers.
(2)	Statement in lieu of prospectus.	Prior to commencing business or exercising borrowing powers.
110	Notice of place where register of members is kept and of any change in that place, unless register always has been kept at registered office.	Within 14 days of change.
116	Notice of rectification of register.	As directed by court.
119	Notice of situation, change of situation or discontinuance of dominion register.	Within 14 days of opening of office or change or discontinuance.
124, 126 & 127	Copy of annual return and summary (including certified copy of balance sheet, etc.) duly signed.	Within 42 days after the annual general meeting.
125	If no share capital, annual return as to address of registered office and directors and statement of indebtedness in respect of mortgages.	Within 42 days after the annual general meeting.

Section.	Nature of Return.	When to be filed.
128	Certificate as to non-issue of invitations to public if a private company and certificate that members in excess of 50 need not be included in reckoning.	With the annual return.
129	Additional certificate in case of exempt private company.	With annual return.
130	Copy of statutory report, if not a private company.	14 days before meeting.
131	Copy of resolution that general meeting be treated as annual general meeting.	Within 15 days of passing resolution.
143	Copy of ordinary resolution (in case of increase of capital) or of special or extraordinary resolution, etc.	Within 15 days after passing of resolution.
181 (1)	Consent and undertaking by director.	Before appointment.
(4)	List of persons who have consented to be directors.	On application for registration.
200	Names, addresses, nationality, occupations, other directorships held and date of birth of directors and any changes therein and name and address of secretary and any change therein.	Within 14 days from appointment of first directors or from any change.
206	Copy of order of court sanctioning compromise with creditors and members.	Before compromise can take effect.
208	Copy of order of court relating to amalgamations, etc.	Within 7 days after making of order.
210	Copy of alteration or addition to memorandum or articles under court order.	Within 14 days after making of order.
230	Copy of winding up order.	Forthwith.
240	Notification of appointment of liquidator (other than the official receiver) by the court.	Before he can act.
256	Copy of order of court to stay winding up proceedings.	Forthwith.

Section.	Nature of Return.	When to be filed.
274	Notification of order for dissolution.	Within 14 days of date of order.
283	Declaration of solvency in members' voluntary winding up.	Before date of passing of resolution winding up the company.
290 (3)	Copy of account of liquidation and return of holding of final meeting.	Within 7 days after meeting.
(5)	Copy of order of court deferring date of dissolution. (Members' voluntary winding up.)	Within 7 days after making order.
300 (3)	Copy of account of liquidation and return of holding of final meetings.	Within 7 days after date of meetings, or if not held on same day, after date of later meeting.
(5)	Copy of order of court deferring date of dissolution. (Creditors' voluntary winding up.)	Within 7 days after making order.
305	Notice by liquidator in voluntary winding up of his appointment.	Within 14 days after appointment.
307	Copy of order of court to stay voluntary winding up proceedings.	Forthwith.
342	Statement by liquidator of proceedings in and position of liquidation.	Prescribed intervals. (See Winding up Rules, 197.)
352	Copy of order of court declaring dissolution void.	Within 7 days after making of order.
353	Copy of court order made on application of aggrieved party restoring company to register.	No stated period.
355	Notice of disclaimer of Crown's title to property of dissolved company.	No stated time.
372 (1) (c)	Copy of statement and summary thereof on affairs of company.	Within two months of receipt of statement.

Section.	Nature of Return.	When to be filed.
372 (2)	Copy of abstract of receiver's receipts and payments.	Within 14 months of receiver's appointment, or such longer period as court allows, and thenceforward annually; within two months of receiver's ceasing to act.
374	Accounts of receivers and managers.	Within one month after the expiration of each 6 months and within one month after ceasing to act.
384, 385	List of members or directors, copy of instrument constituting company and other particulars.	Before registration.
386	Statutory declaration verifying lists of members and directors, and other particulars.	Before registration.
395	Printed copy of memorandum and articles substituted for deed of settlement by special resolution, altering form of constitution.	Within 15 days from date of resolution.
407	Companies incorporated outside Great Britain to deliver copy of charter, etc.	Within 1 month from establishment of place of business in Great Britain.
409	Notice of alteration in charter, directors, secretary or other particulars, by oversea company.	Within 21 days after date of alteration or 21 days after date on which notice could reasonably be received in Great Britain.
410	Copy of balance sheet and profit and loss account of oversea company.	Annually

Section.	Nature of Return.	When to be filed.
410	Companies registered in Northern Ireland, which, if registered in Great Britain, would be entitled to rank as a private company are exempt, if a certificate is sent, duly signed, that it would be an exempt private company.	No stated time.
413	Oversea company ceasing to have place of business in Great Britain.	Forthwith.
416	Company incorporated in Channel Islands or Isle of Man which establishes a place of business in England or Scotland to file documents as if registered in England or Scotland.	On establishment of place of business.
420	Copy of prospectus of issue of shares by company incorporated outside Great Britain.	Before circulation or distribution.
432	Statement of places of business of banking companies.	With annual return.

APPENDIX C

Penalties under the Companies Act, 1948

Section.	Offence.	Maximum Penalty.	Persons Liable.
5	Failure to deliver to Registrar copy of order of court as to alteration of memorandum.	£10 a day.	The company and every officer in default.
7	Failure to notify increase of members to Registrar where company has no share capital.	£5 a day.	The company and every officer in default.
18	Failure to change name on direction of Board of Trade.	£5 a day.	The company.
19	Failure to change name when Board of Trade licence to use words 'Chamber of Commerce' is revoked.	£50 a day.	The body in default.
24	Failure to supply on request, and on payment (if any), copy of memorandum and of articles (if any) and of any Act altering memorandum.	£1 for each offence.	The company and every officer in default.
25	Issue of copies of memorandum without embodying alterations when alterations to memorandum have been made.	£1 a copy.	The company and every officer in default.
30	Failure to deliver to Registrar prospectus or statement in lieu of prospectus where company by alteration of articles ceases to be a private company.	£50 a day.	The company and every officer in default.

Section.	Offence.	Maximum Penalty.	Persons Liable.
30	Untrue statement in statement in lieu of prospectus.	On indictment: imprisonment for 2 years and £500; on summary conviction: imprisonment for 3 months and £100.	Any person authorising delivery of statement for registration.
31	Carrying on business for more than six months with less than statutory number of members.	Liability for debts.	Every member cognisant of the facts.
38	Issuing application form without proper prospectus.	£500.	Person issuing.
40	Issuing prospectus containing statement by expert without his consent.	£500.	The company and every person knowingly a party to the issue.
41	Failure to deliver prospectus to Registrar before issue.	£5 a day until delivered.	The company and every person knowingly a party to issue of prospectus.
43, 45 & 42²	Untrue statement in prospectus or in offer for sale of shares or debentures.	Compensation to all subscribers.	Every director, every person named or consenting to be named as future director, every promoter and every person authorising issue of prospectus.[1]

[1] Liability is not incurred when a person has withdrawn his consent before issue, or if the prospectus is issued without his knowledge or consent and he immediately gives reasonable public notice, or if he withdraws his consent after the issue but before the allotment.
Where an expert has authorised the issue, he is only liable in respect of an untrue statement made by him as an expert.

Section.	Offence.	Maximum Penalty.	Persons Liable.
43, 45 & 422	Prospectus containing name of person as director or as having agreed to become a director, when person has not consented or has withdrawn his consent. Prospectus containing statement by expert without his consent.		Directors knowing and consenting to issue, and any person authorising issue.
44, 45 & 423	Mis-statements in prospectus.	On indictment: imprisonment for 2 years and £500; on summary conviction: imprisonment for 3 months and £100.	Any person authorising issue.
47	Allotment before minimum subscription received.	Repayment of application money with interest at 5% p.a. from expiration of 48th day.	The directors, jointly and severally.
48	Allotment before delivery of statement in lieu of prospectus in certain cases.	£100.	The company and every director knowingly and wilfully at fault.
	Untrue statement in statement in lieu of prospectus.	On indictment: imprisonment for 2 years and £500; on summary conviction: imprisonment for 3 months and £100.	Any person authorising delivery of statement.

Section.	Offence.	Maximum Penalty.	Persons Liable.
49	Allotment in contravention of s. 47 or s. 48.	Liability to compensate the company and allottee for loss, damages or costs.	Any director knowingly at fault.
50	Allotment of shares before 3 days after issue of prospectus.	£500.	The company and every officer in default.
51	Money not repaid within 8 days after the company becomes liable to repay.	Repayment of money with interest at 5% p.a.	The directors, jointly and severally.
52	Money received not kept in separate bank account.	£500.	The company and officers in default.
53	Failure to deliver return of allotments, etc.	£50 a day.	Every officer in default.
54	Failure to deliver statement in prescribed form as to commissions.	£25.	The company and officers in default.
57	Providing financial assistance for purchase of the company's shares.	£100.	The company and officers in default.
62	Failure to state in prospectus particulars of discount allowed on issue of shares.	£5 a day.	The company and officers in default.
63	Failure to give notice of consolidation, division, conversion, redemption or cancellation of shares, or of re-conversion of stock.	£5 a day.	The company and officers in default.
	Failure to notify increase of capital to Registrar.	£5 a day.	The company and officers in default.

Section.	Offence.	Maximum Penalty.	Persons Liable.
71	Concealing name of a creditor or misrepresenting his interests or aiding or abetting any such concealment or misrepresentation.	Prosecution for misdemeanour.	Every officer in default.
72	Failure to forward order of court as to variation of special rights.	£5 a day.	The company and officers in default.
78	Failure to send transferee notice of refusal to register transfer of shares, etc.	£5 a day.	The company and officers in default.
80	Failure to issue certificates for shares, etc., within 2 months after registration of allotment or transfer.	£5 a day.	The company and officers in default.
84	Personation of shareholder, etc.	Penal servitude for life.	Any person.
85*	In Scotland forging or altering or uttering, etc., share warrant.	Penal servitude for life.	Any person.
85*	As to engraving document purporting to be share warrant, etc., in Scotland.	Penal servitude for 14 years.	Any person.
87	Refusing inspection and copies of debenture register and trust deed.	£5 and £2 a day.	The company and officers in default.
96	Failure to register issue of debentures and charges created.	£50 a day.	The company and officers in default.
97	Failure to register mortgages and charges existing on property acquired.	£50 a day.	The company and officers in default.

* These offences in England are dealt with by the Forgery Act, 1913.

Section.	Offence.	Maximum Penalty.	Persons Liable.
99	Delivery of debenture not endorsed with certificate of registration.	£100.	Any person knowingly and wilfully authorising or permitting.
102	Failure to register appointment of receiver or manager, or to give Registrar notice on ceasing to act as receiver or manager.	£5 a day.	Any person in default.
104	Failure to make entry in register of charges.	£50.	Any officer knowingly and wilfully authorising or permitting.
105	Refusing inspection of register of mortgages and copies of instruments.	£5 and £2 a day.	Any officer refusing inspection.
107	Failure to notify to Registrar situation and change of registered office.	£5 a day.	The company and officers in default.
108	Failure to paint or affix name or to keep name painted or affixed.	£5 and £5 a day respectively.	The company and officers in default.
	Using seal or issuing documents without name of company.	£50 and liability to holders.	Any officer or person on behalf of company.
	Failure to have name legibly engraved on seal or in legible characters on all notices, etc.	£50.	The company.
109	Commencing business or exercising borrowing powers without obtaining minimum subscription, and without statutory declaration as to shares held for cash and directors' holdings, and statement in lieu of prospectus.	£50 a day.	Every person responsible for contravention.

Section.	Offence.	Maximum Penalty.	Persons Liable.
110	Failure to make statutory entries in register of members, and failure to notify the Registrar, when required, of place at which register is kept and of any change.	£5 a day.	The company and officers in default.
111	Failure to keep proper index of members.	£5 a day.	The company and officers in default.
112	Entry in register of members of name of bearer of share warrant without surrender and cancellation of warrant.	Liability for any loss incurred.	The company.
113	Refusal to allow inspection or give copy of register of members.	£2 and £2 a day.	The company and officers in default.
119	Failure to notify Registrar of situation, change in situation or discontinuance of dominion register.	£5 a day.	The company and officers in default.
120	Failure to transmit to registered office copy of entries in dominion register and to keep duplicate dominion register.	£5 a day.	The company and officers in default, or person at whose office principal register is kept, if in default.
124–6	Failure to make annual return of members and summary or, if no share capital, annual return as to directors, etc.	£5 a day.	The company and every officer in default, including any person in accordance with whose directions or instructions the directors are accustomed to act.
127	Failure to annex documents to annual return.	£5 a day.	The company and officers.

Section.	Offence.	Maximum Penalty.	Persons Liable.
130	Failure to hold statutory meeting and to circulate and deliver to Registrar statutory report.	£50.	Every director knowingly and wilfully guilty; in case of default by company, every officer in default.
131	Failure to hold annual general meeting.	£50	The company and every officer in default.
	Failure to forward copy of resolution to Registrar.	£2 a day.	The company and every officer in default.
132	Failure to convene meeting on requisition.	Liability to reimburse requisitionists' reasonable costs of convening meeting.	The company, with right of recovery from director(s) responsible.
136	Failure to mention entitlement to appoint proxy in notice calling meeting.	£50.	Every officer in default.
	Invitation to appoint proxies issued to some members only.	£100.	Every officer knowingly and wilfully authorising or permitting issue.
140	Failure to circulate copy of resolution to be moved or proposed at general meeting.	£500.	Every officer in default.
143	Failure to send copy of special or extraordinary resolution, etc., to Registrar.	£2 a day.	The company and officers (including the liquidator).
	Failure to embody special resolution, etc., in articles and to supply to members when required.	£1 a copy.	The company and officers (including the liquidator).

Section.	Offence.	Maximum Penalty.	Persons Liable.
145	Failure to enter minutes of proceedings of general meetings, directors' or managers' meetings.	£5 a day.	The company and officers.
146	Failure to allow inspection or give copies of minutes of general meetings to members.	£2 and £2 a day.	The company and officers.
147	Failure to keep proper books of account or otherwise to comply with section.	Imprisonment for 6 months or £200.	Any director wilfully at fault.
148	Failure to lay before annual general meeting profit and loss account and balance sheet.	Imprisonment for 6 months or £200.	Any director failing to take reasonable steps to comply.
149	Failure to comply with statutory provisions as to contents and form of accounts.	Imprisonment for 6 months or £200.	Any director failing to take reasonable steps to secure compliance.
150	Failure to lay group accounts before company in general meeting.	Imprisonment for 6 months or £200.	Any director failing to take reasonable steps to secure compliance.
155	Issuing balance sheet not properly signed.	£50.	The company and officers in default.
156	Issuing balance sheet without profit and loss account or auditors' report annexed.	£50.	The company and officers in default.
157	Failure to attach directors' report to every balance sheet.	Imprisonment for 6 months or £200.	Any director failing to take reasonable steps to comply.
158	Failure to circulate balance sheet.	£20.	The company and officers in default.
	Failure to furnish within 7 days of request balance sheet to members.	£5 a day.	The company and officers in default.

Section.	Offence.	Maximum Penalty.	Persons Liable.
159	Failure to give notice to Board of Trade that no auditor was appointed or re-appointed.	£5 a day.	The company and officers in default.
161	Body corporate acting as auditor.	£100.	The body corporate.
167 & 169	Failure to produce books and documents and answer questions in investigation.	Punishment as for contempt of court	Officers and agents refusing to comply.
173	Failure to give information concerning ownership of shares or debentures.	Imprisonment for 6 months and £500.	Any person so acting.
174	Exercising of rights over shares restricted by imposition of Board of Trade.	Imprisonment for 6 months and £500.	Any person so acting.
	Issue of shares in contravention of restriction.	£500.	The company and officers in default.
181	Delivery to Registrar of false list of consents to act as director.	£50.	The applicant for registration.
182	Acting as director after failure to obtain qualification within 2 months or shorter time if specified or after ceasing to hold qualification.	£5 a day.	Any person so acting.
186	Failure to give notice of age or to retire from directorship on reaching age limit.	£5 a day.	Any person so doing.
187	Undischarged bankrupt acting as director, etc., without leave of court.	On indictment: imprisonment for 2 years; on summary conviction: imprisonment for 6 months and £500.	Any person so acting.

Section.	Offence.	Maximum Penalty.	Persons Liable.
188	Contravention of order restraining fraudulent persons from managing companies.	On indictment: imprisonment for 2 years; on summary conviction: imprisonment for 6 months and £500.	Any person acting in contravention.
190	Failure to obtain approval of company to make loan.	Liability to indemnify company against loss.	Any directors authorising loan.
193	Failure to include in notice of offer made for shares particulars of compensation to directors for loss of office.	£25.	Any director and any person failing to take reasonable steps to include the particulars required by the section.
195	Failure to produce register of directors' shareholdings at annual general meeting.	£50.	The company and officers in default.
	Failure to keep register of directors' shareholdings and any transactions relating thereto.	£500 and £2 a day.	The company and officers in default.
	Refusal to permit inspection of register.	£500 and £2 a day.	The company and officers in default.
196–8	Failure to disclose remuneration of directors and loans to directors and officers.	£50.	The director or officer failing to disclose.
199	Failure by director to disclose interest in contracts.	£100.	The directors failing to disclose.

Section.	Offence.	Maximum Penalty.	Persons Liable.
200	Failure to keep register of directors and secretaries and send copy or notify changes to Registrar, or refusal to permit inspection.	£5 a day.	The company and officers in default.
201	Failure to state particulars as to directors in trade catalogues, etc.	£5.	Any officer, and where corporation is an officer of the company, any officer of the corporation.
202	Failure to add to proposal for election of director a statement that his liability is unlimited.	£100 and damages (if any).	The directors, managers and proposers.
	Failure to notify the fact of his unlimited liability to any director or manager appointed on that condition.	£100 and damages (if any).	The promoters, directors, managers and secretary.
206	Failure to deliver to Registrar and to annex to memorandum copy of order of court sanctioning compromise with creditors and members.	£1 a copy.	The company and officers in default.
207	Failure to disclose compromises with creditors and members.	£500.	The company and officers (to include liquidators and trustees of deed for securing issue of debentures).
	Failure to disclose personal matters necessary under this section.	£50.	The directors and the trustees for the debenture holders.
208	Failure to deliver to Registrar copy of order of court relating to amalgamation, etc.	£5 a day.	The company and officers in default.

Section.	Offence.	Maximum Penalty.	Persons Liable.
210	Failure to deliver copy of order of court making alteration or addition to memorandum or articles.	£5 a day.	The company and officers in default.
235	Failure after winding up order to submit to Official Receiver statement of affairs and affidavit.	£10 a day.	Any person in default.
	Untruthfully stating oneself to be a creditor or contributory.	Punishment for contempt of court.	Any person in default.
248	Liquidator retaining sum in excess of amount authorised.	Interest at 20% per annum on excess, payment of expenses, disallowance of remuneration, removal from office.	The liquidator.
274	Failure to report dissolution to Registrar.	£5 a day.	The liquidator.
279	Failure to advertise in *Gazette* resolution for voluntary winding up.	£5 a day.	The company and officers (including liquidator) in default.
283	Declaration of solvency on insufficient grounds.	Imprisonment for 6 months and £500.	Any director making declaration without reasonable grounds.
288	Failure to summon meeting of creditors in case of insolvency.	£50.	The liquidator.
289	Failure in voluntary winding up to call general meeting annually.	£10.	The liquidator.

Section.	Offence.	Maximum Penalty.	Persons Liable.
290	Failure to send to Registrar copy of account, and return of holding final meeting.	£5 a day.	The liquidator.
	Failure to deliver copy of order of court deferring date of dissolution.	£5 a day.	The person on whose application the order was made.
	Failure to call general meeting as required by section.	£50.	The liquidator.
293	Failure in creditors' voluntary winding up to advertise and hold meeting of creditors, or to lay statement, etc., before meeting or to appoint chairman or (when so appointed) to attend and preside thereat.	£100.	The company, directors and officers in default.
299	Failure in creditors' voluntary winding up to call general meeting annually.	£10.	The liquidator.
300	Failure in creditors' voluntary winding up to deliver to Registrar copy of account and holding of final meeting.	£5 a day.	The liquidator.
	Failure in creditors' voluntary winding up to deliver copy of order of court deferring date of dissolution.	£5 a day.	The person on whose application order was made.
	Failure in creditors' voluntary winding up to call general meeting of company or meeting of creditors when affairs of company finally wound up.	£50.	The liquidator.

Section.	Offence.	Maximum Penalty.	Persons Liable.
305	Failure to deliver notice of appointment as liquidator.	£5 a day.	The liquidator.
328	Various offences relating to the property of a company in liquidation.	On indictment: penal servitude for 5 years on summary conviction: imprisonment for 12 months.	Any past or present officer in default, including any person in accordance with whose directions or instructions the directors have been accustomed to act.
	Knowingly taking in pawn or pledge or receiving property of a company in liquidation obtained on credit.	In England, penal servitude for 7 years. In Scotland, on indictment: penal servitude for 7 years; on summary conviction: imprisonment for 6 months and £100.	Any person in default.
329	Falsification of books.	Imprisonment for 2 years with hard labour.	Any officer or contributory falsifying.
330	Frauds by officers of company in liquidation.	On indictment: imprisonment for 2 years; on summary conviction: imprisonment for 12 months.	Any officer in default.

Section.	Offence.	Maximum Penalty.	Persons Liable.
331	Failure to have kept proper books of account.	On indictment: imprisonment for 1 year; on summary conviction: imprisonment for 6 months.	Any officer in default.
332	Fraudulent trading.	On indictment: imprisonment for 2 years and £500.	Any person knowingly a party.
333	Delinquent directors.	Liability to restore money or property at interest rate fixed by court.	Promoters, past or present directors, manager, liquidator or any officer.
335	Body corporate acting as liquidator.	£100.	The body corporate.
336	Offer of consideration to secure appointment or nomination as liquidator.	£100.	Any person giving or offering consideration.
338	Failure to state on invoices, etc., that company being wound up or receiver or manager appointed.	£20.	The company, officers, liquidators, and receiver or manager.
341	Contravening rules of Board of Trade relating to books of dissolved company.	£100.	Any person so contravening.
342	Failure to send to Registrar statement of proceedings in liquidation at prescribed intervals.	£50 a day.	The liquidator.
352	Failure to deliver copy of order of court declaring dissolution void.	£5 a day.	The person on whose application order was made.

Section.	Offence.	Maximum Penalty.	Persons Liable.
366	Body corporate acting as receiver.	£100.	The body corporate.
367	Undischarged bankrupt acting as receiver or manager.	On indictment: imprisonment for 2 years; on summary conviction: imprisonment for 6 months and £500.	Any undischarged bankrupt so acting.
370	Failure to state on invoice, etc., that receiver or manager has been appointed.	£20.	The company, any officer, liquidator, receiver or manager knowingly and wilfully authorising or permitting the default.
372	Failure to notify company of appointment as receiver.	£5 a day.	The receiver.
	Failure to deliver copy of statement of affairs of company.	£5 a day.	The receiver.
	Failure to deliver to Registrar, the company and trustees for debenture holders abstract of receipts and payments.	£5 a day.	The receiver.
373	Failure to give necessary information in statement of affairs of company.	£10 a day.	Any person in default.
374	Failure to deliver accounts to Registrar.	£5 a day.	The receiver or manager in default.
414	Failure by company incorporated outside Great Britain to comply with any provision of Part X of the Act.	£50 or £5 a day.	The company, officers and agents.

Section.	Offence.	Maximum Penalty.	Persons Liable.
420 & 421	Unlawfully offering shares of foreign companies for sale, etc.	£500.	Any person in default.
426	Unlawfully stating in writing to be member or creditor.	£50.	Any person in default.
433	Failure of limited banking or insurance company to issue periodical statement.	£5 a day.	The company and officers in default.
436	Failure to make adequate precautions against falsification of register, index, etc.	£50 and £5 a day.	The company and officers in default.
438	Making false statements in documents specified in 13th Schedule of the Act.	In Scotland, on indictment: imprisonment for 2 years with hard labour[1]; in England, on indictment: imprisonment for 2 years with hard labour and a fine[2]; in England and Scotland, on summary conviction: imprisonment for 4 months and £100.	Any person in default.
439	Improper use of the word 'Limited.'	£5 a day.	Any person in default.

[1] See False Oaths (Scotland) Act, 1933.
[2] See Perjury Act, 1911, s. 5.

APPENDIX D
Stock Exchange Regulations
Governing the Requirements
for Quotation

[*Reproduced by permission of the Council of the Stock Exchange, London.*]

Applications for quotation in the Official List must be made to the Secretary of the Share & Loan Department and must comply with the requirements of the Council as contained in Appendix 34 *or, in the case of Unit Trusts, with the requirements of the Council as contained in Appendix 35.* [*Rule* 159 (2)].

The following are the main provisions of Appendix 34 of the Rules and Regulations of the Stock Exchange, 1946. Reference should be made to Appendix 34 for particulars as to government, municipalities, local authorities and statutory bodies.

NOTE.—These regulations incorporate amendments confirmed by the Council on 2nd October, 1950, and will come into force on 3rd January, 1951.

SECTION A. COMPANIES.

PART I.
ORIGINAL ISSUES BY PROSPECTUS OR OFFER FOR SALE.

Cases in which the security which is offered to the Public by Prospectus or Offer for Sale is new to The Stock Exchange and will not be identical with any security already quoted.

I. Application should be made to the Department at the earliest possible date in the form set out in Schedule I.

II. The Prospectus or Offer for Sale must be advertised in full in at least two leading London newspapers, unless the issue is made only to existing shareholders or debentureholders of a Company whose Capital is already quoted. The Prospectus or Offer for Sale must comply with the requirements of Part 1 of Schedule II, whether or not required by Law.

Applicants must submit 4 copies of the draft Prospectus or Offer for Sale to the Department for initial approval at least 14 days prior to insertion in the Press; and where the Issue or Offer is in addition to be advertised in the Press by means of Abridged Particulars or Preliminary Announcement, applicants must submit 4 copies of such draft advertisements to the Department for approval at least 4 days prior to insertion in the Press.

III. The following documents must be lodged with the Department at least 2 days prior to the hearing of the application by the Committee:—

(a) A formal application in the form issued by the Department, signed by the Broker appointed by the Company and supported by at least two Dealers in the Market concerned *together with payment of the appropriate charge for quotation in accordance with Schedule X.*

(b) A copy of the Prospectus or Offer for Sale.

(c) A copy of each of the newspapers in which any advertisement of the issue appeared.

(d) A certified copy of the Board Resolution authorising the issue or Offer for Sale.

(e) A certified copy of every Letter, Report, Balance Sheet, Valuation, Contract or other document any part of which is extracted or referred to in the Prospectus or Offer for Sale.

(f) A certified copy of the written consent by any expert to the inclusion in the Prospectus or Offer for Sale of a statement purporting to be a copy of or extract from a summary of a report or valuation or other statement by such expert.

(g) A specimen (or 2 advance proofs) of the Allotment Letter or Acceptance Letter. This must comply with Schedule III.

(h) A specimen (or 2 advance proofs) of the Definitive Certificate. This must comply with Schedule IV.

(i) A statement in the form set out in Schedule V.

(j) An undertaking to submit as soon as possible after the grant of quotation the Statutory Declaration set out in Part 1 of Schedule VI.

(k) Where any scrip is to be issued by any person other than the Company whose scrip it is, a certified copy of the Resolution or other document, evidencing the authority to issue the scrip, must be supplied.

(l) Where the vendor of a Security offered for sale has not paid in full for that Security at the date of the offer:—

(i) a certified copy of an irrevocable authority given by the vendor to the Bankers to the offer authorising the Bankers to earmark the proceeds of the offer to discharge the obligation of the vendor to make payment for the security on the date or dates for payment as laid down in the Contract for the acquisition of the security by the Vendor, and

(ii) a certified copy of the Bankers' acknowledgment of this authority and an agreement to act on it.

IV. The following documents may be required:—

(a) *The Certificate of Incorporation.

(b) *The Certificate (if any) entitling the Company to commence business.

(c) †Two copies of the Memorandum and Articles of Association or other corresponding document. These must comply with Part 1 of Schedule VII.

(d) †Two copies of the Trust Deed or Debenture (if the Debentures are not secured by a Trust Deed). These must comply with Part 2 of Schedule VII.

(e) The general undertaking in the form set out in Part 1 of Schedule VIII.

(f) Where the promoter or other interested party is a limited company or a firm, a Statutory Declaration as to the identity of those who control it or are interested in its profits or assets.

(g) A statement giving the following particulars of every Director:—

    (i) any former christian names and surnames;

    (ii) his nationality, if not British;

    (iii) his nationality of origin, if his present nationality is not the nationality of origin.

(h) A copy of the sub-underwriting letter, together with a list containing the names, addresses and description of the sub-underwriters and the amounts sub-underwritten by each of them.

PART II.

ORIGINAL ISSUES BY PLACING OR INTRODUCTION.

Cases in which the security to be placed or introduced is new to The Stock Exchange and will not be identical with any security already quoted.

I. Application should be made to the Department at the earliest possible date in the form set out in Schedule I.

II. An Advertisement stating the matters specified in the appropriate Section of Part 2 of Schedule II must be prepared for circulation by the Exchange Telegraph Co. Ltd. and Moodys Services Ltd. in their statistical services and must be inserted in at least two leading London newspapers.

---

* Where the Company is registered abroad, a notarially certified copy or translation will be required.

† In the event of any of these documents not complying with the requirements of the Committee and if it is impracticable for the Company to alter them before making the application for quotation, the Committee may accept an undertaking to amend these documents at the earliest possible opportunity.

Applicants must submit 4 copies of the draft Advertisement to the Department for initial approval at least 14 days prior to insertion in the Press, and where Abridged Particulars or a Preliminary Announcement are to be advertised in the Press, Applicants must submit 4 copies of such draft advertisements to the Department for approval at least 4 days prior to insertion in the Press.

III. The following documents must be lodged with the Department at least 2 days prior to the hearing of the application by the Committee:—

(a) A formal application in the form issued by the Department, signed by the Broker appointed by the Company and supported by at least two Dealers in the Market concerned *together with payment of the appropriate charge for quotation in accordance with Schedule X.*

(b) A copy of the Advertisement dated and signed by every person who is named therein as a director or proposed director of the Company, or by his agent authorised in writing.

(c) A copy of the Exchange Telegraph and Moodys Services cards and of each newspaper in which the Advertisement appeared.

(d) A certified copy of the Board Resolution authorising the Advertisement and/or any issue of Capital.

(e) A certified copy of every Letter, Report, Balance Sheet, Valuation, Contract or other document any part of which is extracted or referred to in the Advertisement.

(f) A certified copy of the written consent by any expert to the inclusion in the Advertisement of a statement purporting to be a copy of or extract from or summary of a report or valuation or other statement by such expert.

(g) A specimen (or 2 advance proofs) of the Allotment Letter or Scrip. This must comply with Schedule III.

(h) A specimen (or 2 advance proofs) of the Definitive Certificate. This must comply with Schedule IV.

(i) A statement in the form set out in Schedule V.

(j) An undertaking to submit as soon as possible after the grant of quotation the Statutory Declaration set out in Part 1 of Schedule VI.

(k) A marketing statement by the Broker in the form set out in Schedule IX or as near thereto as circumstances admit.

IV. The following documents may be required:—

(a) *The Certificate of Incorporation.

(b) *The Certificate (if any) entitling the Company to commence business.

* Where the Company is registered abroad, a notarially certified copy or translation will be required.

(c) *Two copies of the Memorandum and Articles of Association or other corresponding document. These must comply with Part 1 of Schedule VII.

(d) *Two copies of the Trust Deed or Debenture (if the Debentures are not secured by a Trust Deed). These must comply with Part 2 of Schedule VII.

(e) The general undertaking in the form set out in Part 1 of Schedule VIII.

(f) Where the promoter or other interested party is a limited company or a firm a Statutory Declaration as to the identity of those who control it or are interested in its profits or assets.

(g) A statement giving the following particulars of every Director:—

  (i) any former christian names and surnames;

  (ii) his nationality, if not British;

  (iii) his nationality of origin, if his present nationality is not the nationality of origin.

PART III.
ORIGINAL ISSUES BY CIRCULAR.

Cases in which the security has been or will be offered in the terms of a circular by way of Right or Bonus or as an open or conversion offer to shareholders; and some part of the Capital of the Company is already quoted on The Stock Exchange.

I. Application should be made to the Department at the earliest possible date in the form set out in Schedule I.

II. †Applicants must submit 4 copies of the draft of any circular, notice or resolution to the Department for initial approval at least 14 days prior to the intended date of issue.

III. The following documents must be lodged with the Department at least 2 days prior to the hearing of the application by the Committee:—

  (a) A formal application in the form issued by the Department, signed by the Broker appointed by the Company and (except in the case of issues by way of Right or Bonus) supported by at least two Dealers in the Market concerned *together with payment of the appropriate charge for quotation in accordance with Schedule X.*

---

* In the event of any of these documents not complying with the requirements of the Committee and if it is impracticable for the Company to alter them before making the application for quotation, the Committee may accept an undertaking to amend these documents at the earliest possible opportunity.

† Application for quotation of a security issued by way of Right or Bonus may be made before the issue of the relative circular, in which case the Committee will, if it thinks fit, grant the application from a future date subject to the issue of the circular.

(b) A copy of any circular stating the terms of the issue and containing full details of any underwriting arrangements; and estimate of the net proceeds of the issue and how such proceeds are to be applied; and where the proceeds or any part of the proceeds of the issue are or is to be applied directly or indirectly in the purchase of a business or shares in a company which is, or will by reason of such purchase become, a subsidiary company of the Company a report made by qualified accountants:—

(i) with respect to the profits or losses of the business or as the case may be to the profits or losses attributable to the interest acquired or being acquired by the Company in the subsidiary in respect of each of the 10 completed financial years preceding the issue of the circular or in respect of each of the years since the commencement of the business or the incorporation of such subsidiary company if this occurred less than 10 years prior to the issue of the circular: and if in respect of a period ending on a date earlier than three months before issue of the circular no accounts had been made up, a statement of that fact. In making such report the accountants shall make such adjustments, if any, as are in their opinion necessary for the purposes of the circular:

Provided that where any such subsidiary is itself a holding company the report shall be extended to the profits or losses of that company and its subsidiary companies so far as such profits or losses are attributable to the interests of the Company:

(ii) with respect to the assets and liabilities of the business or of the subsidiary and where such subsidiary is itself a holding company the report shall be extended to the assets and liabilities of that company and of its subsidiary companies so far as attributable to the interests of the Company. In making such report the accountants shall make such adjustments as are in their opinion necessary for purposes of the circular.

In addition to the foregoing provisions, any circular offering Debentures or Debenture Stock to be issued by way of conversion or replacement of Debentures or Debenture Stock previously issued shall state all material differences between the security for the old Stock and the security for the new Stock or (if such be the case) shall state that the security for the new Stock is identical with the security for the old Stock, and shall contain a statement of any provisions of the Trust Deed for the indemnification of the Trustees and/or their relief from responsibility.

(c) A certified copy of the Board Resolution authorising the issue.

(d) A certified copy of every Letter, Report, Balance Sheet, Valuation, Contract, or other document any part of which is extracted or referred to in the circular.

(e) A specimen (or 2 advance proofs) of any Allotment Letter, Provisional Allotment Letter or Letter of Rights, which must comply with Schedule III.

(f) A statement in the form set out in Schedule V.

(g) An undertaking to submit as soon as possible after the grant of quotation the Statutory Declaration set out in Part 1 of Schedule VI.

IV. The following documents may be required:—

(a) Two copies of the Memorandum and Articles of Association or other corresponding document. These must comply with Part 1 of Schedule VII.

(b) Two copies of the Trust Deed or Debenture (if the Debentures are not secured by a Trust Deed). These must comply with Part 2 of Schedule VII.

(c) A specimen (or 2 advance proofs) of the Definitive Certificate. This must comply with Schedule IV.

(d) The general undertaking in the form set out in Part 1 of Schedule VIII.

V. If required by the Committee provision must be made for any documents referred to in the circular to be open for inspection for a reasonable time (being not less than 14 days) at a place in the City of London.

PART IV.

FURTHER ISSUES.

Cases in which the security has not been issued to the Public or offered in the terms of a circular to shareholders of the Company; and the security is or will become identical with a quoted security.

I. Application should be made to the Department at the earliest possible date in the form set out in Schedule I.

II. A formal application in the form issued by the Department signed by the Broker appointed by the Company and supported by at least two Dealers in the Market concerned must be lodged with the Department at least 2 days prior to the hearing of the application by the Committee *together with payment of the appropriate charge for quotation in accordance with Schedule X.*

III. The application must be accompanied by a copy or specimen of any Resolution, Circular, Order of the Court, Agreement, Allotment Letter, Definitive Certificate and any other document or information relative to the issue of the security.

IV. The following documents may be required:—

    (a) A statement in the form set out in Schedule V.

    (b) An undertaking to submit as soon as possible after the grant of quotation the Statutory Declaration set out in Part 2 of Schedule VI.

    (c) The general undertaking in the form set out in Part 1 of Schedule VIII.

    (d) A marketing statement by the Broker in the form set out in Schedule IX or as near thereto as circumstances admit.

PART V.

PROVINCIAL ISSUES.

Cases in which the security is already quoted on a Stock Exchange affiliated to the Council of Associated Stock Exchanges, and no further issue being made.

    I. Application should be made to the Department at the earliest possible date in the form set out in Schedule I.

    II. The following documents must be lodged with the Department at least 2 days prior to the hearing of the application by the Committee:—

    (a) A formal application in the form issued by the Department, signed by the Broker appointed by the Company and supported by at least two Dealers in the Market concerned *together with payment of the appropriate charge for quotation in accordance with Schedule X.*

    (b) A certified copy of any Advertisement formerly published or statement compiled by the Company to comply with the requirements of the Stock Exchange on which the security is already quoted.

    (c) A letter from the Secretary of that Stock Exchange stating the number of shares quoted at the date of the application.

    (d) A specimen of the Definitive Certificate. This must comply with Schedule IV.

    (e) An undertaking to submit as soon as possible after the grant of quotation the Statutory Declaration set out in Part 1 of Schedule VI.

    (f) *Two copies of the Memorandum and Articles of Association or other corresponding document. These must comply with Part 1 of Schedule VII.

    (g) *Two copies of the Trust Deed or Debenture (if the Debentures are not secured by a Trust Deed). These must comply with Part 2 of Schedule VII.

* In the event of any of these documents not complying with the requirements of the Committee and if it is impracticable for the Company to alter them before making the application for quotation, the Committee may accept an undertaking to amend these documents at the earliest possible opportunity.

(h) The general undertaking in the form set out in Part 1 of Schedule VIII.

(i) A marketing statement (if required) by the Broker in the form set out in Schedule IX or as near thereto as circumstances admit.

(j) A copy of the audited accounts of the Company for each of the 10 completed financial years preceding the date of the application for which the accounts have been made up.

SECTION B.

SCHEDULE I.

LETTER OF APPLICATION.

To the Secretary,
  The Share & Loan Department.

....19..........

Dear Sir,

We are instructed by...
....

to make application for permission to deal and for quotation in :—

(1)..

(2)..
....

(3)..
....

We shall be glad to receive in due course a note of the requirements of the Department.

We are,

Yours faithfully,

....*Brokers.*

(1) Set out the securities for which application is made.

(2) State how it is proposed to issue the securities, *i.e.* whether by Prospectus, Offer for Sale, Circular or Placing; or if the securities have already been issued, state when, how and to whom, and whether it is intended to make an offer for Sale or a Placing, or merely to introduce them.

(3) If a Placing is intended a request to that effect should be included, supported by reasons for desiring this procedure, including an outline of the contemplated marketing arrangements.

SCHEDULE II.

PART 1.

PROSPECTUS OR OFFER FOR SALE.

The following information and requirements must be given or dealt with:—

1.   The time of the opening of the Lists.

2.   A statement that an application for permission to deal and for quotation has been made to the Council of The Stock Exchange, London.

3.   The authorised share capital, the amount issued or agreed to be issued, the amount paid up and the description and nominal value of the shares.

4.   The authorised loan capital, the amount issued and outstanding or agreed to be issued, or if no loan capital is outstanding, a statement to that effect.

5.   (i) The full name, address and description of every Director and, if required by the Committee, particulars of (*a*) any former christian name and surname and (*b*) of present and former nationality, if not British.

   (ii) The full name and professional qualification of the Secretary and situation of Registered Office.

6.   The names and addresses of the Bankers, Brokers, Registrars, Solicitors and Trustees (if any).

7.   The professional qualification of the Auditors.

8.   If the application is in respect of shares and if there is more than one class of share, a statement as to the consents necessary for the variation of the rights of such shares.

9.   The provisions or a sufficient summary of the provisions of the Articles of Association or other corresponding document with regard to the borrowing powers exercisable by the Directors and how such borrowing powers can be varied.

10.   If the issue is in respect of loan capital, the date of the Board Resolution creating any loan capital, the rights conferred upon the holders thereof, the obligations undertaken by the Company in respect thereof, and short particulars of any mortgages and charges subsisting on any part of the Company's assets.

Any Prospectus or Offer for Sale relating to Debentures or Debenture Stock issued by way of conversion or replacement of Debentures or Debenture Stock previously issued shall state all material differences between the security for the old Stock and the security for the new Stock or (if such be the case) shall state that the security for the new Stock is identical with the security for the old Stock.

11.   A Statement of any provisions, excluding any invalidated by law, of the Articles of Association and/or Trust Deed for the indemnification of the Directors and/or Trustees and/or their relief from responsibility.

12. The date and country of incorporation. The authority under which the Company was incorporated and the date (if any) of conversion into a public company. In the case of a company not incorporated in the United Kingdom, the address of the principal place of business and the place of business in the United Kingdom (if any).

13. A statement of:—
  (i) any alterations in the share capital within the preceding 2 years, and
  (ii) the names of the holders of any substantial or controlling beneficial interest in the capital of the Company and the amount of their holdings.

14. The principal objects of the Company. The situation, area and tenure of the factories (if any) and in the case of lease-hold property the unexpired term and rent of such lease.

15. The name, date and country of incorporation, and capital of any subsidiary company, together with details of capital held by the parent company. The principal objects and situation of factories (if any) of any such subsidiary.

16. A statement as to the financial and trading prospects of the Company, together with any material information which may be relevant thereto.

17. A statement by the Directors that in their opinion the working capital available is sufficient, or, if not, how it is proposed to provide the additional working capital thought by the Directors to be necessary.

18. A report by the Auditors of the Company or qualified Accountants with respect to the profits and losses of the Company and, where the proceeds or any part of the proceeds of the issue are to be applied directly or indirectly in the purchase of a business or of shares in a company which is or will by reason of such purchase become a subsidiary company, with respect to the profits and losses of such business or subsidiary, in respect of the 10 completed financial years preceding the issue of the prospectus or in respect of the years since the commencement of the business or the incorporation of the Company or the subsidiary if this occurred less than 10 years prior to such issue as the case may be. Such report shall include a statement of the aggregate emoluments paid to the Directors by the Company during the last period for which the accounts have been made up and the amount (if any) by which such emoluments would differ from the amounts payable under the arrangements in force at the date of the Prospectus.

19. In the case of capital issued or agreed to be issued for cash within twelve months of the date of the Prospectus or Offer for Sale, the price and terms upon which the same has been or is to be issued and (if not already fully paid) the dates when instalments are payable with the amount of all calls or instalments in arrear.

20. Particulars of any discounts, brokerages or other special terms granted to any persons in connection with the issue or sale of any capital of the Company.

21. A reasonable time (being not less than 14 days) during which and a place in the City of London at which the following documents (or copies thereof) where applicable may be inspected:— The Memorandum and Articles of Association, Trust Deed, all material contracts or in the case of a contract not reduced into writing, a memorandum giving full particulars thereof, all reports, letters, balance sheets, valuations, and statements by any expert, any part of which is extracted, or referred to in the Prospectus or Offer for Sale, a written statement signed by the Auditors or Accountants setting out the adjustments made in the report on the profits and giving the reasons therefor and the audited accounts of the Company for each of the two financial years preceding the date of the Prospectus or Offer for Sale, together with all notes, certificates or information required by the Companies Act.

NOTE.—The requirements stated above are in general applicable to an industrial company. The Committee will require additional or alternative information for companies engaged in other enterprises, e.g. mining.

SCHEDULE II.

PART 2 (a).

ADVERTISED STATEMENTS.

In the case of a Company (a) no part of whose capital is already quoted on The Stock Exchange, and (b) whose annual accounts for at least two years have not been made up and audited, the statement required to be advertised must contain the following information giving all material particulars relating to the formation of the Company and to the flotation of the issue, including the following:—

1. The full name of the Company.

2. A statement as follows:—

'This Advertisement is issued in compliance with the Regulations of the Council of The Stock Exchange, London, for the purpose of giving information to the Public with regard to the Company. The Directors collectively and individually accept full responsibility for the accuracy of the information given and confirm, having made all reasonable enquiries, that to the best of their knowledge and belief there are no other facts, the omission of which would make any statement in the Advertisement misleading.

3. A statement that an application for permission to deal and for quotation has been made to the Council of The Stock Exchange, London.

4. The authorised share capital, the amount issued or agreed to be issued, the amount paid up and the description and nominal value of the shares.

5. The authorised loan capital, the amount issued and outstanding or agreed to be issued, or if no loan capital is outstanding, a statement to that effect.

6. The full name, address and description of every Director and, if required by the Committee, particulars of (a) any former christian name and surname and (b) of present and former nationality, if not British.

7. The full name and professional qualification of the Secretary and situation of Registered Office.

8. The names and addresses of the Bankers, Brokers, Registrars, Solicitors and Trustees (if any).

9. The name, address and professional qualification of the Auditors.

10. If the application is in respect of shares:—

   (a) The voting rights of shareholders.

   (b) If there is more than one class of share, the rights of each class of share as regards dividend and capital, and

   (c) a statement as to the consents necessary for the variation of such rights.

11. The provisions or a sufficient summary of the provisions of the Articles of Association, contract or other corresponding document with regard to:—

   (a) Qualification of Directors.

   (b) Remuneration of Directors or other similar body.

   (c) Any power enabling the Directors to vote remuneration to themselves or any members of their body.

   (d) The borrowing powers exercisable by the Directors and how such borrowing powers can be varied.

12. The date of the Board Resolution creating any loan capital, the rights conferred upon the holders thereof, the obligations undertaken by the Company in respect thereof, and short particulars of any mortgages and charges subsisting on any part of the Company's assets.

Any Advertisement relating to Debentures or Debenture Stock issued by way of conversion or replacement of Debentures or Debenture Stock previously issued shall state all material differences between the security for the old Stock and the security for the new Stock or (if such be the case) shall state that the security for the new Stock is identical with the security for the old Stock.

13. A statement of any provisions, excluding any invalidated by law, of the Articles of Association and/or Trust Deed for the indemnification of the Directors and/or Trustees and/or their relief from responsibility.

14. The date and country of incorporation. The authority under which the Company was incorporated and the date (if any) of conversion into a public company. In the case of a company not incorporated in the United Kingdom, the address of the principal place of business and the place of business in the United Kingdom (if any).

15. A statement of:
 (i) any alterations in the share capital within the preceding 2 years; and
 (ii) the names of the holders of any substantial or controlling beneficial interest in the capital of the company and the amount of their holdings.

16. The principal objects of the Company. The situation, area and tenure of the factories (if any) and in the case of lease-hold property, the unexpired term and rent of such lease.

17. The name, date and country of incorporation, and capital of any subsidiary company, together with details of capital held by the parent company. The principal objects and situation of factories (if any) of any such subsidiary.

18. A statement as to the financial and trading prospects of the Company, together with any material information which may be relevant thereto.

19. A statement by the Directors that in their opinion the working capital available is sufficient, or, if not, how it is proposed to provide the additional working capital thought by the Directors to be necessary.

20. A report by the auditors of the Company:—
 (i) with respect to the profits or losses of the company in respect of each of the years since the incorporation of the Company, and, if in respect of a period ending on a date earlier than three months before the publication of the Advertisement no accounts have been made up, a statement of that fact. In making such report the auditors shall make such adjustments (if any) as are in their opinion necessary for the purposes of the Advertisement;
 (ii) in the case of an issue by a holding company, in lieu of the report in (i), a like report with respect to the profits or losses of the Company and of its subsidiary companies, so far as such profits or losses are attributable to the interests of the holding company. For the purposes of this report the financial years of each company shall mean as regards that company the financial years immediately preceding the publication of the Advertisement;
 (iii) with respect to the rates of the dividends, if any, paid by the Company in respect of each class of shares in the Company in respect of each of the said years giving particulars of each such class of shares on which such dividends have been paid and particulars of the cases in which no dividends have been paid in respect of any class of shares in respect of any of those years;
 (iv) with respect to the assets and liabilities of the Company and in the case of an issue by a holding company, a like report with respect to the assets and liabilities of the Company and of its subsidiary companies so far as attributable to the interests of the Company. In making such reports the auditors shall make such adjustments as are in their opinion necessary for the purposes of the Advertisement;

(v) with respect to the aggregate emoluments paid to the Directors by the Company during the last period for which the accounts have been made up and the amount (if any) by which such emoluments would differ from the amounts payable under the arrangements in force at the date of the Advertisement.

21. If the proceeds, or any part of the proceeds, of the issue of the shares or debentures are or is to be applied directly or indirectly in the purchase of a business or of shares in a company which is, or will by reason of such purchase become, a subsidiary company of the Company, a report made by qualified accountants who shall be named in the Advertisement:—

(i) with respect to the profits or losses of the business or to the profits or losses attributable to the interests acquired or being acquired by the Company in the subsidiary in respect of each of the 10 completed financial years preceding the publication of the Advertisement or in respect of each of the years since the commencement of the business or the incorporation of such subsidiary if this occurred less than 10 years prior to such Advertisement; and, if in respect of a period ending on a date earlier than three months before the publication of the Advertisement no accounts have been made up, a statement of that fact. In making such report the accountants shall make such adjustments (if any) as are in their opinion necessary for the purposes of the Advertisement:

Provided that where any such subsidiary is itself a holding company the report shall be extended to the profits or losses of that company and its subsidiary companies which shall be ascertained in the manner laid down in sub-paragraph (ii) of paragraph 20;

(ii) with respect to the assets and liabilities of the business or of the subsidiary and where such subsidiary is itself a holding company, the report shall be extended to the assets and liabilities of that company and of its subsidiary companies in the manner laid down in sub-paragraph (iv) of paragraph 20.

22. Particulars of the capital which has been issued or is proposed to be issued fully or partly paid up otherwise than in cash and the consideration for which the same has been issued or is proposed to be issued.

23. In the case of capital issued or agreed to be issued for cash, the price and terms upon which the same has been or is to be issued and (if not already fully paid) the dates when instalments are payable with the amount of all calls or instalments in arrear.

24. Particulars of any capital which is under option, or agreed conditionally or unconditionally to be put under option, with the price and duration of the option and consideration for which the option was granted, and the name and address of the grantee.

Provided that where an option has been granted or agreed to be granted to all the members or debentureholders or to any class thereof, it shall be sufficient, so far as the names are concerned, to record that fact without giving the names and addresses of the grantees.

25. (i) Particulars of any preliminary expenses incurred or proposed to be incurred and by whom the same are payable.

   (ii) The amount or estimated amount of the expenses of the issue and of the application for quotation so far as the same are not included in the statement of preliminary expenses and by whom the same are payable.

26. Particulars of any commissions, discounts, brokerages or other special terms granted in connection with the issue or sale of any capital of the Company.

27. (i) The names and addresses of the vendors of any property purchased or acquired by the Company or any subsidiary company within two years preceding the publication of the Advertisement or proposed to be purchased or acquired on capital account and the amount paid or payable in cash, shares or securities to the vendor and, where there is more than one separate vendor or the Company is a sub-purchaser, the amount so paid or payable to each vendor and the amount (if any) payable for goodwill;

   (ii) Short particulars of all transactions relating to any property falling within the immediately preceding sub-paragraph which have taken place within two years of the date of the Advertisement and in which any vendor or Director or proposed Director or promoter was or is directly or indirectly interested;

   (iii) The amount of any cash or securities paid or benefit given within the two preceding years or proposed to be paid or given to any promoter and the consideration for such payment or benefit.

28. The name of any promoter; and (if a company) a statement of the issued share capital; the amount paid up thereon; the date of its incorporation; the names of its Directors, Bankers and Auditors; and such other particulars as the Committee think necessary in connection therewith.

29. Full particulars of the nature and extent of the interest direct or indirect (if any) of every Director in the promotion of, or the property proposed to be acquired by, the Company.

30. A statement of all sums paid or agreed to be paid to any Director or to any firm of which he is a member in cash or shares or otherwise by any person either to induce him to become or to qualify him as a Director or otherwise for services rendered by him or by the firm in connection with the promotion or formation of the Company.

31. Where an Advertisement includes a statement purporting to be made by an expert, a statement that the expert has given and has not withdrawn his written consent to the issue of the

Advertisement with the statement included in the form and context in which it is included.

32. The dates of and parties to all material contracts entered into within two years with a description of the general nature of the contracts not being contracts entered into in the ordinary course of the business carried on or intended to be carried on by the Company.

33. A reasonable time (being not less than 14 days) during which and a place in the City of London at which the following documents (or copies thereof) where applicable may be inspected: The Memorandum and Articles of Association, Trust Deed, all material contracts or in the case of a contract not reduced into writing, a memorandum giving full particulars thereof, all reports, letters, balance sheets, valuations and statements by any expert any part of which is extracted or referred to in the Advertisement, a written statement signed by the Auditors or Accountants setting out the adjustments made in the report on the profits and giving the reasons therefor and the audited accounts since the incorporation of the Company, together with all notes, certificates or information required by the Companies Act.

NOTE 1.—In the case of foreign companies, the documents to be offered for inspection will be the documents corresponding to those above mentioned in the case of British companies, and where such documents are not in the English language notarially certified translations thereof must be available for inspection.

NOTE 2.—In cases where it is contended that contracts cannot be offered for inspection without disclosing to trade competitors important information the disclosure of which might be detrimental to the Company's interests, application may be made to the Committee to dispense with the offering of such documents for inspection.

NOTE 3.—In any case where information is not given under any of the above heads Nos. 22, 24, 25, 26, 27, 29 and 30, the Advertisement must state that no such payments etc. have been made or explain why the information is not given.

NOTE 4.—The requirements stated above are in general applicable to an industrial company. The Committee will require additional or alternative information for companies engaged in other enterprises, *e.g.* mining.

SCHEDULE II.

PART 2 (*b*).

ADVERTISED STATEMENTS.

In the case of a Company (a) no part of whose capital is already quoted on The Stock Exchange, and (b) whose annual accounts for at least two years have been made up and audited, the statement required to be advertised must contain the following information giving all material particulars relating to the formation of the Company and to the flotation of the issue, including the following:—

Clauses 1–19 inclusive as in Part 2 (*a*) above.

20. A report by the auditors of the Company:—

    (i) with respect to the profits or losses of the Company in respect of each of the 10 completed financial years immediately preceding the publication of the Advertisement or in respect of each of the years since the incorporation of the Company, if this occurred less than 10 years prior to the publication of such Advertisement; and, if in respect of a period ending on a date earlier than three months before the publication of the Advertisement no accounts have been made up, a statement of that fact. In making such report the auditors shall make such adjustments (if any) as are in their opinion necessary for purposes of the Advertisement;

    (ii) in the case of an issue by a holding company, in lieu of the report in (i), a like report with respect to the profits or losses of the Company and of its subsidiary companies, so far as such profits or losses are attributable to the interests of the holding company. For the purposes of this report the financial years of each company shall mean as regards that company the financial years immediately preceding the publication of the Advertisement;

    (iii) with respect to the rates of the dividends, if any, paid by the Company in respect of each class of shares in the Company in respect of each of the said 10 years or shorter period as the case may be, giving particulars of each such class of shares on which such dividends have been paid and particulars of the cases in which no dividends have been paid in respect of any class of shares in respect of any of those years;

    (iv) with respect to the assets and liabilities of the Company and in the case of an issue by a holding company, a like report with respect to the assets and liabilities of the Company and of its subsidiary companies so far as attributable to the interests of the Company. In making such reports the auditors shall make such adjustments as are in their opinion necessary for the purposes of the Advertisement;

    (v) with respect to the aggregate emoluments paid to the Directors by the Company during the last period for which accounts have been made up and the amount (if any) by which such emoluments would differ from the amounts payable under the arrangements in force at the date of the Advertisement.

21. If the proceeds, or any part of the proceeds, of the issue of the shares or debentures are or is to be applied directly or indirectly in the purchase of a business or of shares in a company which is, or will by reason of such purchase become, a subsidiary company of the Company, a report made by qualified accountants who shall be named in the Advertisement:—

    (i) with respect to the profits or losses of the business or to the profits or losses attributable to the interests acquired or being acquired by the Company in the subsidiary in respect of each of the 10 completed financial years preceding the publication of the Advertisement or in respect of each of the years since the commencement of the business or the incorporation of such subsidiary company if this occurred less than 10 years prior to such Advertisement; and, if in respect of a period ending on a date earlier than three months before the publication of the Advertisement no accounts have been made up, a statement of that fact. In making such report the accountants shall make such adjustments (if any) as are in their opinion necessary for purposes of the Advertisement:

Provided that where any such subsidiary is itself a holding company the report shall be extended to the profits or losses of that company and its subsidiary companies which shall be ascertained in the manner laid down in sub-paragraph (ii) of paragraph 20;

(ii) with respect to the assets and liabilities of the business or of the subsidiary and where such subsidiary is itself a holding company, the report shall be extended to the assets and liabilities of that company and of its subsidiary companies in the manner laid down in sub-paragraph (iv) of paragraph 20.

22.   Particulars of the capital which has within two years preceding the publication of the Advertisement been issued or is proposed to be issued fully or partly paid up otherwise than in cash and the consideration for which the same has been issued or is proposed to be issued.

23.   In the case of capital issued or agreed to be issued for cash within two years of the publication of the Advertisement, the price and terms upon which the same has been or is to be issued and (if not already fully paid) the dates when instalments are payable with the amount of all calls or instalments in arrear.

24.   Particulars of any capital which is under option, or agreed conditionally or unconditionally to be put under option, with the price and duration of the option and consideration for which the option was granted, and the name and address of the grantee.

Provided that where an option has been granted or agreed to be granted to all the members or debentureholders or to any class thereof, it shall be sufficient, so far as the names are concerned, to record that fact without giving the names and addresses of the grantees.

25.   The amount or estimated amount of the expenses of the issue and of the application for quotation and by whom the same are payable.

26.   Particulars of any commissions, discounts, brokerages or other special terms granted within two years preceding the publication of the Advertisement in connection with the issue or sale of any capital of the Company.

27. (i) The names and addresses of the vendors of any property purchased or acquired by the Company or any subsidiary company within two years preceding the publication of the Advertisement or proposed to be purchased or acquired on capital account and the amount paid or payable in cash, shares or securities to the vendor and, where there is more than one separate vendor or the Company is a sub-purchaser, the amount so paid or payable to each vendor and the amount (if any) payable for goodwill;.

(ii) Short particulars of all transactions relating to any property falling within the immediately preceding sub-paragraph which have taken place within two years of the publication of the Advertisement and in which any vendor or Director or proposed Director was or is directly or indirectly interested.

28. Full particulars of the nature and extent of the interest direct or indirect (if any) of every Director in any property proposed to be acquired by the Company.

29. Where an Advertisement includes a statement purporting to be made by an expert, a statement that the expert has given and has not withdrawn his written consent to the issue of the Advertisement with the statement included in the form and context in which it is included.

30. The dates of and parties to all material contracts with a description of the general nature of the contracts entered into within two years preceding the publication of the Advertisement not being contracts entered into in the ordinary course of the business carried on or intended to be carried on by the Company.

31. A reasonable time (being not less than 14 days) during which and a place in the City of London at which the following documents (or copies thereof) where applicable may be inspected: The Memorandum and Articles of Association, Trust Deed, all material contracts or in the case of a contract not reduced into writing, a memorandum giving full particulars thereof, all reports, letters, balance sheets, valuations, and statements by any expert any part of which is extracted or referred to in the Advertisement, a written statement signed by the Auditors or Accountants setting out the adjustments made in the reports on the profits and giving the reasons therefor and the audited accounts of the Company for each of the two financial years preceding the publication of the Advertisement, together with all notes, certificates or information required by the Companies Act.

NOTE 1.—In the case of foreign companies, the documents to be offered for inspection will be the documents corresponding to those above mentioned in the case of British companies, and where such documents are not in the English language notarially certified translations thereof must be available for inspection.

NOTE 2.—In cases where it is contended that contracts cannot be offered for inspection without disclosing to trade competitors important information the disclosure of which might be detrimental to the Company's interests, application may be made to the Committee to dispense with the offering of such documents for inspection.

NOTE 3.—In any case where information is not given under any of the above heads Nos. 22, 24, 25, 26, 27 and 28, the Advertisement must state that no such payments etc. have been made or explain why the information is not given.

NOTE 4.—The requirements stated above are in general applicable to an industrial company. The Committee will require additional or alternative information for companies engaged in other enterprises, *e.g.* mining.

SCHEDULE II.

PART 2 (c).

ADVERTISED STATEMENTS.

In the case of a Company part of whose Capital is already quoted on The Stock Exchange, the statement required to be advertised must contain the following information:—

Clauses 1–5 inclusive as in Part 2 (a) above.

6. The full name, address and description of every Director.

7. The full name and professional qualification of the Secretary and situation of Registered Office.

8. The names and addresses of the Bankers, Brokers, Registrars, Solicitors and Trustees (if any).

9. The name, address and professional qualification of the Auditors.

10. If the application is in respect of shares:—

(a) The voting rights of shareholders.

(b) If there is more than one class of share, the rights of each class of share as regards dividend and capital and a statement as to the consents necessary for the variation of such rights.

11. The provisions or a sufficient summary of the provisions of the Articles of Association, contract or other corresponding document with regard to:—

(a) Remuneration of Directors or other similar body.

(b) Any power enabling the Directors to vote remuneration to themselves or any members of their body.

(c) The borrowing powers exercisable by the Directors and how such borrowing powers can be varied.

12. If the application is in respect of loan capital, the date of the Board Resolution creating any loan capital, the rights conferred upon the holders thereof, the obligations undertaken by the Company in respect thereof, and short particulars of any mortgages and charges subsisting on any part of the Company's assets.

Any Advertisement relating to Debentures or Debenture Stock issued by way of conversion or replacement of Debentures or Debenture Stock previously issued shall state all material differences between the security for the old Stock and the security for the new Stock or (if such be the case) shall state that the security for the new Stock is identical with the security for the old Stock.

13. A statement of any provisions, excluding any invalidated by law, of the Articles of Association and/or Trust Deed for the indemnification of the Directors and/or Trustees and/or their relief from responsibility.

14. A statement as to the financial and trading prospects of the Company, together with any material information which may be relevant thereto.

15. A statement by the Directors that in their opinion the working capital available is sufficient, or, if not, how it is proposed to provide the additional working capital thought by the Directors to be necessary.

Clauses 16 to 27 inclusive and Notes 1, 2, 3 and 4 as in clauses 20 to 31 and Notes 1 to 4 in Part 2 (b) above except that, in clause 21, for 'paragraph 20' read 'paragraph 16' and, in Note 3, for 'Nos. 22, 24, 25, 26, 27 and 28' read 'Nos. 18, 20, 22, 23 and 24.'

SCHEDULE III.
LETTERS OF ALLOTMENT, ACCEPTANCE OR RIGHTS.

1. Where the right of renunciation is given:—
 (i) The period for renunciation for fully-paid shares must not exceed six weeks and for partly-paid shares must not exceed one month from the date of the final call;
 (ii) When, at the same time as an allotment is made for shares issued for cash, shares of the same class are also allotted, credited as fully-paid, to vendors or others, the period for renunciation may be the same as, but not longer than, that allowed in the case of shares issued for cash;
 (iii) The form of renunciation must be printed on the back of, or attached to the document in question.

2. The documents must be serially numbered, printed on good quality paper and must be examined and autographically initialled by a responsible official of the Company.

3. Letters of Allotment and Acceptance must, wherever possible, contain the distinctive numbers of the shares to which they relate.

4. When a security is offered in conversion of another security and is also offered for subscription in cash the Allotment Letters must be marked 'Conversion' and 'Cash' respectively.

5. Renounceable Allotment Letters and Letters of Rights must contain a provision for splitting and Split Letters must be certified by an official of the Company.

6. Letters must state how the next payment of interest or dividend on the security will be calculated.

SCHEDULE IV.

DEFINITIVE CERTIFICATES.

A. Debenture Stock Certificates, Debentures and Notes must:—

1. State the authority under which the Company is constituted.

2. State on the face the dates when interest is payable and on the back all conditions of issue as to redemption, conversion and transfer; and further, when the security is not constituted by a Trust Deed or Deed Poll, all conditions as to meetings and voting rights.

3. State on the face the minimum amount and multiples thereof in which the security is transferable.

4. If registered, bear a footnote stating that no transfer of the security or any portion thereof represented by the Certificate can be registered without production of the Certificate.

5. Be under seal and bear the requisite autographic signatures. (See Schedule VII, Part 1, paragraph (179)).

6. If an application is to be made to deal in units of stock, state in the top right-hand corner the amount of the stock and the number and denomination of units represented by the Certificate.

B. Share Certificates must:—

1. State the authority under which the Company is constituted.

2. State the authorised capital of the Company and the nominal amount and denomination of each class if more than one class of shares.

3. If registered, bear a footnote stating that no transfer of the security or any portion thereof represented by the Certificate can be registered without production of the Certificate.

4. If representing a Preference Security must bear (preferably on the face) a statement of the conditions both as to capital and dividends and redemption (if any) under which the security is issued.

5. Be under seal and bear the requisite autographic signatures. (See Schedule VII, Part 1, paragraph (179)).

6. If an application is to be made to deal in units of stock, state in the top right-hand corner the amount of the stock and the number and denomination of units represented by the Certificate.

7. When applicable state on the face the minimum amount and multiples thereof in which the stock is transferable.

C. Bonds must:—

1. Specify the amount and conditions of the Loan and powers under which it has been contracted.

2. If issued by a company incorporated in the United Kingdom, be under seal and bear the requisite autographic signatures. (See Schedule VII, Part 1, paragraph (179)).

3. If issued in London by a company not incorporated in the United Kingdom, bear autographic signatures on behalf of the London Agent or Contractors.

4. If already listed, quoted or dealt in on a Dominion, Colonial or Foreign Stock Exchange, bear the autographic counter-signature of a duly authorised person.

SCHEDULE V.

PARTICULARS OF NUMBERS OF SHARES TO BE QUOTED.

....Company, Limited.

SHARES AND/OR STOCK FOR WHICH QUOTATION IS TO BE APPLIED.

1. Number and Distinctive numbers of shares and/or amount of stock for which application is now made.	....
2. Number and Distinctive numbers of shares and/or amount of stock (a) which have been allotted for cash or in conversion;	....
(b) which have been allotted to vendors or others for a consideration other than cash or in exchange for cash;	
(c) which have been allotted in pursuance of an option.	....

The shares/stock are/is not identical in all respects and are/is not identical in all respects with existing shares/stock. (If not identical it must be stated at what date, if ever, the shares/stock will become identical and the Definitive Certificates must be enfaced with a note to this effect.)

Letters of Rights/Allotment Letters may be renounced up to.....................and split up to.....................

The Definitive Certificates will be ready on ....
have been issued.

I undertake to lodge with you the required Statutory Declaration in due course.

Signed............................

NOTE.—A statement that shares are in all respects identical is understood to mean that:—
    (1) They are of the same nominal value, and that the same amount per share has been called up.
    (2) They are entitled to dividend at the same rate and for the same period, so that at the next ensuing distribution the dividend payable on each share will amount to exactly the same sum net and gross.
    (3) They carry the same rights as to unrestricted transfer attendance and voting at meetings, and in all other respects.
A statement that stock is in all respects identical is understood to bear a corresponding meaning.

SCHEDULE VI.

PART 1.

STATUTORY DECLARATION (ORIGINAL ISSUES).

(The following is a suggested form of declaration which will need amendment to meet individual cases.)

WE,   and
a Director and the Secretary respectively of   Limited (hereinafter called "the Company"), do solemnly and sincerely declare as follows:—

1. THAT all documents required by the Companies Acts to be filed with the Registrar of Companies in respect of the Company have been duly filed and that compliance has been made with all other legal requirements in connection with the formation of the Company and the issue/offer of any of its Shares, Debenture Stock or other securities.

2. THAT   Shares of   Nos.   to   (inclusive)
     (Number and Class)
     Shares Nos.   to (inclusive) £   Debenture
     (Number and Class)
Stock   Debentures/Notes Nos.   to   (inclusive) have been subscribed/purchased for cash and duly allotted/transferred to the Subscribers/Purchasers (and that the said Shares have been converted into £   Stock).

3. THAT the issue/offer price was as follows (and all money due to the Company in respect thereof has been received by it):—

	Shares	per Share
	Shares	per Share
£	Debenture Stock	per £100 of Stock
	Debentures/Notes	per £ nominal amount.

4. THAT   Shares of   Nos.   to (inclusive)   Shares Nos.   to   (inclusive) £ Debenture Stock   Debentures/Notes Nos.   to (inclusive) have been issued credited as fully paid by way of conversion/exchange/consideration for property acquired/other consideration not being cash and have been duly allotted/transferred to the persons entitled thereto (and that the said Shares have subsequently been converted into £   Stock).

5. THAT the Share/Stock Certificates/Debenture Stock Certificates/Debentures/Notes have been/are ready to be delivered.

6. THAT completion has taken place of the purchase by the Company of all property shown in any Prospectus, Offer for Sale, Advertised Statement or Circular to Members to have been purchased or agreed to be purchased by it and the purchase consideration for all such property has been duly satisfied.

7. THAT the Trust Deed/Deed Poll relating to any Debenture Stock or Notes issued by the Company has been completed and executed and that a copy thereof has (if so required by the Companies Acts) been filed with the Registrar of Companies and a further copy has been lodged with the Share and Loan Department.

8

8.   THAT all the Shares/Debentures/Debenture Stock/Notes of each class for which quotation exists are in all respects identical.*

9.   THAT there are no other facts bearing on the Company's application for quotation which, in our opinion, should be disclosed to the Stock Exchange.

AND we made this solemn declaration conscientiously believing the same to be true and by virtue of the Statutory Declarations Act, 1835.

DECLARED at

SCHEDULE VI.

PART 2.

STATUTORY DECLARATION (FURTHER ISSUES).

(The following is a suggested form of declaration which will need amendment to meet individual cases.)

WE,   and
a Director and the Secretary respectively of
Limited (hereinafter called "the Company"), do solemnly and sincerely declare, as follows:—

1.   THAT all documents required by the Companies Acts to be filed with the Registrar of Companies in respect of the Company have been duly filed and that compliance has been made with all other legal requirements in connection with the formation of the Company and the issue/offer of any of its Shares, Debenture Stock or other securities.

2.   THAT   Shares of   Nos.   to
             (Number and Class)
(inclusive)   Shares Nos.   to   (inclusive)
                                        (Number and Class)
£   Debenture Stock   Debentures/Notes Nos.
to   (inclusive) have been subscribed/purchased for cash and duly allotted/transferred to the Subscribers/Purchasers (and that the said Shares have been converted into £   Stock).

3.   THAT the issue/offer price was as follows (and all money due to the Company in respect thereof has been received by it):—

	Shares	per Share
	Shares	per Share
£	Debenture Stock	per £100 of Stock
	Debentures/Notes	per £ nominal amount.

4.   THAT   Shares of   Nos.   to
(inclusive)   Shares Nos.   to   (inclusive)
£   Debenture Stock   Debenture/Notes Nos.
to   (inclusive) have been issued credited as fully paid by way of conversion/exchange/consideration for property acquired/other consideration not being cash and have been

* See Note to Schedule V.

duly allotted/transferred to the persons entitled thereto (and that the said Shares have subsequently been converted into £   Stock).

5.   THAT the Share/Stock Certificates/Debenture Stock Certificates/Debentures/Notes have been/are ready to be delivered.

6.   THAT the Supplemental Trust Deed/Deed Poll relating to any Debenture Stock or Notes issued by the Company has been completed and executed and that a copy thereof has (if so required by the Companies Acts) been filed with the Registrar of Companies and a further copy has been lodged with the Share and Loan Department.

7.   THAT all the further Shares/Debentures/Debenture Stock/Notes of each class for which quotation has been granted are in all respects identical* with those that were already quoted.

AND we make this solemn declaration conscientiously believing the same to be true and by virtue of the Statutory Declarations Act, 1835.

DECLARED at

SCHEDULE VII.

PART 1.

MEMORANDUM AND ARTICLES OF ASSOCIATION.

(i)   The Company must not by its Memorandum of Association or other corresponding document reserve power to itself to act as Brokers or to deal in shares.

(ii) The Articles of Association or other corresponding document must contain provisions to the following effect:—

A. as regards Transfer and Registration;

1.   That the common form of transfer shall be used;

2.   That fully-paid shares shall be free from any restriction on the right of transfer and shall also be free from all lien;

3.   That where the Company takes power to refuse to register more than three persons as joint holders of a share such power shall not apply to the Executors or Trustees of a deceased holder; and that where a member has sold part of the shares comprised in his holding, he shall be entitled to a certificate for the balance without charge;

B. as regards Definitive Certificates;

1.   That all forms of Certificate for Shares, Stock, Debenture Stock, or representing any other form of security (other than Letters of Allotment or Scrip Certificates) shall be issued under the Common Seal of the Company, and shall bear the autographic signatures of one or more Directors and the Secretary.   This

* See Note to Schedule V.

requirement so far as it relates to the signatures of the Directors may be relaxed in cases where the Directors being so authorised by the Articles have resolved to adopt some method of mechanical signature which is controlled by the Auditors, Transfer Auditors or Bankers of the Company;

2. That the charge for a new Certificate issued to replace one that has been worn out, lost or destroyed shall not exceed one shilling;

3. Where power is taken to issue Share Warrants to Bearer, that no new Share Warrant shall be issued to replace one that has been lost, unless it is proved to have been destroyed;

C. as regards Dividends;

1. That any amount paid up in advance of calls on any share shall carry interest but shall not entitle the holder of the share to participate in respect thereof in a dividend subsequently declared;

2. That unclaimed dividends cannot be forfeited before the claim becomes barred by law;

D. as regards Directors;

1. That Directors must hold a share qualification which must not be merely nominal;

2. That the borrowing powers of the Board are limited so that the aggregate amount at any time owing by the company and its subsidiary companies (exclusive of inter-company borrowings) shall not exceed a reasonable amount except with the consent of the Company in General Meeting by Ordinary Resolution;

3. That a Director shall not vote on any contract in which he is interested and if he do so vote, his vote shall not be counted;

4. That the Directors shall have power at any time and from time to time to appoint any other person as a Director either to fill a casual vacancy or as an addition to the Board, but so that the total number of Directors shall not at any time exceed the maximum number authorised by the Articles of Association; but that any Director so appointed shall hold office only until the next following Ordinary General Meeting of the Company, and shall then be eligible for re-election;

5. That where not otherwise required by law the Company in General Meeting shall have power by Ordinary Resolution to remove any Director (including a Managing Director, but without prejudice to any claim for damages under any contract) before the expiration of his period of office;

E. as regards Accounts;

That a printed copy of the Report, accompanied by the Balance Sheet (including every document required by law to be annexed thereto) and Profit and Loss Account or Income and Expenditure Account, shall, at least 14 days* previous to the General Meeting,

---

* In the case of a Company registered abroad, this period must be extended to such a time as will enable the members who have a registered address within the United Kingdom to be represented at the Meeting at which the accounts are considered.

be delivered or sent by post to the registered address of every member, and that three copies of each of these documents shall at the same time be forwarded to the Secretary of the Share and Loan Department, The Stock Exchange, London;

F. as regards Rights;

1. That adequate voting rights are in appropriate circumstances secured to Preference Shareholders;

2. That the rights attached to any class of shares may not be varied without the reasonable consent of the holders of such shares;

G. as regards Investment Trusts;

Where it is desired that the securities of the Company be classified under the 'Investment Trusts' Section of the Official List, that all moneys realised in the sale or payment off of any capital assets in excess of book value of the same and all other moneys in the nature of accretion to capital shall be treated for all purposes as capital moneys, and not as profits available for dividend;

H. as regards Notices;

1. That where power is taken to give notice by advertisement such advertisement shall be inserted in at least one leading London daily newspaper;

2. That a Company incorporated outside the United Kingdom shall give notice sufficient to enable members, whose registered addresses are within the United Kingdom, to exercise their rights or comply with the terms of the notice;

3. That where it is provided that notices will be given only to those members whose registered addresses are within the United Kingdom, any member, whose registered address is not within the United Kingdom, may name an address within the United Kingdom which, for the purposes of notice, shall be considered as his registered address;

I. as regards Redeemable Securities;

That, where power is reserved to purchase a redeemable security, purchases, if not made through the Market, shall be limited to a maximum price.

SCHEDULE VII.

PART 2.

TRUST DEEDS AND DEBENTURES.

Trust Deeds and Debentures not secured by a Trust Deed must contain provisions to the following effect:—

A. as regards Redemption;

1. That, where provision is made that the security shall be repayable at a premium either at a fixed date or at any time upon notice having been given, the security shall not in the event of the

Company going into voluntary liquidation be repayable at less than the premium then current;

2. That, where power is reserved to purchase a redeemable security, purchases, if not made through the Market, shall be limited to a maximum price;

3. That where stock is subject to redemption by drawings, the amount (or unit) into which the issue is to be divided for the purpose of the drawing shall not exceed £100;

B. as regards Trustees;

1. That there shall be at least two Trustees provided that a Trust Corporation may be appointed Sole Trustee;

2. That where there is more than one Trustee, one at least of the Trustees must be a Corporation;

3. That the Trustee or Trustees must have no interest in or relation with company which might conflict with the position of Trustee;

4. That a new Trustee appointed under any statutory or other power must prior to appointment be approved by an Extraordinary Resolution of the Debenture (or Debenture Stock) holders;

C. as regards Meetings and Voting Rights;

1. That a meeting of debenture (or debenture stock) holders must be called on a requisition in writing signed by holders of at least one-tenth of the nominal amount of the Debentures (or Debenture Stock) for the time being outstanding;

2. That the quorum for passing an Extraordinary Resolution shall be the holders of a clear majority in value of the whole of the outstanding Debentures (or Debenture Stock) present in person or by proxy. If such a quorum be not obtained, provision may be made for the adjournment of the meeting for not less than 14 days; in that event, notice of the adjourned meeting shall be sent to every debenture (or debenture stock) holder and shall state (if it be the case) that if a quorum as above defined shall not be present at the adjourned meeting, the debenture (or debenture stock) holders then present will form a quorum;

3. That the necessary majority for passing an Extraordinary Resolution shall be not less than three-fourths of the persons voting thereat on a show of hands and if a poll is demanded then not less than three-fourths of the votes given on such a poll;

4. That on a poll, each holder of Debentures or Debenture Stock shall be entitled to at least one vote in respect of every £10 of Debentures or Debenture Stock held by him, except that where the lowest denomination in which such securities can be transferred is more than £10, such denomination may be substituted for the £10 above referred to;

D. as regards Transfer;

That in the case of a registered security the common form of transfer shall be used;

E. as regards Definitive Certificates;

1. That the fee for a new registered Debenture or Debenture Stock Certificate to replace one that has been worn out, lost or destroyed shall not exceed one shilling;

2. That on any payment off of part of the amount due on the security, unless a new document is issued, a note of such payment shall be enfaced (not endorsed) on the document;

F. as regards Security;

1. That in the case of securities which are entitled 'Mortgage,' the same shall be secured to a substantial extent by a direct specific mortgage on freehold or long leasehold estate or other immovable property or on ships. In the case of Debentures or Debenture or Loan Stocks which will constitute an unsecured liability it is essential that the same should be entitled 'unsecured';

2. That the aggregate of the borrowings of any subsidiary company shall be limited to a reasonable amount except with the consent of an Extraordinary Resolution of the debenture (or debenture stock) holders.

SCHEDULE VIII.

PART 1.

GENERAL UNDERTAKING (COMPANIES).

1. To issue all Letters of Allotment and of Right simultaneously and in the event of its being impossible to issue letters of regret at the same time to insert in the Press a notice to that effect, so that the notice shall appear on the morning after the Allotment Letters have been posted.

2. To issue the Definitive Certificates within one month of the date of the expiration of any Right to Renunciation or the lodgment of a transfer and to issue Balance Certificates without charge if required within the same period.

3. To certify transfers against Allotment Letters, Definitive Certificates and Balance Receipts.

4. (a) To notify the share or stockholder as soon as a transfer out of his name has been certified by the Company's officials or notification of Certification has been received from the Share and Loan Department or any Associated Stock Exchange.

(b) To send out proxy forms to shareholders and debenture holders in all cases where proposals other than those of a purely routine nature are to be considered; and to provide that such proxy forms are so worded that a shareholder or debenture holder may vote either for or against each Resolution.

5. Where power has been taken in the Articles to issue Share Warrants to Bearer, in the event of the Company deciding to make such an issue: (i) to issue such Warrants in exchange for

registered shares within three weeks of the deposit of the Share Certificates; and (ii) to certify transfers against the deposit of Share Warrants to Bearer.

6. To notify the Share and Loan Department without delay:—

    (a) of any changes in the Directorate;

    (b) of any proposed change in the general character or nature of the business of the Company or of any subsidiary thereof; ·

    (c) of any extension of time granted for the currency of temporary documents;

    (d) of intention to make a drawing of any securities, intimating at the same time the date of the drawing and, in the case of a registered security, the period of the closing of the transfer books (or the date of the striking of the balance) for the drawing;

    (e) of the amount of the security outstanding after any drawing has been made;

    (f) of the date of the Board Meeting at which the declaration of a dividend will be considered.

7. To notify the Share and Loan Department by letter (or telegram or telephone*) immediately the Board Meeting has been held to consider or decide the same:—

    (a) of all dividends and/or cash bonuses recommended or declared or the decision to pass any dividend or interest payment;

    (b) of the net profit figures for the year (with comparison with previous year) even if this calls for the qualification that such profit figures are provisional, or subject to audit;

    (c) of short particulars of any issue of new capital whether to be issued as a bonus or by way of right to shareholders or debenture holders;

    (d) of any other information necessary to enable the shareholders to appraise the position of the Company and to avoid the establishment of a false market in the shares.

8. To forward to the Share and Loan Department:—

    (a) Three copies of the Statutory and Annual Report and Accounts as soon as issued;

    (b) †Through the Company's Brokers, four copies of the proofs of all circulars to shareholders or debentureholders prior to their despatch;

    (c) Three copies of all Resolutions increasing the capital and all notices relating to further issues of capital, call letters or any other circular at the same time as sent to the shareholders; and

---

* The Department should be consulted respecting the method of transmitting advices to be sent by telegram or telephone.

† In cases where it is contended that the submission of confidential proof documents might be detrimental to the Company's interest, application may be made to the Committee to waive compliance with this provision.

(*d*) Three copies of all Resolutions passed by the Company in General Meeting other than Resolutions passed at an Ordinary General Meeting for the purpose of adopting the Report and Accounts, declaring dividends, and re-electing Directors and Auditors.

9. Where a Company is either a holding company or conducts its business through one or more subsidiary companies to make up and circulate a Consolidated Balance Sheet and Profit and Loss Account.

SCHEDULE IX.
MARKETING STATEMENT
(PLACINGS).

1. Name of Company..

2. Description of Security...

3. Total amount involved in marketing operation..............................
   at ....

4. State how allocated, whether subject to quotation or not, and at what price, *e.g.*
   Retained by Issuing House (if any)..
   Placed with Issuing House's Clients...
   at ....
   Retained by Broker..
   Placed with Broker's Clients...
   at ....
   Placed with Country Brokers..
   at ....
   Placed with Market...
   at ....

                                                          Total

5. State how allocated by Market and at what price to:—
   Broker applying for quotation..
   at ....
   Other Brokers ....
   at ....
   Retained by Market for free dealings at opening of the Market..

6. Description of pooling arrangements, if any...............................

7. Anticipated 'opening price' when free dealings commence (*i.e.* apart from all placing arrangements)..

8. Details of proposed orders to repurchase at opening óf Market..

9. Details of further selling limits and whether left firm with Market..

10. General statement that these arrangements have been completed and no other arrangements at other prices have been made ....

11. Details of any other circumstances attending this placing which the Committee should know before giving their decision with regard to granting of quotation...

(See question 4)

Name of Jobber(s) .... Amount.......................

....

....

....

....Brokers.

Dated................................19................

SCHEDULE X.

TABLE OF CHARGES FOR QUOTATION TO BE MADE BY THE COUNCIL.

(No fee is charged for stock unit applications, un-numbering of shares, or applications arising out of change of name, denomination, dividend rights, or exercise of conversion or option rights.)

1. For all Quotations granted up to £100,000 money value other than those indicated above:

Up to £4,999	.. ..	Nil
£5,000 to £9,999	..	5 guineas
£10,000 to £19,999	..	10 ,,
£20,000 to £49,999	..	25 ,,
£50,000 to £100,000	..	50 ,,

2. Quotations involving a money value in excess of £100,000 are divided into two categories as under:—

Category I. Prospectuses, Offers for Sale, Placings and Introductions.

Category II. Rights, Bonuses, Open Offers, Conversions, Reconstructions, and further issues of identical securities.

For Category I Quotation charges are in accordance with the following scale:—

For Category II Quotation charges are at half the following scale:—

SCALE OF CHARGES.

Money value not exceeding	£200,000	..	100 guineas.
" " " "	£300,000	..	150 "
" " " "	£400,000	..	200 "
" " " "	£500,000	..'	250 "
" " " "	£600,000	..	300 "
" " " "	£700,000	..	350 "
" " " "	£800,000	..	400 "
" " " "	£900,000	..	450 "
" " " "	£1,000,000	..	500 "
" " exceeding	£1,000,000	..	500 "

NOTES.

1. No charge is made in the case of issues to be quoted in the following sections of the Official List:—

> British Funds.
> Securities guaranteed under the Trade Facilities and other Acts.
> Corporation and County Stocks—Great Britain and Northern Ireland.
> Public Boards, etc.—Great Britain and Northern Ireland.
> Dominion, Provincial and Colonial Government Securities.
> *Corporation Stocks—Dominion and Colonial.*

2. Where the money value of an issue is in doubt it will be fixed by the Council for the purposes of this Schedule.

Reproduced by permission of the Council of the Stock Exchange, London.

PRELIMINARY ANNOUNCEMENTS.*

Requirements of the Share and Loan Department of the Stock Exchange, London.

It is requested that in the absence of any special circumstances the following minimum information should be included when a preliminary announcement in respect of any year (or accounting period, is made in relation to:—

1. A Holding Company (within the meaning of the Companies Act, 1948).

(a) Group profit (or loss) of the year after all charges including taxation.

(b) United Kingdom taxation charged in arriving at (a).

(c) Amount of (a) attributable to members of Holding Company, *i.e.* after deduction of outside interests.

(d) If material, extent to which (a) has been affected by special credits (including transfers from reserves) and/or debits.

(e) Rates of dividend(s) of Holding Company paid and proposed and net amount absorbed thereby.

* This note was drawn up in co-operation with the Institute of Chartered Accountants, the Society of Incorporated Accountants and the Chartered Institute of Secretaries.

(*f*)   Comparative figures of (*a*) to (*e*) inclusive for the preceding year.

(*g*)   Any supplementary information which in the opinion of the Directors is necessary for a reasonable appreciation of the results of the year or of other material changes in the aggregate of the balances on profit and loss account and other reserves of the Group.

NOTE.—Where in the opinion of the Directors of a Holding Company the amounts involved in respect of one or more subsidiary companies are insignificant, they need not be included in a preliminary announcement, and where the Directors are of such an opinion in respect of each of the subsidiary companies, the information contained in a preliminary announcement may be restricted to that requested in 2 below.

     2.   A Company which is not a Holding Company.

(*a*)   Profit (or loss) of the year after all charges including taxation.

(*b*)   United Kingdom taxation charged in arriving at (*a*).

(*c*)   If material, extent to which (*a*) has been affected by special credits (including transfers from reserves) and/or debits.

(*d*)   Rates of dividend(s) paid and proposed and net amount absorbed thereby.

(*e*)   Comparative figures of (*a*) to (*d*) inclusive for the preceding year.

(*f*)   Any supplementary information which in the opinion of the Directors is necessary for a reasonable appreciation of the results of the year or of other material changes in the aggregate of the balance on profit and loss account and other reserves.

II.   The Share and Loan Department will continue to welcome preliminary announcements which contain information additional to that set out above.

APPENDIX E

Practice of the Board of Trade in relation to the Names of Companies

Reproduced by permission of the Board of Trade

NAMES OF COMPANIES (EXPLANATORY LEAFLET)

Section 17 of the Companies Act, 1948, provides that 'No company shall be registered by a name which in the opinion of the Board of Trade is undesirable.'

The following notes are given for the guidance of the public though it must be understood that they are in no way exhaustive.

1. A name will not be allowed if it is misleading; for example, if it suggests that a company with small resources is trading on a great scale or over a wide field.

2. Names cannot ordinarily be allowed which suggest connection with the Crown or members of the Royal Family or suggest royal patronage (including names containing such words as 'Royal,' 'King,' 'Queen,' 'Princess,' 'Crown').

3. Names cannot ordinarily be allowed if they suggest connection with a Government department or any municipality or other local authority or any society or body incorporated by Royal Charter or by Statute or with the government of any part of the British Commonwealth or of any foreign country.

4. Only in exceptional circumstances and for valid reasons will names be allowed which include any of the following words:— 'Imperial,' 'Commonwealth,' 'National,' 'International.'

5. Names must not include the word 'Co-operative' or the words 'Building Society.'

6. Names including the following words will be allowed only where the circumstances justify it: 'Bank,' 'Banking,' 'Investment,' 'Trust.'

7. Names which include a proper name which is not the surname of the proprietor(s) or of a director as the case may be will not be allowed except for valid reasons.

8. If the proposed name includes a registered trade mark, the consent of the owner of the trade mark should be produced to the Registrar of Companies or the Registrar of Business Names as the case may be.

APPENDIX F

Forms Appendix

INDEX

FORM No. I

Number of⎫
Company ⎭ ....

THE STAMP ACT, 1891
(54 and 55 Vict. Ch. 39).

AND FINANCE ACTS, 1896 AND 1933.

COMPANY LIMITED BY SHARES.

STATEMENT OF NOMINAL CAPITAL

OF

....

LIMITED

Presented by ....

Pursuant to Section 112 of The Stamp Act, 1891,
Section 12 Finance Act, 1896, and Section 41, Finance Act, 1933

[*NOTE.—The Stamp Duty on the Nominal Capital is Ten Shillings for
every £100 or fraction of £100.*

This Statement is to be filed with a Memorandum of Association, or
other Documents, when a Company is registered.]

The Nominal Capital

of

.... Limited,

is .... Pounds,

(£..........................) divided into..

....

....

....

....

....

Signature..
*..

Dated the..day of
....19..........

State whether Director or Secretary.

FORM No. 2

No. of Company...........................

Form No. 4.

THE COMPANIES ACT, 1948.

A 5s. Companies Registration Fee Stamp must be impressed here.

NOTICE OF SITUATION OF REGISTERED OFFICE OR OF ANY CHANGE THEREIN

OF

Name
of   { ....
Company   { .... Limited.

Pursuant to Section 107 (2) of The Companies Act, 1948.

Presented by ....

[This Notice should be signed by a Director or Secretary of the Company, and must be forwarded to the Registrar of Companies within 14 days after the date of the incorporation of the Company or of the change, as the case may be.

If default is made in complying with this Section, the Company and every officer of the Company who is in default shall be liable to a default fine.]

NOTICE

OF THE

SITUATION OF THE REGISTERED OFFICE

OF

....
.... Limited,

or of any change therein.

To the Registrar of Companies

....

....

.... Limited,

hereby gives you notice, in accordance with Section 107 of The Companies Act, 1948, that the Registered Office of the Company is situate at

....

....

Signature..

* ....

Dated the...day

of.. 19..........

*State whether Director or Secretary.

FORM No. 3

No. of Company..................................   Form No. 9.

THE COMPANIES ACT, 1948.

O *A 5s. Companies Registration Fee Stamp must be impressed here.*

PARTICULARS OF DIRECTORS AND SECRETARIES.
Pursuant to Section 200.

Name
of   { ....
Company   { .... Limited.

Presented by   ....

[*This notice should be signed by a Director or Secretary of the Company.*]

NOTES.

*Director includes any person who occupies the position of a Director by whatsoever name called, and any person in accordance with whose directions or instructions the Directors of the Company are accustomed to act.

†*Christian name* includes a forename, and *surname*, in the case of a peer or person usually known by a title different from his surname, means that title.

‡*Former Christian name* and *former surname* do not include—
(a) in the case of a peer or a person usually known by a British title different from his surname, the name by which he was known previous to the adoption of or succession to the title; or
(b) in the case of any person, a former Christian name or surname where that name or surname was changed or disused before the person bearing the name attained the age of eighteen years or has been changed or disused for a period of not less than twenty years; or
(c) in the case of a married woman the name or surname by which she was known previous to the marriage.

§*Directorships.* The names of all bodies corporate incorporated in Great Britain of which the Director is also a director, should be given, except bodies corporate of which the Company making the Return is the wholly-owned subsidiary or bodies corporate which are the wholly-owned subsidiaries either of the Company or of another company of which the Company is the wholly-owned subsidiary. A body corporate is deemed to be the wholly-owned subsidiary of another if it has no members except that other's wholly-owned subsidiaries and its or their nominees. If the space provided in the form is insufficient, particulars of other directorships should be listed on a separate statement attached to this form.

‖*Dates of birth* need only be given in the case of a Company which is subject to section 185 of The Companies Act, 1948, namely, a Company which is not a Private Company or which, being a Private Company, is the subsidiary of a body corporate incorporated in the United Kingdom which is neither a Private Company nor a company registered under the law relating to companies for the time being in force in Northern Ireland and having provisions in its constitution which would, if it had been registered in Great Britain, entitle it to rank as a Private Company.

¶Where all the partners in a firm are *joint Secretaries*, the name and principal office of the firm may be stated.

FORM No. 3 (continued)

PARTICULARS OF THE PERSONS WHO ARE DIRECTORS* OF THE COMPANY AT THE DATE OF THIS RETURN.

NAME (In the case of an individual, present Christian name† or names and surname. In the case of a corporation, the corporate name)	Any former Christian name or names and surname‡	Nationality	Usual residential address (In the case of a corporation, the registered or principal office)	Business occupation and particulars of other directorships§	Date of birth‖

PARTICULARS OF THE PERSON WHO IS SECRETARY OF THE COMPANY AT THE DATE OF THIS RETURN.

NAME (In the case of an individual, present Christian name or names and surname†. In the case of a corporation or a Scottish firm, the corporate or firm name)¶	Any former Christian name or names and surname‡	USUAL RESIDENTIAL ADDRESS (In the case of a corporation or a Scottish firm, the registered or principal office)

Date................................ 19........

Signed _____

(State whether Director or Secretary)

Note.—For explanation of symbols used above, see previous page.

FORM No. 4

No. of Company.................................   Form No. 41.

THE COMPANIES ACT, 1948.

A 5s. Companies Registration Fee Stamp must be impressed here.

DECLARATION OF COMPLIANCE WITH THE REQUIREMENTS OF THE COMPANIES ACT, 1948, ON APPLICATION FOR REGISTRATION OF A COMPANY. *Pursuant to Section 15 (2).*

Name of Company } .... Limited.

Presented by ....

I, ...

of ....

....

Do solemnly and sincerely declare that I am*...

....

....

....

of ....

....

Limited, and that all the requirements of The Companies Act, 1948, in respect of matters precedent to the registration of the said Company and incidental thereto have been complied with. And I make this Solemn Declaration conscientiously believing the same to be true and by virtue of the provisions of the Statutory Declarations Act, 1835.

Declared at..

....

the.. day of

....one thousand

nine hundred and ....

before me,

....

A Commissioner for Oaths.†

* "A Solicitor of the Supreme Court" (*or in Scotland* "a Solicitor") "engaged in the formation" *or* "A person named in the Articles of Association as a Director" (*or* "Secretary").

† *or* Notary Public *or* Justice of the Peace.

FORM No. 5

THIRD SCHEDULE.

FORM OF STATEMENT IN LIEU OF PROSPECTUS TO BE DELIVERED TO
REGISTRAR BY A PRIVATE COMPANY ON BECOMING A PUBLIC COMPANY
AND REPORTS TO BE SET OUT THEREIN.

PART I.

FORM OF STATEMENT AND PARTICULARS TO BE CONTAINED THEREIN.
THE COMPANIES ACT, 1948.

Statement in lieu of Prospectus delivered for registration by
[*Insert the name of the company.*]

Pursuant to section 30 of the Companies Act, 1948.

Delivered for registration by	
The nominal share capital of the company.	£
Divided into	Shares of £ each.
	,, ,, ,,
	,, ,, ,,
Amount (if any) of above capital which consists of redeemable preference shares.	Shares of £ each.
The earliest date on which the company has power to redeem these shares.	
Names, descriptions and addresses of directors or proposed directors.	
Amount of shares issued	Shares
Amount of commissions paid in connection therewith.	
Amount of discount, if any, allowed on the issue of any shares, or so much thereof as has not been written off at the date of the statement.	
Unless more than one year has elapsed since the date on which the Company was entitled to commence business:—	
Amount of preliminary expenses By whom those expenses have been paid or are payable.	£
Amount paid to any promoter ..	Name of promoter:— Amount £ .
Consideration for the payment..	Consideration:—
Any other benefit given to any promoter.	Name of promoter:— Nature and value of benefit:—
Consideration for giving of benefit.	Consideration:—
If the share capital of the company is divided into different classes of shares, the right of voting at meetings of the company conferred by, and the rights in respect of capital and dividends attached to, the several classes of shares respectively.	

FORM No. 5 (*continued*)

Number and amount of shares and debentures issued within the two years preceding the date of this statement as fully or partly paid up otherwise than for cash or agreed to be so issued at the date of this statement.	1. shares of £ fully paid. 2. shares upon which £ per share credited as paid.
Consideration for the issue of those shares or debentures.	3. debenture £ 4. Consideration :—
Number, description and amount of any shares or debentures which any person has or is entitled to be given an option to subscribe for, or to acquire from a person to whom they have been allotted or agreed to be allotted with a view to his offering them for sale.	1. shares of £ and debentures of £
Period during which option is exercisable.	2. Until
Price to be paid for shares or debentures subscribed for or acquired under option.	3.
Consideration for option or right to option.	4. Consideration :—
Persons to whom option or right to option was given or, if given to existing shareholders or debenture holders as such, the relevant shares or debentures.	5. Names and addresses :—
Names and addresses of vendors of property (1) purchased or acquired by the company within the two years preceding the date of this statement or (2) agreed or proposed to be purchased or acquired by the company, except where the contract for its purchase or acquisition was entered into in the ordinary course of business and there is no connection between the contract and the company ceasing to be a private company or where the amount of the purchase money is not material.	
Amount (in cash, shares or debentures) paid or payable to each separate vendor.	

FORM No. 5 (continued)

Amount paid or payable in cash, shares or debentures for any such property, specifying the amount paid or payable for goodwill.

Total purchase price	£	
Cash	£	
Shares ..	£	
Debentures ..	£	
Goodwill ..	£	

Short particulars of any transaction relating to any such property which was completed within the two preceding years and in which any vendor to the company or any person who is, or was at the time thereof, a promoter, director or proposed director of the company had any interest direct or indirect.

Dates of, parties to, and general nature of every material contract (other than contracts entered into in the ordinary course of business or entered into more than two years before the delivery of this statement).

Time and place at which the contracts or copies thereof may be inspected or (1) in the case of a contract not reduced into writing, a memorandum giving full particulars thereof, and (2) in the case of a contract wholly or partly in a foreign language, a copy of a translation thereof in English or embodying a translation in English of the parts in a foreign language, as the case may be, being a translation certified in the prescribed manner to be a correct translation.

Names and addresses of the auditors of the company.

Full particulars of the nature and extent of the interest of every director in any property purchased or acquired by the company within the two years preceding the date of this statement or proposed to be purchased or acquired by the company or, where the interest of such a director consists in being a partner in a firm, the nature and extent of the interest of the firm, with a statement of all sums paid or agreed to be paid to him or to the firm in cash or shares, or otherwise, by any person either to induce him to become or to qualify him as, a director, or otherwise for services rendered or to be rendered to the company by him or by the firm.

FORM No. 5 (continued)

Rates of the dividends (if any) paid
  by the company in respect of each
  class of shares in the company in
  each of the five financial years
  immediately preceding the date of
  this statement or since the incorporation of the company whichever
  period is the shorter.

Particulars of the cases in which no
  dividends have been paid in respect
  of any class of shares in any of these
  years.

(Signatures of the persons above-named
  as directors or proposed directors or
  of their agents authorised in writing.)   ———————————————

                                           ———————————————

Date.

PART II.

REPORTS TO BE SET OUT.

1. If unissued shares or debentures of the company are to be applied
in the purchase of a business, a report made by accountants (who shall be
named in the statement) upon—

(a) the profits or losses of the business in respect of each of the five
     financial years immediately preceding the delivery of the statement
     to the registrar; and

(b) the assets and liabilities of the business at the last date to which
     the accounts of the business were made up.

2.—(1) If unissued shares or debentures of the company are to be
applied directly or indirectly in any manner resulting in the acquisition
of shares in a body corporate which by reason of the acquisition or anything to be done in consequence thereof or in connection therewith will
become a subsidiary of the company, a report made by accountants
(who shall be named in the statement) with respect to the profits and
losses and assets and liabilities of the other body corporate in accordance
with sub-paragraph (2) or (3) of this paragraph, as the case requires,
indicating how the profits or losses of the other body corporate dealt
with by the report would, in respect of the shares to be acquired, have
concerned members of the company, and what allowance would have
fallen to be made, in relation to assets and liabilities so dealt with, for
holders of other shares, if the company had at all material times held the
shares to be acquired.

(2) If the other body corporate has no subsidiaries, the report referred
to in the foregoing sub-paragraph shall—

(a) so far as regards profits and losses, deal with the profits or losses of
     the body corporate in respect of each of the five financial years
     immediately preceding the delivery of the statement to the registrar;
     and

(b) so far as regards assets and liabilities, deal with the assets and
     liabilities of the body corporate at the last date to which the
     accounts of the body corporate were made up.

FORM No. 5 *(continued)*

(3) If the other body corporate has subsidiaries, the report referred to in the sub-paragraph (1) of this paragraph shall—

(*a*) so far as regards profits and losses, deal separately with the other body corporate's profits or losses as provided by the last foregoing sub-paragraph, and in addition deal either—

    (i) as a whole with the combined profits or losses of its subsidiaries, so far as they concern members of the other body corporate; or

    (ii) individually with the profits or losses of each subsidiary, so far as they concern members of the other body corporate;

or, instead of dealing separately with the other body corporate's profits or losses, deal as a whole with the profits or losses of the other body corporate and, so far as they concern members of the other body corporate, with the combined profits or losses of its subsidiaries; and

(*b*) so far as regards assets and liabilities, deal separately with the other body corporate's assets and liabilities as provided by the last foregoing sub-paragraph and, in addition, deal either—

    (i) as a whole with the combined assets and liabilities of its subsidiaries, with or without the other body corporate's assets and liabilities; or

    (ii) individually with the assets and liabilities of each subsidiary;

and shall indicate as respects the assets and liabilities of the subsidiaries the allowance to be made for persons other than members of the company.

Part III.

Provisions applying to Parts I and II of this Schedule.

3. In this Schedule the expression "vendor" includes a vendor as defined in Part III of the Fourth Schedule to this Act, and the expression "financial year" has the meaning assigned to it in that Part of that Schedule.

4. If in the case of a business which has been carried on, or of a body corporate which has been carrying on business, for less than five years, the accounts of the business or body corporate have only been made up in respect of four years, three years, two years or one year, Part II of this Schedule shall have effect as if references to four years, three years, two years or one year, as the case may be, were substituted for references to five years.

5. Any report required by Part II of this Schedule shall either indicate by way of note any adjustments as respects the figures of any profits or losses or assets and liabilities dealt with by the report which appear to the persons making the report necessary or shall make those adjustments and indicate that adjustments have been made.

6. Any report by accountants required by Part II of this Schedule shall be made by accountants qualified under this Act for appointment as auditors of a company which is not an exempt private company and shall not be made by any accountant who is an officer or servant, or a partner of or in the employment of an officer or servant, of the company, or of the company's subsidiary or holding company or of a subsidiary of the company's holding company; and for the purposes of this paragraph the expression "officer" shall include a proposed director but not an auditor.

FORM No. 6

FIFTH SCHEDULE.

FORM OF STATEMENT IN LIEU OF PROSPECTUS TO BE DELIVERED TO REGISTRAR BY A COMPANY WHICH DOES NOT ISSUE A PROSPECTUS OR WHICH DOES NOT GO TO ALLOTMENT ON A PROSPECTUS ISSUED, AND REPORTS TO BE SET OUT THEREIN.

PART I.

FORM OF STATEMENT AND PARTICULARS TO BE CONTAINED THEREIN.
THE COMPANIES ACT, 1948.

Statement in lieu of Prospectus delivered for registration by
[*Insert the name of the company.*]

Pursuant to section 48 of the Companies Act, 1948.

Delivered for registration by

The nominal share capital of the company. £

Divided into .. .. Shares of £ each.
„ „ „
„ „
Shares of £ each.

Amount (if any) of above capital which consists of redeemable preference shares.

The earliest date on which the company has power to redeem these shares.

Names, descriptions and addresses of directors or proposed directors.

If the share capital of the company is divided into different classes of shares, the right of voting at meetings of the company conferred by, and the rights in respect of capital and dividends attached to, the several classes of shares respectively.

Number and amount of shares and debentures agreed to be issued as fully or partly paid up otherwise than in cash.

The consideration for the intended issue of those shares and debentures.

1.   shares of £ fully paid.
2.   shares upon which £ per share credited as paid.
3.   debenture £
4. Consideration:—

1.   shares of £ and debentures of £

Number, description and amount of any shares or debentures which any person has or is entitled to be given an option to subscribe for, or to acquire from a person to whom they have been allotted or agreed to be allotted with a view to his offering them for sale.

Period during which option is exercisable.

2. Until

FORM No. 6 *(continued)*

Price to be paid for shares or debentures subscribed for or acquired under option.	3.
Consideration for option or right to option.	4. Consideration:—
Persons to whom option or right to option was given or, if given to existing shareholders or debenture holders as such, the relevant shares or debentures.	5. Names and addresses:—
Names and addresses of vendors of property purchased or acquired, or proposed to be purchased or acquired by the company except where the contract for its purchase or acquisition was entered into in the ordinary course of the business intended to be carried on by the company or the amount of the purchase money is not material.	
Amount (in cash, shares or debentures) payable to each separate vendor.	
Amount (if any) paid or payable (in cash or shares or debentures) for any such property, specifying amount (if any) paid or payable for goodwill.	Total purchase price £ Cash .. .. £ Shares .. £ Debentures .. £ Goodwill .. £
Short particulars of any transaction relating to any such property which was completed within the two preceding years and in which any vendor to the company or any person who is, or was at the time thereof, a promoter, director or proposed director of the company had any interest direct or indirect.	
Amount (if any) paid or payable as commission for subscribing or agreeing to subscribe or procuring or agreeing to procure subscriptions for any shares or debentures in the company; or	Amount paid. ,, payable.
Rate of the commission	Rate per cent.
The number of shares, if any, which persons have agreed for a commission to subscribe absolutely.	
Estimated amount of preliminary expenses.	£
By whom those expenses have been paid or are payable.	
Amount paid or intended to be paid to any promoter.	Name of promoter Amount £ .
Consideration for the payment ..	Consideration:—

FORM No. 6 (continued)

Any other benefit given or intended to be given to any promoter.	Name of promoter:—
	Nature and value of benefit:—
Consideration for giving of benefit ..	Consideration:—
Dates of, parties to and general nature of every material contract (other than contracts entered into in the ordinary course of the business intended to be carried on by the company or entered into more than two years before the delivery of this statement).	
Time and place at which the contracts or copies thereof may be inspected or (1) in the case of a contract not reduced into writing, a memorandum giving full particulars thereof, and (2) in the case of a contract wholly or partly in a foreign language, a copy of a translation thereof in English or embodying a translation in English of the parts in a foreign language, as the case may be, being a translation certified in the prescribed manner to be a correct translation.	
Names and addresses of the auditors of the company (if any).	
Full particulars of the nature and extent of the interest of every director or in the promotion of or in the property proposed to be acquired by the company, or where the interest of such a director consists in being a partner in a firm, the nature and extent of the interest of the firm, with a statement of all sums paid or agreed to be paid to him or to the firm in cash or shares, or otherwise, by any person either to induce him to become, or to qualify him as, a director, or otherwise for services rendered by him or by the firm in connection with the promotion or formation of the company.	

Signatures of the persons above-named
as directors or proposed directors, or
of their agents authorised in writing.)

Date

FORM No. 6 (*continued*)

PART II.

REPORTS TO BE SET OUT.

1. Where it is proposed to acquire a business, a report made by accountants (who shall be named in the statement) upon—

(*a*)   the profits or losses of the business in respect of each of the five financial years immediately preceding the delivery of the statement to the registrar; and

(*b*)   the assets and liabilities of the business at the last date to which the accounts of the business were made up.

2.—(1) Where it is proposed to acquire shares in a body corporate which by reason of the acquisition or anything to be done in consequence thereof or in connection therewith will become a subsidiary of the company, a report made by accountants (who shall be named in the statement) with respect to the profits and losses and assets and liabilities of the other body corporate in accordance with sub-paragraph (2) or (3) of this paragraph, as the case requires, indicating how the profits or losses of the other body corporate dealt with by the report would, in respect of the shares to be acquired, have concerned members of the company, and what allowance would have fallen to be made, in relation to assets and liabilities so dealt with, for holders of other shares, if the company had at all material times held the shares to be acquired.

(2) If the other body corporate has no subsidiaries, the report referred to in the last foregoing sub-paragraph shall—

(*a*)   so far as regards profits and losses, deal with the profits or losses of the body corporate in respect of each of the five financial years immediately preceding the delivery of the statement to the registrar; and

(*b*)   so far as regards assets and liabilities, deal with the assets and liabilities of the body corporate at the last date to which the accounts of the body corporate were made up.

(3) If the other body corporate has subsidiaries, the report referred to in sub-paragraph (1) of this paragraph shall—

(*a*)   so far as regards profits and losses, deal separately with the other body corporate's profits or losses as provided by the last foregoing sub-paragraph, and in addition deal either—

  (i)   as a whole with the combined profits or losses of its subsidiaries, so far as they concern members of the other body corporate; or

  (ii) individually with the profits or losses of each subsidiary, so far as they concern members of the other body corporate;

or, instead of dealing separately with the other body corporate's profits or losses, deal as a whole with the profits or losses of the other body corporate and, so far as they concern members of the other body corporate, with the combined profits or losses of its subsidiaries; and

(*b*)   so far as regards assets and liabilities, deal separately with the other body corporate's assets and liabilities as provided by the last foregoing sub-paragraph and, in addition, deal either—

  (i)   as a whole with the combined assets and liabilities of its subsidiaries, with or without the other body corporate's assets and liabilities; or

  (ii) individually with the assets and liabilities of each subsidiary;

and shall indicate as respects the assets and liabilities of the subsidiaries the allowance to be made for persons other than members of the company.

FORM No. 6 (continued)

PART III.

Provisions applying to Parts I and II of this Schedule.

3. In this Schedule the expression "vendor" includes a vendor as defined in Part III of the Fourth Schedule to this Act, and the expression "financial year" has the meaning assigned to it in that Part of that Schedule.

4. If in the case of a business which has been carried on, or of a body corporate which has been carrying on business, for less than five years, the accounts of the business or body corporate have only been made up in respect of four years, three years, two years or one year, Part II of this Schedule shall have effect as if references to four years, three years, two years or one year, as the case may be, were substituted for references to five years.

5. Any report required by Part II of this Schedule shall either indicate by way of note any adjustments as respects the figures of any profits or losses or assets and liabilities dealt with by the report which appears to the persons making the report necessary or shall make those adjustments and indicate that adjustments have been made.

6. Any report by accountants required by Part II of this Schedule shall be made by accountants qualified under this Act for appointment as auditors of a company which is not an exempt private company and shall not be made by any accountant who is an officer or servant, or a partner of or in the employment of an officer or servant, of the company or of the company's subsidiary or holding company or of a subsidiary of the company's holding company; and for the purposes of this paragraph the expression "officer" shall include a proposed director but not an auditor.

T

FORM No. 7

No. of Company..................................   Form No. 42.

THE COMPANIES ACT, 1948.

A 5s. Companies Registration Fee Stamp must be impressed here.

CONSENT TO ACT AS DIRECTOR OF A COMPANY

Name
of   { ....
Company { .... Limited,

[to be signed and delivered pursuant to S. 181 (1) (a) of the Companies Act, 1948.]

Presented by ....

To the Registrar of Companies.

(a)   , the undersigned hereby testify (b)   consent to act as Director of ....

....

.... Limited,

pursuant to S. 181 (1) (a) of the Companies Act, 1948.

Signature*	Address	Description

Dated this.......................................day of.........................19..........

(a) Here insert "I" or "We."
(b) Here insert "My" or "Our."
* If a Director signs by "his agent authorised in writing," the authority must be produced.

FORM No. 8

No. of Company............................. Form No. 43.

THE COMPANIES ACT, 1948

A 5s. Companies Registration Fee Stamp must be impressed here.

LIST OF THE PERSONS WHO HAVE CONSENTED TO BE DIRECTORS OF A COMPANY.

Name
of   ....
Company .... Limited,

[to be delivered to the Registrar pursuant to S. 181 (4) of the Companies Act, 1948.]

Presented by ....

List of the Persons who have consented to be Directors of...........................
.... Limited, delivered to the Registrar of Companies, pursuant to Section 181 (4) of the Companies Act, 1948, by..

of ....

the applicant(s) for Registration of the Memorandum and Articles of the Company.

Surname	Christian Name	Address and Description

[*Signature of Applicant(s)*]..

Dated the...day of..........................19.........

FORM No. 9

THE COMPANIES ACT, 1948.
Section 181 (1) (b) (iii).

UNDERTAKING BY THE DIRECTORS TO TAKE AND PAY FOR
QUALIFICATION SHARES IN

....

.... Limited.

Presented by ....

To the REGISTRAR OF COMPANIES.

We, the Undersigned, having consented to act as Directors of........................

....

.... Limited,

do hereby severally Agree to take from the said Company and to pay for

....Shares of..each, being the prescribed

number of Qualification Shares for the office of Director of the Company.

Name	Address

Dated the..day of....................................19..........

Witness to the above Signatures—

FORM No. 10

No. of Company..............................

THE COMPANIES ACT, 1948.

Consent to Take the Name of an Existing Company.

Name
of   {
Company   { ....

.... Limited.

Presented by   ....

To the Registrar of Companies.

I (or We)..

....

....

of   ....

....

....

....

being the Liquidator(s) of...

....

.... Limited.

a Company in the course of being dissolved, hereby, and on behalf of the
said Company, testify its consent to the Registration of a new Company
by the name of..

....

....

....

Signature...

(a) ....

Dated the.................................day of...............................19..........

(a) *To be signed by each Liquidator if more than one.*

FORM No. II

No. of Company................................   Form No. 44.

THE COMPANIES ACT, 1948.

◯   *A 5s. Companies Registration Fee Stamp must be impressed here.*

DECLARATION THAT THE CONDITIONS OF SECTION 109 (1) (a), (b) AND (c) OF THE COMPANIES ACT, 1948, HAVE BEEN COMPLIED WITH.

Pursuant to Section 109 (1) (d).

(To be used by a company which issued a prospectus on or with reference to its formation.)

Name of Company..Limited.

Presented by   ....
....
....

I, ...
of   ....
being   (a)...of...
Limited, do solemnly and sincerely declare:—

That the amount of the share capital of the company offered to the public for subscription is £...

That the amount stated in the prospectus as the minimum amount which in the opinion of the directors must be raised by the issue of share capital in order to provide for the matters specified in paragraph 4 of Part I of the Fourth Schedule to the Companies Act, 1948, is £.............

That the shares held subject to the payment of the whole amount thereof in cash have been allotted to the amount of £.............................

That every director of the company has paid to the company on each of the shares taken or contracted to be taken by him and for which he is liable to pay in cash a proportion equal to the proportion payable on application and allotment on the shares offered for public subscription, except the following director(s) namely...who has/have not taken or contracted to take any shares for which he is/they are liable to pay in cash.

*That no director of the company has taken or contracted to take any shares for which he is liable to pay in cash.

That no money is or may become liable to be repaid to applicants for any shares or debentures which have been offered for public subscription by reason of any failure to apply for or to obtain permission for the shares or debentures to be dealt in on any stock exchange.

And I make this solemn declaration conscientiously believing the same to be true, and by virtue of the provisions of the Statutory Declarations Act, 1835.

Declared at   ....
the   .... day of
.... one thousand
nine hundred and   ....
before me.

....
Commissioner for Oaths (b).

* Delete words not applicable.
(a) "the secretary" *or* "a director."
(b) *or* Notary Public *or* Justice of the Peace.

FORM No. 12

No. of Company.................................   Form No. 44A.

THE COMPANIES ACT, 1948.

◯ *A 5s. Companies Registration Fee Stamp must be impressed here.*

DECLARATION THAT THE PROVISIONS OF SECTION 109 (2) (*b*) OF THE
COMPANIES ACT, 1948, HAVE BEEN COMPLIED WITH.
Pursuant to Section 109 (2) (*c*).

(*To be used by a company which has delivered to the Registrar of Companies a statement in lieu of prospectus.*)

Name of Company... Limited.

Presented by ....

....

....

_____

I, ...

of ....

being (*a*) .... of

.... Limited,

do solemnly and sincerely declare:—

That every director of the company has paid to the company on each of the shares taken or contracted to be taken by him and for which he is liable to pay in cash, a proportion equal to the proportion payable on application and allotment on the shares payable in cash, except the following director(s) namely...
who has/have not taken or contracted to take any shares for which he is/they are liable to pay in cash.

*That no director of the company has taken or contracted to take any shares for which he is liable to pay in cash.

And I make this solemn declaration conscientiously believing the same to be true, and by virtue of the provisions of the Statutory Declarations Act, 1835.

Declared at ....⎫
the.. day ⎪
.... one thousand ⎪
nine hundred and .... ⎬ ....
before me. ⎪
    A Commissioner for Oaths (*b*) ⎭

* Delete words not applicable.
(*a*) "the secretary" *or* "a director."
(*b*) *or* Notary Public *or* Justice of the Peace.

FORM No. 13

No. of Company....................................   Form No. 11.

THE COMPANIES ACT, 1948.

NOTICE OF INCREASE IN NUMBER OF MEMBERS.
Pursuant to Section 7 (3).

Name of Company...Limited.

Presented by

....

....

....

Notice of increase in the Number of Members of.......................................
.... Limited.

To the Registrar of Companies.

....
.... Limited,
hereby gives you notice, pursuant to Section 7 (3) of the Companies Act,
1948, that by (*a*)..resolution of the company
dated the...........................day of...............................19........ the number of
members in the company has been increased by the addition thereto of
....members beyond the present registered number of...............

(*Signature*)..

(*State whether Director or Secretary*)...

Dated the..day of.................................19..........

(*a*) "Ordinary," "extraordinary" *or* "special."

FORM No. 13a

No. of Company.............................   Form No. 17.

THE COMPANIES ACT, 1948.

APPLICATION BY AN EXISTING COMPANY FOR REGISTRATION AS A LIMITED COMPANY.

Pursuant to Sections 384, 385 and 386

Name of Company...

Presented by

....

....

....

Application by (*a*)..
for registration as a limited company under the Companies Act, 1948.

(*a*) ....

....

constituted by..
dated the...day of......................................19..........
desires to register itself as a company limited by..
under the Companies Act, 1948, by the name of ....

....

Limited, and, for that purpose, delivers the under-mentioned documents for registration under the said Act.

(*Signature*)..

(*State whether Director or Secretary*)..

Dated the.....................................day of..............................19..........

Documents delivered for registration with the foregoing application (*b*).

1. Copy of the...
   constituting or regulating the company.
2. List of the members of the company made up to the................................
   day of...................................19..........
3. Statement specifying particulars required by section 384 (*c*).
4. List showing names, addresses and occupations of the directors or other managers and the secretary of the company.
5. Copy of resolutions of the company assenting to its registration as a limited company, and adding the word "Limited" to its name.
6. Declaration by (*c*)...
   of the company, verifying the particulars set forth in the document above mentioned.

(*a*) *Insert name of company.*
(*b*) *See Forms officially numbered 19, 21, 22 and 23.*
(*c*) *This declaration to be by any two directors or other principal officers of the company.*

FORM No. 13b

No. of Company............................   Form No. 18.

THE COMPANIES ACT, 1948.

APPLICATION BY AN EXISTING COMPANY FOR REGISTRATION AS AN UNLIMITED COMPANY.
Pursuant to Sections 384, 385 and 386.

Name of Company..

Presented by

....

....

....

Application by (*a*)..

....

for registration as an unlimited company under the Companies Act, 1948.

   (*a*) ....

....

constituted by..

dated the .... day of .... 19......

desires to register itself under the Companies Act, 1948, and for that purpose delivers the under-mentioned documents for registration under the said Act.

                   (*Signature*)..

(*State whether Director or Secretary*)..

   Dated the..day of............................19........

Documents delivered for registration with the foregoing application (*b*).

1. Copy of the..
      constituting or regulating the company.
2. List of the members of the company made up to the............................
      day of..19........
3. Statement of the registered office of the company.
4. List showing names, addresses and occupations of the directors or other managers and the secretary of the company.
5. Copy of resolutions of the company assenting to its registration.
6. Declaration by (*c*)..
      of the company verifying the particulars set forth in the documents above mentioned.

   (*a*) *Insert name of company.*
   (*b*) *See Forms officially numbered* 19 *and* 23.
   (*c*) *This declaration to be by any two directors or other principal officers of the company.*

FORM No. 13c

No. of Company.................................   Form No. 19.

THE COMPANIES ACT, 1948.

A 5s. Companies Registration Fee stamp must be impressed here.

REGISTRATION OF AN EXISTING COMPANY.
LIST OF MEMBERS.

Pursuant to Section 384.

Name of Company..

Presented by

....

....

....

List of Members of..

....

made up to the (a).................................day of...................19..........

1 Surname	2 Christian name	3 Address	4 Occupation	5 Number of shares, or amount of stock, held	6 Distinctive numbers of the Shares (if any)

(To be signed and dated at the end).

(*Signature*)...

(*State whether Director or Secretary*)...

Dated the.................................day of...................19..........

(a) *Not more than six clear days before delivery for registration.*

FORM No. 13d

No. of Company................................   Form No. 21

THE COMPANIES ACT, 1948.

REGISTRATION OF AN EXISTING COMPANY AS A LIMITED COMPANY.
STATEMENT SPECIFYING PARTICULARS REQUIRED BY SECTION 384 (c).

Name of Company...

Presented by

....

....

....

Amount of nominal capital   ..
Number of shares into which it is
    divided, and amount of each
    share   ..   ..   ..
Amount of stock of which it con-
    sists   ..   ..
Number of shares or amount of
    stock taken up to the...............day
    of.......................19..........(a)   ..
Amount paid on each share   ..

Name of the company   ..   ..   Limited.
Registered office   ..   ..   ..
Resolution declaring the amount
    of the guarantee (b)   ..   ..

(*Signature*)...

(*State whether Director or Secretary*)...

Dated the..day of...............................19..........

(a) *Not more than six clear days before delivery for registration.*
(b) *To be completed by a company intending to be registered as a company
limited by guarantee.*

FORM No. 13e

No. of Company............................   Form No. 22.

THE COMPANIES ACT, 1948.

REGISTRATION OF AN EXISTING COMPANY AS A LIMITED COMPANY.
COPY RESOLUTIONS ASSENTING TO REGISTRATION WITH LIMITED LIABILITY.
Pursuant to Sections 382 (1) (v) and (vii) and 384 (c) (iv).

Name of Company..

Presented by

....

....

....

Copy Resolutions passed at a general meeting of...

....

held on the...........................day of...19........

assenting to its being registered with limited liability.

(The Resolutions to be written or printed here.)

(*Signature*)....................................

(*State whether Director or Secretary*)....................................

FORM No. 13f

No. of Company...............................   Form No. 23.

THE COMPANIES ACT, 1948.

REGISTRATION OF AN EXISTING COMPANY.

DECLARATION VERIFYING DOCUMENTS DELIVERED TO THE REGISTRAR OF
COMPANIES WITH APPLICATION FOR REGISTRATION.

Pursuant to Section 386.

Name of Company...

Presented by

....

....

....

    We, ...

of ....

and ....

of ....

being two of the...

of (a)..

Do solemnly and sincerely declare that the particulars set forth in the
several documents accompanying this Declaration, and marked respec-
tively with the letters...
....are   true;
And we make this solemn Declaration conscientiously believing the same
to be true, and by virtue of the provisions of the Statutory Declarations
Act, 1835.

Declared at..⎫
....⎪
the.....................day of..........................⎪
.... one thousand ⎬   (b)..
nine hundred and.............................⎪   ....
before me.   ⎪
....⎭

    A Commissioner for Oaths (c)

(a) *Insert name of company.*
(b) *To be signed by two or more directors or other principal officers.*
(c) *or* Notary Public *or* Justice of the Peace.

FORM No. 14

No. of Company..   Form No. 9A.

THE COMPANIES ACT, 1948.

A 5s. Companies Registration Fee Stamp must be impressed here.

NOTIFICATION OF CHANGE OF DIRECTORS OR SECRETARY
OR IN THEIR PARTICULARS.

Pursuant to Section 200

Name
of   { ....
Company   .... Limited.

Presented   by...

[*This notice should be signed by a Director or Secretary of the Company.*]

NOTES.

* *Director* includes any person who occupies the position of a Director by whatsoever name called, and any person in accordance with whose directions or instructions the Directors of the Company are accustomed to act.

† *Christian name* includes a forename, and *surname*, in the case of a peer or person usually known by a title different from his surname, means that title.

‡ *Former Christian name* and *former surname* do not include—

(a) In the case of a peer or a person usually known by a British title different from his surname, the name by which he was known previous to the adoption of or succession to the title; or

(b) in the case of any person, a former Christian name or surname where that name or surname was changed or disused before the person bearing the name attained the age of eighteen years or has been changed or disused for a period of not less than twenty years; or

(c) in the case of a married woman the name or surname by which she was known previous to the marriage.

§ *Directorships.* The names of all bodies corporate incorporated in Great Britain of which the Director is also a director, should be given, except bodies corporate of which the Company making the Return is the wholly-owned subsidiary or bodies corporate which are the wholly-owned subsidiaries either of the Company or of another company of which the Company is the wholly-owned subsidiary. A body corporate is deemed to be the wholly-owned subsidiary of another if it has no members except that other and that other's wholly-owned subsidiaries and its or their nominees. If the space provided in the form is insufficient, particulars of other directorships should be listed on a separate statement attached to this form.

‖ *Dates of birth* need only be given in the case of a Company which is subject to section 185 of The Companies Act, 1948, namely, a Company which is not a Private Company or which, being a Private Company, is the subsidiary of a body corporate incorporated in the United Kingdom which is neither a Private Company nor a company registered under the law relating to companies for the time being in force in Northern Ireland and having provisions in its constitution which would, if it had been registered in Great Britain, entitle it to rank as a Private Company.

¶ Where all the partners in a firm are *joint Secretaries*, the name and principal office of the firm may be stated.

FORM No. 14 (continued)

NOTIFICATION OF CHANGE OF DIRECTORS OR SECRETARY OR IN THEIR PARTICULARS.

To the Registrar of Companies.

.... Limited, hereby notifies you in accordance with Section 200 of the Companies Act, 1948, that:—

(Here specify nature and date of change. If change consists of the appointment of a new Director* or Secretary fill in also particulars below).

PARTICULARS OF NEW DIRECTOR* OR SECRETARY (Columns 1, 2 and 4 only need be completed for a Secretary)

NAME (In the case of an individual, present Christian name† or names and surname. In the case of a corporation, the corporate name)‖	Any former Christian names and surname‡	Nationality	Usual residential address (In the case of a Corporation, the registered or principal office)	Business occupation and particulars of other directorships§	Date of birth‖

Date .... 19......

Signed ....

(State whether Director or Secretary)

Note.—For explanation of symbols used above, see previous page.

FORM No. 15

REGISTER OF DIRECTORS' SHAREHOLDINGS.

REGISTER OF DIRECTORS' SHAREHOLDINGS, ETC.   Pursuant to Section 195 of the Companies Act, 1948.

Name of Director...............

NAME OF COMPANY	STOCK—SHARES—DEBENTURES			How held (i.e. Holder; In trust; Right to become Holder)	INTEREST OR RIGHT ACQUIRED		CESSATION OF INTEREST OR RIGHT		If required by Director Details of nature and extent of interest or right
	Number	Description	Amount		Date of Agreement	Price or other con-sideration	Date of Agreement	Price or other con-sideration	

FORM No. 16

REGISTER OF DIRECTORS AND SECRETARIES.

REGISTER OR DIRECTORS* AND SECRETARIES Pursuant to Section 200 of the Companies Act, 1948.

of .... Limited. Entered .... 19......

DIRECTORS

NAME (In the case of an individual, present Christian name† or names and surname. In the case of a corporation, the corporate name)	Any former Christian name or names and surname‡	Nationality	Usual residential address (In the case of a corporation, the registered or principal office)	Business occupation and particulars of other directorships§	Date of birth‖	CHANGES specifying nature and date**

SECRETARIES

NAME (In the case of an individual, present Christian name or names and surname.† In the case of a corporation or a Scottish firm, the corporate or firm name)¶	Any former Christian name or names and surname†	USUAL RESIDENTIAL ADDRESS (In the case of a corporation or a Scottish firm, the registered or principal office)	CHANGES specifying nature and date

NOTES.

* "Director" includes any person who occupies the position of a Director by whatsoever name called, and any person in accordance with whose directions or instructions the Directors of the Company are accustomed to act.

† "Christian name" includes a forename, and "surname" in the case of a Peer or person usually known by a title different from his surname, means that title.

‡ "Former christian name" and "former surname" do not include—

(a) In the case of a peer or person usually known by a British title different from his surname, the name by which he was known previous to the adoption of or succession to the title; or

(b) in the case of any person, a former christian name or surname where that name or surname was changed or disused before the person bearing the name attained the age of eighteen years or has been changed or disused for a period of not less than twenty years; or

(c) in the case of a married woman the name or surname by which she was known previous to the marriage.

§ Directorships—The names of all bodies corporate incorporated in Great Britain of which the Director is also a Director, should be given, except bodies corporate of which the Company making the Return is the wholly-owned subsidiary or bodies corporate which are the wholly-owned subsidiaries either of the Company or of another company of which the Company is the wholly-owned subsidiary. A body corporate is deemed to be the wholly-owned subsidiary of another if it has no members except that other and that other's wholly-owned subsidiaries and its or their nominees.

‖ Dates of birth need only be given in the case of a Company which is subject to Section 185 of The Companies Act, 1948, namely, a Company which is not a Private Company or which, being a Private Company, is the subsidiary of a body corporate incorporated in the United Kingdom which is neither a Private Company nor a Company registered under the law relating to companies for the time being in force in Northern Ireland and having provisions in its constitution which would, if it had been registered in Great Britain, entitle it to rank as a Private Company.

** A complete list of the Directors shown as existing in the last particulars filed should always be given. A note of changes specifying dates since the last Return was made should be given in this column, e.g. by placing against a new Director's name the words "in place of ....", and adding the word "resigned," "deceased," or as the case may be.

¶ Where all the partners in a firm are joint secretaries, the name and principal office of the firm may be stated.

FORM No. 17

FORM OF APPLICATION FOR SHARES.
(PRIVATE COMPANY)

No............................

To the Directors of

.... Limited.

Gentlemen,

    I enclose..for £........................., being a

deposit / payment in full   of .... per share on...........................

....................................:. shares of £...................................each in the above-named Company, and I request you will allot me that number of shares, which I hereby agree to accept or any less number that you may allot to me upon the terms of the Memorandum and Articles of Association of the Company, and I authorise you to place my name in the Register of Members of the Company in respect of the shares allotted to me.

    Important.—To comply with the provisions of the Exchange Control Act, 1947, the Applicant(s) must make the Declaration contained in the following paragraph, or if unable to do so must delete such paragraph and consult his/their Bankers in order to have the appropriate Declaration and Certificate completed. No application will be considered unless this condition is fulfilled.

    I/we hereby declare that I am not/no one of us is resident outside the Scheduled Territories,* nor shall I/we be acquiring the shares as the nominee(s)† of any person(s) resident outside those Territories.

Dated the........................day of....................................19..........

      Signature ....

      Name (in full)..

      Address (in full)...

      ....

    * The Scheduled Territories. Here insert reference to the current definition of Scheduled Territories.
    † The definition of "nominee" is given in the Bank of England's Notice E.C. (Securities) 1, as amended.

.... [PERF.] ....

....

Limited.

RECEIPT
(To be returned to the Applicant)

No............................

Received the........................*day of*....................................19.........., *from*

M ....

of .... • ....

the sum of..*being a deposit of*

....................................*per share of*....................................*each in the above*

Company.

      For .... Limited.

£ : :   .... | 2d. Stamp | ....

                                                    Secretary.

This Form of Application should be sent entire to the Office of the Company at

FORM No. 18

LETTER OF ALLOTMENT.
(PRIVATE COMPANY.)

.... Limited.

Allotment No..................................

....

.... 19.........

To..

Dear Sir,

     In answer to your application I have to inform you that the Directors have allotted to you..Shares of..each in this Company.

The total amount payable up to and on allotment is (at ....per share)   ..   .. £

You have deposited on application (at.........per share) ..   .. £

Leaving still to be paid by you   ..   .. £

which sum is now due, and I have to request be paid to me on or before ....19..........accompanied by this form which will be duly receipted and returned.

     The relative Share Certificates will be ready for delivery on or after ....19.......... in exchange for Letters of Allotment.

Yours faithfully,

....

Secretary.

REQUEST FOR SHARE CERTIFICATE.

To the Secretary of...Limited.

Please ⎰ send by post at my risk to the address below ⎱ Share Certificate in
        ⎱ hand to the bearer hereof

exchange for this Allotment Letter.

Signature ....

Name   ....

Address..

Date.........

.... [PERF.] ....

Allotment No...................................

RECEIPT.   ....19..........

     Received of ....

the sum of..

being the amount payable on Allotment of the above-mentioned Shares.

┌──────┐
│ 2d. │
│Stamp │
└──────┘

....*Secretary.*

This form to be sent entire to the Company with the payment on allotment.

FORM No. 19

FORM OF APPLICATION.
(PUBLIC COMPANY.)

††*Allotment Letter No.*..............................

Serial No.............
(*inserted by Bank*).

....LIMITED.
(*Incorporated under the Companies Act*, 1948).

Issue of   Redeemable Preference Shares of £1 each at

FORM OF APPLICATION.

To THE DIRECTORS,

...................................LIMITED,

...................................London, W.C.2.

GENTLEMEN,

Having paid to your Bankers the sum of £......................., being a deposit of 10s. per share on application for .... per cent Cumulative Redeemable Preference Shares of £1 each in the aboved-named Company, I/we hereby apply for and request you to allot to me/us that number of such shares, and I/we hereby undertake and agree to accept such shares or any less number that may be allotted to me/us, upon the terms of the prospectus dated the ....day of ....19......, and subject to the Memorandum and Articles of Association of the Company, and I/we agree to pay the further instalment as provided by the said prospectus; and I/we hereby authorise you to place my/our name(s) on the Register of Members of the Company as holder(s) of the shares so allotted.

IMPORTANT.—To comply with the provisions of The Exchange Control Act, 1947, the Applicant(s) must make the Declaration contained in the following paragraph, or if unable to do so must delete such paragraph and consult his/their Bankers in order to have the appropriate Declaration and Certificate completed. No application will be considered unless this condition is fulfilled.

I/We hereby declare that I am not/no one of us is resident outside the Scheduled Territories,* nor shall I/we be acquiring the shares as the nominee(s)‡ of any person(s) resident outside those Territories.

Dated this........................day of ...., 19....

In the case of Joint Holdings all Joint Holders must sign.

A Corporation should complete under hand by an official who should state his capacity. If however the seal is affixed, unless in Scotland, a 10s. stamp should be impressed.

Applications in the name of a firm cannot be accepted.

Signature ....
Name in full......................................
  (Block letters)
Address in full..................................

Occupation ....
(A woman should state whether she is a Spinster, Married Woman or Widow).

Signature ....
Name in full......................................
  (Block letters)
Address (in full)................................

Occupation ....
(A woman should state whether she is a Spinster, Married Woman or Widow).

Cheques should be made payable to "................ Bank Limited or Bearer" and crossed "Not Negotiable." Any alteration from "Order" to "Bearer" must be signed by the drawer. This Application Form, together with cheque, should be sent to .... Bank Limited, Issue Department, ... Street, London, E.C.3, or to any branch of .... Bank Limited.

No receipt will be issued for the payment on application, but an acknowledgment will be forwarded in due course, either by Allotment Letter in whole or in part, or by return of the deposit.

*The Scheduled Territories. "Here insert reference to the current definition of Scheduled Territories."
‡The definition of "nominee" is given in the Bank of England's Notice E.C. (Securities) 1, as amended.
††This information is necessary in cases where a *separate* List of Applications and Allotments is not desired. (See Form 26.)

[Machine punched to fit perfectly in files.]

††THIS SPACE FOR COMPANY'S USE ONLY				
Shares Allotted	Total Cash Due	Already Paid	Cash Now	Payable / Returnable
	£ : :	£ : :	£ : :	
Cert. No.	Plate	Posted		

FORM No. 20

ALLOTMENT LETTER.
(PUBLIC COMPANY.)

....Limited
(*Incorporated under the Companies Act, 1948*).

Issue of   Cumulative Redeemable Preference Shares of £1 each at

To	*Transfer Office:*
.... Street,
London, W.C.2.
.....th ...., 19....
No..............

ALLOTMENT LETTER.

DEAR SIR(S) (OR MADAM),

In response to your application I am directed to inform you that the Directors have allotted you............. per cent. Cumulative Redeemable Preference Shares of £1 each, on the terms of the Prospectus as filed with the Registrar of Companies, dated ....19........., and subject to the Memorandum and Articles of Association of the Company.

The total amount payable on the number of Shares allotted, at........is   ..   .. £   :   :

You have paid   ..   .. £   :   :

Leaving a balance now due from you of   ..   .. £   :   :

or

Leaving a balance returnable to you, for which a cheque is attached, of ..   .. £   :   :

The sum due from you must be paid forthwith to.......................... Bank Limited, Issue Department, ... Street, London, E.C.3, or Branches, accompanied by this Letter, which will be receipted by the Bankers and returned to you.

These shares will rank for dividend as from ....inst., and the first dividend, for the period ending ....19........., will be.............. (gross) per share, payable on........................19..........

Renunciation of the above shares can be effected by the use of forms X and Y overleaf, in accordance with the instructions there set out.

Renunciation must deal with the whole of the shares included in this Allotment Letter, but Allotment Letters will be split once only on application at the Transfer Office of the Company, above mentioned, up to and including the ....19......... in which case you should lodge this Letter, specifying the denominations in which you require the Letter split, with the form of Renunciation (Form "X") and Declaration 1 or 1A duly completed. A fee of 1s. od. for each split Letter required must be paid when this Letter is lodged for splitting.

After the ....19........and pending the issue of the Definitive Certificates, instruments of transfer will be certified against delivery of fully paid Allotment Letters at the Transfer Office of the Company, above mentioned.

This Letter of Allotment should be carefully retained intact and should be lodged without further request on or before the ....19.......... with the Company, when a Share Certificate will be issued in exchange therefor. Before lodgment, form Y overleaf must be completed.

By Order of the Board,

....Secretary.

Exd...........................

BANKERS' RECEIPT (not to be detached).

RECEIVED *the above-mentioned sum, being the amount due on Allotment.*

For.................Bank Limited.

......................19..........   .... | 2d.
Stamp | ....Cashier.

.... [PERF.] ....

..........................Limited.   No...........

Issue of.............................Cumulative Redeemable Preference Shares of One Pound each at..........

Balance due on Allotment.

£   :   :

| 2d.
Stamp | ....Cashier.

..........................19..........

To be retained by the Bankers on payment of amount due on Allotment.

FORM No. 20 (continued)

IMPORTANT.

INSTRUCTIONS WITH REGARD TO RENUNCIATION.

The Shares to which this Letter of Allotment relates will (subject to the completion of Form "Y") be registered in the name(s) of the original Allottee(s) unless Form "X" is filled in and signed by the original Allottee(s) and Form "Y" below is completed by the party or parties in whose name(s) the Shares are to be registered, and lodged at the Company's Transfer Office, ..., London, W.C.2, on or before the........................19............ Thereafter the Shares will only be transferable by instruments of transfer in the common form.

No renunciation will be registered until the amount due on allotment has been paid.

* The original allottee(s) will remain liable for the amount due on allotment notwithstanding renunciation in favour of some third party.

In cases where it is desired to renounce to more than one nominee (other than Joint Nominees) or to renounce part of the allotment only, this Letter of Allotment will be split once only on application at the Transfer Office of the Company above mentioned, up to and including the........................19............ A charge of 1s. 0d. for each split Letter of Allotment will be made.

Surrender of this Letter of Allotment with the Form of Renunciation purporting to be signed by the Allottee(s) shall be conclusive evidence in favour of the Company of the title of the party or parties surrendering this Letter of Allotment to deal with the same and to receive split Letters and also the Share Certificate.

In the case of a split, the Form of Renunciation will be endorsed "Original duly Renounced and where applicable, Declaration lodged."

Form X.   FORM OF RENUNCIATION.

To the Directors of........................Limited.

I/We hereby renounce my/our right to the within-mentioned Shares allotted to me/us in favour of the party or parties signing the Registration Application Form below.

Dated this........................day of........................19............

All Joint Holders must sign.
    A Corporation should complete under hand by an official who should state his capacity. If however the seal is affixed, unless in Scotland, a 10s. stamp should be impressed.

Signature(s) of Allottee(s) ....

IMPORTANT.—In cases of Renunciation, Declaration 1 or 1A must also be duly completed on behalf of the allottee(s).

Form Y.   REGISTRATION APPLICATION FORM.

To be completed by the person(s) in whose name(s) the shares are to be registered.

To the Directors of........................Limited.

I/We hereby request and authorise you to register the within-mentioned Preference Shares in my/our name(s) in the Register of Members of the Company and I/we agree to accept the same subject to the Memorandum and Articles of Association of the Company. I/We authorise you to send the Definitive Certificate to me/us at the first address given below by post at my/our risk.

IMPORTANT.—In cases of renunciation, Declaration 2 of Form D or Declaration 2A, certificate and authorisation must be completed on behalf of renouncee(s).

Dated this........................day of........................19............

* This instruction is necessary if the Shares are not fully paid on application.

FORM No. 20 (*continued*)

In the case of Joint Holdings all Joint Holders must sign.

A Corporation should complete under hand by an official who should state his capacity. If however the seal is affixed, unless in Scotland, a 10s. stamp should be impressed.

Applications in the name of a firm cannot be accepted.

Signature ....
Name in full...
   (Block letters)
Address (in full)...
....

Occupation ....
  (A woman should state whether she is a Spinster, Married Woman or Widow.)

Signature ....
Name in full...
   (Block letters)
Address (in full)...
....

Occupation ....
  (A woman should state whether she is a Spinster, Married Woman or Widow.)

EXCHANGE CONTROL ACT, 1947.

FORM D

1. TO BE COMPLETED ON BEHALF OF THE RENOUNCER(s).
(*If this Declaration cannot be made, Declaration 1A must be completed.*)

The holder(s)* of the within-mentioned security is/are not resident outside the Scheduled Territories†† and from the facts known to us or from enquiries we have made is/are not to the best of our belief holding the security as the nominee(s)* of any person(s) resident outside those Territories.

Stamp and Signature of
  *Authorised Depositary***
  or Temporary Recipient†*..* Date........

Address ....

1A. TO BE COMPLETED ONLY IF DECLARATION 1 ABOVE CANNOT BE MADE.

Licence.. No.. examined.
Stamp and Signature of
  *Authorised Depositary*** .... Date........

---

2. TO BE COMPLETED ON BEHALF OF THE RENOUNCEE(s).
(*If this declaration cannot be made, Declaration 2A must be completed.*)

The transferee(s) is/are not resident outside the Scheduled Territories†† and from facts known to us or from enquiries we have made is/are not to the best of our belief acquiring the security as the nominee(s)* of any person(s) resident outside those Territories.

Stamp and Signature of
  *Authorised Depositary***
  or Temporary Recipient†*...*
Address .... Date........

2A. TO BE COMPLETED ONLY IF DECLARATION 2 ABOVE CANNOT BE MADE.

The renouncee(s) is/are permanently resident in.............................(country) and, from facts known to us or from enquiries we have made, to the best of our belief
Delete   (a) is/are not a nominee(s).*
(a) or (b) (b) is/are a nominee(s)* of a person(s) permanently resident in.............................(country),
    (c) the renunciation is not made to or for the benefit of an enemy subject(s) resident outside the Scheduled Territories††

Stamp and Signature of
  *Authorised Depositary***
  or Temporary Recipient†*...* Date........
Address ....

FORM No. 20 (continued)

WE CERTIFY that this transaction is a *bona fide* purchase for full value in the ordinary course of business and that the full consideration money:—

Delete   (i) has been/will be debited to, or is eligible for credit, to a............................Account.

(i) or (ii)   (ii) has been provided by the realisation of other securities sold for that purpose under Licence.

...........................No.........

Stamp and Signature§... *Date*...............

§Where (i) is completed, the above Certificate must be signed by a bank in the United Kingdom, the Isle of Man or the Channel Islands, or by the Public Trustee.

Where (ii) is completed, the Certificate must be signed by an Authorised Depositary** or Temporary Recipient.*†

AUTHORISED for the purposes of the Exchange Control Act, 1947.

(*Authorisation is not required when Declaration* 1 *or* 1A *and Declaration* 2 *have been completed.*)

Date.....................*Stamp and Signature of Authorised Depositary**.....................

Enquiries must be made, where necessary, as to the true ownership of the securities before these declarations are made.

*The definitions of "holder" and "nominee" are given in the Bank of England's Notice E.C. (Securities) 1.

††The Scheduled Territories. Here insert reference to the current definition of Scheduled Territories.

**Authorised Depositaries include:—
  (i) The Bank of England.
  (ii) The Share and Loan Department of The Stock Exchange, London.
  (iii) Offices in the United Kingdom of the Banks listed in Appendix II of the Bank of England's Notice E.C. (Securities) 1.

*†Temporary Recipients include:—
  (i) Members of the Stock Exchange, London.
  (ii) Members of Associated Stock Exchanges listed in Appendix III of the Notice above referred to.
  (iii) Firms of Solicitors in the United Kingdom.
  (iv) The Public Trustee and the Accountant-General of the Supreme Court.
  (v) Persons, firms and corporations listed in Appendix III of the Notice above referred to.

*†Temporary Recipients must indicate their classification (*e.g.* "Members of the Birmingham Stock Exchange," "Exempted Dealers in securities under the Prevention of Fraud (Investments) Act, 1939"). Stockbrokers and Solicitors must sign the firm's name

.... [PERF.] ....

Important.—Please detach, endorse and pay into your Bank immediately.

....Limited Bank National No..........

London..................19........ No.........

To............ Bank Limited,
.... Street,
London, E.C.3.

& Co.
NOT NEGOTIABLE

2d. Stamp

Pay.....................................*or order*

the sum of .... £

.....................*Signature of Payee* For and on behalf of

.....................Limited.

.....................*Secretary*

FORM No. 21

PROVISIONAL ALLOTMENT LETTER.
(Public Company.)

No.......................

This Document is valuable and should not be destroyed. If in doubt you are advised to consult your Stockbroker or Banker immediately.

(*Consent of the Treasury has been obtained to the issue in compliance with the Order made under Section 1 of the Borrowing (Control and Guarantees) Act, 1946; it must be distinctly understood that in giving this consent the Treasury does not take any responsibility for the financial soundness of any schemes or for the correctness of any of the statements made or opinions expressed with regard to them.)

A copy of this document, having attached thereto a print of the Circular Letter therein referred to, has been delivered to the Registrar of Companies for registration.

Application has been made to the Council of The Stock Exchange, London, for permission to deal in and quotation for the Ordinary shares now being issued.

....Company Limited.

(Incorporated under the Companies Act, 1948).

Transfer Office:..Street, London, W.C.2.

To:	Holding of Ordinary and Deferred stock at the close of business on..............19.........	Number of Ordinary shares of £1 each provisionally allotted	Amounts payable
			First Instalment
			£........:.......:...........
			Final Instalment
	£....................	....	£........:.......:...........

Issue to ordinary and deferred stockholders of ....Ordinary Shares of £1 each at .... per share payable as follows:—

On or before................19.........   ..   .. per share (including ....premium)
On or before................19.........   ..   .. per share (including ....premium)

PROVISIONAL ALLOTMENT LETTER.

Dear Sir (or Madam), ...19.........

With reference to the Company's Circular Letter dated.....................19........, the Directors have provisionally allotted to you shares of this issue as indicated above, being in the proportion of three Ordinary shares for every £10 Ordinary or Deferred stock registered in your name at the close of business on.........19......., fractions of a new share being disregarded.

The new Ordinary shares will rank *pari passu* with the existing Ordinary stock of the Company, except that they will not participate in any interim dividend in respect of the Company's financial year ending ....19.........; they will be entitled, however, to the full amount of such final dividend as may be declared in respect of that year. When fully paid the new shares will be converted into stock and will be transferable in amounts and multiples of £1.

First Instalment and Acceptance.—If this Provisional Allotment is accepted, Form "A" on page 2 must be completed by or on behalf of the person(s) making payment, and this Letter must be lodged entire with ....Bank Limited, New Issue Department, London, E.C.2, accompanied by a remittance of ....per share, not later than the close of business on ....19.......... This Letter will be receipted and returned by the Bank. If payment is not received on or before that date, this Provisional Allotment will be deemed to have been declined and will be cancelled. The payment of such first instalment will constitute the acceptance of the Allotment on the terms of this Provisional Allotment Letter and subject to the Memorandum and Articles of Association of the Company.

Cheques should be made payable to "...............Bank Limited or Bearer" and crossed "Not Negotiable." Any alteration from "Order" to "Bearer" must be signed by the Drawer.

Renunciation of this Provisional Allotment can be effected up to and including ....19........., by the use of Form "C" on page 3. In the event of Renunciation, Form "B" on page 2 and Form "E" on page 3 must be completed by the person(s) in whose name(s) the stock is to be registered.

If it is desired to take up part only of the shares to which you are entitled, or to renounce the whole of the allotment to more than one nominee (other than to joint nominees), you must obtain Split Allotment Letters which will be issued upon application on or before ....19......... at the Company's Transfer Office, as above, against surrender of this Provisional Allotment Letter, provided Form "C" on page 3 is duly completed. Allotment Letters may be split, once only nil paid, up to ....19......... and once only partly paid, up to and including................19......... provided the amount payable as set out above has been paid on or before the due date. A fee of 1s. od. will be charged for each Split Allotment Letter issued.

The Final Instalment is payable on or before ....19......... when payment thereof, together with this Allotment Letter with Form "E" on page 3 duly completed, should be lodged with ....Bank Limited as above who will receipt and return pages 1 and 2 of this Allotment Letter.

Failure to pay the final instalment when due will render any amount previously paid liable to forfeiture and the allotment to cancellation. Payment of the first or final instalment may be made in full before their due dates, but no interest will be allowed on any such pre-payment. Interest at the rate of 5 per cent. per annum may be charged on overdue instalments if accepted after their due dates.

*(Where applicable this wording or such other wording as may be ordered. Where consent is necessary the Capital Issues Committee does not always give consent under the Act named.)

FORM No. 21 (continued)

When this Provisional Allotment Letter is fully paid, it should be carefully retained so as to be exchanged for the stock certificate at the Company's Transfer Office, as above, on or after................19........ After................19........, and pending the issue of stock certificates, the Company will certify transfers against delivery of fully paid Provisional Allotment Letters at its Transfer Office.

By Order of the Board,

Exd.....................................   ....Secretary.

NOT TO BE DETACHED		NOT TO BE DETACHED	
Payment of final instalment due on ....19........ *Received the amount due* For............Bank Limited (New Issue Department),	2d. Stamp	Payment of first instalment due on ....19........ *Received the amount due* For............Bank Limited (New Issue Department),	2d. Stamp
Date............ 19........		Date............ 19........	

....[PERF.]...

To be retained by the Bank.

No..............

....Company Limited.

First instalment due on ....19........

£   :   :

Page 2.

....Company Limited.

Notes Regarding Renunciation and Registration.

1. If the original allottee(s) desire(s) all the shares to be registered in his/their name(s) it is not necessary in the first instance to complete either Form "C" or Form "E." The allottee(s) must, however, complete Form "A" upon making payment of the first instalment, and Form "E" upon making payment of the final instalment.

2. If the original allottee(s) desire(s) to dispose of all or part of the shares he/they must complete Form "C" on page 3. The shares comprised in this Provisional Allotment Letter when fully paid as provided therein will be converted into stock and the stock will be registered in the name(s) of the original allottee(s), unless Form "C" has been completed and signed by the original allottee(s) and Forms "B" and "E" have been completed by the person(s) in whose name(s) the stock is to be registered, and this Provisional Allotment Letter is lodged at ....Bank Limited, New Issue Department, London, E.C.2, on or before ....19........, together with remittance for the final instalment of ....per share. After that date or prior payment in full the stock will be transferable only by transfer in the common form.

3. Surrender of this Provisional Allotment Letter duly completed shall be conclusive evidence in favour of the Company of the title of the person(s) depositing this Provisional Allotment Letter to deal with the same and to receive Split Allotment Letters (or definitive certificates). Allotment Letters and definitive certificates will be sent through the post at the risk of the party entitled thereto.

A   TO BE COMPLETED BY THE PERSON(S) MAKING PAYMENT, OR HIS/THEIR AGENT(S), ON OR BEFORE ...., 19........

To the Directors,

....Company Limited.

I/We declare that the person(s) making payment or on whose behalf the payment is made is/are not resident outside the Scheduled Territories†† and is/are not acquiring the shares as nominee(s)* of any person(s) resident outside those Territories.††

(*If this Declaration cannot be signed a separate Declaration 2A Form D and Certificate as on page 4 must be completed and signed by an Authorised Depositary** or Temporary Recipient *† as indicated therein. The Declaration on page 4 should not be used for this purpose.*)

Signature of person(s) or agent(s) making payment..

Address of person(s) or agent(s) making payment..

Date.. 19........

B   IN THE CASE OF RENUNCIATION FULL NAME(S) AND ADDRESS(ES) OF RENOUNCEE(S) MUST BE ENTERED HERE.

FORM No. 21 (continued)

Page 3.

C

FORM OF RENUNCIATION.

No............

(Available until ....19........)

To the Directors,

....Company Limited.

I/We hereby renounce my/our right to the shares comprised in this Provisional Allotment Letter in favour of the person(s) accepting the same and signing the Registration Application Form in relation to such shares.

All joint holders must sign. Renunciations by corporate bodies must be sealed. {

Signature(s) of Allottee(s)..

....

....

Date.............................19.......

In the case of renunciation Declaration 1 or 1A set out on page 4 must also be duly completed on behalf of the allottee(s).

In the case of a split Allotment Letter Declaration 1 or 1A may be completed either on the original or on the split Allotment Letter. Form of Renunciation will be endorsed "Original duly renounced and (when applicable) Declaration lodged."

E

REGISTRATION APPLICATION FORM

(To be completed by the person(s) in whose name(s) the shares are to be registered.)

To the Directors,

....Company Limited.

I/We request you to register the..............................shares comprised in the within Allotment Letter *and in the several Allotment Letters attached hereto, the definitive numbers whereof and the number of shares comprised wherein are detailed below*† (or the stock into which they have become converted) in my/our name(s), on the terms embodied in the within Allotment Letter and subject to the Memorandum and Articles of Association of the Company. I/We authorise you to send the definitive stock certificate to me/us at the first address given below at my/our risk.

IMPORTANT.—Allottee(s) who desire(s) to be registered must make the Declaration contained in the following paragraph, or, if unable to do so must delete such paragraph and consult his/their Bankers in order to have Declaration 2A and Certificate on page 4 completed and Authorised.

In the case of renunciation the appropriate Declaration on page 4 must be completed on behalf of the renouncee(s), and where necessary Authorised.

I/We declare that I am/we are not resident outside the Scheduled Territories†† and am/are not acquiring the security as the nominee(s)* of any person(s) resident outside those Territories.

†*Delete words in italics if not applicable.*

* †† *See page* 4.   *Date*..............................19.......

In the case of joint holdings all joint holders must sign.

Applications by corporate bodies must be signed by duly authorised officials of the Company. If this form is sealed (unless it is sealed in Scotland or by the Public Trustee) it must bear a 10s. impressed stamp.

Applications in the name of a firm cannot be accepted. {

Usual signature ....

Name in full..
(Block letters)
Address in full..

Description..
(A woman should state whether she is a Spinster, Married Woman or Widow)

Usual signature ....

Name in full..
(Block letters)
Address in full..

Description..
(A woman should state whether she is a Spinster, Married Woman or Widow)

(Consolidation of Allotment Letters)

†Insert here details of any additional Allotment Letters referred to above				(For company's use only)		
No of Allotment Letter	No. of shares	No. of Allotment Letter	No. of shares	Cert. No.	Plate	Posted
				(For company's use only)		

Page 4.

EXCHANGE CONTROL ACT, 1947.

For Declarations and explanation of symbols, see Allotment Letter, page 590.

FORM No. 22

FORM OF APPLICATION ON OFFER FOR SALE.

....Limited

(Incorporated under the Companies Act, 1948)

FORM OF APPLICATION.
(PUBLIC COMPANY.)

Offer for Sale of

................Ordinary Shares of £1 each at 26/6 per Share

To: .... FINANCE LIMITED,

LONDON, E.C.2.

GENTLEMEN,

Having paid to your Bankers the sum of £........................ being the amount payable in full on application for .... of the above Ordinary Shares of £1 each at............ per Share, I/we apply for and request you to accept my/our application to purchase such Shares from you upon the terms of your Offer for Sale dated ....19....., and to procure the transfer to me/us of such Ordinary Shares or the right for myself/ourselves to be registered as the proprietor(s) of such Shares. I/We agree to accept such Ordinary Shares or any less number in respect of which you may accept my/our application upon the terms of the said Offer for Sale and subject to the Memorandum and Articles of Association of the Company, and authorise you in my/our name(s) and on my/our behalf to sign any transfer of Ordinary Shares that may be necessary in order that the Ordinary Shares in respect of which this application is accepted may be registered in my/our name(s) in the Ordinary Share Register of the Company. I/we authorise you to procure my/our name(s) to be placed on the Ordinary Share Register of the Company as the holder(s) of such Ordinary Shares.

I/We declare that I/we am/are not resident outside the Scheduled Territories* and I/we am/are not acquiring the security as the nominee(s)‡ of any person(s) resident outside those Territories.

(If this Declaration cannot be made it should be deleted and a Declaration 2A and Certificate as in Form D must be completed and attached to this Application as required by Notice E.C. (Securities) 1 issued by the Bank of England.)

Dated this........................day of....................19...........

FOR OFFICE USE ONLY.
1. No. of Letter of Acceptance
2. No. of Shares applied for
3. No. of Shares accepted
4. Amount Received on Application (...........per Share)
£ : :
5. Amount paid on Shares accepted
£ : :
6. Amount Returned
£ : :

7. Amount payable on application:—

50 Shares ..	£66 5 0
100 Shares ..	£132 10 0
150 Shares ..	£198 15 0
200 Shares ..	£265 0 0
250 Shares ..	£331 5 0
300 Shares ..	£397 10 0
400 Shares ..	£530 0 0
500 Shares ..	£662 10 0
600 Shares ..	£795 0 0
700 Shares ..	£927 10 0
800 Shares ..	£1,060 0 0
900 Shares ..	£1,192 10 0
1000 Shares ..	£1,325 0 0

And so on in proportion.

In the case of Joint Applicants, the signature and particulars of each must be given.

*The Scheduled Territories: Here insert current definition of Scheduled Territories.

‡As defined in Bank of England's Notice E.C. (Securities) 1, as amended.

FORM No. 22 (continued)

	1. *Usual Signature* .... (See Notes below)	3. *Usual Signature* ....
Block Letters	*Surname* .... *Christian Names* .... (in full) *Postal Address* .... (in full)	*Surname* .... *Christian Names* .... (in full) *Postal Address* .... (in full)
	2. *Usual Signature*	4. *Usual Signature* ....
Block Letters	*Surname* .... *Christian Names* .... (in full) *Postal Address* .... (in full)	*Surname* .... *Christian Names* .... (in full) *Postal Address* .... (in full)

Please state whether Mr., Mrs., or Miss

This form should be filled up and forwarded to ....Bank Limited, New Issue Department, London, E.C.2, or Branches; together with a remittance for the amount payable on application. Cheques should be made payable to "The ....Bank Limited or Bearer" and crossed "& Co." Any alteration from "Order" to "Bearer" must be signed by the Drawer.

No receipt will be issued for the payment on application, but an acknowledgment will be forwarded in due course, either by Letter of Acceptance or return of application money.

FORM No. 23

LETTER OF ACCEPTANCE.

IMPORTANT.—This document is negotiable.   You may sell the Acceptance, and for this purpose you should consult your Stockbroker or Banker.

This Letter of Acceptance must be lodged entire with ....Bank Limited.

....LIMITED.

(Incorporated under the Companies Act, 1948.)

To..

....

OFFER FOR SALE by The................Trust Limited of .... 5½ per cent. Cumulative Preference Shares of £1 each at 22s. per Share.

No.....................

................STREET,
LONDON, E.C.4.

................19........

LETTER OF ACCEPTANCE.

DEAR SIR (OR MADAM),

ACCEPTANCE.—I beg to inform you that your application to purchase 5½ per cent. Cumulative Preference Shares of ....Limited has been accepted to the extent indicated below in conformity with the terms of the Offer for Sale dated ....19........, and subject to the Memorandum and Articles of Association of the Company.

Number of Preference Shares of £1 each for which Application is accepted	Amount payable on application and acceptance (namely 22s. per share) on shares for which Application is accepted	Amount paid on Application (10s. per share)	Amount now due from you	Amount due to you for which cheque is enclosed
£	£	£	£

PAYMENT.—Payment of the amount due should be made forthwith to ....Bank Limited, ...Street, London, E.C.2, or any Branch of ....Bank Limited, accompanied by this Letter of Acceptance, which will be receipted and returned to you.   Cheques should be made payable to "................Bank Limited or Bearer" and crossed "Not Negotiable."   Any alteration from "Order" to "Bearer" must be signed by the Drawer.   Where a Declaration 2A and certificate, as in Form D, was furnished at the time of application a further similar Declaration and certificate must accompany this Letter when payment of the amount now due is made.

Failure to pay the amount due on Acceptance by the ...., 19........, will render the Acceptance liable to cancellation and the previous payment to forfeiture.   Interest at the rate of 6 per cent. per annum will be chargeable on the amount due on Acceptance if accepted after the................, 19..........

DIVIDEND.—The first dividend on the Preference Shares comprised in this Letter of Acceptance will be ....d. per share, less tax, payable on the ...., 19.........

RENUNCIATION, SPLITTING AND REGISTRATION.—Your attention is drawn to the instructions regarding renunciation, splitting, registration and definitive Share Certificates which are set out on page 2 and are to be regarded as forming part of this Letter.

Yours faithfully,

For and on behalf of THE................TRUST LIMITED,

Examined..

....Secretary.

NOT TO BE DETACHED

RECEIVED *payment on*
Acceptance as above stated.

(2d. Stamp)

For ....BANK LIMITED.

....Cashier.

(To be retained by Bankers)

....LIMITED.

Payment on Acceptance.

£ .... :

(2d. Stamp)

No....................

FORM No. 23 (continued)

Page 2.

Consolidated Listing Form—Carbon Copy (see page 4 for Top Copy).
(For instructions as to use see bottom of page 3.)

Serial No.	No. of Shares	Serial No.	No. of Shares	Serial No.	No. of Shares	Serial No.	No. of Shares	Total of Consolidation
								No. of Shares
								....
								No. of Letters
								....

INSTRUCTIONS.

RENUNCIATION IN WHOLE. *(Until the ...., 19..........)*

If you are the person(s) named at the top of page 1 and wish to dispose of all the shares comprised herein, you should complete the Form of Renunciation (Form X on page 3) and have Declaration 1 or 1A (as appropriate) on page 4 completed on your behalf and should hand this Letter to the person(s) through or to whom you are disposing of your shares. No renunciation can be recognised until payment of the amount due on acceptance has been made.

RENUNCIATION IN PART AND SPLITTING. *(Until the ...., 19..........)*

If you wish to dispose of part of the shares comprised herein or to dispose of all the shares to more than one person (other than joint holders), you may have this Letter of Acceptance split, provided that it is lodged with ....Bank Limited, ...Street, London, E.C.2, not later than the ...., 19......, with the Form of Renunciation (Form X in page 3) completed and accompanied by a remittance of 1s. for each split Letter of Acceptance required to be issued.

Split Letters of Acceptance will be endorsed "Original duly renounced" and, where applicable, "Declaration lodged." If no declaration has been made on the original Letter of Acceptance, Declaration 1 or 1A must be made on the split Letters.

REGISTRATION.

If you are the person(s) named on the top of page 1 and wish to have the shares comprised in this Letter of Acceptance registered in your name(s), once the amount due on Acceptance has been paid, you need do nothing further with this Letter until the ...., 19........... . *(See* Definitive Share Certificates below.)

To enable the shares comprised herein to be registered free of stamp duty and registration fees in the name(s) of any person(s) other than the person(s) named at the top of page 1, this Letter of Acceptance fully paid and duly renounced must be surrendered to ....Bank Limited, ...Street, London, E.C.2, for recording not later than the ...., 19......, with the Registration Application Form (Form Y on page 3) completed by the person(s) in whose name(s) the shares are to be registered; and with

   (a) Declaration 1 or 1A (on page 4) duly completed, unless the Form of Renunciation (Form X on page 3) is endorsed "Original duly renounced" and "Declaration lodged";

   (b) Declaration 2 and 2A (on page 4) duly completed together, with the Certificate and necessary authorisation form signed by an *Authorised Depositary or *Temporary Recipient;

   (c) Form Z below completed.

After the ...., 19........., the shares (which will then be registered either in the name(s) of the person(s) named at the top of page 1 or, if this Letter has been renounced, of the person(s) who has/have duly completed Forms Y and Z and lodged this Letter with ....Bank Limited by that date) can only be transferred by Transfer in the usual common form.

DEFINITIVE SHARE CERTIFICATES.

On surrender of Renounced Letters of Acceptance for registration as above, ...Bank Limited will retain pages 3 and 4 and return pages 1 and 2. In such cases pages 1 and 2 and in all other cases the entire Letter of Acceptance should be carefully preserved to be exchanged for a Definitive Share Certificate which will be available for issue by the Registered Office of the Company, ...London, W.C., on or after the ...., 19....... . Pending the issue of Definitive Share Certificates, the Registered Office of the Company will certify Transfers against production of Letters of Acceptance or, in cases of renunciation, pages 1 and 2 thereof.

Surrender of this Letter of Acceptance to ....Bank Limited, or to the Registrars, with the Form of Renunciation purporting to have been signed by the person(s) named at the top of this Letter of Acceptance shall be conclusive evidence of the title of the party surrendering it to deal with the same and to receive split Letters of Acceptance or a Definitive Share Certificate.

Form Z.

To be completed in cases of Renunciation at the time of Registration, by or on behalf of the person(s) completing Form Y on page 3.

Block letters

{ Name (in full)..........................   Name (in full)..........................
   Address ....   Address ....

{ Name (in full)..........................   Name (in full)..........................
   Address ....   Address ....

FORM No. 23 (continued)

Page 3.

FORM OF RENUNCIATION.

Form X.

Available until the ...., 19.........

To THE ....TRUST LIMITED.

I/We hereby renounce my/our right to the shares to the extent which my/our application has been accepted, as shown on page 1, in favour of the party or parties signing the Registration Application Form (Form Y) in relation to or including such shares.

Dated this.................................day of................................19.........

Signatures

In the case of joint holdings all such joint holders must sign.

Declaration 1 or 1A, as appropriate, on page 1 must be completed on behalf of the person(s) named at the top of page 4 unless the Form of Renunciation is endorsed "Original Duly Renounced" and "Declaration Lodged" (see instructions with regard to "Splitting" on page 2).

Form Y.

REGISTRATION APPLICATION FORM.

To THE ....TRUST LIMITED, and ....LIMITED.

I/We accept the shares comprised in the within-mentioned Letter of Acceptance (and in the several Letters of Acceptance attached hereto and amounting in all to .... shares, the serials number whereof and the number of shares comprised wherein are tabulated in the Consolidated Listing Form on page 4 of this Letter) subject to the several conditions contained in the Offer for Sale dated ....19....., and subject to the Memorandum and Articles of Association of the Company and request you to procure that the shares be registered in my/our name(s). Completion of this form shall be a full and irrevocable Authority to the Company to place my/our name(s) on the Register of Members of the Company in respect of the within-mentioned shares and shall be deemed to be my/our execution of the relative document of title.

I/We authorise you to send the Certificate for the Shares to me/us at the first address given below by post at my/our risk.

Yours faithfully,

Dated this ....day of...................., 19.........

1. *Usual Signature* ....

Block letters
- *Surname* ....
- *Christian Name*(s) ....
  (In full)
- *Address* ....
- *Description* ....
  (A Lady should state whether Spinster, Married Woman or Widow.)

2. *Usual Signature* ....

Block letters
- *Surname* ....
- *Christian Name*(s) ....
  (In full)
- *Address* ....
- *Description* ....
  (A Lady should state whether Spinster, Married Woman or Widow.)

3. *Usual Signature* ....

Block letters
- *Surname* ....
- *Christian Name*(s) ....
  (In full)
- *Address* ....
- *Description* ....
  (A Lady should state whether Spinster, Married Woman or Widow.)

4. *Usual Signature* ....

Block letters
- *Surname* ....
- *Christian Name*(s) ....
  (In full)
- *Address* ....
- *Description* ....
  (A Lady should state whether Spinster, Married Woman or Widow.)

When this Form is completed Form Z, on page 2, must also be completed.

Where Shares are to be registered in the names of joint holders, the names, address, occupation and signature of each holder is required in the order in which their names are to be registered.

In the case of a Corporation this form should be signed under the hand of a duly authorised officer who should state his capacity.

In all cases of renunciation Declaration 2 or 2A and Certificate as appropriate, on page 4, must be completed on behalf of the final purchaser(s), *i.e.* the person(s) completing the Registration Application Form. Where the latter Declaration, 2A and Certificate are completed the authorisation appended thereto must also be signed by an *Authorised Depositary.

LODGED FOR REGISTRATION BY...................

V

FORM No. 23 (continued)

Instructions for use of Consolidated Listing Form.

Where the facilities for Consolidation are utilised the total number of shares included in a Consolidation must also be inserted in the space provided in the Consolidated Listing Form on page 4. The appropriate Declaration in Form D must also be marked to the effect that it relates to the whole of the shares entered in the Consolidated Listing Form.

Where the shares included in more than one Letter of Acceptance are to be registered in the name(s) of the same renouncee(s), it is not necessary to complete the Consolidated Listing Form, provided the Registration Application Forms on the separate Letters of Acceptance are completed.

Page 4.

Consolidated Listing Form.—Top Copy (See page 2 for Carbon Copy).
(For instructions as to use see bottom of page 3.)

Serial No.	No. of Shares	Serial No.	No. of Shares	Serial No.	No. of Shares	Serial No.	No. of Shares	Total of Consolidation
								No. of Shares
								No. of Letters

If this space is insufficient the particulars may be listed on foolscap sheets in duplicate and attached.

Exchange Control Act, 1947.

* For Declarations, Form of Certificate, definitions of Scheduled Territories and Temporary Recipient, see Allotment Letter, page 590.

FORM No. 23a

[NOTE.—The routine work of the preparation and despatch of Letters of Rights is frequently undertaken by the Secretary and his staff without the assistance of a Bank (or Issuing House). In such cases the wording of the Letter of Rights would be arranged accordingly.]

LETTER OF RIGHTS.

A copy of this Letter of Rights has been delivered to the Registrar of Companies for registration.

Application has been made to the Council of The Stock Exchange, London, and to the Committee of the Stock Exchanges in Birmingham, Liverpool and Manchester for permission to deal in and for quotation for the whole of the Ordinary Shares now offered.

This document is of value. If you are in any doubt as to the course you should follow, you should consult your Stockbroker or Banker.

LETTER OF RIGHTS

.... COMPANY LIMITED.
(Incorporated under the Companies Act, 1948)

*No...........................

*All enquiries in connection with this Issue should be addressed to the New Issue Department, ...Bank Limited, London, E.C.2, quoting the number above.

Address:...........................

To Shareholder

London, E.C.2.

.........................1950

ISSUE OF

..................................Ordinary Shares of.........each at............per Share.

Dear Sir (or Madam),

As recently announced in the Press, your Directors have decided to issue.............Ordinary Shares of ....each and to offer them for subscription at............per share to the holders of Ordinary Shares on the Register at the close of business on..........................19........, in the proportion of one new share for every five existing Ordinary Shares then held, fractions of a new share being disregarded. Accordingly, as the registered holder on that date of.....................Ordinary Shares you are entitled to subscribe for................ new Ordinary Shares of...........each at............per share.

Examined.......................

The amount of...............is payable as follows:—

On acceptance £...............(including a premium of ....per share).

On...............19........... £............... „ „ „ ....„ „

£...............

The new Ordinary Shares will not rank for any interim dividend payable in respect of the year ending ....19........., but will rank for the full amount of any final dividend and in all other respects _pari passu_ with the existing Ordinary Shares.

If you intend to take up the shares to which you are entitled you must fill up and sign the Form of Acceptance marked "Z" on page 3 and forward this Letter of Rights ENTIRE to the Company's Bankers, ...Bank Limited, New Issue Department......................., London, E.C.2, together with a cheque for the amount payable on acceptance, so as to arrive not later than the close of business on................ day, ...19......... . Cheques should be made payable to "...................Bank Limited or Bearer" and crossed "& Co., Not Negotiable." Any alteration from "Order" to "Bearer" must be signed by the Drawer.

No receipt will be issued for such payment on acceptance, but a partly-paid Renounceable Letter of Allotment will be forwarded by post in due course to the first address filled in on the Form of Acceptance. Failure to pay promptly the amount due on..................19........., will render the previous payment liable to forfeiture and the allotment to cancellation. Interest at the rate of 5 per cent. per annum may be charged on any instalment accepted after its due date.

If you desire to dispose of or renounce your "Rights" in favour of not more than one nominee or joint nominees you must sign the Form of Renunciation marked "Y" on page 3 and have Declaration 1 or 1A, on page 4, completed on your behalf. The party or parties in whose favour this Letter is renounced must then fill up and sign the Form of Acceptance marked "Z" on page 3 and have Declaration 2 or 2A, on page 4 completed and forward this document entire, together with a cheque for the amount payable on acceptance to................... Bank Limited, New Issue Department, ..., London, E.C.2, so as to arrive not later than the close of business on ....day, the...............19........

If you wish to take up a smaller number of shares than those to which you are entitled as above and to nominate some other person to take up the remainder, or to transfer all your "Rights" in favour of more than one nominee (other than joint nominees) you must sign the Form of Renunciation marked "Y" and this Letter should then be returned to reach......................, Bank Limited, New Issue Department, ... London, E.C.2, not later than........................., 19......, when it will be split in the proportions required, which should be stated when the Letter is sent for splitting. A charge of 1s. for each split Letter required must be forwarded with the application for splitting.

FORM No. 23a (*continued*)

Page 2.

If the Form of Acceptance and the amount Payable on Acceptance are not received by the close of business on................................19........ as indicated in this Letter, you will be deemed to have declined the Shares now offered and the "Rights" conferred hereunder will lapse.

The holders of Ordinary Shares on the Register at the close of business on................................19........, are also given the opportunity of applying, at the same price of................per share, for any of the................ Ordinary Shares which are not required to meet acceptances under the Letters of Rights. Shareholders desiring to apply for any such excess should complete and sign the pink Form of Application, enclosed herewith, for the number of Excess Shares for which they wish to apply, and should forward the same to the Company's Bankers, ...Limited, New Issue Department, ..., London, E.C.2, together with a remittance of................per share in respect of such Shares, so as to arrive not later than ...., 19.......... If you wish to make use of the Form of Application and to take up Shares under the Letter of Rights, one cheque only to cover the amount due under both documents should be sent.

Definitive Share Certificates in respect of the new Ordinary Shares will be available in exchange for Letters of Allotment on and after................................, 19.........

Messrs................................, of................................, London, E.C.2, have underwritten this Issue for an underwriting commission of 4½d. per share and an overriding commission of 1½d. per share.

By Order of the Board,

Registered Office.

................................Secretary.

Consolidated Listing Form.

Please enter Serial Numbers in numerical order.

Serial Number	Number of Shares	Serial Number	Number of Shares	Serial Number	Number of Shares
1		Carried Forward		Carried Forward	
2					
3				98	
				99	
				100	Total number of Shares comprised in attached Letters of Rights.
					Number of Allotment Letters

NOTE.—Where the Consolidation method is used the whole of the Letters of Rights included therein should be lodged in one batch, with the one containing the particulars in the Form of Acceptance (Form Z) and in the Consolidation List on top, the others sorted in serial order as recorded in the List.

Care should also be taken to ensure that the appropriate Number of Shares is inserted at the top of Form D, on page 4, and that the Forms of Acceptance (Form Z) not used are appropriately stamped and completed in accordance with the regulations issued by the Stock Exchange.

Page 3.

FORM Y.

FORM OF RENUNCIATION.

(To be signed by the Shareholder only if wishing to renounce his rights to the within-mentioned Shares.)

To the Directors of................................Company Limited.

I/We hereby renounce my/our right to the within-mentioned Ordinary Shares in favour of the party/parties signing the Acceptance Form "Z" in respect of such Shares.

†All Joint Holders must sign. } Signature(s) of Shareholder(s) {
....
....
....

Dated................................, 19.......

FORM No. 23a (*continued*)

In cases of Renunciation:—

(i) Declaration 1 or 1A must be completed on behalf of the first seller, *i.e.* the person in whose name this Letter is issued. Where, however, the Letter of Rights is to be split the declaration may be given either on the original or on the "split."

(ii) Declaration 2 or 2A and Certificate must be completed on behalf of the final purchaser, *i.e.* the person in whose name the final registration is to be made and in the case of the latter Declaration (2A) the form marked "Authorised" by an Authorised Depositary.

In the case of a split the Form of Renunciation will be endorsed by the Bank "Original duly renounced" and, where applicable, "and Declaration Lodged."

FORM Z.
FORM OF ACCEPTANCE.
(This Form must be signed by the person(s) accepting the Shares.)

To the Directors of...Company Limited.

Having paid to your Bankers the sum of £................., being the amount of............ per share payable on acceptance for *.................Ordinary Shares of .... each in your Company being those comprised in the within-written Letter of Rights (‡and also those in the several Letter of Rights attached hereto, the serial numbers whereof and the numbers of Shares comprised wherein are tabulated in the Consolidated Listing Form on page 2), I/we hereby accept the said Shares upon the terms and conditions of the within-written Letter of Rights and subject to the Memorandum and Articles of Association of the Company. I/We hereby agree to pay the balance due on the said Shares on ...., 19........., and I/we request you to allot to me/us the said Shares, and I/we hereby authorise you to place my/our name(s) on the Register of Members as the holder(s) of the said Shares, and to send an Allotment Letter by post at my/our risk to the first address written below.

IMPORTANT.—To comply with the provisions of the Exchange Control Act, 1947, the acceptor(s) must make the Declaration contained in the following paragraph, or, if unable to do so, must delete such paragraph and consult his/their Bankers in order to have the appropriate Declaration and Certificate completed. No acceptance can be considered unless this condition is fulfilled.

I/We declare that I/we am/are not resident outside the Scheduled Territories†† and am/are not acquiring the above-mentioned Shares as the nominee(s)†† of any person(s) resident outside those Terrritories.

Dated this........................day of......................, 19.........

Please indicate title, if any, or state whether Mr., Mrs. or Miss.

(1) Usual Signature .... (2) Usual Signature ....
Block letters { Surname... Christian Names... Permanent Address... Description... }   Block letters { Surname... Christian Names... Permanent Address... Description... }

(3) Usual Signature................... (4) Usual Signature...................
Block letters { Surname... Christian Names... Permanent Address... Description... }   Block letters { Surname... Christian Names... Permanent Address... Description... }

† All Joint Holders must sign. In the case of a Corporation this Form should be signed by a duly Authorised Official who should state his capacity. If, however, the Form is completed under Seal, unless in Scotland, a 10s. stamp should be impressed.
* Insert the number of Shares accepted which must not exceed the number on page 1 or the total entered in the Consolidated Listing Form on page 2.
‡ Delete if not required.
†† Refer to current definitions.

FOR OFFICE USE ONLY.

Shares Accepted	Excess Shares Applied For	Excess Shares Allotted	Total Shares Allotted	Amount Returned	Certificate Number

Page 4.

FORM D.
EXCHANGE CONTROL ACT.
(See Form 20, page 590.)

FORM No. 23b

FORM OF APPLICATION FOR EXCESS SHARES.

[PRINTED ON PINK TINT PAPER—Refer to Form 23A (page 2)]

For use by Ordinary Shareholders on the Register at the close of business on........................, 19........ who desire to apply for any of the new Ordinary Shares that may be available after providing for acceptance by Ordinary Shareholders under the Offer contained in the Letter of Rights dated........................, 19........ .

....COMPANY LIMITED.
(Incorporated under the Companies Act, 1948.)

No........................

To Shareholder

ISSUE OF....................ORDINARY SHARES of............each at............per Share, payable as follows:—

On Application   ..   ..   .. £........   (including a premium of ....)
On ...., 19....   ..   .. £........   "   "   "   "

£........

To the Directors of........................Company Limited.

Gentlemen,

*Having paid to your Bankers the sum of £........, being the amount payable on application at the rate of............ per share for............of the above Ordinary Shares of............ each in your company, I/we hereby apply for and request you to allot to me/us that number of Ordinary Shares, and I/we hereby undertake and agree to accept such shares or any smaller number that may be allotted to me/us upon the terms of the Letter of Rights dated........................, 19........, and subject to the Memorandum and Articles of Association of the Company, and I/we hereby agree to pay the balance due thereon as provided by the said Letter of Rights, and I/we authorise you to register me/us as the holder(s) of the shares so allotted and to send an Allotment Letter in respect thereof by post at my/our risk to the first address written below.

IMPORTANT.—To comply with the provisions of the Exchange Control Act, 1947, the Applicant(s), if unable to make the Declaration contained in the following paragraph, must delete such paragraph and consult his/their Bankers in order to have Declaration 2A and relative Certificate completed. No application will be considered unless this condition is fulfilled.

I/We declare the I/we am/are not resident outside the Scheduled Territories† and am/are not acquiring the security as the nominee(s)‡ of any person(s) resident outside those Territories.

Dated........................, 19........ .

Usual Signature........................   Usual Signature........................
Block letters { Surname........................   Christian Name(s)........................ (In full)   Address........................ (In full)   Description........................
Block letters { Surname........................   Christian Name(s)........................ (In full)   Address........................ (In full)   Description........................
(A Lady should state whether she is a "Spinster," "Married Woman" or "Widow.")

Usual Signature........................   Usual Signature........................
Block letters { Surname........................   Christian Name(s)........................ (In full)   Address........................ (In full)   Description........................
Block letters { Surname........................   Christian Name(s)........................ (In full)   Address........................ (In full)   Description........................
(A Lady should state whether she is a "Spinster," "Married Woman" or "Widow.")
In case of joint applicants all must sign.

This form, when completed, should be sent, together with the amount payable on application (namely ....per share), to the Company's Bankers, ...Bank Limited, New Issue Department, ..., London, E.C.2, SO AS TO ARRIVE NOT LATER THAN THE CLOSE OF BUSINESS ON............day, ... 19........ .

Cheques should be made payable to "........................Bank Limited or Bearer" and crossed "& Co., Not Negotiable." If altered from "Order" to "Bearer" the alteration should be signed by the Drawer.

Where a Letter of Rights and this Form of Application are lodged together, one cheque should be tendered to cover the total amount payable.

No receipt for payment will be given but an acknowledgement will be forwarded in due course either by a partly paid Renounceable Letter of Allotment, in whole or in part, or by the return of subscription moneys or the surplus paid.

†The Scheduled Territories comprise (here insert reference to the current definition of Scheduled Territories).

‡Defined in Bank of England's Notice E.C. (Securities) 1, as amended.

	SHARES ALLOTTED	CASH RETURNED	CERTIFICATE NUMBER
For Office use only			

[* If payment is to be made direct to the Company, arrange wording accordingly; see Note at the head of Form 23A.]

FORMS   605

FORM No. 24

FULLY PAID ALLOTMENT LETTER.

....Trust Limited

(Incorporated under the Companies Act, 1948.)

Issue of £................... 3½ per cent. First Debenture Stock, 19......... - 19.........

No..........................

To..   *Transfer Office:*

of..   ....Street,
                                                                  LONDON, W.C.2.
                                                                  ....19.......

Sir,

I am directed to inform you that, having received payment therefor in full, the Directors have allotted you £......................... 3½ per cent. First Debenture Stock 19......... – 19......... in this Company, on the terms of the Company's Advertisement dated ....19...........

This Debenture Stock will rank for interest as from ....19......... and the first payment for the three months ending ....19......... will be ....(less tax) per £100 Stock, payable on ....19...........

Allotment Letters will be split once only on application at the Transfer Office of the Company above-mentioned up to and including ....19.......... A fee of 1s. od. is payable for each split letter required.

The Stock to which this Letter of Allotment relates will (subject to the completion of Form "Y" below) be registered in the name(s) of the original Allottee(s) unless Form "X" below is filled in and signed by the original Allottee(s) and Form "Y" is completed by the renouncee(s) in whose name(s) the Stock is to be registered, and this Allotment Letter is lodged at the Company's Transfer Office, ..., London, W.C.2, on or before the ....19.......... Thereafter the Stock will only be transferable by instruments of transfer in the ordinary form.

After the...................19......... and pending the issue of the Stock Certificates, instruments of transfer will be certified against delivery of Allotment Letters at the Transfer Office of the Company, above mentioned.

This Letter of Allotment should be carefully retained and should be lodged without further request on or after the ....19......... with the Company, when a Stock Certificate will be issued in exchange therefor.   Before lodgment, Form "Y" below must be completed.

By Order of the Board,

....Secretary.

Exd.............................,........................

Form X.   FORM OF RENUNCIATION.

To the Directors of..........................Trust Limited.

I/We hereby renounce my/our right to the above-mentioned Debenture Stock allotted to me/us in favour of the party or parties signing the Registration Application Form below.

Dated this...................day of...................19..........

All Joint Holders must sign. { *Signature(s) of Allottee(s)* ....

....

Important.—In cases of Renunciation, Declaration 1 or 1A overleaf on behalf of the first seller(s), *i.e.* the person(s) in whose name(s) the letter is issued, must also be completed.   In case of splits, the Form of Renunciation will be endorsed "Original duly Renounced and where applicable Declaration lodged."

Form Y.   REGISTRATION APPLICATION FORM.

To be completed by the person(s) in whose name(s) the Debenture Stock is to be registered.

To the Directors of..........................Trust Limited.

I/We hereby request and authorise you to register the above-mentioned Debenture Stock in my/our name(s) in the Register of Debenture Stockholders of the Company and I/we agree to accept the same on the terms of the Company's Advertisement dated ....19.........., and the Memorandum and Articles of Association of the Company. I/We authorise you to send the Stock Certificate to me/us at the first address given below by post at my/our risk.

FORM No. 24 (continued)

IMPORTANT.—In cases of renunciation, Declaration 2 of Form D, Certification and Authorisation must be completed on behalf of renouncee(s).

Dated this................................day of................19........

In the case of Joint Holdings all Joint Holders must sign.

Applications made by Corporate Bodies must be signed by duly authorised officials of the Company.

If the form is sealed (unless it is sealed in Scotland or by the Public Trustee) it must bear a 10s. impressed stamp.

Applications in the name of a firm cannot be accepted.

Signature ....

Name in full..
    (Block Letters) ·

Address (in full)...

A woman should state here whether she is a Spinster, Married Woman or Widow............

Signature ....

Name in full..
    (Block Letters)

Address (in full)...

A woman should state here whether she is a Spinster, Married Woman or Widow............

EXCHANGE CONTROL ACT, 1947.
(For Declarations, etc., see Allotment Letter, page 590.)

EXPLANATORY NOTE ON FORM No. 25 (p. 607)

This form of acceptance would be used in the case of an offer by 'X' Company to purchase shares (usually a majority holding) in 'Y' Company. The circular letter sent to the shareholders of 'Y' Company would explain in detail the terms of the offer and the advantages accruing therefrom.

Frequently alternative offers are made, *e.g.*:—

    (a) For each one £1 Ordinary Share of 'Y' Company one Ordinary Share of in 'X' Company and ....in cash.

    (b) For each 20 £1 Ordinary Shares of 'Y' Company 23 Ordinary Shares of £1 each in 'X' Company.

To render the allotment of shares in 'X' Company to members of 'Y' Company valid, a contract showing title to the shares is required to be filed with the Registrar of Companies pursuant to s. 52 of the Companies Act, 1948.

Regarding Stamp Duty, refer to s. 35 (1) (b) of the Finance Act, 1949. The Inland Revenue Authorities should be given a copy of the circular letter relating to the scheme together with relevant facts so that the question of Stamp Duty liability can be determined.

FORM No. 25

FORM OF ACCEPTANCE.

(MERGER SCHEME.)

No.............................

To

The.. Company Limited.

I/We the undersigned being the Holder(s) of the number of Ordinary Shares in 'X' Company Limited specified below hereby accept your offer to purchase my/our said Shares on the terms set out in the Circular dated the ....day of ...., 19........., issued to me/us by 'Y' Company Limited.

I/We accept the alternative offer set out in:—

Paragraph (a)
Paragraph (b)

(Please strike out the alternative which you do NOT wish to accept.)

on the first page of the said circular issued to me/us.

I/We authorise you to enter my/our name(s) on your Register of Members as the Holder(s) of the Shares in your capital to which I/we shall become entitled in accordance with the terms of your offer and I/we agree to accept the same subject to your Memorandum and Articles of Association, and I/We authorise each Director of 'Y' Company Limited to execute on my/our behalf any contract required to be filed pursuant to the provisions of Section 52 of the Companies Act, 1948.

The Shares which I/We hold in 'X' Company Limited are as follows:—

ORDINARY SHARES

....

(Here set out the number of shares held.)

Dated............................*day of* ....19..........

In case of joint holdings this form must be signed by every holder.

Signature..

Signature..

Signature..

Signature..

NAME AND ADDRESS PANEL.

IMPORTANT.

This Form, when signed, must be returned, together with Transfer Deed duly completed and your Share Certificate(s), in the enclosed envelope to 'X' Company Limited, ...W.C.2, on or before the ....19..........

FORM No. 26

APPLICATION AND ALLOTMENT LIST.

APPLICATION AND ALLOTMENT LIST.

ALLOTMENT OF ....Co. LIMITED.

SHARES OF £......... EACH IN ....

No. of Application	Name	Address	Description	Renunciation and Splits (Date) (No.)	Number of Shares Applied for	Amount of Deposit at .... per Share	Number of Shares Allotted	Distinctive Numbers* (From) (To)	Total Amount in respect of Shares Allotted at .... per Share	FURTHER INSTALMENTS PAYABLE — 1 On Allotment (Rec'd) (£ s. d.)	2 (Rec'd) (£ s. d.)	3 (Rec'd) (£ s. d.)	Amount Returnable (£ s. d.)	Share Reg. Folio	Share Cert. No.

List of Applications — WRITTEN — CHECKED

Letters of Allotment

Letters of Regret

Cheque for Amount Returnable

* If all the issued shares are fully paid up and rank *pari passu* for all purposes with all the shares of the same class such shares need not have a distinguishing number.

FORM No. 27

LETTER OF ALLOTMENT AND INTERIM CERTIFICATE.
(This form should be printed on stout paper.)

THE..........COMPANY, LIMITED.
Registered Office: ...., London.

To A. B. No..............

THIS is to Certify that in accordance with your application you have been allotted and registered as the holder of .... Shares of .... each in The..........Company, Limited, numbered from ...... to ...... inclusive, upon which you have paid the sum of .... per Share.

The remaining instalments are payable as follows:

£..... *per share on*.. 19......

£........ ” ” .... 19......

£........ ” ” .... 19......

Subject to due payment of instalments this interim certificate will be exchanged for a definitive certificate. It should, therefore, be carefully preserved.

Seal of Co.

.... *Director.*

.... *Secretary.*

(Address of Company)

...., 19......

RECEIVED *on Account of* The..........Company, Limited, *for* The ....Bank.

Instalment due..........19......, £ : : ....Cashier..... | 2d. Stamp | ...19......

” ” ....19......, £ : : ....Cashier..... | 2d. Stamp | ...19......

” ” ....19......, £ : : ....Cashier..... | 2d. Stamp | ...19......

.... **[PERF.]** ....

THE..........COMPANY, LIMITED.

Instalment due..........................19......, £ : : *Date*....................19......

Allotment Letter No.......................... *Cashier's Initials*........................

.... **[PERF.]** ....

THE..........COMPANY, LIMITED.

Instalment due..........................19...... £ : : *Date*....................19......

Allotment Letter No.......................... *Cashier's Initials*........................

.... **[PERF.]** ....

THE..........COMPANY, LIMITED.

Instalment due..........................19......, £ : : *Date*....................19......

Allotment Letter No.......................... *Cashier's Initials*........................

EXCHANGE CONTROL ACT.

On payment of each instalment an Exchange Control Act Declaration of Residence must be completed by the person making the payment.

This Form must accompany each Remittance, and all Cheques, etc., must be made payable to the Bankers.

All Remittances must be sent to ....Bank, ...Street, London, E.C., drawn to bearer and crossed 'not negotiable.'

To be detached by the Bankers.

FORM No. 28

THE COMPANIES ACT, 1948.

LETTER OF NOMINATION OF SHARES.

To the Directors of...

.... Limited

I,...

of ....

hereby request you to allot...

fully paid Shares of £... each, being part of the Shares

due to me or my nominees by virtue of an Agreement (or Particulars in

lieu of Contract) dated the..day

of...19......, to the persons and in the pro-

portions stated hereunder, namely:—

| | | | No. of Shares | |
NAME	ADDRESS	Description	Preference	Ordinary

Dated this...*day of*...............................19..........

Signature...

FORM No. 29

SUB-UNDERWRITING LETTER.

....COMPANY LIMITED.

Issue of ....Shares of £1 each at .... per Share.

To....................TRUST LIMITED,
LONDON, W.C.

GENTLEMEN,

I/We hereby agree to underwrite £.................. of the above issue of shares, and I/We hand you herewith a cheque for £.................. being .... per share payable on application in respect thereof, and I/we agree to accept an allotment of any shares that may be alloted to me/us in respect of such underwriting and to pay all subsequent instalments due in respect thereof in accordance with and on the terms mentioned in the Prospectus as issued to the public.

I/We hereby irrevocably authorise you or any Director of your Company in my/our name and on my/our behalf to sign and put in an application for the same or any smaller number of shares and to conclude on my/our behalf an agreement with the Company to take the said shares or any part thereof and to pay all moneys that may become due in respect of the same which moneys I/we undertake to repay to you on demand with interest thereon at the rate of.................. per cent. per annum from date of payment to date of repayment.

It is understood that to the extent to which allotments are made to the public I am/we are to be relieved of my/our underwriting obligations hereunder proportionately as nearly as may be with the other sub-underwriters of the said issue for which purpose you yourselves are to be treated as sub-underwriters for any part of the issue for which you have not procured sub-underwriters.

Firm applications by me/us or other sub-underwriters are not to be treated as applications by the public but allotments made thereon are to be applied exclusively in relief of the sub-underwriters by whom they were put in.

In the event of a general allotment of the said shares being made you are within .... days of such allotment to pay or procure the Company to pay me/us a commission of.................. per cent. in cash on the nominal amount of the shares underwritten by me/us and it is understood that I/we shall not claim any brokerage in respect of the shares allotted to me/us in response to my/our application above referred to.

I/We hereby authorise you to agree with the Company the form of the Prospectus which is to be issued to the public offering the said shares for subscription and my/our obligations hereunder are to hold good notwithstanding any alteration that may be made in the draft Prospectus that has been shown to me/us provided that the total amount of the shares offered for subscription and the price of issue are not altered.

If a Prospectus offering the said shares for subscription has not been issued within .... days from the date hereof you are to return me/us my/our application and cheque and this Agreement will thereupon become void.

Any notice to me/us may be served by sending the same through the post to the subjoined address, and shall be deemed to be served on the day when in the ordinary course of post the letter would reach such address.

Unless written notice of non-acceptance is received by me/us from you this contract shall be deemed to have been accepted and your signature at the foot hereof shall be sufficient notice to me/us of your acceptance.

You may accept my/our underwriting for a less amount than the whole, but in that case you are to notify me/us of the amount for which my/our underwriting has been accepted.

Dated..................19....

Signature(s) .... | 6d. Stamp |

Name(s) in full..................

Address(es)..................

....

Description(s) ....

We accept the above underwriting for £..................

FORM No. 30

LETTER OF REGRET.

....LIMITED.

Issue of .... 4½ per cent. Second Cumulative Redeemable Preference Shares of £1 each at Par.

```
+------------------------------------+      Transfer Office:
|  ................................  |      ....................STREET,
|                                    |      LONDON, W.C.2.
|  ................................  |      ....................19.....
|                                    |
|  ................................  |
+------------------------------------+
```

DEAR SIR(S), or MADAM,

   I am instructed by the Directors of the above Company to express regret that they are unable to allot any of the above Preference Shares to you in response to your application.

   I therefore attach a cheque in refund of the amount paid by you on application.

                         Yours faithfully,

                                   ....Secretary.

.... [PERF.] ....

....LIMITED.

                                                  No. R.............

....................................BANK LIMITED,

....Street, London, E.C.3.

                                                  2d.
                                                  Stamp

Pay..& Co.| or order

the sum of ....£

                         For and on behalf of

                                   ....LIMITED

                                   ....Secretary.

....Signature of Payee.

FORM No. 31

No. of Company............................   Form No. 52.

THE COMPANIES ACT, 1948.

◯ *A 5s. Companies
Registration Fee
Stamp must be
impressed here.*

PARTICULARS OF A CONTRACT RELATING TO SHARES.

Pursuant to Section 52 (2).

Name of Company.. Limited.

*The particulars must be stamped with the same stamp duty as would have
been payable if the contract had been reduced to writing.*

Presented by

....

....

....

Particulars of contract relating to shares allotted as fully or partly
paid up otherwise than in cash by..
....Limited.

(1) The number of shares allotted as fully or partly paid up otherwise than in cash	
(2) The nominal amount of each such share	£
(3) The amount to be considered as paid up on each such share otherwise than in cash	£
(4) If the consideration for the allotment of such shares is services, or any consideration other than that mentioned below in (5), state the nature of such consideration, and the number of shares so allotted	

FORM No. 31 (continued)

(5) If the allotment is made in satisfaction or part satisfaction of the purchase price of property, give a brief description of such property, and full particulars of the manner in which the purchase price is to be satisfied.

(1) Brief description of property.

(2) Purchase price   £ _____

(a) Total amount considered as paid on .... shares allotted otherwise than in cash.   £

(b) Cash.   £

(d) Amount of debt released or liabilities assumed by the purchaser (including mortgages on property acquired).   £

Total purchase price £ _____

(6) Give full particulars, in the form of the following table, of the property which is the subject of the sale, showing in detail how the total purchase price is apportioned between the respective heads:—

Legal Estates in Freehold Property and Fixed Plant and Machinery and other Fixtures thereon (a)................................   £   s.   d.

Legal Estates in Leasehold Property (a)................................

Fixed Plant and Machinery on Leasehold Property (including Tenants', Trade and other Fixtures) ....

Equitable Interests in Freehold or Leasehold Property (a)......

Loose Plant and Machinery, Stock-in-Trade and other Chattels (b) ....

Goodwill and Benefit of Contracts................................

Patents, Designs, Trade Marks, Licences, Copyrights, etc......

Book and other Debts ....

Cash in Hand and at Bank on Current Account, Bills, Notes, etc. ....

Cash on Deposit at Bank or elsewhere................................

Shares, Debentures and other investments................................

Other property, viz. ....

£ _____

(Signature)................................

(State whether Director or Secretary) ....

Dated the................................day of................................19..........

(a) Where such properties are sold subject to mortgage, the gross value should be shown.

(b) No plant and machinery which was not in actual state of severance on the date of the sale should be included under this head.

FORM No. 32

No. of Company................................   Form No. 45.

THE COMPANIES ACT, 1948.

RETURN OF ALLOTMENTS from the

(a) ....
of..
19.......... to the.................................of
.... 19............... of
.... Limited.

A 5s. Companies Registration Fee Stamp must be impressed here.

Pursuant to Section 52 (1) of The Companies Act, 1948.

(To be delivered to the Registrar of Companies within one month after the allotment is made.)

(b) Number of the..........shares allotted payable in cash ....

Number of the..........shares allotted payable in cash ....

Nominal amount of the..........shares so allotted   . . ..

Nominal amount of the..........shares so allotted   . . ..

Amount paid or due and payable on each such share . .   . .

Amount paid or due and payable on each such share . .   . .

*Number of..........shares allotted for a consideration other than cash   . .   . .

Nominal amount of the..........shares so allotted   . . ..

Amount to be treated as paid on each such..........share ....

*The consideration for which such shares have been allotted is as follows:—

....
....
....
....
....
....
....

(a) *Note.—In making a return of Allotments it is to be noted that:—*

   1. *When a return includes several allotments made on different dates, the dates of only the first and last of such allotments should be entered at the top of the front page and the registration of the return should be effected within one month of the first date,*

   2. *When a return relates to one allotment only, made on one particular date, that date only should be inserted and the spaces for the second date struck out, and the word "made" substituted for the word "from" after the word "Allotments."*

(b) *Distinguish between Preference, Ordinary, Redeemable Preference, etc.*

Presented by ....

FORM No. 32 (continued)

Names, Descriptions and Addresses of the Allottees.

Name and Description	Address	Number of Shares allotted		
		Prefer-ence	Ordi-nary	
	TOTAL			

Signature...

(*State whether Director or Secretary*) ....

FORM No. 33

CALL LETTER.

[Size 13 in. by 8¼ in., the docket one quarter of the total length of form.]

No.........................

| Space for Name and Address of Shareholder, to be filled in by the Company. | THE...........COMPANY, LIMITED, LONDON, E.C. |

....19......

CALL OF   PER SHARE ON ISSUE OF   SHARES.
1st, 2nd or 3rd
call as case may be.]
MAKING THE SHARES   PAID.

I have to inform you that the Directors, by a Resolution of the Board dated.., have made a Call as set forth above.

The amount due from you in respect of the......................................Shares registered in your name is £............................. which must be sent on or before ...., together with this *entire* Notice, to the Company's Bankers, the.............................Bank, ... who will return the Notice duly receipted.

[Particulars should be given here if the Certificate requires endorsement, or the Articles of Association provide for any penalty for failure to pay on due date.]

By Order of the Board,

Secretary.

Cheques should be made payable to *Bearer* and crossed 'NOT NEGOTIABLE'

If altered from 'Order' to 'Bearer' the alteration should be signed by the Drawer.

RECEIVED for account of The...........Company, Limited, the amount of the above-mentioned Call as stated.

| 2d. Receipt Stamp |

For ....BANK,

....

Cashier.

Date......................................19......

.... [PERF.] ....

No..................

THE...........COMPANY, LIMITED.

CALL OF   PER SHARE ON ISSUE OF   SHARES.

....   £   :   :

Date......................................19..........

On payment of the Call an Exchange Control Act Declaration of Residence must be completed by the person making the payment.

FORM No. 34

No. of Company.................... Form No. 58.

THE COMPANIES ACT, 1948.

◯ *A 5s. Companies Registration Fee Stamp must be impressed here.*

STATEMENT OF THE AMOUNT OR RATE PER CENT. OF THE COMMISSION PAYABLE IN RESPECT OF SHARES AND OF THE NUMBER OF SHARES FOR WHICH PERSONS HAVE AGREED FOR A COMMISSION TO SUBSCRIBE ABSOLUTELY.

Pursuant to Section 53 (1) (c) (ii) *and* (d).

Name of Company... Limited.

Presented by

....

....

....

Name of Company .. .. { ....
.... LIMITED.

Article of association authorising commission. No...................

Particulars of amount payable as commission for subscribing, or agreeing to subscribe, or for procuring or agreeing to procure, subscriptions for any shares in the Company; or, } £...................

Rate of such commission.................. Rate per cent..................

Date of circular or notice (if any), not being a prospectus, inviting subscriptions for the shares and disclosing the amount or rate of the commission } Date ....

Number of shares for which persons have agreed for a commission to subscribe absolutely. No. ....

(*Signatures of all the Directors or of their agents authorised in writing.*) ....
....
....

Dated the.................................day of.................19........

FORM No. 35

Share Certificate where there is more than one class of shares.
(For Stock Exchange requirements, see Appendix D.)

Certificate No.
Number of Preference shares

THE ...... COMPANY LIMITED.
Incorporated under the Companies Act, 1948.
Registered Office: ......, London.

AUTHORISED SHARE CAPITAL £

Divided into ...... Ordinary shares of £ ...... each, numbered ...... to ...... inclusive, and ...... Five per cent. Cumulative Preference shares of £ ...... each, numbered ...... to ...... inclusive.

The Preference shares carry a fixed Cumulative Preferential Dividend at the rate of 5 per cent. per annum and rank as to dividend and capital in priority to the Ordinary shares, but convey no further right to participate in profits or assets. (If the conditions are lengthy they can if preferred be printed on the back of the Certificate.)

THIS IS TO CERTIFY that ......

of ......
is/are registered as the holder/s of ......
Five per cent. CUMULATIVE PREFERENCE SHARES of ...... Pounds each, fully paid up, numbered as in margin, in THE ...... COMPANY, LIMITED, subject to the Memorandum and Articles of Association of the Company.

Given under the Common Seal of the Company, this ...... day of ...... 19...

.... Director.

.... Secretary.

Seal of Co.

Exd.

Note.—No transfer of the above shares can be registered unless accompanied by the relative share certificate.

(Endorsement as Form 36.)

PARTICULARS OF SHARES HEREIN REFERRED TO		
No. of Shares	DISTINCTIVE NUMBERS FROM	TO

[PREF.]

Signature of Shareholder or Broker

THE COMPANY, LIMITED, in the name of

RECEIVED the ...... day of 19

Certificate No. ...... for ...... Shares in

[PREF.]

THE ...... COMPANY, LIMITED.

5% CUMULATIVE PREFERENCE SHARE CERTIFICATE.

No.
Name.
Address.
No. of Shares.
Date.
No. of transfer.

FORM No. 36

Share Certificate for partly paid shares.
(Where there is only one class of shares.)

Certificate No.............

Number of Shares.............

THE ......COMPANY, LIMITED.

Incorporated under the Companies Act, 1948.

Registered Office: ...., London, E.C.

Authorised Share Capital: £   in   shares of £   each.

This is to certify that.............

of.............

is/are registered as the holder(s) of .... shares

of................Company, Limited, subject to the Memorandum and Articles of Association of the Company, and that there has been paid up on each of the said shares the sum of................each numbered as in margin in the

Given under the Common Seal of the Company, this .... day of .... 19.......

(Seal of Co.)

Director.

Secretary.

Exd.............

Note.—No transfer of the above shares can be registered unless accompanied by the relative share certificate.

(Counterfoil as on Form 35, which see.)

PARTICULARS OF SHARES HEREIN REFERRED TO		
No. of Shares	DISTINCTIVE NUMBERS	
	FROM	TO

FORM No. 36 (continued)

Share Certificate (*continued*)
[*Endorsement on Share Certificate.*]

This is to certify that the further sum of..
has been paid on each of the within-mentioned shares making the amount
paid up per share..

Dated this .... day of..19..........

....

Secretary.

TRANSFERS CERTIFIED OR LODGED.

NOTE.—This Endorsement is reserved for the Company's purposes only, and must not be written upon.

Date of certification or lodgment	NAME OF TRANSFEREE	No. of Shares	DISTINCTIVE NUMBERS		Transfer No.	New Certificate No.	Auditors' Initials	Name of Broker presenting Transfer
			FROM	TO				

FORM No. 37

Share Certificate for fully paid shares
(where there is only one class of shares).
(No distinctive numbers.)

Certificate No._____ Number of Shares._____

THE_____COMPANY, LIMITED.

Incorporated under the Companies Act, 1948.

Registered Office: _____, London.

Authorised Share Capital: £_____ in _____ Shares of £_____ each.

THIS IS TO CERTIFY that_____

of_____

is registered as the holder of_____

Shares of_____ each, fully paid in THE_____COMPANY, LIMITED, subject to the Memorandum and Articles of Association of the Company.

Given under the Common Seal of the Company, this_____ day of_____ 19____

_____ Director.

_____ Secretary.

(Seal of Co.)

Exd._____

Note.—No transfer of the above shares can be registered unless accompanied by the relative share certificate.

[PERF.]

[PERF.]

RECEIVED the_____ day of_____ 19____ for Certificate No._____ in the name of THE_____COMPANY, LIMITED,_____ Shares in

_____
Signature of Shareholder or Broker.

THE
_____COMPANY, LIMITED.

SHARE CERTIFICATE.

No._____

Name_____

Address_____

No. of Shares_____

Date_____

Posted to_____

No. of transfer_____

FORM No. 37 (*continued*)

TRANSFERS CERTIFIED OR LODGED.

[Endorsement on Share Certificate]

NOTE.—This Endorsement is reserved for the Company's purposes only, and must not be written upon.

Date of certification or lodgment	NAME OF TRANSFEREE	No. of Shares	Transfer No.	New Certificate No.	Auditors' Initials	Name of Broker presenting Transfer

FORM No. 38

ORDINARY STOCK CERTIFICATE
(with Duplicate).

Certificate No.   Amount of Stock

£.................................

(Represented by units
of £1 each)

....LIMITED.

(Incorporated under The Companies Act, 1948)

Registered Office: ....Street, London, W.C.2.

Authorised Share Capital £.........................

Divided into £......... 6 per cent. First Cumulative Preference Stock,
£.................5½ per cent. Second Cumulative Preference Stock, and £...............
Ordinary Stock and ....Ordinary Shares of £1 each.

THIS IS TO CERTIFY that..is/are the Registered
Holder(s) of...Pounds Ordinary Stock in
....LIMITED subject to the Memorandum and
Articles of Association thereof, and that the said Stock is fully paid.

GIVEN under the Common Seal of the Company this.........................day
of.........................19.........

(Seal
of Co.)

.... Director.

.... Secretary.

NOTE.—No transfer of any portion of the stock comprised in this certificate
will be registered until this certificate has been lodged at the Transfer
Office of the Company, ..., London,
W.C.2.   The stock is transferable in amounts and multiples of £1.

---

*DUPLICATE

THIS FORM TO BE SIGNED AND RETURNED TO COMPANY INTACT.

Ordinary Stock Certificate   Amount of Stock
No.........................   £.........................

....LIMITED

Transfer Office—

.........................STREET,
LONDON, W.C.2.

....19.........

DEAR SIR(S),

I have pleasure in enclosing Certificate.........................
in favour of.........................
for.........................Pounds Ordinary Stock, fully paid.

Kindly acknowledge receipt by signing this form at foot and returning
it to the Company's Office, as above, promptly.

Certificate dated.........................day of.........................19.........

Yours faithfully,

.........................for Registrar.

RECEIVED the above-mentioned Certificate
Signature.........................
Date.........................

* By completing a carbon copy of the details of the Stock Certificate the duplicate as above is
arranged to provide (1) Copy details, (2) a Stock Certificate Enclosure Letter, (3) Stock Certificate
Receipt, the latter for signature and return by the Stockholder for retention by the Secretary.

FORM No. 39

FRACTIONAL CERTIFICATE.

THE..........COMPANY, LIMITED.

Registered Office: ...., London.

Issue of.................... Shares of £.... each.

FRACTIONAL CERTIFICATE No...........

Representing ONE..............th of a
.................................SHARE.

I HEREBY CERTIFY that the Bearer of this Certificate, upon presenting the same, together with .... other similar Certificates, will be entitled to an allotment of One Fully-paid ....Share of £.... in the Capital of the above-named Company, subject to the following stipulation:

That within three months from the date hereof, this Fractional Certificate, together with similar Certificates, making up one or more whole .... Shares, shall be lodged at the Company's Office with the Application Form endorsed on the back hereof duly signed.

Dated the.................................19

By order of the Board,

Secretary.

Entered..

N.B.—This Fractional part of a Share cannot be Registered, nor can it bear any Dividend until exchanged with other Fractional Certificates for an entire Share.

FORM No. 40

ENDORSEMENT ON FRACTIONAL CERTIFICATE.

FORM OF APPLICATION.

To The............Company, Limited.

As the Bearer of this Fractional Certificate, and the ....
similar Fractional Certificates attached, I (or we) request the
allotment to me (or us) of .... whole .... (Share(s) of
..............., and authorise the Company to place my (or our)
name(s) on the Register of Members in respect thereof.

Signature..

Name in full..

Address ....

Description ....

Signature..

Name in full..

Address ....

Description ....

Date..

N.B.—This application is only to be signed by the holder(s)
when presenting the Fractional Certificate (with others,
making one or more complete Shares) for registration at the
Company's Office.

FORM No. 41

INDEMNITY FOR DUPLICATE CERTIFICATE.

I, the above-named *A. B.*, do hereby request The............COM-
PANY, LIMITED, to issue to me a duplicate Certificate of the
.... shares (stock) of the Company registered in my name
the original Certificate numbered .... being mislaid,
destroyed or lost, and in consideration of the Company so doing, I hereby, for myself, my heirs, executors or
administrators, indemnify the said Company against all claims
and demands, moneys, losses, damages, costs, and expenses
which may be brought against, or be paid, incurred, or sustained by the said Company by reason or in consequence of the
said Certificate having been mislaid, destroyed or lost, or by
reason or in consequence of the issuing to me of the said duplicate Certificate or otherwise howsoever in relation thereto
respectively. I further undertake and agree, if the said
Certificate shall hereafter be found, forthwith to deliver up
the same or cause the same to be delivered up to the..........
Company, Limited, their successors and assigns without cost,
fee or reward.

Dated this .... day of .... 19..........

Signed by the said *A. B.*
in the presence of   6*d.*

Witness's Name ⎰   *X.Y.Z.*   . STAMP.
and Address ⎱   ....   *A. B.*

Note.—The Indemnity must bear a 6*d.* Stamp, either impressed or adhesive. The Company may (and will if the
account be of any magnitude) require a guarantee or indemnity
by a person of standing as follows:—

And I .... of .... concur in the above request and
guarantee the performance by the said............ of the above
undertaking.

(*Signature*)... ....

FORM No. 42

CERTIFICATE OF IDENTITY.

The............Company, Limited.

(To be made by a Solicitor, Broker, or other authorised Agent.)

I, the undersigned, *A. B.*, of ...., state that I have known and been well acquainted for .... years and upwards with *C. D.*, who is registered in the books of The............Company, Limited, in the name of

....

of ....

as the Proprietor of............................Shares of............................ each, and that *C. D.*, mentioned in the*............................

.... herewith exhibited, and of which an Abstract is hereto subjoined, is the same person as the said ....

....

Signature, A. B.

Address ....

Date..19............

---

*Deed of transfer, probate, certificate of death or marriage, or other document requiring identification.

FORM No. 43

STATUTORY REPORT.

No. of Company...

THE COMPANIES ACT, 1948.

A 5s. Companies Registration Fee Stamp must be impressed here.

REPORT

(*Pursuant to Section* 130 (3) *of the Companies Act,* 1948)

of .... Limited.

1. The total number of shares allotted is.......................................

2. Of the shares so allotted.................................have been allotted on the footing that they are to be paid for in cash on the terms mentioned in the Prospectus, and £................... has already been paid up on each share. The residue of such shares viz:...................have been allotted (¹) ....

....

in consideration of (²) ....

....

(¹) Here state as "fully paid up" or "paid up otherwise than in cash to the extent of................ per share."
(²) Here state consideration for which they have been allotted.

3. The total amount of cash received by the Company in respect of the........................ shares issued wholly for cash is £........................... and on the ....shares issued partly for cash is £...............................

4. The following are the Receipts and Payments of the Company to within seven days of the date of this Report:—*

Particulars of Receipts				Particulars of Payments		

* The receipts from shares and Debentures and other sources and the payments thereout must be shown under distinctive headings and particulars must be given concerning the balance remaining in hand.

Presented by

....

....

....

FORM No. 43 (*continued*)

5. The following is an Account or Estimate of the Preliminary Expenses of the Company.

6. The following are the Names, Addresses and Descriptions of the Directors, Auditors (if any), Manager (if any), and Secretary of the Company.

DIRECTORS

Christian Name	Surname	Address	Description

AUDITORS

Christian Name	Surname	Address	Description

MANAGER

Christian Name	Surname	Address	Description

SECRETARY

Christian Name	Surname	Address	Description

FORM No. 43 (*continued*)

7. The following Contract   to be submitted to the meeting for modifications and approval, viz.

(^{1})

($_1$) Here state shortly particulars of agreement.

The proposed modification   as follows:—(^{2})

($_2$) Here state shortly the proposed modification.

We hereby certify that this Report is correct.

.... }*Directors.*
....

We hereby certify that so much of this Report as relates to the shares allotted by the Company and to the cash received in respect of such Shares and to the receipts and payments of the Company on Capital Account is correct.

.... }*Auditors.*
....

Dated this....................................day of...................................19..........

NOTE.—This Report must be certified by not less than two Directors of the Company, and so far as it relates to the shares allotted by the Company, and to the cash received in respect of such shares and to the receipts and payments on capital account by the Auditors if any, and must be forwarded at least fourteen days before the day on which the Statutory Meeting is to be held to every member of the Company, and a copy must be filed with the Registrar of Companies forthwith after it is so forwarded. See Section 130 of the Companies Act, 1948.

W

FORM No. 44

LIST OF MEMBERS TO BE SUBMITTED TO STATUTORY MEETING.

No. of Company...

THE COMPANIES ACT, 1948.

....LIMITED.

List of Members to be submitted to the Statutory Meeting of the Company, pursuant to Section 130 (6) of the Companies Act, 1948.

Names of Members	Addresses	Descriptions	Number of Shares held by each Member

FORM No. 45

NOTICE OF ANNUAL GENERAL MEETING.

....LIMITED.

(*Address*)..

....

NOTICE IS HEREBY GIVEN that the *.. ANNUAL GENERAL MEETING of the Shareholders of the above-named Company will be held at..
.... on.. day
the ....day of..19
at..o'clock for the following purposes:—

1. To receive and consider the annual Statement of Accounts and Balance Sheet for the year ended..and the Directors' and Auditors' Reports thereon, and to declare a dividend.
2. To elect Directors.
3. To fix the remuneration of the Auditors.
4. To transact any other ordinary business of the Company.

Dated this..................................day of..................................19..........

By Order of the Board,

....
Secretary.

Note.—A member entitled to attend and vote at the above meeting may appoint a proxy to attend and vote on his behalf and such proxy need not also be a member of the company.

The Transfer Books of the Company will be closed from the................19......
to the ....19.......... both days inclusive.

* "First," "Tenth" or as the case may be.

FORM No. 46

NOTICE OF EXTRAORDINARY GENERAL MEETING.

....Limited.

Address...

*Notice is hereby given that an Extraordinary General Meeting of Shareholders of the above-named Company, will be held at........................

....

.... on................................... day

the...day of.....................................19...........

at....................a.m./p.m., for the purpose of considering and, if thought fit, passing as an †   Resolution the Resolution following that is to say:—

Dated this...day of...................19...........

By Order of the Board,

....

Secretary.

N.B.—If you are unable to attend the Meeting, please fill up the enclosed Form of Proxy, with the name of one of the Directors, or any Member of the Company or other person whom you think fit to appoint as your Proxy; sign it in accordance with the provisions of the Articles of Association and return the Form to the Secretary on or before the.................
19...........

Note.—A member entitled to attend and vote is entitled to appoint a proxy to attend and vote instead of him and the proxy need not also be a member.

* In the case of convening a meeting of a class of Shareholders, *e.g.* "Preference," "Deferred," the Notice will read: "Notice is hereby given that a separate meeting of the holders of....................Shares in the capital of the above-named Company will be held, etc., etc."
† "Ordinary" or "Extraordinary" as the case may be.

FORM No. 47

NOTICE OF EXTRAORDINARY GENERAL MEETING
TO PASS A SPECIAL RESOLUTION.

....LIMITED.

Address...

NOTICE IS HEREBY GIVEN that an EXTRAORDINARY GENERAL MEETING of the members of the above-named Company, will be held at...........................

....

.... on ....day

the.. day of...............................19...........

at....................a.m./p.m., for the purpose of considering and, if thought fit, passing as a SPECIAL RESOLUTION the resolution following that is to say:—

SPECIAL RESOLUTION.

Dated this..day of...............................19......

By Order of the Board,

....
Secretary.

N.B.—If you are unable to attend the Meeting, please fill up the enclosed Form of Proxy, with the name of one of the Directors, or any Member of the Company or other person whom you think fit to appoint as your Proxy; sign it in accordance with the provisions of the Articles of Association and return the form to the Secretary on or before the.................19...........

Note.—A member entitled to attend and vote is entitled to appoint a proxy to attend and vote instead of him and the proxy need not also be a member.

FORM No. 48

NOTICE OF BOARD MEETING.

....Limited.

Address...

To.. Date................................

Dear Sir,

    You are hereby requested to attend a Board Meeting of this Company at the above address on...at.....................a.m./p.m.

Yours faithfully,

....

Secretary.

Business:

FORM No. 49

PROXY—GENERAL FORM.

....Limited.

I/We, ...

of ....

....being a Member(s) of the above-named

Company, hereby appoint..

.... of..

.... or failing him,

....

of ....

as my/our proxy, to vote for me/us and on my/our behalf at the *.........................

General Meeting of the said Company, to be held on..day

the...day of...19............,

and at any adjournment thereof.

Signed this...day of.................................19............

Signature..

If executed by a Corporation, the Proxy should be sealed.

N.B.—This Proxy must be deposited at the Registered Office of the

Company ....

not less than †................................hours before the time for holding the meeting.

* Annual, Extraordinary, or as the case may be.
† The limit is forty-eight hours.

FORM No. 50

PROXY—WITH INSTRUCTIONS "FOR" OR "AGAINST" A RESOLUTION.

....Limited.

I/We ....

of ....

....being a Member(s) of the above-named

Company, hereby appoint..

.... of ....

.... or failing him,

....

of ....

as my/our proxy, to vote for me/us and on my/our behalf at the *....................

General Meeting of the said Company, to be held on.................................... day

the..day of................................19..........,

and at any adjournment thereof.

This form to be used †$\frac{in\ favour\ of}{against}$ *the resolution.*

	For	Against
††[or alternatively]		
Resolution No. 1	....	....
Resolution No. 2	....	....
Resolution No. 3	....	....

Signed this...day of....................19..........

Signature........................

N.B.—This Proxy must be deposited at the Registered Office of the Company ....

not less than ‡....................................hours before the time for holding the meeting.

* Annual, Extraordinary, or as the case may be.

† Strike out whichever is not desired.   Unless otherwise instructed, the Proxy will vote as he thinks fit.   A direction to vote for any Resolution authorises the Proxy to vote in favour of the Resolution with or without modification as the Proxy may approve.

†† Indicate by inserting X in the appropriate spaces the manner in which the Proxy is to vote.

‡ The limit is forty-eight hours.

If executed by a Corporation, the Proxy should be sealed.

FORM No. 51

ORDINARY

Form of Proxy to be used for the Meeting of Holders of Ordinary Stock pursuant to a Scheme of Arrangement under s. 206.

IN THE HIGH COURT OF JUSTICE.   No................. of 19..........
   CHANCERY DIVISION.
     GROUP............

      IN THE MATTER of..LIMITED
and
      IN THE MATTER of the Companies Act, 1948.

  (*a*) I/We (*b*)...
(IN BLOCK LETTERS)
of (*c*) ....
....

being the holder(s) of Ordinary Stock of the above Company do hereby appoint *A B...of..
or failing him, C D..of.....................................
as (*a*) my/our Proxy to act for (*d*) me/us at the Meeting of the holders of Ordinary Stock of the said Company to be held at...
...., on ....the........................day of ....19......, at..............o'clock, or so soon thereafter as the preceding meeting shall be concluded for the purpose of considering, and, if thought fit, approving, with or without modification, the proposed Scheme of Arrangement referred to in the Notice convening the said Meeting, and at such meeting, and at any adjournment thereof, to vote for (*d*) me/us and in (*a*) my/our name(s) (*e*).............................the said Scheme, either with or without modification as (*a*) my/our Proxy may approve.

     Dated this..............................day of......................................19..........

(Signature).....................................

NOTES.

(1) You are requested to lodge this Form of Proxy with the Secretary at the registered office of the Company, ..., not later than 12 o'clock noon on ....day of ....19....., but if this form is not so lodged it must be handed to the Chairman at the meeting.

(2) Any alteration made in this Form of Proxy should be initialled by the person who signs it.

(3) In the case of joint holders, the vote of the senior who tenders a vote whether in person or by proxy will be accepted to the exclusion of the vote of the other joint holders. For this purpose seniority will be determined by the order in which the names stand in the register of members.

(4) The person to whom this Proxy is given need not be a member of the Company but must attend the Meeting in person to represent you.

(*a*) Delete "I" or "we," "my" or "our" throughout as the case may be.
(*b*) Fill in your full name(s).
(*c*) Fill in your address.
 * NOTE.—If any other Proxy be preferred, strike out the names here inserted and add name of proxy desired and initial alteration.
(*d*) Delete "me" or "us."
 IMPORTANT.—(*e*) If for, insert "for"; if against, insert "against." If against, strike out the words after "Scheme" and initial such alteration.

FOLD HERE

Postage
1d. Stamp

The Secretary,

.............., LIMITED,

LONDON, E.C.

FOLD HERE

FOLD HERE

FORM No. 52

THE COMPANIES ACT, 1948.
(Section 133 (3))

....Limited.

AGREEMENT OF MEMBERS TO A SPECIAL RESOLUTION BEING PASSED AT A MEETING OF WHICH LESS THAN 21 DAYS' NOTICE HAS BEEN GIVEN.

I/We, the undersigned, being a Majority of Members holding together 95 per cent. of nominal value of Shares of the above-named Company and entitled to attend and vote at the meeting hereinafter mentioned hereby agree to the Resolution set out in the Notice of the Meeting dated the ....day of..19..........
and proposed to be passed as a Special Resolution at an Extraordinary General Meeting of the said Company to be held on the...................................day of...19.........., being passed as a Special Resolution notwithstanding that less than twenty-one days' notice of such meeting has been given.

Signature	Address

Dated this..day of.......................................19..........

FORM No. 53

THE COMPANIES ACT, 1948.

REQUISITION FOR EXTRAORDINARY GENERAL MEETING.

OF

....LIMITED.

(Date)..............................19..........

To the Directors of..

....Limited.

We, the undersigned Members of the above-named Company, hereby request you to convene an Extraordinary General Meeting pursuant to Section 132 of the Companies Act, 1948.

The Objects of the Meeting are:—

Signature	Address

FORM No. 54

ANNUAL RETURN.

No. of Company.................................

THE COMPANIES ACT, 1948.

(6th Schedule, Part 2.)

A 5s. Companies Registration Fee Stamp must be impressed here.

FORM OF ANNUAL RETURN OF A COMPANY HAVING A SHARE CAPITAL AS REQUIRED BY PART IV OF THE COMPANIES ACT, 1948 (SECTION 124).

ANNUAL RETURN OF...

....Limited, made up to

the...........................day of............................19....... (being the Fourteenth day after the date of the Annual General Meeting for the Year 19.........).

The Address of the Registered Office of the Company is as follows—

....

Situation of Registers of Members and Debenture Holders—

(a) (*Address of place at which the Register of Members is kept, if other than the Registered Office of the Company*)—

....

(b) (*Address of any place in Great Britain other than the Registered Office of the Company, at which is kept any register of holders of debentures of the Company or any duplicate of any such register or part of any such register which is kept outside Great Britain*)—

....

Presented by...

SUMMARY OF SHARE CAPITAL AND DEBENTURES

(a) *Nominal Share Capital (insert Number and Class)*

Nominal Share Capital, £.................Divided into   ..   { ....shares of ....each
...................shares of ....each
...................shares of ....each

(b) *Issued Share Capital and Debentures.*

	Number	Class
Number of shares of each class taken up to the date of this Return (which number must agree with the total shown in the list as held by existing members)	....	.........shares
	....	.........shares
	....	.........shares
Number of shares of each class issued subject to payment wholly in cash	....	.........shares
	....	.........shares
	....	.........shares
Number of shares of each class issued as fully paid up for a consideration other than cash ..	....	.........shares
	....	.........shares
	....	.........shares

Number of shares of each class issued as partly paid up for a consideration other than cash and the extent to which each such share is so paid up

{ Issued as paid up to the extent of £...........per share
Issued as paid up to the extent of £...........per share
Issued as paid up to the extent of £...........per share }

{ ....shares
..........shares
..........shares }

	Number	Class
Number of shares (if any) of each class issued at a discount	....	.........shares
	....	.........shares
	....	.........shares

Amount of discount on the issue of shares which has not been written off at the date of this Return ..   ..   £..........

	Number	Class
Amount called up on number of shares of each class £.......per share on	....	.........shares
„ „ „ „ £.......per share on	....	.........shares
„ „ „ „ £.......per share on	....	.........shares

Total amount of calls received, including payments on application and allotment and any sums received on shares forfeited   ..   ..   £..........

FORM No. 54 (continued)

SUMMARY OF SHARE CAPITAL AND SHARES (continued)

		Number	Class
Total amount (if any) agreed to be considered as paid on number of shares of each class issued as fully paid up for a consideration other than cash	} £............on	{	shares shares shares
Total amount (if any) agreed to be considered as paid on number of shares of each class issued as partly paid up for a consideration other than cash	} £............on	{	shares shares shares
Total amount of Calls unpaid	£............		
Total amount of the sums (if any) paid by way of Commission in respect of any Shares or Debentures	{ £............		
Total amount of the sums (if any) allowed by way of discount in respect of any Debentures since the date of the last return..	{ £............		

		Number	Class
Total number of shares of each class forfeited	{	....	shares shares shares
Total amount paid (if any) on Shares forfeited	£............		
Total amount of Shares for which Share Warrants to bearer are outstanding	{ £............		
Total amount of Share Warrants to bearer issued and surrendered respectively since date of last Return	{ Issued .. \ Surrendered	£............ £............	
Number of Shares comprised in each Share Warrant to bearer, specifying in the case of Warrants of different kinds, particulars of each kind	{		

PARTICULARS OF INDEBTEDNESS

Total amount of indebtedness of the Company in respect of all mortgages and charges which are required (or in the case of a Company registered in Scotland, which, if the Company had been registered in England, would be required) to be registered with the Registrar of Companies under The Companies Act, 1948, or which would have been required so to be registered if created after 1st July, 1928 ..	£............

CERTIFIED COPIES OF ACCOUNTS.

Except where the Company is either an Exempt Private Company as defined by Section 129 (4) of The Companies Act, 1948, which sends with this Return a certificate in the form set out hereafter or an assurance company which has complied with the provisions of Section 7 (4) of the Assurance Companies Act, 1909, there must be annexed to this Return a written copy, certified both by a Director and by the Secretary of the Company to be a true copy of every balance sheet laid before the Company in General Meeting during the period to which this Return relates (including every document required by law to be annexed to the balance sheet) and a copy (certified as aforesaid) of the report of the auditors on, and of the report of the Directors accompanying, every such balance sheet. If any such balance sheet or document required by law to be annexed thereto is in a foreign language there must also be annexed to that balance sheet a translation in English of the balance sheet or document certified in the prescribed manner to be a correct translation. If any such balance sheet as aforesaid or document required by law to be annexed thereto did not comply with the requirements of the law as in force at the date of the audit, with respect to the form of balance sheets or documents aforesaid, as the case may be, there must be made such additions to and corrections in the copy as would have been required to be made in the balance sheet or document in order to make it comply with the said requirements, and the fact that the copy has been so amended must be stated thereon.

We certify that there is annexed hereto a true copy of every Balance Sheet laid before the Company in General Meeting during the period to which this Return relates (including every document required by law to be annexed to the Balance Sheet) and a true copy of the report of the Auditors on, and of the report of the Directors accompanying, each such Balance Sheet.

(Signed)..Director

(Signed).. Secretary

Banking Companies.

A Banking Company, in order to avail itself of the benefit of Section 432 of The Companies Act, 1948, must add to this Return a statement of the names of the several places where it carries on business.

This return must be signed, at the end, by a Director and Secretary of the Company.

Certificates applicable to a Private Company and additional Certificate applicable to an Exempt Private Company (see page 646).

FORM No. 54 (*continued*)

PARTICULARS OF THE PERSONS WHO ARE DIRECTORS* OF THE COMPANY AT THE DATE OF THIS RETURN.

Name (In the case of an individual, present Christian name† or names and surname. In the case of a corporation, the corporate name)	Any former Christian name or names and surname‡	Nationality	Usual residential address (In the case of a corporation, the registered or principal office)	Business occupation and particulars of other directorships§	Date of birth||

*N.B.—Refer to page 646 for NOTES relating to Particulars of Directors and Secretary. If there is not sufficient space for entries in above columns, particularly column 5, complete and attach a separate sheet.

PARTICULARS OF THE PERSON WHO IS SECRETARY OF THE COMPANY AT THE DATE OF THIS RETURN.

Name (In the case of an individual, present Christian name or names and surname. In the case of a corporation, or a Scottish Firm, the corporate name)¶	Any former Christian name or names and surname	USUAL RESIDENTIAL ADDRESS (In the case of a corporation or Scottish firm, the registered or principal office)

FORM No. 54 (continued)

Indicate whether
(a) Full List ....
(b) Changes only ....

LIST OF PAST AND PRESENT MEMBERS.

List of Persons holding Shares or Stock in the Company on the 14th day after the Annual General Meeting for 19........ and of Persons who have held Shares or Stock therein at any time since the date of the last Return, or in the case of the first Return of the incorporation of the Company.

Folio in Register Ledger containing particulars	Names and Addresses	ACCOUNT OF SHARES				Remarks
		Number of Shares held by Existing Members at date of Return*†	Particulars of Shares Transferred since the date of the last Return, or in the case of the first Return of the incorporation of the Company by (a) persons who are still members and (b) persons who have ceased to be members‡			
			Number†	Date of Registration of Transfer		
				(a)	(b)	

(Signed) .... *Director*

(Signed) .... *Secretary*

NOTES.

1. If the return for either of the two immediately preceding years has given, at the date of that return, the full particulars as to past and present members and the shares and stock held and transferred by them, only such of the particulars need be given as relate to persons ceasing to be or becoming members since the date of the last return and to shares transferred since that date, or to changes as compared with that date in the amount of stock held by a member.

2. If the names in the list are not arranged in alphabetical order, an index sufficient to enable the name of any person to be readily found must be annexed.

* The aggregate number of shares held by each member must be stated, and the aggregates must be added up so as to agree with the number of shares stated in the summary of Share Capital and Debentures to have been taken up.

† When the shares are of different classes these columns may be sub-divided so that the number of each class held, or transferred, may be shown separately. Where any shares have been converted into stock the amount of stock held by each member must be shown.

‡ The date of Registration of each Transfer should be given as well as the number of shares transferred on each date. The particulars should be placed opposite the name of the transferor, and not opposite that of the Transferee, but the name of the transferee may be inserted in the "REMARKS" column, immediately opposite the particulars of each Transfer.

In the case of the larger Companies the List of Members is completed by typewriting or "address plates." The size of sheet is normally 14 inches by 9 inches, which can conveniently be accommodated in the normal file covers at Bush House. The Registrar does not refuse a larger size provided not less than ¾ inch is allowed for securely binding the sheets, but it is urged that these should not exceed 16 inches by 11⅜ inches to fit the larger stock covers at the Registry.

FORM No. 54 (continued)

CERTIFICATES AND OTHER DOCUMENTS ACCOMPANYING ANNUAL RETURN.

Certificate to be given by a Director and the Secretary of every Private Company (whether an Exempt Private Company or not).

We certify that the Company has not, since the $\dfrac{\text{date of the incorporation of the Company}}{\text{last Annual Return}}$ (a) issued any invitation to the public to subscribe for any shares or debentures of the Company.

Signed .... Director

Signed .... Secretary

Further certificate to be given as aforesaid if the number of members of the Company exceeds fifty.

We certify that the excess of the number of members of the Company over fifty consists wholly of persons who, under paragraph (b) of sub-section (1) of Section 28 of The Companies Act, 1948, are not to be included in reckoning the number of fifty.

Signed .... Director

Signed .... Secretary

Additional certificate to be given in the case of an exempt Private Company by the persons signing the above-mentioned certificates.

We certify, that to the best of our knowledge and belief, the conditions mentioned in sub-section (2) of Section 129 of The Companies Act, 1948, are satisfied at the date of this Return and have been satisfied at all times since..(b).

Signed .... Director

Signed .... Secretary

(a) Strike out whichever is inapplicable.
(b) Insert "1st July, 1948" (the date of the commencement of The Companies Act. 1948) or, if the Company was registered after that date, the date on which it was registered, or, if the proviso to Section 129 (1) of The Companies Act, 1948, has effect in relation to the Return, the time at which it was shown to the Board of Trade that the conditions mentioned in the certificate were satisfied.

Notes relating to Particulars of Directors and Secretary referred to on page 644.

* "Director" includes any person who occupies the position of a Director by whatsoever name called and any person in accordance with whose directions or instructions the Directors of the Company are accustomed to act.

† "Christian name" includes a forename, and "surname," in the case of a peer or person usually known by a title different from his surname, means that title.

‡ "Former Christian name" and "former surname" do not include—
    (a) In the case of a peer or person usually known by a British title different from his surname, the name by which he was known previous to the adoption of or succession to the title; or
    (b) in the case of any person, a former christian name or surname where that name or surname was changed or disused before the person bearing the name attained the age of eighteen years or has been changed or disused for a period of not less than twenty years; or
    (c) in the case of a married woman the name or surname by which she was known previous to the marriage.

§ Directorships—The names of all bodies corporate incorporated in Great Britain of which the Director is also a Director, should be given, except bodies corporate of which the Company making the Return is the wholly-owned subsidiary or bodies corporate which are the wholly-owned subsidiaries either of the Company or of another company of which the Company is the wholly-owned subsidiary. A body corporate is deemed to be the wholly-owned subsidiary of another if it has no members except that other and that other's wholly-owned subsidiaries and its or, their nominees. If the space provided in the form is insufficient particulars of other directorships should be listed on a separate statement attached to this Return.

‖ Dates of birth need only be given in the case of a Company which is subject to Section 185 of The Companies Act, 1948, namely, a Company which is not a Private Company or which, being a Private Company, is the subsidiary of a body corporate incorporated in the United Kingdom which is neither a Private Company nor a Company registered under the law relating to companies for the time being in force in Northern Ireland and having provisions in its constitution which would, if it had been registered in Great Britain, entitle it to rank as a Private Company.

¶ Where all the partners in a firm are joint secretaries, the name and principal office of the firm may be stated.

FORM No. 55

ANNUAL RETURN: NO SHARE CAPITAL.

No. of Company...............................   Form No. 7.

THE COMPANIES ACT, 1948.

◯ *A 5s. Companies Registration Fee Stamp must be impressed here.*

ANNUAL RETURN OF A COMPANY NOT HAVING A SHARE CAPITAL.
Pursuant to Sections 125 to 127.

Annual Return of...

.... Limited,

made up to the..day of.........................19..........

(being the fourteenth day after the date of the Annual General Meeting

for the year 19..........).

1.   Address of the registered office of the Company:—

....

....

2.   Situation of Registers of Members and Debenture Holders:—

    (*a*)   (*Address of place at which the Register of Members is kept, if other than the Registered Office of the Company*)—

....

    (*b*)   (*Address of any place in Great Britain other than the Registered Office of the Company, at which is kept any register of holders of debentures of the Company or any duplicate of any such register or part of any such register which is kept outside Great Britain*)—

....

3.   Total amount of indebtedness of the Company in respect of all mortgages and charges which are required (or, in the case of a Company registered in Scotland, which, if the Company had been registered in England, would be required) to be registered with the Registrar of Companies under The Companies Act, 1948, or which would have been required so to be registered if created after 1st July, 1908.

£..........................

Presented by

....

....

....

FORM No. 55 (continued)

PARTICULARS OF THE PERSONS WHO ARE DIRECTORS* OF THE COMPANY AT THE DATE OF THIS RETURN.

NAME (In the case of an individual, present Christian name† or names and surname. In the case of a corporation, the corporate name)	Any former Christian name or names and surname‡	Nationality	Usual residential address (In the case of a corporation, the registered or principal office)	Business occupation and particulars of other directorships§	Date of birth‖

PARTICULARS OF THE PERSON WHO IS SECRETARY OF THE COMPANY AT THE DATE OF THIS RETURN.

NAME (In the case of an individual, present Christian name or names and surname.‡ In the case of a corporation or a Scottish firm, the corporate or firm name)¶	Any former Christian name or names and surname	USUAL RESIDENTIAL ADDRESS (In the case of a corporation or a Scottish firm, the registered or principal office)

Signed............... *Director.*
Signed............... *Secretary.*

The return must be signed, by a Director and Secretary of the Company.

* "Director" includes any person who occupies the position of a Director by whatsoever name called, and any person in accordance with whose directions or instructions the Directors of the Company are accustomed to act.

† "Christian name" includes a forename, and "surname" in the case of a peer or person usually known by a title different from his surname, means that title.

‡ "Former christian name" and "former surname" do not include—
(a) In the case of a peer or person usually known by a British title different from his surname, the name by which he was known previous to the adoption of or succession to the title; or
(b) in the case of any person, a former christian name or surname where that name or surname was changed or disused before the person bearing the name attained the age of eighteen years or has been changed or disused for a period of not less than twenty years; or
(c) in the case of a married woman the name or surname by which she was known previous to the marriage.

§ Directorships—The names of all bodies corporate incorporated in Great Britain of which the Director is also a Director, should be given, except bodies corporate of which the Company making the Return is the wholly-owned subsidiary or bodies corporate which are the wholly-owned subsidiaries either of the Company or of another company of which the Company is the wholly-owned subsidiary. A body corporate is deemed to be the wholly-owned subsidiary of another if it has no members except that other and that other's wholly-owned subsidiaries and its or their nominees. If the space provided in the form is insufficient, particulars of other directorships should be listed on a separate statement attached to this Return.

‖ Dates of birth need only be given in the case of a Company which is subject to Section 185 of The Companies Act, 1948, namely, a Company which is not a Private Company or which, being a Private Company, is the subsidiary of a body corporate incorporated in the United Kingdom which is neither a Private Company nor a Company registered under the law relating to companies for the time being in force in Northern Ireland and having provisions in its constitution which would, if it had been registered in Great Britain, entitle it to rank as a Private Company.

¶ Where all the partners in a firm are joint secretaries, the name and principal office of the firm may be stated.

FORM No. 55 (continued)

CERTIFICATES AND OTHER DOCUMENTS ACCOMPANYING ANNUAL RETURN.

Certified copies of Accounts.

Except where the Company is either an Exempt Private Company as defined by Section 129 (4) of The Companies Act, 1948, which sends with this Return certificates as required by Sections 128 and 129 (1) (*b*) of that Act or an assurance company which has complied with the provisions of Section 7 (4) of The Assurance Companies Act, 1909, there must be annexed to this Return a written copy, certified both by a Director and by the Secretary of the Company to be a true copy, of every balance sheet laid before the Company in General Meeting during the period to which this Return relates (including every document required by law to be annexed to the balance sheet) and a copy (certified as aforesaid) of the report of the auditors on, and of the report of the Directors accompanying, each such balance sheet. If any such balance sheet or document required by law to be annexed thereto is in a foreign language there must also be annexed to that balance sheet a translation in English of the balance sheet or document certified in the prescribed manner to be a correct translation. If any such balance sheet as aforesaid or document required by law to be annexed thereto did not comply with the requirements of the law as in force at the date of the audit, with respect to the form of balance sheets or documents aforesaid, as the case may be, there must be made such additions to and corrections in the copy as would have been required to be made in the balance sheet or document in order to make it comply with the said requirements, and the fact that the copy has been so amended must be stated thereon.

Banking Companies.

A Banking Company, in order to avail itself of the benefit of Section 432 of the Companies Act, 1948, must add to this Return a statement of the names of the several places where it carries on business (Form No. 56).

FORM No. 56

THE COMPANIES ACT, 1948.

STATEMENT OF PLACES OF BUSINESS OF BANKS.
Pursuant to Section 432.

To be attached to the Annual Return of a banking company wishing to avail itself of the benefit of Section 432 of the Companies Act, 1948.

Statement pursuant to Section 432 of the Companies Act, 1948, of the names of the several places of business of...with the counties in which they are situate.

Address	County

(To be signed at the end.)

(Signature)..

(State whether Director or Secretary)..

Dated the...day of...............................19...........

FORM No. 57

No. of Company...

THE COMPANIES ACT, 1948.

NOTICE OF INCREASE IN NOMINAL CAPITAL.
Pursuant to Section 63

Name
of   {..
Company   {.. Limited.

This Notice, accompanied by a printed copy of the resolution authorising the Increase, must be forwarded to the Registrar of Companies within 15 days after the passing of the said resolution.

Presented by

....

....

....

To the Registrar of Companies.

.... Limited
hereby gives you notice, pursuant to Section 63 of The Companies Act, 1948, that by (a)...Resolution of the Company dated the...............day of.....................................19.........the nominal capital of the Company has been increased by the addition thereto of the sum of £...............
beyond the registered capital of £.................................

The additional capital is divided as follows:—

No. of Shares	Class of Share	Nominal amount of each Share

The conditions (*e.g.* voting rights, dividend rights, winding up rights, etc.) subject to which the new shares have been or are to be issued are as follows:—

(If any of the new shares are Preference Shares state whether *they are redeemable or not.*)

Signature..

(b)..

Dated the..day of.....................................19...........

(a) "Ordinary," "Extraordinary" or "Special."
(b) State whether Director or Secretary.

FORM No. 58

No. of Company...

THE COMPANIES ACT, 1948.

STATEMENT OF INCREASE OF NOMINAL CAPITAL OF

.... Limited.

Pursuant to s. 112 of 54 and 55 Vict., ch. 39 (Stamp Act, 1891) as amended by s. 41 of 23 and 24 Geo., 5 ch. 19 (Finance Act, 1933).

NOTE.—The Stamp Duty on an increase of Nominal Capital is Ten Shillings for every £100 or fraction of £100.

This Statement is to be filed with the Notice of Increase registered under Section 63 of The Companies Act, 1948.

Presented by

....

....

THE NOMINAL CAPITAL *of*..

.... *Limited*

has been increased by the addition thereto of the sum of.........................*Pounds,*

(£........................*) divided into*..

....

Shares of..*each beyond the Registered*

Capital of ....

Signature ....

Officer ....

Dated the..*day of*........................19..........

This Statement should be signed by a Director or Secretary of the Company

FORM No. 59

No. of Company.. (Form No. 28)

THE COMPANIES ACT, 1948.

◯ *A 5s. Companies Registration Fee Stamp must be impressed here.*

NOTICE OF CONSOLIDATION, DIVISION, SUB-DIVISION, OR CONVERSION INTO STOCK OF SHARES, SPECIFYING THE SHARES SO CONSOLIDATED, DIVIDED, SUB-DIVIDED, OR CONVERTED INTO STOCK OR OF THE RE-CONVERSION INTO SHARES OF STOCK, SPECIFYING THE STOCK SO RE-CONVERTED, OR OF THE REDEMPTION OF REDEEMABLE PREFERENCE SHARES OR OF THE CANCELLATION OF SHARES (OTHERWISE THAN IN CONNECTION WITH A REDUCTION OF SHARE CAPITAL UNDER SECTION 66 OF THE COMPANIES ACT, 1948).

Pursuant to Section 62.

Name
of
Company { ....
....Limited

Presented by

....
....
....

To the Registrar of Companies.

The..
.... Company, Limited, hereby gives you notice in accordance with Section 62 of the Companies Act, 1948, that

(Signature)..

(State whether Director or Secretary)..

Dated the...day of..................................19..........

FORM No. 60

No. of Company............................   (Form No. 101)

THE COMPANIES ACT, 1948.

A 5s. Companies
Registration Fee
Stamp must be
impressed here.

NOTICE OF APPLICATION MADE TO THE COURT FOR THE CANCELLATION OF
AN ALTERATION MADE BY SPECIAL RESOLUTION TO THE PROVISIONS
OF THE MEMORANDUM OF THE COMPANY.

Pursuant to Section 5 (7).

Name of Company...Limited

Presented by..

....

....

To the Registrar of Companies.

.... Limited

hereby gives you notice, pursuant to sub-section (7) of Section 5 of the
Companies Act, 1948, that an application has been made to the Court
under that section for the cancellation of the alteration made to the
provisions of the memorandum of the company by a special resolution
dated the...day of..19.....,
of which a copy was forwarded to you on the...day
of...19..........

(*Signature*)...

(*State whether Director or Secretary*)..

Dated the...day of......................................19..........

FORM No. 61

DIVIDEND NOTICE AND WARRANT.

(The details required by s. 33 of the Finance Act, 1924, which are set out below* must be stated by companies incorporated in Great Britain, including those of them making 'free of tax' payments.)

Serial Number.............................   No......................

THE..........COMPANY, LIMITED.

LONDON, E.C....................................19...........

Dear Sir (or Madam),

I enclose Warrant for $\frac{\text{FINAL}}{\text{INTERIM}}$ DIVIDEND of..per share in respect of the year ended........................19....., on...........................

shares of ....each held by you.

$$\begin{array}{llll}
\text{Dividend} & .. & .. & \pounds \quad : \quad : \\
\textit{Less } \text{Income Tax at} & & & \\
\qquad\qquad ....\text{in } \pounds 1 & .. & \pounds \quad : \quad : \\
& & & \pounds \\
\end{array}$$

Name

....

....

I certify that Income Tax on the profits out of which the above-mentioned dividend is paid, has been, or will be, duly accounted for by the Company to the proper Officer for the receipt of Taxes.

N.B.—Proprietors claiming exemption from or abatement of Income Tax are informed that the Inland Revenue Commissioners will accept this statement as a Certificate of the deduction of Income Tax. It should therefore be carefully preserved. A charge of (1/-) will be made for each duplicate issued.

....

Secretary.

.... [PERF.] ....

[*Continued on next page.*

* (a) The gross amount which, after deduction of the Income Tax appropriate thereto, correspononds to the net amount actually paid; and

(b) The rate and the amount of Income Tax appropriate to such gross amount; and

(c) The net amount actually paid.

FORM No. 61 (continued)

*......................

....LIMITED,

LONDON, E.C. ....19..........

No.................................

....................................SHARES/STOCK DIVIDEND WARRANT.

To................................BANK LIMITED,........................E.C.2.

PAY .... | & Co. NOT NEGOTIABLE | or Order | Revenue Stamp

.... £ _____

For and on behalf of

THE................................LIMITED

....*Secretary*

Signature of Payee................................

Exd.............................

†T[C]*Signature of Payee*................................ .

NOTE.—This Warrant must be signed by the Payee and presented to the Company's Bankers within six months of the date hereof.

[†Enter:—T (town), or C (country), whichever letter is applicable, and the *Bank's "National" number.]

[The Committee of the London Clearing Bankers dealing with the standardisation of Cheque Forms, Dividend Warrants, Tax Deduction Certificates, recommend the following sizes:—

Minimum length 6 inches.   Maximum length 8 inches.
„   depth 3   „   „   depth 4   „

To accord with a request of the Chartered Institute of Secretaries it has been agreed in certain cases that the permissible *length* of Dividend Warrants can be amended to minimum 5¾ inches, maximum 8½ inches.]

FORM No. 61a

DIVIDEND WARRANT FOR USE WITH MACHINE ACCOUNTANCY SYSTEMS.

....Limited

Dear Sir (or Madam),

    I enclose Warrant for Dividend for the ....year ended.................19.....
on the ......per cent. Cumulative Preference Shares held by you on the
..........................instant as per Statement below.

    I certify that Income Tax on the profits out of which the above-
mentioned Dividend is paid, has been, or will be, duly accounted for by the
Company to the proper officer for the receipt of Taxes.

Yours faithfully,

....Secretary.

No. of Shares	Gross Dividend at the Rate of......% per annum	Less Income Tax at.................in the £	Net Dividend
†			

To | | *No.........................../...............................

Date.......................19..........

Address of Company.

THIS VOUCHER TO BE RETAINED BY THE SHAREHOLDER

This Certificate will be accepted by the Inland Revenue Authorities in
connection with any claim for Allowance or Relief of Income Tax.

.... [PERF.] --

(Bank National Number)

......per cent. Cumulative Preference Share Dividend Warrant

....Limited,

London,...19............

*No.........................../....................

....Bank Limited ....London, W.C.

Pay *the sum of* £ | £   s.   d. | Revenue Stamp

To | |

                  or Order

For and on behalf of
...............................Limited

‡
T[C] | |

....Secretary.

Shareholder's Signature...

    * For recording the consecutive number of the Dividend and of the Warrant.
    † Carbon strip on back of form of the shaded portion enables details to be listed on Dividend
Sheets, etc.
    ‡ Enter:—T (town) or C (country), whichever is applicable.

FORM No. 62

AUTHORITY TO PAY INTEREST OR DIVIDENDS.

To the Secretary of

....LIMITED.

Transfer Office:

....STREET, LONDON, W.C.2.

I/We hereby request and authorise you to pay all interest and dividends from time to time falling due and becoming payable on any stock or shares now or hereafter registered in my/our name(s) in the books of the company to*.......................

....or to any branch of that Bank to which my/our account may be transferred whose receipt shall be your sufficient discharge for the same.

Dated this.........................day of.................................19..........

† *Signature* ....
Name in full...............................
((Block letters)
Address ....

....

† *Signature* ....
Name in full...............................
(Block letters)
Address ....

....

For Company's Use only			
Ack'd.............. *By*........			
	6%	5½%	Ord.
Holding			
Plate-work			
Ledgers			

† *Signature* ....
Name in full...............................
(Block letters)
Address ....

....

† *Signature* ....
Name in full...............................
(Block letters)
Address ....

* Name, full address and National Bank number.
† In Joint Account this form must be signed by all the registered holders.

The company cannot accept any instructions that a warrant shall be paid to any particular account with the Bank. Such instructions must be communicated to the Bank direct.

AUTHORITY TO PAY DIVIDENDS TO BANKERS.

Stockholders are recommended to have their dividends paid direct to their Bankers. This course ensures the prompt crediting of the payments in the stockholders' banking accounts, eliminates the risk of warrants being lost in the post or mislaid, and effects economies in postage, stationery, stamp duty and labour.

Income tax vouchers for the dividends so paid are sent to the Bankers for inclusion in stockholders' pass books.

Kindly complete above form of request by inserting the name and branch of your Banker, appending your signature and full name and address, thereafter returning to the company. An envelope is not required, as this form, bearing the company's address, can be fastened by inserting flange in slot.

NOTE.—It is the practice of many companies, to insert on the back of a Dividend Warrant, a Form of Request to pay Interest or Dividend direct to a banking account, for completion by a Stock/Shareholder.

FORM No. 63

SPECIMEN SIGNATURE AND DIVIDEND REQUEST.

*(This Form may be sent out with Certificate in the case
of all new holdings.)*

THE..........COMPANY, LIMITED,

No.................

..............................., LONDON, E.C............................... 19.........

To...

(Address)..

For Office Use Only	
No. of Certificate	No. of Shares or Amount of Stock

Please favour me with a specimen of your ordinary signature below, returning this form to me.

If you desire that Dividends [or Interest] on your Shares [or Stock] should be paid to your Bankers direct, please also fill up and sign the form at foot hereof.

Secretary.

*Ordinary Signature of
Shareholder or Stockholder* {

....

....

To THE..........COMPANY, LIMITED.

I/We hereby request and authorise you to pay all interest and Dividends from time to time falling due and becoming payable on any stock or shares now or hereafter registered in my/our name(s) in the books of the Company to*..
Bank at..or to any Branch of that Bank to which my/our account may be transferred whose receipt shall be a sufficient discharge for the same.

Date................................19.........

(Signature) ....

Name in full................................
(Block letters)

Address ....

NOTE.—In the case of a joint account all holders must sign.

* Insert name, full address and National number of Bank.

FORM No. 64

DEBENTURE STOCK INTEREST WARRANT.

No.....................

....LIMITED.
..........................LONDON, E.C.2.
..................................19..........

Sir (or Madam),

...... PER CENT. FIRST MORTGAGE REDEEMABLE DEBENTURE STOCK.

I send you subjoined a Warrant in payment of Interest at the rate of ...... per cent. per annum (less Income Tax at....s. in the £) for the half-year to.....................19........., on your holding of the above-mentioned Stock, according to the Register of Stockholders which was closed on the.........................19..........

The Net Amount of Interest on your holding of £.......................Stock is £................................

For the gross amount of Interest and the amount of Income Tax appropriate thereto see table printed on the back hereof.

I hereby certify that the Income Tax deducted from this Interest has been, or will be, accounted for by me to the proper Officer for the receipt of Taxes.

N.B.—Stockholders claiming exemption from or abatement from Income Tax are informed that the Inland Revenue Commissioners will accept this statement as a Certificate of the deduction of Income Tax. It should therefore be carefully preserved. A charge of (1s.) will be made for each duplicate issued.

Yours faithfully,

....
Secretary.

This portion to be retained by the Proprietor.

Stockholders are particularly requested to give signed notification of any change of address.

.... [PERF.] ....

....LIMITED †..............
No.......................   LONDON, E.C....................................19..........

...... PER CENT. MORTGAGE REDEEMABLE DEBENTURE STOCK.

Interest Warrant for Half-Year to....................19..........

To....................BANK LIMITED, ..., E.C.2.

PAY .... *or Order* | Revenue Stamp |

& Co.
NOT NEGOTIABLE

....   £ ══════════
For and on behalf of

THE...LIMITED.
....*Secretary.*

Exd....................   *Signature of Payee*...
*T[C]

[NOTE.—This Warrant remains in force for six months only; after that period it must be presented at the Registered Office of the Company, ..., London, E.C.2, for verification.]

*[Enter—T (town) or C (country), whichever letter is applicable, and the †Bank's National number.]

FORM No. 65

INDEMNITY AND REQUEST FOR DUPLICATE DIVIDEND WARRANT.

To THE............COMPANY, LIMITED.

IN consideration of The............Company issuing to me a duplicate Warrant for the [Interest or Dividend] to the [30 June or 31 December, 19......], amounting to £.................... on the [amount of holding, *e.g.* £100 ordinary stock] registered in my name, in lieu of the original Warrant No...... dated.............. which has been lost, destroyed, or mislaid, I hereby undertake and engage for myself, my Executors, Administrators and Assigns, to hold the said Company, and the Directors and Officers thereof, harmless and indemnified against all losses and expenses which may be incurred in the event of the said original Warrant being paid or forthcoming at any future time, or otherwise in consequence of the said Company issuing a duplicate to me as aforesaid, and I request that such duplicate Warrant may be issued to me accordingly and I engage to return the original should it be found.

Dated this............*day of*...................., 19......

Signature..

6d. Stamp unless under £5

Address..

Witness:

Signature..

Address..

Occupation ....

NOTE.—Where there are circumstances involving the slightest suspicion or the amount involved is substantial, the holders' bankers should be requested to join in the indemnity.

For Company's Use Only
Bank Notified....................
Checked Unpaid ....
Entered....................
Duplicate Issued....................

FORM No. 66

DIVIDEND LIST.

Name	Stockholding	Gross Dividend	Less Income Tax at........	Net Dividend	Warrant Number

DIVIDEND No..........................

CONTENTS........................

LEDGER No.........................

FORM No. 67

STOP NOTICE RE DIVIDEND WARRANT.

THE ....COMPANY LIMITED.

....

LONDON, E.C.2.

............................19............

The Manager,
..............................Bank Limited,
.... Street,
London, E.C.3.

Dear Sir,

Dividend Account No............................

Please stop payment of the undermentioned Warrant(s) payable on the..on the........................Shares of this Company.

No. of Warrant	Amount	Name of Payee
....	£..............................	....

Yours faithfully,

....

Secretary.

FORM No. 68

DIVIDEND PROGRAMME.

Company.. Stock............... No...................

Period..

Gross per cent actual ....

„ „ £1 unit ....

Less Income Tax at...........................

Co.'s Net U.K. Tax rate....................

Board Meeting ....

S/E Advices ....

Press Advices....................................

Post Reports and Speeches....................

Close Books ....

Send Banks Bulk
   Cheques and Vouchers...............

Post Private Warrants..........................

Payable ....

General Meeting ....

Annual Return due ....

Amount of Stock in issue £

	£	s.	d.
Total Gross Payment			
„ Income Tax			
„ Net Payment			
£			

No. Reports
and Speeches } .... from ....

Dividend Sheets check stock ....

Report envelopes „ „ ....

Window „ „ „ ....

Warrant Details.

Supplier............... Ordered............... in..........

.....................Coupons No'd............ to..........

.....................Warrants No'd............ to..........

.....................Warrants not numbered.

RECONCILIATION OF WARRANTS.

Nod.

Used as per sheets — Big Banks ..

„ „ „ — Small Banks {
    and Privates

Total warrants used .. ..

Surplus and spoils .. .. ..

Available for re-issues .. ..

Total printed as per order ..

Stockholders
Big Banks
Small Banks
Privates

FORM No. 69

DEBENTURE AND CONDITIONS.

....LIMITED.

Registered Office..

| No. | £ |

DEBENTURE.

1. For valuable consideration already received.............................Limited, (hereinafter called "the Company") will on the...day of..19........., or on such earlier day as the Principal Moneys hereby secured become payable in accordance with the conditions endorsed hereon, pay to—

....

of ....

or other Registered Holder for the time being hereof, his Executors, Administrators or Assigns, the sum of..pounds.

2. The Company will in the meantime pay to such Registered Holder interest thereon at the rate of...........................pounds per centum per annum, by equal half-yearly payments on the.......................................day of...............................and the...........................day of................................in each year, the first of such half-yearly payments to be made on the...................................day of...............................next.

3. The Company as benficial owner hereby charges its undertaking and all its property whatsoever and wheresoever both real and personal, present and future, including its uncalled capital for the time being, with the payment of the said principal sum and interest hereby secured.

4. This Debenture is issued subject to the conditions endorsed hereon, which shall be deemed part of and incorporated therewith.

Given under the Common Seal of the Company this

....day of..............................19...........

The Common Seal of the Company was affixed hereto in the presence of—

....
.... } Directors.

.............................Secretary.

FORM No. 69 (continued)

THE CONDITIONS BEFORE REFERRED TO.

*1. This Debenture is one of a series of Debentures issued or to be issued by the Company for securing principal Sums not exceeding in the aggregate the sum of_____Pounds. The Debentures of the said series are all to rank *pari passu* as a first charge on the property hereby charged without any preference or priority one over another, and such charge is to be a floating security, but so that the Company is not to be at liberty to and hereby undertakes that it will not create any other mortgage, charge or incumbrance or confer any lien on or pledge any of its property or assets in priority to or *pari passu* with the said Debentures, and the Company shall not be at liberty to sell, convey, assign or dispose of the undertaking and assets of the Company, or any part or parts thereof to any person or persons or to any subsidiary or other company for cash or for fully or partly paid up shares or debentures or debenture stock or other securities of any company or for any other consideration. Provided always that the Company may until the principal money hereby secured becomes payable, sell and otherwise deal with its ordinary trading goods, wares and manufactures in the customary course of its business, and for the purpose of carrying on the same, but immediately on the principal money hereby secured becoming payable such permission shall forthwith cease.

2. A Register of the Debentures will be kept at the Company's Registered Office, wherein there will be entered the names, addresses and descriptions of the registered holders and particulars of the Debentures held by them respectively, and such Register will at all reasonable times during business hours be open to the inspection of the registered holder hereof and his legal personal representatives and any person authorised in writing by him or them.

3. The registered holder or his legal personal representative will be regarded as exclusively entitled to the benefit of this Debenture, and all persons may act accordingly, and the Company shall not be bound to enter in the Register notice of any trust, or to recognise any right in any other person save as herein provided.

4. Every transfer of this Debenture must be in writing under the hand of the registered holder or his legal personal representatives.   The transfer must be delivered at the Registered Office of the Company with a fee of 2s. 6d., and such evidence of identity or title as the Company may reasonably require, and thereupon the transfer will be registered and a notice of such registration will be endorsed hereon.   The Company shall be entitled to retain the transfer.

5. In the case of joint registered holders, the principal money and interest hereby secured shall be deemed to be owing to them upon a joint account.

6. No transfer will be registered during the seven days immediately preceding the days by this Debenture fixed for payment of interest.

7. The principal money and interest hereby secured will be paid without regard to any equities between the Company and the original, or any intermediate holder hereof, and the receipt of the registered holder for such principal money and interest shall be a good discharge to the Company for the same.

8. The Company may at any time give notice in writing to the registered holder hereof, his executors or administrators, of its intention to pay off this Debenture, and upon the expiration of six calendar months from such notice being given the principal money hereby secured shall become payable.

9. The principal money hereby secured shall immediately become payable—

   (a) If the Company makes default for a period of six calendar months in the payment of any interest hereby secured, and the registered holder hereof before such interest is paid by notice in writing to the Company calls in such principal money.

   (b) If an order be made or an effective resolution be passed for the winding up of the Company.

   (c) If a receiver be appointed of the Company's undertaking or any part thereof.

   (d) If a judgment against the Company for any sum exceeding £50 or an order involving the payment by it of £50 or more without the necessity of a judgment shall be obtained in any Court, and shall remain unsatisfied for fourteen days.

   (e) If a distress or execution shall be levied or enforced upon or against any of the chattels or property of the Company and shall not be satisfied within seven days of the levy or enforcement of such distress or execution.

   (f) If the Company shall stop payment or cease to carry on its business, or threaten to cease to carry on the same.

   (g) If the Balance Sheet of the Company shall not be duly made out in accordance with the Company's Articles of Association and be certified by the Auditor of the Company.

* In the case of a single Debenture this condition would read "This Debenture is a first charge on the property hereby charged and such charge is to be a floating security but so that the Company is not to be at liberty to create any mortgage or charge on any of its property and assets ranking *pari passu* with or in priority to this Debenture."

FORM No. 69 (continued)

(h) If the Company shall without the consent of the registered holders of the majority in value of the outstanding Debentures of this series make or attempt to make any alterations in the provisions of the Memorandum and Articles of Association of the Company, which might in the opinion of such majority prejudicially affect the interests of the Debenture holders.

(i) If the Company shall assign any of its book debts, or pledge any of its goods, or create or purport or attempt to create any charge or mortgage ranking or which by any means may be made to rank *pari passu* with or in priority to this Debenture.

10. At any time after the principal money hereby secured becomes payable the registered holder of this Debenture with the consent in writing of the holders of the majority in value of the outstanding Debentures of the same series may by writing appoint any person or persons to be a receiver or receivers of the property charged by the Debentures and may fix his or their remuneration and such appointment shall be as effective as if all the holders of the Debentures of the same series had concurred in such appointment.

And a receiver so appointed shall have power—

1. To take possession of, collect, and get in the property charged by the Debentures and for that purpose to take any proceedings in the name of the Company or otherwise as may seem expedient.

2. To carry on or concur in carrying on the business of the Company and for that purpose to appoint, employ or dismiss managers, servants and agents and to fix and pay their remuneration.

3. To sell or concur in selling any of the property charged by the Debentures without giving any notice whatever to the Company of intention to sell and to carry any such sale into effect by conveying in the name and on behalf of the Company.

4. To make any arrangement or compromise which he or they shall think expedient in the interests of the Debenture holders.

And all money received by such receiver or receivers shall be applied—

(a) In discharge of all rents, taxes, rates and outgoings affecting the mortgaged premises and

(b) In satisfying all incumbrances (if any) ranking in priority to the Debentures of this series and

(c) In paying his or their remuneration, costs and expenses, premiums on fire or other insurances (if any) and the cost of executing necessary or proper repairs and

(d) In paying the interest accruing due upon the Debentures of this series and

(e) In paying the principal money secured by the Debentures of this series

and shall pay the balance (if any) to the Company, its successors or assigns. And such receiver or receivers shall be the agent or agents of the Company which shall alone be responsible for his or their acts and defaults, and such receiver or receivers shall conform to all lawful directions given to him or them in writing by such majority of Debenture holders as aforesaid and any such majority may by writing under their hands remove any receiver or receivers appointed as aforesaid and appoint another or others in his or their places. And the foregoing conditions shall take effect by way of variation and extension of the provisions of The Law of Property Act, 1925.

11. The principal money hereby secured will when due be paid at the Registered Office of the Company, or at the Company's bankers for the time being.

12. A notice may be served by the Company upon the holder of this Debenture by sending it through the post in a prepaid letter addressed to such person at his registered address.

13. Any notice served by post shall be deemed to have been served at the expiration of twenty-four hours after it was posted, and in proving such service it shall be sufficient to prove that the letter containing the notice was properly addressed and put into the Post Office.

14. The holders of three fourths in value of the outstanding Debentures of this series may sanction any agreement with the Company for any modification or alteration of the rights of the holders of Debentures of this series as a class, including any release of any property charged thereby and any postponement of the time for payment of any moneys secured thereby, and any increase or reduction of the rate of interest; and an agreement so sanctioned shall be binding on all the holders of Debentures of this series, and notice thereof shall be given to each Debenture holder, and each Debenture holder shall be bound thereupon to produce his Debentures to the Company, and to permit a notice of such agreement and the sanction thereof aforesaid to be placed thereon.

[Conditions Applicable to Meetings of Debenture Holders.

The Company may at any time convene a meeting of the Debenture Holders and the Company shall do so forthwith upon a requisition in writing (deposited at the Registered Office of the Company) of Holders of (one tenth) or more of the Nominal amount of Debentures for the time being outstanding.

Fourteen days' notice at least to the Debenture Holders specifying the place day and hour of meeting shall be given previously to any meeting of the Debenture Holders. It shall not be necessary to specify in any such notice the nature of the business to be transacted at the meeting thereby convened.

At any such meeting persons present in person or by proxy and holding (one tenth) of the nominal amount of the Debentures for the time being outstanding shall form a quorum for the transaction of business and no business shall be transacted at any meeting unless the requisite quorum be present at the commencement of business.

FORM No. 69 (continued)

Some person nominated by the Company shall be entitled to take the chair at every such meeting and if no such person is nominated or if at any meeting the person nominated shall not be present within fifteen minutes after the time appointed for holding the meeting the Debenture Holders present shall choose one of their number to be Chairman.

Any Directors of the Company may attend any such meeting.

If within half-an-hour from the time appointed for any meeting of the Debenture Holders a quorum is not present the meeting shall stand adjourned to the same day in the next week at the same time and place and if at such adjourned meeting a quorum is not present the Debenture Holders present shall form a quorum and may transact any business which a meeting of the Debenture Holders is competent to transact.

Every question submitted to a meeting of the Debenture Holders shall be decided in the first instance by a show of hands and in case of equality of votes the Chairman shall both on a show of hands and on a poll have a casting vote in addition to the vote or votes (if any) to which he may be entitled as a Debenture Holder.

At any Meeting of the Debenture Holders unless a poll is demanded by the Chairman or by (................) persons holding in the aggregate at least (................) Debentures a declaration by the Chairman that a resolution has been carried or carried by a particular majority or lost or not carried by a particular majority shall be conclusive evidence of the fact.

If at any such meeting a poll is demanded as aforesaid it shall be taken in such manner and either at once or after an interval or adjournment or otherwise as the Chairman directs and the result of such poll shall be deemed to be the resolution of the meeting at which the poll was demanded, but any poll demanded at any such meeting on the election of a Chairman or on any question of adjournment shall be taken at the meeting without adjournment.

The Chairman may with the consent of any such meeting adjourn the same from time to time and from place to place.

At any such meeting as aforesaid the registered holder of each Debenture or in the case of joint holders that one whose name stands first on the register as one of the holders thereof shall be entitled to vote in respect of such Debenture either in person or by proxy but every instrument appointing a proxy must be in writing under the hand of the appointor or in case of a corporation under its common seal and must be delivered to the Chairman of the meeting and every such proxy must be in the terms or to the effect following that is to say:—

I.............. of ...., a Debenture Holder of ....Company Limited, hereby appoint ....of.............., or failing him.............. of..............

to vote on my behalf at the meeting of the Debenture Holders of the said Company which is to be held on the ....day of..............19......, and at any adjournment of such meeting.

As witness my hand.

On a poll each Debenture Holder whether present in person or by proxy shall be entitled to one vote in respect of every Debenture of which he shall be the holder.

A meeting of the Debenture Holders shall in addition to the powers hereinbefore given have the following powers exercisable by Extraordinary Resolution namely:—

(1) Power to sanction the release of any of the mortgaged property.

(2) Power to sanction any modification or compromise of the rights of the Debenture Holders against the Company or against its property whether such rights shall arise under these presents or otherwise.

(3) Power to assent to any modification of the provisions contained in these presents which shall be proposed by the Company.

An Extraordinary Resolution passed at a Meeting of the Debenture Holders duly convened and held in accordance with these presents shall be binding upon all the Debenture Holders whether present or not present at such meeting and each of the Debenture Holders shall be bound to give effect thereto accordingly and the passing of any such resolution shall be conclusive evidence that the circumstances justify the passing thereof the intention being that it shall rest with the meeting to determine without appeal whether or not the circumstances justify the passing of such resolution.

The expression "Extraordinary Resolution" means a resolution when it has been passed by a majority of not less than three-fourths of such holders as, being entitled so to do, vote in person or, where proxies are allowed, by proxy, at a Meeting of which notice specifying the intention to propose the resolution as an extraordinary resolution has been duly given.]

COPY OF CERTIFICATE OF THE REGISTRATION OF A SERIES OF DEBENTURES

(Pursuant to Section 98 (2) of the Companies Act, 1948.)

(Royal Arms.)

I HEREBY CERTIFY that a series of debentures created by ....LIMITED and securing or intending to secure £..............was this day registered pursuant to Section 95 of the Companies Act, 1948.

Given under my hand at London, this.............. day of .... one thousand nine hundred and..............

....

Registrar of Companies.

FORM No. 70

DEBENTURE STOCK CERTIFICATE.

[For Stock Exchange regulations as to Debenture Stock Certificates, see Appendix D.]

No. ....

£ ....

THE .... COMPANY, LIMITED.

Incorporated under the Companies Act, 1948.

Registered Office: ...., London.

CAPITAL £ ....

Divided into .... % Cumulative Preference Shares of £ ....
each, and .... Ordinary Shares of £ .... each.

£ .... % FIRST MORTGAGE DEBENTURE STOCK.

Interest payable 1st February and 1st August.

Issued pursuant to Article .... of the Articles of Association and a Resolution of the Directors dated the .... day of .... 19........

This is to Certify that ....

of ....

is/are the registered holder/s of .... Pounds of .... % FIRST
MORTGAGE DEBENTURE STOCK, which Stock is constituted by
a Trust Deed dated the .... day of .... 19........, and made between
the Company of the one part, and .... of the
other part, and issued subject to the provisions contained in such deed.

Given under the Common Seal of the Company this .... day of
.... 19........

(Seal of Co.)

.... Director.

Exd. .... Secretary.

Note.—No transfer of the above stock can be registered unless
accompanied by the relative stock certificate. No fraction of £1 can be
transferred.

[PERF.]

(*Signature of Stockholder or Broker*)

in the .... Company, Limited, in the name of

Certificate No. .... for £ .... % Mortgage Debenture Stock

RECEIVED the .... day of .... 19........

[PERF.]

THE .... COMPANY
LIMITED.

.... % MORTGAGE DEBENTURE
STOCK CERTIFICATE.

No. ....

£ ....

Name ....

Address ....

No. of Transfer ....

FORM No. 71

DEBENTURE STOCK SCRIP CERTIFICATE.

No.....................................

....Trust Limited.

(*Incorporated under the Companies Act, 1948*)

———

Issue of £...............................

...............per cent. First Debenture Stock 19........./...........

Interest payable 1st March and 1st September.

———

Scrip Certificate to Bearer for £1,000

———

This is to certify that the sum of £........................... has been paid on allotment in respect of One Thousand Pounds............................... Limited .... per cent. First Debenture Stock.

This Scrip Certificate, with the form on the back duly completed, must be lodged for Registration not later than.............19....., at the Transfer Office of the Company, ... Street, London, W.C.2.

On Registration a scrip receipt will be issued which will be exchangeable for a definitive Debenture Stock Certificate on or after ....19...........

By Order of the Board,

....

Secretary.

.............................19...........

FORM No. 71 (*continued*)

This Form to be filled up and lodged not later than ....19.........., at the
Transfer Office of the Company, ...Street, London, W.C.2.

To the Directors of

.................................Trust Limited.

Please issue a Registered Debenture Stock Certificate for £........................... in exchange for Scrip attached hereto and listed below, in the name(s) of:—

Full Name (BLOCK LETTERS)..

Full Postal Address..

....

Description ....

These spaces only to be utilised when stock is to be registered in names of holders in joint account

Full Name (BLOCK LETTERS)..

Full Postal Address..

....

Description ....

Full Name (BLOCK LETTERS)..

Full Postal Address..

....

Description

I/We declare that I/We am/are not resident outside the Scheduled Territories* and I/We am/are not acquiring the Security as the nominee(s)† of any persons resident outside those Territories.

(If this Declaration cannot be made it should be deleted and a Declaration 2A and Certificate as in Form D must be completed and attached to this application as required by Notice E.C. (Securities) 1, issued by the Bank of England.)

NOTE.—If more than one Scrip Certificate is to be registered in the same name(s), it is only necessary to fill in particulars on the back of one Form, but the Numbers of the Scrip must be inserted in the respective columns at the foot of that Form, in numerical order.

Numbers of £5,000 Scrip Series A	Numbers of £1,000 Scrip Series B	Numbers of £500 Scrip Series C	Numbers of £100 Scrip Series D

In the case of Joint Accounts all parties must sign

Usual Signature...

Usual Signature...

Usual Signature...

Date...19..........

Lodged by...

* The Scheduled Territories—Here insert reference to the current definition of Scheduled Territories.
† As defined in Bank of England's Notice E.C. (Securities) 1 as amended.

FORM No. 72

No. of Company................................   (Form No. 47)

THE COMPANIES ACT, 1948.

Fee Stamp   *See below.*

PARTICULARS OF A MORTGAGE OR CHARGE CREATED BY A COMPANY
REGISTERED IN ENGLAND.
Pursuant to Section 95.

Name of Company {..
.... Limited.

The fee payable on registration of a Mortgage or Charge is 10s. if the amount secured does not exceed £200, and £1 if it exceeds £200.

Presented by...

PARTICULARS OF A MORTGAGE OR CHARGE CREATED BY
....LIMITED,
A COMPANY REGISTERED IN ENGLAND.

(1) Date and description of the Instrument creating or evidencing the Mortgage or charge. (a)	(2) Amount secured by the Mortgage or Charge.	(3) Short particulars of the Property Mortgaged or Charged.	(4) Names, addresses and descriptions of the Mortgagees or Persons entitled to the Charge.	(5) The amount or rate per cent. of the Commission, Allowance or Discount (if any) paid or made either directly or indirectly by the Company to any person in consideration of his subscribing or agreeing to subscribe, whether absolutely or conditionally, or procuring or agreeing to procure subscriptions, whether absolute or conditional, for any of the debentures included in this return. (b)

(*Signature*)...

(*Designation of position in relation to the Company*)...

Dated the.........................day of.........................19.........

(a) A description of the Instrument, *e.g.* "Trust Deed," "Mortgage," "Debenture," etc., as the case may be, should be given.

NOTE.—As to delivery of the Instrument itself with these Particulars—see Section 95 (1) of The Companies Act, 1948.

As to delivery in certain cases of (a) a copy of the Instrument, or (b) a copy of the Instrument and a prescribed form of certificate—see Section 95 (3) and (5).

(b) The rate of interest payable under the terms of the Debentures should *not* be entered.

FORM No. 73

No. of Company.................................... (Form No. 47A.)

THE COMPANIES ACT, 1948.

PARTICULARS OF A SERIES OF DEBENTURES CONTAINING, OR GIVING BY REFERENCE TO ANY OTHER INSTRUMENT, ANY CHARGE, TO THE BENEFIT OF WHICH THE DEBENTURE HOLDERS OF THE SAID SERIES ARE ENTITLED PARI PASSU, CREATED BY A COMPANY REGISTERED IN ENGLAND.

Pursuant to Section 95.

Fee Stamp

See below.

Name of Company { ....

.... Limited.

The fee payable on the registration of these Particulars is 10s. if the amount of the whole series does not exceed £200, and £1 if it exceeds £200.

Presented by ....

....

....

PARTICULARS OF A SERIES OF DEBENTURES CREATED BY
....LIMITED,
A COMPANY REGISTERED IN ENGLAND.

(1) Total amount secured by the whole series.	(2) Amount of the present issue of the series.	(3) Dates of Resolutions authorising the issue of the series.	(4) Date of the Covering Deed (if any) by which the security is created or defined; or, if there is no such Deed, the date of the first execution of any Debenture of the series.	(5) General Description of the Property charged.	(6) Names of the Trustees (if any) for the Debenture holders.	(7) (a) Amount or rate per cent. of the Commission, Allowance or Discount (if any) paid or made either directly or indirectly by the Company to any person in consideration of his subscribing or agreeing to subscribe, whether absolutely or conditionally, or procuring or agreeing to procure subscriptions, whether absolute or conditional, for any of the Debentures included in this return.

(Signature)..

(Designation of position in relation to the Company)................................

Dated the....................................day of........................19..........

(a) The rate of interest payable under the terms of the Debentures should *not* be entered.

NOTE.—The Deed, if any, containing the charge must be delivered with these particulars to the Registrar within 21 days after the execution of such Deed; or, if there is no such deed, one of the Debentures must be so delivered within 21 days after the execution of any Debentures of the series.

This form is to be used for registration of particulars of an *entire* series of Debentures. For registering particulars of any issue in the series subsequent to the first, Form No. 76 is to be used.

FORM No. 74

No. of Company.....................   (Form No. 47B.)

THE COMPANIES ACT, 1948.

Fee
Stamp

See
below.

PARTICULARS OF A MORTGAGE OR CHARGE SUBJECT TO WHICH PROPERTY
HAS BEEN ACQUIRED BY A COMPANY REGISTERED IN ENGLAND.
Pursuant to Section 97.

Name of Company...Limited

The fee payable on registration of a Mortgage or Charge is 10s. *if the
amount secured does not exceed £200, and £1 if it exceeds £200.*

Presented by

....

....

....

Particulars of a Mortgage or Charge subject to which property has been
acquired by .... Limited,
a company registered in England.

(1) Date and description of the instrument creating or evidencing the mortgage or charge. (a)	(2) Date of the acquisition of the property.	(3) Amount owing on security of the mortgage or charge.	(4) Short particulars of the property mortgaged or charged.	(5) Names, addresses and descriptions of the mortgagees or persons entitled to the charge.

(*Signature*)...

(*Designation of position in relation to the company*)..

Dated the...day of..........................19..........

(*a*) *A description of the instrument,* e.g. "Trust Deed," "Mortgage,"
"Debenture," *etc., as the case may be, should be given.*

FORM No. 74 (continued)

A copy of the instrument, certified as prescribed in paragraph 4 of the Companies (Forms) Order, 1949, must be delivered with these Particulars.

A Certificate in the following terms satisfies the requirements of the Order:—

We certify this to be a true and correct copy of a (Mortgage) dated the........................day of............................19.......... and made between the within mentioned parties.

* Given under the Common Seal of the Company this.............day of.................... 19...........

```
 ____
/      \
| Seal |        ..................................................................... Director
| of Co.|
_____/        ..................................................................... Secretary
```

[Or if the Certificate is given under the hand of some person interested otherwise than on behalf of the Company,]

*Signature   ....

Description (*e.g.* Solicitor to...................................)

FORM No. 75

No. of Company........................   (Form No. 47c.)

THE COMPANIES ACT, 1948.

A 5s. *Companies Registration Fee Stamp must be impressed here.*

CERTIFICATE OF REGISTRATION IN SCOTLAND OR NORTHERN IRELAND OF A CHARGE COMPRISING PROPERTY SITUATE THERE.

Pursuant to Section 95 (5).

Name of Company... Limited.

Presented by

....

....

....

CERTIFICATE.

....

....

I *or* We, ...

of ....

....

being (*a*) ....

hereby certify that the charge (*b*)..

of which a true copy is annexed hereto was presented for registration

on..day of..19.....

at (*c*) ....

(*Signature*)..

(*a*) *This certificate must be given by a director or secretary of the company or by a person interested in the charge otherwise than on behalf of the company or by a solicitor acting on behalf of the company or of some person so interested as aforesaid. The capacity in which the certificate is given must be stated.*

(*b*) *Give date and parties to charge.*

(*c*) *State description and situation of office of registration.*

FORMS

FORM No. 76

No. of Company............................... (Form No. 48)

THE COMPANIES ACT, 1948.

◯ *A 5s. Companies Registration Fee Stamp must be impressed here.*

PARTICULARS OF AN ISSUE OF DEBENTURES IN A SERIES BY A COMPANY REGISTERED IN ENGLAND.
Pursuant to Section 95 (8).

Name of Company..Limited.

For registration of the entire series Form No. 73 must be used.

Presented by
....
....
....

Particulars of an issue of Debentures in a series when more than one issue in the series is made by..Limited, a company registered in England.

(1) (a) Date of registration of the series	(2) Date of present issue	(3) Amount of present issue	(4) Particulars as to the amount or rate per cent. of the commission, allowance, or discount (if any) paid, or made, either directly, or indirectly, by the company, to any person in consideration of his subscribing or agreeing to subscribe, whether absolutely or conditionally, or procuring or agreeing to procure subscriptions, whether absolute or conditional, for any of the debentures included in this return (b)

(*Signature*)..
Designation of position in relation to the company)..
Dated the........................day of........................19..........

(*a*) *The date of registration may be confirmed from the certificate of registration.*
(*b*) *The rate of interest payable under the terms of the debentures should* not *be entered.*

FORM No. 77

DEBENTURE TRANSFER.

I/We ....

of ....

in consideration of the sum of..

paid to me/us by..

of ....

do hereby transfer to the said ....

a certain Debenture [or Debentures] numbered..........[or numbered..........to ....inclusive] issued by..Limited

to ....

bearing date the ....day of ....

for securing the sum of...

and interest, and all my right, estate, and interest in and to the money thereby secured on the property and securities thereby assigned.

As WITNESS our Hands (and Seals) the ....day of............................

One Thousand Nine Hundred and...

*Signed,   by the **above-named** ....

in the Presence of

Witness's { Signature ....

Address..

Occupation ....

*Signed,   by the **above-named** ....

in the Presence of

Witness's { Signature ....

Address..

Occupation ....

*Signed,   by the **above-named** ....

in the Presence of

Witness's { Signature ....

Address..

Occupation ....

* If under Seal insert "sealed and delivered."

[Add Declarations under Exchange Control Act, 1947; see Form 92.]

MEMORANDUM OF TRANSFER FOR INDORSEMENT ON DEBENTURE(S)

On the........................day of..19..........

A.B. (and C.D) of...was/were registered as the holder(s) of this Debenture.

For .... Limited.

....*Secretary.*

FORM No. 78

No. of Company............................... . (Form No. 102.)

THE COMPANIES ACT, 1948.

◯ *A 5s. Companies Registration Fee Stamp must be impressed here.*

NOTICE OF PLACE WHERE A REGISTER OF HOLDERS OF DEBENTURES OR A DUPLICATE THEREOF IS KEPT OR OF ANY CHANGE IN THAT PLACE.

Pursuant to Section 86 (3).

Name of Company { ....
.... Limited.

This notice should be signed by a Director or Secretary of the Company.

Presented by...

To the Registrar of Companies:—

....
....
.... Limited,

hereby gives you notice, in accordance with sub-section (3) of Section 86 of The Companies Act, 1948, that a Register of Holders of Debentures of the Company is kept at...
....

Signature...

*...

Dated the................................day of................................19..........

* *State whether Director or Secretary.*

FORM No. 79

No. of Company............................. .   (Form No. 49.)

THE COMPANIES ACT, 1948.

(No Revenue Stamp Duty chargeable.)

DECLARATION VERIFYING MEMORANDUM OF SATISFACTION OF A REGISTERED MORTGAGE OR CHARGE.
Pursuant to Section 100.

Name of Company { ....
.... Limited.

Presented by...

We,.. of................................

....

a Director of..Limited,

and ....

of ....

the Secretary thereof do solemnly and sincerely declare that the particulars contained in the Memorandum of Satisfaction annexed hereto are true to the best of our knowledge, information and belief. And we make this solemn Declaration, conscientiously believing the same to be true, and by virtue of the provisions of the Statutory Declarations Act, 1835.

Declared at...

....

the...............day of.......................................

....one thousand

nine hundred and.......................................

before me

....
A Commissioner for Oaths. *(a)*

(a) or Notary Public *or* Justice of the Peace.

FORM No. 79 (continued)

Memorandum of Complete Satisfaction of Mortgage or Charge

◯ *A 5s. Companies Registration Fee Stamp must be impressed here.*

....

.... Limited

hereby gives notice that the registered charge being (b)........................

....

....

....

of which Particulars were registered with the Registrar of Companies on

the (c)........................day of....................................19.......... was wholly satisfied

on the........................day of....................................19..........the debt for which

the charge was given having been paid or satisfied.

In witness whereof the common seal of the Company was hereunto

affixed the..day of....................................19.........

....

.... } Directors.

◯ Seal of Co.

....Secretary.

(b) A description of the Instrument(s) creating or evidencing the charge, *e.g.* "Mortgage," "Charge," "Debenture," etc., with the date thereof should be given. If the registered charge was a "Series of Debentures" or "Debenture Stock," the words "authorised by resolution" together with the date of the resolution should be added.

(c) The date of registration may be confirmed from the Certificate of Registration and (except in the case of a series of debentures) from the registration stamp affixed to the instrument(s) registered.

FORM No. 80

No. of Company...................................   (Form No. 49A.)

THE COMPANIES ACT, 1948.

(No Revenue Stamp Duty chargeable.)

DECLARATION VERIFYING MEMORANDUM RELATING TO A REGISTERED MORTGAGE OR CHARGE.

Pursuant to Section 100.

Name of Company { ....
.... Limited.

Presented by...

We,.. of..

....

a Director of...Limited,

and ....

of ....

the Secretary thereof do solemnly and sincerely declare that the particulars contained in the Memorandum annexed hereto, are true to the best of our knowledge, information and belief. And we make this solemn Declaration, conscientiously believing the same to be true, and by virtue of the provisions of the Statutory Declarations Act, 1835.

Declared at...

....

the...............day   of..

....one thousand

nine hundred and...

before me

....

A Commissioner for Oaths. (*a*)

(*a*) *or* Notary Public *or* Justice of the Peace.

FORM No. 80 (continued)

Memorandum of (1) Partial Payment or Satisfaction of Mortgage or Charge, (2) Release of Part of Property or Undertaking from Mortgage or Charge.

◯ *A 5s. Companies Registration Fee Stamp must be impressed here.*

....
.... Limited

hereby gives notice that the registered charge being (b)...

....

....

....

of which Particulars were registered with the Registrar of Companies on

the (c).............................day of..19.......... was satisfied on

the...............................day of..19.......... to the extent of

£..

*(i) the debt for which the charge was given having been partly paid or satisfied and

(ii) part of the property or undertaking charged having been released from the charge.

†Short particulars of the property or undertaking no longer charged:—

In witness whereof the common seal of the Company was hereunto

affixed the...day of..19..........

....
.... } Directors.

◯ Seal of Co.

....Secretary.

* Delete (i) or (ii) as necessary.
† Delete if necessary.

(b) A description of the Instrument(s) creating or evidencing the charge, e.g. "Mortgage," "Charge," "Debenture," etc., with the date thereof should be given. If the registered charge was a "Series of Debentures" or "Debenture Stock," the words "authorised by resolution" together with the date of the resolution should be added.

(c) The date of registration may be confirmed from the Certificate of Registration and (except in the case of a series of debentures) from the registration stamp affixed to the instrument(s) registered.

FORM No. 81

No. of Company...........................   (Form No. 49B.)

THE COMPANIES ACT, 1948.

(No Revenue Stamp duty chargeable.)

DECLARATION VERIFYING MEMORANDUM RELATING TO A REGISTERED MORTGAGE OR CHARGE.
Pursuant to Section 100.

Name
of
Company {..
.... Limited.

Presented by

....

....

_____

We,.................................. of ....

a Director of.. Limited,

and ....

of ....

the Secretary thereof do solemnly and sincerely declare that the particulars contained in the Memorandum annexed hereto are true to the best of our knowledge, information and belief. And we make this solemn declaration conscientiously believing the same to be true and by virtue of the provisions of the Statutory Declarations Act, 1835.

Declared at.................................... ⎫
.... ⎪
the.............day of.................................. ⎪
....................................one thousand ⎬
nine hundred and.................................. ⎪
before me. ⎪
.... ⎪
A Commissioner for Oaths. (a) ⎭

(a) *or* Notary Public *or* Justice of the Peace.

FORM No. 81 (continued)

MEMORANDUM OF FACT THAT PART OF PROPERTY OR UNDERTAKING
MORTGAGED OR CHARGED HAS CEASED TO FORM PART OF PROPERTY
OR UNDERTAKING OF COMPANY.

*A 5s. Companies
Registration Fee
Stamp must be
impressed here.*

..............................Limited hereby gives notice that on the.............................
day of..............................19........., part of the property or undertaking
secured by the registered charge being (b)..............................of which
particulars were registered with the Registrar of Companies on the (c)...........
day of ....19........., ceased to form part of the company's
property or undertaking.

Short particulars of such property:—

In witness whereof the common seal of the Company was hereunto
affixed the..............................day of..............................19...........

....
.... } *Directors.*

..............................*Secretary.*

Seal
of Co.

(b) *A description of the instrument(s) creating or evidencing the charge,*
e.g. "Mortgage," "Charge," "Debenture," etc., *with the date thereof should
be given. If the registered charge was a* "Series of Debentures," *or* "Debenture Stock," *the words* "authorised by resolution," *together with the date
of the resolution should be added.*

(c) *The date of registration may be confirmed from the Certificate of Registration and (except in the case of a series of debentures) from the registration
stamp affixed to the instrument(s) registered.*

FORM No. 82

REGISTER OF CHARGES.

(All charges specifically affecting property of the Company and all Floating Charges on the undertaking or any property of the Company.)

Date and description of the Instrument creating or evidencing the Charge		Amount of charge	Short particulars of the Property Charged	Name and Address of Mortgagee	Rate of Interest per annum	Remarks
Date	Description					

FORM No. 83

NOTICE OF REDEMPTION BY DRAWING OF DEBENTURE STOCK.

....LIMITED.

Registered Office.

....19...........

Dear Sir (or Madam),

.... PER CENT. FIRST MORTGAGE DEBENTURE STOCK.

This is to inform you that in accordance with the terms of the Trust Deed dated the.................................19........... a drawing of Debenture Stock was made at the offices of the Trustees, on the.................................19..........., the Stock so drawn being redeemable on the.............................19........... at par.

As a result of such drawing, £...................... Stock registered in your name has been drawn for redemption and will be repaid to you on the........... ....19..........., and interest thereon will cease to accrue from that date.

In accordance with the Trust Deed, you are required to deliver to the Company the Certificate of your Stock, in order that the same may be cancelled. In respect of the balance of the Stock (if any) registered in your name and not drawn for redemption, you will receive a fresh Certificate in your name.

A Form of Receipt and instructions for payment is enclosed for your signature. In the case of joint holdings the Form should be signed by all holders.

When signed the document should be returned accompanied by the Certificate so as to reach me at the Registered Office of the Company, ..., not later than ....19...........

The half-year's interest due on................................19........... will be paid by separate warrant on that day in the usual way.

Yours faithfully,

For..LIMITED.

....

Secretary.

FORM No. 84

DEBENTURE STOCK REDEMPTION RECEIPT.

....LIMITED.

Transfer Office:

....STREET,
LONDON, W.C.2.

RECEIPT TO ACCOMPANY CERTIFICATE(S) FOR REDEEMED .... PER CENT.
FIRST MORTGAGE DEBENTURE STOCK.

Received of..Limited the sum of........................
pounds, being the sum secured by £.................................. of the above mentioned
Debenture Stock the Certificate in respect of which is herewith delivered up to
the Trustees for the Debenture Stockholders to be cancelled in pursuance of the
provisions of the Debenture Trust Deed.

£...

Dated this..day of................................19..........

NOTE.—In the case
of joint holdings *all*
the joint holders
must sign.

Signature ....

Corporate Bodies;
signatures of at least
two duly authorised
officers.

Signature ....

Signature ....

2d.
Stamp

EXCHANGE CONTROL ACT, 1947.
TRADING WITH THE ENEMY ACT, 1939.

I/We declare that no persons who directly or indirectly are entitled to the
redemption proceeds of the holding of £..................................Limited.........% First
Mortgage Debenture Stock now standing in my/our name(s) are enemies within
the meaning of the Trading with the Enemy Act, 1939, and that since 3rd September, 1939, no enemy within the meaning of that Act has directly or indirectly
owned or had any interest in the said Stock.

I/We request that the warrant for the redemption monies be forwarded

NOTE.—If the ad-
dress inserted here
is outside the Sched-
uled Territories* you
should consult your
banker as special
permission of the
Bank of England
may be necessary.

to: ....

....

NOTE.—In the case
of joint holdings *all*
the joint holders
must sign and in the
case of Corporate
Bodies, signatures
of at least two duly
authorised officers,
are required.

Signature ....

Signature ....

Signature ....

IMPORTANT.—This Form, duly completed, must be returned, together with the
relevant Stock Certificate(s), in the enclosed envelope to the Company's Transfer
Office, so as to reach there not later than..

* Defined in Bank of England's Notice E.C. (Securities) 1 as amended.

FORM No. 85

REGISTER OF MEMBERS AND SHARE LEDGER (fast bound with Index).

Name ....

Address ....

Dividends to ....

Date of entry as a member .... 19 ......

Date of ceasing to be a member .... 19 ......

Memoranda—

SHARES ACQUIRED									SHARES TRANSFERRED OR REDEEMED								Balance of Shares Held
Date of Entry	No. of Allotment or Transfer	Transferor's Folio	Description of Shares	Number of Shares	Distinctive Numbers* From	Distinctive Numbers* To	Share Certificate No.	Amount per share paid or agreed to be considered as paid	Date of Entry of Transfer	No. of Transfer	Transferee's Folio	Description of Shares	Number of Shares	Distinctive Numbers* From	Distinctive Numbers* To	Amount per share paid or agreed to be considered as paid	Number of shares

* If all the issued shares are fully paid up and rank *pari passu* for all purposes with all the shares of the same class, such shares need not have a distinguishing number.

FORM No. 86

*REGISTER OF MEMBERS AND SHARE REGISTER.

Sheet No. of this account...........................

Name(s) ....

Address ....

Date of Entry as a Member ....

Date of Ceasing to be a Member ....

Amount per share paid or agreed to be considered as paid...........................

MEMORANDA

Dividends to—

Date of Entry	Number of Allotment or Transfer	Transferor's Folio	Number of Shares	†Distinctive Numbers		Date of Entry of Transfer	Number of Transfer	Transferee's Folio	Number of Shares	†Distinctive Numbers		Balance Shares Held
				From	To					From	To	Number of Shares
	SHARES ACQUIRED						SHARES TRANSFERRED					

* A company of more than 50 members must keep an Index of Members (Sec. 111). A Register of Members in loose leaf form can be arranged so as to constitute itself an Index.

† If all the issued shares are fully paid up and rank *pari passu* for all purposes with all the shares of the same class, such shares need not have a distinguishing number.

FORM No. 87

*REGISTER OF STOCKHOLDERS WITH DIVIDEND CALCULATIONS.

*REGISTER OF STOCKHOLDERS WITH DIVIDEND CALCULATIONS (Loose leaf).

PAGE.........

| Name | Address | | | | | | | | | | | | | | | |

Date of Allotment or Registration	Allotment or Transfer No.	Amount of Stock		Balance	Dividend Calculations							Balance†	Dividend Calculations						
		Acquired	Transferred		Gross		Income Tax		Net				Gross		Income Tax		Net
					Rate	Amount	Rate	Amount					Rate	Amount	Rate	Amount	

This Form is designed for use where a machine system for payment of Dividends is used. The operator prepares the Dividend Warrants direct from the particulars given in the Stockholder's Account.
† The second column is not used until the first column is filled up.

FORM No. 88

INDEX TO SHARE [STOCK] REGISTER.

NOTE.—The loose-leaf ledger makes this system obsolete, as the former if properly kept is an index in itself, and may be so arranged as to contain most of the information which this form provides.

Surname	Christian Name		Holding				
			Debenture Stock	Folio	Preference Shares	Folio	Ordinary Shares	Folio

FORM No. 89

CARD INDEX TO SHARE REGISTER.

Holding	Folio
5% Deb. £	
4½ do. £	
Pref. Shares	
Ord. do.	

DIVIDEND INSTRUCTIONS:

REMARKS:

Name

Address

Register Folio

*Share/Stock holder's Specimen Signature:—

PLEASE SIGN
(USING YOUR ORDINARY SIGNATURE)
IN SPACE PROVIDED.

[*NOTE.—In the cases where a specimen signature is required the Secretary will send the Card to the Share/Stockholder with a request that it be signed and returned to the Company.]

FORM No. 90

No. of Company..................................   (Form No. 103.)

THE COMPANIES ACT, 1948.

◯ *A 5s. Companies Registration Fee Stamp must be impressed here.*

NOTICE OF PLACE WHERE REGISTER OF MEMBERS IS KEPT OR OF ANY CHANGE IN THAT PLACE.

Pursuant to Section 110 (3).

Name
of   { ....
Company   .... Limited.

This notice should be signed by a Director or Secretary of the Company.

Presented by...

To the Registrar of Companies:—

....

....

.... Limited,

hereby gives you notice, in accordance with sub-section (3) of Section 110 of The Companies Act, 1948, that the Register of Members of the Company is kept at..

....

Signature..

* ....

Dated the...day of...............................19..........

* *State whether Director or Secretary.*

FORM No. 91

REGISTER OF TRANSFERS.

REGISTER OF TRANSFERS†

Date	No. of Transfer	Share Reg. Fo.	TRANSFERORS			TRANSFEREES			Number of Shares Transferred	*Distinctive Nos.		Remarks
			Name	Address	Description of Shares	Name	Address	Share Reg. Fo.		From	To	

* If all the issued shares are fully paid up and rank *pari passu* for all purposes with all the shares of the same class, such shares need not have a distinguishing number.

† See Forms 93 and 100.

Y

FORM No. 92

Transfer No.......................

TRANSFER FORM.

....

Insert "I" *or* "We"

....

of ....

....

in *consideration of the sum of ....

....

paid by ....

....(hereinafter called "the said Transferee.....")

Do hereby bargain, sell, assign and transfer to the said Transferee.................................

....

....of and in the undertaking called

....

To HOLD unto the said Transferee.....................Executors, Administrators and Assigns, subject
to the several conditions on which.................held the same at the time of the execution hereof;
and..................the said Transferee.........do hereby agree to accept and take the said................
subject to the conditions aforesaid.

As WITNESS our Hands (and Seals) this ....day of.................
One thousand nine hundred and.................................

† Signed,   by the above-named

Witness's   in the presence of
Signature.................
Address
Occupation ....

† Signed,   by the above-named

Witness's   in the presence of
Signature.................
Address
Occupation ....

† Signed,   by the above-named

Witness's   in the presence of
Signature.................
Address
Occupation ....

† Signed,   by the above-named

Witness's   in the presence of
Signature.................
Address
Occupation ....

*The Consideration money set forth in a transfer may differ from that which the first Seller will receive, owing to sub-sales by the original buyer. The Stamp Act, 1891, requires that in such cases the Consideration money paid by the sub-purchaser shall be the one inserted in the Deed, as regulating the *ad valorem* Duty. The following is the Clause in question:—

"Where a person, having contracted for the purchase of any property, but not having obtained a Conveyance thereof, contracts to sell the same to any other person and the Property is in consequence conveyed immediately to the sub-purchaser, the conveyance is to be charged with *ad valorem* Duty in respect of the consideration for the sale by the original purchaser to the sub-purchaser."—54 & 55 Vic., cap. 39 (1891) Section 58, sub-section 4.

When a transfer is executed out of Great Britain it is recommended that the signatures be attested by H.M. Consul or Vice-Consul, a Clergyman, Magistrate, Notary Public or by some other person holding a public position, as most companies refuse to recognise signatures not so attested. When a witness is a female she must state whether she is a Spinster, Wife or Widow, and if a wife must give her husband's name, address and quality, profession or occupation. The date must be inserted in words and not in figures.

A wife must not witness the signature of her husband and *vice versa*.

† If under Seal insert "sealed and delivered."

FORM No. 92 (*continued*)

For use as indicated below.**

EXCHANGE CONTROL ACT, 1947.

Title of Security**_____

Nominal Amount_____, say, _____

_____

TO BE COMPLETED ON BEHALF OF THE TRANSFEROR(S)   1.
(If this declaration cannot be made, Declaration 1A must be completed.)

The holder(s)* of the above-mentioned security is/are not resident outside the Scheduled Territories* and from facts known to us or from enquiries we have made is/are not to the best of our belief holding the security as the nominee(s)* of any person(s) resident outside those Territories.

Stamp and Signature of Authorised
Depositary*or Temporary Recipient*†_____

Address_____ Date_____

TO BE COMPLETED ONLY IF DECLARATION 1 ABOVE CANNOT BE MADE.   1A.

Licence_____ No._____examined.

Stamp and Signature of
Authorised Depositary*_____ Date_____

TO BE COMPLETED ON BEHALF OF THE TRANSFEREE(S)   2.
(If this declaration cannot be made, Declaration 2A must be completed.)

The transferee(s) is/are not resident outside the Scheduled Territories* and from facts known to us or from enquiries we have made is/are not to the best of our belief acquiring the security as the nominee(s)* of any person(s) resident outside those Territories.

Stamp and Signature of Authorised
Depositary* or Temporary Recipient*†_____

Address_____ Date_____

TO BE COMPLETED ONLY IF DECLARATION 2 ABOVE CANNOT BE MADE.   2A.

The transferee(s) is/are permanently resident in_____(*country*)
and, from facts known to us or from enquiries we have made, to the best of our belief—

Delete (*a*) or (*b*)   (*a*) is/are not a nominee(s).*
               (*b*) is/are a nominee(s)* of a person(s) permanently resident in_____(*country*).
               (*c*) the transfer is not made to or for the benefit of an enemy subject(s) resident outside the Scheduled Territories.*

Stamp and Signature of Authorised
Depositary* or Temporary Recipient*†_____

Address_____ Date_____

WE CERTIFY that this transaction is a *bona fide* purchase for full value in the ordinary course of business and that the full consideration money—

Delete (i) or (ii)   (i)   has been/will be debited to, or is eligible for credit to, a_____Account.
              (ii)   has been provided by the realisation of other securities sold for that purpose under
                   Licence_____ No._____

Stamp and Signature‡_____ Date_____

‡ Where (i) is completed, the above certificate must be signed by a bank in the United Kingdom, the Isle of Man or the Channel Islands, or by the Public Trustee.
Where (ii) is completed, the certificate must be signed by an Authorised Depositary* or Temporary Recipient.*†

AUTHORISED
for the purposes of the Exchange Control Act, 1947.

(Authorisation is not required when Declaration 1 or 1A and Declaration 2 have been completed.)

Stamp and Signature of

Date_____   Authorised Depositary* _____

_____

** This Form is to be used for securities which are—
    (*a*) registered in the Scheduled Territories* otherwise than in a Subsidiary Register* and on which interest or dividends are not payable by coupon, and
    (*b*) not Prescribed Securities.*
 * Defined in Notice E.C. (Securities) 1 issued by the Bank of England as amended.
 † Temporary Recipients must indicate their classification, *e.g.* "Members of the Birmingham Stock Exchange," "Exempted dealers in securities under the Prevention of Fraud (Investments) Act, 1939."

FORM No. 92 (continued)

FORM OF CERTIFICATE REQUIRED WHERE TRANSFER IS MADE FOR A NOMINAL CON-
SIDERATION AND IS NOT LIABLE TO *AD VALOREM* STAMP DUTY.

Instruments of Transfer are liable to a Deed Stamp of 10s. when the transaction falls within one of the following categories:—

(a) Transfers vesting the property in trustees on the appointment of a new trustee of a pre-existing trust, or on the retirement of a trustee.

(b) Transfers, where no beneficial interest in the property passes. (i) to a mere nominee of the transferor; (ii) from a mere nominee of the transferee; (iii) from one nominee to another nominee of the same beneficial owner.

(c) Transfers by way of security for a loan or re-transfer to the original transferor on repayment of a loan.

(d) Transfers to a residuary legatee of stock, etc., forming part of the residue divisable under a Will.

(e) Transfers to a beneficiary under a Will of a specific legacy of stock, etc. (Note.—Transfers by executors in discharge, or partial discharge, of a pecuniary legacy are chargeable with *ad valorem* duty on the amount of the legacy so discharged).

(f) Transfers of stock, etc., forming part of an intestate's estate to the person entitled to it.

(g) Transfers to a beneficiary under a settlement on distribution of the trust funds of stock, etc., forming the share or part of the share of those funds to which the beneficiary is entitled in accordance with the terms of the settlement.

(h) Transfers, on the occasion of a marriage, to trustees of stocks, etc., to be held on the terms of a settlement made in consideration of marriage.

(i) Transfers by the liquidator of a company of stocks, etc., forming part of the assets of the company to the persons who were shareholders, in satisfaction of their rights on a winding up.

The evidence necessary to establish that a transfer is liable to the fixed duty of 10s. should take the form of a certificate setting forth the facts of the transaction. In cases falling within (b) or (c) such a certificate should be signed by (i) both transferor and transferee or (ii) a member of a Stock Exchange or a solicitor acting for one or other of the parties or (iii) an accredited representative of a bank; in the last case when the bank or its official nominee is a party to the transfer the certificate, instead of setting out the facts, may be to the effect that "the transfer is excepted from Section 74 of The Finance (1909-10) Act, 1910." A certificate in other cases should be signed by a solicitor or other person (*e.g.* a bank acting as trustee or executor) having a full knowledge of the facts.

N.B.—A transfer on sale or by way of a gift *inter vivos* or in liquidation of a debt or in exchange for other securities, is chargeable with *ad valorem* duty.

(1) "I" or "We." (2) Insert (a), (b) or appropriate Clause. (3) Detail briefly the facts explaining the transaction,	(1) .... hereby certify that the transaction in respect of which this transfer is made is one which falls within the description set out in Clause (2) .... above, the facts being as follows: (3).. ....

Date.. 19........   Signature ....

                                                           Description ....

Signatures of all Transferors and Transferees—

FORM No. 92a

FORM OF ATTESTATION WHERE DEED HAS BEEN EXECUTED BY A MARK.

SIGNED, sealed and delivered by the above-named *A.B.* in our presence, he having signed by a mark in consequence of being unable [*e.g.* through physical infirmity] to sign his name, the deed having first been read over and explained to him and he appearing fully to understand the effect thereof.

[Two Witnesses should attest, one of whom should be a Doctor, Justice of the Peace, Minister of Religion, Barrister, Solicitor, or other person of standing.]

FORM No. 93

RUBBER STAMP ON TRANSFER, FOR RECORD OF OPERATIONS.

[*By using this form on transfer deeds the need for a separate Register of Transfer is avoided.*]

THE............Co., LTD.	
Transfer Receipt No. ..	
Date lodged ..	
Signature checked ..	
Notice Sent ..	
Date Passed ..	
Old Cert. No. ..	
Transferor's Fo.	
New Cert. No.	
Transferee's Fo.	
Date Cert. sent.	
Entered in Share Register	

FORM No. 94

RECEIPT FOR TRANSFER.

(Bound interleaved for carbon copy.)

No. ....

19 ....

THE .... COMPANY, LIMITED.

Registered Office: ...., London, E.C.

RECEIVED from ....

the undermentioned .... Transfer Deed .... of .... SHARES

[£ .... stock] for registration, subject to the approval of the directors.

Transferee. ....

No. of Shares, or Amount of Stock	*Share Numbers	
	From	*To*

The Certificate .... in respect of the above Transfer .... will be ready for delivery in exchange for this Receipt on ....

Registration Fee paid ....

(*for*) *Secretary.*

* If the Shares bear distinguishing numbers.

.... [PEER.] ....

NOTE

It is the practice of many Companies to issue a NON-RETURNABLE Transfer receipt. This may take the form of a detailed acknowledgment or a printed post card. Acknowledgments are sent in the case of postal transactions but for "counter transactions" Companies issue "counter tickets" (serially numbered). These, however, have to be surrendered in exchange for new Share/Stock Certificates. The counterfoil of the Ticket follows the Transfer through the Company's Transfer routine, finally being attached to the new Certificate to "match" the issued half when the latter is surrendered.

FORM No. 95

NOTICE OF CERTIFICATION.

No.......................

THE...........COMPANY, LIMITED,

........................., LONDON, E.C.

....19...........

To A.B.

Please note that the undermentioned Deed(s) of Transfer, purporting to be signed by you, $\frac{has}{have}$ been presented for certification, together with the relative Certificate(s) :—

No. of Shares.	Amount of Stock	Transferee(s)

Unless I hear from you to the contrary by return of post, I shall assume the same to be in order, and the said Transfer(s), which $\frac{has}{have}$ been certified, will be duly submitted to the Directors for registration when presented for that purpose.

(for) Secretary.

Delete words not applicable.

[Note.—This notice should be sent in a plain envelope and addressed in handwriting.]

FORM No. 96

BALANCE RECEIPT.

THE.......CO., LTD.
...................., LONDON, E.C.

No........ ....19....

BALANCE RECEIPT for........ Shares/Stock.

Issued to Messrs. ....

| *Distinctive Nos. | | Name of Share/Stockholder |
From	To	

Old Certificate No........

New Certificate to be ready........

................for Registrar.

NOTE.—This receipt does not in any way constitute a title to the shares (stock) therein referred to and is not negotiable. The Company will not be in any way responsible for any purpose for which it may be used other than the Certification of further Deeds of Transfer or exchange for a Definitive Balance Certificate.

No Transfer for any of the Balance of Shares/Stock above referred to will be certified, neither will a Balance Certificate be issued, without the production of the relative receipt.

* If the Shares bear distinguishing numbers.

[PERF.]

N.B.—This form can be printed on thin paper and bound interleaved with plain paper for use with carbons, in which case the counterfoil is unnecessary.

THE.......COMPANY, LIMITED.

No........ ....19....

No. of Certificate ...... for £......stock [......shares].

Name

Amount of Balance £......stock [......shares].

Issued to ....

FORM No. 97

NOTICE OF REGISTRATION.

_____

THE............COMPANY, LIMITED,

..............................., LONDON, E.C.

....19...........

To A.B.

Please note that the undermentioned Deed(s) of Transfer purporting to be signed by you $\frac{has}{have}$ been lodged for registration, together with relative certificate(s).

Delete words not applicable.

No. of Shares	Amount of Stock	Transferee(s)

Unless I hear from you to the contrary by return of post I shall assume the same to be in order, and the said Stock/Shares will, subject to the approval of the Directors, be registered in the name(s) of the Transferee(s).

(for) Secretary.

[NOTE.—This notice should be sent in a plain envelope and addressed in handwriting.]

FORM No. 98

REQUEST TO BE PLACED ON DOMINION REGISTER WITH DIRECTORS' CERTIFICATE ATTACHED.

THE..........COMPANY, LIMITED.

FORM OF REQUEST.

For Transfer of Shares from London Register to Dominion Register.

No................................

To the Directors of

..........COMPANY, LIMITED.

For Office use only.
Receipt No. ....
Share Reg. Fo. Lon. ......
Share Reg. Fo. Dom ......
Old Cert. No. ....

I, the undersigned..
request that you will transfer...Shares
numbered†...
now standing in my name on the London Register to the Dominion
Register, in the State of *———, entering same in my name at the
following address, viz:—

....

....

I enclose the London Share Certificate representing such Shares.

AS WITNESS my hand this .... day of ....19........

Witness to the Signature of —

....
                             Signature of Shareholder.

Name ....
Address ....
                                   Address of Shareholder.
Occupation ....

[The provisions respecting the keeping of a Dominion Register are
contained in ss. 119 and 120 of the Companies Act, 1948.]

CERTIFICATE OF DIRECTORS.

LONDON.

WE CERTIFY *that the above-named*........................*is entered on
the London Register as the Proprietor of the Shares referred to above, and
that the London Certificate in respect of the said Shares has been received
by us and duly cancelled.*

.... } *Directors*
....

Date...........................   ....*Secretary.*

Received in *———...........................   ....19*
Passed by the Dominion Agents...19
Entered on Dominion Register and Certificate issued on 19
Entered...
Folio..

† If the Shares bear distinguishing numbers.

FORM No. 99

RECEIPT FOR CERTIFICATE LODGED ON TRANSFER FROM LONDON TO DOMINION REGISTER.

THE............COMPANY, LIMITED.

RECEIPT FOR CERTIFICATE LODGED TO BE
FORWARDED TO————

Number of Shares	*Shares Numbered	
	From	To

London, E.C.

....19......

RECEIVED from ....

of ....

.... *Certificate No.* ....

for............*Shares [numbered as per*

margin], for Transfer from London

Register to the Dominion Register.

..............................*Registrar.*

New Certificate for............................*Shares will be exchanged for this*
Voucher on or after ....*19*......

* If the Shares bear distinguishing numbers.

FORM No. 100

REGISTER OF TRANSFERS (FOR BOARD MEETING).

[See alternative Form 91.]

Consolidated Ordinary Stock.   *Date of Registration,*

...., 19...........

Transfer Ledger.

No.	Folio	Transferor	Amount	Transferee	Folio	Total Consideration
2204	918	....	1000	....	90 n	nom.
2205	2290	....	800	....	91	£804
2206	1000	....	200	....	209 n	£198
			2000			

Transfers Nos.   to   , both inclusive, passed

...................................., 19...........

['n' means New Account. The name opposite which it appears has not previously been entered on the register.]

FORM No. 101

PARTICULARS OF CERTIFICATES SIGNED AND SEALED.

Particulars of Certificates signed and sealed.................... 19......

Cancelled Certificates		New Certificates to be signed and sealed against transfers		Balance Certificates to be signed and sealed		Certificates in lieu of old Certificates to be signed and sealed		Balance to be held for further instructions	Transfers *Certified* against Certificates, but *not Registered*	Certificates sealed at previous Meetings relating to same cancelled Certificates	No. of Certificate Carried forward
No. of Cert.	No. of Shares*	No. of Cert.	No. of Shares*	No. of Cert.	No. of Shares*	No. of Cert.	No. of Shares*				

* Or amount of stock.

FORM No. 102

REGISTRATION STAMP FOR PROBATES, ETC.

.... Limited

Registered .... 19...........

....

for Secretary.

........................Fee Paid

FORM No. 103

SHARE CERTIFICATE MARKING STAMP FOR REGISTRATION OF MARRIAGE AND DEATH CERTIFICATES

.... Limited

.... Certificate

of ....

Registered .... 19...........

........................Fee Paid   *for Secretary.*

FORM No. 104

Request by Executors/Administrators to be placed on Register.

To the Secretary and Directors of

....Limited,

....Street,

London, W.C.2.

I/We the undersigned, the Executor(s) of the Will/Administrator(s) of the Estate of.. deceased, late of ....

....

hereby request you to register me/us in the books of the Company as the holder(s) of the ....

now standing registered in the name of the said deceased.

Dated this ....day of ....19..........

Signature .... Name in full .... Address .... Description	

	For Company's Use Only
Signature .... Name in full .... Address .... Description	Receipt .... Checked .... Old Cert. .... New Cert. ....
Signature .... Name in full .... Address .... Description	Posted Out.. Plate(s) ,, ... Mandate ,, ... Ex. Bank ....
Signature .... Name in full .... Address .... Description	Posted In .... New Index.. ,, Plate .... ,, Tab .... Bank .... Control

Lodged by ....

Address ....

Note.—If not already in Company's possession, Stock Certificates *must* be lodged with this request.

FORM No. 105

....*Limited.*

REGISTER OF PROBATES OF WILLS AND LETTERS OF ADMINISTRATION.

Name, address and description of ⎧ ....
the deceased Member   ..   ⎩ ....
....

Number of Shares held and ⎧ ....Preference, Nos.....................
distinctive Nos.   ..   .. ⎩   Ordinary, Nos.....................
....

Date of Death ..   ..

Date of Will and Codicil   .. ..

.   ⎧ Executors   ⎧ ....
       ⎩ Administrators .. .. ⎨ ....
                                ⎨ ....
                                ⎨ ....
                                ⎩ ....

* Date of proving the Will at ⎧
  Probate Registry or of Grant ⎨ ....
  of Letters of Administration.. ⎩

* Whether the above Shares ⎧ ....
  devolve upon—   ....
  (1) Specified Legatees, or   ....
  (2) Beneficiaries under Let- ⎨ ....
  ters of Administration   ....
  and if so, their name   ....
  or names   ..   .. ⎩ ....

* Date of Probate (or of Admin- ⎧ ....
  istration Grant) left at Office.. ⎩ ....

By whom left ..   ..   .. ⎧ ....
                            ⎩ ....

*Strike out words which do not apply.

	Examined by	Entered in Share Register		Fees paid	Remarks
		Pref. folio	Ordy. folio		
FOR OFFICE USE ONLY.					Date {probate grant} returned............ To whom ....

FORM No. 106

FORM OF REPLY TO BANKERS AND OTHERS
RE NOTICE OF LIEN.

THE............COMPANY, LIMITED,

..................................LONDON, E.C.

..................................19.....

DEAR SIR,

    With reference to your communication dated the
.............................., which purports to be a notice of the deposit
of certain Certificates of Stock [Shares] of this Company
with your Bank, I beg to inform you that the Company
is unable to recognise, or in any way to act upon, the said
communication.

    I return it herewith.

Secretary.

To the Manager

..................................Bank

(Per Registered Post.)

FORM No. 107

GENERAL REGISTER OF DOCUMENTS (INDEXED).

No.	Date of registration	Name of stock or shareholder	Document registered		Short particulars	Share ledger fol.
			Date of Document	Nature of Document		

FORM No. 108

REGISTER OF SEALS.

Document Sealed	Date of Resolution or Order to Seal	Date of Sealing	Sealed in Presence of	How Disposed of

FORM No. 109

(Form No. 100.)

THE COMPANIES ACT, 1948.

NOTICE TO DISSENTING SHAREHOLDERS.

Pursuant to Section 209 (1).

re (a)..Limited
(hereinafter called 'the transferor Company')

Notice by (b)..Limited
(hereinafter called 'the transferee Company')

To (c)...

....

....

Whereas on the....................day of ....19......... the transferee
Company made an offer to all the holders of (d)......................shares in the
transferor Company (*state shortly the nature of the offer*)......................; and

Whereas up to the....................day of........................19......... being a
date within four months of the date of the making thereof such offer was
approved by the holders of not less than nine-tenths in value of the said
(d)............... shares (other than shares already held at the date of the offer by
or by a nominee for the transferee company or its subsidiary).

Now therefore the transferee Company in pursuance of the provisions of
Section 209 (1) of the Companies Act, 1948, hereby gives you notice that it
desires to acquire the (d)......................shares held by you in the transferor
Company.

And further take notice that unless upon an application made to the
Court by you the said (c)......................on or before the......................day
of......................19.........being one month from the date of this notice
the Court thinks fit to order otherwise, the transferee Company will be
entitled and bound to acquire the (d)......................shares held by you in
the transferor Company on the terms of the above-mentioned offer approved
by the approving (d)......................
shareholders in the said Company.

(*Signature*)......................

for (b)......................
(*State whether Director or Secretary*)

Dated the......................day of......................19.........

(a) *Name of transferor Company.*
(b) *Name of transferee Company.*
(c) *Name(s) and address(es) of dissenting shareholder(s).*
(d) *If the offer is limited to a certain class or classes of shareholders state
description of that class or those classes.*

FORM No. 110

(Form No. 100A.)

THE COMPANIES ACT, 1948.

NOTICE TO NON-ASSENTING SHAREHOLDERS.
Pursuant to Section 209 (2).

re (a)...Limited
(hereinafter called 'the transferor Company')

Notice by (b)..Limited
(hereinafter called 'the transferee Company')

To (c)...

Whereas a scheme or contract involving the transfer of the (d)..................
shares in the transferor Company to the transferee Company was up to the
.............................day of...................19........., being a date within four months
of the making of the offer in that behalf by the transferee Company
approved by the holders of not less than nine-tenths in value of those
shares (other than shares already held at the date of the offer by or by a
nominee for the transferee Company or its subsidiary), and

Whereas in pursuance of that scheme or contract (e)...........................shares
were on the..day of..19......
transferred to the transferee Company or to its nominee.

Now therefore the transferee Company in pursuance of Section 209 (2)
of the Companies Act, 1948, hereby gives you notice that those shares
together with such other shares in the transferor Company as were held by
or by a nominee for the transferee Company or its subsidiary on the said
date comprise or include nine-tenths in value of the (d)...........................shares
in the transferor Company.

And further take notice that you may within three months from the
giving of this notice give notice that you require the transferee Company to
acquire your holding of (d).............................shares in the transferor
Company, and that if you give such notice the transferee Company shall
be entitled and bound to acquire those shares on the terms on which under
the said scheme or contract the shares of the approving shareholders were
transferred to it, or on such other terms as may be agreed or as the Court
on the application of either the transferee Company or yourself/yourselves
think fit.

(*Signature*)...

for (b)..
(*State whether Director or Secretary*)

Dated this....................................day of..19........

(a) *Name of transferor Company.*
(b) *Name of transferee Company.*
(c) *Name(s) and address(es) of non-assenting shareholder(s).*
(d) *If the offer is limited to a certain class or classes of shareholders state
description of that class or those classes.*
(e) *State amount of shares transferred.*

FORM No. III

(Form No. 100B.)

THE COMPANIES ACT, 1948.

NOTICE TO TRANSFEREE COMPANY BY NON-ASSENTING SHAREHOLDER.

Pursuant to Section 209 (2).

re (a)..Limited
(hereinafter called 'the transferor Company')

Notice by (b)...
To (c)..Limited
(hereinafter called 'the transferee Company')

Whereas on the................................day of..............................19........., (c)...........................
gave notice to me/us that on the................................day of...........................19.........,
by reason of the (d)..........................shares in the transferor Company having
that day been transferred to the transferee Company or its nominee in
pursuance of a scheme or contract approved in accordance with the
provisions of Section 209 (1) of the Companies Act, 1948, those shares
together with other shares in the transferor Company held by or by a
nominee for the transferee Company or its subsidiary at that date comprised
or included nine-tenths in value of the said (d)..........................shares.

Now I/we the said................................being the holder(s) of (e)....................shares
in the transferor Company hereby give notice in accordance with the
provisions of subsection (2) of Section 209 of the Companies Act, 1948,
to the transferee Company that I/we require it to acquire the said shares
held by me/us.

Dated this................................day of................................19..........

(*Signature*)...

NOTES.

1. Strike out 'I' or 'we,' 'me' or 'us' as the case may be.

2. If the shares are not acquired on the terms on which, under the
scheme or contract, the shares of the approving shareholders were transferred, or on agreed terms, either party may apply to the Court to fix the
terms.

    (a) *Name of transferor Company.*
    (b) *Name of non-assenting shareholder.*
    (c) *Name of transferee Company.*
    (d) *If the offer is limited to a certain class or classes of shareholders state
description of that class or those classes.*
    (e) *State the number and description of shares held by the non-assenting
shareholder.*

FORM No. 112

NOTICE TO A LIMITED COMPANY ACQUIRING SHARES IN ANOTHER LIMITED COMPANY.

....LIMITED

Transfer Office:

................................STREET,

LONDON, W.C.2.

....19.........

The Secretary,

....................Limited.

With reference to Shares/Stock of this Company recently acquired by your Company, please let me have a certified excerpt from the Articles of Association of your Company governing the use of the seal.

* Please also send a certified excerpt from the Memorandum of Association governing your Company's powers to invest in Stocks of other Companies.

* (*The second paragraph is deleted in the case of investment trusts and bank nominee companies.*)

Yours faithfully,

Secretary.

FORM No. 113

SHARE WARRANT.

THE............COMPANY, LIMITED.
....LONDON, E.C.

Registered under the Companies Act, 1948.

Authorised Share Capital £

[numbers]   No. of   [numbers]
                       shares

Share warrant for

....

shares of...................sterling each.

Nos. ....

| This is to certify that the Bearer of this Warrant is the Proprietor of [TWENTY-FIVE.] fully paid shares numbered as above in the Capital of the............Company, Limited, subject to the Memorandum and Articles of Association and other Regulations of the Company for the time being. | *Repeat wording in French or other language of the foreign country where the warrants circulate extensively. |

Given under the Common Seal of the Company this.....................................day

of ....19...........

.... *Director*

(Seal of Co.)

.... *Secretary*

-------------------------------- [PERF.] --------------------------------

THE............COMPANY, LIMITED.

Share Warrant No............

Talon for Fresh Supply of Coupons for Share Warrant to Bearer representing

....

Shares.

The Bearer of the above Warrant will receive in exchange for this Talon a fresh supply of Coupons when those below have fallen due.

....*Secretary.*

-------------------------------- [PERF.] --------------------------------

† THE............COMPANY, LIMITED.

Dividend Coupon No....... on   Shares.

[PERF.] Included in the Share Warrant numbered as below for Dividend payable according to Advertisement to be issued by the Company. [PERF.]

No............   *Secretary.*

-------------------------------- [PERF.] --------------------------------

[* NOTE.—Should the Warrants circulate extensively abroad a translation should be printed.
† A set of dividend coupons (e.g. 30 coupons) is attached to the Share Warrant. All coupons are perforated so as to be readily detachable.]

FORM No. 114

RECEIPT FOR DEPOSITED SHARE WARRANT.

No.........................

THE..........COMPANY, LIMITED,

....LONDON, E.C.

THIS is to Certify that ....

of ....

has, in accordance with the regulations of the Company, deposited the under-mentioned Share Warrant(s) in respect of which he is entitled to attend the Extraordinary (or Annual) General Meeting of the Company to be held at ....

on the .... day of ....19..........

Dated the .... day of ....19......

For THE..........COMPANY, LIMITED,

....*Secretary.*

Denomination	Distinctive Nos. of Warrants	No. of Warrants (in words)	No. of Shares
One	A		
Five	B		
Twenty-five	C		
One Hundred	D		
	Total No. of Warrants ..		
	Total No. of Shares ..		

IMPORTANT.—The Warrants named herein will only be delivered in exchange for this Certificate, which must be carefully preserved.

FORM No. 115

APPLICATION FOR SHARE WARRANTS.

No..............................

..................SHARES.   *Date lodged*..............................

To the Directors of

THE..........COMPANY, LIMITED,

..............................London, E.C.

I/We, the undersigned, being the Holder(s) of..............................
registered Shares of your Company, as per particulars at back hereof,
the Certificates whereof I/we enclose, hereby request you to issue to
me/us the following Share Warrant(s) to Bearer in respect thereof, and
I/we enclose remittance for £..............................to defray the
charges for same as undernoted.

No.	PARTICULARS OF SHARE WARRANTS REQUIRED. Description.	APPLICATION FEE. 1 to 5 Shares, 1/-; over 5 Shares, 2/6 per 100 or fraction thereof.	WARRANT FEES. 1/6 for each Warrant.	STAMP DUTY.‡		TOTAL.
	*1 Share ..					
	5 Shares ..					
	25 Shares ..					
					£	

* Only 5 per cent. of the number of Shares to be converted will be
issued in Warrants of 1 Share each at the usual fee. Shareholders desiring a larger proportion can obtain them on payment of 6d. per Warrant extra.

Dated this..............................day of..............................19..........

Witness: Shareholder's Signature†..............................

....   Name in full ....

                    Address in full ....

Address ....

† The Signa-
ture must be at-
tested by a Wit-
ness who must
add his Postal
Address after the
name. When the
Signature is af-
fixed out of Great
Britain it must
be attested by
H.M. Consul or
Vice-Consul, No-
tary Public, or
by some other
person holding
a public position.

[‡ Three times the amount of *ad valorem* Stamp Duty chargeable on deed transferring
the share(s) if consideration for transfer be nominal value of shares.]

FORM No. 115 (continued)

[BACK OF FORM]

DIRECTIONS AS TO DELIVERY OF SHARE WARRANTS.

Please deliver the Share Warrants referred to overleaf, when ready, to the Bearer of the Voucher given by the Company on lodgment of this application, whose receipt shall be a sufficient discharge to the Company for the same.

....Shareholder's Signature.

One of these forms of Directions must be signed by the Shareholder.

DIRECTIONS TO TRANSMIT THE SHARE WARRANTS BY POST

Please forward to...

at ....

at my risk, the Share Warrants referred to above, when ready, by

....

....Shareholder's Signature.

Left by (Name)   ....

(Address)   ....

The following particulars to be filled in before this form is lodged at the Company's Office.

Nos. of Certificates	Number of Shares.	Distinctive Numbers of Shares.		Nos. of Certificates.	Number of Shares.	Distinctive Numbers of Shares.	
		From	To			From	To
						Forward	
	Forward						

FORM No. 116

SHARE WARRANT APPLICATION RECEIPT.

THE .... COMPANY, LIMITED.

(Incorporated under the Companies Act, 1948).

Registered Office: .... London, E.C.2.

No. ....

Company's Charges £ ....

English Stamp Duty £ ....

The documents applied for will be delivered to the bearer in exchange for this voucher on .... or any following day between ....

The Bearer must be prepared to state full particulars of the documents he is to receive.

This voucher is issued subject to the approval of the application by the Directors.

[PERF.]

The .... COMPANY, LIMITED.

(Incorporated under the Companies Act, 1948).

Registered Office: .... London, E.C.2.

No. .... 19....

RECEIVED from ....

(Share Warrants for) ....

(Shares for exchange into Warrants of ...... denominations as undernoted) ....

(Registered Shares in the name of ......)

with an application for the following Share Warrants:—

	Application Fee	Warrant Fee	English Stamp Duty	TOTAL
of 1 Share each				
" 5 Shares "				
" 25 " "				
TOTAL				

Signed ....

Warrants to be ready on ....

FORM No. 117

RECEIPT FOR TALONS.

THE .... COMPANY, LIMITED.

(Incorporated under the Companies Act, 1948)

Registered Office: .... London, E.C.2.

No. T. ....

PRESENT *on* ....

or any following week-day between 11 *and* 2; *Saturdays excepted.*

The Bearer must be prepared to state full particulars of the documents he is to receive.

[PERF.]

THE .... COMPANY, LIMITED.

[Incorporated under the Companies Act, 1948.]

TALONS.

No. T. ....

.... 19 ....

RECEIVED from ....

New Talons and Coupons ready on

FORM No. 118

RECEIPT FOR SHARE WARRANTS LODGED FOR REGISTRATION.

RECEIPT FOR SHARE WARRANTS LODGED FOR REGISTRATION.

THE .... COMPANY, LIMITED.

No. ....

LONDON, E.C. .... 19......

RECEIVED from .... Share Warrants, as under:—

.... Warrants of 1 Share each.

,, ,, 5 Shares each.

,, ,, 25 ,,

Total .... Shares left for Registration in the name

of ....

If the application is accepted the Certificate will be ready for delivery at this Office, on or after .... between 11 and 3 o'clock, Saturdays 11 and 12 o'clock, but may be sent by post, at Shareholder's risk, on receipt of stamped registered envelope. In either case the Certificate will be delivered only in exchange for this Receipt.

Fees paid £ : :

Secretary.

.... [PERF.] ....

[N.B.—This form can be printed on thin paper and bound interleaved with plain paper for use with carbons, in which case 11 counterfoil can be dispensed with.]

THE .... COMPANY, LIMITED.

No. .... 19......

RECEIVED of .... NUMBERED

.... Warrants of 1 Share ....

,, 5 Shares ....

,, 25 ,, ...

Total .... Shares for Registration in the

name of M ....

Certificate to be ready ....

Fees paid £ : :

FORM No. 119

REGISTER FOR ISSUE OF SHARE WARRANTS IN EXCHANGE FOR REGISTERED SHARES.

Appn. No.	Name of Shareholder	Folio Register of Members	No. of Shares	Distinctive Numbers From	To	No. of Warrants	Distinctive Numbers A From	To	No. of Shares	No. of Warrants	Distinctive Numbers B From	To	No. of Shares	Remarks

REGISTERED SHARES EXCHANGED — SHARE WARRANTS ISSUED — Denomination of Warrants...... — Denomination of Warrants......

FORM No. 120

REGISTER FOR ISSUE OF REGISTERED SHARES IN EXCHANGE FOR SHARE WARRANTS.

	SHARE WARRANTS SURRENDERED							REGISTERED SHARES EXCHANGED					
		One			Five								
Appn. No.	No. of Warrants	Distinctive Numbers A		No. of Shares	No. of Warrants	Distinctive Numbers B		No. of Shares	Name of Shareholder	Folio Register of Members	No. of Shares	Distinctive Numbers of Shares	Remarks
		From	To			From	To					From	To	

FORM No. 121

SHARE WARRANTS REGISTER.
(One book for each denomination.)

(Denomination), *e.g.* FIVE SHARES.

No. of Warrant	Coupons attached Nos.	Date of Issue	Distinctive Nos. of relative registered shares	Directors' initials	Date of cancellation

FORM No. 122

APPLICATION FOR REGISTERED SHARES IN EXCHANGE FOR SHARE WARRANTS.

Application No. ....

New Share Cert. No. ....

To THE............COMPANY, LIMITED,

I, the undersigned, being the holder of the under-mentioned Share Warrants to Bearer of your Company, representing ....Shares, hereby surrender the same to be cancelled, and request that you will enter my name in the Register of Members as the proprietor of the said Shares.

Please forward the new Share Certificate by post, at my risk, to .... at ....

Enclosed is 2s. 6d., being the fee required in accordance with the Conditions of Issue of Share Warrants.

Signature..

Name in full ....

Address ....

....

Date..19..........

No. of Warrants	Distinctive* No. of Shares	Denomination	No. of Shares
....	A	One	....
....	B	Five	....
....	C	Twenty-five	....
		Total Shares	

* If the Shares have distinctive numbers.

Z

FORM No. 123

APPLICATION FOR EXCHANGE OF SHARE WARRANTS FOR OTHER SHARE WARRANTS.

To the............COMPANY, LIMITED.

I, the undersigned, being the holder of the under-mentioned Share Warrants to Bearer of your Company, representing ....Shares, hereby surrender the same to be cancelled, and request that you will issue to me Share Warrants to Bearer as under-noted in respect of the said Shares.

A remittance for £.................., being 2s. 6d. Application Fee, 1s. per new Warrant, and Stamp Duty, is enclosed.

Please deliver or forward the Warrants at my risk by registered post to...at...

Dated this................................ day of ....19......

Usual Signature ....

Name (in full)..

Address ....

....

PARTICULARS OF SHARE WARRANTS SURRENDERED.

							Warrants numbered	Shares numbered From To
..........Warrants each for	1 Share of £	=	.... Shares	A				
.... "	"	"	5	"	" "	=	.... " B	
.... "	"	"	25	"	" "	=	.... " C	
Total Warrants.						Total Shares.		

PARTICULARS OF SHARE WARRANTS REQUIRED.

							Stamp Duty per Warrant
..........Warrants each for	1 Share of £	=	..........Shares	1 Share =			s.
.... "	"	"	5	"	" "	=	.... " 5 " = s.
.... "	"	"	25	"	" "	=	.... " 25 " = £ s.
Total Warrants.						Total Shares.	

FORM No. 124

NOTICE TO PARTY ON WHOSE BEHALF NOTICE IN LIEU OF DISTRINGAS HAS BEEN LODGED.

(This form can be modified, as requisite, where payment of dividends has been restrained.)

THE............COMPANY, LIMITED,

....LONDON, E.C.

....19.........

Dear Sir(s),

I beg to inform you that deed(s) transferring the.................. Stock [........Shares] registered in the joint names of *O. P. &* *R. S.*, the Stock (..............Shares) referred to in the Affidavit and Notice of Restraint dated .... and lodged at this Office on the ...., has(ve) been presented here for (certification/registration), and I have to give you notice on behalf of the Company that such transfer(s) will* [when presented for registration] be duly passed by the Directors after the expiration of eight days from the date hereof, unless in the meantime proceedings are taken to prevent the registration of the said transfer(s).

Yours faithfully,

Secretary.

* In the case of a transfer already lodged for registration cross out the words 'when presented for registration.'

[*This notice should be sent by registered post.*]

FORM No. 125

NOTICE TO PARTY WHO LODGED THE NOTICE IN LIEU OF DISTRINGAS.

THE............COMPANY, LIMITED,

....LONDON, E.C.

....19.........

Dear Sir(s),

Referring to the Affidavit and Notice dated............................ filed..................... and lodged by you at the Company's Office on................restraining the transfer of £..... Stock [....Shares] registered in the joint names of *O. P. & R. S.*, I beg to send you herewith copy of a letter forwarded to-day to......................... ....on whose behalf the restraint was placed, notifying them that the Stock (Shares) is (are) about to be transferred.

Please acknowledge receipt.

Yours faithfully,

Secretary.

[*This notice should be sent by registered post.*]

FORM No. 125a

NOTICE IN LIEU OF DISTRINGAS AND AFFIDAVIT IN SUPPORT.

To the............................Company Limited.

Take notice that the stock comprised in and now subject to the trusts of the (settlement or will) referred to in the affidavit to which this notice is annexed consists of the following (that is to say) (here specify the stock, stating the name or names in which it stands).

This notice is intended to stop the transfer of the stock only, and not the receipt of dividends (or, the receipt of the dividends on the stock as well as the transfer of the stock).

Signed, etc.,

[*Note.—This notice must in every case be signed by the deponent to the affidavit to which it is annexed.*]

In the High Court of Justice,
        Chancery Division.

In the matter of (here state the nature of the document comprising the stock, and add the date and other particulars, so far as known to the deponent, sufficient to identify the document)

and

In the matter of the Act of Parliament, 5 Vict. c. 5.

I,..............of.............., make oath and say that according to the best of my knowledge, information, and belief, I am beneficially interested in the stock comprised in the (settlement or will) above-mentioned, which stock, according to the best of my knowledge and belief, now consists of the stock specified in the notice hereto annexed.

Sworn, etc.,

This affidavit is filed on behalf of   whose address is

FORM No. 126

No. of Company...   (Form No. 108.)

THE COMPANIES ACT, 1948.

◯ *A 5s. Companies Registration Fee Stamp must be impressed here.*

MEMBERS' VOLUNTARY WINDING UP.

DECLARATION OF SOLVENCY EMBODYING A STATEMENT OF
ASSETS AND LIABILITIES.

(*Pursuant to Section* 283.)

Name
of   { ....
Company   { .... Limited.

Presented by..

Declaration of Solvency.

We, ...

of ....

....

being ───*all the───── Directors of .... Limited
      the majority of the

do solemnly and sincerely declare that we have made a full enquiry into the affairs
of this Company, and that, having so done, we have formed the opinion that this
Company will be able to pay its debts in full within a period of.................................†
months, from the commencement of the winding up, and we append a statement
of the Company's assets and liabilities as at...19...........,
being the latest practicable date before the making of this Declaration. And we
make this solemn Declaration conscientiously believing the same to be true, and
by virtue of the provisions of The Statutory Declarations Act, 1835.

Declared at ....⎫

the .... day of ⎪

..................................one thousand   ⎬

nine hundred and ....   ⎪

before me,   ⎪

....   ⎭

A Commissioner for Oaths(*a*) *or* Notary
Public *or* Justice of the Peace.

* *Delete as necessary.*
† *Insert a period of months not exceeding twelve.*
(*a*) *Delete as necessary.*

FORM No. 126 (*continued*)

Statement as at...19.......... showing Assets at estimated realisable values and Liabilities expected to rank.

Assets and Liabilities	Estimated to Realise or to Rank for Payment (to nearest £)
Assets:—	
Balance at Bank	
Cash in hand	
Marketable Securities	
Bills receivable	
Trade Debtors	
Loans and Advances	
Unpaid Calls	
Stock-in-Trade	
Work in Progress	
....	
....	
....	
Freehold Property	
Leasehold Property	
Plant and Machinery	
Furniture, Fittings, Utensils, etc.	
Patents, Trade Marks, etc.	
Investments other than marketable securities ..	
Other property, viz.:—	
....	
....	
Estimated realisable value of Assets .. ..£	
Liabilities:—	
Secured on specific Assets, viz.:— £	
....	
Secured by Floating Charge(s)	
Estimated cost of liquidation and other expenses, including interest accruing until payment of debts in full..	
Unsecured Creditors (amounts estimated to £ rank for payment):—	
Trade Accounts	
Bills payable	
Accrued expenses	
Other Liabilities:—	
....	
....	
Contingent Liabilities:—	
....	
....	
....	
Estimated surplus after paying debts in full .. £	

Remarks:—

FORM No. 127

No. of Company............................   (Form No. 39C.)

THE COMPANIES ACT, 1948.

◯ *A 5s. Companies Registration Fee Stamp must be impressed here.*

MEMBERS' VOLUNTARY WINDING UP.

NOTICE OF APPOINTMENT OF LIQUIDATOR.
Pursuant to Section 305.

Name
of   { ....
Company { .... Limited.

Nature of Business ....

[NOTE.—This notice must be delivered to the Registrar of Companies within fourteen days of the appointment.]

Presented by...

Members' Voluntary Winding Up.

To the Registrar of Companies.

I (*or* We) .... of...............................

....

....

....

....

hereby give you notice that I (*or* We) have been appointed Liquidator(s) of

....

.... Limited,

by (*a*) Resolution of the Company dated the.......................................day of

.... 19..........

....

(*Signature*)...

(*b*)...

Dated the..day of...........................19..........

(*a*) *State how appointed, whether by Resolution of the Company, or how otherwise, and adapt if necessary.*

(*b*) *To be signed by each Liquidator, if more than one.*

FORM No. 128

No. of Company...........................   (Form No. 39D.)

THE COMPANIES ACT, 1948.

A 5s. Companies Registration Fee Stamp must be impressed here.

CREDITORS' VOLUNTARY WINDING UP.

NOTICE OF APPOINTMENT OF LIQUIDATOR.
Pursuant to Section 305.

Name
of   { ....
Company { .... Limited.

Nature of Business..

[NOTE.—This notice must be delivered to the Registrar of Companies within fourteen days of the appointment.]

Presented by..

Creditors' Voluntary Winding Up.

To the Registrar of Companies.

I (*or* We)...of..........................

....

....

....

hereby give notice that I (*or* We) have been appointed liquidator(s) of

....

....Limited.

by (*a*) ....

....

....

(*Signature*)...

(*b*)...

Dated the..day of.............................19.......

(*a*) *State how appointed, whether by the creditors of the Company or how otherwise. If appointed by Company, state whether such appointment was confirmed by creditors.*

(*b*) *To be signed by each Liquidator, if more than one.*

FORM No. 129

(Form No. 39E.)

(For insertion in London Gazette.)

THE COMPANIES ACT, 1948.

*Members'/Creditors' Voluntary Winding Up.

Notice of Appointment of Liquidator.
Pursuant to Section 305.

Name
of
Company
{ ....
....Limited.

Nature of Business...

Address of Registered Office..

....

....

....

Liquidator(s) name(s) and address(es) :—

....

....

....

....

Date of Appointment...

By whom Appointed..

....

....

†*Signed*...

———————————————————
Liquidator(s).

†Witness to the Signature(s) of

....

....

....

Name ....

Address ....

———————————————————
Solicitor.

* Delete as necessary.

FORM No. 130

(Form No. 92.)

LIQUIDATOR'S STATEMENT OF RECEIPTS AND PAYMENTS.

THE COMPANIES ACT, 1948, AND THE COMPANIES WINDING-UP RULES, 1949.
(Rules 197, 198 and 201.)

No. of Company..................   *(No Registration Fee payable.)*

(Re)

This is the Exhibit marked B referred to in the affidavit of...

sworn before me this..day of..19.........

.... Commissioner for Oaths.

STATEMENT OF RECEIPTS AND PAYMENTS AND GENERAL DIRECTIONS AS TO STATEMENTS.

Name of Company...

(1) Every statement must be on sheets 13 inches by 16 inches.	Size of sheets.
(2) Every statement must contain a detailed account of all the liquidator's realisations and disbursements in respect of the Company. The statement of realisations should contain a record of all receipts derived from assets existing at the date of the winding up resolution and subsequently realised, including Balance in Bank, Book Debts and Calls collected, Property Sold, etc., and the account of disbursements should contain all payments for costs and charges, or to creditors or contributories. Where property has been realised the gross proceeds of sale must be entered under realisations, and the necessary payments incidental to sales must be entered as disbursements. These accounts should not contain payments into the Company's Liquidation Account (except unclaimed dividends —*see paragraph* 5) or payments into or out of Bank, or temporary investments by the liquidator, or the proceeds of such investments when realised, which should be shown separately:—	Form and Contents of Statement.

    (*a*)   By means of the Bank Pass Book;
    (*b*)   By a separate detailed statement of moneys invested by the liquidator,
        and investments realised.

Interest allowed or charged by the Bank, Bank Commission, etc., and profit or loss upon the realisation of temporary investments should, however, be inserted in the accounts of realisations or disbursemments, as the case may be. Each receipt and payment must be entered in the account in such a manner as sufficiently to explain its nature.   The receipts and payments must severally be added up at the foot of each sheet *and the totals carried forward from one account to another without any intermediate balance, so that the gross totals shall represent the total amounts received and paid by the liquidator respectively.*

(3) When the liquidator carries on a business, a trading account must be forwarded as a distinct account, and the totals of receipts and payments on the trading account must alone be set out in the statement.	Trading Account.
(4) When dividends or instalments of compositions are paid to creditors, or a return of surplus assets is made to contributories, the total amount of each dividend, or instalment of composition, or return to contributories, actually paid must be entered in the statement of disbursements as one sum; and the liquidator must forward separate accounts showing in lists the amount of the claim of each creditor, and the amount of dividend or composition payable to each creditor and of surplus assets payable to each contributory, distinguishing in each list the dividends or instalments of composition and shares of surplus assets actually paid and those remaining unclaimed. Each list must be on sheets 13 inches by 8 inches.	Dividends, etc.

(5)   When unclaimed dividends, instalments of composition or returns of surplus assets are paid into the Companies Liquidation Account, the total amount so paid in should be entered in the statement of disbursements as one sum.

(6)   Credit should not be taken in the statement of disbursements for any amount in respect of liquidator's remuneration, unless it has been duly allowed by resolution of the Committee of Inspection or of the creditors, or of the Company in General Meeting, or by order of Court, as the case may require.

LIQUIDATOR'S STATEMENT OF ACCOUNT.
(Pursuant to Section 342 of the Companies Act, 1948.)

Name
of   }...
Company

Nature of proceedings (whether a Members'
    or Creditors' voluntary winding up or a
    winding up under the supervision of the   }
    Court)

Date of commencement of Winding Up...
Date to which Statement is brought down...
Name and address of Liquidator...

This Statement is required in duplicate.

FORM No. 130 (continued)

LIQUIDATOR'S STATEMENT OF ACCOUNT
Pursuant to Section 342 of the Companies Act, 1948.

REALISATIONS

Date	Of whom received	Nature of Assets realised	Amount £ s. d.
		Brought forward	
		*Carried forward	

DISBURSEMENTS

Date	To whom paid	Nature of Disbursements	Amount £ s. d.
		Brought forward	
		*Carried forward	

* NOTE.—No Balance should be shown on this Account, but only the total Realisations and Disbursements which should be carried forward to the next Account.

FORM No. 130 (continued)

ANALYSIS OF BALANCE.

	£	s.	d.
Total Realisations		,,	,,
,, Disbursements		,,	,,
Balance ..		,,	,,

The Balance is made up as follows:—

1. Cash in hands of Liquidator .. .. ,, ,,

	£	s.	d.
2. Total payments into Bank, including balance at date of commencement of winding up (*as per Bank Book*)		,,	,,
Total withdrawals from Bank		,,	,,

Balance at Bank .. ..

3. Amount in Companies Liquidation Account ... . ,, ,,

	£	s.	d.
*4. Amounts invested by Liquidator		,,	,,
Less amounts realised from same		,,	,,

Balance .. .. ,, ,,

Total Balance as shown above   £   ,,   ,,

(*Note.—Full details of Stocks purchased for investment and realisation thereof should be given in a separate statement.*)

* The investment or deposit of money by the Liquidator does not withdraw it from the operation of Section 343 of the Companies Act, 1948, and any such investments representing money held for six months or upwards must be realised and paid into the Companies Liquidation Account, except in the case of investments in Government securities, the transfer of which to the control of the Board of Trade will be accepted as a sufficient compliance with the terms of the section.

NOTE.—The Liquidator should also state:—

(1) The amount of the estimated assets and liabilities at the date of the commencement of the winding up .... } Assets (after deducting amounts charged to secured creditors and debenture holders) £

Liabilities { Secured Creditors .. £
Debenture Holders .. £
Unsecured Creditors .. £

(2) The total amount of the capital paid up at the date of the commencement of the winding up .... { Paid up in cash .. .. .. £
Issued as paid up otherwise than for cash .. .. £

(3) The general description and estimated value of outstanding assets (if any) ....

(4) The causes which delay the termination of the winding up ....

(5) The period within which the winding up may probably be completed ....

FORM No. 131

No. of Company.............................   (Form No. 93.)

THE COMPANIES ACT, 1948, AND
THE COMPANIES (WINDING-UP) RULES, 1949.
(Rules 197, 198 and 201.)

No Registration Fee payable.

AFFIDAVIT VERIFYING STATEMENT OF LIQUIDATOR'S ACCOUNT
UNDER SECTION 342.

Name
of
Company .... Limited.

I, ...

of ....

the Liquidator of the above-named Company, make oath and say:—
That *the account hereunto annexed marked B contains a full and true
account of my receipts and payments in the winding up of the above-named
Company*, from the...day of
....19.........., to the...................................day of
....19.........., inclusive *and that* I have not nor has any
other person by my order or for my use during such period received or
paid any monies on account of the said Company *other than, and except
the items mentioned and specified in the said account*.

I further say that the particulars given in the annexed Form 92 marked
B with respect to the proceedings in and position of the liquidation, are
true to the best of my knowledge and belief.

SWORN at...⎫
in the County of...⎪
this...................................day of...................................19......⎬
Before me, ...⎪
    A Commissioner for Oaths.⎭

* NOTE.—If no receipts or payments, strike out words in italics.

[The Affidavit is *not* required in duplicate, but it must in every case be
accompanied by a statement on Form 92 in duplicate.]

FORM No. 132

No. of Company..............................   (Form No. 94.)

THE COMPANIES ACT, 1948.

THE COMPANIES (WINDING-UP) RULES, 1949.
(Rules 197 and 201.)

LIQUIDATOR'S TRADING ACCOUNT.

Under Section 342.

Name
of
Company.   { ....
                { .... Limited.

Insert here the ⎫
name of the   ⎬ ....
Liquidator.   ⎭

the Liquidator of the above-named Company in account with the Estate.

This Account is required in *duplicate* in addition to Form No. 92.

	RECEIPTS.				PAYMENTS		
DR.							CR.
Date		£	s.	d.	Date	£	s.	d.

(*Date*)..............................   .... *Liquidator*

FORM No. 133

No. of Company.................................... (Form No. 96.)

THE COMPANIES ACT, 1948.
THE COMPANIES WINDING-UP RULES, 1949.
(Rules 197 and 201.)

LIST OF AMOUNTS PAID OR PAYABLE TO CONTRIBUTORIES.

Name
of   {...
Company   ....

I hereby certify that a return of surplus assets was declared payable to contributories on and after the.............................day of...............................19..........., at the rate of...............................per share, and that the Contributories, whose names are set forth below are entitled to the amounts set opposite their respective names, and have been paid such amounts except in the cases specified as unclaimed.

....*Liquidator.*

Dated the..day of...............................19..........
To the Board of Trade.

Surname	Christian Name	No. of Shares	Amount returned on Shares					
			Paid			Unclaimed		
			£	s.	d.	£	s.	d.

Date.. ....*Liquidator.*

This List is required in duplicate.

FORM No. 134

No. of Company................................   (Form No. 95.)

THE COMPANIES ACT, 1948, AND
THE COMPANIES WINDING UP RULES, 1949.
(Rules 197 and 201.)

LIST OF DIVIDENDS OR COMPOSITION.

Name
of   { ....
Company   ....

I hereby certify that a Dividend (or Composition) of................................
in the £ was declared payable on and after the...............................day of
....19......... and that the Creditors whose names
are set forth below are entitled to the amounts set opposite their respective
names, and have been paid such amounts except in the cases specified as
unclaimed.

....*Liquidator.*

Dated the...day of...................................19..........
To the Board of Trade.

Surname	Christian Name	Amount of Proof			Amount of Dividend (or Composition)					
					Paid			Unclaimed		
		£	s.	d.	£	s.	d.	£	s.	d.
Total £										

This List is required in Duplicate.

FORM No. 135

No. of Company...........................   (Form No. 111.)

THE COMPANIES ACT, 1948.

◯ *A 5s. Companies
Registration Fee
Stamp must be
impressed here.*

MEMBERS' VOLUNTARY WINDING UP.

RETURN OF FINAL WINDING UP MEETING.
Pursuant to Section 290.

Name
of   { ....
Company   ....Limited.

[NOTE.—This Return must be made within one week after the Meeting,
and must be accompanied by a Copy of the Liquidator's account of the
Winding Up.]

Presented by..

Members' Voluntary Winding Up.

To the Registrar of Companies.

I (or We)..of....................................

....

being the Liquidator(s) of...

....Limited

have to inform you that a General Meeting of the Company was duly

(a) $\dfrac{\text{held on}}{\text{summoned for}}$ the.........................day of.......................19.........

pursuant to Section 290 of the Companies Act, 1948, for the purpose of
having an Account (of which a copy is attached hereto) (b) laid before
it showing how the Winding Up of the Company has been conducted
and the property of the Company has been disposed of, and that

(a) $\dfrac{\text{the same was done accordingly.}}{\text{no quorum was present at the Meeting.}}$

(Signature) (c) { ....
                    ....

Dated the.............................day of.......................19.........

(a) *Strike out that which does not apply.*
(b) *The copy account accompanying this Return must be authenticated by
the written signature(s) of the Liquidator(s).*
(c) *To be signed by each Liquidator if more than one.*

FORM No. 136

No. of Company.............................. (Form No. 112.)

THE COMPANIES ACT, 1948.

◯ *A 5s. Companies Registration Fee Stamp must be impressed here.*

CREDITORS' VOLUNTARY WINDING UP.

RETURN OF THE FINAL WINDING UP MEETINGS OF MEMBERS AND CREDITORS.

Pursuant to Section 300.

Name
of ⎰ ....
Company ⎱ .... Limited.

[NOTE.—This return must be made within one week after the date of the Meetings or, if the Meetings are not held on the same date, after the date of the later Meeting and must be accompanied by a Copy of the Liquidator's account of the Winding Up.]

Presented by...

Creditors' Voluntary Winding Up.

To the Registrar of Companies.

I (or We) ....

of.. being the Liquidator(s) of..........................
....Limited

have to inform you

(1) that a General Meeting of this Company was duly (*a*) $\frac{\text{held on}}{\text{summoned for}}$

the..............................day of............................, 19........., pursuant to Section 300 of the Companies Act, 1948, for the purpose of having an Account (of which a copy is attached hereto) (*b*) laid before it showing how the Winding Up of the Company has been conducted and the property of the Company has been disposed of, and that

(*a*) $\frac{\text{the same was done accordingly;}}{\text{no quorum was present at the Meeting;}}$

(2) that a Meeting of the Creditors of this Company was duly

(*a*) $\frac{\text{held on}}{\text{summoned for}}$ the..............................day of..............................19...........

pursuant to Section 300 of the Companies Act, 1948, for the purpose of having the said Account laid before it showing how the Winding Up of the Company has been conducted and the Property of the Company

has been disposed of, and that (*a*) $\frac{\text{the same was done accordingly.}}{\text{no quorum was present at the Meeting.}}$

(*Signature*) (*c*) ⎰ ....
⎱ ....

Dated the..............................day of..............................19...........

(*a*) *Strike out that which does not apply.*
(*b*) *The copy account accompanying this Return must be authenticated by the written signature(s) of the Liquidator(s).*
(*c*) *To be signed by each Liquidator if more than one.*

FORM No. 137

No. of Company...........................   (Form No. 110.)

THE COMPANIES ACT, 1948.

(Rule 182)

LIQUIDATOR'S STATEMENT OF ACCOUNT
(MEMBERS' OR CREDITORS' VOLUNTARY WINDING UP).

Pursuant to Sections 290 *and* 300.

STATEMENT SHOWING HOW THE WINDING UP HAS BEEN CONDUCTED AND THE
PROPERTY OF THE COMPANY HAS BEEN DISPOSED OF.

.... Limited

(in liquidation)

Presented by..

1. Assets, including..shown in the statement of
Assets and Liabilities and estimated to be of the value of £.....................have proved
to be unrealisable.

2. State amount paid into the Companies Liquidation Account in respect of:—

   (a) Unclaimed dividends payable to Creditors in the
       winding up   ..   ..   £..............................

   (b) Other unclaimed distributions in the winding up ..   £..............................

   (c) Monies held by the Company in trust in respect of
       dividends or other sums due before the commence-
       ment of the winding up to any person as a member
       of the Company   ..   ..   £..............................

3. Add here any special remarks the Liquidator thinks desirable:—

   ....

   Dated this..day of..19..........

        Signature of Liquidator(s)..

        ....

            Address..

            ....

FORM No. 137 (continued)

LIQUIDATOR'S STATEMENT OF ACCOUNT
[MEMBERS]*[CREDITORS] VOLUNTARY WINDING UP.

From..19.......... (*Commencement of winding up*) to

	Statement of Assets and Liabilities	Receipts		
	£	£	s.	d.
RECEIPTS:—				
Cash at Bank				
Cash in Hand				
Marketable Securities				
Sundry Debtors				
Stock-in-Trade				
Work in Progress				
Freehold Property				
Leasehold Property				
Plant and Machinery				
Furniture, Fittings, Utensils, etc.				
Patents, Trade Marks, etc.				
Investments, other than marketable securities ..				
Surplus from Securities				
Unpaid Calls at commencement of winding up ..				
Amounts received from Calls on Contributories made in the winding up				
Receipts, per Trading Account				
Other property, viz.:—				
....				
....				
....				
	£			
Less—				
Payments to redeem Securities				
Cost of execution				
Payments, per Trading Account				
NET REALISATIONS .. .. £				
	£			

* Delete as necessary.

FORM No. 137 (continued)

....19.......... (*Close of winding up*).

	Payments
	£ s. d.

	£ s. d.	Payments £ s. d.
Costs of Solicitor to Liquidator		
Other Law costs		
Liquidator's remuneration:—		
Where {........% on £........realised		
Applicable {........% on £........distributed ..		
By whom fixed		
Auctioneer's and Valuer's charges		
Costs of possession and maintenance of estate		
Cost of notices in *Gazette* and local papers		
Incidental outlay		
TOTAL COSTS AND CHARGES	£	

	£ s. d.	
(i) DEBENTURE HOLDERS:—		
Payment of £		
per £ debenture		
Payment of £		
per £ debenture		
Payment of £		
per £ debenture		
(ii) CREDITORS:—		
................‡Preferential		
................‡Unsecured:—		
Dividend(s) of........s........d. in £ on		
£........................... ..		
(*The estimate of amount expected to rank for dividend*		
was £...........................)		
(iii) RETURNS FOR CONTRIBUTORIES:—		
........s........d. per £........†share		
........s........d. per £........†share		
........s........d. per £........†share		
	BALANCE ..	
	£	

‡*State number. Preferential creditors need not be separately shown if all creditors have been paid in full.*
†*State nominal value and class of share.*

FORM No. 138

PETITION FOR WINDING UP.

IN THE MATTER OF.., LIMITED,
AND IN THE MATTER OF THE COMPANIES ACT, 1948.

To (a) .... (a) Insert title of
                                                                                                     Court.
    The humble Petition of (b)...

.... (b) Insert full
                                                                                                     name, title, etc.,
.... of Petitioner.

showeth as follows:—

1. ...., Limited
(hereinafter called "the Company"), was in the month of........................
incorporated under the Companies Acts.

2. The Registered Office of the Company is at (c)............................. (c) State the full
                                                                                                     address of the
....   Registered Office
3. The Nominal Capital of the Company is £ ...., so as sufficiently
divided into............................Shares of £............................each. The to show the
amount of the Capital paid up or credited as paid up is £.................... district in which
                                                                                                     it is situate.
4. The Objects for which the Company was established are as
follows:—

    To

and other objects set forth in the Memorandum of Association thereof.

    (d)   (d) Here set out
                                                                                                     in paragraphs
                                                                                                     the facts on
                                                                                                     which the
    NOTE.—If the Petition is by an Unpaid Creditor on Simple Contract the Petitioner relies.
paragraphs should be as follows:—

5. The Company is indebted to your Petitioner in the sum of †State considera-
£   :   :   for †... tion for the debt,
                                                                                                     with particulars
6. Your Petitioner has made application to the Company for pay- so as to establish
ment of his debt, but the Company has failed and neglected to that the debt
pay the same or any part thereof.   claimed is due.

7. The Company is [insolvent and] unable to pay its debts.

8. In the circumstances it is just and equitable that the Company
should be wound up.

Your Petitioner therefore humbly prays as follows:—

(1) That ...., Limited,
may be wound up by the Court under the provisions of the
Companies Act, 1948; or
(e) [That the Voluntary Winding Up of............................... (e) Add words in
...., Limited, [ ] if Supervision
may be continued, but subject to the supervision of the Order is asked
Court.]   for.

(2) That such other Order may be made in the premises as shall
be just.

NOTE.—(f) It is intended to serve this Petition on—   (f) This note will
                                                                                                     be unnecessary
....   if the Company
                                                                                                     is Petitioner.
....(Signature).

FORM No. 139

ESTATE CASH BOOK RULING.

THE COMPANIES ACT, 1948, AND THE COMPANIES (WINDING-UP) RULES, 1949.

In the .... Court.   Companies Liquidation No. .... of .... 19......

In the matter of .... LIMITED   CASH BOOK.

RECEIPTS.

Date	Particulars	Total	Drawn from Bank	Debts Collected	Property Realised	Receipts from Securities held by Creditors	Calls	Other Receipts

PAYMENTS.

Date	Particulars	Voucher Nos. (in red)	Total	Paid into Bank	COSTS OF REALIZATION											Preferential Creditors and Rent	Payments to redeem Securities	Dividends Paid	Repayments to Contributories	Other Payments

Costs of Realization columns: Board of Trade and Court Fees; Law Costs of Petition; Law Costs after Winding up Order; Remuneration of Manager and Liquidator; Official Receiver's Commission on Assets Realised and Amount Distributed in Dividend or paid to Contributories; Charges of Auctioneer, Accountant, Shorthand Writer, etc., as taxed; Notices in *Gazette* and Local Paper; Incidental Expenses, including Possession.

FORM No. 140

No. of Company F.............................   (Form No. 1 F.)

THE COMPANIES ACT, 1948.

LIST OF DOCUMENTS DELIVERED FOR REGISTRATION BY AN OVERSEA COMPANY.

Pursuant to Section 407.

Name of Company ....

Presented by

....

....

List of documents delivered to the Registrar of Companies for registration, pursuant to Section 407 of the Companies Act, 1948, by

....

a company incorporated in (a)...

and which has a place of business within Great Britain at..............................

....

(A)

(B)

(C)

(A) *A certified copy of the Charter, Statutes, or Memorandum and Articles of the company, or other instrument constituting or defining the constitution of the company, and, if the instrument is not written in the English language, a certified translation thereof.*

The copies and translations (if any) above mentioned must be certified in the manner prescribed in paragraphs 2 and 5 of the Companies (Forms) Order, 1949.

(B) *A list of the directors and secretary of the company, containing with respect to the directors and secretary the particulars required by Section 407 (2) of the Companies Act, 1948.*

(C) *The names and addresses of some one or more persons resident in Great Britain authorised to accept on behalf of the company service of process and any notices required to be served on the company.*

Signatures of the persons auth-   ....
orised under Section 407 (1) (c) of   ....
the Companies Act, 1948, or of   ....
some other person in Great   ....
Britain duly authorised by the   ....
Company.   ....

Dated the..day of.................................19..........

(a) *Country of origin.*

FORM No. 141

No. of Company F. ....

(Form No. 2 F.)

A 5s. Companies Registration Fee Stamp must be impressed here.

THE COMPANIES ACT 1948.

LIST AND PARTICULARS OF THE DIRECTORS AND SECRETARY OF AN OVERSEA COMPANY.
Pursuant to Section 407.

Name of Company...

Where incorporated ....

Address of place of business in Great Britain...

Presented by

....

....

PARTICULARS OF THE PERSONS WHO ARE DIRECTORS* OF THE COMPANY AT THE DATE OF THIS RETURN.

1 Name (In the case of an individual, present Christian name or names and surname.† In the case of a corporation, the corporate name)	2 Any former Christian name or names and surname‡	3 Nationality	4 Usual residential address (In the case of a corporation, the registered or principal office)	5 Other business occupation or directorships, if any. If none, state so§

PARTICULARS OF THE PERSON WHO IS THE SECRETARY OF THE COMPANY AT THE DATE OF THIS RETURN.

1 Name (In the case of an individual, present Christian name or names and surname.† In the case of a corporation or a Scottish firm, the corporate or firm name)¶	2 Any former Christian name or names and surname‡	3 Usual residential address (In the case of a corporation or a Scottish firm, the registered or principal office)¶

Date............................19........

Signatures of the persons authorised under Section 407 (1) (c) of the Companies Act, 1948, or of some other person in Great Britain duly authorised by the company.

{ ....
....
....
....
....

NOTES.

* "*Director*" includes any person who occupies the position of a director by whatsoever name called, and any person in accordance with whose directions or instructions the directors of the company are accustomed to act.

† "*Christian name*" includes a forename, and "*surname*" in the case of a peer or person usually known by a title different from his surname means that title.

‡ "*Former Christian name*" and "*former surname*" do not include—

  (a) in the case of a peer or a person usually known by a British title different from his surname, the name by which he was known previous to the adoption of or succession to the title; or

  (b) in the case of any person, a former Christian name or surname where that name or surname was changed or disused before the person bearing the name attained the age of eighteen years or has been changed or disused for a period of not less than twenty years; or

  (c) in the case of a married woman the name or surname by which she was known previous to the marriage.

§ In the case of an individual who has no business occupation but holds any other directorship or directorships, particulars of that directorship or some one of those directorships must be entered.

¶ Where all the partners in a firm are *joint secretaries*, the name and principal office of the firm may be stated.

FORM No. 142

No. of Company F. ....

(Form No. 3 F.)

◯ A 5s. *Companies Registration Fee Stamp must be impressed here.*

THE COMPANIES ACT, 1948.

LIST OF THE NAMES AND ADDRESSES OF PERSONS RESIDENT IN GREAT BRITAIN AUTHORISED TO ACCEPT SERVICE ON BEHALF OF AN OVERSEA COMPANY.

Pursuant to Section 407.

Name of Company ....

Presented by

....

....

....

List of persons resident in Great Britain authorised to accept on behalf of the company service of process and any notices required to be served on ....

....

a company incorporated in (a)..

and which has established a place of business in Great Britain at

....

Surname	Christian Name	Address

Signatures of the persons authorised under Section 407 (1) (c) of the Companies Act, 1948, or of some other person in Great Britain duly authorised by the company.

....

....

....

....

....

Dated the..day of................................19.........

(a) *Country of Origin.*

FORM No. 143

INCOME TAX

| District Refce. |
| / |

NOTICE TO EMPLOYER OF AMENDED CODE NUMBER FOR THE YEAR 19—.

Name of employee..

Nature of employment..

Works No...

Branch, dept., contract, etc..

The Code Number of the above
employee has been amended to—

The amended Code Number and the date from which it is applied should be entered in the spaces provided on the employee's Tax Deduction Card and the previous Code Number should be crossed out. If the previous Code Number has been entered on both sides of the Card, amend both sides.

As from the first pay day after this form is received, the free pay figures to be entered on the Tax Deduction Card are those shown in Table A of the Tax Tables for the amended Code Number.

Keep this form as your authority.

Issued by
H.M. Inspector of Taxes
(................................ District),
...., E.C.3.

P6   ....Date

SECRETARIAL PRACTICE

FORM No. 144

EMERGENCY CARD INCOME TAX YEAR ENDING 5 APRIL, 19___*

* To be completed by employer.

	Address of employee—
Works No. (if any)	....

	Enter "W" if paid weekly or "M" if paid monthly	Date employment commenced
	Employer	
Spaces above for employer's use	District	

Date of Payment (1)	Gross Pay (2)			Tax deducted (*See Emergency Card Table*) (3)		Date of Payment (1)	Gross Pay (2)			Tax deducted (*See Emergency Card Table*) (3)	
	£	s.	d.	£	s.		£	s.	d.	£	s.

(Left margin labels: Branch, Dept., Contract, etc. — Nature of employment — Name of employee)

If this card is in use at 5th April, state the amount
of the employee's Superannuation Contributions
(if any) from the date employment commenced   } £ : s.
to 5th April   ..   ..

P 13   Follow the instructions on the PINK EMERGENCY CARD TABLE (P 15).

FORM No. 145

INCOME TAX PAY AS YOU EARN
EMPLOYER'S ANNUAL RETURN
Year 19......-......, ended 5th April, 19......

Reference Number
P................/...........

To M..
    (Employers)

You are required to make a return of the pay and tax deductions of every employee for whom you have received or prepared a Tax Deduction Card or Emergency Card for the year ended 5th April, 19....... The return is to be made by sending the completed Tax Deduction Cards and Emergency Cards to the Collector of Taxes after 5th April, 19......, and not later than 19th April, 19......, accompanied by this form.

Directions for completing the cards are given in paragraphs 101 to 112 and 114 to 117 of the Employer's Guide and, as regards payments for expenses and benefits in kind, in the March, 1949, Supplement to the Employer's Guide and in leaflet No. P7H. The "pay" returned must include all salaries, wages, fees, commissions, bonuses, overtime, holiday pay or other emoluments whatever paid by you to such employees in the year ended 5th April, 19......

Part I overleaf should be completed in respect of every employee in whose case tax was deducted or refunded during 19......-....... Particulars need not be given in respect of employees in whose cases you did not deduct or refund tax but the Cards must be sent to the Collector (see Part I (*b*) below).

(1) Column 1. Enter in column 1 the name (and/or identifying number) of every employee in whose case you deducted or refunded tax, whether or not he was still in your employment at 5th April, 19......, for whom—

    (*a*) you have received or prepared a Tax Deduction Card P9 or P11, at any time during the year, or

    (*b*) you have prepared an Emergency Card P13 the particulars on which have not been transferred to a Tax Deduction Card.

(2) Column 2. For every employee from whose pay net tax was deducted by you during the year, enter in column 2 the net tax so deducted as shown on the completed Card (*i.e.* the total tax deducted by you less the amount of any refunds made by you).

(3) Column 3. If you have refunded to an employee more tax than you have deducted from him, do not make any entry in column 2 but enter in column 3 the net amount refunded by you (which you should have marked "R" on the Tax Deduction Card.

(4) Do not include in column 2 any tax in respect of a previous employment.

(5) Add up columns 2 and 3 and deduct the total of column 3 from the total of column 2.

Where the particulars on an Emergency Card have been transferred to a Tax Deduction Card, the Emergency Card should not be listed in Part I overleaf. The same applies where the particulars on a Tax Deduction Card have been transferred to another Tax Deduction Card (*e.g.* on a change from weekly to monthly payment).

If an employer finds it unduly onerous to list all the names he may arrange with the Tax Office to identify the cases by numbers or alternatively may arrange to supply a machine list of the tax deductions (see paragraph 117 of the Employer's Guide).

FORM No. 145 (continued)

After completing the list overleaf, complete Parts I (*b*), II and III and the Declaration below. Send the completed form to the Collector with all the Tax Deduction Cards and Emergency Cards whether or not they are required to be listed in Part I overleaf. Please arrange the listed Cards in the order in which they appear in the list.

The balance of tax due as shown in Part II should be remitted to the Collector.

Collector of Taxes,

.... Collection,

.... Street,

....................................., E.C.3.

....Date

PART I.   19......–...... TAX DEDUCTION CARDS AND EMERGENCY CARDS

   (*a*)   List of Cards for employees in whose cases tax was deducted or refunded by me during 19......–...... as shown overleaf.

   (*b*)   Number of cards for employees not included in the list overleaf in whose cases no tax was deducted or refunded by me during 19......–.......

PART II. SUMMARY OF TAX DEDUCTED AND REMITTED.	£	s.	d.
Total net tax deducted by me in 19......–...... (brought forward from Part I overleaf) ..			
Add, total of amounts (if any) advanced or reimbursed by the Tax Office for refunds to employees			
Deduct, total tax already remitted to the Collector on account of 19......–......			
Balance due to the Collector			

PART III.   (Please answer "Yes" or "No" to each question)

   (1)   Apart from the cases in Part I have you at any time during the year 19......–...... employed any person at a rate of pay of £3 or more a week or £12 10s. or more a month?   ..   ..

   (2)   Apart from the cases in Part I have you employed any person part-time or casually whose earnings with you exceeded £10 in the year?   ..   ..

   (3)   Was any remuneration paid "free of tax," that is, did you undertake to bear any part of the tax liability of any employee?   ..   ..

DECLARATION TO BE SIGNED BY EMPLOYER.

I declare that all Tax Deduction Cards and Emergency Cards which have been received or prepared by me during the year 19......–...... are forwarded herewith.

I also declare that all the particulars required to be entered on the Cards and all the particulars required in this notice to be returned are in every respect fully and truly stated according to the best of my knowledge and belief.

This declaration covers any documents corresponding to Tax Deduction Cards which I have been authorised by the Commissioners of Inland Revenue to supply.

Signature of Employer..

Address

....

Date..............................

P 35

FORM No. 145 (continued)

PART I.   LIST OF 19....... TAX DEDUCTION CARDS AND EMERGENCY CARDS.

	To be completed by employer			For official use					
Name of Employee and/or identifying number	[Where total deductions exceeded total refunds] Total tax deducted by me (*less* refunds) as shown on the Card	[Where total refunds exceeded total deductions] Net tax refunded by me as shown on the card (marked "R")	District Refce.	A	T	R	U	Notes	
(1)	(2) £ s. d.	(3) £ s. d.	(4)	(5) £ s. d.	(6) £ s. d.	(7) £ s. d.	(8) £ s. d.	(9)	
From Continuation Sheets									
Totals									
Deduct total of column 3 from total of column 2									
Total net tax deducted, carried to Part II overleaf									

Note.—If there is not sufficient space above to list all the Cards, continuation sheets may be used but the totals of the amounts shown on those sheets should be entered above.

FORM No. 146

INCOME TAX.   Part 3.
NEW EMPLOYEE.

Particulars of old employment—

1. Name of employee...
2. Date of leaving   ..   ..   (Shown on Part I only)
3. District refce. (not for entry on
    Tax Deduction Card) or entry "E"............................/............................/...........................
4. Code No. at date of leaving ☐
5. Last entries on Tax Deduction Card (except where Week 1 (or Month 1)
    basis applies)—
    (a) Week No...........................or Month No...
    (b) Total gross pay to date ..   ..   ..   £   :   s.   d.
    (c) Total tax to date   ..   ..   £   :   s.

The new employer should complete the following items—

6. Branch, Dept., Contract, etc...
7. Nature of employment...
8. Works No...
9. Date employment commenced...
10. Private address of employee..
    ....
    ....

11. If the total tax entered on the Tax Deduction ⎧
Card from Table B of the Tax Tables does not agree ⎬   £   :   s.
with the total tax shown at item 5 (c) above, state the ⎫
Tax Table figure here.   ⎭

DECLARATION.

I have prepared a*...........................Tax Deduction Card in accordance
with the particulars given above.

                    Employer...
                    Address   ....
                              ....
Date...

P 45.   * State whether "Weekly," "Monthly," or "Emergency."

FOR OFFICIAL USE ONLY.

Issued by .... District

Receiving District Date Stamp.

Items 1–5 verified....................................Initials.

FORM No. 147

INCOME TAX.

PARTICULARS OF EMPLOYEE FOR WHOM NO CODE NUMBER HAS BEEN NOTIFIED TO EMPLOYER.

The particulars overleaf should be given and this form sent immediately to the Inspector of Taxes—

(1) for any employee who at 6th April is being paid by you at a rate of £3 a week or more (or £12 10s. a month or more) and for whom you have not received a Tax Deduction Card from the Inspector of Taxes; or

(2) for any new employee who is engaged at a rate of pay of £3 a week or more (or £12 10s. a month or more) and who does not produce a certificate from a previous employer (Parts 2 and 3 of form P45); or

(3) when the pay of an employee to whom you have previously paid less than £3 a week (or £12 10s. a month) and for whom you do not hold a Tax Deduction Card, is increased to £3 a week or more (or £12 10s. a month or more) for the first time; or

(4) when a new employee who has other employment is engaged at a rate of pay exceeding £1 a week (or £4 a month) but less than £3 a week (or £12 10s. a month).

For any case under heading (1) or (2) you must prepare an Emergency Card and deduct tax by reference to the Emergency Card Table (P15). For any case under (3) or (4) do not prepare an Emergency Card and do not deduct tax unless further instructions are received.

Surname ....
(in BLOCK CAPITALS)

Christian Names..

If a woman state, if known, ⎫
whether married, widow or spinster ⎭ ....

Which of the headings (1) to (4) overleaf applies?..

If employment commenced after ⎫
5th April last, date of commencement.....⎭ ....

Private address ....

....

Nature of employment..

Works No...

Branch, Dept., Contract, etc...

Will the remuneration be paid at intervals of less than a month?..................

If a new employee, state name ⎰ ....
    and address of previous ⎨ ....
    employer, if known. ⎱ ....

For Official use only.	Employer ....
	Address ....
	....

P 46.   Date....................................

A 2

FORM No. 148

INCOME TAX YEAR 19......-......
CERTIFICATE OF PAY AND TAX DEDUCTED.

....
(Name of employee and Works No., if any)

Code No. at 5th April, 19......
(Enter "E" if an Emergency
Card is in use at 5th April, 19.....)

District
Refce.
(if any) ....…/.............../................

	Gross pay			Tax		
	£	s.	d.	£	s.	d.
1. Pay and tax in respect of previous employment(s) in 19......-...... taken into account in arriving at the tax deductions made by me/us						
2. Pay and tax in my/our employment..						

I/We certify that the particulars given above include the total amount of pay (including overtime, bonus, commission, etc.) paid to you by me/us in the year ended 5th April, 19....., and the total tax deducted by me/us (less any refunds) in that year.

Employer..

Date..

TO THE EMPLOYEE. Keep this certificate. It will help you to check any Notice of Assessment which the tax office may send you in due course.

INSTRUCTIONS TO EMPLOYER.

1. A certificate must be given to each employee who was in your employment on 5th April, 19......, and whose Tax Deduction Card or Emergency Card shows that tax has been deducted at any time during the year either by you or any previous employer.

2. The certificate should be prepared from the Tax Deduction Card or Emergency Card, after the card has been completed to show the pay and tax for the year.

3. Item 2 of the certificate should be completed in every case in which a certificate is required to be given.

4. In addition, Item 1 of the certificate should be completed in the case of an employee engaged during the year if any pay and tax in respect of previous employments have been deducted from the year's totals at the end of the Tax Deduction Card.

If in such a case the "tax in respect of this employment" as shown on the Tax Deduction Card is a refund (marked "R"), the word "refund" should be entered after the figure of tax at Item 2.

P 60.

FORM No. 149

(a)

(b)		Address of employee		Code§	Date applied
Spaces above for employer's use					
Employer					
District		District Refce. .... /	/	§ If amended cross out previous Code.	

Week No. (1)	Gross pay in the week (2)			Total gross pay to date (3)			Total free pay to date as shown by Table A (4)			* Total taxable pay to date (5)			Total tax due to date as shown by Table B (6)		Tax deducted in the week (7)		Tax refunded in the week (8)	
	£	s.	d.	£	s.	d.	£	s.	d.	£	s.	d.	£	s.	£	s.	£	s.
1									—									
2									—									
3									—									
4									—									
5									—									
6									—									
7									—									
8									—									
9									—									
10									—									
11									—									
12									—									
13									—									
14									—									
15									—									
16									—									
17									—									
18									—									
19									—									
20									—									
21									—									
22									—									
23									—									
24									—									
25									—									
26									—									

Works No.

Branch, Dept., Contract, etc.

Nature of employment

Name of employee

Follow the instructions on the BLUE CARD.

* If in any week the amount in col. (4) is more than the amount in col. (3) make no entry in col. (5).

P 9 (19.....).

FORM No. 149 (continued)

Works No.			Name						Amended codes						Code	
									Dates applied							

Week No. (1)	Gross pay in the week (2)			Total gross pay to date (3)			Total free pay to date as shown by Table A (4)			Total taxable pay to date (5)			Total tax due to date as shown by Table B (6)		Tax deducted in the week (7)		Tax refunded in the week (8)	
	£	s.	d.	£	s.	d.	£	s.	d.	£	s.	d.	£	s.	£	s.	£	s.
B.F. from Wk. No. 26	-	-	-				-	-	-	-	-	-			-	-	-	-
27									—									
28									—									
29									—									
30									—									
31									—									
32									—									
33									—									
34									—									
35									—									
36									—									
37									—									
38									—									
39									—									
40									—									
41									—									
42									—									
43									—									
44									—									
45									—									
46									—									
47									—									
48									—									
49									—									
50									—									
51									—									
52									—									
53									—									
If employee engaged during year, deduct pay and tax in respect of previous employment(s).				-	-	-	-	-	-									
Pay and tax deducted (or refunded†) in respect of this employment.				-	-	-	-	-	-									

† If a refund, mark entry in col. (6) "R"

Amount of employee's Superannuation Contributions (if any) for the year in respect of this employment } £   :   s.

Holiday pay paid in full (where authorised—see Employer's Guide) } £   :   s.

19......-....

FORM No. 150

INSTRUCTIONS TO EMPLOYERS—WEEKLY TAX DEDUCTION CARDS.

19......

HOW TO FILL UP THE TAX DEDUCTION CARD P9.

1. The card must be written up each time a payment is made to the employee (unless it is obvious that no tax will be deductible—see Employer's Guide).

Column 1: Week 1 covers any pay day within the period from 6th April to 12th April inclusive, Week 2 any pay day within the period from 13th April to 19th April inclusive, and so on as shown in the Tax Tables. The week in which a payment is made determines the line on which entries should be made. Throughout these instructions "Week" means a week as shown in the Tax Tables.

Column 2: Enter the gross amount of the pay (including overtime, bonus, commission, etc.) before any deductions, regardless of the period in which the pay was earned. If in doubt whether a particular item should be included in the gross pay, see Employer's Guide.

Column 3: Enter the total to date of the figures in column 2. In Week 1 the amount will be the same as that in column 2. In each subsequent week the figure for column 3 is obtained by adding the week's pay in column 2 to the previous total in column 3.

Column 4: Enter the total free pay to date as shown by Table A of the Tax Tables. Be sure you look up the right Week and the right Code as shown on the Tax Deduction Card.

Column 5: Subtract the figure in column 4 from the figure in column 3 and enter the difference in column 5. If the amount in column 4 is more than the amount in column 3, make no entry in column 5.

Column 6: From Table B of the Tax Tables find the amount of tax which applies to the figure of total net pay to date which you have entered in column 5. If Table B shows no tax enter "Nil." Be sure you look up the right Week.
  If no entry has been made in column 5 because the amount in column 4 is greater than the amount in column 3, enter "Nil" in column 6.

Columns 7 and 8: In Week 1 the figure you have just entered in column 6 will be the figure to be entered in column 7, and this is the amount of tax to be deducted from the pay that week.
  In Week 2 and each subsequent week, subtract from the figure which you have just entered in column 6 the figure entered in column 6 for the previous week. The difference is the amount to be deducted and should be entered in column 7.
  If the figure you have entered in column 6 is less than the figure in column 6 for the previous week, the difference is to be refunded to the employee. Enter the amount to be refunded in column 8, leaving column 7 blank. This tax refund must be included in the payment made to the employee. No refund exceeding £5 should be given to a new employee on his first pay day—see paragraph 11.

2. If there is more than one pay day in any Week, the same Week's Tables should be used for all pay days in that Week and all the figures should be inserted on the card against that Week.

3. If the intervals between pay days are more than a week but less than a calendar month, the Tax Tables for Weeks other than those in which the pay days fall may have to be used—see Employer's Guide.

4. Where there are 53 Weekly pay days in the year ending 5th April, the entries against Week 53 should be made as follows—

Column 2: As explained in paragraph 1.

Columns 4, 5 and 7: For this Week only, columns 4, 5 and 7 must be completed before columns 3 and 6. Find in Table A for Week 1 the free pay for the Code shown on the Tax Deduction Card. Enter this figure in column 4, subtract it from the figure of pay in column 2 and enter the difference in column 5. If the amount in column 4 is more than the amount in column 2 make no entry in column 5.
  Find in Table B for Week 1 the tax for the taxable pay entered in column 5 for Week 53. Enter this figure of tax in column 7 and deduct it from the pay. (If no tax is deductible, leave column 7 blank.)

Column 3: Now add the figure in column 2 of Week 53 to the last total in column 3 and enter the total in column 3 for Week 53.

Column 6: Add the figure in column 7 for Week 53 to the figure in column 6 for Week 52 and enter the total in column 6 for Week 53.

Column 8: Leave blank. No refund will be made by the employer for Week 53.

WHERE NO TAX DEDUCTION CARD IS HELD.

5. If the pay of an employee for whom you have not received a Tax Deduction Card exceeds £2 11s. in any week, send form P46 to the tax office at once. If the pay received in Week 1 (6th to 12th April) exceeds £2 11s. you should also prepare an Emergency Card P13 and deduct tax in accordance with the directions on the Emergency Card Table P15.

EMPLOYEE LEAVING.

6. When an employee for whom you hold a Tax Deduction Card leaves your employment, mark the card "Left ... (date)" after the last entries of pay and tax. Retain the card—see paragraph 15.
  Fill up form P45 in accordance with the directions thereon; take care NOT to enter the figures of "total free pay" or "total taxable pay" on the form by mistake. Hand Parts 2 and 3 to the employee when he leaves and send Part 1 to the tax office at once.
  If any payment is made to the employee after he has left, deduct tax in accordance with the Tax Tables for Week 1, without regard to the total gross pay to date. Enter the figures separately on the card.
  This paragraph does not apply to an employee who joins H.M. Forces—see Employer's Guide.

FORM No. 150 (continued)

NEW EMPLOYEE.

7. A new employee taken on by you after 5th April should be asked for Parts 2 and 3 of form P45.

8. Where Parts 2 and 3 of form P45 are not produced. If the earnings will exceed £2 11s. a week, send form P46 to the tax office at once, prepare an Emergency Card P13 and deduct tax from the employee's pay in accordance with the directions on the Emergency Card Table P15. If he has other employment and his earnings with you will exceed £1 a week but will not exceed £2 11s. a week, send form P46 to the tax office, but do not prepare an Emergency Card P13 or deduct tax unless further instructions are received.

9. Where Parts 2 and 3 of form P45 are produced. Follow the instructions on that form and prepare a Tax Deduction Card P9 as follows—

(a) Enter the employee's name, address, works no., etc., but put nothing in the spaces for District and District Reference.

(b) Enter the employee's code number as shown on form P45.

(c) Enter against the Week number as shown on form P45—
  (i) In column 2, the date the employee was taken on.
  (ii) In column 3, the total pay to date from previous employers.
  (iii) In column 4, the total free pay to date from Table A of the Tax Tables for the Code and Week shown on form P45.
  (iv) In column 5, the excess of the figure in column 3 over the figure in column 4. If there is not an excess, make no entry.
  (v) In column 6, the correct figure of total tax due to date as shown by Table B of the Tax Tables for the Week shown on form P45.

The figures which you have just entered in columns 3, 4, 5, and 6 should be taken into account for the purpose of all tax to be deducted or refunded by you.

10. Follow the directions in paragraph 1 overleaf for all payments you make to the new employee and deduct or refund tax for each week of employment with you as necessary. No refund should however be given to a new employee on his first pay day if it exceeds £5—see next paragraph.

11. Refund exceeding £5 to New Employee. If the Tax Tables show that a refund exceeding £5 is due to a new employee on his first pay day—

(a) enter in column 8 of the Tax Deduction Card the amount repayable, mark the entry "N", but do not make the refund.

(b) complete form P47 and send it to the tax office at once.

(c) make the refund on receipt of the authority from the tax office on form P48. (If you cannot do so because the employee has left, see Employer's Guide.)

Tax deductions on the second and subsequent pay days should proceed as though the refund had actually been made, and any refund which may become due on those pay days should be made whether or not the authority to make the refund due on the first pay day has been received from the tax office.

AMENDMENT OF CODE NUMBER.

12. If an employee's code number is amended you will be notified by the tax office on form P6, P6A, P6B or P153. Tax is to be deducted under the previous code number until this authority has been received.

On receipt of the authority, enter the amended code number and the date from which it applies in the space provided on the card, and cross out the previous code number. If the previous code number has been entered on both sides of the card, amend both sides.

Deduct or refund tax by reference to the amended code number as from the first pay day after form P6, P6A, P6B or P153 is received.

PAYMENT OF TAX TO COLLECTOR.

13. Tax deducted is to be paid to the Collector of Taxes monthly in accordance with the instructions on the Remittance Card.

ERRORS IN DEDUCTING OR REFUNDING TAX.

14. It is very important that the entries on the card should be made correctly and a check of the additions and subtractions on the card is desirable.

The tax which you are liable to pay over is the total tax deductible as shown in Table B of the Tax Tables. If at the end of the year this amount differs from the total of the amounts deducted by you less any amounts refunded by you, you will still be liable to account to the Collector for the correct amount as shown by the Tax Tables.

The Employer's Guide tells you what to do if an error is discovered.

RETURN OF CARDS TO COLLECTOR.

15. Retain all the cards until after 5th April. They should then be returned to the Collector in accordance with the instructions in the Employer's Guide.

EMPLOYER'S GUIDE.

16. Information on special points is contained in the Employer's Guide.

P8 (BLUE CARD) (19......).

FORM No. 151

(a)

| MONTHLY TAX DEDUCTION CARD 19....-....

(b)	Address of employee		Code§	Date applied
Spaces above for employer's use				
Employer				
District	District Refce. / /		§ If amended, cross out previous Code	

(left margin, rotated: Branch, Dept., Contract, etc. · Nature of employment · Name of employee)

Month in which payment made (1)	Gross pay in the month (2)			Total gross pay to date (3)			Total free pay to date as shown by Table A (4)			* Total taxable pay to date (5)			Total tax due to date as shown by Table B (6)		Tax deducted in the month (7)		Tax refunded in the month (8)	
	£	s.	d.	£	s.	d.	£	s.	d.	£	s.	d.	£	s.	£	s.	£	s.
Month 1 6 Apr. to 5 May									—									
Month 2 6 May to 5 June									—									
Month 3 6 June to 5 July									—									
Month 4 6 July to 5 Aug.									—									
Month 5 6 Aug. to 5 Sept.									—									
Month 6 6 Sept. to 5 Oct.									—									
Month 7 6 Oct. to 5 Nov.									—									
Month 8 6 Nov. to 5 Dec.									—									
Month 9 6 Dec. to 5 Jan.									—									
Month 10 6 Jan. to 5 Feb.									—									
Month 11 6 Feb. to 5 Mar.									—									
Month 12 6 Mar. to 5 Apr.									—									
If employee engaged during year, deduct pay and tax in respect of previous employment(s)																		
Pay and tax deducted (or refunded†) in respect of this employment ..																		

† If a refund mark entry in col. (6) "R."   * If in any month the amount in col. (4) is more than the amount in col. (3), make no entry in col. (5).

Follow the instructions on the YELLOW CARD.

Amount of employee's Superannuation Contributions { (if any) for the year in respect of this employment { £ : s.

P11 (19....)

FORM No. 151 (continued)

Before the card is sent to the Collector please complete any of the sections below which apply—see Employer's Guide.

I. EXPENSES PAYMENTS, ETC.

(A) Directors and certain employees (Part IV, Finance Act, 1948).

If this card is for a Director (whatever his rate of pay) or for an employee whose remuneration including pay, expenses allowance and the value of any benefits was not less than £2,000 for the year—

    (i) Nature of expenses.. Amount   £

    (ii) Nature of Benefits.. Value   £

    (iii) Amount (if any) included in total gross pay overleaf   ..   ..   ..   £

(B) Other persons.

If this card is not for a person described in (A) above—

    (i) Amount of expenses payments included in total gross pay overleaf   ..   ..   £

    (ii) Amount not included in total gross pay overleaf if more than £25 in the year (including any round sum allowance but excluding reimbursement of expenditure actually incurred in performance of duties)   ..   ..   £

II. FEES, BONUSES, COMMISSIONS, ETC., PAID AFTER END OF YEAR FOR WHICH EARNED.

    (i) Payments included in total gross pay overleaf relating to a period commencing before 6th April, 19——

       Description.. Amount   £

    (ii) Payments relating to 19—— which will be made after 5th April, 19——

       Date payment will be made (if known) .... Amount (or approximate amount)   £

III. REMUNERATION NOT SHOWN ABOVE FROM WHICH TAX COULD NOT BE DEDUCTED.

    Description.. Amount or Value   £

FORM No. 152

19......

INSTRUCTIONS TO EMPLOYERS—MONTHLY TAX DEDUCTION CARDS.

How to fill up the Tax Deduction Card P11.

1. The Monthly Tax Deduction Card is to be used where the salary, etc., is paid monthly or at longer intervals. The card must be written up in accordance with these instructions each time a payment is made to the employee (unless it is obvious that no tax will be deductible—see Employer's Guide).

Column 1: Month 1 covers any pay day within the period from 6th April to 5th May inclusive, Month 2 any pay day within the period from 6th May to 5th June inclusive, and so on as shown in the Tax Tables. The month in which a payment is made determines the spaces in which entries should be made. Throughout these instructions "Month" means a month as shown in the Tax Tables and on the Monthly Tax Deduction Card.

Column 2: Enter the gross amount of the pay (including overtime, bonus, commission, etc.) before any deductions, regardless of the period in which the pay was earned. If in doubt whether a particular item should be included in the gross pay, see Employer's Guide.

Column 3: Enter the total to date of the figures in column 2. On the first pay day after 5th April the amount will be the same as that in column 2. At each subsequent pay day the figure for column 3 is obtained by adding the pay on that day in column 2 to the previous total in column 3.

Column 4: Enter the total free pay to date as shown by Table A of the Tax Tables. Be sure you look up the right Month and the right Code as shown on the Tax Deduction Card.

Column 5: Subtract the figure in column 4 from the figure in column 3 and enter the difference in column 5. If the amount in column 4 is more than the amount in column 3, make no entry in column 5.

Column 6: From Table B of the Tax Tables find the amount of tax which applies to the figure of total net pay to date which you have entered in column 5. If Table B shows no tax enter "Nil." Be sure you look up the right Month.

If no entry has been made in column 5 because the amount in column 4 is greater than the amount in column 3, enter "Nil" in column 6.

Columns 7 and 8: In Month 1 the figure you have just entered in column 6 will be the figure to be entered in column 7, and this is the amount of tax to be deducted from the pay that month.

In Month 2 and each subsequent month, subtract from the figure which you have just entered in column 6 the figure entered in column 6 for the previous month. The difference is the amount to be deducted and should be entered in column 7.

If the figure you have entered in column 6 is less than the figure in column 6 for the previous month, the difference is to be refunded to the employee. Enter the amount to be refunded in column 8, leaving column 7 blank. This tax refund must be included in the payment made to the employee. No refund exceeding £5 should be given to a new employee on his first pay day—see paragraph 10.

2. If there is more than one payment in any Month, the same Month's Tables should be used for all payments in that Month and tax should be deducted or refunded at the time of each payment.

Exception.—Where a payment which is small in relation to the main pay for the Month, e.g. for overtime, is made before the main pay day in the Month, enter the amount in column 2 and the total to date in column 3. Make no entries in columns 4, 5, 6, 7 or 8, and do not deduct or refund tax at the time of that payment. When the main payment in the Month is made, the entry in column 3 will include all payments to date, so that the total tax due to date entered in column 6 will automatically include the tax on the overtime, etc., paid earlier in the Month.

3. If the regular pay days are at intervals of more than one month, the Tax Tables for Months other than those in which the payments are made may have to be used—see Employer's Guide.

Where no Tax Deduction Card is Held.

4. If the pay of an employee for whom you have not received a Tax Deduction Card exceeds £11 in any month, send form P46 to the tax office at once. If the pay received in Month 1 (6th April to 5th May) exceeds £11, you should also prepare an Emergency Card P13 and deduct tax in accordance with the directions on the Emergency Card Table P15.

Employee Leaving.

5. When an employee for whom you hold a Monthly Tax Deduction Card leaves your employment, mark the card "Left ... (date)" after the last entries of pay and tax. Retain the card—see paragraph 14.

Fill up form P45 in accordance with the directions thereon; take care NOT to enter the figures of "total free pay" or "total taxable pay" on the form by mistake. Hand Parts 2 and 3 to the employee when he leaves and send Part 1 to the tax office at once.

If any payment is made to the employee after he has left, deduct tax in accordance with the Tax Tables for Month 1, without regard to the total gross pay to date. Enter the figures separately on the card.

This paragraph does not apply to an employee who joins H.M. Forces—see Employer's Guide.

FORM No. 152 (continued)

NEW EMPLOYEE.

6. A new employee taken on by you after 5th April should be asked for Parts 2 and 3 of form P45.

7. Where Parts 2 and 3 of form P45 are not produced. If the earnings will be at a rate exceeding £11 a month, send form P46 to the tax office at once, prepare an Emergency Card P13 and deduct tax from the employee's pay in accordance with the directions on the Emergency Card Table P15. If he has other employment and his earnings with you will be at a rate exceeding £4 a month but not exceeding £11 a month, send form P46 to the tax office, but do not prepare an Emergency Card P13 or deduct tax unless further instructions are received.

8. Where Parts 2 and 3 of form P45 are produced. Follow the instructions on that form and prepare a Monthly Tax Deduction Card P11 as follows—
    (a) Enter the employee's name, address, etc., but put nothing in the spaces for District and District Reference.
    (b) Enter the employee's code number as shown on form P45.
    (c) Enter against the Month number as shown on form P45—
        (i) In column 2, the date the employee was taken on.
        (ii) In column 3, the total pay to date from previous employers.
        (iii) In column 4, the total free pay to date from Table A of the Tax Tables for the Code and Month shown on form P45.
        (iv) In column 5, the excess of the figure in column 3 over the figure in column 4. If there is not an excess, make no entry.
        (v) In column 6, the correct figure of total tax due to date as shown by Table B of the Tax Tables for the Month shown on form P45.
The figures which you have just entered in columns 3, 4, 5 and 6 should be taken into account for the purpose of all tax to be deducted or refunded by you.

9. Follow the directions in paragraph 1 overleaf for all payments you make to the new employee and deduct or refund tax for each month of employment with you as necessary. No refund should however be given to a new employee on his first pay day if it exceeds £5—see next paragraph.

10. Refund exceeding £5 to New Employee. If the Tax Tables show that a refund exceeding £5 is due to a new employee on his first pay day—
    (a) enter in column 8 of the Tax Deduction Card the amount repayable, mark the entry "N," but do not make the refund.
    (b) complete form P47 and send it to the tax office at once.
    (c) make the refund on receipt of the authority from the tax office on form P48. (If you cannot do so because the employee has left, see Employer's Guide.)
Tax deduction on the second and subsequent pay days should proceed as though the refund had actually been made, and any refund which may become due on those pay days should be made whether or not the authority to make the refund due on the first pay day has been received from the tax office.

AMENDMENT OF CODE NUMBER.

11. If an employee's code number is amended you will be notified by the tax office on form P6, P6A, P6B or P153. Tax is to be deducted under the previous code number until this authority has been received.
On receipt of the authority, enter the amended code number and the date from which it applies in the space provided on the card, and cross out the previous code number.
Deduct or refund tax by reference to the amended code number as from the first pay day after form P6, P6A, P6B or P153 is received.

PAYMENT OF TAX TO COLLECTOR.

12. Tax deducted is to be paid to the Collector of Taxes monthly in accordance with the instructions on the Remittance Card.

ERRORS IN DEDUCTING OR REFUNDING TAX.

13. It is very important that the entries on the card should be made correctly and a check of the additions and subtractions on the card is desirable.
The tax which you are liable to pay over is the total tax deductible as shown in Table B of the Tax Tables. If at the end of the year this amount differs from the total of the amounts deducted by you less any amounts refunded by you, you will still be liable to account to the Collector for the correct amounts as shown by the Tax Tables.
The Employer's Guide tells you what to do if an error is discovered.

RETURN OF CARDS TO COLLECTOR.

14. Retain all the cards until after 5th April. They should then be returned to the Collector in accordance with the instructions in the Employer's Guide.

EMPLOYER'S GUIDE.

15. Information on special points is contained in the Employer's Guide.

P10 (YELLOW CARD) (19——).

APPENDIX G

Registration of Business Names Act, 1916

[6 & 7 Geo. V, c. 58] [22nd December, 1916]

as amended by

The Companies Act 1947

[10 & 11 Geo. VI, c. 47] Sections 58 and 116.

ARRANGEMENT OF SECTIONS.

BE it enacted by the King's most Excellent Majesty, by and with the advice and consent of the Lords Spiritual and Temporal, and Commons, in this present Parliament assembled, and by the authority of the same, as follows:

Firms and persons to be registered.

1.—Subject to the provisions of this Act—

(a) Every firm having a place of business in the United Kingdom and carrying on business under a business name which does not consist of the true surnames of all partners who are individuals and the corporate names of all partners who are corporations without any addition other than the true Christian names of individual partners or initials of such Christian names;

(b) Every individual having a place of business in the United Kingdom and carrying on business under a business name which does not consist of his true surname without any addition other than his true Christian names or the initials thereof;

(c) Every individual or firm having a place of business in the United Kingdom, who, or a member of which, has either before or after the passing of this Act changed his name, except in the case of a woman in consequence of marriage;

(d) *Every company as defined in the Companies Act, 1929, carrying on business under a business name which does not consist of its corporate name without any addition**

shall be registered in the manner directed by this Act:

Provided that—

(i) where the addition merely indicates that the business is carried on in succession to a former owner of the business, that addition shall not of itself render registration necessary; and

(ii) where two or more individual partners have the same surname, the addition of an *s* at the end of that surname shall not of itself render registration necessary; and

(iii) where the business is carried on by a trustee in bankruptcy or a receiver or manager appointed by any court registration shall not be necessary; and

(iv) a purchase or acquisition of property by two or more persons as joint tenants or tenants in common is not of itself to be deemed carrying on a business whether or not the owners share any profits arising from the sale thereof.

Registration by nominee, etc.

2.—Where a firm, individual, or corporation having a place of business within the United Kingdom carries on the business wholly or mainly as nominee or trustee of or for another person, or other persons, or another corporation, or acts as general agent for any foreign firm, the first-mentioned firm, individual, or corporation shall be registered in manner provided by this Act,

---

* Added by Companies Act, 1947, s. 58.

and, in addition to the other particulars required to be furnished and registered, there shall be furnished and registered the particulars mentioned in the schedule to this Act:

Provided that where the business is carried on by a trustee in bankruptcy or a receiver or manager appointed by any court, registration under this section shall not be necessary.

3.—(1) Every firm or person required under this Act* to be registered shall furnish by sending by post or delivering to the registrar at the register office in that part of the United Kingdom in which the principal place of business of the firm or person is situated a statement in writing in the prescribed form containing the following particulars:— *Manner and particulars of registration.*

(a) The business name;

(b) The general nature of the business;

(c) The principal place of the business;

(d) Where the registration to be effected is that of a firm, the present Christian name and surname, any former Christian name or surname, the nationality [and if that nationality is not the nationality of origin, the nationality of origin],* the usual residence, and the other business occupation (if any) of each of the individuals who are partners, and the corporate name and registered or principal office of every corporation which is a partner;

(e) Where the registration to be effected is that of an individual, the present Christian name and surname, any former Christian name or surname, the nationality [and if the nationality is not the nationality of origin]† the nationality of origin, the usual residence, and the other business occupation (if any) of such individual;

(f) Where the registration to be effected is that of a corporation, its corporate name and registered or principal office;

(g) If the business is commenced after the passing of this Act, the date of the commencement of the business.

(2) Where a business is carried on under two or more business names, each of those business names must be stated.

4.—The statement required for the purpose of registration must in the case of an individual be signed by him, and in the case of a corporation by a director or secretary thereof, and in the case of a firm either by all the individuals who are partners, and by a director or the secretary of all corporations which are partners or by some individual who is a partner, or a director or the secretary of some corporation which is a partner, and in either of the last two cases must be verified by a statutory declaration made by the signatory: Provided that no such statutory declaration stating that any person other than the declarant is a partner, or omitting to state that any person other than as aforesaid is a partner, shall be evidence for or against any such other person in respect of his liability or non-liability as a partner, and that the *Statement to be signed by persons registering.*

* Deleted by Companies Act, 1947, s. 116 (3).
† By virtue of Companies Act, 1947, s. 58 (2), s. 3 (1) applies to companies.

High Court or a judge thereof may on application of any person alleged or claiming to be a partner direct the rectification of the register and decide any question arising under this section.

Time for
registration.

5.—The particulars required to be furnished under this Act shall be furnished within fourteen days after the firm or person commences business, or the business in respect of which registration is required, as the case may be: *Provided that if such firm or person has carried on such business before the passing of this Act or commences such business within two months thereafter, the statement of particulars shall be furnished after the expiration of two months and before the expiration of three months from the passing of this Act, and that if at the expiration of the said two months the conditions affecting the firm or persons have ceased to be such as to require registration under this Act, the firm or person need not be registered so long as such conditions continue.

This section shall apply, in the case where registration is required in consequence of a change of name, as if for references to the date of the commencement of the business there were substituted references to the date of such change.

Registration of
changes in firm.

6.—Whenever a change is made or occurs in any of the particulars registered in respect of any firm or person such firm or person shall, within fourteen days after such change, or such longer period as the Board of Trade may, on application being made in any particular case, whether before or after the expiration of such fourteen days, allow, furnish by sending by post or delivery to the registrar in that part of the United Kingdom in which the aforesaid particulars are registered a statement in writing in the prescribed form specifying the nature and date of the change signed, and where necessary verified, in like manner as the statement required on registration.

Penalty for
default in
registration.

7.—If any firm or person by this Act required to furnish a statement of particulars or of any change in particulars shall without reasonable excuse make default in so doing in the manner and within the time specified by this Act, every partner in the firm or the person so in default shall be liable on summary conviction to a fine not exceeding five pounds for every day during which the default continues, and the court shall order a statement of the required particulars or change in the particulars to be furnished to the registrar within such time as may be specified in the order.

Penalty for
carrying on
business under
name if registra-
tion refused.

It is provided by the Companies Act, 1947, s. 116 (2), that where registration of a business name is refused under s. 14 of the Act, any person carrying on business under that name in such circumstances as to require registration under the Act, shall be liable under s. 7 (supra) to the same penalties as if he had without reasonable excuse made default in furnishing a statement of particulars with respect to that name.

Disability of
persons in
default.

8.—(1) Where any firm or person by this Act required to furnish a statement of particulars or of any change in particulars shall

* By virtue of the Companies Act, 1947, s. 58 (2), the proviso to s. 5 includes companies.

have made default in so doing, then the rights of that defaulter under or arising out of any contract made or entered into by or on behalf of such defaulter in relation to the business in respect to the carrying on of which particulars were required to be furnished at any time while he is in default shall not be enforceable by action or other legal proceeding either in the business name or otherwise:

Provided always as follows:—

(a) The defaulter may apply to the court for relief against the disability imposed by this section, and the court, on being satisfied that the default was accidental or due to inadvertence, or some other sufficient cause, or that on other grounds it is just and equitable to grant relief, may grant such relief either generally, or as respects any particular contracts, on condition of the costs of the application being paid by the defaulter, unless the court otherwise orders, and on such other conditions (if any) as the court may impose, but such relief shall not be granted except on such service and such publication of notice of the application as the court may order, nor shall relief be given in respect of any contract if any party to the contract proves to the satisfaction of the court that, if this Act had been complied with, he would not have entered into the contract;

(b) Nothing herein contained shall prejudice the rights of any other parties as against the defaulter in respect of such contract as aforesaid;

(c) If any action or proceeding shall be commenced by any other party against the defaulter to enforce the rights of such party in respect of such contract, nothing herein contained shall preclude the defaulter from enforcing in that action or proceeding, by way of counterclaim set off or otherwise, such rights as he may have against that party in respect of such contract.

(2) In this section the expression 'court' means the 'High Court' or a judge thereof:

Provided that, without prejudice to the power of the High Court or a judge thereof to grant such relief as aforesaid, if any proceeding to enforce any contract is commenced by a defaulter in a county court, the county court may, as respects that contract, grant such relief as aforesaid.

9.—If any statement required to be furnished under this Act contains any matter which is false in any material particular to the knowledge of any person signing it, that person shall, on summary conviction, be liable to imprisonment with or without hard labour for a term not exceeding three months, or to a fine not exceeding twenty pounds, or to both such imprisonment and fine. *Penalty for false statements.*

10.—(1) The Board of Trade may require any person to furnish to the Board such particulars as appear necessary to the Board for the purpose of ascertaining whether or not he or the firm of which *Duty to furnish particulars to Board of Trade.*

he is partner should be registered under this Act, or an alteration made in the registered particulars, and may also in the case of a corporation require the secretary or any other officer of a corporation performing the duties of secretary to furnish such particulars, and if any person when so required fails to supply such particulars as it is in his power to give, or furnishes particulars which are false in any material particular, he shall on summary conviction be liable to imprisonment with or without hard labour for a term not exceeding three months or to a fine not exceeding twenty pounds or to both such imprisonment and fine.

(2) If from any information so furnished it appears to the Board of Trade that any firm or person ought to be registered under this Act, or an alteration ought to be made in the registered particulars, the Board may require the firm or person to furnish to the registrar the required particulars within such time as may be allowed by the Board, but, where any default under this Act has been discovered from the information acquired under this section, no proceedings under this Act shall be taken against any person in respect of such default prior to the expiration of the time within which the firm or person is required by the Board under this section to furnish particulars to the registrar.

Registrar to file statement and issue certificate of registration. 11.—On receiving any statement or statutory declaration made in pursuance of this Act the registrar shall cause the same to be filed, and he shall send by post or deliver a certificate of the registration thereof to the firm or person registering and the certificate or a certified copy thereof shall be kept exhibited in a conspicuous position at the principal place of business of the firm or individual, and if not kept so exhibited, every partner in the firm or the person, as the case may be, shall be liable on summary conviction to a fine not exceeding twenty pounds.

Index to be kept. 12.—At each of the register offices hereinafter referred to the registrar shall keep an index of all the firms and persons registered at that office under this Act.

Removal of names from register. 13.—(1) If any firm or individual *or company*,* registered under this Act ceases to carry on business, it shall be the duty of the persons who were partners in the firm at the time when it ceased to carry on business or of the individual or if he is dead his personal representative (*and in the case of a company the director or any liquidator of the company*)* within three months after the business has ceased to be carried on, to send by post or deliver to the registrar notice in the prescribed form that the firm or individual *or company*,* has ceased to carry on business, and if any person whose duty it is to give such notice fails to do so within such time as aforesaid, he shall be liable on summary conviction to a fine not exceeding twenty pounds.

(2) On receipt of such a notice as aforesaid the registrar may remove the firm or individual *or company*,* from the register.

(3) Where the registrar has reasonable cause to believe that any firm or individual *or company*,* registered under this Act is not carrying on business he may send to the firm or individual *or company*,* by registered post a notice that, unless an answer is

* Words in italics have been in effect added by the Companies Act, 1947, s. 58 (3).

received to such notice within one month from the date thereof, the firm or individual *or company** may be removed from the register.

(4) If the registrar either receives an answer from the firm or individual *or company** to the effect that the firm or individual *or company** is not carrying on business or does not within one month after sending the notice receive an answer, he may remove the firm or individual *or company** from the register.

14.—(1) Where any business name under which the business of a firm or individual is carried on contains the word 'British' or any other word which, in the opinion of the registrar is calculated to lead to the belief that the business is under British ownership or control, and the registrar is satisfied that the nationality of the persons by whom the business is wholly or mainly owned or controlled is at any time such that the name is misleading, the registrar shall refuse to register such business name or, as the case may be, remove such business name from the register, but any person aggrieved by a decision of the registrar under this provision may appeal to the Board of Trade, whose decision shall be final. Misleading business names.

(2) The registration of a business name under this Act shall not be construed as authorising the use of that name if apart from such registration the use thereof could be prohibited.

The Companies Act, 1947, s. 116 (1), provides that the power conferred by s. 14 on the registrar to refuse registration of a business name under the Act shall extend (without prejudice to the specific provision of s. 14) to any name which is in his opinion undesirable.†

15.—There shall be offices in London, Edinburgh, and Dublin for the registration of firms and persons whose principal places of business are respectively situated in England and Wales, Scotland, and Ireland, and the registrar of companies in each of those cities or such other person as the Board of Trade may determine shall be the registrar for the purposes of this Act. Registrar.

16.—At any time after the expiration of six months from the passing of this Act or of such longer period, not being more than nine months from the passing of this Act, as the Board of Trade may by order direct, any person may inspect the documents filed by the registrar on payment of such fees as may be prescribed not exceeding one shilling for each inspection; and any person may require a certificate of the registration of any firm or person, or a copy of or extract from any registered statement to be certified by the registrar or assistant registrar, and there shall be paid for such certificate of registration, certified copy, or extract such fees as may be prescribed not exceeding two shillings for the certificate of registration, and not exceeding sixpence for each folio of seventy-two words, or in Scotland for each sheet of two hundred words, of the entry, copy, or extract. Inspection of statements registered.

A certificate of registration, or a copy of or extract from any statement registered under this Act, if duly certified to be a true copy or extract under the hand of the registrar or one of the

* Words in italics have been in effect added by the Companies Act, 1947, s. 58 (3).
† For penalties for carrying on business under name after registration refused see s. 7 (*supra*).

assistant registrars (whom it shall not be necessary to prove to be the registrar or assistant registrar), shall, in all legal proceedings, civil or criminal, be received in evidence.

Power for Board of Trade to make rules.

17.—(1) The Board of Trade may make rules (but as to fees with the concurrence of the Treasury) concerning any of the following matters—

(*a*) The fees to be paid to the registrar under this Act, so that they do not exceed the sum of five shillings for the registration of any one statement;

(*b*) The forms to be used under this Act;

(*c*) The duties to be performed by any registrar under this Act;

(*d*) The performance by assistant registrars and other officers of acts by this Act required to be done by the registrar;

(*e*) Generally the conduct and regulation of registration under this Act, and any matters incidental thereto.

(2) All fees payable in pursuance of any such rules shall be applied as the Treasury may direct.

Publication of true names, etc.

18.—(1) After the expiration of three months from the passing of this Act every individual and firm required by this Act to be registered shall, in all trade catalogues, trade circulars, showcards, and business letters, on or in which the business name appears and which are issued or sent by the individual or firm to any person in any part of His Majesty's dominions, have mentioned in legible characters—

(*a*) in the case of an individual, his present Christian name or the initials thereof and present surname, any former Christian name or surname, his nationality if not British [and if his nationality is not his nationality of origin his nationality of origin];* and

(*b*) in the case of a firm, the present Christian names, or the initials thereof and present surnames, any former Christian names and surnames, and the nationality if not British [and if the nationality is not the nationality of origin the nationality of origin]* of all the partners in the firm or, in the case of a corporation being a partner, the corporate name.

(2) If default is made in compliance with this section the individual or, as the case may be, every member of the firm shall be liable on summary conviction for each offence to a fine not exceeding five pounds.

Provided that no proceedings shall in England or Ireland be instituted under this section except by or with the consent of the Board of Trade.

Offences by corporations.

19.—Where a corporation is guilty of an offence under this Act every director, secretary, and officer of the corporation who is knowingly a party to the default shall be guilty of a like offence and liable to a like penalty.

* Deleted by Companies Act, 1947, s. 116 (3).

20.—Anything required or authorised by this Act to be done by the Board of Trade may be done by the President or a Secretary or Assistant Secretary of the Board, or any other person authorised in that behalf by the President of the Board.

Mode of action by the Board of Trade.

21.—There shall be paid out of moneys to be provided by Parliament such remuneration in respect of the duties performed under this Act as the Treasury may assign.

Remuneration for duties under this Act.

22.—In the construction of this Act the following words and expressions shall have the meanings in this section assigned to them, unless there be something in the subject or context repugnant to such construction:—

Interpretation of terms.

'Firm' shall mean an unincorporated body of two or more individuals, or one or more individuals and one or more corporations, or two or more corporations, who have entered into partnership with one another with a view to carrying on business for profit, but shall not include any unincorporated company which was in existence on the second day of November eighteen hundred and sixty-two:

'Business' shall include profession:

'Individual' shall mean a natural person and shall not include a corporation:

'Christian name' shall include any forename:

'Initials' shall include any recognised abbreviation of a Christian name:

In the case of a peer or person usually known by a British title different from his surname, the title by which he is known shall be substituted in this Act for his surname:

References in this Act to a former Christian name or surname shall not [in the case of natural-born British subjects]* include a former Christian name or surname where that name or surname has been changed or disused before the person bearing the name had attained the age of eighteen years, and in the case of a married woman, shall not include the name or surname by which she was known previous to the marriage:

* The words in brackets have been deleted by Companies Act, 1947, s. 116 (4). That sub-section also provides (a) that a former Christian name or surname shall not include a former Christian name or surname where that name or surname has been changed or disused before the person having the name had attained the age of eighteen years or has been changed or disused for a period of not less than twenty years; and (b) that an individual or firm shall not require to be registered under the Act by reason only of a change of his name, or of the name of a member of the firm, if the change has taken place before the person who has changed his name has attained the age of eighteen years or if not less than twenty years have elapsed since it took place.

Section 116 (5) provides that where under s. 116 (4) (supra) an individual or firm registered under the Act no longer requires to be registered: (a) the registrar, if so required by the individual or firm, shall remove him or it from the register; (b) the individual firm need no longer keep exhibited the certificate of registration or a copy thereof required by s. 11 of the Act.

Finally, where the particulars registered under the Act include a former name or surname which under s. 116 (4) (supra) no longer needs to be included among those particulars, the registrar, if so requested by the individual or firm, shall amend the particulars by leaving out that name or surname.

References in this Act to a change of name shall not include, in the case of natural born British subjects, a change of name which has taken place before the person whose name has been changed has attained the age of eighteen years; or, in the case of a peer or a person usually known by a British title different from his surname, the adoption of or succession to the title:

'Business name' shall mean the name or style under which any business is carried on, whether in partnership or otherwise:

'Foreign firm' shall mean any firm, individual, or corporation whose principal place of business is situate outside His Majesty's dominions:

'Showcards' shall mean cards containing or exhibiting articles dealt with, or samples or representations thereof:

'Prescribed' shall mean prescribed by rules made in pursuance of this Act.

Application to Scotland.

23.—(1) In the application of this Act to Scotland—

'Court of Session' shall be substituted for 'High Court';

'Sheriff court' shall be substituted for 'county court';

'Trustee on a sequestrated estate' shall be substituted for 'trustee in bankruptcy';

'Receiver or manager appointed by any court' shall include 'judicial factor'; and

'Joint tenants' and 'tenants in common' shall mean pro indiviso proprietors.

Application to Ireland.

24.—In the application of this Act to Ireland the expression 'trustee in bankruptcy' shall be construed as including an assignee in bankruptcy and a trustee of the estate of an arranging debtor.

Short title.

25.—This Act may be cited as the Registration of Business Names Act, 1916.

Schedule

Description of Firm, etc.	The additional Particulars
Where the firm, individual, or corporation required to be registered carries on business as nominee or trustee.	The present Christian name and surname, any former name, nationality [and, if that nationality is not the nationality of origin, the nationality of origin],* and usual residence, or, as the case may be, the corporate name, of every person or corporation on whose behalf the business is carried on: Provided that if the business is carried on under any trust and any of the beneficiaries are a class of children or other persons, a description of the class shall be sufficient.
Where the firm, individual, or corporation required to be registered carries on business as general agent for any foreign firm.	The business name and address of the firm or person as agent for whom the business is carried on: Provided that if the business is carried on as agent for three or more foreign firms it shall be sufficient to state the fact that the business is so carried on, specifying the countries in which such foreign firms carry on business.

Section 2.

* Deleted by Companies Act, 1947, s. 116 (3).

APPENDIX H

Prevention of Fraud (Investments) Act, 1939

2 & 3 GEO. 6.   CH. 16

Provisions for regulating the business of dealing in securities.

1.—(1) Subject to the provisions of the next following section, no person shall, on or after the appointed day,—

    (*a*) carry on or purport to carry on the business of dealing in securities except under the authority of a principal's licence, that is to say, a licence under this Act authorising him to carry on the business of dealing in securities, or

    (*b*) in the capacity of a servant or agent of any person carrying on or purporting to carry on that business, deal or purport to deal in securities except under the authority of a representative's licence, that is to say, a licence under this Act authorising him to deal in securities as a servant or agent of any holder of a principal's licence for the time being in force.

(2) Any person who contravenes this section shall be liable, on conviction on indictment, to imprisonment for a term not exceeding two years or to a fine not exceeding five hundred pounds or to both such imprisonment and such fine or, on summary conviction, to imprisonment for a term not exceeding six months or to a fine not exceeding one hundred pounds or to both such imprisonment and such fine.

(3) Proceedings for an offence under this section shall not, in England, be instituted except by, or with the consent of, the Board of Trade or the Director of Public Prosecutions:

Provided that this sub-section shall not prevent the arrest, or the issue or execution of a warrant for the arrest, of any person in respect of such an offence, or the remanding, in custody or on bail, of any person charged with such an offence, notwithstanding that the necessary consent to the institution of proceedings for the offence has not been obtained.

*   *   *

General provisions for the prevention of fraud.

12.—(1) Any person who, by any statement, promise or forecast which he knows to be misleading, false or deceptive, or by any dishonest concealment of material facts, or by the reckless making of any statement, promise or forecast which is misleading, false or deceptive, induces or attempts to induce another person—

(a) to enter into or offer to enter into—

    (i) any agreement for, or with a view to, acquiring, disposing of, subscribing for or underwriting securities or lending or depositing money to or with any industrial and provident society or building society, or

    (ii) any agreement the purpose or pretended purpose of which is to secure a profit to any of the parties from the yield of securities or by reference to fluctuations in the value of securities, or

(b) to acquire or offer to acquire any right or interest under any arrangements the purpose or effect, or pretended purpose or effect, of which is to provide facilities for the participation by persons in profits or income alleged to arise or to be likely to arise from the acquisition, holding, management or disposal of any property other than securities, or

(c) to enter into or offer to enter into an agreement the purpose or pretended purpose of which is to secure a profit to any of the parties by reference to fluctuations in the value of any property other than securities,

shall be guilty of an offence, and liable to penal servitude for a term not exceeding seven years.

(2) Any person guilty of conspiracy to commit an offence under the preceding sub-section shall be punishable as if he had committed such an offence.

13.—(1) Subject to the provisions of this section, no person shall, on or after the appointed day,— *Restriction on distribution of circulars relating to investments.*

(a) distribute or cause to be distributed any documents which, to his knowledge, are circulars containing—

    (i) any invitation to persons to do any of the acts mentioned in paragraphs (a) to (c) of sub-s. (1) of the last preceding section, or

    (ii) any information calculated to lead directly or indirectly to the doing of any of those acts by the recipient of the information, or

(b) have in his possession for the purpose of distribution any documents which, to his knowledge, are such circulars as aforesaid, being documents of such a nature as to show that the object or principal object of distributing them would be to communicate such an invitation or such information as aforesaid.

(2) The preceding sub-section shall not apply—

(a) in relation to any distribution of a prospectus to which s. 35 or s. 354 of the Companies Act, 1929, applies, or in relation to any distribution of a document relating to securities of a corporation incorporated in Great Britain which is not a registered company, being a document which—

(i) would, if the corporation were a registered company, be a prospectus to which the said s. 35 applies, and

(ii) contains all the matters which, by virtue of the said s. 354, it would have to contain if the corporation were a company incorporated outside Great Britain and the document were a prospectus issued by that company, or

(b) in relation to any issue of a form of application for shares in, or debentures of, a corporation, together with—

(i) a prospectus which complies with the requirements of s. 35 or Part XII of the Companies Act, 1929, or

(ii) in the case of a corporation incorporated in Great Britain which is not a registered company, a document containing all the matters mentioned in sub-paragraph (ii) of paragraph (a) of this subsection,

or in connection with a bona fide invitation to a person to enter into an underwriting agreement with respect to the shares or debentures, or

(c) in relation to any distribution of documents which is required or authorised by or under any Act other than this Act or by or under any enactment of the Parliament of Northern Ireland,

and shall not apply in relation to any distribution of documents which is permitted by the Board of Trade.

(3) This section shall not prohibit the distribution or possession of any document by reason only—

(a) that it contains an invitation or information—

(i) made or given with respect to any securities by or on behalf of a member of any recognised stock exchange or recognised association of dealers in securities, or by or on behalf of the holder of a principal's licence, or

(ii) made or given with respect to any securities by or on behalf of the Bank of England or any exempted dealer, or

(iii) made or given by or on behalf of a corporation to holders of securities of, or to persons employed by, or to creditors of, that corporation or any other corporation which, in relation to the first-mentioned corporation, is a subsidiary company as defined by s. 127 of the Companies Act, 1929, with respect to securities of the first-mentioned corporation or of any such other corporation as aforesaid, or

(iv) made or given by or on behalf of the manager under an authorised unit trust scheme with respect to any securities created in pursuance of that scheme, or

(v) made or given by or on behalf of the Government of any part of His Majesty's dominions or the Government of any foreign state, or by or on behalf of any statutory corporation or municipal corporation, with respect to securities of that Government or corporation, or

(vi) made or given by or on behalf of any industrial and provident society or building society with respect to shares of the society, or loans or deposits which may be made to or with the society, or

(vii) made or given to beneficiaries under a trust by or on behalf of a person acting in the capacity of a trustee of that trust, or

(viii) made or given with respect to any securities in connection only with a sale or proposed sale of those securities by auction, or

(b) that it contains an invitation or information which a person whose ordinary business or part of whose ordinary business it is to buy and sell any property other than securities (whether as a principal or as an agent) may make or give in the course of the business of buying and selling such property:

Provided that nothing in paragraph (a) of this sub-section shall authorise the doing of anything in respect of securities created in pursuance of any unit trust scheme which is not an authorised unit trust scheme; and nothing in paragraph (b) of this sub-section shall authorise any person to do anything in pursuance of, or for the purpose of, any arrangements the purpose or effect, or pretended purpose or effect, of which is to provide facilities for the participation by persons in profits or income alleged to arise or to be likely to arise from the acquisition, holding, management or disposal of any property other than securities.

(4) Documents shall not, for the purposes of this section, be deemed not to be circulars by reason only that they are in the form of a newspaper, journal, magazine or other periodical publication; but a person shall not be taken to contravene this section by reason only that he distributes, or causes to be distributed, to purchasers thereof, or has in his possession for the purpose of distribution to purchasers thereof, copies of any newspaper, journal, magazine or other periodical publication.

(5) A person shall not be taken to contravene this section by reason only that he distributes documents to persons whose business involves the acquisition and disposal, or the holding, of securities (whether as principal or as agent), or causes documents to be distributed to such persons, or has documents in his possession for the purpose of distribution to such persons.

(6) Any person who contravenes this section shall be liable, on conviction on indictment, to imprisonment for a term not exceeding two years or to a fine not exceeding five hundred pounds or

to both such imprisonment and such fine or, on summary conviction, to imprisonment for a term not exceeding six months or to a fine not exceeding one hundred pounds or to both such imprisonment and such fine.

(7) Proceedings for an offence under this section shall not, in England, be instituted except by, or with the consent of, the Board of Trade or the Director of Public Prosecutions:

Provided that this sub-section shall not prevent the arrest, or the issue or execution of a warrant for the arrest, of any person in respect of such an offence, or the remanding, in custody or on bail, of any person charged with such an offence, notwithstanding that the necessary consent to the institution of proceedings for the offence has not been obtained.

(8) If a justice of the peace is satisfied by information on oath that there is reasonable ground for suspecting that, at any such premises as may be specified in the information, a person has any documents in his possession in contravention of this section, the justice may grant a warrant under his hand empowering any constable to enter the premises, if necessary by force, at any time or times within one month from the date of the warrant, and to search for, and seize and remove, any documents found therein which he has reasonable ground for believing to be in the possession of a person in contravention of this section.

(9) Any document seized under this section may be retained for a period of one month or, if within that period there are commenced any proceedings for an offence under this section to which the document is relevant, until the conclusion of those proceedings.

(10) Where any person is convicted of an offence under this section, the court dealing with the case may make an order authorising the destruction, or the disposal in any other specified manner, of any documents produced to the court which are shown to its satisfaction to be documents in respect of which the offence was committed:

Provided that an order under this sub-section shall not authorise the destruction of a document, or the disposal of a document in any other manner, until the conclusion of the proceedings in the matter of which the order is made.

60 & 61 Vict.
c. 30.

(11) Subject to the provisions of the last two preceding sub-sections, the Police (Property) Act, 1897 (which makes provision with respect to the disposal of property in the possession of the police), shall apply to property which has come into the possession of the police in consequence of a seizure under this section, as it applies to property which has come into the possession of the police in the circumstances mentioned in that Act.

*   *   *

APPENDIX J

The Finance Act, 1927, Section 55

with subsequent amendments

And The Finance Act, 1930, s. 42, and

The Finance Act, 1938, s. 50

I. The Finance Act, 1927, s. 55, as amended.

(1) If in connection with a scheme for the reconstruction of any company or companies or the amalgamation of any companies it is shown to the satisfaction of the Commissioners of Inland Revenue that there exist the following conditions, that is to say— *Relief from capital and transfer stamp duty in case of reconstructions or amalgamations of companies.*

(a) that a company with limited liability is to be registered, or that since the commencement of this Act a company has been incorporated by letters patent or Act of Parliament, or the nominal share capital of a company has been increased;

(b) that the company (in this section referred to as 'the transferee company') is to be registered or has been incorporated or has increased its capital with a view to the acquisition either of the undertaking of, or of not less than ninety per cent. of the issued share capital of, any particular existing company;

(c) that the consideration for the acquisition (except such part thereof as consists in the transfer to or discharge by the transferee company of liabilities of the existing company) consists as to not less than ninety per cent. thereof—

  (i) where an undertaking is to be acquired, in the issue of shares in the transferee company to the existing company or to holders of shares in the existing company; or

  (ii) where shares are to be acquired, in the issue of shares in the transferee company to the holders of shares in the existing company in exchange for the shares held by them in the existing company;

then, subject to the provisions of this section,—

(A) The nominal share capital of the transferee company, or the amount by which the capital of the transferee company has been increased, as the case may be, shall, for the purpose of computing

785

the stamp duty chargeable in respect of that capital, be treated as being reduced by either—

(i) an amount equal to the amount of the share capital of the existing company [in respect of which stamp duty has been paid],* or, in the case of the acquisition of a part of an undertaking, equal to such proportion of the said share capital as the value of that part of the undertaking bears to the whole value of the undertaking; or

(ii) the amount to be credited as paid up on the shares to be issued as such consideration as aforesaid *and on the shares, if any, to be issued to creditors of the existing company in consideration of the release of debts (whether secured or unsecured) due or accruing due to them from the existing company or of the assignment of such debts to the transferee company,*†

whichever amount is the less; and

F.A. 1928, s. 31.
(B) Stamp duty under the heading 'Conveyance or Transfer on Sale' in the First Schedule to the Stamp Act, 1891, shall not be chargeable on any instrument made for the purposes of or in connection with the transfer of the undertaking or shares, *or on any instrument made for the purposes of or in connection with the assignment to the transferee company of any debts, secured or unsecured, of the existing company,*† nor shall any such duty be
58 & 59 Vict. c. 16.
chargeable under section twelve of the Finance Act, 1895, on a copy of any Act of Parliament, or on any instrument vesting, or relating to the vesting of, the undertaking or shares in the transferee company:

Provided that—

(a) no such instrument shall be deemed to be duly stamped unless either it is stamped with the duty to which it would but for this section be liable or it has in accordance with the provisions of section twelve of the Stamp Act, 1891, been stamped with a particular stamp denoting either that it is not chargeable with any duty or that it is duly stamped; and

8 Edw. 7, c. 69.
(b) in the case of an instrument made for the purposes of or in connection with a transfer to a company within the meaning of the Companies (Consolidation) Act, 1908, the provisions of paragraph (B) of this subsection shall not apply unless the instrument is either—

(i) executed within a period of twelve months from the date of the registration of the transferee company or the date of the resolution for the increase of the nominal share capital of the transferee company, as the case may be; or

(ii) made for the purpose of effecting a conveyance or transfer in pursuance of an agreement which has been filed, or particulars of which have been filed, with the

---

* The words in brackets were deleted by Finance Act, 1930, s. 41. It was further provided by s. 41 that up to the commencement of the 1930 Act the words in brackets were deemed to have had effect as if the words 'or relief has been allowed under the provisions of this section' were added thereto.

† The revisions to the section incorporated by Finance Act, 1928, s. 31, are printed in italics.

registrar of companies within the said period of twelve months; *and (c) the foregoing provision with respect to the release and assignment of debts of the existing company shall not, except in the case of debts due to banks or to trade creditors, apply to debts which were incurred less than two years before the proper time for making a claim for exemption under this section.* *

(2) For the purposes of a claim for exemption under paragraph (B) of subsection (1) of this section, a company which has, in connection with a scheme of reconstruction or amalgamation, issued any unissued share capital shall be treated as if it had increased its nominal share capital.

(3) A company shall not be deemed to be a particular existing company within the meaning of this section unless it is provided by the memorandum of association of, or the letters patent or Act incorporating, the transferee company that one of the objects for which the company is established is the acquisition of the undertaking of, or shares in, the existing company, or unless it appears from the resolution, Act or other authority for the increase of the capital of the transferee company that the increase is authorised for the purpose of acquiring the undertaking of, or shares in, the existing company.

(4) In a case where the undertakings of or shares in two or more companies are to be acquired, the amount of the reduction to be allowed under this section in respect of the stamp duty chargeable in respect of the nominal share capital or the increase of the capital of a company shall be computed separately in relation to each of those companies.

(5) Where a claim is made for exemption under this section, the Commissioners of Inland Revenue may require the delivery to them of a statutory declaration in such form as they may direct, made in England by a solicitor of the Supreme Court or in Scotland by an enrolled law agent, and of such further evidence, if any, as the Commissioners may reasonably require.

(6) If—

(a) where any claim for exemption from duty under this section has been allowed, it is subsequently found that any declaration or other evidence furnished in support of the claim was untrue in any material particular, or that the conditions specified in subsection (1) of this section are not fulfilled in the reconstruction or amalgamation as actually carried out; or

(b) where shares in the transferee company have been issued to the existing company in consideration of the acquisition, the existing company within a period of two years from the date, as the case may be, of the registration or incorporation or of the authority for the increase of the capital, or the transferee company ceases, otherwise than in consequence of reconstruction, amalgamation or liquidation, to be the beneficial owner of the shares so issued to it; or

* The revisions to the section incorporated by Finance Act, 1928, s. 31, are printed in italics.

(c) where any such exemption has been allowed in connection with the acquisition by the transferee company of shares in another company, the transferee company within a period of two years from the date of its registration or incorporation or of the authority for the increase of its capital, as the case may be, ceases, otherwise than in consequence of reconstruction, amalgamation or liquidation, to be the beneficial owner of the shares so acquired;

the exemption shall be deemed not to have been allowed, and an amount equal to the duty remitted shall become payable forthwith, and shall be recoverable from the transferee company as a debt due to His Majesty, together with interest thereon at the rate of five per cent. per annum in the case of duty remitted under paragraph (A) of subsection (1) of this section from the date of the registration or incorporation of the transferee company or the increase of its capital, as the case may be, and in the case of duty remitted under paragraph (B) of the said subsection from the date on which it would have become chargeable if this Act had not passed.

(7) If in the case of any scheme of reconstruction or amalgamation the Commissioners of Inland Revenue are satisfied that at the proper time for making a claim for exemption from duty under subsection (1) of this section there were in existence all the necessary conditions for such exemption other than the condition that not less than ninety per cent. of the issued share capital of the existing company would be acquired by the transferee company, the Commissioners may, if it is proved to their satisfaction that not less than ninety per cent. of the issued capital of the existing company has under the scheme been acquired within a period of six months from the earlier of the two following dates, that is to say—

(a) the last day of the period of one month after the first allotment of shares made for the purposes of the acquisition; or

(b) the date on which an invitation was issued to the shareholders of the existing company to accept shares in the transferee company;

and on production of the instruments on which the duty paid has been impressed, direct repayment to be made of such an amount of duty as would have been remitted if the said condition had been originally fulfilled.

(8) In this section, unless the context otherwise requires—

References to the undertaking of an existing company include references to a part of the undertaking of an existing company:

The expression 'shares' includes stock.

II. The Finance Act, 1930, s. 42.

Relief from transfer Stamp Duty in case of transfer of property as between associated companies. 54 & 55 Vict. c. 39.

(1) Stamp duty under the heading 'Conveyance or Transfer on Sale' in the First Schedule to the Stamp Act, 1891, shall not be chargeable on an instrument to which this section applies:

Provided that no such instrument shall be deemed to be duly stamped unless either it is stamped with the duty to which it would but for this section be liable, or it has in accordance with the provisions of section twelve of the said Act been stamped with a particular stamp denoting either that it is not chargeable with any duty or that it is duly stamped.

(2) This section applies to any instrument as respects which it is shown to the satisfaction of the Commissioners of Inland Revenue—

(a) that the effect thereof is to convey or transfer a beneficial interest in property from one company with limited liability to another such company; and

(b) that either—

   (i) one of the companies is beneficial owner of not less than ninety per cent. of the issued share capital of the other company; or

   (ii) not less than ninety per cent. of the issued share capital of each of the companies is in the beneficial ownership of a third company with limited liability.

(N.B. The granting of relief under Finance Act, 1930, s. 42, is dependent upon the fulfilment of the conditions imposed by Finance Act, 1938, s. 50.)

III. The Finance Act, 1938, s. 50.

(1) Section forty-two of the Finance Act, 1930 (which relieves from stamp duty any instrument the effect whereof is to convey or transfer a beneficial interest in property from one associated company to another, in this section respectively referred to as the 'transferor' and 'transferee') shall not apply to any such instrument, unless it is shown to the satisfaction of the Commissioners of Inland Revenue that the instrument was not executed in pursuance of or in connection with an arrangement whereunder— *(Restriction of relief from Stamp Duty on transfers from one associated company to another.)*

(a) the consideration for the transfer or conveyance has to be provided directly or indirectly by a person other than a company which at the time of the execution of the instrument was associated with either the transferor or the transferee; or

(b) the beneficial interest in the property was previously conveyed or transferred directly or indirectly by such a person as aforesaid.

(2) For the purpose of this section, a company shall be deemed to be associated with another company if, but not unless, both are companies with limited liability, and either—

   (i) one of them is the beneficial owner of not less than ninety per cent. of the issued share capital of the other; or

   (ii) not less than ninety per cent. of the issued share capital of each of them is in the beneficial ownership of a third company with limited liability.

APPENDIX K

*Permission has been given for this reprint, but it does not
purport to be published 'by authority.'*

Extract from Law of Property Act,
1925

[SECTION 74]

Execution of
instruments
by or on
behalf of
corporations.

(1) In favour of a purchaser a deed shall be deemed to have been
duly executed by a corporation aggregate if its seal be affixed
thereto in the presence of and attested by its clerk, secretary or
other permanent officer or his deputy, and a member of the board
of directors, council or other governing body of the corporation,
and where a seal purporting to be the seal of a corporation has
been affixed to a deed, attested by persons purporting to be
persons holding such offices as aforesaid, the deed shall be deemed
to have been executed in accordance with the requirements of
this section, and to have taken effect accordingly.

(2) The board of directors, council or other governing body of a
corporation aggregate may, by resolution or otherwise, appoint an
agent either generally or in any particular case, to execute on
behalf of the corporation any agreement or other instrument not
under seal in relation to any matter within the powers of the
corporation.

(3) Where a person is authorised under a power of attorney or
under any statutory or other power to convey any interest in
property in the name or on behalf of a corporation sole or aggregate, he may as attorney execute the conveyance by signing the
name of the corporation in the presence of at least one witness,
and in the case of a deed by affixing his own seal, and such execution shall take effect and be valid in like manner as if the corporation had executed the conveyance.

(4) Where a corporation aggregate is authorised under a power
of attorney or under any statutory or other power to convey any
interest in property in the name or on behalf of any other person
(including another corporation), an officer appointed for that
purpose by the board of directors, council or other governing body
of the corporation by resolution or otherwise, may execute the
deed or other instrument in the name of such other person; and
where an instrument appears to be executed by an officer so
appointed, then in favour of a purchaser the instrument shall be
deemed to have been executed by an officer duly authorised.

(5) The foregoing provisions of this section apply to transactions wherever effected, but only to deeds and instruments
executed after the commencement of this Act, except that, in the

case of powers or appointments of an agent or officer, they apply whether the power was conferred or the appointment was made before or after the commencement of this Act or by this Act.

(6) Notwithstanding anything contained in this section, any mode of execution or attestation authorised by law or by practice or by the statute, charter, memorandum or articles, deed of settlement or other instrument constituting the corporation or regulating the affairs thereof, shall (in addition to the modes authorised by this section) be as effectual as if this section had not been passed.

NOTE:—

A 'corporation aggregate' is composed of many persons acting on all solemn occasions by the medium of their common seal, including joint stock companies, in contradistinction to a 'corporation sole' which is composed only of one person, such as a bishop or a beneficed clergyman, the Treasury Solicitor, or the Public Trustee.

APPENDIX L

Company Legislation in Australia, Canada, New Zealand, the Union of South Africa, Northern Rhodesia, Southern Rhodesia, the Irish Republic, India and Pakistan

AUSTRALIA

Each State and the Australian Capital Territory has its own separate legislation for regulating companies.

QUEENSLAND

Statutes.

The statutes governing company law in Queensland are as follows:—

Companies Acts, 1931–1942.
Companies Acts, 1863 to 1913, s. 6 (1) (*b*).
Companies Act Amendment Act of 1909, s. 99 (6).
Life Assurance Companies Act of 1901, ss. 6 (1) (*a*); 6 (2); 120 (3); 141 (6).
Mining Act of 1898, s. 5.
Foreign Companies Act of 1867, s. 4 (*g*).
Companies Act, 1863, ss. 4 (*a*) (ii); 5; 6 (1) (*a*); 342 (4).
Banking Companies Act of 1840, s. 139 (3).

Copies of these statutes may be obtained from the Agent General for Queensland, 409/410, Strand, London, W.C.2.

The address of the Registrar of Companies is Treasury Buildings, Queen Street, Brisbane, from whom further information can be obtained.

The following points relating to foreign companies, to which Part X of the Act applies, should be noted:

Registration of Foreign Companies.

1. The Companies Act Amendment Act, 1942, requires the registration of every company incorporated outside Queensland which establishes a place of business or commences to carry on business within the State after 1st January, 1943, or which has established such place of business and has commenced to carry on business before that date and continues to carry on that business thereafter.

2. Within one month from the date of the establishment of a place of business or the commencement to carry on business in Queensland, a foreign company must (under s. 322) file:—

(*a*) A copy certified by the Registrar of Joint Stock Companies or other proper officer of the country of incorporation of the memorandum and articles of association, deed of settlement, or other instrument declaring the constituion and functions of the company together with a copy certified

792

by such registrar or proper officer of the certificate of incorporation of the company; and if the instrument is not written in the English language, a certified translation thereof; or

(b) If the company is a company incorporated within a British Dominion other than in Queensland and the company is incorporated in the country of incorporation by an Act or Ordinance, a copy of such Act or Ordinance purporting to be printed by the King's Printer or the official printer for the government of the country of incorporation; or

(c) If the company is incorporated by royal charter, a copy of such royal charter certified by a notary public; or

(d) If the company is a company incorporated according to the laws of a country other than His Majesty's Dominions and the company is incorporated in the country of incorporation by an Act or Ordinance or by charter, a copy of such Act, Ordinance, or charter certified under the hand of a Secretary of State of the country of incorporation and under the seal (if any) of his office or certified under the hand of a British ambassador, envoy, minister, chargé d'affaires, secretary of embassy or legation, consul-general, consul, vice-consul, acting consul, pro-consul, consular agent, or notary public and under the seal of his office, and if the instrument is not written in the English language a certified translation thereof; or

(e) Such other evidence of incorporation as the Registrar may require,

together with, in any of the four last-mentioned cases, a copy of every deed of settlement or other instrument declaring the constitution and functions of the company.

(f) A list of the directors of the company in the country in which it is incorporated, and also of any local directors in this State, containing with respect to the directors such particulars as are required by the Act to be given of directors of a local company. Where there are local directors in the State, a memorandum stating the powers of the local directors is required.

(g) A memorandum of appointment under the seal of the company or executed in such manner as to be binding on the company, and, in either case, verified in the prescribed manner stating the name and address of some one or more persons resident in this State authorised to accept on behalf of the company service of process and any notices required to be served on the company, which person or persons shall be deemed to be the agent or agents of such company for the purposes of this Act. The memorandum of appointment required by this paragraph may be by power of attorney.

(h) Notice of the situation of its registered office and of the days and hours during which it is accessible to the public, and of the place of abode or of business of the agent of the company.

(i) A statutory declaration made and signed by the agent of the company as prescribed in the Act. (Form A, Schedule 12.)

Alterations to Constitution.

Within three months (or such further time as the Registrar of Companies may allow in a particular case) of the making of any alterations in:—

(a) the charter, statutes or memorandum and articles of association or like document;

(b) the directors of the company, or the particulars contained in the list of directors;

(c) the names and places of abode or business of the persons authorised to accept service on behalf of the company;

(d) the situation of the company's registered office or the hours when it is accessible to the public; or

(e) the name of the company;

a return must be filed, setting out particulars of such alterations [s. 324 (2)].

Balance Sheets.

Every company to which Part X of the Act applies (i.e. every company incorporated outside the State) shall, at least once in every year, and at intervals of not more than fifteen months, file with the Registrar a true copy, signed by the agent, of the last general balance sheet of the company, and post up, and keep posted up until the filing of a true copy of the next following balance sheet, in a conspicuous place at the registered office of the company, a true copy of such balance sheet signed as aforesaid.

Such balance sheet shall be in such form and contain the particulars required by s. 327 of the Act.

The provisions of the Act respecting the filing of the balance sheet do not apply to a company incorporated in Great Britain or in any of the British Dominions or possessions as a private or proprietary company, which, by the law of the place in which it is incorporated, is not required to publish its balance sheet or lodge the same in a public office [s. 327 (3)].

Publicising Name of Company.

Every foreign company must conspicuously exhibit on every place where it carries on business in the State, the name of the company and the country in which the company is incorporated. It must also cause the name of the company and of the country in which it is incorporated to be stated in legible characters in all billheads, letter-paper, notices, advertisements and other official publications of the company. If the liability of the members of the company is limited it must, unless the last word of the name of the company is the word 'limited,' cause notice of the fact to be stated in legible characters in every prospectus inviting subscriptions in Queensland for its shares or debentures, in all billheads, letter paper, notices, advertisements, and other official publications of the company in the State, and to be affixed on every place where it carries on its business (s. 330).

In every prospectus inviting subscriptions for shares or debentures in a foreign company which is circulated in Queensland, there must also be set forth the name of the company, and the situation of its registered office in Queensland and country in which the company is incorporated [s. 330 (a)].

If any foreign company which has been registered under Part X of the Act ceases to carry on business in the State, it must immediately file notice of the fact with the Registrar and from the date of such notice the obligation of the company to file any document with the Registrar ceases (s. 340). *Notice of Discontinuance of Business.*

NEW SOUTH WALES

The statutes governing company law in New South Wales are as follows:—

Companies Act, 1936 (No. 33) (The Principal Act).
Assurance Companies Management Act, 1938 (No. 2).
Companies Amendment Act, 1940 (No. 56).

Copies of these statutes may be obtained from the Official Secretary, New South Wales Government Office, 56/57, Strand, London, W.C.2.

Further information may be obtained from the Registrar General at Chancery Square, Sydney, New South Wales.

The following points relating to foreign companies (to which Part VI of the Act applies) should be noted:

1. Section 61 of the Principal Act requires the registration of every company incorporated outside New South Wales which establishes a place of business or commences to carry on business within the State after 1st January, 1937, or which has established such place of business or has commenced to carry on business before that date and continues to carry on that business thereafter. *Registration of Foreign Companies.*

2. Within one month from the date of the establishment of a place of business or the commencement to carry on business in New South Wales, a foreign company must (under s. 62) file:—

(a) A certified copy of the certificate of incorporation. This is deemed to be duly certified if certified in the manner provided by sub-s. (2) of the s. 32 of the Evidence Act, 1898, and in the case of a document to which that section does not apply, if it purports to be certified by an official of the government of the country in which the company is incorporated, holding or purporting to hold a similar office to that of a registrar or an assistant registrar of companies.

(b) A certified copy of the charter, statute or memorandum and articles of the company, or other instrument constituting or defining the constitution of the company, and, if the instrument is not written in the English language, a certified translation thereof.

The instrument constituting or defining the constitution of the foreign company should be:—

(i) duly certified as a true copy by an official of the government to whose custody the original is committed; or

(ii) duly certified as a true copy by a notary public; or

(iii) duly declared to be a true copy by a director or the manager or secretary of the company before a notary public, or before any person authorised to administer an oath under the law of the country where the declaration is made.

(c) A list of the directors of the company in the country in which it is incorporated, and also of any local directors in the State, containing with respect to the directors such particulars as are required by the Act to be given of directors of a local company.

(d) Where there are local directors in the State, a memorandum stating the powers of the local directors or a certified copy of any instrument conferring and defining such powers. The certification should be by a notary public or by a director or the manager or secretary of the company before a notary public, or before any person authorised to administer an oath under the law of the country in which the copy is so certified.

(e) A certified copy of a memorandum of appointment of agent or of a power of attorney under the seal of the company or executed in such a manner as to be binding on the company, authorising the agent to accept service of process and any notices required to be served on the company.

The documents must be verified by a statutory declaration made by the agent appointed by the memorandum of appointment or power of attorney, or by a director or manager or secretary of the company, in or to the effect of Form 16 in the Companies Regulations, 1936.

Where the declaration is made outside New South Wales it must be declared before a notary public or other person authorised by the law of the country, where the declaration is made, to administer oaths.

(f) Notice of the situation of its registered office in New South Wales.

(g) A statutory declaration made and signed by the agent of the company as prescribed in the Act. (Form A, Schedule 5.)

Alteration to Constitution. Within three months (or such further time as the Registrar-General may allow in a particular case) of the making of any alterations in:—

(a) the memorandum and articles of association or like document;

(b) the directors of the company, or the particulars contained in the list of directors;

(c) the names and places of abode or business of the persons authorised to accept service on behalf of the company;

(d) the situation of the company's registered office and the hours and days when it is accessible to the public; or

(e) the name of the company;

a return in Form 17 of the Companies Regulations, 1936, must be filed, setting out particulars of such alterations [s. 67 (1)].

A return pursuant to paragraphs (d) and (e) is required to be advertised by the Registrar-General at the cost of the company [s. 67 (2)].

Foreign companies are required to make out a balance sheet **Balance Sheets.** in every calendar year in such form and containing such particulars and including such documents, as, under the provisions of the Act, a local company is required to make out and lay before its general meeting of members. Within three months of the making out of the balance sheet of a foreign company a copy must be filed with the Registrar-General [s. 68 (1)].

If the balance sheet is not written in the English language, a certified translation must be annexed [s. 68 (2)].

The provisions of the Act respecting the filing of the balance sheet do not apply to a company incorporated in Great Britain, or in any of the British Dominions or possessions as a private or proprietary company, which, by the law of the place in which it is incorporated, is not required to publish its balance sheet. The provision also does not apply where the only business carried on in New South Wales by the foreign company is the selling of goods, wares, and merchandise by an agent [s. 68 (3) (4)].

Every foreign company must conspicuously exhibit, on every **Publicising** place where it carries on business in New South Wales, the name **Name of** of the company and the country in which the company is in- **Company.** corporated. It must also cause the name of the company and of the country in which it is incorporated to be stated in legible characters in all billheads, letter-paper, notices, advertisements and other official publications of the company. If the liability of the members of the company is limited it must, unless the last word of the name of the company is the word 'limited,' cause notice of the fact to be stated in legible characters in every prospectus inviting subscriptions in New South Wales for its shares or debentures, in all billheads, letter-paper, notices, advertisements and other official publications of the company in New South Wales, and to be affixed on every place where it carries on its business (s. 69).

In every prospectus inviting subscriptions for shares or debentures in a foreign company which is circulated in New South Wales, there must also be set forth the name of the company, and the situation of its registered office in New South Wales and the country in which the company is incorporated [s. 69 (a)].

The provisions of the Act in regard to the registration of certain **Registration of** classes of mortages or charges in relation to local companies **Foreign** apply with equal force to foreign companies where such mort- **Companies.** gages or charges have been created over the property in New South Wales after 1st January, 1937 (s. 198).

If any foreign company which has been registered under **Notice of Dis-** Part VI of the Act ceases to carry on business in New South **continuance of** Wales, it must immediately file notice of this fact with the **Business.** Registrar-General, and from the date of such notice the obligation of the company to file any document with the Registrar-General ceases [s. 72 (1)].

SOUTH AUSTRALIA

The statutes governing company law in South Australia are as follows:—

The Companies Acts, 1934–1939.
Life Assurance Companies Amendment Act, 1931.
Life Assurance Companies Amendment Act, 1899.
Life Assurance Companies Act, 1882.
Banking Companies Amendment Act, 1919.
Banking Companies Act, 1863.

Copies of these statutes may be obtained from the Agent General for South Australia, South Australia House, Marble Arch, London, W.1.

Further information may be obtained from the Registrar of Companies, 13, Grenfell Street, Adelaide, South Australia.

The following points relating to foreign companies (to which Part XII of the Act applies) should be noted:

Registration of Mortgages or Charges.
1. Section 351 of the principal Act requires the registration of every company incorporated outside South Australia which establishes a place of business or commences to carry on business within the State after 1st March, 1935, or which has established such place of business or has commenced to carry on business before that date and continues to carry on that business thereafter.

2. Within one month from the date of the commencement to carry on business in South Australia a foreign company must (under s. 352) file:—

(a) A certified copy of the certificate of incorporation or other document of similar effect.

(b) A certified copy of the charter, statute, or memorandum and articles of the company, or other instrument constituting or defining the constitution of the company, and if the instrument is not written in the English language a certified translation thereof.

(c) A list of directors in the State or country in which it is incorporated and of local directors (if any), giving such particulars as are required by the Act to be given of directors of a local company. Where there are local directors, a memorandum stating the powers of the local directors must be filed.

(d) A verified copy of the memorandum of appointment of agent or of a power of attorney under the seal of the company (or executed in such manner as to be binding on the company) authorising the agent to accept service of process and any notices required to be served on the company.

(e) Notice of the situation of the registered office.

(f) A statutory declaration by the agent, as prescribed in the Act. (Form A, Eleventh Schedule).

Where any alteration is made in:—

(a) the charter, statutes, or memorandum and articles of the company or any such instrument as aforesaid; or

(b) the directors of the company, or the particulars contained in the list of the directors; or

(c) the names or addresses of the persons authorised to accept service on behalf of the company; or

(d) the situation of the company's registered office, or the hours when such office is accessible to the public,

the company must, within one month after the date on which particulars of the alteration if despatched with due diligence could in due course of post have been received in South Australia file with the Registrar a return containing particulars of the alteration (s. 359).

Registered foreign companies are required to file with the   Registrar a copy of their last general balance sheet every year and at intervals of not more than fifteen months. This balance sheet must be signed by the agent and it must be conspicuously displayed at the registered office of the company. The particulars to be included in the documents attaching to such balance sheets must be those in accordance with the law applicable to such company in its place of incorporation, but the Registrar may require the balance sheet to be in such form and include such documents as are required of balance sheets of local companies. These provisions as to balance sheets do not apply to any company which, by the law in force in the country or State where it is incorporated, is not required to publish its balance sheet (s. 358).

Every company to which Part XII of the Act applies (i.e. every   company registered outside the State) must under s. 360:—

(1) in every prospectus inviting subscriptions for its shares or debentures in South Australia, state the country in which the company is incorporated; and

(2) cause the name of the company and of the country in which the company is incorporated:

(a) to be affixed on every place where it carries on business; and

(b) to be stated in legible characters in all billheads and letter papers and in all notices, advertisements, and other official publications of the company; and

(3) if the liability of the members of the company is limited, cause notice of that fact:—

(a) to be stated in legible characters in every such prospectus as aforesaid, and in all billheads, letter-paper, notices, advertisements, and other official publications of the company in the State; and

(b) to be affixed on every place where it carries on its business:

Provided that in the case of a company to which s. 358 of this Act (companies to file balance sheets) applies, it shall be sufficient compliance with the provisions of paragraphs 2 (b) and 3 (a) if such company duly complies with the provisions of that section.

Registration of Mortgages or Charges. The provisions of the Act in regard to the registration of certain classes of mortgages or charges in relation to local companies, apply with equal force to foreign companies where such mortgages or charges have been created over the property in South Australia after 1st March, 1935 (s. 113).

Notice of Discontinuance of Business. Before any foreign company which has been registered under Part XII of the Act voluntarily ceases to carry on business in the State it must give at least three months' notice of its intention to do so to the Registrar and advertise the same in the Government *Gazette* and in one South Australian daily newspaper circulating in Adelaide (s. 361).

TASMANIA

The statutes governing company law in Tasmania are as follows:—

> The Companies Act, 1920, No. 66. As amended by
>> The Companies Act, 1922, No. 77.
>> The Companies Act, 1923, No. 23.
>> The Companies Act, 1927, No. 89.
>> The Companies Act, 1935, No. 23.
>> The Companies Act, 1939, No. 52.
>> The Companies Act, 1940, No. 56.
>> The Companies Act, 1945, No. 45.
> Mining Companies Act, 1884, No. 15.
> The Co-operative Industrial Societies Act, 1928, No. 49.
> The Criminal Code Act, 1924, No. 69. Also amends the Companies Act, 1920.

Copies of these statutes may be obtained from the Agent General for Tasmania, 457, Strand, London, W.C.2.

Further information may be obtained from the Registrar of Companies at Crown Law Office, Hobart, Tasmania.

The following points relating to foreign companies (to which Part X of the Act applies) should be noted:

Registration of Companies Incorporated outside Tasmania. 1. Every company formed or incorporated outside Tasmania, which carries on business in Tasmania, must register under Part X of the Companies Act, 1920, s. 264. A company is not deemed to carry on business in Tasmania, by reason only of investing its funds or other property in the State. 'Carrying on business' includes establishing or using a share transfer or share registration office. A company formed and incorporated in the United Kingdom or in a British possession, which has duly registered as a 'foreign' company in the State, has the same power to hold land as if it were a company incorporated under the Companies Act of the State (s. 265).

2. Within one month from the date of commencement to carry on business in Tasmania, a foreign company must, under s. 264 (1), file:—

> (a) A certified copy of the charter, memorandum and articles of association or other instrument constituting or defining the constitution of the company, duly certified as a true copy by a notary public, or by an official of the government to whose custody the original is committed.

(b) List of directors of the company in the State or country in which it is incorporated, and of any local directors.

(c) The name and address of some person resident in Tasmania authorised to accept service of process, etc., who will be the registered agent of the company in Tasmania.

(d) A statutory declaration as prescribed by the Act (Second Schedule).

See sub-ss. (6) and (15) of s. 264, for special provisions relating to trustee and executor companies.

In the event of any alteration being made in any instrument *Alterations to* constituting or defining the constitution of a company, or in the *Constitution.* directors, or in the name or address of the agent of the company there must be filed with the Registrar a notice of the alteration. [s. 264 (1)].

A registered foreign company must, at least once in every year *Balance Sheets.* and at intervals of not more than fifteen months, file with the Registrar a true copy, signed by the agent, of the last general balance sheet of the company prepared prior to such filing. A copy of such balance sheet must be posted in a conspicuous place at the address of the agent and kept so posted until the filing of the next balance sheet. These provisions do not apply to the life insurance business of any company which is subject to the Life Assurance Companies Act, 1874, or to any proprietary company [s. 264 (5)]. A foreign company which does not do any business other than selling goods, wares, or merchandise through an agent, is not required to file or post or keep posted its balance sheet [s. 264 (13)].

Every foreign company with the word 'limited' as part of its *Publicising* name, must state the country of incorporation in every prospectus *Name of* inviting subscriptions for its shares or debentures in Tasmania *Company.* [s. 264 (9)].

When a foreign company ceases to carry on business in Tas- *Ceasing to* mania it must, within three months of its ceasing to carry on such *Carry on* *Business.* business, file with the Registrar a notice that it has ceased to carry on business [s. 264 (16)].

A foreign company may be wound up in the same way as if it *Liquidation.* were an unregistered company within the meaning of Part IX of the Companies Act, 1920. This does not apply to a foreign company which carries on the business of selling goods, wares or merchandise through an agent [s. 264 (17)].

VICTORIA

The statutes governing company law in Victoria are as follows:

Companies Act, 1938, No. 4602.
Investment Companies Act, 1938, No. 4621.
Companies (Special Investigations) Act, 1940, No. 4790.
Registrar General's Fees Act, 1928, No. 3263.

Copies of these statutes may be obtained from the Government Printer, Government Printing Offices, Melbourne: reference may be made to office copies of the statutes at the office of the Agent General for Victoria, Melbourne Place, Strand, London, W.C.2.

Further information may be obtained from Registrar-General and Registrar of Titles of Victoria, 283, Queen Street, Melbourne.

The following points relating to companies incorporated outside Victoria should be noted:—

1. Every company or society formed or incorporated outside Victoria, which after the 1st May, 1939, establishes a place of business within Victoria, and every company or society formed or incorporated outside Victoria which had before such date established a place of business within Victoria and continues to have an established place of business within the State, must register under Division 12 of Part I of the 1938 Act (s. 343). It should be noted that the Act does not use the word 'foreign' when referring to such companies. For the sake of convenience, however, the word 'foreign' will be used in that context in these notes. 'Place of business' includes a share transfer or share registration office [s. 352 (1)].

A company by reason only of investing its funds or other property in Victoria, is not deemed to have established a place of business in Victoria, within the meaning of Division 12 of Part I [s. 352 (2)].

2. Within one month from the date of the establishment of a place of business within Victoria, a 'foreign' company must register under Division 12 of Part I of the Act, and file with the Registrar-General for registration:—

(a) a certified copy of the certificate of incorporation or a document of similar effect;

(b) a certified copy of the charter, statute or memorandum and articles of the company or society or other instrument constituting or defining the constitution of the company or society and if the instrument is not written in the English language a certified translation thereof;

(c) a list of the directors of the company or society containing such particulars with respect to the directors as are required to be contained in the register of the directors of a local company;

(d) The name and address of some person resident in Victoria authorised to accept on behalf of the company or society, service of process and any notices required to be served on the company or society, which person is deemed to be the agent of the company;

(e) notice of the situation of its registered office and of the days and hours during which it is accessible to the public; and

(f) a statutory declaration by the agent (see Eleventh Schedule under Part 14).

The instrument constituting or defining the constitution of the foreign company should be:—

(i) duly certified as a true copy by an official of the government to whose custody the original is committed; or

(ii) duly certified as a true copy by a notary public; or

   (iii) duly declared to be a true copy by a director or the manager or secretary of the company on oath before a notary public.

Where any alteration is made in:— Alterations to
Constitution.

   (a) the charter, statutes or memorandum and articles or like instrument; or

   (b) the directors of the company or society or the particulars contained in the list of directors; or

   (c) the address of the person authorised to accept service on behalf of the company or society; or

   (d) the name of the company or society;

the company or society must, within the prescribed time, file with the Registrar-General a return in Form 60 of the Regulations under the Companies Act, 1938, setting out the particulars of the alteration (s. 346).

Notice of any change in the situation of the registered office or of the days or hours during which it is accessible to the public, must, within twenty-one days after the date of the change, be filed with the Registrar-General [s. 344 (2) (b)].

A foreign company must keep proper books of accounts in Accounts and
Balance Sheets. Victoria, in which there must appear full, true and complete accounts of its affairs and transactions in Victoria. These books must be kept at the principal place of business in Victoria or at such other place in Victoria as the company or society thinks fit, must at all times be open to inspection by the directors or agent of the company, and (for the purposes of any law relating to the investigation of the affairs or transactions of such companies in Victoria) by a law officer or any person appointed by him [s. 347 (1) (2)].

A balance sheet must be made out at least once in every calendar year and at intervals of not more than fifteen months. A copy of this balance sheet must be filed with the Registrar-General and a further copy posted up in a conspicuous place at the registered address of the company [s. 347 (3)].

The particulars to be shown in the balance sheet and the documents to be attached thereto must conform with the law of the place where the foreign company is incorporated. A statutory declaration stating that such law has been complied with must accompany the balance sheet. The Registrar-General may, in any case in which he thinks proper, require the balance sheet to contain certain particulars and include certain documents, but he cannot require the foreign company to do more than is required of a local company [s. 347 (5)].

The above provisions relating to particulars in a balance sheet, documents to be attached thereto and the filing of the same, do not apply to any proprietary company, which, by the law in force in the country or State where it is incorporated, is not required to publish its balance sheet. Under the Act, a 'proprietary' company for this purpose means:—

    Any company, which, by the law in force in the country or State where it was formed or incorporated, is, in regard to companies in that country or State which are not proprietary companies, in a substantially similar position to that in which a proprietary company incorporated in Victoria is in regard to companies incorporated under this Part or any corresponding previous enactment, which are not proprietary companies; and includes a private company [s. 347 (6) (*b*)].

Where the company is a proprietary company formed or incorporated in Great Britain or any part of His Majesty's Dominions, or Ireland, and is registered as a 'foreign' company in Victoria, it must in a similar manner to a local company make and file an annual return and summary [s. 347 (7)].

Publicising Name of Company.

Every 'foreign' company to which Division 12 applies, must:—

(*a*)   in every prospectus inviting subscriptions for its shares or debentures in Victoria state the name of the company or society, the situation of its registered office in Victoria, and the country in which the company or society is formed or incorporated;

(*b*)   conspicuously exhibit on every place of business established by it in Victoria the name of the company or society and the country in which the company or society is formed or incorporated;

(*c*)   cause the name of the company or society and of the country in which the company or society is formed or incorporated to be stated in legible characters in all billheads and letter-paper and in all notices, advertisements and other official publications of the company or society; and

(*d*)   if the liability of the members of the company or society is limited (unless the last word of the name of the company or society is the word 'limited'), cause notice of the fact to be stated in legible characters in every such prospectus as aforesaid and in all billheads, letter-paper, notices, advertisements and other official publications of the company or society in Victoria and to be affixed on every place of business established by it in Victoria (s. 348).

Registration of Mortgages or Charges.

The provisions of the Act (Division 4) in regard to the registration of certain classes of mortgages or charges in relation to local companies apply to a 'foreign' company which has at the time of the creation of the charge or the acquisition of the property (over which the charge was given) an established place of business in Victoria [s. 79 (11)].

Notice of Discontinuance of Business.

If any company or society to which this Division applies ceases to have an established place of business in Victoria, it shall forthwith file notice of the fact with the Registrar-General, and as from the date on which notice is so filed the obligation of the company or society to file any document (not being a document that ought to have been filed before that date) with the Registrar-General shall cease, and the Registrar-General shall forthwith remove the name of such company or society from the register [s. 350 (1)]. Section 350 makes provision for liquidation, removal from register and striking off register, and s. 351 provides penalties for infringement of the provisions of Division 12.

The statutes governing company law in Western Australia are as follows:—

Companies Acts, 1943–1949.

Copies of these statutes may be obtained from the Agent General for Western Australia, 115/116, Strand, London, W.C.2.

Further information may be obtained from the Agent General for Western Australia and from the Registrar of Companies, Supreme Court, St. George's Terrace, Perth, Western Australia.

1. The principal Act requires the registration of every company incorporated outside Western Australia which establishes a place of business or commences to carry on business within the State after 31st December, 1947, or which has established such place of business or has commenced to carry on business before that date and continues to carry on that business thereafter. 'Carrying on business' includes establishing or using a share transfer or share registration office. *Registration of Companies Incorporated outside Western Australia.*

2. Within 28 days from the date of commencement to carry on business in Western Australia, a foreign company must register under this Part and file under s. 329:—

(a) A certified copy of the certificate of incorporation or document of similar effect.

(b) A certified copy of the charter, statute or memorandum and articles of the company, or other instrument constituting or defining the constitution of the company, and, if the instrument is not written in the English language, a certified translation thereof.

A copy of the charter, statute or memorandum and articles of a foreign company or other instrument constituting or defining its constitution shall be deemed to be certified as required by s. 329 of the Act if it is:—

(i) duly certified as a true copy by an official of the government to whose custody the original is committed; or

(ii) duly certified as a true copy by a notary public; or

(iii) duly declared to be a true copy by a director or the manager or secretary of the company.

(c) A list of the directors of the company normally resident in the Commonwealth of Australia and of the directors in the State, if any, containing such particulars with respect to the directors as are by the Act required to be contained with respect to directors in the register of the directors of the company.

(d) A memorandum of appointment under the seal of the company or executed in such manner as to be binding on the company and, in either case, verified in the prescribed manner stating the name and address of some one or more persons resident in the State authorised to accept on behalf of the company service of process and any notices required to be served on the company, which person shall be deemed to be the agent of such company for the purposes of the Act. The memorandum of appointment required by this paragraph may be by power of attorney. Where the appointment is made by some person duly authorised in manner aforesaid in that behalf by the company an original copy of the deed granting such power or authority shall be produced to the Registrar, who shall retain the same or a copy thereof certified under the hand and seal of the Registrar to be a true copy, and such copy shall for all purposes be deemed to be an original.

(e) Notice of the situation of its registered office in Western Australia.

(f) A statutory declaration made and signed by the agent of the company in the form contained in the Form D of the Thirteenth Schedule to the Act, or to the like effect.

Alterations to Constitution.

Alterations in the following must, under s. 335, be advised to the Registrar :—

(a) the charter, statutes, memorandum and articles of association or like document;

(b) the directors of the company, or the particulars contained in the list of directors;

(c) the names or addresses of the persons authorised to accept service on behalf of the company;

(d) the situation of its registered office or the hours on which such office is accessible to the public;

(e) the name of the company;

(f) the nominal capital of the company.

Registered Office.

Every company must have a registered office which must be accessible to the public at least twice a week for at least four hours between the hours of 8 a.m. and 10 p.m. (s. 330). All communications and notices to the company may be addressed to the company at its registered office. Notice of the situation of the registered office and the days and hours on which it is open to the public and of any change therein must be filed with the Registrar before commencement of business by the company or within the prescribed time of the change (s. 330).

On the registration of a foreign company a certificate is issued, and this certificate is *prima facie* evidence on all legal proceedings that the company is formed and incorporated and is duly registered under Part XI of the Act, that the person named as the agent, is the agent of the company in the State, and that the address of such agent is situate as therein stated and of all matters therein mentioned (s. 331). On every appointment by the company of a new agent, or on the filing of a notice of alteration in the name of the company or the address of the person authorised to accept service on behalf of the company, or the situation of the registered office, a fresh certificate of registration altered to meet the case is issued by the Registrar.

Power to Hold Land.

Any company incorporated within the British dominions and which is registered in the State has the same power to hold land as a company incorporated in the State (s. 332).

Under s. 334 of the Act every company to which Part XI of the Balance Sheets. Act applies must at least once in every year and at intervals not exceeding 15 months file with the Registrar a true copy, signed by the agent, of the last general balance sheet of the company prepared prior to the filing.

Such balance sheet shall be in such form and contain such particulars and include such documents as the company is required to make out and lay before the company in general meeting by the law for the time being applicable to such company in the country or State where it was incorporated, and shall be accompanied by a statutory declaration in a form prescribed by regulations that such law has been complied with: provided that the Registrar may, in any case in which he thinks proper, require the balance sheet to be in such form and to contain such particulars and to include documents of such a nature as the Registrar requires by notice in writing to the company, but this proviso shall not authorise the Registrar to require a balance sheet to contain any particulars or include any documents other than are required in the balance sheet of any class of public company under Part IV of the Act.

If any such balance sheet is not written in the English language, there shall be annexed to it a certified translation thereof.

This section shall not apply to any company, which by the law in force in the country or State where it was incorporated is not required to file with a Registrar its balance sheet.

Every foreign company must conspicuously exhibit on every Publicising Name of Company. place where it carries on business in Western Australia the name of the company and the country in which the company is incorporated. It must also cause the name of the company and the country in which it is incorporated to be stated in legible characters in all billheads, letter-paper, notices and other official publications of the company. If the liability of the members of the company is limited it must, unless the last word of the name of the company is the word 'limited,' cause notice of the fact to be stated in legible characters in every prospectus inviting subscriptions in Western Australia for its shares or debentures, in all billheads, letter-paper, notices and other official publications of the company in Western Australia, and to be affixed on every place where it carries on its business (s. 336). It is, however, provided that with regard to stating the name of the company in legible letters on all billheads, letter-paper, notices and other official publications of the company that s. 336 shall be deemed to have been complied with if the company is one to which s. 334 applies, and if it has lodged a balance sheet under that section.

In every prospectus inviting subscriptions for shares or debentures in a foreign company which is circulated in Western Australia, there must be set forth the name of the company and the country in which the company is incorporated.

The provisions of the Act relating to charges extend to charges Registration of Mortgages or Charges. on property in Western Australia which are created, and to charges on property in Western Australia which is acquired after the 31st December, 1947, by a foreign company (s. 98).

(1) Before any company registered under this Part shall Notice of Discontinuance of Business. voluntarily cease to carry on business in this State it shall give at least three months' notice of the intention so to do.

Such notice shall be filed with the Registrar and advertised in three consecutive issues of the *Government Gazette* and in one daily newspaper published in Western Australia and circulating in Perth.

(2) Upon being satisfied that three months have expired since the filing and the last publication of the notice referred to in sub-section (1) of this section, the Registrar shall remove the name of the company from the register.

(3) Until removal of the name of the company from the register any process or notice may be served on the company as provided by section three hundred and thirty-three of the Act (s. 337).

Liquidation and Dissolution. If a foreign company goes into liquidation or is dissolved in the country or State of its incorporation, the person appointed as its agent under s. 329 of the Act must within seven days of receiving notice of the liquidation or dissolution, as the case may be, give notice thereof to the Registrar (ss. 338 and 339). In any case where the Registrar has reason to believe that a company has ceased to carry on business in the State, he must take action under s. 340.

Agent. The position of the person appointed as agent of the company under s. 329 is governed by the provisions of ss. 342 to 344, inclusive, of the Act.

Inspection. Every document deposited with the Registrar under the provisions of Part XI of the Act is open to inspection by any person on the payment of one shilling.

Local Register. Section 347 of the Act (as amended by s. 14 of the Companies Act Amendment Act, 1947) provides that every company carrying on business in the State and having any shareholders who are resident in the State, must within two months of the deposit in the office of the Registrar of the memorandum of appointment of the agent under s. 329 of the Act, open and keep a local register of members. This local register must be kept in the manner provided by Part 4 of the Act in the case of the register of members. There are heavy penalties for non-compliance with this provision. The registration of transfers is regulated by ss. 348 to 352, inclusive, of the Act. The local register is open to inspection by members free of charge, and by non-members on the payment of a sum which shall not exceed one shilling. Both members and non-members are entitled to copies of the local register on the payment of one shilling for every hundred words. The local register may be closed for a period not exceeding 28 days in any year, but not for longer than 14 days at any one time.

Notice of dividends must be given to all shareholders on the local register at their registered address and by advertisement within 14 days of the declaration of such dividends (s. 357).

On the reconstruction of a foreign company by a sale by the liquidator of the company of its assets, the liquidator is bound to reserve for shareholders on the local register a proportion of the cash consideration passing to the reconstructing company, and notice of such reservation must forthwith be published in the *Gazette*. The liquidator must forward to the Registrar a statutory declaration stating that this has been done (s. 358).

Where a foreign company issues debentures or additional shares to be received or taken up by its members, the company is bound to reserve a part of such issue proportionate to the interests of shareholders on the local register. Notice of such reservation must be published in the same manner as in the case of reconstruction (*supra*) (s. 359). A similar reservation must be made where a foreign company carrying on business in the State has passed any resolution or entered into any arrangement whereby any right or option accrues to the members of the company (s. 360). In the case of non-observation of the provisions of s. 359 or 360 and if a statutory declaration has not been made and filed by the company in the manner prescribed by these sections, the company is debarred from bringing or maintaining, either directly or indirectly, any action, set-off or counterclaim, or other legal proceeding and shall so remain debarred until the statutory declaration has been filed.

Section 361 provides for general penalties for the non-compliance with the provisions of Part XI of the Act.

AUSTRALIAN CAPITAL TERRITORY

The statutes governing company law in the Federal Capital Territory are as follows:—

Companies Ordnance, 1931–1938.
Companies (Liquidation) Ordnance, 1935–1938, as amended by No. 14 of 1936 and by No. 28 of 1938.
Companies (Receiver and Manager) Ordnance, 1934.
Companies (Investigation of Affairs) Ordnance, 1934–1936, as amended by No. 23 of 1936 and by No. 25 of 1936.

Copies of these statutes may be obtained from the Intelligence Department, Australia House, Strand, London, W.C.2.

Further information may be obtained from the Registrar of Companies in Canberra and the Intelligence Department, Australia House, Strand, London, W.C.2.

CANADA

Reference may be made to 'Canadian Secretarial Practice,' published in Toronto by Sir Isaac Pitman & Sons (Canada) Limited, under the aegis of the Council of the Chartered Institute of Secretaries.

In Canada, the Dominion Government and each of the nine Provincial governments has the power to create companies. In general, a Dominion company is empowered to carry on business in any part of Canada, whereas a Provincial company is restricted to the province wherein it was incorporated unless it obtains a licence as a foreign or extra-provincial company from every other province into which its operations extend. Between certain provinces (*i.e.* Ontario and Quebec) there are reciprocal agreements in virtue of which such licences are not required.

A Dominion charter is usually advisable for a company formed for the purpose of carrying on business throughout Canada or in foreign countries. Similarly, it is generally to the advantage of a foreign company which wishes to extend its operations throughout Canada to be re-incorporated in Canada with a Dominion charter. Otherwise, it must qualify as a foreign or extra-provincial company in each province where it does business. The total fees may easily exceed the cost of a Dominion incorporation and it will have at best a string of powers as granted by each province. Provincial incorporation is cheaper and usually advisable where the company's activities are to be confined to a single province. Mining and other companies which exploit the resources of a particular province usually obtain provincial charters.

A Dominion company may be subject to certain provincial laws and regulations but these cannot be enforced so as to frustrate the general Dominion powers. A province has the right to impose income and other direct taxes. It may require Dominion companies to register, to file reports and to take out certain licences, such as a mortmain licence for the holding of land in that Province.

Under both the Dominion and the Provincial laws, companies may be incorporated either by a special Act of Parliament or in virtue of the provisions of a general Companies Act. Most commercial and trading companies are incorporated pursuant to a general Companies Act. The system of incorporation by Letters Patent exists under the Dominion Companies Act and under the Companies Acts of Quebec, Ontario, New Brunswick, Prince Edward Island and Manitoba. Companies are incorporated by registration of a memorandum of association under the Companies Acts of Nova Scotia, Saskatchewan, Alberta and British Columbia.

Canadian commerce and industry are somewhat concentrated in Ontario and Quebec, and the large majority of its companies is incorporated under the Dominion Companies Act, the Ontario Companies Act or the Quebec Companies Act.

Dominion Legislation

The principal statutes affecting Dominion companies are, The Companies Act, 1934, The Winding Up Act and The Bankruptcy Act. Railways, banks, insurance, loan and trust companies are governed by special legislation. The vast majority of Dominion companies comes under Part I of The Companies Act, 1934.

The official in charge of Dominion companies is the Secretary of State, Ottawa.

Copies of all Federal and Provincial statutes may be consulted at any time at the office of the High Commissioner for Canada, Canada House, London, S.W.1. Information as to fees, etc., and copies of Acts and amendments can be obtained from the Secretary of State, Ottawa, for Dominion incorporated companies, or from the Provincial Secretaries for the various Provinces for corporations under Provincial law. The official title and address of the Registrar of Companies in each province is the Registrar of Companies, Department of the Provincial Secretary, Government of........................ (insert the appropriate province, followed by the name of the capital city of that province).

The Dominion Companies Act

The (Dominion) Companies Act, 1934 (24–25 Geo. V. c. 33), as amended by the Companies Act Amendment Act, 1935 (25–26 Geo. V. c. 55), in most respects follows the English Companies Act, 1929.

The Dominion Companies Act, as amended, differs from the English Companies Act, 1929, in some respects, the more important of which are set out below.

Incorporation is obtained by application for letters patent to the Secretary of State, by not less than three persons. This procedure does not apply to companies whose objects include construction of railways, telegraph or telephone lines, or the business of an insurance, trust, loan or banking company (s. 5). The applicants, who must be over the age of 21 years, must file in the Department of the Secretary of State an application in accordance with Form 1 in the Schedule to the Act, as well as a memorandum of agreement in duplicate, in accordance with Form 2 of the Schedule, signed and sealed by the applicants, of whom each must subscribe for at least one share (s. 7). The company is deemed in existence from the date of its letters patent. It may commence business immediately (s. 11). *Incorporation and Commencement of Business.*

The fee for incorporation depends on the amount of authorised capital as follows (s. 137):

$50,000 or less	$100.
$50,000 to $200,000 ..	$100 plus $1 per $1,000 over $50,000.
$200,000 to $500,000 ..	$250 plus $.40 per $1,000 over $200,000.
Over $500,000	$400 plus $.20 per $1,000 or fraction.

Section 14 provides that a company shall possess as incidental and ancillary to the powers set out in the letters patent or supplementary letters patent, a large number of general powers unless expressly excluded. An extension or reduction of powers contained in the company's letters patent or supplementary letters patent may be sought by the directors provided a by-law for such variation has been sanctioned by a two-thirds majority of shareholders at a special general meeting called for the purpose (s. 17). *Extension an Alteration of Company's Powers.*

The company must have a head office in Canada, which shall be its domicile in Canada. Change of head office can be effected by by-law sanctioned by two-thirds votes of a special general meeting, filed with the Secretary of State and published in the *Canada Gazette* (s. 21). *Registered Office.*

Change of name may be effected by supplementary letters patent confirming a by-law which has been sanctioned by a two-thirds majority at a special general meeting (s. 26). *Name.*

Shares may be allotted by resolution of directors in the absence of contrary provisions in the charter or by-laws (s. 32). *Capital and Shares.*

Subject to confirmation by supplementary letters patent a company may from time to time by by-law increase, decrease or otherwise alter its share capital (s. 48). Provision may be made in letters patent for creation of preferred shares or they may be created by by-law of the company (s. 59).

There must be at least three directors of a company (s. 84). Directors may elect an executive committee if their number exceeds six, provided they are authorised by by-law sanctioned by two-thirds majority of a special general meeting of shareholders (s. 94). *Directors.*

Accounts and Auditors.

Section 112 requires that certain accounts be submitted at the annual meeting, including the balance sheet, which must be drawn up to distinguish severally the assets and liabilities under the headings detailed in that section. The balance sheet must be signed by two directors (s. 116).

No director or officer of the company or a person who is a partner of, or in the employment of, any director or officer of the company is qualified for appointment as auditor of any company except a private company (s. 119).

Annual Return.

Every company must, on or before the 1st of June in every year, make a summary of particulars specified in the section, made up to the 31st March preceding, and file it in duplicate in the department of the Secretary of State on or before the 1st June. Each duplicate must be signed by the President or a Vice-President and by the secretary or treasurer or by one of them and a director, and shall be duly verified by their affidavits (s. 121).

Section 106 requires the keeping of minutes of shareholders, directors and executive committee meetings.

An investigation of the affairs of a company may be directed by the Secretary of State (s. 108).

Winding up.

The company may surrender its charter and be dissolved upon compliance with the requirements of the Secretary of State (s. 29).

ALBERTA

The principal Act is the Companies Act, Chapter 240, Revised Statutes of Alberta, 1942, which includes provisions for winding up. Other legislation affecting companies also found in R.S.A., 1942, include: The Trust Companies Act, Chapter 241; The Insurance Act, Chapter 201; The Companies Information Act, Chapter 242; The Securities Act, Chapter 243. Copies of the Acts and other information may be obtained from the Registrar of Companies, Edmonton, Alberta.

The principal Act is based largely on the English Companies Act of 1929.

Incorporation.

Any three or more persons (or in the case of a private company two) may form a company by subscribing to a memorandum of association, which must be filed with the Registrar, together with articles of association, if desired, and the required fee. The Act provides for three types of company: (*a*) a company limited by shares; (*b*) a company limited by guarantee; and (*c*) a specially limited company (s. 15).

Incorporation fees depend upon the amount of nominal capital and are, for example:—

	$			$
Up to	20,000	..	..	50
,,	50,000	..	..	80
,,	100,000	..	..	130
,,	500,000	..	..	250
,,	1,000,000	..	..	350

In addition, there are small charges for publication in the *Alberta Gazette*, filing articles of association, certification of incorporation, filing annual statements, etc.

Foreign companies must be registered in Alberta within thirty days after commencing to carry on business in the Province (s. 134). The fee payable will vary according to the amount of capital employed in the Province. To register, the company must file a certified copy of its charter and various other documents required by the Registrar. Every foreign company must have an attorney in the Province authorised to accept service of process on its behalf. The Registrar must be notified of any change in such attorney (s. 142). *Registration of Foreign Companies.*

BRITISH COLUMBIA

The principal Act is The Companies Act, 1929, Chapter 42, Revised Statutes of British Columbia, 1936. Other legislation affecting companies also found in R.S.B.C., 1936, includes: The Companies Clauses Act, Chapter 46, and The Securities Act, Chapter 282. The administrative officer under the Companies Act is The Registrar of Companies, Parliament Buildings, Victoria, B.C.

The Companies Act is based on the English Companies Act, 1929.

Five or more persons (two or more, if a private company) may form an incorporated company by subscribing to a memorandum of association and otherwise complying with the requirements of the Act in respect of registration (s. 19). Incorporation fees based on the authorised capital are as follows:— *Incorporation.*

	$			$
Up to	10,000	..	..	25
"	20,000	..	..	35
"	50,000	..	..	52.50
"	100,000	..	..	77.50
"	500,000	..	..	277.50
"	1,000,000	..	..	402.50

Every public company must have at least two directors, one of whom must reside in the Province (s. 99). *Directors.*

Every extra-provincial company which carries on business in the Province must be registered under the Act within thirty days after commencing to carry on business in the Province (s. 179). Every extra-provincial company must have an attorney resident in the place where the head office in the Province is situated (s. 180). The fees for registration are the same as for incorporation. *Registration of Extra-Provincial Companies.*

MANITOBA

The principal Act is the Companies Act, Chapter 36, Revised Statutes of Manitoba, 1940. The Act, so far as it relates to joint stock companies, follows in the main the English Companies Act of 1929. The chief administrative officer in the matter of companies is the Provincial Secretary, Parliament Buildings, Winnipeg, Manitoba.

Incorporation is obtained by application for letters patent by not less than three persons, setting out: (a) the proposed name of the company; (b) the objects for which it is incorporated; (c) the chief place of business; (d) the amount of capital stock; (e) the *Incorporation.*

number of shares and amount of each; (*f*) the names in full, addresses and occupations of the applicants and names of not less than three who are to be the first directors; (*g*) the amount of stock taken by each applicant and amount paid thereon; and (*h*) whether the amount so paid was paid in cash or by the transfer of property or otherwise (s. 18). The fees for letters patent are based on the amount of capital, for example:—

	$			$
Not exceeding	20,000	..	..	25
"	50,000	..	..	55
"	100,000	..	..	105
"	500,000	..	..	285
"	1,000,000	..	..	385

There are also other fees for services under the Companies Act.

Licences for Foreign Companies. Foreign companies require a licence before carrying on business in the Province. The fees are the same as for incorporation (s. 440). A foreign company cannot hold land unless licensed by the Province.

NEW BRUNSWICK

The principal Act is the New Bruswick Companies Act, Chapter 88, Revised Statutes of New Brunswick, 1927. It is founded on the Dominion Companies Act (*supra*). The chief administrative officer for companies is the Provincial Secretary, Parliament Buildings, Fredericton, N.B.

Incorporation. The Provincial Secretary may, by letters patent under his seal of office, grant a charter to not less than three persons for any purposes to which the legislature of the Province extends except railways, insurance, trade unions, friendly societies, building societies or other associations of like nature. The incorporation fees are based upon the amount of capital; the following are examples:—

	$			$
Not over	5,000	..	..	50
"	20,000	..	..	70
"	50,000	..	..	100
"	100,000	..	..	150
"	500,000	..	..	350
"	1,000,000	..	..	600

Registered Office and Meetings. The company must have its head office in the Province, but the Provincial Secretary may grant permission in the letters patent for directors' and shareholders' meetings to be held outside the Province (s. 35).

Extra-Provincial Corporations Holding Land. An extra-provincial corporation may, subject to the provisions of its own charter, acquire, hold, mortgage, alienate and otherwise dispose of real estate in the Province to the same extent as if it had been incorporated under the New Brunswick Companies Act [s. 28 (*a*)].

Licences for Foreign Companies. Foreign companies must be authorised to do business in the Province and pay an annual fee equivalent to 1 per cent. of the capital used in the Province, minimum fee $100, maximum $400.

Annual Return. All corporations doing business in the Province must file an annual return on or before 1st June in each year. Forms may be obtained from the Provincial Secretary (s. 117).

Nova Scotia

The principal Act is the Nova Scotia Companies Act, No. 6 of 1935. The Act follows closely the English Companies (Consolidation) Act of 1908. It contains, however, no provisions for winding up or for the registration of foreign companies, which are dealt with in separate Acts. The main administrative official with regard to companies is the Registrar of Joint Stock Companies, Parliament Buildings, Halifax, N.S.

Incorporation. Any three or more persons may form a company, except a banking, loan, trust or insurance company, by subscribing to a memorandum of agreement and otherwise complying with the Act in respect of registration (s. 8). Incorporation fees based on the amount of capital are:—

$				$
5,000 or less	..	..		50
20,000 "	..	..		85
50,000 "	..	..		115
100,000 "	..	..		152.50
500,000 "	..	..		390
1,000,000 "	..	..		515

Registration of Foreign Companies. Foreign companies are dealt with by the Dominion, Domestic and Foreign Corporations Act, No. 173 of 1923 (amended 1924, 1928, 1931, 1936, 1941, 1942). A foreign company must be granted a certificate of registration by the Registrar of Joint Stock Companies. It must appoint an attorney in the Province for the service of process. The annual fee payable by a foreign company depends upon its authorised capital and the amount of capital used in the Province.

Ontario

The principal Act is the Companies Act, Chapter 251, Revised Statutes of Ontario, 1937. Copies of the Act and other information respecting companies may be obtained from The Provincial Secretary, Toronto.

Incorporation. Incorporation is obtained by application to the Lieutenant-Governor for letters patent by not less than three persons for any lawful objects, except those of a railway or of corporations within the meaning of the Loan and Trust Corporations Act (s. 2). The application must show: the proposed name of the company; the objects for which incorporated; the location in Ontario of the head office; the amount of capital stock; the number of shares and amount of each share; the name, residence and calling of each applicant; the names of at least three applicants who are to be the provisional directors. The application is accompanied by a memorandum of agreement signed by the applicants, whereby each contracts to take an agreed number of shares (specimen forms may be found in the Act) (s. 4). Fees for letters patent depend upon the proposed capital, for example:—

$				$
40,000 or less	..	..	..	100
100,000 "	..	..	..	160
500,000 "	..	..	..	260
1,000,000 "	..	..	..	385

Mining Companies.

Sections 132–9 contain special provisions for mining companies. A mining company, duly authorised by by-law, may issue shares at a discount.

Insurance Companies.

Sections 218–314 contain special provisions for insurance companies.

Foreign and Extra-Provincial Companies.

The Extra-Provincial Corporations Act, Chapter 252, R.S.O., 1937, governs foreign and extra-provincial companies. Generally speaking, all foreign or extra-provincial companies must obtain a licence to do business in Ontario. Application is made to the Lieutenant-Governor. Forms may be obtained from the Provincial Secretary. Fees are the same as for domestic corporations, but are based on the amount of capital employed in the Province. A licensed extra-provincial company, subject to the limitations of the licence and its own charter of incorporation, may acquire and dispose of real estate in Ontario to the same extent as if it had been incorporated under the Companies Act.

Prospectus.

The Companies Information Act, Chapter 253, R.S.O., 1937. Under s. 2 of this Act a prospectus must be filed with the Provincial Secretary by every company upon establishing an office, commencing business or selling its securities in Ontario (fee $5).

Annual Return.

Under s. 3 an annual return must be filed on or before 1st June each year. Forms are obtained from the Provincial Secretary.

PRINCE EDWARD ISLAND

The principal Act is the Joint Stock Companies Act, Chapter 7 of 1939. Copies of the Act may be obtained from the Provincial Secretary, Parliament Buildings, Charlottetown, Prince Edward Island.

Incorporation.

The Lieutenant-Governor in Council may by letters patent grant a charter to not less than five persons who shall petition therefor, for any purposes to which the legislative authority of the Province extends except railways, insurance, or for the management of trade unions, friendly societies, building societies and other like associations (s. 3). The applicants must give two weeks' previous notice of their intention to seek incorporation by a notice in the *Royal Gazette*.

Extra-Provincial Companies.

Extra-provincial companies are not required to take out a licence but must file certain documents with the Provincial Secretary before commencing business in the Province and continue to file certain returns thereafter.

Companies Domicil for the Purposes of Taxations.

Special provisions is made under the Domiciled Companies Act, Chapter 23 of 1940, whereby companies may become domiciled in the Province for tax purposes. The Act does not apply to companies which carry on business in the Province.

QUEBEC

The principal Act is the Quebec Companies Act, Chapter 276, Revised Statutes of Quebec, 1941. Copies of the Act and other information respecting companies may be obtained from The Provincial Secretary, Quebec City.

Incorporation.

Incorporation is by letters patent granted by the Lieutenant-Governor to not less than three persons who have also subscribed to the memorandum of agreement (s. 6). The applicants must be at least 21 years of age.   The application to the Lieutenant-Governor in Council must set out: the proposed corporate name; the purposes for which incorporation is sought; the location in Quebec of its head office; the proposed capital; number of shares and amount of each share; the names, addresses and callings of the applicants and the names of at least three of their number who are to be the first or provisional directors; and the amount of stock to be taken by each applicant (s. 7).   The application may ask for embodiment in the letters patent of any provision which might be made a by-law.   Such provision can then be altered only by supplementary letters patent (s. 8).

Incorporation fees, based on the authorised capital, are as follows (Order in Council 402 of 8th February, 1946):—

(1) When the authorised capital stock is $40,000 or less—$75.00.

(2) When the authorised capital is more than $40,000—$75.00 plus:—

   (a) $1.00 for each $1,000 or fraction in excess of $40,000 up to $200,000;

   (b) $0.50 for each $1,000 or fraction in excess of $200,000 up to $1,000,000;

   (c) $100 for each $1,000,000 or fraction in excess of $1,000,000.

The following are other statutes affecting companies also found in Revised Statutes of Quebec, 1941.

Chapter 279, The Extra-Provincial Companies Act.

In general, all companies not incorporated in virtue of Quebec or Dominion legislation must obtain a license from the Lieutenant-Governor in order to carry on business in the Province.   The fee is based on the amount of capital employed in the Province (minimum $100).

Foreign and Extra-Provincial Companies.

Chapter 281, Companies Information Act.

A prospectus must be filed with the Provincial Secrtary upon commencing business in Quebec or upon the sale therein of any of the company's securities.   On or before 1st September in each year every company incorporated in Quebec and every other company doing business in the Province must file with the Provincial Secretary a detailed return containing particulars (as at 30th June) of its incorporation, capital, officers and directors, etc. (fee $10).

Prospectus.

Chapter 283, The Mortmain Act.

Every company incorporated and existing in Great Britain, U.S.A., or in Canada has the right to hold land and immoveable property for its occupation or the prosecution of its business, but cannot acquire or hold land for any other purpose without a licence from the Lieutenant-Governor in Council (fee $10 for a particular licence; $100 for a general licence).

Mortmain.

SASKATCHEWAN

The principal Act is the Companies Act, 1933, Chapter 113, Revised Statutes of Saskatchewan, 1940. The Act is based on the English Companies Act of 1929. The chief administrative officer in the matter of companies is the Registrar of Joint Stock Companies, Parliament Buildings, Regina, Saskatchewan.

Incorporation.   Any three or more persons, or in the case of a private company any two or more, may form a company for any lawful purpose, by subscribing their names to a memorandum of association and otherwise complying with the requirements of the Act in respect of registration. (This does not apply to railway, telegraph, loan, trust or insurance companies.) Incorporation fees based on the amount of capital are as follows:—

		$			$
Not exceeding	20,000		..	..	40
,,	50,000		..	..	70
,,	100,000		..	..	120
,,	500,000		..	..	270
,,	1,000,000		..	..	370

Foreign Companies.   Foreign companies must register within thirty days of carrying on business in the Province. Every foreign company must file a certified copy of its charter, by-laws and other documents, and must also appoint an attorney in the Province to receive service of process. Fees for registration are practically the same as for incorporation.

NEWFOUNDLAND

The principal Act is the Companies Act, 1916, and follows the English Act of 1908. The chief administrative officer is the Registrar of Companies, St. Johns, Newfoundland.

Three or more persons may form a company by filing a memorandum and articles of association together with the required fees. Fees are based on the amount of capital.

Foreign corporations need not be registered in order to carry on business in Newfoundland. They may also hold land without a special licence.

NEW ZEALAND

Company law in New Zealand is governed by the Companies Act, 1933 (the Principal Act) as amended by the Statutes Amendment Acts, 1939, 1940, 1941 and 1945. The Principal Act closely follows the English Companies Act of 1929 and the amending Acts are of minor importance.

Statutes for the time being in force may be purchased from the New Zealand Government Offices, 415, Strand, London, W.C.2, and bound copies thereof may also be consulted in the library at that address at any time.

Further general information may be obtained

(i) From the New Zealand Government Offices (*supra*).

(ii) From the Bank of New Zealand, 1, Victoria Street, London, E.C.

(iii) From the National Bank of New Zealand, 8, Moorgate, London, E.C.

The address of the Registrar of Companies is National Bank Chambers, Featherstone Street, Wellington, New Zealand.

1. Section 331 of the principal Act requires the registration of every company incorporated outside New Zealand (hereinafter called a 'foreign company), which establishes a place of business within New Zealand after 1st April, 1934, or, which has prior to that date established and continues to have such place of business thereafter. *Registration of Companies incorporated outside New Zealand.*

2. Within one month from the date of the establishment of a place of business in New Zealand a foreign company must, under s. 332, file the following documents with the Registrar:— *Documents to be delivered to the Registrar.*

(a) A certified copy of the charter, statutes, or memorandum and articles of the company, or other instrument constituting or defining the constitution of the company, and, if the instrument is not written in the English language, a certified translation thereof.

(b) A list of the directors of the company, containing the following particulars with respect to the directors:—

(1) In the case of an individual, his full name, his usual residential address, and his business occupation, if any, or, if he has no business occupation but holds any directorships, particulars of such directorships.

(2) In the case of a corporation, its corporate name and registered or principal office.

(c) The names and addresses of some one or more persons resident in New Zealand authorised to accept on behalf of the company service of process and any notices required to be served on the company. Any subsequent alterations which are made to any of these documents must be filed with the Registrar within the prescribed time (s. 334).

An annual licence must be obtained. The fee payable in the case of overseas companies is 1s. per cent. with a minimum of £10 and a maximum of £300. In the case of companies incorporated in some other part of His Majesty's Dominions the duty is at the rate of 6d. per cent. with a minimum of £10 and a maximum of £150. In the case of banking and insurance companies there is a uniform fee of £300. *Annual Licence.*

A certificate of incorporation duly executed under the law of the country of the foreign company and verified by a declaration made by one of its directors or its manager before a mayor, provost, notary public, British consul or vice-consul (or other person authorised to take such declaration) is conclusive evidence that the company is duly incorporated. Such certificate may be filed with the above-mentioned documents, but this is not necessary if it appears from the documents already filed that the company is incorporated. *Certificate of Incorporation.*

Power to hold Land.

A foreign company which has filed with the Registrar the necessary documents under s. 332 (*supra*), may hold any quantity of land, except in the case of companies which are not carried on for the acquisition of gain. Such companies, *e.g.* companies formed for the purpose of promoting art, science, religion, etc., may not hold more than two acres without a licence from the Governor-General [s. 333 (1)].

Balance Sheets.

Foreign companies must in every calendar year, and at intervals of not more than fifteen months, make out a balance sheet in the prescribed manner, containing such particulars and including such documents as a local company is required to make out and lay before its members in general meeting. A copy of such balance sheet must be delivered to the Registrar for registration. If any such balance sheet is not written in the English language a certified translation must be annexed [s. 335 (1)]. A profit and loss account need not be filed.

Books of Account.

Foreign companies must keep proper books of account in respect of:—

    (a)   particulars of all sums of money received and expended by the company in relation to its New Zealand business,

    (b)   all sales and purchases of goods by the company in relation to its New Zealand business,

    (c)   the assets and liabilities of the company in relation to its New Zealand business.

Prospectus.

In addition to the requirements of the Act relating to the prospectuses of local companies which apply also to foreign companies, s. 336 of the principal Act requires that a statement as to the country of incorporation be included.

Publicising Name of Company.

In every place at which a foreign company carries on business in New Zealand the name of the company and the country of its incorporation must be conspicuously exhibited. The name of the company and the country of its incorporation must also be stated in legible characters in all bill-heads and letter paper and in all notices, advertisements, and other official publications of the company.

Limited Liability.

If the liability of the members of the company is limited, notice of this fact must be given in legible characters in every prospectus and in all bill-heads, letter paper, notices, advertisements and other official publications of the company. Notice of limited liability must be affixed also in every place where the company carries on business.

Notice of ceasing to carry on Business.

If a foreign company decides to cease to have a place of business in New Zealand, it must first of all publish in three successive issues of the *Gazette*, and of some newspaper circulating at each place of business in New Zealand, notice of its intention to cease to have a place of business in New Zealand. When the foreign company ceases to have a place of business in New Zealand, it must immediately file notice of this fact with the Registrar, and from the date of such notice, the obligation of the company to file any document with the Registrar ceases. The notice to the Registrar, however, will not take effect for three months after the date of the first publication in the *Gazette*.

A declaration endorsed upon or annexed to any instrument appointing an attorney of a foreign company made by one of its directors before a mayor, provost, notary public, British consul or vice-consul or other person authorised to take such declaration, if any, of the following facts, is conclusive evidence of those facts:— *Powers of Attorney.*

(a) the company is incorporated under the style mentioned in the instrument, in accordance with the law of the country where it is so incorporated, the name of the country being specified in the declaration;

(b) the seal affixed thereto is the common seal of the company;

(c) the seal has been affixed, and the instrument executed, and the powers and authorities purporting to be conferred upon the attorney are authorised to be conferred under the constitution of the company, or in pursuance of the Act or instrument under which the company is incorporated, or by the regulations for the time being thereof;

(d) the declarant is a director or general manager of the company.

If under the law of the relevant foreign country no seal is necessary, the existence of such law, or the fact that the company has no seal, may be stated in the declaration. If a declaration has been made in the foregoing manner and containing the above-mentioned particulars, the power of attorney will be receivable in evidence without further proof of the sealing, signature, or other execution thereof. A power of attorney may, together with the declaration, be delivered to the Registrar for registration with any of the documents registered under s. 332 (*supra*).

The law as to powers of attorney in New Zealand is governed by Part XI of the Property Law Act, 1908.

THE UNION OF SOUTH AFRICA

The Companies Act, 1926, set up a uniform company law for all the Provinces of the Union of South Africa. All the old Provincial Acts have accordingly been repealed.

The Act applies to all companies in every part of the Union, and was based on the English Companies (Consolidation) Act, 1908.

The 1926 Act was amended by the Companies Amendment Act, 1939, which brought the Union Act into line with the English Act, 1929, and came into operation on 1st January, 1940. It is, however, expected that in the near future a new Companies Act will be passed, incorporating most of the recommendations of the Commission on Company Law Amendment, which published its report in November, 1948. The effect of this will be to bring Union company law more or less into line with the English Companies Act, 1948, although with many important differences in detail. (See *The Secretary*, 1949, pp. 330, *et seq*.) The Companies Registration Office is situated in Pretoria.

Further information may be obtained from the Standard Bank of South Africa, 10, Clements Lane, London, E.C.4.

A foreign company means a company or other association of persons, which has for its object the acquisition of gain, and which *Definition of Foreign Company.*

is incorporated under the laws of any state, country or territory other than the Union, whether or not included in the British Commonwealth.

Filing of Documents by Foreign Company.

Every foreign company establishing a place of business in the Union must within one month lodge with the Registrar in quadruplicate:—

(a) a certified copy of the charter, statutes, memorandum and articles of the company, or other instrument defining the constitution of the company. Such copy must be in, or be accompanied by, a translation into, one of the official languages of the Union;

(b) a list of the names and addresses of the directors of the company;

(c) the names and addresses of some one or more persons resident in the Union authorised to accept service of process and notices on behalf of the company. Notice in quadruplicate of any alteration in these documents must be lodged with the Registrar within three months of such alteration.

Balance Sheets.

Every foreign company having a place of business in the Union must in every year prepare a balance sheet in the manner prescribed for a Union company, and a copy thereof in quadruplicate must be lodged with the Registrar.

Every foreign company which uses the word 'Limited' as part of its name must:—

Limited Liability.

(a) state the country of incorporation in every prospectus inviting subscriptions for shares or debentures in the Union;

(b) exhibit conspicuously outside all its places of business in the Union the name of the company and the country of its incorporation;

(c) state in legible characters the name of the company and the country of its incorporation in all bill-heads, letter paper, and in all notices, advertisements and other official publications of the company.

Exemption from Transfer Duty.

If a foreign company carrying on its principal business within the Union is being wound up for the purpose of transferring its undertaking to a company to be registered under the principal Act, the court may order that the foreign company be exempt from the transfer duty on the immovable property transferred.

Books of Account.

A foreign company must keep books of record in the manner provided for Union companies.

Prospectuses.

No prospectus may be issued in the Union by a foreign company (whether or not having a place of business in the Union) unless a duly certified copy has been lodged for registration with the Registrar. The prospectus must, of course, contain the particulars and comply with the provisions required by the Union Act as to prospectuses.

Licences.

Every company, including every foreign company, must obtain from the Receiver of Revenue of the district in which the principal office of the company is situated a licence in respect of each and every year. The licence costs five shillings for each £1,000 or part thereof, of capital subscribed, subject to a minimum payment of £1. If a company is registered on or after 1st July in any year, half duty only will be charged in respect of the licence for that year. The licence duty chargeable will not exceed £5 in respect of any year during which no active operations in connection with the principal business of a company are carried on within the Union, or during which the only business carried on is the registration of transfers of shares in the company. An application for a licence must be accompanied by a declaration setting out the subscribed capital of the company as at the first day of January of the year in respect of which the licence is to be issued, or, in the case of registration after the first day of January, or in the case of a foreign company within one month from the date when it establishes a place of business in the Union, the subscribed capital at the date when the company first commenced business within the Union or first established a place of business there as the case may be. Every company failing to take out a licence before 31st January in any year or within a month of the day on which it commenced business within the Union, will be obliged to pay as additional licence duty a further amount calculated at the rate of 10 per cent. of the annual licence duty for each month or part of the month for which the company is in default. All licence moneys due under this section will be a debt due to the Government of the Union. Associations not for profit will be exempt from the duty chargeable under this section. There is no similar provision regarding licences in the English Act of 1948.

In addition to the annual licence, trading licences must be taken out in the case of certain specified trades. *Trading Licences.*

Capital duty on incorporation or on increase of capital is 5s. per cent. of the nominal capital. *Capital Duty.*

If a foreign company ceases to have a place of business in the Union, it must forthwith give notice of this fact to the Registrar, and from the date on which such notice is given, the obligation of the company to lodge any documents with the Registrar ceases. *Notice on ceasing to have Place of Business.*

NORTHERN RHODESIA

The law relating to joint stock companies operating in Northern Rhodesia is contained in a principal Ordinance, Chapter 113 of 1921, and in the following amending Ordinances:—

No. 6 of 1931 and No. 4 of 1933.

The Office of the Registrar of Companies is: High Court Offices, Livingstone, Northern Rhodesia, from whom copies of these Ordinances can be obtained.

SOUTHERN RHODESIA

The law relating to joint stock companies in Southern Rhodesia is still governed by a principal Ordinance No. 2 of 1895 as amended by Companies Amendment Ordinances No. 11 of 1907, No. 11 of 1910, and High Commissioner's Notices No. 7 of 1915, No. 8 of 1918 and No. 4 of 1920. The amendment and modernisaton of company law is under consideration by the Southern Rhodesian Government and an amending and/or an amending and consolidating Act may be expected before long. If it is intended to form a company or open a place of business in Southern Rhodesia an enquiry should be made as to the stage which the new legislation has reached.

Copies of the statute law and of the Joint Stock Companies Ordinances can be obtained from the Office of the High Commissioner for Southern Rhodesia, 429, Strand, London, W.C.2. Further information can be obtained from the Secretary for Justice, P.O. Box 92 Causeway, Salisbury, Southern Rhodesia, the Law Society of Southern Rhodesia, c/o Messrs. Sonnenberg & Bartels, P.O. Box 190, Bulawayo, and the Standard Bank of South Africa, Ltd., 10, Clements Lane, London, E.C.4. The address of the Registrar of Joint Stock Companies is P.O. Box 84 Causeway, Salisbury, Southern Rhodesia.

Company Law.   Under the law subsisting in 1950 the following points should be noted:—

(1) There are no special provisions as to the registration of foreign companies.

(2) Every joint stock company having a place of business in Southern Rhodesia must take out an annual licence in addition to any trading licences rendered necessary by the nature of the company's business. The fee is 6d. for every £100 or fraction of £100 of the issued capital and the minimum fee is £5.

(3) Capital duty is payable on the formation of a company, or on increase of capital, at the rate of 2s. 6d. for every £100 or fraction of £100 of the nominal capital and the minimum payable is £5.

(4) There is no distinction between private and public companies, all companies being what English law would regard as public companies.

(5) Special resolutions have to be confirmed, as was the rule under the law in England before 1929.

(6) There are no restrictions as to the nationality of directors and the names of directors do not have to appear in official documents of the company.

(7) Stamp duty on share certificates originally issued in respect of shares allotted is at the rate of 3d. for every £10 of the nominal value of the shares, but there is no stamp duty on share certificates issued after transfer.

(8) Stamp duty on transfers is at the rate of 1d. for every £10 of the nominal value of the shares transferred.

(9) The 1895 ordinance as amended contains no provision for the issue of debentures, but mortgage debentures are issued and secured by the mortgage of immovable property in favour of trustees.

(10) Duty on the conveyance of immovable property is 4 per cent. on the total value of the purchase consideration (including improvements and fixtures, if any).

Taxation.   The law of income tax in Southern Rhodesia is contained in Act No. 15 of 1948 (The Income Tax Consolidation Act, 1948) as amended by No. 20 of 1949. (2) Sur-tax is imposed by Act No. 18 of 1948 on individuals and certain companies. (3) A gold industry contribution on individuals and companies is imposed by Act No. 19 of 1948. (4) An undistributed profits tax is imposed by Act No. 17 of 1949. Repealed since Devaluation.

The Southern Rhodesian income tax year runs from 1st April until 31st March.

THE REPUBLIC OF IRELAND

The law relating to companies in the Irish Republic is governed by four English statutes and one Irish statute.

The English statutes are:—

The Companies (Consolidation) Act, 1908.
The Companies Act, 1913.
The Companies (Foreign Interest) Act, 1917.
The Companies (Particulars as to Directors) Act, 1917.

The Irish statute is:—

The Companies (Constitution of Records) Act, 1924.

The law applies only to companies incorporated before 26th May, 1921. All these Acts together are referred to as the Companies Acts, 1908–24.

Copies of Irish statutes and other official publications may be obtained from the Government Publications Sale Office, at 3 and 4, College Street, Dublin.

The address of the Registrar of Companies is: Dublin Castle, Dublin.

Further information may be obtained from the Department of Industry and Commerce, Kildare Street, Dublin, which department exercises the functions of the Board of Trade under the 1908 Act.

The Companies Acts, 1908–17 must, in their application to the Irish Republic, be read in the light of the (Irish) Adaptation of Enactments Act, 1922. Section 3 of that Act provides that for the purpose of construction of any British statute, the name 'Ireland' whether used alone or in conjunction with the expression 'Great Britain' or by the implication as being included in the expression 'United Kingdom' so named 'Saorstateirean.' In s. 4 of the same Act references to the *Dublin Gazette* are to be construed as referring to the Irish publication 'Irish Oifigiuil.' Interpretation of the Margin.

An English company which contemplates carrying on business in Ireland may either:— Particulars of Colonial Register.

(i) merely furnish the particulars required by s. 274 of the Companies (Consolidation) Act, 1908, which are dealt with in the next following paragraph; or

(ii) in addition establish in Ireland a colonial register under s. 34 of the Act of 1908; or

(iii) promote a subsidiary company incorporated in Ireland.

If any appreciable number of shares is held by persons domiciled in the Irish Republic, it is advisable in the interests of those shareholders to establish a colonial register in order that the duties payable on these shares, on the death of the shareholder of Irish domicil, may be at the Irish rate (see s. 35 of the Act of 1908). Apart from this benefit to shareholders, the company also gains certain advantages in the rate of corporation profits tax payable in Ireland if such a register is kept (see s. 31 (i) of the Finance Act, 1928, s. 47 of the Finance Act, 1932, and s. 12 of the Finance Act, 1943).

Non-Irish Companies. A non-Irish company which seeks to establish a place of business in Ireland must comply with the requirements of s. 274 of the Companies (Consolidation) Act, 1908. That section requires certain particulars to be lodged with the Registrar of Companies within one month after the establishment of a place of business in the country, the filing of an annual balance sheet and (in the case of limited companies) publication in any prospectus, with a notice to be exhibited at its place of business and on all bill-headings and stationery, with the name of the company and the name of the country in which the company is incorporated.

Mortmain. It should be noted that apart from the penalties laid down by s. 274 for failure to comply with these provisions any conveyance of lands in Ireland to a company which is not registered in Ireland is probably voidable at the suit of the Irish Attorney General under the Irish Mortmain Acts.

The Control of Manufacturers Acts, 1932–34. Any company or individual contemplating setting up any manufacturing business in Ireland should consider the provisions of the Control of Manufacturers Acts, 1932 and 1934. Under s. 19 of the 1934 Act, no person may as part of a business carried on for gain make, alter, repair, ornament, finish or adapt for sale any article, material or substance, unless certain provisions are complied with. These statutory provisions are complicated, but the general scheme is to prevent non-Irish persons, who were not carrying on business in Ireland before 2nd July, 1934, from setting up any kind of manufacturing business (with certain exceptions) in the country without first obtaining a licence from the Ministry of Industry and Commerce. Such a licence is not required:

(i) if a business is owned by a corporation in respect of which more than half (in nominal value) of the issued shares are beneficially owned by Irish nationals; and

(ii) at least two-thirds (in nominal value) of the shares carrying voting rights are so owned; and

(iii) a majority of the directors are Irish nationals.

For further details the Acts themselves must be consulted.

Tax Relief. Certain taxation reliefs are available when the company is Irish-controlled and owned. Reference may be made to Finance Act, 1932, s. 7, Finance Act, 1933, s. 43, and Finance Act, 1935, s. 7, and to the book *Irish Corporation Profits Tax*, by Lionel Winder, published by Morris, 1 and 2, Rutland Place, Dublin. The Irish Finance Acts, in so far as they relate to income tax, are illustrated in Shawcross and Armstrong's *Law of Income Tax in the Irish Free State*, and Grogan's *Principles and Practice of Irish Income Tax*.

Corporations and private individuals are affected by the recent increase in stamp duty payable on conveyances and transfers of land and house property in Ireland. Under the Finance No. 2 Act, 1947, the general rate of duty was raised to 25 per cent. of the purchase price on all conveyances executed after 1st December, 1947. The rate is, however, reduced to 5 per cent. where the purchaser is: (i) an Irish citizen; (ii) a company incorporated in Ireland before 15th October, 1947; or (iii) a company incorporated in Ireland after that date where the issued shares of each class, to an extent exceeding one half in nominal value, are in the beneficial ownership of Irish citizens or companies incorporated in Ireland before 15th October, 1947. The conveyance must contain a certificate to this effect to escape the higher rate. There is no increase in duty where a lease or contract of tenancy is taken without a fine.

The rules as to winding up of companies have long been different in England and Ireland and reference may be made to Quin on winding up of companies in Ireland. Text Books.

INDIA AND PAKISTAN

The principal Act regulating company law is The Indian Companies Act No. 7, of 1913. This Act was based on the English Act of 1908 and was extensively amended by an Amending Act No. 22 of 1936 which adopted in part the changes in English company law introduced by the English Act of 1929 and in part introduced a number of new provisions not found in the English Act. Further amendments were introduced by No. 36 of 1940, No. 26 of 1941, No. 17 of 1942, No. 30 of 1943, No. 4 of 1944, and No. 4 of 1945. Some of these new provisions, or provisions similar to them, have now been introduced into English law by the English Act of 1948.

Copies of these statutes and any further information can be obtained from the Registrar of Joint Stock Companies, 21, Mission Row Extension, Calcutta, or the Companies Registration Office, Raja Bahadur Mansions, 32, Apollo Street, Bombay.

While the Indian Act as amended corresponds broadly to the English Companies Act, 1948, there are a great many differences of detail of which the most important are set out below.

Section 17 (2) makes certain regulations of Table A compulsory in articles of every company, and s. 79 also introduces compulsory regulations over-riding the articles as to period of notice of, and voting at, general meetings. The compulsory articles relate to voting at general meetings, lodging of proxies, powers of directors, rotation of directors (public company only), power to declare dividends, inspection of accounts and books, form of profit and loss account, and notices of meetings, including a requirement for registering an address in India. Articles of Association.

Sections 83A and 83B, and ss. 86A to 86I, deal with directors and restrict their powers and provide as to loans, offices of profit, and removal from, and vacation of, office. Sections 87A to 87I deal with managing agents. Sections 131A, 132 and 132A deal with reports of directors and the balance sheet and profit and loss account and the profits and losses of subsidiaries. Sections 277 and 277A to 277E deal with particulars to be filed by foreign companies having a place of business in India.

The Act refers throughout to 'British India.' This will now have to be read in view of s. 18 of the Indian Independence Act, 1947, as meaning the Dominion of India or the Dominion of Pakistan as the case may be.

APPENDIX M

Exchange Control Act, 1947

*Reprinted by kind permission of the Bank of England as current
at the date of publication.*

INSTRUCTIONS TO REGISTRARS AND OTHERS CONCERNED WITH
REGISTERS OF SECURITIES.

This Notice is one of an administrative series issued by the
Bank of England to draw attention in convenient form to the law
contained in the Act and Treasury Orders made thereunder, and
(by virtue of powers delegated by H.M. Treasury under s. 37 of
the Act) to give certain exemptions, permissions, consents,
authorities and directions (including directions imposing certain
requirements on bankers and others under s. 34 of the Act).
It should be construed accordingly.

The Notice announcing the appointed day will contain transitional arrangements regarding:—

(a) the acceptance after that date of Declarations D.1 and
D.2 and authorities given before that date under the
Defence (Finance)Regulations, 1939;

(b) the use after that date of Declarations D.1 and D.2
already printed on forms of transfer.

References in this Notice to the United Kingdom should be
read to include the Isle of Man and the Channel Islands and the
term 'registered' to include 'inscribed.'

The following additional Notice to Registrars has been issued—

E.C. (Securities) 7 .. Instructions to Registrars, Company
Secretaries and Paying Agents in respect
of interest, dividends and capital repayments on securities, and to Banks
and Bankers paying warrants issued in
the United Kingdom.

SUMMARY.

PART I.

Issue of Securities.

Issue and replacement of bearer securities.
Issue of registered securities.

PART II.

Transfer of Securities.

Prescribed Securities.
Securities (other than Prescribed Securities) which are registered
as to both principal and interest or dividends in a Register
which is not a Subsidiary Register.

828

Securities (other than Prescribed Securities) registered as to principal only or registered in a Subsidiary Register.

Transfers to and from Registers outside the United Kingdom.

PART III.

General Information.

Acquisition of securities by operation of law.

Registration of addresses outside the Scheduled Territories.

Recording of mandates for interest or dividends.

Acceptance of signatures.

Trading with the Enemy Act, 1939.

Appendices.

PART I.

ISSUE OF SECURITIES.

Nothing in this Notice affects in any way any need for permission from H.M. Treasury under Regulation 6 of the Defence (Finance) Regulations, 1939, or any Order for the time being in force under s. 1 of the Borrowing (Control and Guarantees) Act, 1946, in respect of an issue or offer of capital. All questions arising therefrom should be addressed to the Secretary, Capital Issues Committee, Treasury Chambers, Whitehall, S.W.1, and not to the Bank of England.

Issue and Replacement of Bearer Securities.

1. Permission is required for the issue for any purpose of a bearer security (including a Letter of Allotment which may be renounced, a Letter of Rights, or a Scrip Certificate to bearer) or a coupon, or for the alteration of any document so that it becomes a bearer security or coupon.

Note.—Letters of Allotment or Rights issued with permission may be 'split' without further authority; declarations are not required for this purpose.

Issue of Registered Securities

2. Registered securities may not be issued unless:—

   (a) on application or subscription (whether or not immediate registration is to be effected), the forms of application are endorsed with or accompanied by:—

   (i) Declaration 2 as in Form D (with the word 'transferee' suitably altered) *signed by the applicant or his agent, or*

   (ii) Declaration 2A as in Form D (with the word 'transferee' suitably altered) *signed by an Authorised Depositary or a Temporary Recipient,* and a certificate as appended to Declaration 2A in Form D provided that:—

(a) where permission to make the issue or offer is not required under Regulation 6 of the Defence (Finance) Regulations, 1939, or any Order for the time being in force under s. 1 of the Borrowing (Control and Guarantees) Act, 1946, the permission of the Bank of England must have been obtained to accept applications or subscriptions by or on behalf of non-residents, and

(b) any address outside the Scheduled Territories entered in the Register must be in the country of residence as shown in the declaration, of the person who is to become the owner.

(b) on presentation for registration of a Letter of Allotment or Rights or Scrip Certificate, the form of request is endorsed with or accompanied by:—

(i) a declaration as in (a) (i) above *signed by the applicant or his agent, or*

(ii) a declaration and certificate as in (a) (ii) above and an 'authorisation' by an Authorised Depositary.

(c) on conversion of a registered security, the address to be entered in the Register in respect of the new security is either within the Scheduled Territories or in the same country as that recorded for the old security; declarations are not required.

(d) on registration of a bearer security (whether on conversion or otherwise except as in (b) above), the form of request is lodged by an Authorised Depositary or a Temporary Recipient and is endorsed with or accompanied by:—

(i) a declaration as in (a) (i) above *signed by an Authorised Depositary or a Temporary Recipient, or*

(ii) a declaration (but not certificate) as in (a) (ii) above and an 'authorisation' by an Authorised depositary.

When a Form BA or BUK is lodged with a bearer security, the form should be marked on the reverse over the Registrar's signature 'Security registered' and returned direct to the delivering Depositary shown thereon.

PART II.

TRANSFER OF SECURITIES.

Prescribed Securities.

1. A transfer may be effected if:—

(a) accompanied by a Form BUK (to be retained by the Registrar) which is marked 'Deposit not required' across the spaces provided for the use of delivering and receiving Depositaries, and

     (i) is authorised by an Authorised Depositary, or

     (ii) if not authorised by an Authorised Depositary, is completed as to Declaration 1 or 1A and Declaration 2, provided that the address to be entered in the Register is in the United Kingdom; or

  (b) authorised by the Bank of England or other Authorised Depositary.

Securities (other than Prescribed Securities) which are Registered as to both Principal and Interest or Dividends in a Register which is not a Subsidiary Register.

2. A transfer may be effected if:—

  (a) accompanied by a revised Form D (attached to or printed on the form of transfer) which:—

     (i) is authorised by an Authorised Depositary, or

     (ii) if not authorised by an Authorised Depositary, is completed as to Declaration 1 or 1A and Declaration 2, provided that the address to be entered in the Register is in the Scheduled Territories; or

  (b) authorised by the Bank of England.

3. Registrars may also give effect to forms of transfer received from any of the Scheduled Territories outside the United Kingdom which are accompanied by declarations substantially in the terms of Declarations 1 and 2 in Form D signed by local banks.

Securities (other than Prescribed Securities) Registered as to Principal only or Registered in a Subsidiary Register.

4. A transfer may be effected only if authorised by the Bank of England or other Authorised Depositary.

Transfers to and from Registers outside the United Kingdom.

5. A security on which interest or dividends are not payable by coupon may be transferred from a Register in the United Kingdom to a Register in another part of the Scheduled Territories and conversely, provided that neither Register is a Subsidiary Register and that the name and address registered for the holder remain unchanged.

6. In all other cases permission of the Bank of England is required in respect of transfers between a Register in the United Kingdom and a Register outside the United Kingdom; where transfer will involve the export of a discharge warrant, exhibition of a Certificate C may be accepted by the Registrar as evidence of such permission.

PART III.

GENERAL INFORMATION.

Acquisition of Securities by Operation of Law.

1. Registrars are permitted to enter in a Register the name of the personal representative, trustee in bankruptcy or other person legally entitled to transfer a security where, by reason of death, bankruptcy, unsoundness of mind or other disability, the

holder of the security becomes incapable of its transfer. An address outside the Scheduled Territories may not, except as permitted under paragraph 2 (c) below, be entered without evidence of the permission of the Bank of England.

Registration of Addresses outside the Scheduled Territories.

2. Permission of the Bank of England is required for the entry in a Register in the United Kingdom of an address outside the Scheduled Territories in respect of any security except:—

(a) where it is the transferee's address in any form of transfer authorised by an Authorised Depositary or accompanied by a Form D or BUK similarly authorised;

(b) where the address appears in a form of application or request which complies with the requirements set out in sub-paragraphs (a) (ii), (b) (ii), (c) or (d) (ii) of paragraph 2 of Part I of this Notice;

(c) on a request to substitute another address in the same country as that already recorded;

(d) on transfer from another Register in the Scheduled Territories, provided the address is the same as that recorded in the other Register.

Recording of Mandates for Interest or Dividends.

3. A Registrar is permitted to record a mandate by a non-resident in favour of:—

(a) another resident in the same country; or

(b) a resident in the Scheduled Territories.

Permission of the Bank of England is required in respect of any other mandate which may be given by or in favour of a non-resident.

Acceptance of Signatures.

4. Signatures which purport to be those of Authorised Depositaries or Temporary Recipients may be accepted where there appears no reason to doubt their authenticity, provided that:—

(a) the signatories are included in the list of Authorised Depositaries or the classification indicated entitles them to sign the declarations or documents concerned;

(b) in the case of a firm, the firm name has been signed;

(c) an official, who has indicated his capacity, has signed on behalf of a company or corporate body.

Trading with the Enemy Act, 1939.

5. While it is to be understood that final responsibility for conforming with Trading with the Enemy legislation continues to rest with the persons concerned, it is considered that conformity with the administrative procedure established under the Exchange Control Act will, in general, provide an adequate safeguard.

APPENDIX I.

DEFINITIONS FOR THE PURPOSES OF E.C. SECURITIES NOTICES.

1. **Authorised Depositaries** ..   persons appointed by order of H.M. Treasury to receive securities into deposit in accordance with the terms of the Act. Authorised Depositaries may also in certain circumstances approve forms and give declarations relating to and otherwise deal in or with securities.

2. **Bearer Securities** ..   ..   securities by the delivery of which, with or without endorsement, the title to the securities is transferable.

3. **Coupon** ..   ..   ..   a coupon representing interest or dividends on a security *but not* a coupon conferring a right to acquire a security (see definition of Securities).

4. **Non-resident** ..   ..   regarded for the purposes of the Act as resident *outside* the Scheduled Territories.

5. **Prescribed Securities** ..   securities on which capital moneys, dividends or interest are payable in Belgian, Congolese, or Luxembourg francs, Canadian dollars, Swiss francs or U.S. dollars, or in respect of which the holder has an option to require payment of any capital moneys, dividends or interest in any of those currencies.

6. **Scheduled Territories** ..   the British Commonwealth (except Canada), the Irish Republic, British Trust Territories, British Protectorates and Protected States, Burma, Iraq, Iceland and the Hashemite Kingdom of the Jordan.

7. **Securities** ..   ..   ..   shares, stock, bonds, notes, debentures, debenture stock, units under a unit trust scheme, shares in an oil royalty, letters of allotment which may be renounced, letters of rights, coupons conferring rights to acquire securities, option warrants and certificates of deposit, *but not* promissory notes or Treasury Bills.

8. Subsidiary Register   ..   a Register in the Scheduled Territories the securities in which can, without the consent of the Registrar, be transferred to or in a Register outside those Territories.

9. Temporary Recipients   ..   persons who may in certain circumstances withdraw Deposited Securities, give declarations relating to and otherwise deal in or with securities.

FORMS TO WHICH REFERENCE IS MADE IN THIS NOTICE.

New or revised Forms, supplies of which may be obtained through banks and brokers:—

Form D   ..   ..   ..   for transfer of—

(which may be attached to or printed on a form of transfer)

(a) securities which are registered in the Scheduled Territories and are *not*—
   (i) in a Subsidiary Register, or
   (ii) payable as to interest or dividends by coupon, or
   (iii) Prescribed Securities.

(b) Letters of Allotment which may be renounced, Letters of Rights and Scrip Certificates to bearer issued in the United Kingdom.

Form BA   ..   ..   ..   for transfer of securities (except Prescribed Securities) which are—

(a) bearer (other than Letters of Allotment which may be renounced, Letters of Rights or Scrip Certificates issued in the United Kingdom), or

(b) payable as to interest or dividends by coupon, or

(c) registered in a Subsidiary Register, or

(d) registered outside the Scheduled Territories.

Form BUK   ..   ..   ..   for transfer of Prescribed Securities.

Certificate C   ..   ..   ..   certificate permitting the export of certain items, including securities and coupons, from the United Kingdom.

Note.—Appendix II and Appendix III which give current details of authorised depositories and temporary recipients respectively have been omitted.

EXCHANGE CONTROL ACT, 1947.

Reprinted by kind permission of the Bank of England as current at the date of publication.

INSTRUCTIONS TO REGISTRARS, COMPANY SECRETARIES AND PAYING AGENTS IN RESPECT OF INTEREST, DIVIDENDS AND CAPITAL REPAYMENTS ON SECURITIES, AND TO BANKS AND BANKERS PAYING WARRANTS ISSUED IN THE UNITED KINGDOM.

This Notice is one of an administrative series issued by the Bank of England to draw attention in convenient form to the law contained in the Act and Treasury Orders made thereunder, and (by virtue of powers delegated by H.M. Treasury under s. 37 of the Act) to give certain exemptions, permissions, consents, authorities and directions (including directions imposing certain requirements on bankers and others under s. 34 of the Act). It should be construed accordingly.

References to the United Kingdom should be read to include the Isle of Man and the Channel Islands and the term 'registered' to include 'inscribed.'

This Notice should be read in conjunction with Instructions to Registrars and Others concerned with Registers of Securities, Notice E.C. (Securities) 6, which lists Authorised Depositaries and Temporary Recipients and explains various terms used herein.

SUMMARY.

Securities registered as to both principal and interest or dividends in a Register which is not a Subsidiary Register.

Securities registered in a Subsidiary Register and capital repayments on securities registered as to principal only.

Bearer securities and coupons.

Interest, dividends or capital repayments by United Kingdom Companies controlled by non-residents.

Extraordinary repayments of capital.

Loan Service Accounts.

Sub-Paying Agents.

1. *Subject to the provisions of paragraphs 13 and 14 of this Notice, Registrars, Company Secretaries, Paying Agents and Paying Banks should follow the instructions set out in paragraphs 2 to 12 below.*

SECURITIES REGISTERED AS TO BOTH PRINCIPAL AND INTEREST OR DIVIDENDS IN A REGISTER WHICH IS NOT A SUBSIDIARY REGISTER.

Despatch of Warrants etc. to addresses within the Scheduled Territories.

2. Warrants etc. for interest, dividends or capital repayments in respect of securities in the names either of residents in the Scheduled Territories or of non-residents may be despatched

without formality to addresses within the Scheduled Territories. Details of such warrants must not be included in the schedules referred to in paragraph 4 below.

Despatch of Warrants etc. to addresses outside the Scheduled Territories.

3. Subject to the requirements of paragraphs 4 to 7 below warrants for interest, dividends or capital repayments may be despatched outside the Scheduled Territories to the address registered for the holder or given in a mandate. The circumstances in which Registrars etc. may enter or alter an address outside the Scheduled Territories or record a mandate with such an address are explained in Notice E.C. (Securities) 6.

Registrars' Schedules.

4. Before any warrants are despatched to addresses outside the Scheduled Territories, Registrars or Company Secretaries should lodge with the paying bank or banks schedules specifying:

> (*a*) the definitive numbers of the warrants (in numerical order);
>
> (*b*) the amount of each warrant;
>
> (*c*) the payee;
>
> (*d*) the country to which the warrant is being despatched.

5. The schedules must be signed by the Registrar or Company Secretary concerned and must embody a declaration that the instructions contained in this Notice regarding the despatch of warrants and in Notice E.C. (Securities) 6 regarding mandates and addresses outside the Scheduled Territories have been complied with.

6. The lodgment of signed schedules with paying banks will be considered as application to H.M. Treasury for permission to effect payment to non-residents of the proceeds of the relative warrants and no other formalities are required from Registrars or Company Secretaries.

7. Warrants listed in a Registrar's schedule may be paid by banks for the credit of the type of non-resident account indicated by the collecting bank's stamp irrespective of the country to which the warrant was despatched, provided that where the schedule does not bear the Bank of England's authorisation, the paying bank has no reason to believe that the payments arise under paragraphs 13 or 14 below.

The terms of this paragraph also apply to the payment of warrants in respect of interest on share, loan or deposit accounts listed in schedules prepared by Building Societies.

SECURITIES REGISTERED IN A SUBSIDIARY REGISTER AND CAPITAL REPAYMENTS ON SECURITIES REGISTERED AS TO PRINCIPAL ONLY.

Interest or Dividends on Securities Registered in a Subsidiary Register.

8. Since interest or dividends on such securities may not be paid if they are required under the Act to be deposited with an

Authorised Depositary and have not been so deposited, *Registrars or Company Secretaries should consult the Bank of England before sending out warrants for interest or dividends on holdings registered with addresses in the United Kingdom.*

9. In the case of holdings registered with addresses outside the United Kingdom Registrars or Company Secretaries should follow the procedure set out in paragraphs 1 to 7 above.

Capital Repayments on Securities Registered in a Subsidiary Register or Registered as to Principal only.

10. Registrars or Company Secretaries should follow the procedure set out in paragraphs 11 and 12 below.

BEARER SECURITIES AND COUPONS.

11. Coupons and drawn or matured securities may be paid only to an Authorised Depositary or a Temporary Recipient. Payment may be made to an Authorised Depositary without formality and to a Temporary Recipient provided the Paying Agent holds or has received from him a general or specific declaration to the effect:—

(a) that the security presented, or the security from which a coupon presented has been detached, is a Deposited Security or has been exempted from deposit; or

(b) provided the Temporary Recipient is a bank or banker, that the security or coupon presented has been received for collection from outside the United Kingdom accompanied by a declaration as to ownership and non-enemy interest as set out in T.W.E.D. Notices to Banks currently in force and signed/countersigned as laid down therein.

12. If a Form BA or BUK is also presented, it should be accepted, marked on the reverse 'Payment made' and signed, dated and forwarded to the delivering Depositary shown thereon.

INTEREST, DIVIDENDS OR CAPITAL REPAYMENTS BY UNITED KINGDOM COMPANIES CONTROLLED BY NON-RESIDENTS.

13. Before making an announcement or despatching any warrants Registrars and Company Secretaries should apply in writing to the Bank of England, Exchange Control (T.C. & I.), London, E.C.2, and should furnish the relevant Balance Sheet and Profit and Loss Account. If permission is given, the procedure described in paragraphs 2–10 above should be followed except that the relative schedules will require to be submitted to the Bank of England for authorisation.

EXTRAORDINARY PAYMENTS OF A CAPITAL NATURE.

14. Where any payments whatsoever of a capital nature, whether in sterling or in foreign currency, are being made, otherwise than as provided in the original terms of issue, by resident borrowers or issuers or where such payments are being made in sterling by any borrower or issuer through the medium of a Paying Agent in the United Kingdom, the Registrar, Company Secretary or Paying Agent concerned should apply in writing to

the Bank of England, Securities Control Office, London, E.C.2, before making any announcement or any payment or despatching any warrants. It is emphasised that the terms of this paragraph cover not only repayments of capital but also payments which are in the nature of a distribution of capital assets, capital reserves or capital gains arising from the realisation of assets.

Loan Service Accounts.

15. Service Accounts in respect of foreign sterling loans are to be regarded as resident accounts. The Bank of England must be advised if such accounts are credited with funds other than Service moneys. Such moneys must be provided either from a sterling account appropriate to the country of residence of the borrower or, alternatively, if the currency of that country is a Specified Currency, by the sale of that currency to an Authorised Dealer in the United Kingdom.

Sub-paying Agents.

16. Except where the Bank of England give permission to proceed otherwise, a principal Paying Agent in the United Kingdom must arrange for Sub-Paying Agents outside the United Kingdom to obtain, before making any payments, a declaration as to ownership and non-enemy interest as set out in T.W.E.D. Notices to Banks currently in force and signed/counter-signed as laid down therein. In addition Sub-Paying Agents outside the Scheduled Territories must be instructed not to make any payment where the declaration shows that the owner of the security is resident in the United Kingdom unless the presenter confirms that collection is for account of an Authorised Depositary or Temporary Recipient.

17. Application for permission to make payments to Sub-Paying Agents should be submitted to the Bank of England on a Sterling Transfer Form or Form E, as appropriate, through the United Kingdom bankers of the principal Paying Agents. The application must contain a statement that the Sub-Paying Agent concerned has been instructed as required under paragraph 16 above.

18. Declarations lodged with a Sub-Paying Agent should be forwarded in due course to the principal Paying Agent who should retain them for inspection if required.

Statutory Instruments.

1950 No. 1072

Permission has been given for this reprint, but it does not purport to be published 'by authority.'

EXCHANGE CONTROL

Payments

The Exchange Control (Payments) Order, 1950

Made	- - -	-	29th June, 1950
Laid before Parliament		-	30th June, 1950
Coming into Operation		-	1st July, 1950

Whereas by s. 5 of the Exchange Control Act, 1947 (*a*), restrictions are placed on certain payments and other transactions in the United Kingdom, but those restrictions are by s. 31 of that Act subject to such exemptions as may be granted by order of the Treasury;

And Whereas by s. 23 of the Exchange Control Act, 1947, payment for goods exported to a destination in any such territory as may be prescribed must be made in such manner as may be prescribed in relation to those territories;

And Whereas by the Exchange Control (Channel Islands) Order, 1947 (*b*), the provisions of the Exchange Control Act, 1947, other than ss. 38 and 43 thereof, are extended, with such modifications as are specified in that Order, to the Channel Islands;

And Whereas it is expedient to amend the exemptions heretofore granted and the provisions heretofore made and, in particular, to make such provision for certain territories outside the scheduled territories as hereinafter appears:

Now, therefore, the Treasury, in pursuance of the said ss. 5, 23 and 31, of those sections as extended to the Channel Islands, and of all other powers enabling them in that behalf, hereby make the following Order:—

1. References in this Order to any provision of the Exchange Control Act, 1947, include references to that provision as extended to the Channel Islands by the Exchange Control (Channel Islands) Order, 1947.

2. There shall be exempted from the provisions of s. 5 of the Exchange Control Act, 1947, anything done for the purpose of the transfer of the whole or any part of an amount standing to the credit of an

(i) an account of a person resident outside the scheduled territories, being a transfer to or to the account of a person resident in the scheduled territories;

(ii) an account of a person resident in any territory specified in the First Schedule to this Order, being a transfer to another account of a person resident in the same territory;

(iii) an account of a person resident in any territory specified in the Second Schedule to this Order, being a transfer to another account of a person resident in that territory, a transfer to the account of a person resident in or to a transferable account relating to any territory specified in the Third Schedule to this Order, or a transfer to the account of a person resident both outside the scheduled territories and outside any of the territories specified in the First, Second or Third Schedules to this Order;

(iv) a transferable account relating to any territory specified in the Third Schedule to this Order, being a transfer to the account of a person resident in or to a transferable account relating to any of the said territories, or a transfer to the account of a person resident both outside the scheduled territories and outside any of the territories specified in the First, Second or Third Schedules to this Order;

(v) an account (not being a transferable account) of a person resident in any territory specified in the Third Schedule to this Order, being a transfer to the account of a person resident in or to a transferable account relating to the same territory;

(vi) an account of a person resident both outside the scheduled territories and outside any of the territories specified in the First, Second or Third Schedules to this Order being a transfer to another such account.

3. There shall be exempted from the provisions of s. 5 of the Exchange Control Act, 1947, any payment made in cash in the United Kingdom or in the Channel Islands to a person resident outside the scheduled territories

(i) by a person resident outside the scheduled territories if that payment is made out of

(a) any notes of a class which are or have at any time been legal tender in the United Kingdom or the Channel Islands or any part of the United Kingdom or the Channel Islands and which have been legally imported into the United Kingdom or the Channel Islands, or

(b) any moneys withdrawn from an account in favour of that person with a banker in the United Kingdom or the Channel Islands, or

(c) any moneys arising from the sale of foreign currency by that person to an authorised dealer, or

(d) any foreign currency which has been legally imported into the United Kingdom or the Channel Islands provided that the payment is not made as consideration for or in association with the receipt by any person of sterling;

(ii) by a person resident in the scheduled territories if that payment

(a) does not exceed £10 sterling in value, and

(b) does not form part of a transaction or series of transactions wherein the aggregate value of the payments exceeds £10 sterling in value;

(iii) by a banker in the United Kingdom or the Channel Islands acting in the course of his business if that payment

(a) is made from moneys standing to the credit of an account in favour of that person with that banker, or

(b) is in respect of the encashment by that person of a travellers' cheque or letter of credit in favour of that person.

4.—(1) Section 23 of the Exchange Control Act, 1947, shall apply to territories outside the scheduled territories.

(2) The prescribed manners of payment for the purposes of the said s. 23 in relation to goods exported to a destination in any of the said territories are the manners specified in relation to those territories respectively in the second column of the Fourth Schedule hereto.

5.—(1) The provisions of this Order shall have effect subject to any restrictions imposed by any direction given by the Treasury under Regulation 2A of the Defence (Finance) Regulations, 1939.

(2)   The exemptions from the provisions of s. 5 of the Exchange Control Act, 1947, granted by this Order, shall not apply in relation to the transfer of the whole or any part of an amount standing to the credit of—

(a)   an account of a person resident in the Argentine Republic, being a transfer to an Argentine Guaranteed Account;

(b)   an account of a person resident in China;

(c)   an account of a person resident in Formosa;

(d)   an account of a person resident in the French Franc Area, which is not a French No. 1 Account, except in so far as the transfer may be from such an account to a French No. 1 Account;

(e)   an Israel No. 2 Account, except in so far as the transfer may be from one such account to another such account.

(3)   The exemptions from the provisions of s. 5 of the Exchange Control Act, 1947, granted by this Order, shall not apply in relation to the transfer of an amount from any account, being a transfer to the account of a person resident in China or to the account of a person resident in Formosa.

6.   In this Order:

(a)   The expression 'account' means a sterling account with a banker in the United Kingdom or the Channel Islands;

(b)   the expression 'transferable account' means any account which is for the time being recognised by the Bank of England for the purposes of this Order as a transferable account relating to any territory specified in the Third Schedule to this Order;

(c)   the expression 'Argentine Guaranteed Account' means an account which is for the time being recognised by the Bank of England as an Argentine Guaranteed Account for the purposes of this Order;

(d)   the expression 'French No. 1 Account' means an account which is for the time being recognised by the Bank of England for the purposes of this Order as an official account of the French Government or of the Government of any other territory comprised in the French Franc Area or of a banque agréée carrying on business in that Area;

(e)   the expression 'Israel No. 2 Account' means an account of a person resident in Israel which is for the time being recognised by the Bank of England as an Israel No. 2 Account for the purposes of this Order;

(f)   the expression 'Turkish Account' means an account of a person resident in Turkey which is for the time being recognised by the Bank of England as a Turkish Account for the purposes of this Order;

(g) the expression 'scheduled territories' has the meaning ascribed to it by s. 1 of the Exchange Control Act, 1947;

(h) where among the territories specified in any of the Schedules to this Order two or more territories are grouped together, the expression 'territory' shall include all the territories in that group.

7. The Exchange Control (Payments) Order, 1948 (c), the Exchange Control (Payments) (Chile) Order, 1948 (d), the Exchange Control (Payments) (Peru) Order, 1948 (e), the Exchange Control (Payments) (Tangier) Order, 1948 (f), the Exchange Control (Payments) (Faroe Islands) Order, 1948 (g), the Exchange Control (Payments) (Italy, Republic of San Marino and Trieste) Order, 1948 (h), the Exchange Control (Payments) (Western Zones of Germany and Saar Territory) Order, 1949 (i), the Exchange Control (Payments) (French Somali Coast) Order, 1949 (j), the Exchange Control (Payments) (Lebanon) Order, 1949 (k), the Exchange Control (Payments) (Czechoslovakia) Order, 1949 (l), and the Exchange Control (Payments) (China and Formosa) Order, 1949 (m), are hereby revoked.

8. This Order shall extend to the Channel Islands.

9.—(1) This Order may be cited as the Exchange Control (Payments) Order, 1950.

(2) The Interpretation Act, 1889 (n), shall apply to the interpretation of this Order as it applies to the interpretation of an Act of Parliament.

10. This Order shall come into force on the first day of July, 1950.

Dated this twenty-ninth day of June, 1950.

> W. A. Wilkins,
> Wm. Hannan,
>
> Two of the Lords Commissioners of
> His Majesty's Treasury.

First Schedule

Group 1. The Argentine Republic.
     " 2. Austria.
     " 3. The Belgian Monetary Area, that is to say, Belgium, Luxembourg, Belgian Congo and the Trust Territory of Ruanda-Urundi.
     " 4. Brazil.
     " 5. Bulgaria.
     " 6. Canada.
     " 7. Denmark, the Faroe Islands and Greenland.

(c) S.I. 1948 (No. 1080) I, p. 928.   (d) S.I. 1948 (No. 1418) I, p. 936.
(e) S.I. 1948 (No. 1736) I, p. 942.   (f) S.I. 1948 (No. 1856) I, p. 943.
(g) S.I. 1948 (No. 2423) I, p. 938.   (h) S.I. 1948 (No. 2628) I, p. 939.
(i) S.I. 1949 (No. 540) I, p. 1625.   (j) S.I. 1949 (No. 890) I, p. 1622.
(k) S.I. 1949 (No. 895) I, p. 1624.   (l) S.I. 1949 (No. 1554) I, p. 1620.
(m) S.I. 1949 (No. 2365) I, p. 1618.   (n) 52 & 53 Vict. c. 63.

Group 8. The French Franc Area, that is to say, Metropolitan France (which includes Corsica and Algeria), the Saar Territory, Monaco, Viet Nam, Laos and Cambodia, French West Africa, French Equatorial Africa, Madagascar and its dependencies, Reunion, French Guiana, Guadeloupe, Martinique, St. Pierre and Miquelon, French Establishments in India, New Caledonia, French Establishments in Oceania, Condominium of the New Hebrides, the Protectorates of Morocco and Tunisia, and the French Trust Territories of Cameroon and Togo.

„   9. The Western Zones of Germany, that is to say, the areas in Germany (including the French, British and United States Sectors of Berlin) for the time being under the authority of the High Commissioners of France, the United Kingdom and the United States of America.

„   10. Greece.
„   11. Hungary.
„   12. Israel.
„   13. Japan, that is to say, the four main islands of Japan (Hokkaido, Honshu, Kyuchu and Shikoku) and the adjacent islands which are under the control of the Supreme Commander for the Allied Powers.
„   14. The Lebanon.
„   15. Paraguay.
„   16. Peru.
„   17. The Portuguese Monetary Area, that is to say, Portugal and the Portuguese Empire.
„   18. Roumania.
„   19. The French Somali Coast.
„   20. Switzerland and Liechtenstein.
„   21. Syria.
„   22. The Tangier Zone of Morocco.
„   23. Turkey.
„   24. Uruguay.
„   25. The Vatican City.
„   26. Yugoslavia.

SECOND SCHEDULE

Group 1. The United States of America, and any territory under the sovereignty of the United States of America; former Japanese Pacific Islands under United States trusteeship and other former Japanese Islands under United States military administration; the Philippine Islands; Bolivia, Colombia, Costa Rica, Cuba, the Dominican Republic, Ecuador, Guatemala, Haiti, Honduras, Mexico, Nicaragua, Panama, el Salvador and Venezuela.

THIRD SCHEDULE

Group 1. Chile.
„   2. Czechoslovakia.

Group 3. Egypt, and that area of the former territory of Palestine at present administered by Egypt.
 „   4. Ethiopia.
 „   5. Finland.
 „   6. Iran.
 „   7. The Italian Republic, the Republic of San Marino and the Free Territory of Trieste.
 „   8. The Netherlands Monetary Area, that is to say, the Netherlands, the Republic of the United States of Indonesia, the Netherlands New Guinea, Surinam and the Netherlands Antilles.
 „   9. Norway.
 „   10. Poland.
 „   11. The Spanish Monetary Area, that is to say, the Peninsular Territories of the Spanish State, the Canary Isles and the Balearic Isles, Ceuta and Melilla, the Spanish Zone of Morocco and the Spanish Colonies.
 „   12. The Anglo-Egyptian Sudan.
 „   13. Sweden.
 „   14. Thailand.
 „   15. The Union of Soviet Socialist Republics.

EXPLANATORY NOTE

(This Note is not part of the Order, but is intended to indicate its general purport.)

With the exception of its provisions relating to the Argentine Republic, Japan and Paraguay, this Order consolidates the provisions of the following Orders:—

The Exchange Control (Payments) Order, 1948 (S.I. 1948 No. 1080);
The Exchange Control (Payments) (Chile) Order, 1948 (S.I. 1948 No. 1418);
The Exchange Control (Payments) (Peru) Order, 1948 (S.I. 1948 No. 1736);
The Exchange Control (Payments) (Tangier) Order, 1948 (S.I. 1948 No. 1856);
The Exchange Control (Payments) (Faroe Islands) Order, 1948 (S.I. 1948 No. 2423);
The Exchange Control (Payments) (Italy, Republic of San Marino and Trieste) Order, 1948 (S.I. 1948 No. 2628);
The Exchange Control (Payments) (Western Zones of Germany and Saar Territory) Order, 1949 (S.I. 1949 No. 540);
The Exchange Control (Payments) (French Somali Coast) Order, 1949 (S.I. 1949 No. 890);
The Exchange Control (Payments) (Lebanon) Order, 1949 (S.I. 1949 No. 895);
The Exchange Control (Payments) (Czechoslovakia) Order, 1949 (S.I. 1949 No. 1554), and
The Exchange Control (Payments) (China and Formosa) Order, 1949 (S.I. 1949 No. 2365).

In the case of the Argentine Republic, this Order modifies the exemptions granted by the Exchange Control (Payments) Order, 1948, which enabled all transfers between the sterling accounts of residents of the Argentine Republic to be made without the specific permission of the Treasury.

In the case of Japan, this Order modifies the prescribed manner of payment for exports from the United Kingdom to Japan.

In the case of Paraguay, this Order varies the arrangements for payments between the United Kingdom and Paraguay.

In addition this Order ceases to apply the provisions of the Exchange Control (Payments) Order, 1948, to the Hashemite Kingdom of the Jordan, as that country is now one of the scheduled territories for the purposes of the Exchange Control Act, 1947.

APPENDIX N

Permission has been given for this reprint, but it does not purport to be published 'by authority.'

Winding-up Rules

Extracts from "The Companies (Winding-up) Rules, 1949, dated 23rd February, 1949, made pursuant to the Companies Act, 1948."

1 to 90 * * * * *

Proofs.

91. In a winding-up by the Court every creditor shall subject as hereinafter provided prove his debt, unless the Judge in any particular winding-up shall give directions that any creditors or class of creditors shall be admitted without proof.

Mode of proof.

92. A debt may be proved in any winding-up by delivering or sending through the post an affidavit verifying the debt. In a winding-up by the Court the affidavit shall be so sent to the Official Receiver or if a Liquidator has been appointed, to the Liquidator; and in any other winding-up the affidavit may be so sent to the Liquidator.

Verification of proof.

93. An affidavit proving a debt may be made by the creditor himself or by some person authorised by or on behalf of the creditor. If made by a person so authorised, it shall state his authority and means of knowledge.

Contents of proof.
Form 59.

94. An affidavit proving a debt shall contain or refer to a statement of account showing the particulars of the debt, and shall specify the vouchers if any, by which the same can be substantiated. The Official Receiver or Liquidator to whom the proof is sent may at any time call for the production of the vouchers.

Statement of security.

95. An affidavit proving a debt shall state whether the creditor is or is not a secured creditor.

Proof before whom sworn.

96. An affidavit proving a debt may in a winding-up by the Court be sworn before an Official Receiver, or Assistant Official Receiver, or any Officer of the Board of Trade or any Clerk of an Official Receiver duly authorised in writing by the Court or the Board of Trade in that behalf.

Costs of proof.

97. A creditor shall bear the cost of proving his debt unless the Court otherwise orders.

Discount.

98. A creditor proving his debt shall deduct therefrom (*a*) any discount which he may have agreed to allow for payment in cash in excess of five per centum on the net amount of his claim and (*b*) all trade discounts.

99. When any rent or other payment falls due at stated periods, Periodical payments. and the order or resolution to wind-up is made at any time other than one of those periods, the persons entitled to the rent or payment may prove for a proportionate part thereof up to the date of the winding-up order or resolution as if the rent or payment grew due from day to day. Provided that where the Liquidator remains in occupation of premises demised to a Company which is being wound up, nothing herein contained shall prejudice or affect the right of the landlord of such premises to claim payment by the Company, or the Liquidator, of rent during the period of the Company's or the Liquidator's occupation.

100. On any debt or sum certain, payable at a certain time or Interest. otherwise, whereon interest is not reserved or agreed for, and which is overdue at the date of the commencement of the winding-up, the creditor may prove for interest at a rate not exceeding four per centum per annum to that date from the time when the debt or sum was payable, if the debt or sum is payable by virtue of a written instrument at a certain time, and if payable otherwise, then from the time when a demand in writing has been made, giving notice that interest will be claimed from the date of the demand until the time of payment.

101. A creditor may prove for a debt not payable at the date of Proof for debt payable at a future time. the winding-up order or resolution, as if it were payable presently, and may receive dividends equally with the other creditors, deducting only thereout a rebate of interest at the rate of five per centum per annum computed from the declaration of a dividend to the time when the debt would have become payable according to the terms on which it was contracted.

102. Unless the Official Receiver or Liquidator shall in any Proof under section 319. special case otherwise direct formal proof of the debts mentioned in paragraph (e) of subsection (1) of section 319 of the Act shall not be required.

103. In any case in which it appears that there are numerous Workmen's wages.
Form 60. claims for wages or accrued holiday remuneration by workmen and others employed by the Company, it shall be sufficient if one proof for all such claims is made either by a foreman or by some other person on behalf of all such creditors. Such proof shall have annexed thereto as forming part thereof, a schedule setting forth the names of the workmen and others, and the amounts severally due to them. Any proof made in compliance with this Rule shall have the same effect as if separate proofs had been made by each of the said workmen and others.

104 and **105**   *   *   *   *   *

ADMISSION AND REJECTION OF PROOFS AND PREFERENTIAL CLAIMS AND APPEAL TO THE COURT.

106.—(1) Subject to the provisions of the Act, and unless other- Notice to Creditors to prove. wise ordered by the Court, the Liquidator in any winding-up may from time to time fix a certain day, which shall be not less than fourteen days from the date of the notice, on or before which the creditors of the Company are to prove their debts or claims, and to establish any title they may have to priority under section 319 of the Act, or to be excluded from the benefit of any distribution made before such debts are proved, or as the case may be from objecting to such distribution.

(2) The Liquidator shall give notice in writing of the day so fixed by advertisement in such newspaper as he shall consider convenient, and in a winding-up by the Court to every person mentioned in the Statement of Affairs as a creditor who has not proved his debt, and to every person mentioned in the Statement of Affairs as a preferential creditor whose claim to be a preferential creditor has not been established and is not admitted, and in any other winding-up to the last known address or place of abode of each person who, to the knowledge of the Liquidator, claims to be a creditor or preferential creditor of the Company and whose claim has not been admitted.

(3) All the Rules hereinafter set out as to admission and rejection of proofs shall apply with the necessary variations to any such claim to priority as aforesaid.

Examination of proof.
Form 61.

107. The Liquidator shall examine every proof of debt lodged with him, and the grounds of the debt, and in writing admit or reject it, in whole or in part, or require further evidence in support of it.   If he rejects a proof he shall state in writing to the creditor the grounds of the rejection.

Appeal by creditor.

108. If a creditor or contributory is dissatisfied with the decision of the Liquidator in respect of a proof, the Court may, on the application of the creditor or contributory, reverse or vary the decision; but, subject to the power of the Court to extend the time, no application to reverse or vary the decision of the Liquidator in a winding-up by the Court rejecting a proof sent to him by a creditor, or person claiming to be a creditor, shall be entertained, unless notice of the application is given before the expiration of twenty-one days from the date of the service of the notice of rejection.

Expunging at instance of Liquidator.

109. If the Liquidator thinks that a proof has been improperly admitted, the Court may, on the application of the Liquidator, after notice to the creditor who made the proof, expunge the proof or reduce its amount.

Expunging at instance of creditor.

110. The Court may also expunge or vary a proof upon the application of a creditor or contributory if the Liquidator declines to interfere in the matter.

111 to 118   *   *   *   *   *

119 and 120   *   *   *   *   *

121 to 126   *   *   *   *   *

GENERAL MEETINGS OF CREDITORS AND CONTRIBUTORIES IN RELATION TO WINDING-UP BY THE COURT AND OF CREDITORS IN RELATION TO A CREDITORS' VOLUNTARY WINDING-UP

Liquidator's meetings of creditors and contributories.

127.—(1) In addition to the first meetings of creditors and contributories and in addition also to meetings of creditors and contributories directed to be held by the Court under section 346 of the Act (hereinafter referred to as Court meetings of creditors and contributories), the Liquidator in any winding-up by the Court may himself from time to time subject to the provisions of the Act and the control of the Court summon, hold and conduct meetings of the creditors or contributories (hereinafter referred to as Liquidator's meetings of creditors and contributories) for the purpose of ascertaining their wishes in all matters relating to the winding-up.

(2) In any creditors' voluntary winding-up the Liquidator may himself from time to time summon, hold and conduct meetings of creditors for the purpose of ascertaining their wishes in all matters relating to the winding-up (such meetings and all meetings of creditors which a Liquidator or a Company is by the Act required to convene in or immediately before such a voluntary winding-up and all meetings convened by a creditor in a voluntary winding-up under these Rules are hereinafter called voluntary liquidation meetings).

128. Except where and so far as the nature of the subject-matter or the context may otherwise require the Rules as to meetings hereinafter set out shall apply to first meetings, Court meetings, Liquidator's meetings of creditors and contributories, and voluntary liquidation meetings, but so nevertheless that the said Rules shall take effect as to first meetings subject and without prejudice to any express provisions of the Act and as to Court meetings subject and without prejudice to any express directions of the Court. *Application of rules as to meetings.*

129.—(1) The Official Receiver or Liquidator shall summon all meetings of creditors and contributories by giving not less than seven days' notice of the time and place thereof in the *London Gazette* and in a local paper; and shall not less than seven days before the day appointed for the meeting send by post to every person appearing by the Company's books to be a creditor of the Company notice of the meeting of creditors, and to every person appearing by the Company's books or otherwise to be a contributory of the Company notice of the meeting of contributories. *Summoning of meetings. Form 75.*

(2) The notice to each creditor shall be sent to the address given in his proof, or if he has not proved to the address given in the Statement of Affairs of the Company, if any, or to such other address as may be known to the person summoning the meeting. The notice to each contributory shall be sent to the address mentioned in the Company's books as the address of such contributory, or to such other address as may be known to the person summoning the meeting.

(3) In the case of meetings under section 297 of the Act the continuing Liquidator or if there is no continuing Liquidator any creditor may summon the meeting.

(4) This Rule shall not apply to meetings under section 293 or section 300 of the Act.

130. A certificate by the Official Receiver or other officer of the Court, or by the clerk of any such person, or an affidavit by the Liquidator, or creditor, or his solicitor, or the clerk of either of such persons, or as the case may be by some officer of the Company *Proof of notice. Forms 76 and 77.*

or its solicitor or the clerk of such Company or solicitor, that the notice of any meeting has been duly posted, shall be sufficient evidence of such notice having been duly sent to the person to whom the same was addressed.

Place of meetings.

131. Every meeting shall be held at such place as is in the opinion of the person convening the same most convenient for the majority of the creditors or contributories or both. Different times or places or both may if thought expedient be named for the meetings of creditors and for the meetings of contributories.

Costs of calling meetings.

132. The costs of summoning a meeting of creditors or con- tributories at the instance of any person other than the Official Receiver or Liquidator shall be paid by the person at whose instance it is summoned who shall before the meeting is summoned deposit with the Official Receiver or Liquidator (as the case may be) such sum as may be required by the Official Receiver or Liquidator as security for the payment of such costs. The costs of summoning such meeting of creditors or contributories, in- cluding all disbursements for printing, stationery, postage and the hire of room, shall be calculated at the following rate for each creditor or contributory to whom notice is required to be sent, namely, two shillings per creditor or contributory for the first 20 creditors or contributories, one shilling per creditor or contribu- tory for the next 30 creditors or contributories, sixpence per creditor or contributory for any number of creditors or contribu- tories after the first 50. The said costs shall be repaid out of the assets of the Company if the Court shall by order or if the credi- tors or contributories (as the case may be) shall by resolution so direct. This Rule shall not apply to .meetings under sections 293 or 297 of the Act.

Chairman of meeting.
Form 78.

133. Where a meeting is summoned by the Official Receiver or the Liquidator, he or someone nominated by him shall be Chair- man of the meeting. At every other meeting of creditors or contributories the Chairman shall be such person as the meeting by resolution shall appoint. This Rule shall not apply to meetings under section 293 of the Act.

Ordinary resolution of creditors and contributories.

134. At a meeting of creditors a resolution shall be deemed to be passed when a majority in number and value of the creditors present personally or by proxy and voting on the resolution have voted in favour of the resolution, and at a meeting of the contribu- tories a resolution shall be deemed to be passed when a majority in number and value of the contributories present personally or by proxy, and voting on the resolution, have voted in favour of the resolution, the value of the contributories being determined according to the number of votes conferred on each contributory by the regulations of the Company.

Copy of resolu- tion to be filed.

135. The Official Receiver or as the case may be the Liquidator shall file with the Registrar a copy certified by him of every resolution of a meeting of creditors or contributories in a winding- up by the Court.

136. Where a meeting of creditors or contributories is summoned by notice the proceedings and resolutions at the meeting shall unless the Court otherwise orders be valid notwithstanding that some creditors or contributories may not have received the notice sent to them.

Non-reception of notice by a creditor.

137. The Chairman may with the consent of the meeting adjourn it from time to time and from place to place, but the adjourned meeting shall be held at the same place as the original meeting unless in the resolution for adjournment another place is specified or unless the Court otherwise orders.

Adjournments. Form 79.

138.—(1) A meeting may not act for any purpose except the election of a chairman, the proving of debts and the adjournment of the meeting unless there are present or represented thereat, in the case of a creditors' meeting, at least three creditors entitled to vote or, in the case of a meeting of contributories, at least three contributories or all the creditors entitled to vote or all the contributories if the number of creditors entitled to vote or the number of contributories as the case may be shall not exceed three.

Quorum.

(2) If within half an hour from the time appointed for the meeting a quorum of creditors or contributories, as the case may be, is not present or represented, the meeting shall be adjourned to the same day in the following week at the same time and place or to such other day or time or place as the chairman may appoint, but so that the day appointed shall be not less than seven or more than twenty-one days from the day from which the meeting was adjourned.

139. In the case of a first meeting of creditors or of an adjournment thereof a person shall not be entitled to vote as a creditor unless he has duly lodged with the Official Receiver, not later than the time mentioned for that purpose in the notice convening the meeting or adjourned meeting, a proof of the debt which he claims to be due to him from the Company. In the case of a Court meeting or Liquidator's meeting of creditors a person shall not be entitled to vote as a creditor unless he has lodged with the Official Receiver or Liquidator a proof of the debt which he claims to be due to him from the Company and such proof has been admitted wholly or in part before the date on which the meeting is held: Provided that this and the next four following Rules shall not apply to a Court meeting of creditors held prior to the first meeting of creditors. This Rule shall not apply to any creditors or class of creditors who by virtue of the Rules or any directions given thereunder are not required to prove their debts or to any voluntary liquidation meeting.

Creditors entitled to vote.

140. A creditor shall not vote in respect of any unliquidated or contingent debt or any debt the value of which is not ascertained, nor shall a creditor vote in respect of any debt on or secured by a current bill of exchange or promissory note held by him unless he is willing to treat the liability to him thereon of every person who is liable thereon antecedently to the Company, and against whom a Receiving Order in Bankruptcy has not been made, as a security

Cases in which creditors may not vote.

in his hands, and to estimate the value thereof, and for the purposes of voting, but not for the purposes of dividend, to deduct it from his proof.

Votes of secured creditors.

141. For the purpose of voting, a secured creditor shall, unless he surrenders his security, state in his proof or in a voluntary liquidation in such a statement as is hereinafter mentioned the particulars of his security, the date when it was given, and the value at which he assesses it, and shall be entitled to vote only in respect of the balance (if any) due to him after deducting the value of his security. If he votes in respect of his whole debt he shall be deemed to have surrendered his security, unless the Court on application is satisfied that the omission to value the security has arisen from inadvertence.

Creditor required to give up security.

142. The Official Receiver or Liquidator may, within twenty-eight days after a proof or in a voluntary liquidation a statement estimating the value of a security as aforesaid has been used in voting at a meeting, require the creditor to give up the security for the benefit of the creditors generally on payment of the value so estimated with an addition thereto of twenty per cent: Provided that where a creditor has valued his security he may at any time before being required to give it up correct the valuation by a new proof and deduct the new value from his debt, but in that case the said addition of twenty per cent. shall not be made if the security is required to be given up.

Admission and rejection of proofs for purpose of voting.

143. The Chairman shall have power to admit or reject a proof for the purpose of voting, but his decision shall be subject to appeal to the Court. If he is in doubt whether a proof shall be admitted or rejected he shall mark it as objected to and allow the creditor to vote subject to the vote being declared invalid in the event of the objection being sustained.

Statement of security.

144. For the purpose of voting at any voluntary liquidation meetings, a secured creditor shall, unless he surrender his security, lodge with the Liquidator or, where there is no Liquidator, at the Registered Office of the Company, before the meeting a statement giving the particulars of his security, the date when it was given and the value at which he assesses it.

Minutes of meeting.

145.—(1) The Chairman shall cause minutes of the proceedings at the meeting to be drawn up and fairly entered in a book kept for that purpose and the minutes shall be signed by him or by the Chairman of the next ensuing meeting.

Form 74.

(2) A list of creditors and contributories present at every meeting shall be made and kept as in Form 74 in the Appendix.

PROXIES IN RELATION TO A WINDING-UP BY THE COURT AND TO MEETINGS OF CREDITORS IN A CREDITORS' VOLUNTARY WINDING-UP

Proxies.

146. A creditor or a contributory may vote either in person or by proxy. Where a person is authorised in manner provided by section 139 of the Act to represent a corporation at any meeting of creditors or contributories such person shall produce to the Official Receiver or Liquidator or other the Chairman of the meeting a copy of the resolution so authorising him. Such copy must either be under the seal of the corporation or must be certified to be a true copy by the secretary or a director of the corporation. The succeeding Rules as to proxies shall not (unless otherwise directed by the Court) apply to a Court meeting of creditors or contributories prior to the first meeting.

147. Every instrument of proxy shall be in accordance with the appropriate form in the Appendix. *Form of proxies. Forms 80 and 81.*

148. General and special forms of proxy shall be sent to the creditors and contributories with the notice summoning the meeting, and neither the name nor description of the Official Receiver or Liquidator or any other person shall be printed or inserted in the body of any instrument of proxy before it is so sent. *Forms of proxy to be sent with notices.*

149. A creditor or a contributory may give a general proxy to any person. *General proxies.*

150. A creditor or a contributory may give a special proxy to any person to vote at any specified meeting or adjournment thereof:— *Special proxies.*

    (*a*) for or against the appointment or continuance in office of any specified person as Liquidator or Member of the Committee of Inspection, and;

    (*b*) on all questions relating to any matter other than those above referred to and arising at the meeting or an adjournment thereof.

151. Where it appears to the satisfaction of the Court that any solicitation has been used by or on behalf of a Liquidator in obtaining proxies or in procuring his appointment as Liquidator except by the direction of a meeting of creditors or contributories, the Court if it thinks fit may order that no remuneration be allowed to the person by whom or on whose behalf the solicitation was exercised notwithstanding any resolution of the Committee of Inspection or of the creditors or contributories to the contrary. *Solicitation by Liquidator to obtain proxies.*

152. A creditor or a contributory in a winding-up by the Court may appoint the Official Receiver or Liquidator and in a voluntary winding-up the Liquidator or if there is no Liquidator the Chairman of a meeting to act as his general or special proxy. *Proxies to Official Receiver or Liquidator.*

153. No person acting either under a general or a special proxy shall vote in favour of any resolution which would directly or indirectly place himself, his partner or employer in a position to receive any remuneration out of the estate of the Company otherwise than as a creditor rateably with the other creditors of the Company: Provided that where any person holds special proxies to vote for an application to the Court in favour of the appointment of himself as Liquidator he may use the said proxies and vote accordingly. *Holder of proxy not to vote on matter in which he is financially interested.*

154.—(1) A proxy intended to be used at the first meeting of creditors or contributories, or an adjournment thereof, shall be lodged with the Official Receiver not later than the time mentioned for that purpose in the notice convening the meeting or the *Proxies. Forms 80 and 81.*

adjourned meeting, which time shall be not earlier than twelve o'clock at noon of the day but one before, nor later than twelve o'clock at noon of the day before the day appointed for such meeting, unless the Court otherwise directs.

(2) In every other case a proxy shall be lodged with the Official Receiver or Liquidator in a winding-up by the Court, with the Company at its Registered Office for a meeting under section 293 of the Act, and with the Liquidator or if there is no Liquidator with the person named in the notice convening the meeting to receive the same in a voluntary winding-up not later than four o'clock in the afternoon of the day before the meeting or adjourned meeting at which it is to be used.

(3) No person shall be appointed a general or special proxy who is a minor.

Use of proxies by deputy.
Form 78.
155. Where an Official Receiver who holds any proxies cannot attend the meeting for which they are given, he may, in writing, depute some person under his official control to use the proxies on his behalf and in such manner as he may direct.

Filling in where creditor blind or incapable.
156. The proxy of a creditor blind or incapable of writing may be accepted if such creditor has attached his signature or mark thereto in the presence of a witness, who shall add to his signature his description and residence: Provided that such witness shall have certified at the foot of the proxy that all such insertions have been made at the request and in the presence of the creditor before he attached his signature or mark.

157 to 159   *   *   *   *   *

LIQUIDATOR AND COMMITTEE OF INSPECTION

Limit of remuneration.
160. Except as provided by the Act or the Rules, a Liquidator shall not under any circumstances whatever make any arrangement for, or accept from any solicitor, auctioneer, or any other person connected with the Company of which he is Liquidator, or who is employed in or in connnection with the winding-up of the Company, any gift, remuneration, or pecuniary or other consideration of benefit whatever beyond the remuneration to which under the Act and the Rules he is entitled as Liquidator, nor shall he make any arrangement for giving up, or give up any part of such remuneration to any such solicitor, auctioneer, or other person.

Dealings with assets.
161. Neither the Liquidator, nor any member of the Committee of Inspection of a Company shall, while acting as Liquidator or member of such committee, except by leave of the Court, either directly or indirectly, by himself or any employer, partner, clerk, agent, or servant, become purchaser of any part of the Company's assets. Any such purchase made contrary to the provisions of this Rule may be set aside by the Court on the application of the Board of Trade in a winding-up by the Court or of any creditor or contributory in any winding-up, and the Court may make such order as to costs as the Court shall think fit.

162. Where the Liquidator carries on the business of the Company, he shall not, without the express sanction of the Court, purchase goods for the carrying on of such business from any person whose connection with him is of such a nature as would result in his obtaining any portion of the profit (if any) arising out of the transaction. *Restriction on purchase of goods by Liquidator.*

163. No member of a Committee of Inspection shall, except under and with the sanction of the Court, directly or indirectly, by himself, or any employer, partner, clerk, agent, or servant, be entitled to derive any profit from any transaction arising out of the winding-up or to receive out of the assets any payment for services rendered by him in connection with the administration of the assets, or for any goods supplied by him to the Liquidator for or on account of the Company. In a winding-up by the Court if it appears to the Board of Trade or in a voluntary winding-up if it appears to the Committee of Inspection or to any meeting of creditors or contributories that any profit or payment has been made contrary to the provisions of this Rule, they may disallow such payment or recover such profit, as the case may be, on the audit of the Liquidator's accounts or otherwise. *Committee of Inspection not to make profit.*

164. In any case in which the sanction of the Court is obtained under the two last preceding Rules, the cost of obtaining such sanction shall be borne by the person in whose interest such sanction is obtained, and shall not be payable out of the Company's assets. *Costs of obtaining sanction of Court.*

165. Where the sanction of the Court to a payment to a member of a Committee of Inspection for services rendered by him in connection with the administration of the Company's assets is obtained, the order of the Court shall specify the nature of the services, and such sanction shall only be given where the service performed is of a special nature. Except by the express sanction of the Court no remuneration shall, under any circumstances, be paid to a member of a Committee for services rendered by him in the discharge of the duties attaching to his office as a member of such Committee. *Sanction of payments to Committee.*

166.—(I) When a Liquidator appointed by the Court has notified his appointment to the Registrar of Companies and has given security to the Board of Trade, the Official Receiver shall forthwith put the Liquidator into possession of all property of the Company of which the Official Receiver may have custody: Provided that such Liquidator, before the assets are handed over to him by the Official Receiver, shall have discharged any balance due to the Official Receiver on account of fees, costs, and charges properly incurred by him, and on account of any advances properly made by him in respect of the Company, together with interest on such advances at the rate of four pounds per centum per annum, and the Liquidator shall pay all fees, costs, and charges of the Official Receiver which may not have been discharged by the Liquidator before being put into possession of the property of the Company, whether incurred before or after he has been put into such possession. *Discharge of costs before assets handed to Liquidator.*

D 2

(2) The Official Receiver shall be deemed to have a lien upon the Company's assets until such balance shall have been paid and the other liabilities shall have been discharged.

(3) It shall be the duty of the Official Receiver, if so requested by the Liquidator, to communicate to the Liquidator all such information respecting the estate and affairs of the Company as may be necessary or conducive to the due discharge of the duties of the Liquidator.

(4) This and the next following Rule shall only apply in a winding-up by the Court.

Resignation of Liquidator.

167. A Liquidator who desires to resign his office shall summon separate meetings of the creditors and contributories of the Company to decide whether or not the resignation shall be accepted. If the creditors and contributories by ordinary resolutions both agree to accept the resignation of the Liquidator, he shall file with the Registrar a memorandum of his resignation and shall send notice thereof to the Official Receiver, and the resignation shall thereupon take effect. In any other case the Liquidator shall report to the Court the result of the meetings and shall send a report to the Official Receiver and thereupon the Court may, upon the application of the Liquidator or the Official Receiver, determine whether or not the resignation of the Liquidator shall be accepted, and may give such directions and make such orders as in the opinion of the Court shall be necessary.

Office of Liquidator vacated by his insolvency.

168. If a Receiving Order in Bankruptcy is made against a Liquidator, he shall thereby vacate his office, and for the purposes of the application of the Act and Rules shall be deemed to have been removed.

Payments Into and Out of a Bank

Payments out of Bank of England.

169. All payments out of the Companies Liquidation Account shall be made in such manner as the Board of Trade may from time to time direct.

Special Bank account.

Forms 82 and 83.

170.—(1) Where the Liquidator in a winding-up by the Court is authorised to have a special bank account, he shall forthwith pay all moneys received by him into that account to the credit of the Liquidator of the Company. All payments out shall be made by cheque payable to order, and every cheque shall have marked or written on the face of it the name of the Company, and shall be signed by the Liquidator, and shall be countersigned by at least one member of the Committee of Inspection, and by such other person, if any, as the Committee of Inspection may appoint.

(2) Where application is made to the Board of Trade to authorise the Liquidator in a winding-up by the Court to make his payments into and out of a special bank account, the Board of Trade may grant such authorisation for such time and on such terms as they may think fit, and may at any time order the account to be closed if they are of opinion that the account is no longer required for the purposes mentioned in the application.

Books

171. In a winding-up by the Court the Official Receiver, until a Record Book. Liquidator is appointed by the Court, and thereafter the Liquidator, shall keep a book to be called the 'Record Book' in which he shall record all minutes, all proceedings had and resolutions passed at any meeting of creditors or contributories, or of the Committee of Inspection, and all such matters as may be necessary to give a correct view of his administration of the Company's affairs; but he shall not be bound to insert in the 'Record Book' any document of a confidential nature (such as the opinion of counsel on any matter affecting the interest of the creditors or contributories), nor need he exhibit such document to any person other than a member of the Committee of Inspection, the Official Receiver, or the Board of Trade.

172. In a winding-up by the Court the Official Receiver, until a Cash Book. Liquidator is appointed by the Court, and thereafter the Liquidator, shall keep a book to be called the 'Cash Book' (which shall be in such form as the Board of Trade may from time to time direct) in which he shall (subject to the provisions of the Rules as to trading accounts) enter from day to day the receipts and payments made by him.

(2) In a winding-up by the Court a Liquidator other than the Official Receiver shall submit the Record Book and Cash Book, together with any other requisite books and vouchers, to the Committee of Inspection (if any) when required, and not less than once every three months.

(3) In a creditors' voluntary winding-up the Liquidator shall keep such books as the Committee of Inspection or if there is no such Committee as the creditors direct and all books kept by the Liquidator shall be submitted to the Committee of Inspection or if there is no such Committee to the creditors with any other books documents papers and accounts in his possession relating to his office as Liquidator or to the company as and when the Committee of Inspection or if there is no such Committee the creditors direct.

Investment of Funds

173.—(1) Where in a winding-up by the Court or in a creditors' Investment of assets in securities and realisation of securities. voluntary winding-up the Committee of Inspection are of opinion that any part of the cash balance standing to the credit of the account of the Company should be invested, they shall sign a certificate and request, and the Liquidator shall transmit Forms 84 and 85. such certificate and request to the Board of Trade.

(2) Where the Committee of Inspection in any such winding-up are of opinion that it is advisable to sell any of the securities in which the moneys of the Company's assets are invested they shall sign a certificate and request to that effect, and the Liquidator shall transmit such certificate and request to the Board of Trade.

(3) Where there is no Committee of Inspection in any such winding-up as is mentioned in paragraphs (1) and (2) of this Rule and in every members' voluntary winding-up whether under the supervision of the Court or not, if a case has in the opinion of the Liquidator arisen under section 362 of the Act for an investment

of funds of the Company or a sale of securities in which the Company's funds have been invested, the Liquidator shall sign and transmit to the Board of Trade a certificate of the facts on which his opinion is founded, and a request to the Board of Trade to make the investment or sale mentioned in the certificate, and the Board of Trade may thereupon, if they think fit, invest or sell the whole or any part of the said funds and securities, as provided in the said section, and the said certificate and request shall be a sufficient authority to the Board of Trade for the said investment or sale.

174 to 181 * * * * *

FINAL ACCOUNT IN VOLUNTARY WINDING-UP

Form 110.

182. The account required by sections 290 and 300 of the Act to be made up by the Liquidator as soon as the affairs of the Company are fully wound up shall be in Form No. 110 in the Appendix.

183 to 195 * * * * *

STATEMENTS BY LIQUIDATOR TO THE REGISTRAR OF COMPANIES

Conclusion of winding-up.

196. The winding-up of a Company shall, for the purposes of section 342 of the Act, be deemed to be concluded:—

(*a*) in the case of a Company wound up by order of the Court, at the date on which the order dissolving the Company has been reported by the Liquidator to the Registrar of Companies, or at the date of the order of the Board of Trade releasing the Liquidator pursuant to section 251 of the Act.

(*b*) in the case of a Company wound up voluntarily, or under the supervision of the Court, at the date of the dissolution of the Company, unless at such date any funds or assets of the Company remain unclaimed or undistributed in the hands or under the control of the Liquidator, or any person who has acted as Liquidator, in which case the winding-up shall not be deemed to be concluded until such funds or assets have either been distributed or paid into the Companies Liquidation Account at the Bank of England.

Times for sending Liquidator's statements, and regulations applicable thereto.

197. In a voluntary winding-up or a winding-up under the supervision of the Court, the statements with respect to the proceedings in and position of the liquidation of a Company winding-up of which is not concluded within a year after its commencement shall be sent to the Registrar of Companies twice in every year as follows:—

(1) The first statement, commencing at the date when a Liquidator was first appointed and brought down to the end of twelve months from the commencement of the winding-up, shall be sent within 30 days from the expiration of such twelve months, or within such extended period as the Board of Trade may sanction, and the subsequent statements shall be sent at intervals of half-a-year, each statement being brought down to the end of the half year for which it is sent. In cases in which the assets of the Company have been fully realised and distributed before the expiration of a half-yearly interval a final statement shall be sent forthwith.

(2) Subject to the next succeeding Rule, Form No. 92, and Forms 92, 94, 95 and 96.
where applicable Forms 94, 95 and 96, with such variations
as circumstances may require, shall be used, and the
directions specified in the Form (unless the Board of Trade
otherwise direct) be observed in reference to every statement.

(3) Every statement shall be sent in duplicate, and shall be Form 93.
verified by an affidavit in the Form No. 93, with such
variations as circumstances may require.

198. Where, in a voluntary winding-up or a winding-up under Affidavit of no receipts or payments.
the supervision of the Court, a Liquidator has not during any
period for which a statement has to be sent received or paid any
money on account of the Company, he shall, at the period when Forms 92 and 93.
he is required to transmit his statement, send to the Registrar of
Companies the prescribed statement in the Form No. 92, in
duplicate, containing the particulars therein required with respect
to the proceedings in and position of the Liquidation, and with
such statement shall also send an affidavit of no receipts or
payments in the Form No. 93.

UNCLAIMED FUNDS AND UNDISTRIBUTED ASSETS IN THE HANDS OF A LIQUIDATOR

199.—(1) All money in the hands or under the control of a Payment of undistributed and unclaimed money into Companies Liquidation Account.
Liquidator of a Company representing unclaimed dividends,
which for six months from the date when the dividend became
payable have remained in the hands or under the control of the
Liquidator, shall forthwith on the expiration of the six months be
paid into the Companies Liquidation Account.

(2) In a voluntary winding-up or a winding-up under the
supervision of the Court, all other money in the hands or under the
control of a Liquidator of a Company, representing unclaimed or
undistributed assets or held by the Company in trust which, under
sub-section (1) of section 343 of the Act, the Liquidator is to pay
into the Companies Liquidation Account, shall be ascertained as
on the date to which the statement of receipts and payments sent
in to the Registrar of Companies is brought down, and the amount
to be paid to the Companies Liquidation Account shall be the
minimum balance of such money which the Liquidator has had in
his hands or under his control during the six months immediately
preceding the date to which the statement is brought down, less
such part (if any) thereof as the Board of Trade may authorise
him to retain for the immediate purposes of the liquidation.
Such amount shall be paid into the Companies Liquidation
Account within fourteen days from the date to which the statement
of account is brought down.

(3) Notwithstanding anything in this Rule, any moneys in
the hands of the Liquidator at the date of the dissolution of the
Company representing unclaimed or undistributed assets or
dividends or held by the Company in trust in respect of dividends
or other sums due to any person as a member of the Company
shall forthwith be paid by him into the Companies Liquidation
Account.

(4) A Liquidator, whose duty it is to pay into the Companies Liquidation Account at the Bank of England money representing unclaimed or undistributed assets of the Company or held by the Company in trust in respect of dividends or other sums due to any person as a member of the Company, shall apply in such manner as the Board of Trade shall direct to the Board of Trade for a paying-in order, which paying-in order shall be an authority to the Bank of England to receive the payment.

(5) In a voluntary winding-up or a winding-up under the supervision of the Court, money invested or deposited at interest by a Liquidator shall be deemed to be money under his control, and when such money forms part of the minimum balance payable into the Companies Liquidation Account pursuant to paragraph (2) of this Rule, the Liquidator shall realise the investment or withdraw the deposit, and shall pay the proceeds into the Companies Liquidation Account: Provided that where the money is invested in Government securities, such securities may, with the permission of the Board of Trade, be transferred to the control of the Board of Trade instead of being forthwith realised and the proceeds thereof paid into the Companies Liquidation Account. If and when the money represented by the securities is required wholly or in part for the purposes of the Liquidation, the Board of Trade may realise the securities wholly or in part and pay the proceeds of realisation into the Companies Liquidation Account and deal with the same in the same way as other monies paid into the said Account may be dealt with.

Liquidator to furnish information to Board of Trade.

Form 97.

200. In a voluntary winding-up or a winding-up under the supervision of the Court, every person who has acted as Liquidator of any Company, whether the liquidation has been concluded or not, shall furnish to the Board of Trade particulars of any money in his hands or under his control representing unclaimed or undistributed assets of the Company or held by the Company in trust in respect of dividends or other sums due to any person as a member of the Company, and such other particulars as the Board of Trade may require for the purpose of ascertaining or getting in any money payable into the Companies Liquidation Account at the Bank of England. The Board of Trade may require such particulars to be verified by affidavit.

Board of Trade may call for verified accounts.

Forms 92, 93 to 96.

201.—(1) In a voluntary winding-up or a winding-up under the supervision of the Court, the Board of Trade may at any time order any such person as is mentioned in the preceding Rule to submit to them an account verified by affidavit of the sums received and paid by him as Liquidator of the Company, and may direct and enforce an audit of the account.

- (2) For the purposes of section 343 of the Act, and the Rules, the Court has and may exercise all the powers conferred by the Bankruptcy Act, 1914 (a), with respect to the discovery and realisation of the property of a debtor, and the provisions of Part I of that Act with respect thereto shall, with any necessary modification, apply to proceedings under section 343 of the Act.

(a) 4 & 5 Geo. 5, c. 59.

202. An application by the Board of Trade for the purpose of ascertaining and getting in money payable into the Bank of England pursuant to section 343 of the Act shall be made by motion and, where the winding-up is by or under the supervision of the Court, shall be made to and dealt with by the Judge, and in a voluntary winding-up shall be made to and dealt with by the Judge of the High Court.

Application to the Court for enforcing an account, and getting in money.

203. An application by a person claiming to be entitled to any money paid into the Bank of England in pursuance of section 343 of the Act, shall be made in such form and manner as the Board of Trade may from time to time direct, and shall, unless the Board of Trade otherwise directs, be accompanied by the certificate of the Liquidator that the person claiming is entitled and such further evidence as the Board of Trade may direct.

Application for payment out by person entitled.

204. A Liquidator who requires to make payments out of money paid into the Bank of England in pursuance of section 343 of the Act, either by way of distribution or in respect of the cost and expenses of the proceedings, shall apply in such form and manner as the Board of Trade may direct, and the Board of Trade may thereupon either make an order for payment to the Liquidator of the sum required by him for the purposes aforesaid, or may direct cheques to be issued to the Liquidator for transmission to the persons to whom the payments are to be made.

Application by Liquidator for payment out.

205 to 230   *   *   *   *   *

Table of Cases

The following abbreviations have been used in the references to the cases cited.

A.C.	= House of Lords and Privy Council Appeal Cases.	Jur.	= 'Jurist.'
All E.R.	= All England Reports.	Jur. (N.S.)	= 'Jurist,' New Series.
B. & Ad.	= Barnwell and Adolphus.	K.B.	= King's Bench.
B. & C.	= Barnwell and Creswell.	Knapp	= Knapp's Reports.
B. & C.R.	= Barnwell and Creswell's Reports.	L.J. (Bcy.)	= 'Law Journal,' Bankruptcy.
B. & S.	= Best and Smith.	L.J.C.P.	= 'Law Journal,' Common Pleas.
B.W.C.C.	= Butterworth's Workmen's Compensation Cases.	L.J.Ch.	= 'Law Journal,' Chancery.
Beav.	= Beavan.	L.J.Ex.	= " " Exchequer.
Bing.	= Bingham.	L.J.K.B.	= " " King's Bench.
Burr.	= Burrows.		
C.B.	= Common Bench.	L.J.P.C.	= 'Law Journal,' Privy Council.
C.P.D.	= Common Pleas Division.		
Ch.	= Chancery.	L.J.Q.B.	= 'Law Journal,' Queen's Bench.
Ch. App.	= Chancery Appeals.		
Ch.D.	= Chancery Division.	L.J.R.	= 'Law Journal' Reports.
Com. Cas.	= Commercial Cases.	L.R.C.P.	= Law Reports, Common Pleas.
Cox C.C.	= Cox's Criminal Cases.		
Cr. App. Rep.	= Criminal Appeal Reports.	L.R.Eq.	= Law Reports, Equity.
		L.R.Ex.	= " " Exchequer.
D. & L.	= Dowling and Lowndes' Reports.	L.R.H.	= " " House of Lords.
De G. & J.	= De Gex and Jones.	L.R.Q.B.	= Law Reports, Queen's Bench.
De G., F. & J.	= De Gex, Fisher and Johnson.	L.T.	= 'Law Times.'
		L.T. (O.S.)	= 'Law Times,' Old Series.
De G., J. & S.	= De Gex, Jones and Smith.	M. & W.	= Meeson and Welsby.
		Mans.	= Manson, Bankruptcy Cases.
De G., M. & G.	= De Gex, Macnaghten and Gordon.	Meg.	= Megone's Company Cases.
		Morr.	= Morrell, Bankruptcy Reports.
Digest	= The Digest.	New Rep.	= New Reports.
Digest Supp.	= The Digest Supplement.	N.I.L.R.	= Northern Ireland Law Reports.
Drew.	= Drewry.	P.	= Probate.
E. & B.	= Ellis and Blackburn.	Q.B.	= Queen's Bench Division.
East	= East's Reports.	Q.B.D.	= " " "
Eden	= Eden's Reports.	R.	= The Reports.
Ex. D.	= Exchequer Division (Law Reports).	Rettie	= Rettie, Court of Sessions.
		Ry. & Can. Cas.	= Railway and Canal Cases.
Exch.	= Exchequer.	S.C.	= Session Cases.
H. & C.	= Hurlstone and Coltman.	S.L.R.	= Scottish Law Reports.
H.B.R.	= Hansell's Bankruptcy Reports.	Smith	= Smith's Reports.
		Sol. J.	= 'Solicitor's Journal.'
H.L.	= House of Lords Cases.	T.L.R.	= Times' Law Reports.
H.L.C.	= " " "	Taunt.	= Taunton.
Hare	= Hare's Reports.	Tax Cas.	= Tax Cases.
Hem. & M.	= Hemming and Miller.	Ves.	= Vesey.
I.R.	= Irish Law Reports.	W.N.	= 'Weekly Notes.'
I.R.C.L.	= Irish Reports, Common Law.	W.R.	= 'Weekly Reporter.'
J.P.	= 'Justice of Peace.'		

Table of Cases

863

PAGE

Index

Board meetings—*continued*
    dissenting directors at, as to minuting, 195
    expenses of attending, 167
    financial statement should be submitted to, 237
    interest in contracts, disclosure of, by directors, 176
    invalid, when, 177
    minutes of, 180, 192 *et seq.*   *And see* Minutes
        alteration of, 192
        circulation of, 180
        duty of secretary to prepare, 192
        formal proceedings at, 196
        inspection of, members not entitled to, 161
            auditors' right, 180
            directors' right, 180
        must be kept, 179
        preceding meeting, minutes of, 192
        reason for keeping, 192
    notice of, 179
        form of, 636
        length of, 179
    outsiders, how affected by invalid, 177
    procedure at, 20, 180, 195
    quorum at, 196
        articles usually prescribe, 176
    ratification of invalid, 177, 178
    resolution in writing signed by all directors, when equivalent to
      resolution of meeting, 176
    routine business at, 195
    secretary, duties of, 178 *et seq.*
    Table A, provisions of, as to, 176
    telephone, by, 175
    time, 179
    votes at, 176, 177, 180
    when held, 179
Board of Trade
    annual general meeting, default in holding, 143
    auditors appointed by, 218
    balance sheet, period up to which to be made up, power to extend,
      143
    capital, interest payable out of; sanction required under s. 65, 242
    consolidated accounts, 212
    damages, recovery of, by, 424
    directors, particulars of, on circulars, etc., exemptions, 175
    enquiries without inspector, 424
    exempt private companies, 369
    expenses of, 424
    investigations by, 423–425
        appointment of inspector, 423
        bankers' disclosures, 424
        books, demand for production of, 424
        examination of officers and agents, 424
        information witheld from members, 424
        inspector, appointment of, 423
            court enforcement of powers of, 424
            powers of, 424
            report by, 424
        powers extended under Companies Act, 1948, 423
        reasons for, 423, 424
        secretary's position in case of, 425
        solicitors' privileged communications, 424
        special resolution for, 423

Canada—*continued*
Provincial Laws, Manitoba, 813
New Brunswick, 814
Newfoundland, 818
Nova Scotia, 815
Ontario, 815
Prince Edward Island, 816
Quebec, 816
Saskatchewan, 818

Cancellation of shares
articles must authorise, 31
unissued shares, only applies to, 31

Canvassing, 60

Capital, 28 *et seq. And see* Issue of shares; Register; Shares
alteration of, how to be carried out, 28 *et seq.*
articles of association, can be authorised by, 19, 28–31
amount of, to be stated in memorandum, 9, 28
appreciation of, capital assets; set off in, 245
'authorised,' 28
'bonus,' 246
cancellation of shares, 31
articles must authorise, 31
capitalisation of profits, 244, 247
circulating, how dividends paid if, 245
what is, 245
classes, divided into, specified on transfer, 81
consolidation of loan capital, 467
stamp duty on, 467
consolidation of share capital, 29
general meeting, must be effected in, 29
notice to registrar, 29
resolutions for, 29
conversion and re-conversion, 29
articles must authorise, 29
effect of, 30
general meeting, must be effected in, 29
notice to registrar, 30
special resolution for, 29
stock, how differs from shares, 30
dividends cannot be paid out of, 242, 244
directors may be liable if so paid, 244
memorandum or articles cannot authorise, 244
dividends, proportion of share capital regulates payment of, 242
duty on, 32, 466, 467. *And see* Stamp duty
loan capital, 467
share, 466
expenditure, taxation of, 406
'fixed,' need not be maintained out of revenue, 245
what is, 245
'floating,' 245
increase of, 28
articles must authorise, 28
duty payable on, 29
general meeting, must be effected in, 28
notice of, to registrar, 29
form of, 651
preference shares, issue of, on, 29
resolutions for, 28, 188
form of, 189
what should define, 188
rights of existing shareholders cannot be prejudiced, 29

Change of name, 15
    approval of Board of Trade, 15
    fee, 101
Charges. *See* Register of charges
    'fixed' and 'floating,' 257
    'floating' (Scotland), 390
    mortgages, word includes, 259
    register of, 686
Charities
    allowance on taxation for donations to, 403
Charter, when not required, 2
Cheques
    application moneys, for, receipt of, 46
    attorney, drawn by, 362
    director signing, when personally liable, 12
    fractional balances, 295
    name of company to appear on all, 12
    receipts for payments by, 466
'Chose in action'
    share is a, 34
Circulars
    invitation to persons to acquire securities illegal, 60
    issue of, to creditors, 60
    restriction of distribution, relating to investments, 60
    scheme of arrangement, explaining, 286, 287
        documents accompanying, 287
    transactions in securities, relating to, 60
Circulating capital, 245
Class meetings, 20, 29, 144
Clergyman
    attest signature, can, 83
    may not be director of trading company, 163
Clerk
    may represent company's secretary, 13
Closing register, 111
Clubs, 3
Colonial probate, 95
Colonial Stock Acts, 362
Commencing business
    certificate of, 47, 251
    contracts prior to company, are provisional, 47
    forms for, 572, 573
    private company, does not require certificate, 372
    statutory restrictions as to, 43 *et seq.*
Commissions, 106 *et seq.* *And see* Underwriting commissions
    absolutely, shares agreed to be subscribed, for, 106, 107
    annual return, particulars of, in, 109
    articles must authorise, 106
    disclosure of, 107
    limit on, 106
    over-riding, 109
    private company may pay, 374
    prospectus must disclose, 106
    shares, on issue of, 37, 106
        form of, 618
        writing off of, 174
    underwriting, 106 *et seq.*
Commissioners of Inland Revenue. *See* Inland Revenue Commissioners
Committee of inspection, 314. *And see* Voluntary winding up
    absence of member from meetings of, 315
    appointment of, 314

Company

alteration of objects, 15

amalgamation of.   *See* Reconstruction

books; directors resolution to close, form of, 189

books of, disposal on winding up, 346, 347

    possession of by liquidator, 319

borrowing power, 14, 19, 47, 251

    business, liquidator and, 324

    implied for ordinary business, 14, 21, 251

    method usually adopted, 251

business, disclosure of change of nature of, 203

control of, may be vested in a manager, 163

controlling interest in, acquisition of complete, how effected, 271, 282

corporate body, when company becomes, 8

creditors and, scheme of arrangement with, 283

debts, deemed unable to pay, 305

definition of, 1

directors may bind although improperly appointed, when, 164

discount, issue of shares at a, 37, 108 *et seq.*

dissolution of, 347

    cannot be sued after, 348

    property vests in Crown after, 348

    setting aside of, 348

    striking off register, by, 348

executor, appointed as, 97

    syndic represents, 97

'existing company,' meaning of, 1

foreign, 4, 394 *et seq.   And see* Oversea company

guarantee, limited by, 2, 3, 4, 18.   *And see* Guarantee companies

    memorandum of association of a, 9

    without share capital, 3, 4

holding, 211

investigation of, by Board of Trade, 423

land, holding by, 8

law, definition of, 2

    case law, 2

limited by shares, 2, 3, 4, 18

loans to directors prohibited, 166

    exceptions, 166

meetings.   *See* Meetings; Ordinary general meetings; Statutory meeting

    how represented at, 157

member of another company, when, may appoint representative, 157

member, can sue and be sued by, 22

membership of a, how constituted, 38

memorandum of association of.   *See* Memorandum of association

mining within the stannaries, 2

minutes, must keep, 161

name of, 5, 11, 12.   *And see* Name of company

not limited by, shares, 3, 4

objects of, 13–15

oversea, 4.   *See* Oversea company

private, 4.   *See* Private company

private company becoming public, 375

profit, not trading for, 203

public company becoming private, 13, 375

purchase of its own shares prohibited, 38

    financial assistance for, provision of, illegal, 38

purchase of business of, 19

Income tax—*continued*
    scientific research, 408, 416
    shipping profits, 410
    statement annexed to warrents, 414
        penalty for omission, 414
    statutory return, responsibility of company, 401
    superannuation, exemptions, 445, 447
        relief from, 445
    surtax, 415
        distribution of income, 416
        to whom applicable, 415
        undistributed profits liable to, 416
    tax credits, 410
    tax deduction card, 761
        instructions to employers, 763, 767
        monthly, 765
    tax reserve certificates, 412
    trade subscriptions on, 403
    trading profits, assessment of, 401
        collection of, 400
        from abroad, 410, 411
    valuation for purposes of, 400
    warrants, deductions on, 414
    wear and tear, 403, 405, 407
        allowance carried forward, 409
    when due, 411
Income Tax Act, 1918, 399, 409, 413
Income Tax Act, 1945, 405, 407
Income Tax (Employment) Regulations, 1944, 225
Incorporation
    certificate of, 8
    how far evidence, 8
Increase of capital, 28, 29
    articles must authorise, 28
    duty payable on, 29
    general meeting, effected in, 28
    ordinary resolution may be sufficient authority for, 28
    preference shares, issue of, on, 29
    resolutions for, 28
        form of, 189
        nature of new shares to be defined, 188
    rights fixed by memorandum cannot be prejudiced on, 29
Indemnity
    for duplicate certificate; form of, 42, 627
Indemnity and request
    for duplicate dividend warrant, 250
        form of, 661
Index. *And see* Filing
    annual return, annexed to, 113
    card, 68
    loose leaf, 67
    register of members, 67
    share register, 68
India and Pakistan
    company legislation in, 827 *et seq.*
Infants
    allotment of shares to, not desirable, 58
        if knowingly, amounts to misfeasance, 58
    application in name of, 57
    articles often prohibit registration of, 116
    calls on shares, liability for, 118

Machinery
    taxation of, 407, 408
Majority
    amalgamation under s. 209, 282
    how computed, 138
    minority, articles if altered must not be oppressive to, 26
    powers of, over minority under debenture trust deeds, 254
    reconstruction, on winding up for purposes of, 273
    scheme meeting, at, 291
        requisite for, 215
    termination of meeting by, 149
Manager. *See* Receiver
Managing director
    not a 'clerk or servant' within s. 264 of Act of 1929, 341
    private company, whether 'in employ of company' in, 368
    what is a, 162
Mandamus
    registrar may be compelled to register by, 5
Mandates, dividend. *See* Dividend mandates
Manitoba
    company legislation in, 813
Mark. *And see* Execution; Illiteracy
    execution by, not valid in Scotland, 388
    form of attestation where deed executed by, 699
Marriage
    of female shareholder, 64
Married woman
    attorney, power to appoint, 349
    memorandum of association, may subscribe to, 7
    National insurance contributions, 230
Meetings. *See also* Annual general meeting; Extraordinary general
    meeting; Meetings of shareholders; Ordinary general meeting;
    Requisitioned meeting; Statutory meeting
    adjourned, 160
    annual general, 3, 142
    attendance list at, 152
    board. *See* Board meeting
    Board of Trade's power, 141
    court's power to convene, 141
    creditors', annual, 333
    creditors', of, in creditors' voluntary winding up, 313, 333
        matters determined at, 314
    debenture holders, of, 254
    final, in winding up, 345
        return of, 743, 744
    general, to cancel shares, 31
        to consolidate shares, 29
        to convert shares into stock and reconvert, 29
        to increase capital, 28
        to subdivide shares, 31
    invalid, when, 135
    liquidation, in, 333, 345
        accounts to be laid before, 333, 346
        notice of, in writing to be given, 333
    meaning of, 130
    notice of, 130–137. *And see* Notices of meeting
        special business if mentioned, nature of, to be stated in, 135
            form of, 137
    requisitioned. *See* Requitioned meetings; Meetings of shareholders
    special or extraordinary resolutions, notice of, should be carefully
      framed, 137

Promoter
    commissions, payment of, 107
    liability for statements in prospectus, 45
    prospectus to state amounts paid to, 106, 107

Property, taxation on investment of, 403

Prospectus, 43 *et seq.*
    accuracy of, 45
    allotment after third day of publication, 50
    amount on application, minimum payable, to apply to subsequent issues, 50
    application for quotation on Stock Exchange, 50, 511 *et seq.*
    application forms must be accompanied by, 52
    auditors' names to appear in, 218
    commissions, must disclose, 106
    contracts, must state particulars, of, 45
    dated, must be, 45
    definition of, 43
    directors, consent of, 45
        copy signed by, to be delivered to registrar, 45
        liability for mis-statements in, 44, 45
        named in, 6
        signing of, 45
        shares to be paid for, 48
    documents to be specified, 45
    expert's consent to, 44, 45
    foreign company, 396
    full information to legal advisers, 44
    issue of, what is, 43
    minimum subscription, 46. *And see* Minimum subscription
    offer for sale, when deemed to be a, 59
    'offer to the public,' 43, 52, 60
    particulars, to be set out, 44
    permission for quotation on Stock Exchange, 50, 511 *et seq.*
    preparation of, 44
    profit to be disclosed, 44
    promoters, liability of, 45
    registrar's certificate, 47
    registration, copy delivered for, 44, 45
    requirements, 44 *et seq.*
    resolution of directors to issue, form of, 188
    restrictions on issue of, 428
        oversea companies, 428
    statement in lieu of, 47. *See* Statement in lieu of prospectus
        delivery to registrar, 47
        not in case of private company, 372
    statutory declaration as to, to be filed by secretary, 47
    statutory requirements of company which issues a, 43, 44, 45
    underwriting commissions should be stated in, 106, 107
    untrue statement in, 45

Proxies, 19, 154 *et seq.*
    articles usually determine, 19, 155
    blank, may be signed in, 156
    class meetings under s. 206 of Act of 1948, 156
    company's regulations provide for, 155
    creditors' meeting at commencement of voluntary winding up, 314
    execution of, name inserted after, 156
    extraordinary resolutions, may be used for, 186
    filling up, implied authority for, 156
    forms of, 155, 637–639
    funds of company may be used in sending out, 156

Resolutions—*continued*
    amendments to—*continued*
      minutes of, 198
        exact words to be recorded, 199
        secretary's duty, 199
      procedure on, 190, 199
    appointment of auditors by, 218
      of directors under single, 147
    articles, under, 185
      when copies to be annexed to or embodied in, 187
    call, to make a, 102
      form of, 188
    capital, form of resolution to increase, 189
    chairman refusing amendment to, 148, 190
    chairman's duty as to proposed amendments, 190, 199
    classes of, 144, 185
    clearly expressed, should be, 188
    debentures, to issue, form of, 189
    definition of, 185
    extraordinary, 137, 186
      form of, to wind up, 190
    forms of, 188 *et seq.*
    if given majority required, fact to be recorded, 199
    invalid, when, 186
      chairman improperly refusing amendment, 148
      failure to receive notice may render, 135
    liquidator, appointing, notice to be given to registrar, 319
    to be advertised, 319
    minutes of, at meetings, 198
    notices of, examples, 135, 136, 191
    notices not received by shareholder, may render invalid, 135
      articles may provide for accidental omissions, 135
    ordinary, how passed, 185
    poll demanded on, 199
    'previous question,' moving the, 344
    printing of, 373
    registrar, resolutions to be filed with, 187
      when copy to be forwarded to, 187
    secretary's duty concerning, 185
    several, put to meeting *en bloc*, 147
    shareholders' consent to, without meeting, 185
    shareholders', definition of, 185
    special, 137, 186.   *And see* Special resolution
    special notice required, 132
    statutory meeting, as to, 142
    winding up, on, 310
    written, validated, 368
Resolution of directors, 190
    articles may give control of company to, 191
      alteration of, if oppressive on shareholders, 191
    casting vote of chairman at, 190
    debentures, for creation of, 252
    de-numbering of shares, 34
    forms
      to allot shares, 188
        close books, 189
        forfeit shares, 188
        issue prospectus, 188
        make call, 188
        pay final dividend, 188
        pay interim dividend, 188

Set off, 332. *See* Winding up
    contributory, by, 333
    what is a, 332
    winding up, in, 333
Share capital
    balance sheet, stated in, 205
    companies limited by guarantee, 3
    companies with, 2
        without, 2
    duty on, 466
    equity, 211
    redemption of, in profit and loss account, 209
    unlimited companies with, 3
Share warrants, 62, 120 *et seq.*
    advertisement of dividends payable, 124
        form of, 124
    alteration of, with intent to defraud, 128
    annual summary, shown in, 126
    application for, 125
        form of, 719
        receipt for, 721
    application for exchange of, for other share warrants, 728
    application for registered shares in exchange for, 126, 727
    articles of association, under, 120
        not in case of private company, 120, 368
        conditions of, to be followed strictly, 121
        seal, conditions of, as to affixing, 125
    auditors of company should examine all applications, etc., 126
        certificate, should give, 126
    bank, how should be shown at, 127
    board of directors' resolution may authorise, 120
    cancellation of, on surrender by holder, 126
    conditions of issue, model form of, 121–124
    conditions of issue separate from, 120
    contract to sell registered shares, delivery of warrants not enough to satisfy, 127
        coupons for dividends, 127
        coupon account at bank, 127
        registers to be kept, 128
    delivery of, 126
        directions as to, 720
    deposited, receipt for, 718
    directors' share qualifications not satisfied by shares represented by, 127, 166
    dividends payable on, form of advertisement of, 124
        payment of, how provided for, 127
    duplicate, 124
    duty on, 125, 467
    exchange of, 126
    exchange for other warrants, register for issue, 728
    fees, 125
    forgery, danger of, 120
        penalties for, 128
    form of, 121, 717
        application for, 719
        application for, form of receipt, 721
    fully paid shares or stock, may be issued in respect of, 120
    holder of, rights on surrendering for cancellation, 126
        whether entitled to notice of statutory meeting, 134
    issue of, what particulars to be entered on register, 125
        unstamped, 125

H 2

Shareholders—*continued*

member, definition of, 38, 39, 56
    who may become a, 40
minimum number, 6
minority, remedy under s. 210, 306
new shares to existing, procedure, 56
non-assenting, notice to, 714
notice to transferee company by, 715
notices to, 132. *And see* Notices of meetings
partnership as, 40
payments to, 221
personal representative's title, 91 *et seq.*
preferential rights of, extending to new issue, 56
private company, of. *See* Private company
reconstruction, rights on, 275
    agreement for sale, rights on, 279
    alteration of rights, 275
    dissent to scheme, 275, 282. *And see* Dissentients
    distribution of new shares, 273
    how affects, 294
    rights fixed by memorandum or articles, 273, 277
    scheme binds, 282
reduction in rate of interest, 295
resolutions of, 185
'rights' issues to, 56
statutory company, of. *See* Statutory company
transmission of interest of (statutory companies), 383
vote, right to, 153
who may be, 39
winding up of company, surplus assets, 341

Shares, 9, 28 *et seq. And see also* Capital; Shareholder; Share warrant; Stock

agreement to take, how may be expressed, 39
allotment of. *See* Allotment
    preparation of certificates, 41
annual return, particulars of, in, 112
application for, 39, 50, 54, 58
    agent, may be made by an, 39, 57
    excess, 604
    forms, 585, 587
    in fictitious name, 57
    legal decisions upon, 56, 57
    withdrawal of, 57
        communicated to clerk or secretary, 57
arbitrator, when value determined by, 277
articles of association may alter rights, 35
balance of unpaid, when may be payable, 102
balance receipt, 75
Bankruptcy Act, 1914, not within, 34
bonus, 37, 246, 247
bonus terms, offered on, 43
calls on. *See* Calls
cancellation of, 31
cash, shares allotted as paid otherwise than in, 51, 278
stamp duty on, adjudication of, 51, 462
cash, shares need not be paid in, 7
certificate, 34, 40, 41. *And see* Certificates
    completion of, time for, 53
    endorsement on death of joint holder, 40
    forms of, 619, 620, 622
    fractional, form of, 625

Shares—*continued*
>   winding up. *See* Winding up
>   writing down, 295
Sheriff
>   goods seized by, in winding up, 327
Show of hands
>   resolutions by, 148
>   voting by, 148
>>   in case of proxy, 155
Signatories, 7
Signature
>   agent, by, 7
>   misrepresentation, induced by, 7
Solicitor
>   appointment of, by articles, not binding, 24
>   attest signature, can, 83
>   certificate of exemption from control of borrowing, 431
>   costs, taxation of, in winding up, 336
>   costs, liquidator not liable for, 343
>   lien claimed by, on company's property, 320
>   liquidator may employ, 318, 325
>   privileged communication, 429
>   statutory declaration by, on formation of company, 6
Solvency, declaration of, 731
South Africa (Union of)
>   company legislation in, 821
South Australia
>   company legislation in, 798
Southern Rhodesia
>   company law relating to, 823
Special business
>   meaning of, 135
>   nature of, to be stated in notices, 135
Special notice, 131
>   auditors, regarding retirement of, 219, 220
>   company, to, and by, 131
>   length of notice required for, 132
>   object of, 131
>   resolutions requiring, 132
Special resolutions, 137, 186
>   alteration of articles, by, 25, 271
>>   form of, 188, 189
>   alteration of conditions in memorandum by, 15
>   alteration of objects of company, required for, 16
>   articles, copy of resolution to be annexed to or embodied in, 187
>   capital increase of, by, 28, 29
>   change of name, first step necessary to, 15
>   characteristics of, 186
>   consolidation of share capital, as to, 29
>   conversion authorised by, 29, 288
>   declaration of chairman, 187
>   definition of, 137
>   extraordinary general meeting, notice to pass, 635
>   increasing capital by, 28, 29
>   length of notice for, 137
>   length of notice for meeting, to pass, 130
>   liquidator, appointment of, not necessary for, 313
>   members, agreement of to pass, 640
>   notice of intention to propose as a, 137, 186
>>   form of, 137
>>   waiver of, 138

Stamp duty—*continued*

Inland Revenue Circular relating to, 462, 463, 474 *et seq.*
  adjudication of stamp duty, 462
Inland Revenue Commissioners, statement delivered to, 463
  discretion as to gifts *inter vivos*, 461
  voluntary dispositions *inter vivos*, as to, 461, 462
instrument relating to several distinct matters, 458
insufficient stamp on instrument of transfer, secretary may take opinion, 462
Irish Republic, documents stamped in, 460
lease of land, agreement for, 469
legal advice, when required, 464
letters of allotment, on, abolished, 464
letters of renunciation, abolished on, 464
liquidation, 468
  transfer of assets, 468
  transfer of specie, 468
loan capital, on, 467
  by whom payable, 467
  consolidation or conversion of, 467
  definition of, 467
  duty, when may be repaid on conversion of, 467
  not to be charged, when, 467
  rate of, 467
loans repayable at a premium, 367
marketable securities, on, 467
marking officer, 463
memorandum of association, on, 6, 7
  as a deed, 6
mortgage, agreement operating as, 464
nominal consideration, transfer made for, 461
Northern Ireland, documents stamped in, 460
order for payment, 465
penalties for evasion of, 459, 460
penalty stamps, 459
postage stamps, when used, 459
powers of attorney, on, 351
production of instrument receivable in evidence, 458
promissory notes, rates of, 466. *And see* bills of exchange *supra*
proxy, on, 464
rates of, 464
  ad valorem, 458
  agreements, 464
  bills of exchange, 465
  consideration, in form of annuity, where, 463
  fixed, 458
  loan capital, 467
  share capital, 466
  transfer of shares, 460
receipts, on, 465 *et seq.*
  bank entries initialled by cashier, 466
  banker's receipt, 465
  bill of exchange, 466
  charitable gifts, 465
  cheque, for payment by, 465
  definition of, 466
  directors' fees, 465
  donation to charity, 465
  duty on, how denoted, 465
  exemptions from duty on, 465
  liability if not duly stamped or refusal, 465

Statutory company—*continued*

    differ from ordinary limited companies, how, 380

    executor, attorney of, registration in case of, 385

        if also a beneficiary registration without transfer, 385

        transfers, execution by all if more than one, 385

    fees on transfer and transmission, 383, 385

    general meetings, business transacted at, 380

        notice, 380

        proxies, 380

        quorum, 380

        shareholder a corporate body, 380

    incorporated by Royal Charter, 377

    infant holding shares in a, 116

    inspection of register, none, 381

    inspection of shareholders' address book, 381

    legal personal representatives, registration of transfers by, 384

    letters of administration, as to fees on, 385

    'limited,' word, not necessary for a, 380

    meetings of, 380

    memorandum, uses in case of, 378

    nationalisation, 377

    particular undertakings, incorporation of special Acts relating to, 379

    preference stock, redemption of, 379

    proxies, blanks in, must be filled up by member, 380

    public utility, 377

    redeeming debenture or preference stock, 379

    register of consolidated stock holders, 382

    register of shareholders, must keep a, 381

        alteration of, evidence, 385

        copy of, but no inspection, 111, 381

        seal of company to be attached, 381

    registered, is not, 380

    registered office, 377

    registration by legal personal representatives, 384

    Scotland, in, 392

    seal on register of stockholders, 381

    secretary, 379, 380

        applications for special Acts, on, 379

            special meeting, to summon, 379

        legislation, should acquire knowledge of, 379

        remuneration of, 381

        special Acts, should have knowledge of, relating to his own company, 379

        transfers of shares, duties on, 382

            endorsement of deed, 383

            issue of new certificate, 383

            legal personal representatives, registration in case of, 383

        transmission, declaration of, to be produced to, 384

            duties on, 383

            entry of name of representative, 384

                consent of board not necessary, 384

            evidence of right of representative, 384

    shares, consolidation of, into stock, 381

        transfers of, 382

    special Act contains the powers of a, 377

        applications for, procedure on, 379

        parliamentary committees consider, 379

        should always be consulted, 379

        what Acts usually incorporated in, 378

    standing orders relating to private bills must be considered, 379